Eighteenth-Century Thought

Eighteenth-Century Thought

Editor: James G. Buickerood
University of Missouri, St. Louis

Editorial Board

Editorial Consultants

Eighteenth-Century Thought

Volume 1

James G. Buickerood
Editor

AMS Press
New York

Eighteenth-Century Thought

Volume 1

ISSN 1545-0449
Set ISBN: 0-404-63760-4
Vol. 1 ISBN: 0-404-63761-2

All AMS books are printed on acid-free paper that meets the guidelines
for performance and durability of the Committee on Production
Guidelines for Book Longevity of the Council on Library Resources.

AMS PRESS, INC.
BROOKLYN NAVY YARD, BLDG. 292, SUITE 417, 63 FLUSHING AVE.
BROOKLYN, NY 11205, USA

MANUFACTURED IN THE UNITED STATES OF AMERICA

Eighteenth-Century Thought
Volume 1 (2003)

Contents

Review Essay

Book Reviews

Editorial Statement

The past two decades have hosted a proliferation of important, widely ramifying research in the intellectual history of the long eighteenth century. As a natural consequence of this development scholars working in pertinent fields have increasingly recognized and emphatically expressed a need for a forum focused especially on research into the various interrelated conceptual endeavors marking this period. Adequate interdisciplinary channels for publication of studies of the eighteenth century with primarily literary, artistic, social and cultural emphases are widely recognized to exist already; until now, however, there has been no organ concentrating on the study of conceptual efforts of the period that have proven so fecund and otherwise significant. This Journal has been conceived to provide such a venue.

Eighteenth-Century Thought has been founded in order to encourage and support inquiry into early modern thought by its annual publication of interdisciplinary research on the philosophy, natural philosophy, medicine, law, historiography, political theory, religion, economics and other emerging human sciences as conceived, practiced and variously related to one another from the second half of the seventeenth century to the first quarter of the nineteenth century. To this end, the Journal will publish essays, substantive discussion notes, review essays and book reviews concentrating solely on this intellectual history. *Eighteenth-Century Thought*'s principal object of fostering understanding of the thought of this period through a comprehensive appreciation of the efforts of its creators will be met by distribution of rigorous study of their texts and the contexts in which they were created. While figures and movements conventionally understood to have principal status will receive due attention, serious consideration will also be offered to less well known authors, movements, controversies and positions not simply in an effort to understand the principals' contexts, but equally importantly to comprehend the merits and limitations of such currently less known subjects.

As *Eighteenth-Century Thought* is an interdisciplinary journal, it strongly encourages interdisciplinary methods and topics. Such an integrative approach will often elicit comprehensive, thoroughly documented, and occasionally longer than conventional essays.

Empiricism and English Political Thought, 1550-1720

Barbara J. Shapiro

University of California, Berkeley

Abstract

This essay traces the development of a neglected genre of political writing that flourished from the Renaissance to the Enlightenment and sought to convey political knowledge by reporting personal observations of empirical political phenomena. The focus is on one of the "ways of knowing" politics and government. This paper traces the importance of this body of writing in shaping early modern English thought by examining publications through which the reading public acquired political information—travel accounts and instructions, diplomatic reports and natural history—arguing that they share both a common set of categories or grid for understanding governmental institutions and a preference for empirical description. These texts are empirical in that they aspire to, and purport to be based on careful and credible firsthand observation or reliable second hand observation. The genres investigated are political or governmental in that they involve observations, descriptions and characterizations of states or kingdoms. Many of the texts discussed do not conform to modern disciplinary boundaries. They were often called chorographies, geographies, natural histories, or *The Present State of ...*, and frequently combined natural and civil topics. Widespread distribution of this material meant that the English were far more familiar with foreign countries than one might think if one concentrates on the well known political theorists or philosophers, or focuses solely on constitutional issues. This essay suggests that empirically derived political observation was an important aspect of early modern English political culture and that this observation, organized around a familiar topical grid, was applicable to all existing states.

The dominant tradition in the history of political thought has been the intensive analysis of the principal writings of one or more major political thinkers, either in the context of traditions of discourse or in the context of contemporary social and political developments. Deviating from that tradition this paper concerns the development of a particular genre of political writing that flourished in the Renaissance and the Enlightenment and sought to convey political knowledge by reporting personal observations of empirical political phenomena. In short the focus here is not on Foucauldian epistemes or "humanist," "scientific" or "Enlightenment" paradigms but on one of the "ways of knowing" politics.

Given the quantity and popularity of works in this empirical political genre throughout the early modern period and beyond, it is surprising that it has received so little scholarly attention.[1] Here I seek to trace the

---

[1] There is no mention of this tradition in J. H. Burns and Mark Goldie, eds., *The Cambridge History of Political Thought 1450-1700* (Cambridge: Cambridge University Press, 1991). For

importance of this tradition in shaping English thought by examining publications through which the English reading public acquired political information about its own and other countries.[2]

I survey three overlapping genres that deal with political information—travel instructions, diplomatic reports and natural history, arguing that they share both a common set of categories or grid for understanding governmental institutions and a preference for empirical description. These texts are "empirical" in that they aspire to, and purport to be, based on careful and credible firsthand observation or the reliable firsthand observations of others. Although it was understood that such observations were subject to error and bias, these empirical reporters believed that accurate accounts of things, events, and practices might be achieved. The very nature of their work implied that subsequent observers would correct errors and record alterations in the conditions and institutions observed. These genres should be considered as species of the early modern "discourses of fact."[3]

The genres I investigate are political or governmental in that they involve observations, descriptions, and characterizations of a particular locale, typically a state or kingdom. We encounter a terminological problem since early modern empirical efforts do not conform to modern disciplinary boundaries. They sometimes bore such now defunct labels as "chorography" or "cosmography" or employed such terms as "geography" or "history" in ways that do not conform to modern usage.[4] Titles such as "The Present State of ... ," "A Description of ...," "An Account of ...," "A Survey of ... ," or even "The Natural History of ..." were prevalent. The focus of these publications varied, some treating extensively of governmental topics, others favoring flora, fauna, natural resources, or antiquities.

I. Origins

These empirical genres were deeply indebted to the natural histories and geographical works of Pliny and Strabo, the firsthand political accounts of ancient historians and the wide-ranging accounts of Herodotus which drew attention to local customs and practices.[5] The revival of

---

an exception see W. H. Greenleaf, *Order, Empiricism and Politics: Two Traditions of English Political Thought* (Oxford: Oxford University Press, 1964).

[2] Information was also gained from newsbooks and newsletters.

[3] See Barbara J. Shapiro, *A Culture of Fact: England 1550-1720* (Ithaca: Cornell University Press, 1999).

[4] Chorographies included both natural and civil information. The term "history" referred to past or present events and phenomena.

[5] See Katherine Clarke, *Between History and Geography: Hellenistic Constructions of the Roman World* (Oxford: Clarendon Press, 1999). Clarke demonstrates that the conventional allocation of space and place to geography and time and event to history is inadequate to describe the work of Ptolemy and Strabo. See also Cristiaan Van Paassen, *The Classical*

classical geography, natural history, and historiographical traditions played a significant role in the shaping of Renaissance and later empirical genres. The revival of descriptive writing in the Renaissance began with Flavio Biondo's description of Italy and various chorographies of German towns and was elaborated in the worldwide treatment of Ortelius.[6] These and later empirical studies typically combine the physical description of place with information on manners, customs, buildings, trade, natural and strategic resources, and government.

II. Travel and political education

I begin with sixteenth- and seventeenth-century English examples that emphasize observation of foreign states as a means of political education. If the reading of history was thought necessary to prepare gentlemen for public service by placing before them the experience of the past, foreign travel, properly pursued, would provide direct encounters with existing states and political systems. Firsthand political observation would complement the vicarious "experience" derived from the reading of history.[7] Though foreign travel was considered a means of creating a politically well-informed and useful political elite, it created the risk of corruption through exposure to alien mores and religion.[8] Travel was often recommended only for the mature well-socialized person. Travel advice typically featured a list of topics to which travelers were to attend in making and recording their observations. This apparatus can show us a good deal about how governments were conceptualized by early modern Englishmen.

The Elizabethan statesman William Cecil insisted that travelers pay particular attention both to the governments of the countries visited, including their courts of justice and parlements, and to their principal commodities and industries. Those visiting France, for example, were to

Tradition of Geography (Groeningen: J. B. Wolters, 1957); Robert J. Mayhew, *Enlightenment Geography: The Political Languages of British Geography 1650-1850* (New York: St. Martin's Press, 2000). Mayhew shows that "geographers" often dealt with "the Laws, Manners, and Customs of nations, their Advantages and Disadvantages" (35).

[6] Flavio Biondo, *Italia Illustrata* (Basel, 1531); Gerard Strauss, *Sixteenth-Century Germany: Its Topography and Topographers* (Madison: University of Wisconsin Press, 1959); Justin Stagl, "The Methodizing of Travel in the Sixteenth Century: A Tale of Three Cities," *History and Anthropology* 4 (1990): 300-338. Stagl suggests that Francesco Sansovino's *Del Governo de I regni et della republiche cosi antiche come moderne* (Venetia, 1561) is "the fountainhead of a stream of descriptions of the different states and nations of the world" (308, 310).

[7] See John Walter Stoye, *English Travellers Abroad 1604-1667* (New York: Octagon Press, 1968); Charles L. Batten, *Pleasurable Instruction: Form and Convention in Eighteenth-Century Travel Literature* (Berkeley: University of California Press, 1978); Justin Stagl, *A History of Curiosity: The Theory of Travel 1550-1800* (Chur, Switzerland: Harwood Academic Publishers, 1995); Sara Warneke, *Images of the Educational Traveller in Early Modern England* (Leiden: Brill, 1995).

[8] See Warneke, *Images, passim.*

acquire knowledge of the court, especially of the king and royal family, the personnel of the privy council, the principal officers of state, state revenues, military and naval preparedness, ordinary revenues, and the principal adherents to the reformed religion. They must also observe the criminal and civil courts and provincial parlements. Such information was to be recorded in a daily or weekly journal.[9]

Robert Dallington, who also advised travel for "ripening in knowledge" and "service of his countryie," directed the traveler to cosmography, that is climate and air, lakes and rivers, ports, geography, as well as provincial divisions, commodities, cites, and fortifications. Under the category "governors," he includes "law," both fundamental and temporary, and "magistrates," supreme and subordinate. The "governed," or "the People," required observation and notation of their "nature and inclination," customs and characteristics.[10]

Francis Bacon treated foreign travel as education for the young and as "experience" for the mature. He recommends keeping a diary, giving special attention to "the courts of princes" and encounters with ambassadorial secretaries that allowed travelers to "suck the experience" of the knowledgeable. Travelers must observe the courts of justice and ecclesiastical consistories as well as military preparedness and strength, with their subcategories "walls and fortifications," "havens and harbours," shipping, navies, armories, and arsenals.[11]

Later seventeenth-century works followed in the same vein. *Profitable Instructions; Describing what special Observations are to be taken by Travellers in all Nations, States and Countries* (1633), again suggests that book learning is insufficient for those wishing to enter "on the stage of publike employment." Personal observation of "men of several humours, factions, and countries" was essential. A complex set of topics, listed under the headings of "the Country," "the People," and "Policy and Government" are presented in diagrammatic form. To comprehend "Country" the traveler observed and recorded data on geographical "scituation," topography, climate, fertility, commodities, and "strength," the last of which focused on defense and fortifications. Information

---

[9] "Memorial of instructions by William Cecil to the Earl of Rutland,"in Warnecke, *Images*, Appendix B, 295-98. Thomas Bodley also emphasized travel as a means of becoming employed "in the public service of the State" (Warneke, *Images*, 46). Thomas Blundeville in 1574 suggests that information on trade, the public revenue, military forces and manner of government should be included in the histories of all states.

[10] Robert Dallington, *A Method of Travel shewed by taking the view of France* (London, 1604), n. pag. See also Pierre d'Avity, *The Estates, Empires and Principalities of the World* trans. Edward Grimstone (London, 1615).

[11] Francis Bacon, "Of Travel," in *The Essays*, ed. John Pitcher (London: Penguin, 1985), 114. For John Cleland, travel was the principle means for the nobility to become serviceable to the state (Warnecke, *Images*, 45).

collected on the "People" included population size, trade, and social divisions. The virtues, vices, and revenues of the nobility, their factional affiliations and participation in government are thought to require special attention. "Policy and Government," was a broadly conceived category, comprehending civil, canon and municipal law and their "conformity with the nature of the people." "Governors" were "sovereign," monarchical, aristocratic or popular, or "subaltern." Travelers should indicate whether monarchical authority was gained by succession, election or usurpation, and how the ruler "doth carry himself in administration," a phrase comprehending the ruler's "wisdom, his inclination to peace, war, how he is beloved or feared by the people and neighbors, his enterprises and designs, his disposition ... his favorites, the confidence or distrust he hath in his people," his revenues, his friends and confederacies. Treatment of "the State" involved an account of those having "the managing of the state" or "Counsell of Estate." These were further subdivided into "ordinary" or "extraordinary," the former included the "Great," "Privy," and "Cabinet" councils, the latter, the "Estates of Parliament." The last required an account of the number of members, their authority and counsel, wisdom, and fidelity, as well as of their credit and favor with prince and people. Information on councils of finance and war, and provincial governments are also to be recorded. "Justice," civil and criminal, must be observed, and the information recorded.[12] If travelers were as diligent as Dallington hoped, they would have a complete and useful description of the chief governmental institutions.

The turmoil of the mid seventeenth-century civil wars and interregnum spurred travel and travel prescriptions but they remained remarkably consistent. James Howell's *Instructions and Directions for Forren Travell; Shewing [how] one may take an Exact Survey of the Kingdoms and States of Christendom* again praises the firsthand "moving Academy" over vicarious or "sedentary" travel, arguing that the "most materiall use" of foreign travel was "to finde out something that may be applyable to the publique utility of one's own country." The traveler, before setting out, should become well versed in the topography, government and history of his own country. Knowledge of France was particularly important because of its proximity, "conformity in

---

[12] *Profitable Instructions* (London, 1633). Letters concerning travel by the Earl of Essex, Sir Philip Sidney, and Secretary Davison were appended to the instructions. Essex in 1596 emphasized "Observations" in understanding "the coherence of causes, effects, counsels and successes, with the proportion ... between Nature and Nature, Fortune and Fortune, Action and Action, State and State" (63-65). For Sidney, knowledge of topography, situation, revenues, forces and fortifications were necessary to assess the strength and defensibility of one's own country (82-85, 91-92, 95-96).

Government ... and necessary intelligence of State." Comparison of different states was recommended.[13]

The Restoration era, which would bring even greater numbers of English gentlemen to the Continent, elicited new guides but familiar advice. In 1665, Edward Waterhouse's *The Gentleman's Monitor* advised those wishing to become informed about foreign governments to "discourse with their Statists, understand the Art of their Manufacturers, and Improvement of their land." Like Howell, he insists that knowledge of "the Laws, Customs and Usages of their [own] Country," prior to foreign exposure was necessary to retain respect for "native English rules and practices."[14] *The Gentleman's Companion* recommends meeting ambassadors and observing "Government of the State and places Civil." The law courts must be observed, particularly the ways in which causes were pleaded, judged and determined. A daily written account of observations, especially those with potential strategic value, was necessary. The importance of knowledge of foreign nations was again underlined by Jean Gailhard in 1678. While Gailhard advised regular visits to Parliament, Westminster, the Exchange and Old Bailey to gain familiarity with English institutions, it was equally necessary to become familiar with the laws and governments of other nations, and it was especially important to understand the "constitutions and interest" of that "potent Monarchy France."[15]

The conventional prescriptions were echoed by the great luminaries of the late seventeenth century. Isaac Newton advised travelers to observe the policies and state of affairs, taxation, trades and commodities, fortifications, and "laws and customs" as well as the "power and respect" given to the nobility and magistrates and "how far" foreign nations differed from England.[16] From John Locke we hear that knowledge and familiarity with the "Laws and Fashions" of England armed the observer to learn the "Customs, Manners, Laws and Government" of other

---

[13] James Howell, *Instructions and Directions for Forren Travell; Shewing [how] one may take an Exact Survey of the Kingdoms and States of Christendom* (London, 1650), 2-5, 14, 66, 112, 117. One of the ten categories to organize observations was "State and Government." Bernard Varen, *Geographica generalis* (Amsterdam, 1650); P. J. Marshal and Glyndwr Williams, *The Great Map of Mankind: British Perceptions of the World in the Age of Enlightenment* (Cambridge: Harvard University Press, 1982), 45.
[14] Edward Waterhouse, *The Gentleman's Monitor* (London, 1665), 346, 347, 348.
[15] [William Ramesey], *The Gentleman's Companion: or, a Character of True Nobility and Gentility* (London, 1672), 55-56; Jean Gailhard, *The Compleat Gentleman* (In the Savoy, 1678) 25, 26, 38, 57, 138-39.
[16] To Aston, May 18, 1668. Stephen Rigaud, *Correspondence of Scientific Men of the Seventeenth Century*, 2 vols. (Oxford: Oxford University Press, 1841), 2: 293.

nations.[17] The pattern was repeated by the late seventeenth-century radical, Robert Molesworth, who suggested that the English were particularly fortunate in that the "middling sort" were often able to travel, making both them and the gentry "useful to their country." Although the English had one of the best constitutions in the world, "exact Accounts of the constitutions, Manners, and Conditions of other nations," were needed so their good Customs could "serve as Models" for England."[18]

Eighteenth-century sentiment was remarkably similar. *An Essay on the Education of a Young British Nobleman* again stresses the importance of looking "abroad into the frame of other States." From this inquiry would "arise a knowledge ... the public interest of Nations or Commonwealths with respect to each other." Josiah Tucker, writing in the mid-eighteenth century again insists that the traveler trace the "various systems of Religion, Government, and Commerce of the world."[19] From the mid-sixteenth to the eighteenth century and beyond, up to date political and strategic information was central to the political education of the early modern English political elite.

III. The empirical description of England, Scotland and Ireland

Surveys or descriptions of England employed virtually the same categories as the foreign traveler in search of political education.[20] The most important early surveys of England were William Harrison's *The Description of England* and Sir Thomas Smith's *De Republica Anglorum*. The former, based on personal experience, eyewitnesses, and "conference ... either at the table or secretly alone," covered the standard chorographical topics—topography, climate, flora and fauna, language, customs, marvels, antiquities and government. Harrison's "description," designed to provide a total picture of England, outlined the division of the country into shires and counties, described the "degrees" of people, the character and authority of the High Court of Parliament, the laws and legal organization. Parliament is characterized as having "the most high and absolute power of the realm, for thereby kings and mighty princes have from time to time been deposed ... laws either enacted or abrogated, offenders of all sorts punished, and corrupted religion either disannulled or reformed." It is "the head and body of all the realm and the place

---

[17] John Locke, *Some Thoughts concerning Education*, in *The Educational Writings of John Locke*, ed. James Axtell (Cambridge: Cambridge University Press, 1958), 321-22; see also 402.

[18] Robert Molesworth, *An Account of Denmark* [1694] (London, 1738), Preface, 252-53, 258.

[19] *An Essay on the Education of a young British Nobleman* (London, 1730), 15-16; see also 21-22; and Josiah Tucker, *Instructions for Travellers* (London, 1758), quoted in Mayhew, *Geography*, 142.

[20] See Stan A. Mendyk, *Speculum Britanniae* (Toronto: University of Toronto Press, 1989).

wherein every particular person is intended to be present, if not by himself, yet by his advocate or attorney." The procedure and functions of each house are surveyed, the role of the Crown in lawmaking described and lists provided of counties and boroughs sending members of Parliament. The law was composed of "statute law, common law, [and] customary law and prescriptions."[21]

Unlike Harrison's multitopic survey, Sir Thomas Smith's *De Republica Anglorum* focuses on government and law. Smith, who served as both Secretary of State and ambassador to France, sought to "sette" a "chart or mappe" before the eyes showing the "forme and manner of the government of England" and how it differed from contemporary European states. English Readers should reject ideal and "feigned" commonwealths devised by "vaine imaginations," and the "phantasies of Philosophers," and judge which states had taken "the righter, truer, and more commodious way to govern," in order to be better positioned to serve prince and commonwealth and to give "counsell for the better administration" of government.[22] Accurate information was superior to political speculation. Smith's account, based on what could "be seen with eyes," described how "England standeth and is governed at this day the xxviii of March, Anno 1565," that is at the time that its present state or condition had been observed. Smith outlines the monarchy, the monarch's relation to the Privy Council, the royal prerogative and the role of the queen in the justice system. He treats the chief legal institutions, among them Parliament, its rules of debate and its relation to the crown, and the common law courts. Justices of the peace are discussed in terms of personnel, duties, organization and procedures and role in the criminal justice system.

The best known Restoration survey of England, Edward Chamberlayne's *Angliae Notitia; or the Present State of England*, was first published in 1669. Chamberlayne too employs the familiar chorographic grid to provide information on the current government and courts of justice, geography, climate, language, religion, attire and diet. Unlike Harrison and Smith he lists current officeholders rather than describing the

---

[21] William Harrison, *The Description of England*, ed. George Edelen (Ithaca: Cornell University Press, 1968), 149, 152-62, 169, 170-71, 180-94. Statute is distinguished from the common law, which is characterized in Cokean terms as "stand[ing] upon sundry maxims or principles ... which do contain such cases as by great study and solemn argument of the judges, sound practice, confirmed by long experience, fetched even from the course of most ancient laws made far before the Conquest, and therefore the deepest each and foundations of reason, are ruled and adjudged for law." For the law, one could use information derived from "general discourse," report, and common hearsay.

[22] Sir Thomas Smith, *De Republica Anglorum*, ed. Mary Dewar (Cambridge: Cambridge University Press, 1982), 144. By 1643, there were eleven English editions and two Latin editions.

functions of offices and institutions. Emphasis on the immediate present and on current data meant that frequent revisions were necessary. By 1738 the eighth edition described the then current condition of trade, class divisions, military strength, crown and government, parliament and the courts of justice.[23]

Socioeconomic topics predominate in Daniel Defoe's early eighteenth-century *Tour Thro' the Whole Island of Great Britain*, a work he characterizes as "A Description of the present state of England." Defoe claims to have been an eyewitness of what he recorded or had relied on others "of undoubted credit" who had themselves been "an eye-witness." He promises a "true and impartial Description" and "the most exact Truth," not romance or panegyrick. He claims to have visited "every Nook and Corner" of England observing and recording agricultural conditions and production, the condition of the poor, manufactures, the nature of the people and natural resources.[24]

The English were also interested in the political and economic conditions of Ireland and Scotland. During the Civil War and Interregnum, extensive land surveys of Ireland were undertaken by William Petty, whose "great Political knowledge ... taught the Age."[25] Petty describes the major institutions of Irish government and their relationship to the English government as well as the Irish political and religious factions. Petty believed that politics required "long, tedious and reiterated Observations and comparisons."[26]

A publication dealing with the "present state" of Scotland contained the standard brief discussion of climate, dimensions, air, soil and commodities as well as a description of its constitution. Scotland is characterized an "Independent Monarchy, and an Imperial Crown" whose "Prerogatives are great." Property in Scotland was secured by law and the people in possession of great "Liberties and Freedoms." Although the author focused on the law and the constitution, like Chamberlayne he lists the more important institutions and offices and their current

[23] Edward Chamberlayne, *Angliae Notitia* (London, 1669). It was modeled on *L'Estat Nouveau de France* (Paris, 1661). See *Dictionary of National Biography*, X, 8-9. Later editions added more political information. In 1708 it was renamed *Magnae Brittanniae Notitia or the Present State of Great Britain*. See also Guy Miege's *The New State of England* (London, 1671). There were editions in 1691,1693, 1699 and 1701.

[24] Daniel Defoe, *A Tour Thro' the Whole Island of Great Britain*, ed. P. Rogers (Harmondsworth: Penguin, 1971), I, 8, 13; II, 520, 664; Preface to XI, 552. See also Clarke, *Between Geography and History*, 45.

[25] William Petty, *The Political Anatomy of Ireland* (London, 1691), "Advertisement." Edmund Spencer's *A View of the Present State of Ireland* (1633) is not written in the descriptive present state genre.

[26] William Petty, *The Economic Writings of Sir William Petty*, ed. Charles Hull (Cambridge: The University Press, 1899), 1: 170-76.

Barbara J. Shapiro

officeholders.[27] This is empiricism that particularized without any concern for analysis or comparison.

IV. Diplomats and empirical political description

Many empirical accounts in the "present state" vein were the work of diplomats who had the opportunity for first hand observation and who wished to bring information to a broader public. Here I ignore periodic, routine diplomatic reports of particular events and negotiations and concentrate on synchronic efforts describing the "present state" of a state. Most reports made by diplomats were unavailable to the public. I focus on the published accounts that contribute to the general availability and circulation of empirically derived information. These publications are typically organized by the same categories as the travel advice genre—geographical features, economic conditions, political and military strength, governmental institutions, current rulers and high officials and political factions.

Diplomatic reporting began as an innovation of resident ambassadors dispatched by the Italian city states and rapidly spread beyond the Italian peninsula. The best known and most admired reports are the Venetian "relazione," initiated in 1425, that often contained a sketch of contemporary government, national characteristics, resources, industry and defenses.[28] Early modern diplomats were thought to need "an observant mind," that pursued knowledge of "the position of various European states, of the principle interests which govern their action, which divide them from one another, of the diverse forms of government which prevail in different parts, and of the character of those princes, soldiers, and ministers who stand in positions of authority." They are required to understand "the material power, revenues and the whole dominion of each prince or each republic."[29] These, of course, were precisely the same duties assigned to the intelligent, observant traveler by travel writers.

Although diplomatic reporting was well developed prior to 1660 in England, we focus primarily on post-Restoration examples because it was

---

[27] A. M. Philopatris, *Scotiae Indiculum: or the Present State of Scotland* (London, 1682), Epistle Dedicatory.

[28] Garrett Mattingly, *Renaissance Diplomacy* (Boston: Houghton Mifflin, 1955), 111-12. Thomas Middleton's play, *A Game of Chess*, indicates that ambassadors were to provide information on fortifications, geographical information of significance for invasion, naval and military strength and state revenues. Mattingly, *Renaissance Diplomacy*, 258.

[29] Monsieur de Calliers, *The Practice of Diplomacy* (London: Constable and Company Limited, 1919), 18, 39, 40-45. See also Phyllis Lachs, *The Diplomatic Corps Under Charles II and James II* (New Brunswick, NJ: Rutgers University Press, 1965), 42-43, 45; Peter Fraser, *The Intelligence of the Secretaries of State and the Monopoly of Licensed News 1660-1668* (Cambridge: Cambridge University Press, 1956).

only then that printed accounts become publically available. Such publications often coincided with significant political developments in the country described or otherwise highlighted their relevance for the English.

One of the best known is Robert Molesworth's *An Account of Denmark*, a publication most often associated with English fear of Continental absolutism and radical political thinking. It is a striking example of how the empirical "Present State" genre might be linked to current political issues. Formerly Envoy Extraordinary to the Court of Denmark, Molesworth claims that his portrayal of the "present state" of Denmark is based on his own observations, those of "sensible grave Persons, or what my own Knowledge and Experience have confirmed to be Truth."[30] In keeping with the conventions of the empirical genres, Molesworth promises to relate the present conditions in Denmark fairly and impartially, "with the greatest exactness possible." Since not everyone was in a position to observe Denmark, Molesworth thought his firsthand account might serve as a surrogate, showing that Danish loss of liberty was an object lesson for the English.

Molesworth stresses the kingdom's formerly elective kingship and frequent meetings of the Estates, with its crucial role in taxation, legislation, decisions about war, peace and foreign alliances, the appointment of great offices, and deliberation concerning royal marriages. Although all these matters once required the "Advice and Consent of the Nation," the role of the Estates vanished when Danish kings became "Absolute and Arbitrary" some thirty-two years earlier. The result of the change was arbitrary taxation, decline in property values, impoverishment of the gentry and peasant misery. Since many living persons remembered its better days, the Danes should be encouraged to "think of methods tending to a Change."[31]

Molesworth suggests that all of Western Europe, once governed by elected kings, developed into "mighty Kingdoms" that had become or were becoming "absolute and arbitrary." Personal observation amply demonstrated that there was "nothing but Misery in the fruitfulest Countries subject to Arbitrary Power."[32]

The Danish legal system is described at length. Among its features favorably commented upon are its one volume vernacular code, low legal fees, efficient legal proceedings, clear jurisdictional boundaries, a salaried judiciary and the bar on removing suits from one court to another. His

---

[30] Molesworth, *Account of Denmark*, 2. Molesworth describes Denmark as it was in 1672.
[31] Molesworth, *Account of Denmark*, 266, 268-69.
[32] Molesworth notes that the current monarch is a "mild and gracious Prince, beloved, if not reverenced by his people." *Account of Denmark*, 42-48, 150.

assessment echoes the Interregnum law reform program and may indicate that Molesworth hoped to revive English interest in law reform.[33]

While Molesworth's condemnation of absolutism has often been noticed, scholars have ignored the fact that he follows the conventions of the empirical descriptive genres, providing information on royal revenues, the army, fleet and fortresses, the royal family, ministers of state and the court. Although Molesworth's account was not the sole example of how the empirical "present state" genre might be combined with a political agenda, it was exceptional in the public response it provoked.[34]

Works by Guy Miege and Gideon Pierreville, both of whom had diplomatic connections, described Denmark's transition to absolutism favorably. Pierreville, General Secretary to the King's Minister at the court of Denmark, following the familiar grid, outlines the powers of the crown, principal councils, provincial government, laws, crown revenues and their sources and military strength.[35] Two "Accounts of Sweden" were also published.[36]

The present state of Poland attracted attention when Polish political developments seemed relevant to the English. Bernard Conner's report on Poland took the form of letters dedicated to important English diplomats. The letter on the "ancient state" of Poland was dedicated to Lord Dartmouth whose "Genius" led him "to inquire not only into the

---

[33] Molesworth, *Account of Denmark*, 233-38. On law reform see B. J. Shapiro, "Law Reform in Seventeenth Century England," *American Journal of Legal History*, 19 (1975): 280-312; S. Prall, *The Agitation for Law Reform During the Puritan Revolution, 1640-1660* (The Hague: Nijhoff, 1966); Donald Veall, *The Popular Movement for Law Reform 1649-1660* (Oxford: Clarendon Press, 1970).

[34] It was soon translated into French and German. The Danish government attempted to have the publication suppressed. William King and Joducus Crull attacked Molesworth in *Animadversions on a Pretended Account of Denmark* (London, 1694), and in *Denmark Vindicated* (London, 1694). The former defends Danish constitutional changes as necessary and as willingly submitted to by the people and rejects Molesworth's maxims as too much like a Commonwealth (58-59, 71). *An Account of Sweden* (London, 1694) notes the "kind reception" of Molesworth's *Account*.

[35] Guy Miege, *The Present State of Denmark* (London, 1682); Gideon Pierreville, *The Present State of Denmark* (London, 1683). Sir William Temple thought the change from elective to hereditary monarch was typical of most Christian Kingdoms. Sir William Temple, *Works*, 4 vols. (New York: Greenwood Press, 1968), 2: 218. See also Jodocus Crull, *Memoirs of Denmark*, (London, 1700); Monsieur Roger, *The Present State of Denmark* (London, 1772).

[36] John Robinson, *An Account of Sweden* (London, 1683); *An Account of Sweden* (London 1694). Robinson was chaplain to the resident in Sweden. The second work, written by a twenty-year resident at the Court of Sweden followed the standard grid, treating natural resources, government state revenue, law and courts, military and naval strength, trade, nature and disposition of the people and the "interest" of Sweden. It emphasized the impact of war on government and characterized the crown as "Absolute a Sovereign, as any Prince in Europe" (97, 109). See also D. B. Horn, *The British Diplomatic Service 1689-1789* (Oxford: Clarendon Press, 1961).

Government, Laws, and Characters of the several Nations you passed through, but likewise to examine nicely into their Maxims of State, and their different Interests; and this, that by discovering the Excellency of some of their Constitutions, and Defects in others, you might likewise and Thinking Patriot, advise our own, Goodness of our Laws, and Wisdom of our Senate of which you are a member." Conner explains how the Poles maintained "liberties, Properties and peculiar manner of Government" as well as their opposition to "any change to the succession of kings without subjecting themselves either to a Despotic or Hereditary Monarchy." Another letter was dedicated to the well-traveled Charles Lord Townsend, who is characterized as giving "constant application to Sciences and Politics," especially to "maxims of State and Forms of Government." Conner's recurrent theme was the value of accurate political information to those engaged in government work. [37]

The Netherlands, as one might expect, given the frequently changing state of its relations with England, elicited firsthand accounts from the sixteenth century onwards. Thomas Overbury's "Observations, in his Travels, upon the State of the United Provinces," recorded during the 1609 peace negotiations, begins with a depiction of the disposition of the people and the country's physical attributes. He suggests that the remoteness of Spain led to the rise and maintenance of the state. The government, which is characterized as "Free State," is described. Attention is given to the Council of State and the Assembly of the States, likened to the British Parliament. "Care" in "Government is very exact and particular," because everyone has "an immediate interest in the State" and this egalitarianism produced democracy. With republican Rome in mind, Overbury writes that the Netherlands exhibited "private poverty and public weal," the signs of a still uncorrupted commonwealth. Like so many on the spot observers, he reports on the justice system, state revenues and expenses and on the strengths and weaknesses of the state. Precisely because it was a "free state," Overbury was uncertain whether it would "subsist in peace, as it hath hitherto done in war." [38]

The well known and highly esteemed diplomat, Sir William Temple, whose diplomatic career centered on the Netherlands, associated empirical knowledge with the government's need "to know and reflect upon the Constitution, Forces, and conjectures among their neighboring States, as

[37] Bernard Conner, *The History of Poland ... giving an Account of the Antient and Present State of that Kingdom, Historical, Geographical, Physical, Political and Ecclesiastical* (London, 1698), 2, 212.
[38] Overbury, "Observations," in *An English Garner, Stuart Tracts 1603-1693*, intro. C. H. Firth (New York: Cooper Square Publishers, 1964). Overbury discussed the reasons for Dutch success against Spain, the framework of Dutch government, the Council of State, the political influence of the towns and the sound administration of justice and finance.

well as the Factions, Humours" and an assessment of the "Interest of the Subjects."[39] His treatment of the Netherlands combines a historical account of their "late Revolutions and Change" with a "Map" or description of "their State and Government."[40] Temple discussed the influence of geography and climate and comments favorably on the policy of religious toleration. He attributes the military disasters of 1672 to a false sense of security and the disloyalty of Holland's burgomasters to the Prince of Orange.[41] Temple's *Survey of the Constitutions and Interests of the Empire, Sweden* (1671) was presented to the Secretary of State at the end of his embassy.[42]

Temple's *Observations upon the United Provinces* make use of his secretary Aglionby's *Present State of the United Provinces*, which traces the origin of the Dutch state to the desire to preserve liberty. The revolution of 1579, according to Aglionby, involved only a change in sovereignty and had not altered the state's ancient laws and customs. Aglionby was interested in the "rise, growth, and grandeur of States and Empires." He remarks on the "marvellous progress of the little State" whose "robust and athletick" constitution "infinitely transcended all the ancient republics" and was little inferior to the "greatest Monarchs of these latter Ages." Aglionby surveys the "State and Government" with a "Variety of Political Reflections," sketching its chief institutions, including the States General and the Council of State as well as the nation's "riches" and "forces." He pays particular attention to Holland's town government and to the East and West India Companies that contributed to the "strength" and "riches" of the Netherlands, and describes the distribution of financial obligations. Aglionby was interested in the conditions that contributing to the "lasting or decay" of commonwealths, speculating that the Dutch "Form and Government, and present felicity" provided some opportunity "to give a guess about its future happiness." Invoking the maxim "Those states that have suffer'd least in their changes, are likely to last longest," he concluded that because there was no domestic interest in political change there was little likelihood of dissolution.[43]

---

[39] Sir William Temple, "A Survey of the Constitutions and Interests of the Empire, Sueden, Denmark. . . in 1671," in *Miscellanea* (London, 1680), 3.

[40] Sir William Temple, *Observations upon the United Provinces* (London, 1673), Preface.

[41] Lachs, *The Diplomatic Corps*, 152.

[42] Temple, *Works*, 2: 218. See Harold Dobson and Kenneth Haley, *An English Diplomat, Sir William Temple* (Oxford: Oxford University Press, 1986). Stoye, *English Travellers*, 278-79.

[43] William Aglionby, *The Present State of the United Provinces* (London, 1669) Preface, 153, 174-75. The Netherlands are characterized as having the most "Liberty" and "Equality" in the world (222-25, 246-48, 250, 252-54). For a negative view see Felltham Owen, *A Brief Character of the Low Countries under the States* (London, 1659). See also Richard Peers, "Description of the Seventeen Provinces," *The English Atlas* (Oxford, 1680-1683), 4; *An*

As one might anticipate, publications describing France and French institutions were popular with the English. Early examples are Robert Dallington's 1604 *The View of France* and Sir Thomas Overbury's "Observations on the State of France, 1609," undertaken during diplomatic negotiations in the Netherlands. Overbury, who reports France as "flourishing with peace," found it "the most absolute of monarchies" because the King made both war and peace, "calls and dissolves Parliaments, pardoneth, naturaliseth, ennobleth, names the value of money [im]presseth to the war; but even makes laws and imposes at his pleasure." The meeting of the three estates is "almost as extraordinary as a General council." As in so much "present state" literature, Overbury provides as assessment of "strengths" and "weaknesses." Overbury describes the French "manner of Government" in typical fashion, paying particular attention to the law. Civil justice in France was "corrupt" due to the venality of offices and because judges were "not bound to judge according to the written Law, but according to the equity drawn out of it," a practice which left judges "without limits."[44]

Royalists traveling in France during the hectic war and Interregnum years had considerable opportunities for observation. John Evelyn, who presented the reader "a succinct Method" for "atomizing" France, insisted on the importance of observing "the mysteries of their Polity." He reports on the nature, powers and resources of the French crown, the officers of state and system of taxation. His anatomy gave special attention to the Council of State, the *parlements*, French forces and fortifications and France's relationships with other European powers.[45] Peter Heylyn, another Royalist exile, dealt with a similar set of topics.[46]

Accurate Description of the United Netherlands and ... Germany, Sweden, and Denmark (London, 1691), 3-4.

[44] "Observations on the State of France, 1609, under Henry IV," in *An English Garner*, 221-32. France, currently the "greatest united force of Christendom" derived from its strength from physical attributes, the multitude of towns and places of strength for armies, financial treasure, arsenals, the size of its army and the "best Generals of Christendom." Weaknesses were lack of infantry and sufficient ships, poor distribution of wealth, the size of church holdings, weak frontiers, and religious differences. For "reason of State" the English were bound to side with France, but France would become dangerous to the English if it controlled the Netherlands. Dallington drew attention to "the pattern of a method of how to discourse of the Cosmography, Policy and Oeconomy of such other Countries wherein you shall travaile." Quoted in Stoye, *English Travellers Abroad*, 38.

[45] John Evelyn, *The State of France as it stood in the ixth yeer of this present Monarch Lewis XIII* (London, 1652), 12-16, 20-27, 38-42, 76-77, 83-85. See also John Lough, *France Observed in the Seventeenth Century by British Travelers* (Boston: Oriel Press, 1985).

[46] Although a staunch Royalist, Heylyn emphasized French tyranny, the subject's lack of liberty, the decline of the Assembly of the Estates, and the misery of the peasantry and praised the mixed government of England. Heylyn wrote that a state without a church was a "Carcass or thing inanimate." *France Painted to the Life* (London, 1656), 136-43, 214-19, 215, 217, 221-29, 231.

The Restoration saw several publications on France. *The Present State of France: Conteining the Orders, Dignities, and Charges of that Kingdom,* first published in 1673, went through several editions. A translation of Nicolas Besongne's *The Present State of France, Containing a General Description of the Kingdom* appeared in 1687. The translator's additions, made "conformable" to Chamberlayne's *Angliae Noticia,* were garnered from observation and "converse in that Magnificent and splendid Court."[47] 1694 saw the publication of *An Historical and Geographical Description of France,* the first portion of which concerned the "French Monarchy and Politics, the Power of their Parliaments, the State of their Nobility and Gentry, and the impact of the Reformation."[48] Still another account of France that included discussion of government and the subject's liberty and property was Thomas Franz's *A Tour Through France, Flanders and Germany.*[49]

The political institutions of the Empire received a modest amount of attention from diplomats. Bernard Gascoigne's *A Description of Germany* criticized the absence of sovereign authority and methods of taxation that enriched the powerful at public expense. An anonymous *Present State of Germany* (1690) was probably written by George Etheridge, who had spent several years in Germany. It too noted the weaknesses of German political arrangements.[50] Abraham Stanyan's 1714 *Account of Switzerland* provided a brief geographical and historical account together with a description of the Swiss government. Stanyon rejects the frequently made comparison between the Swiss Confederation and the Netherlands, suggesting instead similarity to the ancient Greeks. The Swiss, he thought, would be able to preserve their "liberty" as did the Greeks, at least "till such a restless power, as that of the Romans, arise again, and overrun all Europe with its conquests."[51]

---

[47] (London, 1681).

[48] *Popery and Tyranny: or, The Present State of France: in relation to its Government, Trade* .... (London, 1679); J. de la Crose, *An Historical and Geographical Description of France* (London, 1694).

[49] (London, 1735). English travelers often commented on the absolute character of the government, the decline of the estates, the sale of offices, the administration of justice, and the strength of the armed forces. Lough, *France Observed,* 88-89; 91-96, 98-114, 124-161, 162-81.

[50] Lachs, *The Diplomatic Corps,* 154. James Howell's *A Discourse of the Empire of Germany* (London, 1659), which focused on the recent imperial election, does not follow the grid.

[51] Quoted in Horn, *The British Diplomatic Service,* 288-90, from Abraham Stanyon, *Account of Switzerland* (Edinburgh, 1714), 216. Stanyon, a diplomat, lived in Switzerland for eight years. See also Gregorio Leti, *The Present State of Geneva* (London, 1681), 29-37, 64-69; James Howell, *A Discourse of the Empire of Germany* (London, 1659). For Italy see Jean Gailhard, *The Present State of the Princes and Republics of Italy* (London, 1668); Jean Gailhard, *The Present State of the Republick of Venice* (London, 1669). There was little English writing on Spain in the present state genre. Richard Sergier's brief *The Present State*

The Ottoman Empire, of both political and commercial interest to the English, was uniformly characterized as an absolute monarchy, dependent on slavery and a standing army.[52] Richard Knolles's popular *The General History* (1603) described the statecraft, manners, and military system, and concluded with a "brief Discourse of the Greatness of the Turkish Empire." Another early work, Fynes Moryson's *Itinerary* (1617), provided descriptions of the military, finance and government. Henry Marsh's *A New Survey of the Turkish Empire and Government* appeared in 1633 and was reprinted in 1663 and 1664. Henry Blount's *Voyage to the Levant* (1636), which went through eight editions by 1671, described the manner, policies and government of the Turks, while Francis Osborne's more comparative *Political Reflections on the Government* (1656) included "maxims" governing Turkish rule. Paul Rycaut's *The Present State of the Ottoman Empire* (1670) presented a "true System of Model of the Turkish Government and Religion" and "the maxims of the Turkish polities." Rycaut claimed to have utilized documents from the embassy as well as registers and records of the viziers. Sir Thomas Smith's *Remarks upon the manners, religion and Government of the Turks* appeared in 1678.[53]

Although little was known of Russia due to difficulties of language, travel and government surveillance, it, like Turkey, was thought to epitomize autocratic government. Giles Fletcher's *Of the Russe Commonwealth or Maner of Government by the Russe Emperor*, "reduced" the author's observations "to some order," utilized the typical list of topics ranging from physical description to provincial divisions and natural resources. This "tyrannical state" was "without written Lawe, without common justice; save that which procedeth from their Speaking lawe," the magistrate. Fletcher, ambassador to Russia in 1588, compares England, whose "subjects" are not slaves, and are kept "within dutie" by "love, not by fear," to Russia, where the emperor subjugated nobility and people and collected "impositions" and "exactions" at will. All principal matters of state were in the hands of the Emperor and his council. Parliament existed only to ratify the emperor's commands. A corrupt church enhanced imperial power because "superstition and false religion best ... agree with a tyrannical state." Though the current emperor was a

---

of Spain was translated into English in 1594. See also Charles Brockwell, *The Natural and Political History of Portugal* (London, 1726).

[52] Brandon Beck, *From the Rising of the Sun: English Images of the Ottoman Empire to 1715* (New York: P. Lang, 1987), 35-38.

[53] Quotations are from Beck, *Rising*, 78, 79. Rycaut's work, first published in 1666, had eight editions by 1700. His continuation of Knolles's history appeared in 1699, 1701, and 1704. See also Sonia Anderson, *Consul in Smyrna; Paul Rycaut at Smyrna 1667-1678* (Oxford: Oxford University Press, 1989); Aaron Hill, *Full Account of the Ottoman Empire* (London, 1709); Sir James Porter, *Observations on the Religion, Law, Government and Manners of the Turks* (London, 1768); Daniel Goffman, *Britons in the Ottoman Empire, 1642-1660* (Seattle: University of Washington Press, 1998).

fool, a competent empress handled public affairs. He notes that the government fomented noble feuds and points to Russian xenophobia. Fletcher also reports the chief state offices and their functions, and provides information on state revenues, military strength, and conquered territories.[54]

A publication of 1670 viewed Russians as moved by instinct and appetite rather than intellect and reason.[55] Although Collins's 1671 *The Present State of Russia* was the best English account of Russia in several generations, Russia was not treated as a part of Europe in the seventeenth century and, unlike Turkey, was not engaged in expansion threatening to English interests. For these reasons also, the English acquired little accurate information about Russia.[56]

Nor did they have much first hand knowledge of the Far East. What they learned about China they learned from French and Dutch translations. It was generally believed that its huge population was governed with an exceptional degree of centralization, which operated evenly and without obstacles over a vast territory. Its government was thought to be exceptionally stable, open to advice and criticism and staffed by well-qualified officials. Its stability was attributed to Chinese reverence to authority. The Japanese government was characterized as despotic, its population industrious, frugal, cruel and warlike.[57] The English, however, were in no position to determine the accuracy of such descriptive treatments and *An Historical and Geographical Description of Formosa*, which followed the standard pattern, was a complete fabrication.[58]

V. Geography and political information

The "present state" genres we have thus far examined for the most part describe a single state. "Geography," as its name suggests, was

---

[54] Giles Fletcher, *Of the Russe Commonwealth or Maner of Government by the Russe Emperor* (London, 1591). See also *Sir Thomas Smithes voyage and entertainment in Russia* (London, 1605).

[55] *The Present state of Russia* (London, 1671).

[56] M. S. Anderson, *Britain's Discovery of Russia 1553-1815* (London: Macmillan, 1958), 14, 22-25, 28-30, 35-36, 39, 34. See *A Relation of Three Embassies ... to Muscovie ... Sweden and ... Denmark* (London, 1660), an account characterized as more a "survey" than a voyage and treats, among other topics, "Under what Policy they live, and what of Government they had." See also John Milton, *A Brief History of Moscovia* (London, 1682) which contained "a relation of Manners, Religion and Government" (Preface); *A New Description of Moscovy* (London, 1698); J. Crull, *The Present condition of the Muscovite Empire* (London, 1699); Charles Whitworth, *Account of Russia as it was in the year 1710* (London, 1768); Fredrich Weber, *The Present State of Russia* (London, 1722-23).

[57] Marshall and Williams, *The Great Map of Mankind*, 21-24, 87. See also Alvaro Semedo, *The History of the Great and Renowned Monarchy of China* (London, 1655).

[58] George Psalmanazor, *An Historical and Geographical Description of Formosa* (London, 1704).

envisaged as a composite work covering the entire globe, a compilation of material derived from the reports of explorers, navigators and authors of "present state" accounts. "Geography" thus shared many of the aims and characters of the present state genres and frequently offered political descriptions of the included locales. Laurence Echard, who provided "Rules" for a "large and compleat Geography," insisted that it include treatment of "The Government, shewing the Original and Fundamental constitutions, how Absolute or Limited it is, good Properties, Disease or Defect of it, with their Remedies and compared with others." Geographers should cover topics such as military and naval forces and courts of judicature and should provide a general history of the country, "relating all the several Governments, Sovereignties, and Revolutions that ever were." Furthermore the statesman and politician required information on "all the several sorts of Government and Interests in other parts, and by the Knowledge of them is capable of correction of many Faults, and supply Defects of the matters of Policy and State in his own Country" as well as assisting him in matters of war.[59] The English public, from the sixteenth century onward, was offered a variety of "geographies," large and small. Given the need to cover the whole earth, however, geographies, of necessity, drew on the descriptive accounts of earlier observers. These "geographies," which like the descriptions of individual nations were indebted to classical and humanist models, were widely distributed throughout the seventeenth and eighteenth centuries.[60]

VI. Empirical political description, natural history and the Royal Society

Having surveyed the overlapping travel and diplomatic traditions of empirical description and taken note of geography, we are in a better position to investigate the contributions of seventeenth-century naturalists

---

[59] Laurence Echard, *A Most Compleat Compendium of Geography ... Describing all the Empires, Kingdoms and Dominions in the Whole World* (London, 1691) 59, 205, 210-11, 222.

[60] See for example Pierre d'Avity, *Estates, Empires and Principalities* (London, 1615), which dealt "only with politicke and civile matters;" Bernard Varens, *Geographica Generalis* (Amsterdam, 1650); Peter Heylyn, *Cosmographie in Four Books* (London, 1652); Richard Blome, *Geographical Description of the Four Parts of the World* (London, 1680); Sieur Du Val, *Geographia Universalis: The present state of the World; Giving an account of the several Religions, Customes, and Riches of each People: The Strength and Government of each Polity and State enlarged and Englished by Ferrand Spence* (London, 1685); Samuel Clarke, *A New Description of the World or a Compendious Treatise of the Empires, Kingdomes, States....* (London, 1689); Robert Morden, *Geography Rectified: or a Description of the World, in all its Kingdoms, Principalities ... Situations, Histories, Customes, Governments* (London, 1693). See also Mayhew, *Enlightenment Geography*, 19, 26-29, 49-65; Lesley B. Cormack, *Charting an Empire: Geography at the English Universities, 1580-1620* (Chicago: University of Chicago Press, 1997).

and the role of the Royal Society in furthering an empirical approach to government and politics. In this connection, Bacon is an important but ambiguous figure. His "Essay on Travel" is devoid of "scientific" motivation. On the other hand his wide-ranging natural history project, which inspired so much of the research and data collection of the Royal Society, included social as well as physical data. Unlike its ancient and Renaissance predecessors, with their unsubstantiated claims and fables, Baconian natural history was to be built on careful firsthand observation and its participants were to observe, collect and carefully record observations of matters of fact.

Historians of political thought largely have overlooked the Royal Society's interest in and involvement with the collection of political and economic data.[61] From its inception, however, the Society was not only committed to experiment and observation of natural phenomena but to the development of descriptive natural history, an enterprise encompassing the acquisition of political, economic, and anthropological data as well as plants and animals. "Natural history," a much broader term then than now, consisted of a collection of well observed "matters of fact" established by credible eyewitnesses or trustworthy reports.[62] It thus overlapped chorography, geography and the various "present state" genres.

The Royal Society's efforts to gain information was systematized in a series of "articles of inquiry" that provided a set of topics or grid on which to organize observations. These topics overlapped substantially and were sometimes identical to those of Renaissance and later chorographers and travel writers, diplomatic and otherwise. In 1661, and again in 1664, the Society drew up "General Inquiries" to guide the description of "foreign parts."[63] Soon Thomas Sprat was claiming, albeit prematurely, that "The English have describ'd and illustrated, all parts of the Earth."[64] Society members traveling abroad were expected to contribute to the enterprise. Some of these reports included descriptions of political, social and economic conditions along with natural observations; others would not. Members of the Society with diplomatic posts were encouraged to transmit physical and sociopolitical data. The correspondence of Henry Oldenburg, secretary to the Society, is larded with requests for

[61] An exception is the "political arithmetic" of William Petty and John Graunt.
[62] See Shapiro, *A Culture of Fact*.
[63] See D. Carey, "Compiling Nature's History: Travellers and Travel Narratives in the Early Royal Society," *Annals of Science* 54 (1997): 269-92.
[64] Thomas Sprat, *Some Observations on Monsieur de Sorbier's Voyage into England* (London, 1665), 60. When a 1676 letter in the *Philosophical Transactions* complained that the natural history of most countries was still lacking, a correction noted, "now I see very much done in that kind" (11: 552; 12: 816).

information on European and more exotic locales.[65] By 1681 Robert Hooke wished to further regularize the articles of inquiry to insure that observers would record "what is pertinent and considerable to be observ'd."[66]

Sir William Petty's "Method of Enquiring into the State of any Country" perhaps most clearly shows virtuosi attention to economic and political topics. The ideal inquiry, based on firsthand observation, would include information on who held the legislative power and how jurisdictions of the courts were distributed as well as information on agriculture, housing, population, rents and prices. "Matters of fact" relating to money, interest rates, banking, and provisions for the sick and aged were to be observed and recorded. An account of the most flourishing trades, the structure of the professions, typical recreations as well as the pursuit of the arts and sciences would help to fill out the portrait. In keeping with the diplomatic and travel accounts for the instruction of gentlemen, Petty asked that special attention be given to current rulers, their strengths and weaknesses and their friends and foes. State revenues and available military resources were to be recorded as was information concerning who was feared and envied and what alliances and conflicts existed among the powerful in the country. The names of the principal noble families and their interests were to be recorded as were the principal officers of state and reigning court beauties. Although Petty's scheme gave far more detailed attention to political and economic matters than those of Boyle and Woodward, it was not different in kind. Many publications dealing with the "present state" of countries conformed

---

[65] Henry Oldenburg, *The Correspondence of Henry Oldenburg*, 13 vols., ed. and trans. by A. Rupert Hall and Marie Boas Hall (Madison: University of Wisconsin Press, 1965-1986); Thomas Birch, *History of the Royal Society*, 4 vols. (London, 1756-57) 4: 24. Oldenburg translated Francis Bernier's *History of the Late Revolution in the Empire of the Great Mogul* (London, 1671). Oldenburg was ambivalent whether "Moral and Political" information merited the attention of the Society. Carey, "Locke, Travel Literature, and the Natural History of Man," *Seventeenth Century* 11 (1996): 268.

[66] Robert Knox, *A Historical Relation of the Island of Ceylon* [1681] (Glasgow: James MacLehose and Sons, 1911), Preface by Hooke, lxiv. Hooke recommended the collection and translation of all voyages and "Accounts of Countries." Knox, who follows the standard topical grid, acquaints the reader with the "King's way of Governing, Revenues, Military Strength, Wars" (33-60). Boyle's *General Heads for the Natural History of a Country* (London, 1692) did not feature socioeconomic headings. See also John Woodward's tract prepared at the request of the Royal Society: *Brief Instructions for Making Observations in all Parts of the World ... Natural and Civil* (London, 1696), 1, 9. Instructions for travelers included in Awnsham Churchill's early eighteenth-century *Collection of Voyages and Travels* also recommended observation of governments, princely courts, places of strength, trade, manufacturing and "power." (London, 1704), 1: lxxi. See also, Carey, "Compiling Nature's Histories," 272; R. W. Franz, *The English Traveller and the Movement of Ideas 1660-1732* (Lincoln: University of Nebraska Press, 1967).

roughly to Petty's method, though few would cover all the prescribed topics.[67]

Petty, however, wanted more than accurate data suitably arranged. He hoped to learn "How hath the Globe of Earth been divided into Soveraintyes for the 30 last centuryes of the World, & under what formes & species of government." It was necessary to know "the weight and power of each at this day; in People, wealth, territory, shipping, armes, money, reputations, duration, &c." A survey of "all the practiced formes of Civill Governements ... And their Respective durations & achievements" had not, he thought, been yet attempted, let alone completed. Petty hoped for a worldwide series of "Political Anatomyes."[68]

The "political arithmetick" of Petty and John Graunt was also integrated into the Royal Society's research program. Graunt's *Natural and Political Observations* explicitly associates the accurate compilation of information with both the Baconian program of the Royal Society and with policy-making necessities. "The Art of Governing and the true Politiques," required accurate, up to date information dealing with the "land and the hands of the Territory to be governed, according to all their intrinsick and accidental differences." It was necessary to know a country's "Scituation" and geography, its productive capacities and population distribution. A clear knowledge of "particulars" was essential for "good, certain, and easie government, and even to balance Parties, and factions in Church and State."[69]

Richard Blome's *Geographical Description of the Four Parts of the World*,[70] a multisubject, multivolume publication sponsored by several members of the Royal Society, also directed travelers to observe and produce daily written accounts that would include the types of law encountered, their conformity to the nature of the people, who governs, the type of sovereign, and the mode of succession as well as information on the character and aims of specific rulers and their relations with

---

[67] Petty's *Anatomy of Ireland* included information on many of these topics.

[68] William Petty, *The Petty Papers: Some Unpublished Writings of Sir William Petty* (London: Constable and Co., 1927), 1: 144, 175ff.; Petty, *The Economic Writings*, 1: 249. Petty himself focused primarily on wealth and taxation. See *Verbum Sapienti* (appended to *The Political Anatomy of Ireland*). See also Henry Spiegel, *The Growth of Economic Thought* (Durham, NC: Duke University Press, 1971), 124-135; Greenleaf, *Order and Empiricism*, 257-61.

[69] John Graunt, *Natural and Political Observations* (London, 1662), 18, 35. Graunt distinguished political observations, which dealt with "government" and "trade" from natural observations which dealt with disease and longevity. He felt uncertain "whether the information thereof be necessary to many, or fit for others, then the Sovereign, and his chief Ministers." 78-79. John Arbuthnot suggested "true political knowledge" about nations required the subjection of "particulars to calculation." Quoted in Patricia Kline Cohen, *A Calculating People* (Chicago: University of Chicago Press, 1982), 28-29.

[70] (London, 1680).

subjects, favorites and the court. Blome insists on collecting data on
subordinate magistrates, the administration of state business, the strength
of land and sea forces, and the causes and success of past wars. Observers
must itemize the chief officers of state, army and navy and report on the
civil and criminal law and the legal profession. Blome's topical
arrangement indicates how deeply embedded the pattern had become for
conceptualizing states and their governments.

Restoration writers producing "present state" surveys often associated
their work with the Royal Society by noting their membership on the title
page or in prefatory remarks. Bernard Conner, the author of *History of
Poland*, was a member. Edward Chamberlayne, author of the *Anglicae
Notitia*, was an original member and his son, who continued the popular
handbook, also was a member and contributed to the *Philosophical
Transactions*. Aglionby's *The Present State of the United Provinces* was
advertised as coming from "the elegant Pen of a Virtuoso of the Royal
Society." John Evelyn wrote a description of France some years before
the Society was formed. Defoe's *Tour* of England, a "Natural History" in
the Baconian tradition, followed many of the standard topics.[71]

In a sense then the Royal Society was devoted not only to natural
science but to political science and social science more broadly and to
organization of political knowledge and the pursuit of political knowledge
as a means of improving practical political performance. In the language
of the day, however, the words "science" or "natural philosophy" were
more properly reserved for causal explanation and certain knowledge that
had achieved certainty such as mathematical demonstration. The efforts
described here would usually have been labeled natural history,
chorography, geography or "matter of fact."

Although accurate empirical data was proving necessary for both
government and the pursuit of knowledge, English monarchs provided
little financial support to Royal Society projects. They did, however, give
the Society's questionnaires to diplomats leaving for new posts and made
diplomatic channels available to the Society's foreign correspondents.
Letters for Henry Oldenburg, Secretary of the Society, were delivered to
Secretary of State Williamson's office and then copied by Oldenburg who
provided relevant "civil" information to Williamson. The government
rather than the Society paid the postage on these letters. In 1713 the
government ordered that ambassadors, admirals and officers going abroad
should "receive directions for making enquiries relating to the
improvement of natural philosophy."[72] Several issues of the *Philosophical*

[71] For Defoe see Ilse Vickers, *Defoe and the New Sciences* (Cambridge: Cambridge
University Press, 1996).
[72] Lachs, *The Diplomatic Corps*, 154; R. K. Bluhm, "Henry Oldenburg, F. R. S.," in *The
Royal Society: Its Origins and Founders* (London: Royal Society, 1960), 185-86. Reports

Transactions were dedicated to powerful government figures in order to publicize and cement these connections.[73]

The overlapping interests of government and Society in political information or "intelligence" are perhaps best exemplified by Sir Joseph Williamson, the Principal Secretary of State, who, in this capacity, required and sought up to date political and naval information from a wide variety of sources. Williamson, despite a busy political life, was an active member of the Society and served as its president for several years.[74]

If for obvious reasons diplomat members were not active participants in the Society's experimental program, their contribution to knowledge and commitment to Society objectives should not be underestimated because of infrequent attendance at meetings. This group included Sir John Finch, Francis Gailhard, Bernard Gascoigne, Thomas Henshaw, Henry Howard, Duke of Norfolk, Francis Vernon, Sir Peter Wyche, Sir Samuel Tuke, Sir Robert Southwell, Jodocus Crull, Bernard Conner, Robert Molesworth, Gregorio Leti, Alexander Stanhope, and Sir Paul Rycaut.[75] Rycaut provided information on the Ottoman Empire, Finch on Turkey, Italy and Egypt, Gascoigne on the Empire and Sir Peter Winch on Russia.[76] Southwell communicated information to the Society and Lord Henry Howard, Duke of Norfolk, a generous benefactor, whose Arundel House served as the meeting place of the Royal Society for many years, was a diplomat at the Moorish Court.[77] Bernard Conner, a distinguished physician, was elected to membership on his return from Poland in 1695.

VII. Characteristics of the empirical political reporting: of accuracy and policy

The various modes of early modern empirical political reporting shared several common characteristics. The most frequently mentioned norm was reliance on eyewitness observation and credible reports of

---

sent to the Society from foreign sources were sent to Trinity House for use by the Naval board.

[73] Issues were dedicated to the Duke of Buckingham, Lord Henry Howard of Norfolk, Lord Arlington, Lord Ranleigh and Sir Joseph Williamson.

[74] Chamberlayne consulted Williamson when making corrections or additions to the *Angliae Notitia*. H. Leona Rostenburg, *Printing, Publishing and Bookselling in England 1551-1700*, 2 vols. (New York: B. Franklin, 1965), 2: 261.

[75] Several foreign ambassadors resident in England were made members in 1682. *Notes and Records of the Royal Society* 31 (1976): 111-12. See also Stephen Passmore, "Thomas Henshaw, F. R. S. (1618-1700)," *Notes and Records of the Royal Society* 36 (1982): 177-188.

[76] Finch, a professor of anatomy at the University of Pisa and a member of the Accademia del Cimento, was Charles II's Resident at the Grand Ducal court in Florence. Edward Chaney, *The Grand Tour and the Great Rebellion* (Geneva: Slatkine, 1985), 60; Lachs, *The Diplomatic Corps*, 156.

[77] See James E. McClellan III, *Science Reorganized: Scientific Societies in the Eighteenth Century* (New York: Columbia University Press, 1985), 27-34.

earlier firsthand observers, a norm shared by the natural historians describing flora, fauna, experiments and natural curiosities as well as civil historians recording contemporary political events. The priority given to eyewitness testimony was common to all those observing and reporting "matters of fact."[78] One political observer praising the superiority of the "authentique" witnessing of the "Eye" indicated that "ocular view" and personal conversation were the best way to learn about the "genius" of the people, and "the policy and municipal Customes ... It being an Act of Parliament in force among all Nations, That one Eyewitness is of more validity than ten Auricular."[79] Another insisted that "the testimony of senses, and reasoning upon the objects supplied from the senses" was required to "understand the Government and interest of other Nations."[80]

To insure clarity and precision, authors writing in the "present state" and related genres often promised readers a plain writing style, because ornate and highly rhetorical styles were associated with deception and display.[81] A plain style could more accurately represent the truth of what had been observed. For a similar reason diplomatic dispatches were expected to be "stripped of verbiage, preambles, and other vain and useless ornaments."[82]

Reporters of the "present state," like the virtuosi, claimed to make truthful and impartial observation, insisting that truthseekers must try to render themselves "indifferent, free, and disengaged."[83] Petty made it clear that reporters must deal with their observations "without passion or interest, faction or party" according to the "Eternal Laws and measures of Truth."[84] Normative statements about impartiality and impartiality, however, often existed side by side with policy recommendations or pursuit of political agendas and critics of particular travel accounts were quick to charge failures of impartiality.[85]

Reports were obviously not as objective as their authors suggested. A good many were related to current political issues and agendas and relations with foreign powers that inevitably inspired partisanships. Yet

[78] See Shapiro, *A Culture of Fact*.
[79] James Howell, *Instructions and Directions for Forren Travell* (London, 1650), 2-4. See also Theophilis Lavender, *The Travels of certain Englishmen* (London, 1609), To The Reader; Warneke, *Images*, 272.
[80] Walker, *Of Education*, 192, See also 194.
[81] Chamberlayne, *Angliae Noticia* (London, 1669), To the Reader.
[82] Calliers, *The Practice of Diplomacy*, 136.
[83] Walker, *Of Education*, 282.
[84] Edmund Fitzmaurice, *Life of William, Earl of Shelburne* (London: Macmillan and Co., 1875-76), 158.
[85] A critic of Molesworth said he had failed to provide "A true and impartial account" of Denmark and thought it was Molesworth's intention to give us a novel, "whereof of late years some have taken a privilege to intermingle Truth with their own Inventions" instead of "matters of fact." J. Crull, *Denmark Vindicated* (London, 1694), 89, 166-67.

this literature was written and read under the belief that accurate information was important to both foreign and domestic policy initiatives. Those responsible for making and implementing foreign and military policy were concerned with acquiring information on the offensive and defensive capabilities of foreign nations and their current political condition. Appropriate policies in the national interest could only be pursued with accurate up to date information. Thus even when data collection is intermixed with policy considerations, the proclaimed norm is accuracy in matters of fact.

Petty was particularly insistent that accurate data was required for the "Art of Governing"[86] even as his *Political Anatomy of Ireland* contained policy recommendations and his "Report from the Council of Trade in Ireland" provided both information and "inferences" dealing with "remedies and expedients."[87] Petty also drew up "A Register Generall of People, Plantations and Trade of England ... to give the King a True State of the Nation at all Times."[88] Graunt's compilations led him to propose policies pertaining to poverty, beggars, trades, and litigation.[89]

We have already noted how Molesworth's description of Denmark was designed to point out the dangers of continental absolutism and to demonstrate the positive aspects of its legal system. Another publication commented on the unacceptable treatment of commoners in Lithuania, Poland, Bohemia, and some places in Germany and Denmark where the aristocrats and gentry "highly abuse the Commons." These conditions are then contrasted to the "Liberty" and "Equality" of the Netherlands.[90] Descriptions of the Netherlands often considered whether its policies and practices should be adopted by the English and whether it should be treated as friend or foe.

English constitutional issues were also reflected in accounts of Poland. The 1697 *The Ancient and Present State of Poland* was much concerned with issues of royal absolutism, the relations of the Polish monarch to parliament, and the role of the nobility in one the one hand counterbalancing the crown and on the other oppressing the peasantry.[91]

---

[86] Petty, *Economic Writings*, 2: 395-97; *Petty Papers*, 1: 171ff.

[87] Petty, *Petty Papers*, 4: 29, 100.

[88] Information could be used to assess the division of parishes, determine the value of buildings, to order markets and Parliamentary boroughs, assist in quartering solders and victualing armies, tax assessment and adjust the number of justices and other offices. Petty, *Petty Papers*, 1: 171-74.

[89] Graunt, *Natural and Political Observations*, 33-34, 79.

[90] Aglionby, *Present State of the Netherlands* (London, 1669), 350-52.

[91] *The Ancient and Present State of Poland* (London, 1697). The recent death of the King and the "present Election" drew English attention to Polish affairs. Although the monarch could do nothing of importance without the consent of the noble controlled Diet, he could sometimes do "many things not strictly legal" by allying with the clergy or forming a party

Bernard Conner's work on Poland, which followed the "principle Heads upon which we make our Enquiries of any Country and People," raises precisely the same issues.[92]

VIII. Greatness

The question of what conditions were responsible for the "greatness" of nations occupied an important position in the present state genre. Such concerns had, of course, been explored by Machiavelli and also by Botero, whose volume on greatness was translated into English in 1601.[93] Bacon's essay "Of the True Greatness of Kingdoms and Estates" emphasized military strength and argued that Spain, among contemporary states, best embodied the military arts and values necessary to greatness and power. Britain's strength at sea, however, was one of its principal "dowries." Bacon also examines trade and the relations between crown, nobility and commons as relevant to assessments of national power.[94] The author of *Profitable Instructions* (1633) thought "power and strength" were measured by military capabilities. While many continued to emphasize military strength as a source of "greatness," in contemporary European states, growing attention was being given to the role of trade and economic resources. The Ottoman Empire's great military strength, for instance, was seen as undermined by the general impoverishment brought about by Turkish rule.[95] Considering "greatness" in contemporary France and Holland, Petty wrote that in spite of France's vastly greater population and territory its strength was only three times as great, because of Holland's better geographic situation, trade and policy and greater prosperity and sea power. He was confident, however, that England's wealth and strength could overtake that of both France and the Netherlands. On another occasion Petty devised "Ten Tooles making the

from within the nobility. The author followed the "principal Heads upon which we make our Enquiries of any Country and People" (Preface, 3, 13, 16, 18-22).

[92] Connor, *History of Poland*. Conner referred to the current English interest in the Polish election and its "Form of Government" (Preface, iv, vii).

[93] Giovanni Botero, *The World, or a historical description of the most famous Kingdoms and Commonweals therin* (London, 1601). (Reprinted five times by 1630.) See also Botero, *A Treatise Concerning the Causes of the Magnificancy and Greatness of Cities* (London, 1606).

[94] Francis Bacon, *Essays*, 146-55; see also "Of Empire," 116-17. Merchants were a "strength" and a flourishing trade was essential to successful kingdoms. He notes the danger of great prelates and a powerful nobility and suggests that rulers prefer the lesser nobility, who, though they "sometimes discourse high" provide a "counterpoise" to the nobility and could "temper popular commons." Commoners were dangerous only when led by powerful leaders or when religion or customs were tampered with. See Markku Peltonen, "Politics and Science: Francis Bacon and the True Greatness of States," *Historical Journal* 35 (1992) 279-306.

[95] Marshall and Williams, *The Great Map of Mankind*, 16.

Crown and State of England more Powerfull than any other now in Europe."[96]

The contrast between Bacon's and Petty's generations is noteworthy. Both rely on observation and experience, but Bacon's "experience" was to a considerable extent provided by Roman history and only modestly by current economic analysis, while Petty's was focused entirely on observations of the world about him. Roman experience counted for a great deal, but it was being supplemented, and for some replaced, by current observation and current experience.

IX. Interest

Many empirically oriented writers considered something they called "interest."[97] George Stepney's "An Essay on the Present Interest of England" notes the French interest in destroying England and the Netherlands and suggests that interests of king and people were not always identical. Another publication characterized the country in question as having no distinct "interest" separate from that of its king, who encouraged trade and manufacture. There were domestic and well as foreign interests. One reporter thus suggests that it was the domestic interest of the Swedish Crown to preserve the government in its current state and to keep the nobility and gentry "very low." Its foreign interest was to avoid offensive wars, keeping quiet possession of conquered lands, and to maintain friendly relations with France, England and Holland. *The Practice of Diplomacy* distinguished between "the general public interests of the state" and the private and personal interests of princes, ministers and favorites. Diplomats, not surprisingly, were expected to understand the "principal interest of European princes."[98]

Samuel Pufendorf, whose work was translated into English, distinguishes between "Imaginary" and "Real" interest. The first existed

[96] Petty, *Economic Writings* 1: 258-61, 363-73; William Petty, *Political Arithmetick* (London, 1690), 19-23; Petty, *Petty Papers*, 1: 171-74. His "The Weight of the Crown" (1687), which discusses how to compute "the greatness, Force and Wealth of States," emphasizes demography, agricultural production, money supply, the value of exported and imported goods and public revenue. England was already able to defend itself against the "whole power of France." *Petty Papers*, 1: 264-65.

[97] See Albert Hirschman, *The Passions and the Interests* (Princeton: Princeton University Press, 1977); Alan Houston, "Republicanism, the Politics of Necessity, and the Rule of Law," in Alan Houston and Steve Pincus, editors, *A Nation Transformed: England after the Restoration* (Cambridge: Cambridge University Press; 2001), 241-71; Steve Pincus, "From Holy Cause to Economic Interest: the Study of Population and the Invention of the State," in *A Nation Transformed*, 272-98.

[98] Anglionby, *Netherlands*, Preface, 7-10; Robinson, *Sweden*, 159-61, 165; Calliers, *The Practice of Diplomacy*, 45-46. The author recommends the Duc de Rohan's treatise on the interests of European sovereigns (47). See also Temple, "Survey of the Constitutions and Interests," in *Miscellany*.

when princes consented to things that could not be performed without "disquieting and being Injurious to a great many other states." "Real interest" was "perpetual" or "temporary," the former depending on the "Situation and Constitution of the Country and the natural Inclination of the people," the latter on strength and weaknesses of neighboring states. He surveys the "power and strength" and "interest" of various European states.[99]

Considerations of "interest" were to be found in both relatively unbiased and highly politicized accounts. Discussions of "interest" and "greatness," which sometimes resulted in statements of a comparative nature, were increasingly treated in terms of recently acquired information gathered by travelers, diplomats, and naturalists.

X. The grid and empirical observation

Much of this literature both prescribed and employed a pre-existing grid or topical arrangement to organize presentations of matters of fact. One might think of the grid as a frame of reference, a taxonomy or, as Petty and Evelyn did, as an "anatomy." This topical arrangement had a remarkable degree of consistency from the Renaissance onward and was one of the most salient aspects of the empirical genres of early modern political and economic observation. The broadest categories were celestial, terrestrial and subterrestrial. That portion of the terrestrial category that dealt with flora and fauna, topography and geography, easily entered into the European notion of natural history and therefore of what would eventually be labeled natural "science." The material dealing with topography and geography have been similarly absorbed. The portions of the grid that deal with government, customs, and social structure have been largely ignored by those interested in the history of political thought. Governmental topics, like the treatments of plants or animals, might be brief or extensive, according to the interests of the reporter and the size of the report.

The grid provided a conceptual apparatus for thinking about government and politics more generally. Even those travel accounts that were organized chronologically often employed the taxonomy when stopping to survey a particular political entity. The grid often employed the traditional categories of monarchy, aristocracy and democracy and absolute versus limited monarchy.[100] But it emphasized the insertion of

[99] Pufendorf, *An Introduction of the History of the Principal Kingdoms and States of Europe* (London, 1699), Preface, 157-59.
[100] Sir William Temple was unusual in suggesting that neither Britain nor the Netherlands fit traditional governmental designations. Temple believed each country had "a natural constitution or something near it," though many states differed "less in Nature than in

current, concrete and particular data on rulers, advisors, courts and
councils and detailed military and naval information. And it encouraged
multidimensional assessments of the strength and weakness of regimes on
the basis not only of the capacity of rulers and citizenry and actual military
strength but also in terms geographical, trade and population resources.
Although the traditional concern with the greatness and decay of states
remains of central concern, such evaluations are increasingly seen as
dependent upon data, particularly by political, military, and economic
data.

The grid was both a heritage of the ancient world and the Renaissance
revival of ancient letters and a reflection of the worldwide investigations
of the Royal Society. The employment of the grid by educators,
diplomats, and Royal Society reporters suggests how aspects of the
humanist interest in applied knowledge based on experience were
transmitted to naturalists and other empirical writers of the seventeenth
and eighteenth centuries. Despite the myriad changes in political fortunes
of states and the status and interests of the observers of the political and
governmental scene during the early modern era and beyond, the
categories by which observers examined or described what they saw
remained remarkably consistent and created the rudiments of an empirical
political science.

XI. Particulars and generalization

Throughout the early modern era, those of an empirical bent, whether
naturalists or political observers, emphasized the observation of
particulars. Even treatment of "interest" tended to focus on the particular
interests of particular states at particular times rather than on the concept
of national "interest." There was some concern with "maxims"
appropriate to the particular states. Conner's treatment of Poland and both
Osborne's and Rycaut's of Turkey refer to such maxims, often associated
with particular state "interest." Both maxims and interests were assumed
to be subject to modification with changing circumstances rather than seen
as independent variables. Hypothesis and conjecture were sometimes
utilized by natural historians but only rarely employed by those writing in
the present state and related genres. Although there are occasional
statements of the desirability of comparison between states, very few
actually attempted it, and those who did, did so only in a cursorily
manner. The empirical genres of these generations did not produce a
Montesquieu.

Concern with the particular also led observers to emphasize
departures from the norm. If naturalists were attracted to "marvels" and

Name." Like many others, Temple comments on the influence of climate on government.
"Essay on Government," in *Miscellany* (London, 1681), 45-48, 60.

"rarities," political and anthropological observers were similarly attracted to unusual manners, practices and institutions. This concern for the unique meant few political observers would seek political generalizations or maxims common to more than a single political entity. As we have seen, one of the few exceptions was consideration of "greatness" and "strength."

XII. The empirical genres and English political culture

Texts attempting to provide political information on the basis of eyewitness observation were eagerly sought by seventeenth- and eighteenth-century English buyers, and many were produced in multiple editions over considerable periods of time. One of the earliest and surely the best known contribution to the present state genre, ironically, is a work seldom, if ever, associated with empiricism and the truthful description of observed matters of fact. Thomas More's description of "nowhere" or Utopia used the scheme employed by Renaissance geographers and chorographers to provide the matter of fact description of a fictional country. Raphael Hythloday, an intelligent traveler and model observer reports his firsthand observations of a distant land, describing its geography, topography, and cities, and then its manners, customs, education, economic and military institutions and political and legal arrangements. *Utopia*, with its utilization of what would become the increasingly familiar grid adopted by chorographers, geographers, educators, travelers, diplomats and naturalists also mixed description with reform proposals.[101] More's Latin work for a humanist audience highlights the role of the humanists as a bridge between classical and modern genres. Humanists concerned with the education of the political elite, who believed that firsthand experience of foreign nations would have educational value, transmitted the grid to the early modern aristocracy and gentry. Political and economic information gathering also became more directly associated with the needs of early modern governments. Diplomats were pressed for up to date data and their efforts occasionally resulted in publications available to nongovernmental audiences. Their efforts too made use of the grid. The data collection efforts of the Royal Society continued to employ the same categories as government and "virtuosi" cooperated in expanding a growing fund of empirically derived data.

Because this mode of data collection was so widespread over such a lengthy period, we must ask why this immense body of information and the grid on which it was organized has received so little scholarly

---

[101] *Gulliver's Travels* also made good use of the present state and travel writing conventions. See also Francis Godwin, *The Man in the Moone or, a Discourse of a Voyage thither* (London, 1657), 67, 75, 106-107; *The Present State of Bettyland* (London, 1684).

attention. One answer is that the accumulation of political, economic, military and ethnographical data remained scattered among numerous and variously titled accounts. Only a few such as Petty thought in terms of an omnibus compilation of the data. Moreover this widely scattered material was never given collective institutional scrutiny comparable to that given flora and fauna. There was no organization whose primary interest lay in the political, social and economic realm. Nevertheless English audiences, which voraciously purchased descriptive publications of all kinds, were far more familiar with foreign countries, European and otherwise, than one might think if one concentrated on well known political theorists or philosophers, or were primarily focused on the constitutional issues of the seventeenth century and beyond. The English were not uninformed of the institutions and practices of other nations and were not limited to thinking about government and politics solely in terms of the ancient constitution or liberty *versus* absolutism. A vast amount of political information had become the possession of English readers by the end of seventeenth century and that information was organized and classified according to a preexisting grid. While the possibility of error, bias, and even deceit was recognized by observers and readers, there was considerable cultural confidence that the matters of fact described by credible observers and their most reliable informants could not only be believed but put to use. Current empirical information about governments was useful information that supplemented the "experience" derived from reading histories. In practice the "experience" and observation of humanist trained travelers differed little, if at all, from travelers inspired by the norms and goals of the Royal Society.

Empirically derived political observation was an important aspect of early modern political culture. This information, organized around a familiar topical grid, had the advantage of being applicable to all existing states, empires, and colonies. However, the particularizing assumptions of this empirical endeavor did not result either in fruitful comparisons or political generalization. We should recall, however that the accumulation of "particulars" without the search for generalization was characteristic of many naturalists as well. Though some scientific empiricists and experimenters found hypothesis a useful means of deriving generalizations about the operations of the natural world, this practice was not adopted by those surveying political phenomena.

The mode of thinking or knowing about states described here had a lengthy history, and was adopted by humanist educators, diplomats and the scientific community. It was a familiar part of English political writings and thinking. Yet it lies along a vector that intersects the great books by great authors form of history of political thought at only a single point, and then in an atypically fictional version, More's *Utopia*. If we ought to have an interest in the "context" of political thought, this genre is surely part of that context. Indeed, more properly, it was for contemporaries a significant part of political thought itself in that this untheorized piecemeal way of knowing served as the basis for political understanding and political action. Its long history suggests that along with the divisive notions of Foucauldian epistemes and such categories as "Renaissance humanism," and "Restoration science" there are intellectual continuities across time and across disciplines that are as important as cultural discontinuities. The descriptive empirical tradition provided a mode of thinking about political entities for many generations and played a significant role in the way governments, scientists, travelers and educators thought about the political sphere. It must be taken into account by those interested in English political culture and the evolution of political thought and inquiry more generally.

Thus eighteenth-century England received a legacy of a rudimentary, untheorized, deeply and systematically empirical political science. At this point it is tempting to treat the development sketched here as a sort of evolutionary dead end with extinction coming in the eighteenth century and the English social science of the nineteenth century having evolved from a different branch. That conclusion would be premature, however, without further study of eighteenth-century developments that are only adumbrated in this study.

Bossuet, James II and the Crisis of Catholic Universalism

Susan Rosa

Northeastern Illinois University

Abstract

In 1693 the French Catholic bishop Jacques-Bénigne Bossuet, Europe's most articulate defender of Catholic universalism, sent to the papal court a defense of recent demands put forward by James II's Anglican supporters. To facilitate James's restoration, they had insisted that he sign a declaration promising to protect and uphold the privileges and immunities of the Church of England and to uphold the Test Acts. Bossuet's support of the Anglican position constituted an about-face on his part that requires rigorous historical contextualization. Accordingly, this essay first delineates Bossuet's place in seventeenth-century Catholic polemic and his emergence as Europe's most effective spokesman for a Catholic Christendom in order to make clear the unresolvable contradictions between his polemical works on the one hand and his defense of the Anglicans on the other. It then examines specifically Bossuet's relations with England in order to provide an exemplary instance of how his vision of infallible religious authority and international Catholic unity began to lose its cultural appeal, and shows how this process was also reflected in developments on the Continent. By providing a close reading of Bossuet's defense of the Anglicans and an analysis of the political circumstances surrounding it, the essay then attempts to demonstrate the internal collapse of Catholic militancy. Throughout, the essay emphasizes the role of religious factors in the decline of Catholic universalism in order to present a new interpretation of the intellectual upheaval known as "the crisis of the European conscience."

I. Introduction

In April 1693, consigned to exile at Saint-Germain, James II called on the great French bishop Jacques-Bénigne Bossuet, known throughout Europe for a generation as the most eloquent of spokesmen for militant Catholicism, for advice on a question of conscience. At the beginning of the previous January, a proposal had arrived from James's Anglican supporters in England. In order to facilitate his restoration, they were insisting that he agree to sign a declaration promising to protect and uphold the privileges and immunities of the Church of England as by law established; most significantly, the proposed declaration also included promises to implement the Test Acts and under no circumstances to dispense from them.[1]

[1] This essay originated under the auspices of a National Endowment for the Humanities Summer Seminar on the religious origins of the French revolution held at the Newberry Library in Chicago in 1995 under the direction of Dale Van Kley. Without the opportunities afforded by the support of the NEH, the incomparable resources of the Newberry Library and the continuing advice and friendship of Professor Van Kley, whose insightful readings of

Pressed to sign by these supporters and by Louis XIV, James consulted Bossuet as well as several doctors of the Sorbonne, securing from the former an approval of the declaration on February 12. On April 17, James reluctantly signed, despite his own misgivings and the opposition of the English Catholic clergymen advising him, and the declaration was subsequently published in Britain. On May 22, at the behest of James, who continued to be tortured by the pricks of conscience and sought further advice from Pope Innocent XII, Bossuet sent an official defense of the declaration to the papal court. This document exonerates James of any violation of the dictates of conscience on the casuistical grounds that in signing the declaration he is only committing himself to "external" protection of the Anglican Church in order to promote public peace and not adhering to its false doctrine. The implementation of the Test Acts (1673, 1678), which demanded that Catholics who desired to hold public office denounce transubstantiation and take the sacrament according to the rites of the Church of England, and also excluded them from either house of Parliament,[2] is justified on the pragmatic grounds that "the Protestants are the masters," and that in the long run it will be better for the true faith to have a Catholic monarch on the British throne, even if at present he must compromise to get there.[3]

the manuscript have been essential to the construction of the argument in its present form, the essay would not have come to fruition.

During the academic year 1995-96, when a Mellon Fellow at the University of Chicago, I completed the section of the essay that focuses on the correspondence between Bossuet and the Scottish convert James Drummond, Earl of Perth. Entitled "The Mentality of a Persecutor: James Drummond, Earl of Perth, and the Recatholicization of Scotland, 1685-1693," it was subsequently presented as a paper at an international conference on religious conversion held at the cathedral library of Hildesheim, Germany in the fall of 1996 and printed in *Konversionen im Mittelalter und in der Frühneuzeit*, published by the Georg Olms Verlag in 1999. I should like to thank the Mellon Foundation and the members of the Mellon seminar at the University of Chicago for their support. I shall always remember with fondness the kindness and hospitality of the staff at the Dombibliothek, Hildesheim, including especially that of the director, Herr Jochen Bepler and of his assistant, Frau Karin Bury-Grimm. I should also like to thank the Georg Olms Verlag for their permission to reprint this study as part of the present essay. Heartfelt thanks are also due to Gordon Schochet, who shared my original astonishment at the content of Bossuet's defense, and has been a helpful reader of the manuscript ever since, as well as to Orest Ranum, J. H. M. Salmon, and John Woodbridge for their suggestions for revision of an earlier draft.

I have refrained from using "*sic*" in citations; all apparent misspellings reflect the usage of the original text. Unless otherwise indicated, all translations are mine.
[2] On the specific content of the various Test Acts, see John Miller, *James II: A Study in Kingship* (London: Methuen, 1991), 69, 127, 156-57, 181-82; and idem, *Popery and Politics in England, 1660-1688* (Cambridge: Cambridge University Press, 1973), 163.
[3] James's declaration is printed in English and French in Ch. Urbain and E. Levesque, eds., *Correspondance de Bossuet* (Paris, 1910), 5: 527; the contents are summarized in George Hilton Jones, *The Main Stream of Jacobitism* (Cambridge, MA: Harvard University Press, 1954), 33. Bossuet's defense is also printed in F. Lachat, ed., *Oeuvres complètes de Bossuet* (Paris, 1863), 26: 471-77; in Urbain and Levesque, *Correspondance de Bossuet*, 5: 357ff.; and in François Gaquère, *Vers L'Unité Chrétienne: James Drummond et Bossuet, Leur*

It is hardly necessary to point out that Bossuet's defense of James's declaration is not what might have been expected from the great polemicist, who, given the history of his opinions, ought surely to have sustained both the royal prerogative and the cause of Catholicism. Much to the shock and dismay of James, however, it appeared to undermine both. While it might be argued that the defense is not a polemical treatise, but rather a casuistical document produced in response to immediate political realities, I contend that short-term political circumstances are necessary but not sufficient to explain it. Nor do they account for the extent to which the broader cultural and political context of Bossuet's argument in favor of the position of James's Anglican supporters reflected a longer-term transformation in elite mentalities that would drastically weaken the cause of Catholic universalism, which, at least in its papal form, had been moribund for all practical purposes since the Peace of Westphalia, and whose gradual decline as a cultural ideal provides part of the explanation for the failure of James to muster effective Catholic support for his increasingly quixotic attempts to regain his realm.[4]

I further contend that the change in elite habits of thought that marked the last years of the seventeenth century, the period that has been called "the crisis of the European conscience," was not merely a product of growing indifference to religion, but also of alterations in ways of thinking about religion by people who remained religious. In the following pages, therefore, I propose to examine in some detail the trajectory of Bossuet's

---

Correspondance, 1685-1704 (Paris, 1963), 118-22. I use Gaquère's version of this text, which differs insignificantly from that in Urbain and Levesque. On the negotiations surrounding the declaration, see Miller, *James II*, 237-38. On reactions in Great Britain and Ireland, see, e.g., "An Answer to the Late King James's Last Declaration, Dated at St. Germains, April 17, S.N. 1693," (London, 1693); "A Reply to the Answer ... Made to King James's Declaration, Which Declaration Was Dated at St. Germaines, April 17, S.N. 1693 and Published Also in the Paris Gazett, June 20th, 1693," (n.p., n.d.); Narcissus Luttrell, *A Brief Historical Relation of State Affairs from September 1678 to April 1714* (Oxford, 1857), 3: 117; and James MacPherson, ed., *Original Papers, Containing the Secret History of Great Britain, from the Restoration, to the Accession of the House of Hanover. To Which Are Prefixed Extracts from the Life of James II As Written by Himself* (London, 1775), 1: 444-47. For a discussion of the reliability of this collection of documents, whose editor, MacPherson, was responsible for the Ossian hoax, see Miller, *James II*, 243-45; and John Callow, *The Making of King James II: The Formative Years of a Fallen King* (Phoenix Mill: Suton Publishing Ltd., 2000), 5-6. Paul Monod has called the declaration "extraordinary," and though I agree with him about its "Whiggish" character, I cannot accept his conclusion "that [James] was seeking to establish a new image for himself as a promoter of liberty." Promoting this image of James may indeed have been an important part of the strategy of the king's Anglican supporters, but I have seen no evidence that suggests that James himself showed much enthusiasm for it. See Paul Monod, "The Jacobite Press and English Censorship, 1689-95," in Eveline Cruickshanks and Edward Corp, eds., *The Stuart Court in Exile and the Jacobites* (London: Hambledon Press, 1995), 136.
[4] On the declining prestige of the papacy after Westphalia, see Bruno Neveu, "Juge suprême et docteur infaillible: le pontificat romain de la bulle *In eminenti* à la bulle *Auctorem fidei*," in idem, *Érudition et religion aux xviie et xviie siècles* (Paris: A Michel, 1994), 401-403.

relations with England in order to provide an exemplary instance of how the Catholic vision of infallible religious authority and international Christian unity began to lose its cultural appeal. Focusing first on Bossuet's career as a *convertisseur* and representative of Catholic universalism, I examine his correspondence with the Scotsman James Drummond, Earl of Perth, who attributed his conversion in 1686 in great part to Bossuet's polemical argumentation, and set about to transform Scotland into a Catholic country. Here I look closely at both the justification of religious intolerance that informed Perth's vision of a Catholic Scotland, and the phenomenology of his own conversion in order to clarify the ideological and cultural appeal of Catholic infallibility and international Christian unity. With the image of Perth and his reception of the Catholic arguments presented to him by Bossuet in mind, I then show how crucial innovative developments in the Protestant polemic of the 1680s whose origins lie farther back in the history of religious controversy, along with significant negative reactions among educated Protestants and eminent Catholics throughout Europe to Louis XIV's revocation of the Edict of Nantes, began effectively to undermine the cultural and religious attractions of the Catholic ideal.

Finally, I examine Bossuet's defense of James's declaration itself, reviewing in detail its negative implications for the militant Catholic position on a variety of issues, including the justification of religious intolerance, the nature, operations, and rights of conscience, the position of the monarch in the realm, and his duties regarding the preservation of true religion. I also explore the political circumstances of the defense, and attempt to elucidate the reasons for the failure of Louis XIV, the papacy, and Bossuet to support James's hopes of re-establishing Catholicism in England in 1693.

In this context, Gallicanism, considered in terms of its impact on the relations between the papacy and Catholic princes, plays an important role. I conclude that while Louis, who continued on and off to provide concrete and symbolic support for James until 1697, seems in this case to have abandoned him primarily for practical reasons, the papacy had long held James at arm's length because of what it considered to be the Gallican pretensions of the unfortunate king, who, while attracted by the rhetoric of Catholic universalism, had always envisioned himself as the head of a national church.[5] In abandoning James on these grounds, the papacy, while apparently acting in the interests of an ultramontane vision of Catholic universalism against what it perceived as the overweening claims of a secular prince, effectively undermined that cause insofar as it

---

[5] See Paul Kléber Monod, *The Power of Kings: Monarchy and Religion in Europe, 1589-1715* (New Haven and London, 1999), 256-57.

still had any meaning in the world of real politics. Moreover, at the same time, the position of the papacy on James's declaration was equally influenced by an ironic concatenation of circumstances in which Innocent XII, while abandoning one Catholic prince on the grounds of his Gallican pretensions, compromised with another, Louis XIV, in an attempt to repair differences between the papacy and the French king that had divided the two courts for a generation and had undercut the polemical claim of international Catholic unity.

In Bossuet's case, it appears that his admiration for Louis's preservation of Catholic uniformity in France in the wake of the Revocation of the Edict of Nantes contributed to his decision to support Louis's policy toward James by writing the defense. This decision is consistent with a pattern long evident in the relations between monarch and clergy in seventeenth-century France, and constitutes another irony of history: as the French Church became increasingly dependent on the crown to enforce religious uniformity, it lost autonomy, and this state of affairs is reflected in miniature in Bossuet's defense as it moves away from a traditional Gallican argument that envisions the prince as the protector of true religion toward a more Hobbesian conflation of Church and state. And, as has been remarked, it was precisely the identification of Church and state, as carried out in practice by Louis after 1685, that would prove disastrous for the former in the long run, when in eighteenth-century France, "both were associated under a like condemnation."[6] In short, I aim to show how religious factors, including developments in interconfessional controversy, intramural disputes in Catholicism, and the unintended consequences of policies undertaken to preserve Catholic uniformity, contributed to the fragmentation of Catholic universalism.

Finally, as I have indicated, my argument has important implications for how historians have traditionally understood the intellectual upheaval of the late seventeenth century first characterized by Paul Hazard as "the crisis of the European conscience." According to the accepted narrative, European Christianity succumbed during these years to a siege conducted from without, at first subversively, and then ever more openly and aggressively, by the forces of secular rationalism. In contrast, my rigorously contextualized study of Bossuet's defense shows clearly that the change in elite habits of thought that marked the last two decades of the *grand siècle* is equally if not more attributable, as contemporaries

---

[6] See H. G. Judge, "Louis XIV and the Church," in John C. Rule, ed, *Louis XIV and the Craft of Kingship* (Columbus: Ohio State University Press, 1969), 260. For a similar analysis of the churches' loss of autonomy as a result of confessionalization carried out in tandem with princes, primarily in Germany, see Wolfgang Reinhard, "Reformation, Counter-Reformation, and the Early Modern State: A Reassessment," *The Catholic Historical Review* 75, no.3 (July 1989): 402.

frequently noted, to the long-term internecine disputes within European Christendom itself and even within European Catholicism, which, as the century progressed, had undermined confidence in religion and transformed it from a source of consolation into a social, political, and intellectual problem.[7]

II. Bossuet and his place in seventeenth-century religious controversy

It is no exaggeration to say that Jacques-Bénigne Bossuet, Bishop of Meaux (1627-1704), was the most redoubtable Catholic polemicist of the seventeenth century. Born in Burgundy to a *parlementaire* family that had remained staunchly royalist during the Fronde, he began his career as a *convertisseur* in the 1650s, serving the French crown faithfully as it aimed to re-establish religious unity in the realm through persuasion and indirect coercion rather than violence. By 1685, when Louis XIV revoked the Edict of Nantes, and that policy was abandoned in favor of persecution, it was widely acknowledged that the success of Bossuet's arguments in contributing to abjurations among Huguenot aristocrats and scholars was unsurpassed.[8] Despite his stated preference for instruction over violence as

---

[7] See Paul Hazard, *La crise de la conscience européenne* (Paris: A. Fayard, 1961). In challenging Hazard's interpretation, I am indebted to the work of a generation of historians who have interested themselves in the religious origins of the various manifestations of Enlightenment irreligion, though only a few can be mentioned here. Although I disagree with their conclusions, Richard H. Popkin and H. R. Trevor-Roper provided models of inquiry in their studies of the Catholic roots of Humean skepticism and the Erasmian origins of rational theology respectively. I have also benefited from the conclusions of Michael Buckley, S. J., *At the Origins of Modern Atheism* (New Haven: Yale University Press, 1987; and Louise Godard de Donville, *Le libertin des origines à 1665: un produit des apologètes* (Paris: Papers on French Seventeenth-Century Literature/Biblio 17, 1989). Above all, however, I have been inspired by the compelling investigations of Alan Charles Kors and Dale Van Kley, both of whom have shown how internecine disputes among Catholics helped to generate the particularly radical form of disenchantment with religion that marked the French Enlightenment. See Richard H. Popkin, "Skepticism and the Counter-Reformation in France," *Archiv für Reformationsgeschichte* 51 (1960): 58-87; H. R. Trevor-Roper, "The Religious Origins of the Enlightenment," in *Religion, the Reformation and Social Change* (1967; rpt. London: Secker and Warburg, 1984) 193-236; idem, "The Great Tew Circle," in *Catholics, Anglicans and Puritans* (London: Fontana Press, 1989 [1987]), 166-231; idem, "Grotius in England," in *From Counter-Reformation to Glorious Revolution* (Chicago: University of Chicago Press, 1992); Alan Charles Kors, *Atheism in France 1650-1729, Vol. I: The Orthodox Sources of Disbelief* (Princeton: Princeton University Press, 1990); and Dale Van Kley, *The Religious Origins of the French Revolution: From Calvin to the Civil Constitution of the Clergy, 1560-1791* (New Haven: Yale University Press, 1996).

[8] In 1682, for example, in a response to Bossuet's *Exposition de la doctrine de l'Eglise Catholique sur les matières de controverse*, which also ensured its author's international reputation, the Reformed minister Pierre Jurieu complained that this work had been so admired by *convertisseurs* in France since its publication in 1671 that "several bishops have had it printed at their own expense and have distributed it to all Protestants of quality in their dioceses." See Pierre Jurieu, *Préservatif contre le changement de religion, ou Idée juste et véritable, de la religion catholique romaine opposée aux portraits flattés que l'on en fait et*

the most efficacious means of securing conversions among France's Protestant minority, Bossuet welcomed the Revocation and enthusiastically supported its most extreme provisions, including the confiscation of property of Calvinists fleeing France, the abduction of children to insure that they were properly instructed in the Catholic faith, and the billeting of military troops in Protestant households to effect conversions. After 1686, when he proposed that Louis be saluted as a "new Constantine" on account of his willingness to do battle for Catholicism, Bossuet's reputation as Europe's most articulate defender of religious intolerance was assured.[9]

particulièrement à celuy de M. de Condom (The Hague, 1682), Preface. On other contemporary responses to this influential work by Catholics and Protestants in France and abroad, see Amable Floquet, *Bossuet précepteur du dauphin* (Paris, 1864), 302-28; Aimé Georges Martimort, *Le gallicanisme de Bossuet* (Paris: Éditions du Cerf, 1953), 330-41; and Jean Orcibal, "L'Idée d'Église chez les catholiques du xviie siècle," in idem, *Études d'histoire et de littérature religieuses, xvie et xviie siècles*, Jacques Le Brun and Jean Lesaulnier, eds. (Paris: Klincsieck, 1997), 349. For its reception in Rome, see Martimort, *Le gallicanisme de Bossuet,* 333-39.

[9] On the younger Bossuet's preference for instruction over coercion of potential converts, see Martimort, *Le gallicanisme de Bossuet,* 277-91. On his subsequent support of the provisions of the Edict of Fontainebleau, which revoked the Edict of Nantes, see Geoffrey Adams, *The Huguenots and French Opinion, 1685-1787: The Enlightenment Debate on Toleration* (Waterloo, Ontario, Canada: Wilfred Laurier University Press 1991), 23. The epithet "new Constantine" is taken from Bossuet's *Oraison funèbre de Michel Le Tellier* and cited by Adams. On the Edict of Nantes and the revocation more generally, see Janine Garrisson, *L'Edit de Nantes et sa révocation: Histoire d'une intolérance* (Paris: Éditions du Seuil, 1985); Roger Zuber and Laurent Theis, eds., *La révocation de L'Édit de Nantes et le protestantisme français en 1685* (Paris: Société de l'Histoire du Protestantisme Français, 1986); and Philip Benedict, "Un roi, une loi, deux fois: Parameters for the History of Catholic-Reformed Co-Existence in France, 1555-1685," in Ole Peter Grell and Bob Scribner, eds., *Tolerance and Intolerance in the European Reformation* (Cambridge: Cambridge University Press, 1996), 65-93. For the provisions of the Edict of Fontainebleau, see Elisabeth Labrousse, "Calvinism in France, 1598-1685," in Menna Prestwich, ed., *International Calvinism 1541-1715* (Oxford: Oxford University Press, 1985), 285-87.

For Bossuet's biography, see, most recently, Jean Meyer, *Bossuet* (Paris: Plon, 1993); also useful are Jacques Le Brun, *Bossuet* (Paris: Desclée de Brouwer, 1970); and Amable Floquet, *Etudes sur la vie de Bossuet* (Paris, 1855); for an account of Bossuet's background, see Martimort, *Le gallicanisme de Bossuet,* 129-45; for his intellectual formation, see Thérèse Goyet, *L'Humanisme de Bossuet* (Paris: Klincksieck, 1965); for his relations with Louis XIV, see Augustin Gazier, *Bossuet et Louis XIV (1662-1704): Etude historique sur le caractère de Bossuet* (Paris, 1914); for his place in the history of religious controversy, see Owen Chadwick, *From Bossuet to Newman* (Cambridge: Cambridge University Press, 1987), esp. 21-49; and the classic study by Alfred Rébelliau, *Bossuet, Historien du Protestantisme* (Paris, 1891).

Most notable among Bossuet's aristocratic converts were the Maréchal de Turenne (1668) and his nephews, the Maréchal de Duras, the Maréchal de Lorges (1669), and the Prince de Tarente (1670), and his niece, Mlle. de Duras (1678). Other eminent individuals who attributed their conversions to Bossuet included Louis de Courcillon de Dangeau, a descendant of DuPlessis-Mornay, and the Reformed minister and future Catholic polemicist, Isaac Papin. Outside France, Bossuet's converts included the Danish botanist Nicholas Steno, and the Scotsman James Drummond, Earl of Perth, who will be discussed below. On the

Though Bossuet never left France, his polemical writings, as I have indicated, were well known in Protestant countries, where Catholic circles working to obtain conversions among the educated population ensured that they were quickly translated and efficiently circulated.[10] Even before the publication in 1688 of the notorious *Histoire des Variations des Eglises Protestantes*, which was reprinted four times before his death in 1704, and ten times during the eighteenth century, the great bishop's international reputation rested on Latin, Dutch, and English versions of two other masterpieces of controversy, the *Exposition de la doctrine de l'Eglise Catholique sur les matières de controverse*, mentioned above, and the *Conférence avec M. Claude, Ministre de Charenton, sur la matière d'Eglise*, first published in 1678.[11]

These works derived their effect less from Bossuet's originality, than from the consummate skill with which he manipulated polemical strategies developed by his predecessors. The case against the Reformers in the *Histoire des Variations*, for example, depends on arguments elaborated in the earliest years of the Reformation, and deployed with increasing frequency during the second half of the sixteenth century, when controversy between Catholics and Protestants began to focus less on the content of disputed doctrines than on the credibility of the spiritual authority proposing them, and thus on the question of how Christ's true Church can be known. On the Catholic side of this polemic, the need to refute the Protestant charge that Rome could not claim to be the true Church because she had corrupted ancient traditions and introduced novelties in doctrine and worship contributed, among other factors, to a move away from dogmatic toward historical, or positive, theology, especially among Gallicans. Over time this historical emphasis was reinforced and turned in a secularizing direction by the ever more urgent

conversions of Turenne and Tarente, see Susan Rosa, "'Il était possible aussi que cette conversion fût sincère': Turenne's Conversion in Context," *French Historical Studies* 18, no.3 (Spring 1994): 632-67; and idem, "The Conversion of Henri-Charles de la Trémoïlle, Prince de Tarente, 1670," *Historical Reflections/Réflexions Historiques* 21, no.1 (Winter 1995): 57-77. On Steno, see, most recently, Jonathan Israel, *Radical Enlightenment: Philosophy and the Making of Modernity 1650-1750* (Oxford: Oxford University Press, 2001), esp. 43-44 and 507-509.

[10] For an explanation of how this process worked in the United Provinces, Germany, and Sweden, and a contemporary Protestant reaction to its success, see J. A. G. Tans, *Bossuet en Hollande* (Paris: A. G. Nizet, 1949), 61-64, and Jurieu, *Préservatif*, Preface. For the case of England, see below.

[11] Jacques-Bénigne Bossuet, *Histoire des Variations des Eglises Protestantes*, in *Oeuvres complètes*, 14 (entire), and 15: 1-181; *Exposition de la doctrine de l'Eglise Catholique sur les matières de controverse*, in *Oeuvres complètes*, 13: 57-105; *Conférence avec M. Claude, Ministre de Charenton, sur la matière d'Eglise*, in *Oeuvres complètes*, 13: 499-563. On the printing history of the *Histoire des Variations*, see Elisabeth Israels Perry, *From Theology to History: French Religious Controversy and the Revocation of the Edict of Nantes* (The Hague: M. Nijhoff, 1973), 20, n. 24. For the various editions and translations of the *Exposition* and the *Conférence*, see below.

need to confront laymen who tended to be less impressed by formal theological demonstrations than by arguments drawn from worldly contexts.[12] Specifically, the new constraints of controversy encouraged Catholic polemicists to build their defenses of Roman claims to ecclesiological and doctrinal authority more and more exclusively on reason and common sense, on the presentation of historical "facts," and on appeals to other areas of secular experience, such as politics and law, often at the expense of the sources of argumentation, i.e., Scripture and tradition, peculiar to positive theology properly speaking. Strategies that reflected this turn included an increasingly historical emphasis in the rationalized polemic based on the *notae*, or "marks" of the true church, whose origins date to the early years of the Reformation, and the argument of prescription, manipulated most effectively by the seventeenth-century Gallicans and Jansenists Antoine Arnauld and Pierre Nicole, which sought to ground the truth of Roman doctrines in their historical continuity.[13] The *Histoire des Variations* represents the culmination of these developments. As the title indicates, Bossuet presents a battery of historical evidence to substantiate the charge of Protestant "novelty," and appeals to the common sense assumption of educated readers that truth is synonymous with age, unity, and universality in order to suggest that the "separation" of Protestants from the Roman discipline, their disagreements among themselves, and the political rebellions that mark their history are sure signs that they have embraced falsehood. In contrast, only the Roman church—ancient, unchanging, and truly catholic—possesses the "marks" that will enable a believer to identify it as Christ's true church, "outside which there is no salvation."[14]

In the *Exposition*, Bossuet also focuses on the issue of Protestant

[12] On this development, see Barbara Donagan, "The York House Conference Revisited: Laymen, Calvinism, and Arminianism," *Historical Research: The Bulletin of the Institute of Historical Research* 64 (1991): 319.

[13] See for example *La petite perpétuité de la foi de L'Église catholique touchant l'Eucharistie avec la réfutation de l'écrit d'un ministre contre ce traité, divisée en trois parties, Paris, 1672,* in *Oeuvres de Messire Antoine Arnauld,* 12 (Paris, 1777), 75-208. The "ministre" in question was Jean Claude, who will be discussed below.

[14] According to Hubert Jedin, the first monograph on the marks of the true Church was written by the Hessian Franciscan Nikolaus Herborn in 1529. See Hubert Jedin, "Zur Entwicklung des Kirchenbegriffs im 16. Jahrhundert," in *Relazioni del X Congresso Internazionale di Scienze Storiche, 4: Storia Moderna* (Florence, 1955), 67. The indispensable work on the marks of the Church, or *notae*, is Gustave Thils, *Les notes de l'Eglise dans l'apologétique depuis la Réforme* (Gembloux, 1937). On the turn from dogmatic to historical argumentation in sixteenth-century religious controversy, see Pontien Polman, *L'élément historique dans la controverse religieuse du XVIe siècle* (Gembloux, 1932); for the seventeenth century, see Perry, *From Theology to History*; Rémi Snoeks, *L'argument de tradition dans la controverse eucharistique entre catholiques et réformés français au XVIIe siècle* (Louvain, 1951); and René Voeltzel, *Vraie et fausse Eglise selon les théologiens protestants du XVIIe siècle* (Paris, 1956).

"separation," but approaches it from a different angle, employing a two-pronged strategy developed by the Gallican polemicists François Véron (1578-1649) and Cardinal Richelieu.[15] First, following Véron's method exactly, he aims to distinguish the Catholic articles of faith—identified by him with the decrees of the Council of Trent and the doctrines contained in the *Professio fidei* of Pius IV—from "matters disputed in the schools."[16] This distinction enables him to argue further that Protestant "separation" from Rome is the unfortunate and unnecessary result of a series of misunderstandings: in other words, the Reformers have consistently mistaken the unofficial positions of individual theologians on controverted issues like the nature of the pope's spiritual and temporal authority, for the public declarations of the universal Church, which alone are enjoined on believers *de fide*. Second, with this crucial distinction in place, and relying on arguments from the everyday use of language, Bossuet contends that the remaining disagreements among the confessions can be reduced to logomachies. As before, his aim is to show that Protestants had no legitimate cause for abandoning the Roman Church.

In the *Conférence avec M. Claude*, the "separation" of the reformers from the "ancient discipline" once again occupies Bossuet's attention, this time from the perspective of its consequences: in abandoning the Roman Church, he argues, Protestants have developed no spiritual authority adequate to prevent endless sectarian disputes and their inevitable result, civil disorder. With this final claim—reiterated more directly in the *Histoire des Variations*—that religious dissent generates not only schism but political rebellion, Bossuet again exploits a theme that, like a ground bass, had long formed a foundation for the rhetorical and dialectical improvisations of Catholic polemic. During the mid-sixteenth century, Catholic controversialists had relied on the early history of the Reformation to argue that Protestant theology, with its principle of the independent interpretation of Scripture, discouraged respect for spiritual authorities and thereby undermined moral discipline among believers,

[15] François Véron, *Méthodes de traiter les controverses*, Paris, 1638; idem, *Règle générale de la foi catholique separée de toutes autres doctrines* (Paris, 1646); and Cardinal de Richelieu, *Traitté qui contient la méthode la plus facile et la plus asseurée pour convertir ceux qui se sont separez de l'Eglise*: (Paris, 1657 [1651]). Véron's works were extremely influential among Gallican polemicists in England and in the Empire; see for example Serenus Cressy, *Exomologesis or A faithful Narration of the Occasion and Motives of the Conversion unto Catholique Unity of Hugh-Paulin de Cressy* (Paris, 1647); Henry Holden, *Divinae Fidei Analysis seu de fidei christianae resolutione* (Paris, 1652); and Adrian and Peter Walemburch, *Tractatus generales de controversiis fidei* (Cologne, 1669). For Véron's place in the history of polemical theology, see Johannes Beumer S.J., "Zu den Anfängen der neuzeitlichen Kontroverstheologie: Die *Regula fidei* des Franciscus Veronius," *Catholica* 16e année, no.1 (1963): 25-43. On Richelieu's *Traitté*, see Pierre Blet S. J., "Le plan de Richelieu pour la réunion des Protestants," *Gregorianum* 48, no.1 (1967): 100-29.
[16] Bossuet, *Exposition*, 51, 103.

while its "republican" ecclesiology provided a model of government alternative to monarchy, thereby subverting the the authority of secular magistrates by example.[17] And this theme made itself heard all the more aggressively in the seventeenth century as Catholic controversialists attempted to prove to rulers of absolutist inclination that Catholics were better subjects and lovers of monarchy than Protestants, and collectively rushed to repudiate the radical political theories native to their own tradition that had sustained the papal deposing power which in any case had become a dead letter after the Peace of Westphalia. As Bossuet would put it in a letter to cardinal d'Estrées of 1681, "it seems to me that there is nothing that constitutes a greater obstacle to the conversion of heretical kings than ... ultramontane opinions. After all, what sovereign prince would want to give himself over to a master who could take away his kingdom by decree?"[18]

As Bossuet's remark indicates, this polemic had been forged in significant part to encourage the conversion of kings, whose change of religion, it was thought, would insure the recatholicization of their realms. But it also made a remarkable impact on elite publics in Protestant Europe, bringing in converts, as Owen Chadwick has remarked, as did no other arguments of the century.[19] Not only did it provide a convenient procedural means of discovering which church one needed to belong to in order to be saved,[20] it also reassured its audience that truth was accessible,

---

[17] For an excellent discussion of how these themes were exploited by Catholic polemicists in mid-sixteenth-century England, Peter Holmes, *Resistance and Compromise: The Political Thought of the Elizabethan Catholics* (Cambridge: Cambridge University Press, 1982), 70-78. In the context of intramural disputes among Catholics over the nature of ecclesiastical government and the location of authority in the Church, ultramontanes often criticized Gallican conciliarism—i.e, the claim that Catholic infallibility was a product of the decisions of general councils and not of the independent decrees of popes—as amounting to a subversively "aristocratic" model of government. Gallican polemicists, however, as opposed to some Gallican theorists, never completely abandoned the monarchical and hierarchical vision of the Church, whose spiritual unity and strength is embodied and reinforced in the rule of one. For an example, see Bossuet, *Sermon sur l'unité de l'Église*, where, in a common distinction between absolute and despotic rule, the pope is implicitly compared to a monarch whose prerogatives are limited by the fundamental laws of his realm. See Bossuet, *Oeuvres complètes*, 11: 592-601, esp. 600. On the suppression of Gallican/ultramontane hostilities in the international polemic addressed to Protestants, see below.

[18] Bossuet, *Lettre au cardinal d'Estrées*, Dec., 1681, cited in Martimort, *Le gallicanisme de Bossuet*, 287.

[19] Chadwick, *From Bossuet to Newman*, 15. For a discussion of the symbolic and practical effects of international Catholic efforts to return Protestant elites to the Roman fold, see Rosa, "Turenne's Conversion in Context," 635-36.

[20] The attraction of this component of Catholic argumentation is quite evident in the following statement by the Reformed minister Claude Pajon: "The question is ... not precisely to know which are the truths of their religion or ours, but only by what method one can decide this matter without making a mistake and in what way one can distinguish among all the Christian sects, that one where truth is to be found." (Cited in René Voeltzel, *Vraie et*

unchanging, and easily distinguishable from error, and evoked an image of international Christianity that spoke to their preoccupation with unity—that buzzword of the century denoting a metaphysical ideal inherited from humanism which privileged the universal over the particular and permanence over change.[21] In this context, the Gallican polemicists, with Bossuet at their head, proved ironically to be the most effective of foot soldiers in the international Catholic cause. That was because crucial Gallican positions which alienated them from their ultramontane opponents within the Church, such as the conviction that Catholic tradition was limited to the writings of the Fathers of the first few centuries of Christianity and to the decrees of Councils before Trent, and the opposition to the plenitude of papal power based on that understanding of tradition, were the very ones they exploited to appeal to a European-wide audience of potential converts, many of whom considered the claims of the papacy to absolute spiritual—to say nothing of temporal—power an immovable stumbling block, but were willing to accept the Holy See as a symbol of religious unity.[22] Moreover, in the context of polemic, Gallicans set aside their suspicions of the Council of Trent as the work of the papacy. As Bossuet's polemical writings testify, they argued, somewhat paradoxically, that only the decrees of that Council were to be enjoined on new converts *de fide*, and dismissed contested doctrines as merely temporary and contingent disagreements that were the product of "scholastic" disputation, thereby creating an impression of unity in the Church that, while perhaps marked by a potentially subversive tendency toward doctrinal minimalism, could be usefully deployed against the all too evident disagreements among the Protestant confessions. Such was the impact of this polemic that even the papacy, though it had condemned a work by Véron in 1641, extolled the merits of Bossuet's *Exposition* and in 1678 granted an imprimatur to the official Italian translation, which was sent to the bishop accompanied by a congratulatory letter from Innocent XI—an opponent of Gallicanism if there ever was one—praising the work

---

fausse Eglise selon les théologiens protestants du XVIIe siècle, 140.)

[21] On the content of late humanism in Protestant Europe, see R. J. W. Evans, *The Wechel Presses: Humanism and Calvinism in Central Europe, 1572-1627* (Oxford: Oxford University Press, 1975). Evans argues that the late humanist world view was marked not only by a continuing fascination with the classical age, but also by a cosmopolitan ideal that entailed a profound concern with religious unity and harmony, a respect for traditional authority, and a conception of history that regarded it as "the progressive unfolding of what was given and unchanging." (8-10, 12, 39-43.) On the humanist current in early seventeenth-century England, see 25.

[22] For an excellent recent summary of the disagreements between Gallicans and ultramontanes on the issue of tradition, see Henry Phillips, *Church and Culture in Seventeenth-Century France* (Cambridge: Cambridge University Press, 1997), 115-26. For a more complete survey, see George H. Tavard, *La tradition au xviie siècle, en France et en Angleterre* (Paris; Éditions du Cerf, 1969); and idem, *The Seventeenth-Century Tradition: A Study in Recusant Thought* (Leiden: Brill, 1978.)

for "the method and wisdom which make it suitable for instructing readers briefly and efficiently, and for drawing from even the most stubborn of them a firm avowal of the truths of the faith." And later, in 1683, at the height of the dispute between Louis XIV and Innocent XI over the Gallican articles, the French ambassador succeeded in dissuading the pope from condemning the *Exposition* in a fit of pique on the grounds that "the reunion of the Protestants would be compromised."[23]

It is therefore important to consider two contexts when assessing the impact of Gallicanism on the fate of the seventeenth-century Catholic Church, and to understand, as will become evident below, that they occasionally overlapped in complex and unpredictable ways: first, the context of the disputes internal to Catholicism that centered on the claims of royal and episcopal Gallicanism, which supported the cause of the authority of national churches at the expense of that of the papacy; and second, the context of international Catholic polemic. Here, as Bossuet's comment about heretical kings clearly demonstrates, Gallicans proved themselves to be as dedicated as their ultramontane opponents to the aim of Catholic reconquest, combining an aggressive support of absolute monarchy with an equally vociferous commitment to Catholic universalism which, moreover, was frequently espoused by eminent Catholic converts.[24] In short, when it came to the cause of reclaiming lost brethren, intramural contestations were suspended as Gallicans and ultramontanes alike worked to perfect a rhetoric of Catholic unity and universality, and to range the Church on the side of royal and imperial authority.

Years after the publication of the *Histoire des Variations*, the short-lived conversion of the young Edward Gibbon testified to the rhetorical power of Catholic arguments and their continuing attraction to educated people in England, where, in his polemical persona, Bossuet in particular had long been castigated by Protestants as "Goliath."[25] Looking back at

---

[23] On the condemnation of Véron, see Beumer, "Zu den Anfängen der neuzeitlichen Kontroverstheologie," 38-39 and note 58, and Martimort, *Le gallicanisme de Bossuet*, 336; on Innocent XI and the *Exposition*, see Martimort, 334-39.

[24] See for example, *The Discreet Catholic*, by Ernst v. Hessen-Rheinfels, a German princeling who had converted to Catholicism in 1651. In this treatise of 1666, he elaborated a vision of a rehabilitated Christendom composed of national Churches overseen by an international tribunal of Catholic princes, to which Protestants would not be admitted. For a discussion, see Heribert Raab, "Der 'Discrete Catholische' des Landgrafen Ernst von Hessen-Rheinfels (1623-1693): Ein Beitrag zur Geschichte der Reunionsbemühungen und der Toleranzbestrebungen im 17. Jahrhundert," *Archiv für Mittelrheinische Kirchengeschichte* 19 (1967): 175-98.

[25] See for example Jean Claude, *Mr. Claude's Answer to Monsieur de Meaux's Book Intituled A Conference with Mr. Claude. With His Letter to a Friend Wherein He Answers a Discourse of M. de Condom, Now Bishop of Meaux, Concerning the Church* (London, 1687), Translator's Preface, 24; and G. Hicks, Dean of Worcester, to William Wake, 7 July, 1687, cited in G. Lambin, "Les rapports de Bossuet avec l'Angleterre (1672-1704)," *Bulletin du*

his flirtation with Rome, the older Gibbon, writing in 1789, and anxious to distance himself from the callow Oxford student who had succumbed to Bossuet's eloquence, gave the following account of the episode, which despite its ironic attempt to reduce the great bishop's polemical triumph to a mere rhetorical deception, provides a usefully concise statement of the content of his arguments:

> I read, I applauded, I believed: the English translations of two famous works of Bossuet, Bishop of Meaux, *The Exposition of the Catholic Doctrine*, and the *History of the Protestant Variations*, achieved my conversion, and I surely fell by a noble hand. I have since examined the originals with a more discerning eye, and shall not hesitate to pronounce that Bossuet is indeed a master of all weapons of controversy. In the *Exposition*, a specious apology, the orator assumes, with consummate art, the tone of candour and simplicity: and the ten-horned Monster is transformed, at his magic touch, into the milk-white hind, who must be loved as soon as she is seen. In the *History*, a bold and well-aimed attack, he displays with a happy mixture of narrative and argument, the faults and follies, the changes and contradictions of our first reformers; whose variations (as he dextrously contends) are the mark of heretical error, while the perpetual unity of the Catholic Church is the sign and test of infallible truth.[26]

With his evocative reference to the "milk-white hind," Gibbon calls to mind the controversy surrounding the conversion in 1687 of that other eminent British man of letters and reader of the *Exposition*, John Dryden, and in so doing returns us to the atmosphere of confessional clamor that accompanied the rise to power of James II.[27]

Bibliophile (Dec. 1909): 541.

[26] Edward Gibbon, *Memoirs of My Life* (London: Penguin 1990), 85-86. It should be noted that in the *Memoirs* Gibbon generally takes the word "specious" to mean truly "lovely," or "resplendent with beauty" and not, as we do, only apparently or deceptively so. This usage is quite consistent with his intentions in the passage: apologies, in his view, are mere rhetorical exercises, and he means to acknowledge Bossuet's excellence as a rhetorician. Gibbon's youthful conversion took place in 1752.

[27] Gibbon is of course referring to *The Hind and the Panther*, Part I, l.33-34. (See Earl Miner, ed., *The Works of John Dryden*, 3 [Berkeley: University of California Press, 1969].) In this apology for Catholicism masquerading as a beast fable, the Hind represents Catholic truth, which "has such a face and such a meen / As to be loved needs only to be seen." Dryden's famous line echoes Bossuet's argument in the *Exposition* that those who reject Catholic doctrine do not understand it correctly, as well as James II's conviction that a royal declaration of indulgence, by allowing the unfettered practice of Catholicism, would make its

As is well known, James had announced his own conversion to Catholicism in 1672, and in 1680, at the height of the Exclusion Crisis, had written an account of it showing how he had become convinced that the English Church was guilty of schism.[28] Once James became king and had the opportunity to promote his beloved new religion, it was therefore natural for him to supplement his proposed institutional reforms in favor of Catholicism by ensuring that the works of Bossuet, who best expressed the arguments that he himself had found persuasive, were broadly circulated. Although the *Exposition*, for example, had been translated into

superiority apparent to all. In a letter of November 7, 1699 to his Protestant cousin, Elizabeth Steward, Dryden showed that he had also been influenced by the argument that variation was a sign of error:

> I can neither take the Oaths, [he wrote] nor forsake my Religion, because I know not what church to go to if I leave the Catholique; they are all so divided amongst themselves in matters of faith, necessary to salvation: yet all assumeing the name of Protestants. May God be pleased to open your Eyes, as he has open'd mine. Truth is but one; and they who have once heard of it, can plead no Excuse, if they do not embrace it.

(Cited in Philip Harth, *Contexts of Dryden's Thought* [Chicago: University of Chicago Press, 1968], 244.) Harth's *Contexts*—especially 264-91—contains by far the best discussion of Dryden's conversion. But for different views, see Louis I. Bredvold, *The Intellectual Milieu of John Dryden* (Ann Arbor: University of Michigan Press, 1966 [1934]); and idem, "Notes on John Dryden's Pension," *Modern Philology* 30 (1933): 267-74. See also Victor Hamm, "Dryden's *The Hind and the Panther* and Roman Catholic Apologetics," *PMLA* 83 (1968): 400-15; James Anderson Winn, *John Dryden and His World* (New Haven: Yale University Press, 1987), 405-17; and Susan Rosa, "The Conversion of John Dryden," unpublished paper delivered at the annual meeting of the American Society for Eighteenth-Century Studies, Charleston, SC, March 1994. For recent analyses that usefully emphasize the issues of policy and patronage involved in Dryden's conversion and subsequent support of James, see Steven N. Zwicker, "The Paradoxes of Tender Conscience," *ELH* 63 (1996): 851-69, and idem, *Lines of Authority: Politics and English Literary Culture, 1649-1689* (Ithaca, NY: Cornell University Press, 1993), 174-75.

[28] This account is reproduced in The Rev. J. S. Clarke, ed., *The Life of James the Second, King of England, etc. Collected out of Memoirs Writ of His Own Hand* (London, 1816), 2: 629-31. See also John Miller, *James II*, 57; and idem, *Popery and Politics*, 109. For a discussion of the history of James's *Memoirs* and the reliability of Clarke's *Life*, see Miller, *James II*, 243-45; and most recently Callow, *The Making of King James II*, 1-31.

As I have indicated, James's conviction was by no means unique among educated converts, and Protestant polemicists recognized that the issue of separation provided the strongest argument against the Reformers. "Many people," wrote the Reformed minister Jean Claude, "find in our doctrines and forms of Church government nothing inimical to salvation. But this is not the case when it comes to the matter of our separation, which they cannot accept when they compare it with that beautiful word, Church (*ce beau nom d'Eglise*), which ought to held in respect by all people of good will." *La Defense de la Reformation contre le Livre Intitulé Prejugez Legitimes contre les Calvinistes* [1671] (Amsterdam, 1683), 9. For earlier Protestant responses to the charge of separation in the English context, see Anthony Milton, *Catholic and Reformed: The Roman and Protestant Churches in English Protestant Thought, 1600-1640* (Cambridge: Cambridge University Press, 1995), 322-40.

English in 1672,[29] a new translation, by the Benedictine Joseph Johnston, appeared at the end of 1685, and was reprinted twice in the following year, accompanied by two official papal approbations and rave reviews by several illustrious cardinals. The second edition, overseen by James's crony and fellow convert James Drummond, Earl of Perth and Lord Chancellor of Scotland, sold 5000 copies in three months, while the last appeared in its wake bearing the royal imprimatur, "printed by special order of His Majesty." Truly, wrote the French expatriate Saint-Evremond, testifying to the impact of the *Exposition* on polite society in London, "*ce livre coupait le pied à toutes les disputes.*"[30] In addition to the *Exposition*, the *Conférence avec M. Claude* had been translated in 1684, while the *Histoire des Variations*, though not translated in Bossuet's lifetime, provoked a series of polemical responses that kept Bossuet's arguments at the center of the educated public's attention until long after

[29] The translator was Walter Montagu, almoner to Queen Henrietta Maria, and himself a convert to Catholicism. It is interesting to note that Montagu was accused of attempting to convert James during the latter's military service under Turenne in the 1650s. See White Kennett, *A Complete History of England, with the Lives of All the Kings and Queens Thereof* (London, 1719), 3: 320. It is also more than likely that James's thinking about religion was influenced by the conversion in 1668 of Turenne, whom he regarded as "the greatest and most perfect man he had ever known and the best friend he had ever had" and who had an equally negative opinion of schism. (See *The Memoirs of James II, His Campaigns as Duke of York 1652-1660*, tr. A. Lytton Sells [Bloomington: Indiana University Press, 1962], 53.) The depth of the friendship between the two men was also frequently noted by contemporaries. For example, the Scots lawyer Sir John Lauder of Fountainhall, testifying to the great respect in which James was held by Turenne, wrote that the general "was heard say, if he were to conquer the world, he would choise the Duke of York to command his army." (*Historical Observes of Memorable Occurrents in Church and State, from October 1680 to April 1686* [Edinburgh, 1840], 148.) Similarly, Gilbert Burnet, though no friend of James, remarked that Turenne had taken the young Duke of York under his special protection, and "was so much taken with his application, and the heat that he showed, that he recommended him out of measure. He said after of him, There was the greatest prince, and like to be the best general of his time." Gilbert Burnet, *A History of His Own Time* (Oxford, 1833), 3: 4. See also Callow, *The Making of King James II*, 3.

In England, Montagu's translation appears to have elicited only three responses, and two of these were translations of French works. One other response has been attributed to Henry More. With James's accession, however, the *Exposition* came to play an important role in controversy. On the printing history of the *Exposition* in Britain, see Floquet, *Etudes sur la vie de Bossuet*, 362-64; A Joly, *Un converti de Bossuet: James Drummond, Earl of Perth, 1648-1716* (Lille, 1933), 169; G. Lambin, "Les rapports de Bossuet avec l'Angleterre," *Bulletin du Bibliophile* (Sept.-Oct. 1909): 417-32; and F. Cabrol, "Bossuet, ses Relations avec l'Angleterre," *Revue d'Histoire Ecclésiastique* 27 (1931): 551-55. On James's encouragement of the publication of Catholic books, see Miller, *Popery and Politics*, 256; and Eamon Duffy, "'Poor Protestant Flies': Conversions to Catholicism in Early Eighteenth-Century England," in Derek Baker, ed., *Religious Motivation: Biographical and Sociological Problems for the Church Historian* (Oxford: Oxford University Press, 1978), 290.

[30] Floquet, *Etudes sur la vie de Bossuet*, 366. See also the letter of Father Joseph Shirburne to Bossuet, 3 April 1686, which testifies to the popularity of the second edition. (Urbain and Levesque, eds., *Correspondance de Bossuet*, 3: 210.)

James's attempt to reclaim Britain for the Catholic faith had failed.[31]

III. Bossuet and James Drummond, Earl of Perth (1648-1716)

Like Bossuet, James Drummond came from a family of staunch royalists whose traditional devotion to the crown had been intensified by the personal experience of civil unrest.[32] During the winter of 1651-52, Commonwealth troops were billeted in the family's ancestral home of Drummond castle, on the west coast, and James, his younger brother John, later Earl of Melfort, and their parents, were forced to take refuge in the empty and dilapidated country house of Stobhall, where, having "sustained great losse and payed many fynes,"[33] they remained until the Restoration, when James's father, Lord Drummond, was named a privy councillor by Charles II. Like Louis XIV, compelled—so the story goes—to sleep on straw at Saint-Germain during the Fronde, James and John Drummond never forgot their youthful experience of dispossession, and an intense distrust of rebels and rebellion seems to have formed a basic part of their mental equipment, expressing itself subsequently in James Drummond's bloody repression of radical dissenters during the years 1677 to 1684, and reinforcing his unyielding personal loyalty to the Stuart dynasty after 1688.[34] Both brothers were also strong partisans of episcopacy.

According to family custom, James and John were educated at Saint Andrew's and in France, where they attended an academy for young noblemen at Angers. James, who would become Earl of Perth upon the

---

[31] For a chronology of English translations and criticisms of Bossuet's writings, see Edward Gee, D. D., *The Catalogue of All the Discourses Published against Popery, during the Reign of King James II* (London, 1689); William Wake, *The Present State of the Controversy between the Church of England and the Church of Rome* (London, 1687); idem, *A Continuation of the Present State of the Controversy between the Church of England and the Church of Rome* (London, 1688); Lambin, "Les rapports de Bossuet avec l'Angleterre," *Bulletin du Bibliophile* (Nov. and Dec. 1909): 532-45 and 612-21; and *Oeuvres complètes de Bossuet*, 17: 242ff. The response of British Protestants to Bossuet's arguments will be discussed in some detail below.

[32] For James Drummond's biography, see Gaquère, *Vers l'unité chrétienne.*, 15-49; and Joly, *Un converti de Bossuet.*

[33] Robert Sibbald (1641-1722), *Memoirs*, ed. Francis Paget Hett (Oxford, 1932), 65. Sibbald was James Drummond's physician, and, according to Gilbert Burnet, "the most learned antiquary in Scotland." Burnet, *A History of Own Time*, 3: 115.

[34] Much later, John Drummond wrote, "My affections and preferences were formed by the tales of my elders and by conversations with other members of my household. I was brought up to hate rebels and rebellion." Quoted in Joly, *Un converti de Bossuet*, 12. On James Drummond's repressive policies as privy councillor in 1677, Lord Chief Justice in 1680, and Sheriff principal of Edinburgh and Lord Chancellor in 1684, see Joly, *Un converti de Bossuet*, 48, 71, 104-105; Miller, *James II*, 213; and David Ogg, *England in the Reigns of James II and William III* (Oxford: Oxford University Press, 1957), 171. Gilbert Burnet, who had personal and political reasons for disliking Perth, claims that the thumbscrews were introduced into Scotland under his auspices. (Burnet, *A History of His Own Time*, 2: 430.)

death of Lord Drummond in 1675, appears to have been a rather pious
and bookish young man with a love of Anglican ritual, whose literary
preferences and accomplishments reflected the concerns of late northern
humanism. According to his physician, Robert Sibbald, with whom he
conversed at length about his favorite topics, history and religion,

> the Earle was of great partes, and of a serious temper,
> read much, and was very observant of the rites of the
> Church of England, and had the English service always
> in his family. He was temperatte, and was of excellent
> conversation, and very desyrous to learne. I, by his
> order, acquainted him with the curious bookes,
> especially pieces of divinity, history, poemes, memoirs
> of ministers of state, and discoveries in Philosophy....
> He not only wrotte an excellent style of English, but
> upon occasiones made verse, and translated some psalms
> of Buchanan, and some odes of Horace.[35]

While the possibility of a life of *otium cum dignitate* seems briefly to
have appealed to Perth, he was ambitious, and also determined, as Sibbald
remarks, to remedy the low condition of his estate and to improve the
status of his family, which, in his view, had never been adequately
indemnified for its losses during the Interregnum.[36]

Accordingly, in Sibbald's laconic phrase, he began "to goe frequently
to court," where his strong support of the Duke of Lauderdale's repressive
policies against the Covenanters was noted with pleasure by Charles II.
Made a member of the privy council in 1677, Perth was named Lord
Chief Justice of Scotland in 1680, and played an important role in the
1681 parliament at Edinburgh that affirmed James II's right to the
succession in Scotland. In 1683, when Lauderdale died, Perth succeeded
to several of his offices; in the following year, Charles appointed him
Sheriff principal of the County of Edinburgh, and subsequently, Lord
Chancellor. His brother John, now Earl of Melfort, had meanwhile
secured the post of Secretary of State for Scotland. Perth and Melfort
welcomed the succession of James, and at the end of 1685 announced their
conversions to Catholicism, subsequently supporting James's Scottish
policies of strengthening the repressive powers of the crown and
promoting the Catholic faith with all the zeal of true believers. Under
James, who dispensed him from the Test, Perth's activities on behalf of
Catholicism, as I have mentioned, included sponsoring the translation and

---

[35] Sibbald, *Memoirs*, 73. Perth seems also to have been a devoted reader of Sir Thomas
Browne and of Malebranche. (See Joly, *Un converti de Bossuet*, 134.)
[36] Sibbald, *Memoirs*, 73.

publication of Bossuet's *Exposition*, as well as of his notorious *Pastoral Letter* justifying the Revocation of the Edict of Nantes.[37] In his capacity as Lord Chancellor, Perth instituted harsh censorship measures against Protestant printers, and attempted to control the activities of Protestant preachers. In addition, he actively supported the Catholic missions in Scotland, establishing a *caisse des conversions* on the French model to encourage abjurations among the poor, and especially among the clergy of the established church. At the official Chancellor's residence of Holyrood castle in Edinburgh, Perth installed a private printing establishment for the dissemination of Catholic propaganda, and a chapel flamboyantly decorated with religious objects imported from France in violation of Scottish law.[38] The activities of both institutions were supported by funds from the treasury, an intolerable intrusion of Catholicism into the public realm that aroused furious opposition among government officials and provoked popular violence in Edinburgh. Finally, Perth busied himself with the affairs of the Scottish Catholic colleges on the continent, sending one of his sons to the college in Paris and encouraging relatives to follow his example. When James's downfall became imminent in 1688, Melfort fled to France, arriving there in advance of the king. Perth, however, was thwarted in his own rather undignified attempt to escape the revenge of his political enemies and much of the populace by disguising himself as a lackey, and incarcerated in Stirling castle for the next three and a half years. Liberated in the summer of 1693 upon a promise to leave the kingdom, Perth made his way to Rome at the behest of James, where he attempted to plead the Stuart cause to a papacy that had ceased to identify the king's restoration with the cause of Catholicism.[39] He subsequently joined the exiled court at Saint Germain, where James appointed him governor of the Prince of Wales and raised him to a titular dukedom. During the last years of James's life, Perth continued in vain to besiege the pope and the other Catholic princes of Europe on his behalf. When

[37] Bossuet, *Lettre pastorale de Mgr. L'Évêque de Meaux, aux nouveaux catholiques de son diocèse pour les exhorter à faire leurs Pâques, et leur donner des avertissements contre les fausses Lettres pastorales des ministres*, in *Oeuvres complètes de Bossuet*, 17: 242-74.

[38] The lawyer Sir John Lauder of Fountainhall gives a varying account of the decoration of Perth's chapel: "He got from the king 8000 pounds sterling, with which he bought altars, candlesticks, priests' garments, and other ornaments and popish gauds for erecting the Chappell in the Abbey, and brought them home; and, tho ther be Acts of Parliament for seizing such trash, yet our customers past them." Sir John Lauder of Fountainhall, *Historical Observes*, 240.

[39] On the attitude of the papacy toward James after 1689, see Ludwig von Pastor, *The History of the Popes*, tr. Dom Ernst Graf, O. S. B. (London, 1957), 32: 511-15, 540; Ogg, *England in the Reigns of James II and William III*, 365. For more complete views that take in the beginning of James's reign, see Godfrey Anstruther, O.P., "Cardinal Howard and the English Court," *Archivum Fratrum Praedicatorum* 27 (1958): 315-361, and Miller, *Popery and Politics*, 229-39. See also below.

James died in 1701, Perth became the recognized leader of the extreme Catholic faction at Saint Germain. He himself died in 1716, bequeathing to the sons he had left behind in Scotland a fanatical commitment to Catholicism and to the Jacobite cause.[40]

While Perth and Melfort gained unprecedented wealth and prestige in the course of their rapid rise to power, it is clear from what has been said that their reputations did not emerge unscathed. Indeed, Gilbert Burnet seemed to conceive of Perth in particular as a kind of Faustian figure, someone whose rapaciousness had gained him the world, but at the expense of his immortal soul. Dismayed by the Earl's harsh treatment of Presbyterians as Lord Chief Justice, he commented on the outcome of one trial as follows: "Perth ... shewed how ready he was to sacrifice justice and innocent blood to his ambition. And that was yet grosser in this case; because his brother was promised that gentleman's estate, when it should be confiscated." And on the occasion of Perth's accession to the office of Lord Chancellor, "to which he had long been aspiring in a most indecent manner," Burnet paused in his narrative to consider

> how ambition could corrupt one of the best tempered
> men that I had ever known: I mean Lord Perth, who for
> above ten years together seemed to me incapable of an
> immoral or cruel action, and yet was now engaged in the
> foulest and blackest of crimes.[41]

As might be expected, Burnet situates Perth's conversion in the context of his rise to power, and specifically of his rivalry with Lord Treasurer Queensberry for the favor of King James. While Burnet's hostility to

---

[40] On the rise to power of Perth and Melfort, see Burnet, *A History of His Own Time*, 2: 424-35; Fountainhall, *Historical Observes*, 76-77, 129-34, 216-44; and Joly, *Un converti de Bossuet*, 48-204. On Perth's conversion and his attempts to promote Catholicism in Scotland under James, see Burnet, *A History of His Own Time*, 3: 69-71; Fountainhall, *Historical Notices of Scottish Affairs* (Edinburgh, 1848), 2: 699, 764, 816, 829-30; Gaquère, *Vers l'unité chrétienne*, 67, 71-74, 80-82, 84-85; Joly, *Un converti de Bossuet*, 159-203; Miller, *James II*, 210-16; and Rébelliau, *Bossuet historien du protestantisme*, 178. On his attempted escape and imprisonment in Stirling castle, see Joly, *Un converti de Bossuet*, 204ff.; Bruce Lenman, *The Jacobite Risings in Britain 1689-1746* (London: Methuen, 1984), 28-29; and Perth's own account in William Jerdan, ed., *Letters from James Earl of Perth, Lord Chancellor of Scotland etc. to His Sister the Countess of Erroll and Other Members of His Family* (London, 1845), 6-7. On his journey to Rome and activity at the papal court, see Joly, *Un converti de Bossuet*, 249-70, 282ff.; Claude Nordmann, "Louis XIV and the Jacobites," in Ragnhild Hatton, ed., *Louis XIV and Europe* (London: Macmillan, 1976), 87; and Perth's account in Jerdan, *Letters from James, Earl of Perth*, 15-101. On Perth's position at Saint Germain after 1695, see Joly, *Un converti de Bossuet*, 313-487; and Jones, *The Main Stream of Jacobitism*, 76. On Perth's descendants and their Jacobite and Catholic connections, see Lenman, *The Jacobite Risings in Britain*, 63.

[41] Burnet, *A History of His Own Time*, 2: 424.

Perth, to James, and to Catholicism in general needs to be kept in mind, his account is worth quoting at length because it emphasizes the element of self-interest that was frequently, and undeniably, a component of conversions to Catholicism among seventeenth-century elites.

> Some few converts, were made at [the end of 1685]. The chief of these were the Earl of Perth, and his brother the Earl of Melfort. Some differences fell in between the Duke of Queensborough and the Earl of Perth. The latter thought the former was haughty and violent, and that he used him in too imperious a manner. So they broke. At that time the king published two papers found in his brother's strong box.[42] So the Earl of Perth was either

[42] Burnet is referring here to statements purportedly written by Charles II acknowledging the necessity for an infallible authority in matters of religion, and lamenting the "separation" of the Protestant churches from Rome and the dire consequences—civil and religious—of the Protestant principle of the independent interpretation of Scripture. The publication of the papers generated a flurry of pamphlets either attacking or defending their authenticity, of which the best known are those by the Anglican, Edward Stillingfleet, and the Catholic, John Dryden. At this time, James also published his own account of Charles's supposed deathbed conversion, and this was soon supplemented by another, written by the Benedictine Richard Huddleston, who testified that he had given Charles the last sacraments of the Roman Church. As might be expected, Burnet dismisses the authenticity of the "papers," though not denying Charles's sympathy with Catholicism: These papers, he argues,

> were probably writ either by Lord Bristol, or by Lord d'Aubigny, who knew the secret of his religion, and gave him those papers, as abstracts of some discourses they had with him on those heads, to keep him fixed to them. ... [H]e had talked over a great part of them to myself: so that, as soon as I saw them, I remembered his expressions, and perceived that he had made himself master of the arguments, as far as those papers could carry him.

Burnet, *A History of His Own Time*, 2: 485. See also idem, "Six Papers Containing ... Remarks on the Two Papers, Writ by His Late Majesty King Charles II concerning Religion," n. p., 1687. Here, Burnet repeats the arguments he himself had made to the king against the contents of the "papers."

While the nature of Charles's religious sentiments remains a matter of controversy, the question of the authenticity of the "papers" is not what interests me here. Rather, what is important to remember is that the conversion accounts of important people like Charles functioned as *exempla*, whether they reflected the true sentiments of a convert or not: at a time when the credibility of propositions was often enhanced by the status of the person proclaiming them, they constituted an essential part of the Catholic rhetorical arsenal. It is for this reason that James considered their publication a high priority. Indeed, G. Lambin argues that the second edition of Bossuet's *Exposition* was intended by James to enhance the polemical impact produced by the circulation of Charles's papers. (Lambin, "Les rapports de Bossuet avec l'Angleterre," *Bulletin du Bibliophile* (Sept.-Oct. 1909): 426.)

Charles's statements in favor of Catholicism and James's account of his deathbed conversion are printed in Falconer Madan, ed., *Stuart Papers Relating Chiefly to Queen Mary of Modena and the Exile Court of King James II* (London, 1889), 2: 279-88. For recent discussions of Charles's religion, see Ronald Hutton, *Charles II* (Oxford: Oxford University

overcome with the reasons in them, or he thought it would look well at court, if he put his conversion upon these....

Before he declared his change, the king seemed so well satisfied with the Duke of Queensborough, that he was resolved to bring the Earl of Perth to a submission, otherwise to dismiss him. But such converts were to be encouraged.... The Duke of Queensborough was turned out of the treasury.... And now it became soon very visible, that he had the secret no more; but that it was lodged between the two brothers, the Earls of Perth and Melfort. Soon after that, the Duke of Queensborough was not only turned out of all his employments, but design was made to ruin him. All persons were encouraged to bring accusations against him, either with relation to the administration of the government, or of the treasury. And, if any colourable matter could be found against him, it was resolved to have made him a sacrifice. This sudden hatred, after so entire a confidence, was imputed to the suggestions the Earl of Perth had made of his zeal against popery, and of his having engaged all his friends to stick firm in opposition to it.[43]

Press, 1989), 443-44; Miller, *James II*, 40; and idem, *Popery and Politics*, 18, 22, 93, 110, 123. See also Edward Stillingfleet, *An Answer to Some Papers Lately Printed, concerning the Authority of the Catholick Church in Matters of Faith, and the Reformation of the Church of England* (London, 1686); idem, *A Vindication of the Answer to Some Late Papers concerning the Unity and Authority of the Catholick Church, and the Reformation of the Church of England* (London, 1687); John Dryden, *A Defence of the Papers Written by the Late King of Blessed Memory, and the Duchess of York, against the Answer Made to Them* (London, 1686); and John Huddleston, *A Short and Plain Way to the Faith and Church. Composed by Richard Huddleston ... And Now Published by His Nephew Mr. John Huddleston.... To Which Is Annexed His Late Majesty King Charles the Second His Papers ... As Also a Brief Account of What Occurred on His Deathbed in Regard to Religion* (London, 1688). A. Joly, noting that this last work was printed in Edinburgh at Holyrood House, suggests that Perth had a role in its distribution. Dutch and French translations were published in 1689 and 1691. (See Joly, *Un converti de Bossuet*, 137, n. 4.) The role of the "papers" in Perth's conversion will be discussed in more detail below.

[43] Burnet, *A History of His own Time*, 3: 69-71. Burnet also undermines the sincerity of Perth's conversion by invoking his thoroughgoing lack of personal morality and his abuse of canon law in the case of his third marriage to his first cousin, Lady Gordon, with whom he had "lived scandalously" for many years, and whom he had married only weeks after the death of his second wife. According to Burnet, Perth had failed to obtain the papal dispensation required by the Church for marriage within the prohibited degrees of consanguinity, and Cardinal Howard was enlisted to persuade Pope Innocent XI to grant one after the fact:

The pope said, these were strange converts, that would venture on such

While no one denies that Perth played the Catholic card against Queensberry,[44] certain anomalies in his behavior—most notably the emotional and flamboyant religiosity and obsessive proselytizing remarked on by contemporaries that immediately followed his conversion,[45] his devout correspondence with Bossuet while incarcerated at Stirling, and the fervent and unwavering commitment to Catholicism that he exhibited until his death—are simply impossible to reconcile with Burnet's reductive account of his conversion. Consequently, more recent historians, while acknowledging Perth's willingness to profit from his new faith, have been kinder in their assessment of his change of religion,[46] acknowledging that in his case a combination of self-interest and sincerity that twentieth-century observers find improbable marked his conversion.

The ambiguity that characterized Perth's behavior, however, is far from unique; rather, as I have indicated, it is typical of many conversions to Catholicism among European elites of the seventeenth century, a time when the public nature of religion made the distinction that we commonly

> a thing without first obtaining a dispensation. [Cardinal Howard] pretended that new converts did not so soon understand the laws of the Church: but he laid before the pope the ill consequences of offending converts of such importance. So he prevailed at last, not without great difficulty.

Burnet, *A History of His Own Time*, 3: 113; see also Anstruther, "Cardinal Howard and the English Court," 322-40.

On the occasion of Perth's third marriage, Sir John Lauder took the opportunity to repeat a satirical comment on the conduct of both Perth and Melfort that he had recently heard, and one that reflects the hatred they had incurred as a result of their abjurations. It had been said, he wrote, "that they ware the truest brether ever to ther whores, and the falsest to ther God." (Lauder, *Historical Observes*, 244.)

[44] See for example the discussion by Joly, who is usually concerned to paint a flattering portrait of Perth, in *Un converti de Bossuet,* 159.

[45] Dr. Sibbald, whom Perth later persuaded to embrace Catholicism, related that the Earl confessed his change of religion to him as follows:

> one Sunday [when] he had taken physick, he took the opportunity, wee being alone, to tell me, weeping, that he was of [the Romish] persuasion, and that no consideration of worldly interest had induced him thereto, but that he was convinced it was the true and ancient Church.

Sibbald also gives a very brief account of Perth's intense efforts to secure the deathbed conversion of his second wife. Though Sibbald subsequently recanted, has little good to say about Catholicism, and narrates the events in question in an ironic tone, he never calls Perth's sincerity into doubt. (Sibbald, *Memoirs*, 87-88.)

Sir John Lauder of Fountainhall speaks with disdain of Perth's intense and flamboyant religiosity, and his evident love of Catholic ritual, recalling that he was "so bigot" upon his new religion that, "as Collonel Whytfoord a papist observed, [he] would jade the Masse, he caused say it so oft; but omnis apostata est suae sectae osor; and, to expiate and take off suspicion, he most be a slave to the new on." And he goes on to remark that Perth's entourage "ware so childishly fond, that, on Christmas day, the Chancelor rocked a child in the cradle, in memorie of our Savior." Not even the French, he concludes despairingly, indulge in such ceremonies. (Lauder, *Historical Observes*, 240.)

[46] See for example Miller, *James II*, 213; and Lenman, *The Jacobite Risings in Britain*, 29.

draw between self-interest and sincerity more problematic than in our own era. It is of course not the case that contemporaries were not interested in sincerity; on the contrary, "baroque" culture was obsessed with this and related ideas, such as the discrepancy between outward behavior and inward sentiment, which one might see as a subset of its preoccupation with illusion and theatricality. In the context of religion, we have only to recall Calvin's vociferous condemnation of Nicodemism, which justified outward conformity to beliefs that an individual inwardly repudiated, or the terror and disgust experienced by many English Protestants at what they considered to be Jesuit "equivocation," or the suspicion of Leaguer Catholics that Henri IV's conversion was not "sincere," or the objection against Louis XIV's treatment of the Huguenots that paying or bullying potential converts scarcely insured "sincere" conversions.[47] Indeed, it might be said that the seventeenth century saw the triumph of "sincerity" as an ultimate value: when John Locke and Pierre Bayle wrote their influential treatises on toleration at the end of the century, they argued against the view that control of religious behavior touched only the "outer man" precisely on the grounds that, as Locke would put it, "it is vain for an unbeliever to take up the outward show of another man's profession. Faith only, and inward sincerity, are the things that procure acceptance with God."[48] Sincerity then, had come to trump orthodoxy.

At the same time, however, it is quite clear that the question of sincerity ought not to dominate our analysis of early modern conversion, if only because it often oversimplifies the multifaceted character of human motivation, and thus does an injustice to the dead. Moreover, for Perth's contemporaries, sincerity was not always a useful standard for evaluating conversions. Catholic *convertisseurs*, for instance, though they urged claims of sincerity on the part of new converts who publicly profess their faith, were frequently more interested in the exemplary and very public impact of an important conversion than in the quality of that convert's beliefs, which could in theory always be improved by subsequent acculturation once he or she had safely entered the Church. In the present context then, it is important to recall that sincerity gained its current prestige only as religion was privatized and internalized, and that was a process that, while underway, was far from complete at the end of the seventeenth century. Therefore, in the case of elite converts like Perth, it

[47] On Nicodemism, see Carlo Ginzburg, *Il nicodemismo: Simulazione e dissimulazione religiosa nell' Europa del 1500* (Torino: Giulio Einaudi editore, 1970). On the conversion of Henri IV and especially on the Catholic concern with his sincerity, see Michael Wolfe, *The Conversion of Henri IV: Politics, Power, and Religious Belief in Early Modern France* (Cambridge, MA: Harvard University Press, 1993). On reactions to Louis XIV's treatment of the Huguenots, see below.
[48] John Locke, *A Letter concerning Toleration* (1689), in Maurice Cranston, ed., *Locke on Politics, Religion, and Education* (New York: Collier, 1965), 124.

is also essential to consider not only the potential loss of royal patronage incurred by court officials who rejected their sovereign's religion,[49] but also the cultural meanings that such individuals frequently attached to Catholicism, as well as the genuine religious anxiety that informed their attempts to discover the "true Church."

In these last two respects, Perth is typical of the conservative elites throughout Europe to whom the arguments of Bossuet, as they were communicated in the *Exposition* and the *Histoire des Variations*, especially appealed. It is important, therefore, to look at his mentality in some depth. I have already mentioned his intense royalism, and the hatred of rebels and rebellion that he shared with the great bishop, and of course with his master, King James. Like them, he equated monarchy with political stability, and had come to believe that Catholicism better promoted the cause of a divinely sanctioned authority in the state than did Protestantism, whose principle of the independent interpretation of Scripture appeared in his view to generate a fractious spirit that encouraged both religious dissent and civil disorder. On the occasion of Perth's imprisonment at Stirling, Bossuet sought to encourage him by appealing to precisely these convictions: "I am touched," he wrote,

> by your inviolable attachment to the king, your beloved master. Heresy is showing her true colors, everywhere inciting perfidy and rebellion…. [C]onserve the tender love and unalterable fidelity that you have so far shown for your prince; never cease to be an example of such loyalty in the midst of an unfaithful nation; and finally, in life and in death, let the name of the king your master be on your lips, along with those of Jesus Christ and the Catholic Church, as things that are inseparable.[50]

---

[49] Lenman, *The Jacobite Risings in Britain*, 29. On the potential loss of royal patronage as a factor in aristocratic conversions, see Rosa, "The Conversion of Henri-Charles de la Trémoïlle," 73-74.

[50] Bossuet to Perth, Meaux, 14 March 1689, in Gaquère, *Vers l'unité chrétienne*, 111. Bossuet's exhortation echoes the argument of the *Politique tirée des propres paroles de l'Ecriture Sainte*. In this work he contended that while any religion would help to guarantee order and stability in the state, only Catholicism, whose truth can be established with demonstrative certainty, will ground the sovereign's authority in an absolutely unshakeable manner:

> Even though it is true, [he claims,] that false religions, insofar as they contain elements of goodness and truth, contribute necessarily to the stable constitution of states, they nevertheless leave consciences uncertain and doubtful, and therefore are not sufficent to establish a condition of perfect stability.

See Bossuet, *Politique*, ed. Jacques LeBrun (Geneva: Droz, 1967), 217.

The bishop's appeal was well placed, for Perth had held such opinions in the happier days of his ascendancy, and continued to do so throughout his life. For example, in the course of his correspondence with Bossuet regarding the publication of the 1686 translation of the *Exposition*, Perth responded to the bishop's request for English materials to include in his *Histoire des Variations* by lamenting that it was difficult to find such sources. "The Protestants," he wrote,

> have taken great precautions to prevent posterity from informing itself of the secret means whereby religion has been overthrown in this country that was once called "the land of saints," and whereby this kingdom, once so fortunate, has become the theatre of so many horrible tragedies, and an asylum full of madmen where every man pretends to be inspired and thence to instruct others, and where no one wants to listen to reason, or truth.[51]

And he echoed these sentiments in a letter to his sister written nine years later as he traveled to Rome to plead the cause of James at the papal court. Here, he complimented the Venetian authorities on their wise policy of encouraging popular participation in religious festivals, and his remarks continue to reflect a strong sense of the intimate connection between religious dissent and political disorder. "Thus," he observed,

> they direct the people here [in order] to amuse them and keep them from framing conceits of government and religion, such as our giddy people frame to themselves and make themselves the scorn and reproach of mankind, for now all goes under the name of English, and we are said to be so changeable and foolish that nothing from our parts seems strange. Beheading, dethroneing and banishing of kings being but children's

---

[51] Perth to Bossuet, Edinburgh, November 16, 1686, in Gaquère, *Vers l'unité chrétenne*, 81-82. Of Bossuet's reliance on such materials, Gilbert Burnet remarked: "the gentlest censure that can be past on his performances ... is, that some others furnish him with extracts, which he manages to the best advantage, but without examining them." Burnet, "A Censure of Mr. de Meaux's History of the Variations of the Protestant Churches: Together with Some Further Reflections on Mr. LeGrand" (London, 1689).

Perth's letters to Bossuet were translated into French by Eusèbe Renaudot, who had also translated Charles's "papers." (Lambin, "Les rapports de Bossuet avec l'Angleterre," *Bulletin du Bibliophile* [Sept.-Oct. 1909]: 430.) On Renaudot, see Pierre Burger, "Spymaster to Louis XIV: A Study of the Papers of the Abbé Eusèbe Renaudot," in Eveline Cruickshanks, ed., *Ideology and Conspiracy: Aspects of Jacobitism, 1689-1759* (Edinburgh: Atlantic Highlands, 1982), 111-37.

play with us.[52]

As these observations make clear, Perth is convinced that the bond between the temporal and the spiritual realms cannot be severed: in his view, when private persons take it upon themselves to dissent from spiritual authority, the consequences of their behavior are inevitably made manifest in political life. That is because, like many of his contemporaries, he thinks of both realms in terms of a governing organic metaphor inherited from medieval political thought that makes it impossible to conceive of dissent as anything other than destructive: both are conceptualized as bodies, and are therefore subject to the rules of bodily health, including, principally, the proper subordination of members to head.[53] Moreover, the intimate liaison between religious and civil society dictated by the organic metaphor meant that for individuals like Perth, the criteria of truth in the one and of legitimacy in the other were also the same: both could be identified by the degree to which they exhibited unity and continuity, while change, disagreement, inconsistency, or innovation, on the contrary, signaled spiritual and political error. This yoking of the two heterogeneous realms is also evident in their conviction that the proper organization of both is hierarchical. Indeed, for conservatives like Perth, Bossuet, and King James, who continued to reiterate such opinions at a time when changing political and social structures were making them appear increasingly superfluous, the preservation of unity and harmony in church and society cannot be achieved without the maintenance of hierarchy, which itself reflects God's ordering of the cosmos as a whole.[54] In their view, therefore, religious dissent and political rebellion not only undermined human institutions, but amounted to a blasphemous subversion of the divine order. Such convictions evidently informed Perth's

[52] Perth to his sister, Venice, 28 February, 1695, in Jerdan, ed., *Letters from James, Earl of Perth*, 55.

[53] On the metaphor of the body and its application to church and state in European political thought, see Ernst Kantorowicz, *The King's Two Bodies: A Study in Medieval Political Theology* (Princeton: Princeton University Press, 1957). For the persistence of the organic view in seventeenth-century England, see especially James Daly, "Cosmic Harmony and Political Thinking in Early Stuart England," *Transactions of the American Philosophical Society* 69 (1979): 3-40. Daly remarks that to think in terms of the organic metaphor "was to have no intellectual place even to conceive of rebellion" (18). The organic metaphor was first applied to the Church by St. Paul. See I Corinthians 12: 12-31.

[54] For a good discussion of the "world picture" implied by this view, and its increasingly tenuous relation to social and political practice, see Kevin Sharpe, *Politics and Ideas in Early Stuart England: Essays and Studies* (London: Pinter, 1989), 9-44; and David Underdown, *Revel, Riot, and Rebellion: Popular Politics and Culture in England 1603-1660* (Oxford: Oxford University Press, 1985), ch. 2. Paul Monod briefly discusses the persistence of these opinions in the later seventeenth century and their subsequent role in the construction of Jacobite ideology. Monod, *Jacobitism and the English People* (Cambridge: Cambridge University Press, 1993), 20, 43.

partisanship of episcopacy even before his conversion to Catholicism as well as his attitude toward the Presbyterians, whose egalitarian form of church government he held to be subversive of political authority. The Chancellor, wrote Gilbert Burnet in his history of the year 1684, "seemed to set it up for a maxim, that the Presbyterians could not be governed, but with the extremity of rigour; and that they were irreconcilable enemies to the king and the duke, and that therefore they ought to be extirpated."[55]

The hierarchical ecclesiology of Catholicism, in contrast, appealed profoundly to Perth's conceptions of proper religious, political, and social organization, and to his view of the necessity of consistency among them. As Bruce Lenman has argued, both James and Perth held a vision of a Catholic Scotland in which "an absolute King of Scots was to be surrounded by a deferential and strictly graded nobility while a hierarchical Kirk buttressed both throne and social order."[56] This vision informed not only their zealous proselytizing activities, but the imaginary world they created for themselves at court, where James restored the "Most Antient and Most Noble" Order of the Thistle, whose original members included Perth and Melfort.[57] Like other early modern orders of chivalry, the Thistle was a serious form of play that reflected an attempt on the part of the monarchy to secure the loyalty of the great nobility; such an attempt would not have succeeded at all, however, had it not appealed to their cultural preconceptions—most notably a nostalgia for the union of sacred and secular realms exemplified by the imagined activities of the medieval knight—and legitimized their exalted position in the

---

[55] Burnet, *A History of His Own Time*, 2: 426.

[56] Lenman, *The Jacobite Risings in Britain*, 39. This essentially Gallican vision had of course also appealed to James and Perth as Anglicans, and was a legacy of long-term affinities between the political theories of the Gallican and Anglican churches. On this subject, see J. H. M. Salmon, "Gallicanism and Anglicanism in the Age of the Counter-Reformation," in idem, *Renaissance and Revolt: Essays in the Intellectual and Social History of Early Modern France* (Cambridge: Cambridge University Press, 1987), 155-88. See also W. B. Patterson, *King James VI and I and the Reunion of Christendom* (Cambridge: Cambridge University Press, 1997), 94, 103. These affinities also marked the positions of the two churches on the issue of ecclesiastical government, specifically on the question of the authority of bishops. Even Bossuet, in the ecumenical persona he occasionally adopted, considered that it might be possible for the Catholic Church to accept the legitimacy of Anglican episcopal ordinations with a view toward the reunification of the two communions. See Edmond Préclin, *L'Union des Églises Anglicane et Gallicane: Une tentative au temps de Louis XV (P. F. Le Courayer [de 1681 à 1732] et Guillaume Wake)* (Paris, 1928), 1-6. On James II's belief in the claims asserted on behalf of the royal prerogative by the Gallican theorists William Barclay and Jean Bodin, see Salmon, *The French Religious Wars in English Political Thought* (Westport, CT: Greenwood Press, 1981), 147.

[57] Lenman, *The Jacobite Risings in Britain*, 39. See also Matthew Glozier, "The Earl of Melfort, the Court Catholic Party and the Foundation of the Order of the Thistle, 1687," *The Scottish Historical Review* 79, no. 2 (2000): 233-38. Here it is argued that the idea of the Order's restitution originated entirely with Melfort.

secular hierarchy by endowing it with a certain odor of sanctity.

The continuing appeal of Catholicism to other aspects of Perth's aristocratic ethos is evident throughout his correspondence, where he identifies Catholics as people of "the best quality,"[58] and expresses a delight with the city of Rome and a love of Catholic ritual characteristic of many converts of similar social status who, like Perth, had undertaken humanist studies or experienced Catholic culture during their formative years. This reaction to Rome stemmed in part from the cosmopolitan self-image of such individuals, itself a product of their humanist educations, which also encouraged a fascination with the Eternal City as the hub of European civilization and the visible image of a once unified Christendom. Moreover, the internationalist culture of these converts encouraged them to accept the Catholic claim that universality—made manifest in the presence in Rome of representatives of Catholicism from around the world—was a mark of religious truth, while their tendency to identify power with its visible representation, and thus to locate meaning in forms of display, enhanced the attractions of Roman ritual, which they experienced in the Catholic capital in its purest form. All these preconceptions are evident in the enthusiastic description of Rome that Perth sent to his sister in 1695:

> If one should enter, on a particular account of the
> pictures, antiquities, churches, villas, statues, fountains,
> etc. here, 10 volumes would not suffice. Then the
> musick (which surpasses imagination), and the different
> ceremonies and comotions in the churches; and the
> different rites of the different sorts of Christians, who all
> hold the same doctrine and unity, is very edifying. To
> see all nations praise Our Lord is a great joy to me, and
> a confirmation of the Catholic faith from China (where
> there are upwards of 4,000,000 of Christians) to Ireland,
> and from Ireland to China, east and west around the
> globe: you have here Catholicks, Grecians, Turks,
> Siamois, those of Tonquin, Cochin China and China,
> and from Scotland to the Cape of Good Hope the other
> way, so that you see here a college of Blacks, and

---

[58] Perth to his sister, the Countess of Erroll, Rotterdam, 24 November 1693, in Jerdan, ed., *Letters from James, Earl of Perth*, 13. In a character sketch of Charles II written sometime after 1688 and from a quite hostile perspective, the Marquess of Halifax remarked on Charles's distaste "for the ill-bred familiarity of the Scotch divines," as well as on the appeal of the "genteel" aspects of Catholicism to "a prince that had more of the fine gentleman than his governing capacity required." See George Savile, Marquess of Halifax, *Complete Works*, J. P. Kenyon, ed. (Harmondsworth: Penguin, 1969), 247, 249.

amongst them most virtuous, excellent Ecclesiastiques.[59]

For converts like Perth then, it is clear that the ideological and cultural attractions of Catholicism cannot always easily be distinguished from what we might call more genuinely "religious" ones, as Perth's concern with the confirmation of Catholic truth indicates. In this latter context, it is also important to recall his reaction to the international impact of Bossuet's

[59] Perth to the Countess of Erroll, Rome, 30 June 1695, in Jerdan, ed., *Letters from James, Earl of Perth*, 81-82. In contrast, it is important to note the anti-Catholic and anti-foreign components of contemporary British nationalism. As early as 1609, for example, the Scottish parliament had objected to the practice among aristocratic families of sending their sons to France to be educated, lamenting that young men of good lineage frequently returned from their time abroad, "polluted with superstition and heresy, and thus legitimately suspect as dangerous subjects in the state." And in 1669, an English traveler in Scotland remarked with disdain that "the nobility here are no longer Scottish; because as soon as they have left their mothers, their fathers send them to France, where they become fat, [and] acquire new blood and new manners; they learn to stand up straight, to speak properly, to bow, to cultivate women, and to make compliments." (Both statements cited in Joly, *Un converti de Bossuet*, 29.) Taken together, these observations not only reflect the traditional concern that Catholics will prove to be disloyal subjects, but also indicate that the cosmopolitan elements in aristocratic culture were becoming incompatible with an emerging sense of British national character.

For a similar account of a visit to Rome by another aristocratic convert, see Christopher, Count Ranzov, *Epistola ad Georgium Calixtum, Professorem Helmstedensem, Qua sui ad Ecclesiam Catholicam accessus rationes exponit* (Rome, 1652). This enthusiastic description of the Catholic capitol on the occasion of the 1650 Jubilee reads in part as follows:

> where you thought that I would be offended by superstitions, nonsense, and novelties. there appeared to me unexpectedly and plainly, before my eyes in a wondrous spectacle, the universal image of the Catholic Church.... For there I saw, proceeding to the Vatican basilica in a solemn rite of supplication, schools of children, lines of monks, and confraternities of religious men, and thence diverse colleges of clerics and other assemblies of the Church. An immense crowd of the faithful followed this leader and high priest of the Christian people, and in their ardor of spirit they seemed as though they would conquer the heavens.
>
> I saw with what pious striving the pilgrims flowed into the city and into the community of the Church, and how all particular nations are drawn in as its guests.
>
> In such a great number of peoples and nations, I easily perceived that the Church distances itself from all sects and private factions: since here all nations and all languages are united by a single chain of faith and love. (7, 9)

Ranzov's account was actually written by Lucas Holstenius, Vatican librarian and *convertisseur*, but published under Ranzov's name. This was a common practice when princes converted, and reflected the conviction of proselytizers that for the purposes of propaganda, it was not the internal sentiments of the convert that mattered, but the publication and circulation of accounts by eminent individuals that testified to the universality of the Catholic religion. Note finally, however, that for Bossuet too, Rome constituted *"un idéal de chrétienté terrestre."* Bossuet, *Discours sur l'histoire universelle*, cited in Martimort, *Le gallicanisme de Bossuet*, 310.

polemical writings because he considered that it provided just such a confirmation. Writing to the bishop in 1685, he proclaimed exultantly that

> [i]t would be necessary to close one's eyes to the light in order not to recognize the truth, as your excellent pen has exposed it. You are like another St. Paul, whose labors are not confined to just one nation, or just one province: at present, your works are speaking in most of the idioms of Europe, and your converts sing your praises in languages that you cannot understand.[60]

Indeed, I would suggest that the example of Perth's thinking, in which the ideological, cultural and religious attractions of Catholicism are inextricably linked, tends to substantiate the claim that the emergence of systematic ideologies depends upon the differentiation of the secular realm as an autonomous polity, a process which, in seventeenth-century Europe, was far from complete, and would not be so for a long time to come. In Perth's case specifically then, I would further suggest that we are observing two overlapping symbol-systems at work. Reflected in the organic worldview and the unitary and universalist conception of truth that I have described, these symbols, which in his view were best embodied in the ethos of post-tridentine Catholicism, enabled Perth not only to validate the traditional social order and his own place in it, but also to negotiate what he considered to be a proper relationship with a transcendent realm. As he wrote to the Earl of Balcarres in 1694, "To be Catholic is not only to change one's opinion, but to conform oneself to what God requires of those to whom He has revealed what they are to believe of Him, and what they must do to earn His good will."[61]

I should like now to turn to Perth's conversion proper, and to a more detailed discussion of the subsequent activities on behalf of Catholicism in Scotland that he undertook with the support of Bossuet. While I shall continue to emphasize the appeal of Catholic arguments and rhetorical strategies to the spectrum of cultural and religious concerns that marked Perth's thinking in particular, my primary focus will be the theological defense of religious intolerance underlying the vision of a Catholic Scotland that he shared with Bossuet, and the conception of conscience that this entailed.

It is important to understand at the outset that the Catholic polemic brought to perfection by Bossuet often succeeded in persuading an educated audience not only because its argumentation appealed to their conception of proper religious and political order and to their unitary

---

[60] Perth to Bossuet, London, 12 November 1685, in Gaquère, *Vers l'unité chrétienne*, 59.
[61] Cited in Joly, *Un converti de Bossuet*, 256.

conception of truth, but also because its rhetorical strategies took their self-image into account. By offering arguments in favor of Catholic truth, controversialists appeared implicitly to differentiate potential elite converts from their counterparts among the lower orders and to acknowledge their social pre-eminence by proposing to them an active and reasoned submission to Catholic authority rather than a passive, fideistic one.[62] In addition, it appealed to their definition of themselves as public persons by urging them to use their influence to convert others. In this latter project, the strategy they were to follow was twofold: instruction of their social equals and coercion of those whose lesser status, while by no means eliminating catechizing and other forms of persuasion as means of inculcating Catholic truth, made the use of force a more appropriate tactic of religious control. Perth enthusiastically embraced both of these courses of action. In his letters to Bossuet, he pledged to "return great numbers of people to the Church of God,"[63] employing the language of enlightenment or coercion depending on the targets involved. Of Melfort's conversion, for example, he wrote triumphantly, though with becoming modesty,

> Most well-bred men need only to be disabused [of their errors]. Such was certainly my experience in the case of my brother, who, in eight days of conversation with me—though it must be granted that such feeble means could only have been effective because the end was holy—became a very good Catholic.[64]

As far as his countrymen in general were concerned, however, he tacitly acknowledged that instruction must be supplemented by coercion. "The farthest reaches of our land," he wrote,

> where the people are the most violent, have been in great part converted, or at least there are grounds for hoping that when the truth is presented to them, it will, with God's blessing, make rapid strides, because the king is master of all Argyle county, and most of the other lands belong to the Duke of Gordon, the Earl of Stafford, or to

---

[62] The process of reasoned submission is reflected in Perth's conception of what it meant to be Catholic, which I have quoted above. Here, the active verbs to "change one's opinion" and to "conform oneself" indicate that the reconciliation with God implied in a conversion to Catholicism is in significant part the product of an intellectual and moral initiative on the part of the convert. For a different view of Catholic strategies, see Richard H. Popkin, "Skepticism and the Counter-Reformation in France," 58-87.

[63] Perth to Bossuet, Edinburgh, 8 February 1686, in Gaquère, *Vers l'unité chrétienne*, 67.

[64] *Ibid.*

me.[65]

And he further concluded that his brother Melfort's conversion would be of particular advantage to the cause of Catholicism "because he will be most useful in advancing the interests of our holy religion in this country since his position provides him many excellent opportunities to do so."[66]

Like many other converts of high social status, however, Perth aimed primarily to set an example for other eminent individuals, including not only members of his own family, but friends like Dr. Sibbald, whom he urged to repeat the process of reading and study that had led him to the true faith.[67] Bossuet encouraged Perth in this goal, proclaiming that his exemplary conversion signaled a victory for Catholicism in Britain:

> I hope, My Lord, that God, who has wrought such great things in a man of your elevation and merit, will make them work for the salvation of many: on this happy occasion, I am encouraged to redouble the efforts I have so long been making to secure the conversion of Great Britain.... May the spirit of God descend with abundance on all the Catholics in your land ... following your example, let them show their faith by their works, and learn from you an absolute respect for the apostolic order and the holy hierarchy of the Church.[68]

[65] Perth to Bossuet, Windsor, 25 July 1686, in Gaquère, *Vers l'unité chrétienne*, 71-2.

[66] Perth to Bossuet, Edinburgh, 8 February 1686, in Gaquère, *Vers l'unité chrétienne*, 67. It should be noted that Perth and Melfort were exactly the sort of Catholics whose power and influence had long filled English Protestants with fear. In 1642, for example, an M. P. for Dorset told Parliament that what made his entire county fear the suspected Catholic George Lord Digby was "the greatness of his authoritie with us, [and] his large revenues and multiplicitie of tenants who are for the most part Recusants, and impetuous resisters of the Protestant religion." (Cited in Robin Clifton, "The Popular Fear of Catholics during the English Revolution," *Past and Present* 52 (1971): 47.)

[67] For the doctor's account of this conversation, see Sibbald, *Memoirs*, 88. Throughout his life, Perth attempted unsuccessfully to convert his sister, the Countess of Erroll, urging her repeatedly to read and study as he had done. See for example his letters to her of 25 April 1694, 28 November 1694, and 28 March 1695, in Jerdan, *Letters from James, Earl of Perth*, 19, 49, 60.

[68] Bossuet to Perth, Paris, 28 November, 1685, in Gaquère, *Vers l'unité chrétienne*, 63-64. In a letter of 1703, where he thanks Perth for a copy of some devotional writings by King James, Bossuet reiterated his sense of the importance of the example set by eminent converts: "The Church," he proclaimed, "has nothing more precious than ... great examples [like King James], who show that God makes saints whenever he pleases and knows how to inspire adherence to the exalted maxims that the life and teachings of Jesus Christ made evident in the world." (Bossuet to Perth, Paris, 28 March 1703, in Gaquère, *Vers l'unité chrétienne*, 145.) On James's own sense of the value of his personal example, see Miller, *Popery and Politics*, 244. It is perhaps appropriate to recall that the Counter-Reformation cult of saints

The diverse strategies of recatholicization pursued by Bossuet and Perth, including instruction and persuasion by example of the educated classes, and coercion of those of lesser status, were justified, in their view, on both political and religious grounds. Because they believed that the health of the temporal realm was inseparable from that of the spiritual one, a return of "the land of saints" to its former condition of pristine orthodoxy would automatically entail the proper submission of disobedient subjects to their lawful monarch. They also held an objectivist view of religion, believing that religious truths could be known with certainty and that salvation was contingent upon adherence to these truths. Given these assumptions, it became the duty of those in authority, and especially kings, as St. Augustine had proclaimed, to put pressure on those subjects whose erroneous beliefs were endangering the welfare of their immortal souls.[69] Moreover, the insistence of Bossuet and Perth that education and

was based on a similar sense of the importance of outstanding examples in inducing piety among the faithful.

[69] See St. Augustine, Epistle 185, ch.10, where he bases his argument against the Donatist claim that persecution is never justified on the need to inquire into "the reasons which induce anyone ... to persecute," and concludes that persecution for the sake of truth is not only just, but necessary. Following Augustine, Bossuet comments—à propos of the Donatists—"that when their excesses were suppressed by the laws of orthodox emperors, they based the case for their religion on the fact that it was persecuted, and took it upon themselves to attribute to Catholic the name of persecutors." ("*Cinquième Avertissement aux Protestants sur les Lettres du Ministre Jurieu contre l'Histoire des Variations*," in *Oeuvres complètes de Bossuet*, 15: 443.)

In ch. 20 of Epistle 185, Augustine further argues that once Christ's truth was revealed, kings became obligated to act in its service, and he poses the following rhetorical question:

> But after the prophetic words began to be fulfilled, as it is written: "And all the kings of the earth shall adore him; all nations shall serve him," what serious-minded man would say to kings: "Do not trouble to care whether the Church of your Lord is hampered or attacked by anyone in your kingdom; let it not concern you whether a man chooses to practice or to flout religion"? For it would not be possible to say to them: "Let it not concern you whether anyone in your kingdom chooses to be virtuous or shameless."

Epistle 185, in St. Augustine, *Letters*, tr. Sister Wilfred Parsons, S.N.D. (New York, 1955), 4: 150-51; for other references to the duty of kings regarding the preservation of true religion, see Epistle 93, 2: 65, 75.

In the *Politique tirée des propres paroles de l'Ecriture Sainte*, Bossuet follows St. Augustine exactly in this matter, arguing that

> [The prince] is the protector of public order, which rests on religion.... Those who do not believe that [he] should employ a rigourous discipline in matters of religion, because religion ought to be free, are guilty of an impious error. For otherwise he would have to tolerate in all his subjects, and indeed in the entire state, idolatry, Mohammedanism, Judaism, every false religion, blasphemy, even atheism, and the greatest crimes would be exempt from the least punishment.

In this context, according to Bossuet, the marks of the true religion prove to be especially useful, because they allow the sovereign to recognize it without difficulty, and thus to adopt a

argument accompanied by force were the necessary means to inculcate true belief depended on a shared conception of the act of conscience—one in which intellect and will work reciprocally on one another to produce adherence to truth. In this view, inherited from Augustine and Aquinas, coercion can be effective, as Mark Goldie has explained, because it provides "an occasion for the reconsideration of opinions." In other words, the will, which can be constrained, directs the intellect, which cannot, to turn its attention to truths that hitherto it has refused to acknowledge. Pressure—even the infliction of suffering or the deprivation of livelihood—is thus justified because, by bringing about a "change of mental direction, it may motivate a person to listen to new teachings."[70]

The same is true of persuasion by example, a strategy appropriate in the case of potential converts whose high social status precludes direct coercion. To show how this is so, I want to turn to Perth's account of his own conversion, which, in both language and content, communicates a strong sense of the interrelation of intellect and will in the act of conscience. In Perth's case, however, the will, in keeping with his social pre-eminence, is not constrained, but persuaded.

The language of Perth's account reflects a view of conscience inherited from Aquinas that was characteristic not only of Catholics, but also of Anglican supporters of religious intolerance. Aquinas defined conscience in part as the *dictamen rationis*, or "precept of reason," and locating it in the understanding, divided it into two parts: *synderesis*, or knowledge of the moral law by an infallible natural intuition, and *conscientia*, the application of that law to particular situations.[71] In the latter activity,

proper attitude toward falsehood. See Bossuet, *Politique*, 218, 228.

It is also interesting to note that in Epistle 185, Augustine offers a justification for the harsher treatment of the lower orders in cases of religious dissent, arguing that "a hard-hearted slave will not be corrected by words, for if he understandeth, he will not obey" (162). Augustine also justifies compulsion by invoking the example of St. Paul, whom Christ "not only compelled ... by words, but used his power to strike him prostrate, and in order to force him to leave off the savagery of his dark unbelief and to desire the light of his heart He afflicted him with corporeal blindness" (163). I would suggest that this passage helps to explain why St. Paul appears only rarely in the accounts of elite conversions to Catholicism: these individuals distinguished themselves from the lower orders precisely because they thought of themselves as having the capacity to be convinced by argument rather than compelled by force. For a contrasting example, note the title of the sermon preached by Andreas Wigand, a Jesuit who left the order to become a Lutheran in July 1671: "Sermon of Abjuration: In Which He Justifies the Repudiation of His Entire Past as the Result of an Instantaneous Illumination from God Which Overwhelmed Him as It Had Saint Paul." See Wilhelm Kratz, S.J., *Landgraf Ernst von Hessen-Rheinfels und die deutschen Jesuiten: Ein beitrag zur Konvertitengeschichte des 17. Jahrhunderts* (Freiburg im Breisgau, 1914), 70.

[70] Mark Goldie, "The Theory of Religious Intolerance in Restoration England," in Grell *et al.*, eds., *From Persecution to Toleration: The Glorious Revolution and Religion in England* (Oxford: Oxford University Press, 1991), 347.

[71] St. Thomas Aquinas, *Summa Theologiae*, tr. Timothy Suttor (London, 1964), 11: 189 (1a.79, 12), 191-93 (1a.79, 13). See also Mircea Eliade, ed., *The Encyclopedia of Religion*

conscience, though it has a duty to inform itself, can err through invincible ignorance. Such ignorance, however, does not necessarily exempt a person from the sin that may result from following an erroneous conscience. Moreover, the excuse of invincible ignorance can be invoked only in the domain of fact, and never of right. In the latter context, which includes religious truth, the duty of the conscience to enlighten itself is absolute. Given this imperative, heretics are more guilty than infidels because, theoretically at any rate, the truth has been presented to them and they have failed to accept it, either through stubbornness, laziness, self-interest, or mere passivity—forms of ignorance that Aquinas calls either directly or indirectly voluntary.[72] In their case, therefore, the sincerity of their beliefs does not exempt them from coercion; on the contrary, coercion is necessary because it acts on the will, which in turn moves the understanding to reconsider the content of beliefs and the reasons for holding them.

Let us look now at Perth's account of his conversion in light of this conception of conscience and the justification of religious intolerance that it entailed. Like many similar converts, Perth begins his narrative at the point when the will, due to proper persuasion, has begun to move the understanding: in other words, he is concerned to record the moment when he repudiates views passively held in favor of new convictions actively examined, and thus his transition from conventional opinion to right understanding. Deploying the vocabulary of enlightenment to assert both the intellectual respectability of his new beliefs and the active, inquiring manner in which he arrived at them, Perth wrote the following

(New York: Macmillan, 1986), 4: 46-47; and *The New Catholic Encyclopedia* (New York: McGraw-Hill, 1967), 4: 200. On the thomistic view of the objective basis of conscience, see for example Keith Thomas, "Cases of Conscience in Seventeenth-Century England," in John Morrill, Paul Slack, and Daniel Woolf, eds., *Public Duty and Private Conscience in Seventeenth-Century England: Essays Presented to G.E. Aylmer* (Oxford: Oxford University Press, 1993), 31. On the history of the concept of synderesis, see Robert A. Greene, "Synderesis, the Spark of Conscience in the English Renaissance," *Journal of the History of Ideas* 52, no. 2 (June 1991): 195-219, and especially 198. My thanks to Gordon Schochet for acquainting me with Greene's essay.

[72] In his discussion of Aquinas on conscience, Goldie puts the matter this way: Aquinas, he explains, "justified the coercion of conscience by invoking the importance of having good reasons for our beliefs. Most people, however, believe what they do not because they have thought clearly about it, but because they have passively received their views, from their parents, education, and social milieu, or just because (consciously or not) it serves their interests to hold such views." (Goldie, "The Theory of Religious Intolerance," 346.) On the duty of the conscience to inform itself and the relation of this imperative to the domains of fact and right, see Aquinas, *Summa*, 18: 67 (1a2ae.19, 6); Edmund Leites, "Conscience, Casuistry, and Moral Decision: Some Historical Perspectives," *Journal of Chinese Philosophy* 2, no. 1 (Dec. 1974): 44-45; and J. P Massaut, "Les droits de la conscience erronée dans la théologie catholique moderne," in Hans R. Guggisberg *et al.*, eds., *La liberté de conscience (XVIe-XVIIe siècles* (Geneva: Droz, 1991), 239. On the justification of compulsion in the case of heretics, see Aquinas, *Summa*, 32: 63 (2a2ae.10, 8).

to his sister-in-law:

> After the death of the late king, His Majesty presently reigning showed me a paper relating to the true Church, which I believe that you have seen. There I found such strong *arguments* that I was not able to rest until I had *examined* the subject in its entirety by reading books, listening to religious disputations, and *reflecting* a great deal about it. When I was entirely *instructed*, I proceeded to *examine* other points of controversy as objectively as possible. The excellent volume of the bishop of Meaux on the explication of church doctrine was such a great help to me that I would like to express the gratitude that I owe to that worthy prelate by kissing his feet every day.... Thus, I was troubled by only one scruple, which made me delay my return to the Catholic Church: I was afraid that people would believe that because the king professed that same religion, I was converting more to please him than to attain my own salvation, and it angered me to think that I would pass for a hypocrite. However, I finally mastered myself, and resolved to risk my reputation.... [I]f men want to consider me a deceiver, God sees my conscience and knows that it is clear....[73]

It is important to note that this exemplary account serves several polemical functions. First, the emphasis on reading and study, argument and disputation, and the use of "intellectual" verbs to characterize the process of inquiry serve to illustrate the reasonable nature of Catholicism, while the denial of all self-interested motives anticipates and attempts to defuse the attacks of Perth's former coreligionists. For my purposes here, however, both these strategies ought to be considered as means of distinguishing his new beliefs, which are the result of active inquiry and successful self-mastery, generated by a proper inclination of the will, from his previous ones, which he merely inherited, and which, as he subsequently indicates, had served him well in his career.[74]

---

[73] Perth to Mme. de Crolly, n.p., n.d., probably late 1685, in Gaquère, *Vers l'unité chrétienne,* 52-53 (my emphasis).

[74] In summing up the function of such accounts in general, it is useful to turn to Clifford Geertz, who argues that religious discourse, like other symbol systems that he includes in the larger category of cultural patterns, provides models both "of" and "for" reality, expressing the world's climate, and shaping it. Seen in this light, Perth's account offers a model "of" Catholicism, one that, through its emphasis on reasoned inquiry, communicates the characteristic Catholic sense of the continuity between the realms of nature and grace. At the

In this context, the "paper relating to the true Church," and Bossuet's "explication of Church doctrine," like coercion in the case of individuals of lesser status, constitute the occasions for Perth's "change of mental direction." This is because, despite their appeal to the intellect, both also act on the will as vehicles of persuasion. As Bossuet himself informs us, the "paper relating to the true Church" included the exemplary recognitions of Catholic truth written by Anne Hyde, late Duchess of York, and purportedly by King Charles.[75] Such accounts, which all eminent converts were expected to write, were particularly valued by Catholic proselytizers, not only because they reiterated arguments that consistently proved convincing to an educated population, but because the high social status of their authors enhanced the credibility of these arguments to their social equals, thereby exercising an equally effective, but less rational appeal—one that derived its rhetorical power from a deeply felt sense of class solidarity. In this context, it should be remembered that Aristotle had defined the example, along with the enthymeme, as the basic figures of *rhetorical*, as opposed to dialectical, argumentation because both are intended to produce belief by implicitly addressing broadly shared prejudices and preconceptions.[76] In this manner, the exemplary conversion account by an eminent individual not only addresses the intellect, but also appeals to the emotions, and thus to the will—but without constraining it—thereby constituting the perfect vehicle of spiritual shaping for those whose social pre-eminence exempted them from direct coercion.[77] Perth's own account, in the case of his family and friends, was intended to perform a similar function.

It may be objected that Bossuet's "explication of Church doctrine," to which Perth also attributed his conversion, does not fit this pattern. Such a text, it would seem, addresses the intellect exclusively, rehearsing a series

same time, by recording Perth's exemplary search for truth, it presents a model "for" the disposition of mind to be adopted by other potential converts. Geertz's argument is contained in his essay, "Religion as a Cultural System," in *The Interpretation of Cultures* (New York: Basic Books, 1973), 93-95.

In his infamous *Lettre pastorale*, addressed to the *nouveaux convertis* of the diocese of Meaux (1686), Bossuet argues in a fashion similar to Perth—and to Aquinas—that erroneous beliefs are the product of habit: "I have seen you approaching the pulpit, with the same eagerness as the rest of the flock: healthy doctrine entered your hearts when it was presented to you undisguised; and the doubts that habit rather than reason had raised in your minds, yielded gradually to truth" (245).

[75] See n. 22 above. On 28 November 1685, Bossuet wrote to Perth as follows: "The writing of Madame the late Duchess of York, and that of the late king of England, which began to shake you (*qui a commencé à vous ébranler*), are testimonies that God himself has elicited in order to revive the ancient faith." (In Gaquère, *Vers l'unité chrétienne*, 63.)

[76] An enthymeme, it will be recalled, is an incomplete syllogism in which the major premise is not stated because it is thought to be a matter of universal agreement.

[77] The *New Catholic Encyclopedia* emphasizes the emotional component of will, explaining that willing is "usually (but not always) distinguished from knowing in that [it] involves some sort of affective approach to what is cognitively present to consciousness" (14: 909).

of arguments designed to convince the potential convert of the truth of
Catholic doctrine. Significantly, however, Perth seems to conceive of his
encounter with it as another "occasion" that brought about his change of
mental direction. In a letter to Bossuet of 1687, he wrote the following:

> I thank God each day that [your explication] fell into
> my hands, especially because, most surprisingly, it was a
> minister who sent it to me, as a work he considered
> more suitable for one who desired rather to satisfy his
> curiosity than to come to a determination about matters
> of religion. But God is all-powerful, and when men are
> only considering their own amusement, He turns that
> amusement toward their edification; when Saint
> Augustine had no other intention than to listen with
> pleasure to the eloquence of Saint Ambrose, he took
> away with him the seeds of the scruples that the great
> preacher had sown in his heart, which, by a great
> miracle, when they had grown to maturity, produced the
> fruit of a perfect conversion.[78]

This passage appears to reflect Perth's own conviction that the decision
of conscience depends on a reciprocal interaction of intellect and will.
Note by the way here that Perth plays Saint Augustine to Bossuet's Saint
Ambrose, thereby complimenting the great bishop's oratorical talents and
exalting himself. This strategy, however, does not necessarily reflect
excessive pride or slavish flattery: the identification with Saint Augustine
was not at all uncommon among eminent converts in the seventeenth
century, and was often encouraged by Catholic writers and
controversialists. When, for example, Catholic loyalists in England still
nursed hopes that James I would return to the old faith, the poet John
Abbott, writing in 1623, presented Augustine to him as a model whose
conversion was rendered even more glorious by his former heresy.[79] Far
more important to consider in the present context is Perth's emphasis on
the phenomenology of Augustine's conversion, which provides exemplary
confirmation of the claim that the journey toward right understanding
begins with an inclination of the will. In the case of Saint Augustine, and
by implication of all those converted by Bossuet's powerful rhetoric as
well, the origin of true belief, as Perth represents it, lies in the moment
when the will succumbs to the emotional appeal of eloquence and thus
initiates in the understanding a new process of inquiry. Such an analysis, it

[78] Perth to Bossuet, Edinburgh, 15 January 1687, in Gaquère, *Vers l'unité chrétienne,* 84.
[79] See Alison Shell, *Catholicism, Controversy and the English Literary Imagination, 1558-1660* (Cambridge: Cambridge University Press, 1999), 143.

may be pointed out, also underlies Augustine's own theory of preaching.

I have dwelt at length on Perth and his relations with Bossuet in order to show that their policies reflected a shared conviction that the spiritual health of the kingdom determined its temporal well being. I have also argued that, in their case, this conviction entailed a theological justification of intolerance that placed paramount importance on the truth of religious beliefs and posited a reciprocal interaction of intellect and will in the act of conscience. In contrast, Bossuet's defense of James II's 1693 declaration is predicated on an implicit acknowledgment that the temporal health of the realm is *not* dependent on its adherence to religious truth and on a philosophy of conscience that separates understanding from will. Moreover, the religious policies recommended to James by Bossuet in the defense are justified by arguments that appear not only to undermine the universalist values that had attracted converts like Perth to Catholicism, but also to weaken the Catholic defense of royal absolutism. Before discussing the defense proper, however, I should like to situate it further by looking closely at certain innovative Reformed and Anglican arguments of the 1680s that help to set the stage for the declining cultural appeal of the vision of Catholic infallibility and international Christian unity that attracted converts like Perth and James II.

IV. Some interim developments in controversy

It goes without saying that James's departure from Britain in 1688 diminished Bossuet's stature there.[80] And since 1685 the great bishop's reputation had been irreparably tarnished internationally by his support for the Revocation of the Edict of Nantes, as educated public opinion turned

---

[80] Bossuet's credibility had previously sustained a serious attack by the Anglican William Wake, who had purported to show that an early version of the *Exposition* had been condemned by the doctors of the Sorbonne. While this accusation was never proved, the flight of James put an end to the combat, and Wake was left in possession of the polemical field. See William Wake, *An Exposition of the Doctrine of the Church of England in the Several Articles Proposed by Mr. de Meaux, Late Bishop of Condom, in His Exposition of the Doctrine of the Catholic Church* (London, 1686); and the response by Bossuet's defender and translator of the *Exposition*, Father Joseph Johnston, *A Vindication of the Bishop of Condom's Exposition of the Doctrine of the Catholick Church, In an Answer to a Book Entituled, An Exposition of the Doctrine of the Church of England. With a Letter from the Said Bishop* (London, 1686). The polemic between Wake and Johnston continued until the end of 1688. For a complete account, see Lambin, "Les rapports de Bossuet avec l'Angleterre," *Bulletin du Bibliophile* (Nov. 1909): 535-41. In his *Censure of M. de Meaux's History of the Variations of the Protestant Churches* (1689), Gilbert Burnet commented that "some of my countrymen have of late exposed him [Bossuet] in so severe a manner, that his credit in England was so much sunk before this new attempt that he [Wake] has made upon it, that there was no need of this work to destroy it quite" (20). For a detailed account of Wake's attack on the *Exposition* see H. A. Moore, "On the Text of Bossuet's 'Exposition de la doctrine de l'Église Catholoque,'" *Seventeenth-Century French Studies* 12 (1990): 231-49.

emphatically against the ideal of religious unity with a persecuting face.[81] But even before 1685, Bossuet's arguments attacking variation as a sign of error and midwife of political rebellion, and invoking the perpetual unity of the Catholic Church as a mark of its infallible authority had begun to lose some of their clout, succumbing both to the pressure of widely publicized and increasingly articulate defenses of reformed church government, as French Protestants in particular sought from the early 1680s to stave off the imminent Revocation, as well as to longer-term intellectual and cultural changes, including the profound transformation in intellectual values exemplified by the quarrel of the ancients and the moderns, which began to make itself felt in Reformed and Anglican polemics.

To understand this development, let us first return to the organic metaphor linking religious and civil society that had grounded Catholic arguments for the necessity of an absolute authority in both realms. Like their Catholic counterparts, Protestant polemicists and ecclesiologists had long conceived of the Church as a body whose sovereign head was Christ.[82] At the same time, however some had maintained that, given Christ's headship, all authorities within that body possessed only a subordinate jurisdiction and could therefore be legitimately resisted if they deviated from Christ's law as it was expressed in Scripture. As might be expected, this argument also entailed an analogy with the state. The Church, argued the Anglican Whig Gilbert Burnet in 1687 in a response to King Charles's "papers,"

> is a body united together, and by consequence brought under some regulation: and as in all states, there are subalterne judges.... If [these] judges do so manifestly abuse their authority, that they fall into rebellion and treason, the subjects are no more bound to consider

---

[81] See Orcibal, "L'Idée d'Église," 352.

[82] Note for example the following argument of John Calvin:

> We are all in search of the Church of God.... We all admit it to have been so propagated from the beginning as to have continued through an uninterrupted series of ages down to our own day, and to be diffused at present over the whole world. But how may we recognize it? Surely not by the titles of men, but by the truth of Christ.
>
> Who of us, to recognise a man, would look at his shoes or his feet? Why then, do we not begin at its head, seeing that Christ himself invites us to do so?... Wherefore, if we would unite in holding the unity of the Church, let it be by a common consent only to the truth of Christ.

John Calvin, *The True Method of Giving Peace to Christendom and Reforming the Church*, cited in P. D. L. Avis, *The Church in the Theology of the Reformers* (London: Marshall, Morgan, and Scott, 1981), 34.

them; but are obliged to resist them, and to maintain
their obedience to their Sovereign; tho' in either matter,
their judgment must take place, till they are reversed by
the Sovereign. The case of religion being then this, that
Jesus Christ is the Sovereign of the Church; the
Assembly of the Pastors is only a subalterne judge: if
they manifestly oppose themselves to the Scriptures,
which is the Law of Christians, particular persons may
be supposed as competent judges of that, as in civil
matters they may be of the rebellion of the judges, and in
that case they are bound still to maintain their obedience
to Jesus Christ.[83]

Arguments like Burnet's remained vulnerable to the Catholic claim,
brought to perfection by Bossuet, that such principles posed a danger to
political order, especially because they appeared to hold out the possibility
of opposing the king in the king's name.[84] But other more conservative
Protestants were elaborating justifications of reformed church government
that seem designed to elude this charge. The most articulate of these were
written by Bossuet's great antagonist, the Reformed minister, Jean Claude
(1619-1687). By the 1680s, Claude's stature among European Protestants
was unsurpassed, and in Britain, translations of his works would constitute
the core of the Church of England's response to the Catholic polemical
onslaught that began with the accession of James.[85] Writing in France as
Louis XIV's threat to revoke the Edict of Nantes loomed increasingly
large, Claude, who had no quarrel with the notion that an absolute
authority was necessary in the state, was concerned to counteract the
radical pronouncements of ministers like Pierre Jurieu, and thus to
reassure the king that those who professed the Reformed religion in his
realm were indeed loyal subjects. To accomplish this, Claude employed

[83] Burnet, "Six Papers," 44-45 (emphasis in original).
[84] Bossuet had also argued that the reformers had proved to be inconsistent in their view of
Church authority. By even creating synods and other institutions of Church government, he
claimed, they had tacitly undermined the principle of *sola scriptura*. See for example the
Conférence avec M. Claude, in *Oeuvres complètes de Bossuet*, 13: 518-19.
[85] See for example, Jean Claude, *Mr. Claude's Answer to Monsieur de Meaux's Book Intitled
A Conference with Mr. Claude. With His Letter to a Friend Wherein He Answers a Discourse
of M. de Condom, Now Bishop of Meaux, concerning the Church* (London, 1687); and *A
Relation of the Famous Conference Held about Religion at Paris between M. Bossuet, Bishop
of Condom (Late Tutor to the Dauphin) and M. Claude, Minister of the Reformed Church at
Charenton* (London, 1684) For subsequent editions of these works in England, see Gee, *The
Catalogue of All the Discourses against Popery, during the Reign of James II*. A brief French
biography of Claude was translated into English in 1688. See Abel Rodolphe de LaDevize,
The Life and Death of Monsieur Claude, the Famous Minister of Charenton in France
(London, 1688).

two very different strategies, which depended in turn on different manipulations of the organic metaphor. The first of these, implicit in a justification of the reformers' original "separation" that occurs in his *Defense of the Reformation*, translated into English in 1683,[86] consisted in approaching the analogy between the body politic and the body religious from a new angle, through a concentration on the distinction between public and private activities in both church and state. Answering the question, "What right did our fathers as private persons have to reform themselves and others?" Claude argued in the following manner:

> this question will be easily dispatched if we consider that there are two sorts of common actions in all societies, some of which are so common that they only pertain to the body taken *collectively*, as the Schoolmen say, and not to each private person. Thus, in a *Parlement*, to issue a decree, to absolve a man or condemn him, are actions of the entire body, and not of each person who composes it; and in the same manner, to declare war or make peace, are acts of the person or persons who possess the prerogatives of the entire State (*qui ont entre les mains les droits de tout l'Etat*). But there are other actions that are so common in society, that they pertain to every private person (*chaque particulier*), or, as they say, to all *distributively*, and not to all *collectively*. Thus, to express one's opinion in an assembly is not an action of the entire body, but of each private person who composes it; and to live in a kingdom, to marry there, to manage one's resources, to work there, to protect oneself against the discomforts of life, are actions that are so common that they pertain to all private persons. And jurists have drawn this distinction clearly when they say that there are acts that pertain to *omnes ut singulos* and others that regard *omnes ut universos*.
>
> Now, applying this distinction to our subject, I say that in the religious society of the Church, faith, piety, sanctity, and consequently the rejection of errors, false cults, and sins, are common acts that pertain to every private person. *The just man lives by faith*, says the Gospel, and just as it would be ridiculous to demand of a man in civil society what personal calling (*vocation*) he

---

[86] See n. 28, above. Translated as *An Historical Defence of the Reformation* (London, 1683). I shall be quoting from the third French edition (Amsterdam, 1683). For a summary of Claude's historical argument, see Perry, *From Theology to History*, 84-86, 98-99, 103-105.

has to live, to work, to avoid those things harmful to
life, and to have concern for his self-preservation, so is
it absurd to demand of our fathers, what right they had
to believe firmly in God, to serve Him with pure hearts,
and to distance themselves from those whom they
believed were undermining spiritual life, and threatening
their salvation.[87]

In this argument, Claude identified the initiatives a believer may
undertake to protect his salvation with the actions a subject may take to
preserve his life and well being. Just as, in the state, those activities, like
marriage, work, and self-defense, which serve the cause of the subject's
own preservation, may legitimately be carried on by all private persons,
so, in the Church, all believers may equally legitimately question religious
authority in the name of the quality of spiritual life and of salvation. By
arguing in this manner, Claude succeeded in having his cake and eating it
too: in other words, by equating the resistance of believers to authority in
the Church with the legitimate activities of self-preservation of subjects in
the state, he could justify that resistance while consigning it to a private
realm, where, implicitly, it would have no impact on public order.

In his answer to Bossuet's *A Conference with M. Claude*, first
published in 1684 and translated into English in 1687, Claude pursued a
different strategy, one more explicitly congenial with his commitment to
royal absolutism. Here, he repudiated the intimate link between religious
and civil society hitherto dictated by the organic metaphor, and argued
that because Church and society were two very different sorts of bodies,
they therefore required different forms of government. Refining earlier
Protestant arguments centering on the question of the visibility of Christ's
Church,[88] Claude began by attacking the Catholic claim that Christ's
promises had been granted to a Church which "must always subsist after
the manner of a sensible and palpable body, so as to be the object of our
sight, and discernable by all the world."[89] This claim, he continued, has

---

[87] Claude, *La défense de la Réformation*, 294-95 (emphasis in original). Claude's argument
that the act of separation from a Church for reasons of conscience is a legitimate one had
appeared in the writings of earlier Reformed controversialists, but his prudent distinction
between the public and private realms reflects an innovative adaptation to the context of
political absolutism. Moreover, it would have a significant future in the history of toleration.
On the theme of the legitimacy of separation from a corrupt church on the grounds of
conscience in Reformed polemic generally, see Perry, *From Theology to History*, 92.

[88] On the disagreements between Anglicans and Calvinists on the issue of the visible church,
which tended to make some conservative Church of England divines suspicious of Claude,
see Milton, *Catholic and Reformed*, 278.

[89] Claude, *Mr. Claude's Answer*, 2. For previous British Protestant reactions to the Roman
position on this issue, see Milton, 270-300.

led the Catholics to conceive of their Church as a visible society, or, as a twentieth-century commentator has put it, a "sociological reality,"[90] whose members one can point to without difficulty, by remarking their "bare, outward profession" of faith. Moreover,

> carrying these conceptions of theirs still further, they fancied, that as in order to the preservation of civil society, an absolute supreme authority, to which all must bend, is necessary because without such a one there would be no possible means of composing differences ... the same was likewise necessary in the Church.[91]

Thus, Claude concluded, the analogy that Catholics draw between the Church and civil society has given birth either to pretensions to infallibility on the part of popes, or to demands for implicit obedience to the decisions of councils.

In Claude's view, those who argue in this manner have misunderstood the character of the Church. Refuting Bossuet's claim that the term "Church" must be taken in its most "natural" signification, he went on to define it as

> not barely the visible body, or company of the faithful at present upon earth, but that body or company of the faithful, which have been, are, or at any time shall be, from the beginning to the end of the world.... [And this] company ...[is] separated from the world by the Word and the Holy Spirit of God, according to the purpose of His election.... I acknowledge the word *Church*, when used in a civil sense, as for instance when spoken of the people of Israel, does most properly signifie an external and visible company.... But still I assert, that this word when applied to a Christian society, does not properly denote a visible congregation, or an outward profession of the faith, and no more; but chiefly an inward calling, a spiritual communion, and such as that outward is only a consequence of, and does depend upon.[92]

---

[90] See Orcibal, "L'Idée d'Église," 338. For an earlier Reformed version of the argument distinguishing the society of the Church from political society, see Moïse Amyraut, *Du gouvernement de l'Église contre ceux qui veulent abolir l'usage et l'autorité des synodes,* 1653, summarized in René Voeltzel, *Vraie et fausse Église,* 15.

[91] Claude, *Mr. Claude's Answer,* 3.

[92] *Mr. Claude's Answer,* 3, 6 (emphasis in original). The Roman conception of the visible church helps to explain the apparent lack of concern on the part of Catholic proselytizers

The core of Claude's argument here is his distinction between "external ... company" and "inward calling," one that reflects in turn the decisive separation between the realms of nature and of grace that was characteristic of Reformed anthropology. In Claude's view, Christ's Church is a world of being, different in every respect from the world of seeming that human beings have created for themselves. Given this conception, any equivalency between the body of the Church and the body of civil society can only be considered a blasphemy. Moreover, because Christians are held together by an inner bond, the relationship of believers to authority in the Church must be of a different character from that of subjects to authority in the state. "What greater vanity can there be," Claude asked,

> than to go about to form an Idea of the Church after the pattern of a civil society? The Civil Society is a humane contrivance, that owes its birth to natural instinct, under the government of a general Providence, and is kept up and preserved by Rules of Justice and humane policy. The Church is a divine and supernatural work, born only of the Blood of the Son of God, and animated only by His Spirit. His hands have made it, and His particular Providence watches over it, and preserves it. The Laws of the Civil Society do not properly respect any more than the outward man, they never make it any part of their End or business to regulate mens hearts, or alter the inclinations, or inward motivations there; all within, they leave perfectly free, and are satisfied with an outward observation, which comes within the reach of each man's power. The Laws of the Church do chiefly regard the inward man, their design is to sanctifie the heart, and fix themselves especially in the soul, which are effects above any power of Man, and can belong to none but God only.
>
> In the Civil Society, private men ought rather to suffer injuries that are put upon them, than disturb the peace of the whole body, because such injuries may be endured, and yet not approved; and besides if they do it, the evil is not past all redress; for God who protects the innocent and oppressed, is able to right them, and recompense their losses with interest: In the Church it is

about the "sincerity" of potential converts. In their view, the church, considered as a "sociological reality," embraces good and bad individuals, all of whom are capable of transformation, and who will be sorted out, as the wheat is sorted from the chaff, at the end of time.

> far otherwise, where the conscience must acquiesce, and
> a quiet submission cannot be given to a lye, an error, or
> an unjust thing, without approving it; and when it is
> approved, the evil is past redress, for God will avenge
> that fault, and nothing can make us amends for the loss
> of an eternal salvation.[93]

In Claude's two arguments, the organic metaphor and the analogy between Church and state that accompanied it are manipulated in contrasting fashion to support the claim that the resistance of believers to authority in the Church has no consequences for their attitude as subjects toward authority in the state. The second argument, despite its radical rejection of the organic metaphor, is the more congenial to royal absolutism. That is because, while breaking the figurative link between Church and state, it does not repudiate the claim that the prerogative of secular authorities to control the "outward man" may include regulation of religious practice. Therefore, it remains quite compatible with the Erastian argument that religious behavior, as opposed to belief, is indeed a matter of public order, and so falls within the purview of the magistrate.

Claude's first argument, though conservative in its manipulation of the organic metaphor, is the more subversive in content because the analogy it draws between activities like marriage and work and religious commitment and the actions that may result from it appears genuinely to relegate religion to the private realm. Taken together, both arguments look beyond Bossuet: the second argument, though Claude might not have seen it that way, is consistent with a secularized justification of religious intolerance generally identified with Hobbes, one that claims for the magistrate the right to regulate religious practice in the name, not of religious truth, but of public order. Moreover, Claude's decisive separation between the "inward" and the "outward" man is also consistent with the philosophy of conscience that informed the Hobbesian position. In contrast to the augustinian/scholastic conception of the act of conscience, in which intellect and will work reciprocally on one another to effect adherence to truth, the Hobbesian view asserts their mutual independence, arguing that constraint of the will, or of outward behavior, has no effect on the content of belief.[94]

---

[93] *Mr. Claude's Answer*, 3-5.
[94] On the distinction between the augustinian/scholastic and the Hobbesian conceptions of conscience, see Goldie, "The Theory of Intolerance," esp. 358. By identifying conscience with intellect or judgment and denying the will any role in its operations, it was possible to claim that liberty of conscience was not infringed by the regulation of religious practice. See Gordon J. Schochet, "Intending Political Obligation: Hobbes and the Voluntary Basis of Society," in Mary G. Dietz, ed., *Thomas Hobbes and Political Theory*, Lawrence: University Press of Kansas, 1990), 67 and 73, n. 42; and idem, "From Persecution to

Claude's first argument constitutes an even more decisive step beyond Bossuet. By identifying religious behavior with the activities that every private person may legitimately undertake in the name of self-preservation, he anticipates not only the arguments of Locke as they are expressed in the *Letter concerning Toleration* of 1689,[95] but especially those of Bayle, who despite his commitment to absolutism in politics, held a radical conception of religious liberty.[96]

By implicitly relegating religion to the private sphere, Claude's first argument, like the more straightforward ones of Locke and Bayle, begins to sever the bond between the religious and the temporal realms, thereby undermining Bossuet's claim that heresy generates rebellion. At the same time, other developments within religious controversy were proving equally dangerous to Bossuet's contention that variation in religious matters was a sure sign of error. One of these, which had long been in evidence, worked to undermine the objectivist conception of religious truth that informed Bossuet's argument. As I indicated earlier, Bossuet believed that only *one* religious truth existed, and that it could be

---

'Toleration,'" in J. R. Jones, ed., *Liberty Secured? Britain before and after 1688* (Stanford: Stanford University Press, 1992), 137. I shall argue below that Bossuet himself is constrained to adopt the Hobbesian view in his defense of James's declaration.

[95] See for example Locke's discussion of the sorts of religious activities a magistrate may lawfully prohibit:

> Whatsoever is lawful in the commonwealth cannot be prohibited by the magistrate in the Church. Whatsoever is permitted unto any of his subjects for their ordinary use, neither can nor ought to be forbidden by him to any sect of people for their religious uses. If any man may lawfully take bread or wine, either sitting or kneeling, in his own house, the law ought not to abridge him of the same liberty in his religious worship. But those things that are prejudicial to the commonweal of a people in their ordinary use, and are therefore forbidden by laws, those things ought not to be permitted to Churches in their sacred rites. Only the magistrate ought always to be very careful that he do not misuse his authority, to the oppression of any Church, under pretence of public good.

John Locke, *A Letter concerning Toleration*, in *Political Writings of John Locke*, ed. David Wootton (New York: Penguin, 1993), 415.

[96] Bayle's commitment to absolutism, like Claude's, was based on the Reformed conception of fallen man, whose corrupt nature made him incapable of living in society without constraint. In religious matters, however, such constraint, according to Bayle, is superfluous at best because it acts only on the outward man. True religion, on the other hand, is inward, and has nothing to do with external forms of worship. Constraining the latter, therefore, is pointless, because it can have no impact on public morality. The effect of Bayle's argument is to relegate religion decisively to the private sphere. See Miriam Yardeni, "French Calvinist Political Thought, 1534-1715," in *International Calvinism*, ed. Prestwich, 332.

Like Claude, Bayle was concerned, in the wake of the Revocation, to deny the identification of the Protestant cause with rebellion. As Elisabeth Labrousse remarks, he was convinced not only that fidelity to absolutism was a cardinal point of Christian morality, but also that it was an urgent political necessity. See Labrousse, *Pierre Bayle* (The Hague: Nijhoff, 1963), 1: 224).

identified with demonstrative certainty by certain marks—notably, age, unity, and continuity. Against this view, Anglicans had begun to argue as early as the 1630s that a moral, rather than a demonstrative certainty about religious truth was all that was required for salvation.[97] Once this probabilistic opinion gained ground, it succeeded in making the Catholic polemic based on the marks of truth or error superfluous, especially since it appeared to hold out the possibility that more than one religious truth existed, as Locke's famous remark that "every one is orthodox to himself" indicates.[98]

[97] See for example William Chillingworth (1602-1644), *The Religion of Protestants a Safe Way to Salvation* [1638] (London, 1836), esp. 64-65. This radical opinion was vehemently opposed by zealots on both sides of the confessional fence. Among Protestants, the best example of the antipathy aroused by Chillingworth's book is the notorious conduct of the clergyman Francis Cheynell, who interrupted Chillingworth's funeral to fling a copy of *The Religion of Protestants* into his grave, that it might "rot with its author and see corruption." The reception of *The Religion of Protestants* is clearly reflected in the history of its publication: while two editions appeared in 1638, a third did not see the light of day until 1664. A fourth edition appeared in 1674, to be followed by a fifth in 1684. In 1687, a condensed edition appeared, indicating that by this time British Protestants had come to consider that Chillingworth's arguments could constitute part of an effective response to the Catholic polemical onslaught unleashed by the accession of James. (For the publishing history of *The Religion of Protestants*, see the *Dictionary of National Biography* [Oxford: Oxford University Press, 1959-60], 4: 256.) For an important discussion of how Chillingworth's polemic against infallibility in religion contributed to the formulation of the concept of probabilistic knowledge, see Barbara Shapiro, *Probability and Certainty in Seventeenth-Century England* (Princeton: Princeton University Press, 1983), esp. 79-83. For a critical biography of Chillingworth, see Robert R. Orr, *Reason and Authority: The Thought of William Chillingworth* (Oxford: Oxford University Press, 1967). Henry G. Van Leeuwen also provides a brief discussion of Chillingworth in *The Problem of Certainty in English Thought 1630-1690* (The Hague: Nijhoff, 1963), 15-18.

[98] Locke, *A Letter concerning Toleration*, in Wooton, ed., 390. Locke's comment occurs in the context of an attack on the "marks of the true Church" that reads as follows:

> Honoured Sir,
> Since you are pleased to inquire what are my thoughts about the mutual toleration of Christians in their different professions of religion, I must needs answer you freely, that I esteem that toleration to be the chief characteristical mark of the true Church. For whatsoever some people boast of the antiquity of places and names, or of the pomp of their outward worship; others, of the reformation of their discipline; all, of the orthodoxy of their faith (for everyone is orthodox to himself): these things, and all others of this nature, are much rather marks of men striving for power and empire over one another, than of the Church of Christ. Let anyone have never so true a claim to all these things, yet if he be destitute of charity, meekness, and good-will in general towards all mankind, even to those that are not Christians, he is certainly yet short of being a true Christian himself.

It may be noted that in Locke's argument the marks of religious truth are being internalized and individualized: no longer identified with the external features of a corporate body, they are rather to be located in the disposition of mind and heart of each Christian person. In a similar fashion, it may also be argued that the appeal to conscience, as opposed

In the present context, however, I am more interested in another development, one that stemmed directly from Protestant responses to the charge of variation. Throughout the century, representatives of the mainstream reformed churches had attempted to refute this accusation in two primary ways: either they had argued defensively that the changes they had inaugurated in doctrine and worship did not constitute an innovation, but rather represented a return to the pristine belief and practice of the ancient Church, or they had attacked the Catholics by claiming that it was they who were guilty of innovation.[99] In both cases, however, they continued to share with their opponents a unitary conception of truth, one that defined it as ancient and unchanging and entailed the conviction that innovation or variation could only be a mark of error. At the beginning of the century in France, the Reformed theologian John Cameron had put the matter this way:

> Antiquity, say [the Catholics], is venerable and divine; novelty, on the other hand, is damnable and diabolic. We of course readily agree to this. But we do not admit that they are entitled to boast of the antiquity of their doctrines, while we must suffer the reproach of novelty.... If they can prove that they are more ancient than we, then they will have won the battle.[100]

Echoing Cameron as late as 1686, his former coreligionist Aubert de Versé, who had migrated from Catholicism to Calvinism, and subsequently become a Socinian, clearly revealed the high stakes of the debate, proclaiming, though perhaps with some sarcasm, that "when it is shown that the [Roman] Church has always been the same, then all the Protestants will return to it."[101]

Even as Versé wrote, however, some Protestant polemicists were beginning tentatively to formulate arguments that would constitute an effective demurral to the charge of variation. Again, the direction of this new strategy is best exemplified in the work of Claude, and especially in his *Défense de la Réformation*. Here, Claude by no means abandoned the traditional identification of variation with error, vehemently attacking the Catholics for their deviation from the doctrine and practice of the ancient

---

to the reliance on an infallible Church, constituted an internalization of the sources of religious certainty. See Elisabeth Labrousse, "Eléments rationalistes de la controverse huguenote à la veille de la Révocation," in *Recherches sur le XVIIe siècle* (1978), 99.

[99] For other Protestant defenses against the charge of innovation, especially in the British context, see Milton, *Catholic and Reformed*, 229-51, 270-96. For France, see Perry, *From Theology to History*, 132-34.

[100] John Cameron, quoted in Voeltzel, *Vraie et fausse Église*, 88.

[101] Cited in Voeltzel, *Vraie et fausse Église*, 89. On Aubert de Versé, see, most recently, Israel, *Radical Enlightenment*, 352-54.

Church, and remarking on the unfortunate propensity of all men "to alter their earliest institutions by adding or taking away, or by endowing them with new forms and new purposes."[102] At the same time, however, he developed an argument that is structurally similar to his differentiation of the body of the Church from the body of civil society, and one whose consequence is to distinguish religious truth from other kinds, thereby exempting it from the requirements of age, unity, and continuity. This argument took the form of an attack on the Catholic argument of prescription, manipulated to best effect by Claude's Catholic antagonists Antoine Arnauld and Pierre Nicole under the approving eye of Bossuet.[103] Deployed first in religious controversy by Tertullian, who adapted it from Roman law, the argument of prescription was a legal and political principle justifying a right or title on the grounds that it has remained undisputed over a prolonged period of time. As such, this time honored principle was dear to the hearts of seventeenth-century elites, and came to constitute an important foundation of Catholic polemic. Applying this principle to the Catholic doctrine of transubstantiation, Arnauld and Nicole turned to the history of the medieval Church in order to show that opposition to this doctrine can be specifically located in time and place, thereby attempting to demonstrate that the doctrine itself, in contrast, was widely held by believers at the time it was called into question. The attacks on the doctrine must therefore have been innovations *ipso facto* and cannot legitimately claim to be considered the doctrine of Christ's true Church, which alone exhibits antiquity and continuity. And it follows, of course, that the same is also true of later Protestant reforms.

Claude answered this argument in the following manner:

> It might be objected that there existed a prescription in
> favor of the things our Reformers attacked, because they
> had been established in the Church for several centuries,
> just as in civil society the laws prohibit disturbing those
> who have long enjoyed possession of their titles ... even
> if it were to be established that they were usurpers; and
> that therefore the reforms of our fathers could not be
> justified in the face of opinions and practices that time
> had, in one manner or other, consecrated and made
> venerable. But this objection is worthless because even
> without alleging here that most of these dogmas and

---

[102] Claude, *La Défense de la Réformation*, 63.
[103] See Antoine Arnauld, *La perpétuité de la foi de l'Eglise catholique touchant l'Eucharistie* (Paris, 1669); and Pierre Nicole, *Prejugez legitimes contre les calvinistes* (Paris, 1671), with an official approbation by Bossuet. Claude's *Défense de la Réformation* was a direct response to Nicole's polemic.

practices were themselves innovations, as has often been
shown, and without insisting that they were publicly
contested and so were not in peaceful possession of any
title, who does not know that nothing can prescribe in
matters of faith and worship against true religion, which
is all from God, and that neither time, nor custom, nor
possession can bring truth out of falsehood, or make a
divine institution of a human tradition, or a virtue of a
vice? In civil society, the laws reasonably establish
prescription because without it, public order, which is
the purpose of the laws, cannot be preserved; but in
religious society, the principal purpose is the glory of
God and the salvation of the faithful, two things that are
established on a sure, perpetual, and invariable
foundation, and that consequently are not amenable to
prescription, nor to titles contrary [to that foundation],
no matter how ancient they may be. If prescription could
be applied to religion, Christianity would have been
forced to leave Paganism alone, for how long had
Paganism not dominated the belief of men?[104]

Just as he had distinguished the Church from civil society on the
grounds of its nature, so Claude insists here that religious truth, by nature
eternal and unvarying, cannot be measured by human standards, and
therefore transcends any marks—such as antiquity and continuity—that we
may employ to identify it.[105]

While Claude seeks to exempt the Protestant reforms from the charges
of variation and innovation by locating religious truth outside of time,
other Protestant polemicists of the 1680s began to confront these
accusations head on, arguing, though timidly at first, that the accepted

---

[104] Claude, *Défense de la Réformation*, 291-93. While Claude was not the first among
Protestant polemicists to dispute the equation of antiquity and truth by pointing to the
example of paganism, most had been logically constrained to avoid pursuing it because they
themselves had turned to antiquity to justify their own reforms. (See Voeltzel, *Vraie et fausse
Eglise*, 88.) By posing the objection of paganism at the end of his argument, where it
occupies a dominant rhetorical position, Claude shows how far he has moved beyond his
contemporaries in questioning the value of the historical argumentation that had hitherto
constituted the great strength of Reformed polemic.

[105] Claude's refutation of the argument of prescription, it might be noted, is structurally
similar to arguments in philosophy and political theory that preceded and followed it,
including the Cartesian rejection of antiquity as a mark of philosophical truth on the grounds
of the uniformity of nature, and the defense of eternal and unvarying—and therefore
"imprescriptible"—rights that marked political discussion on the eve of the French
Revolution. For a similar argument made by Pierre Bayle, see Perry, *From Theology to
History*, 105-106.

verdict on change and novelty ought perhaps to be reconsidered. As I indicated earlier, this development in controversy can perhaps best be understood by situating it in the context of the transformation in intellectual values exemplified by the quarrel of the ancients and the moderns. As is well known, seventeenth-century philosophy was marked by the beginnings of a reorientation towards antiquity best reflected in the British context in the work of Francis Bacon, and one which would generate the modern idea of progress. In a famous passage of the *Novum Organum*, Bacon had argued that because the moderns have profited from all the knowledge that has been gained by human beings since the classical age, it is they who are the true ancients, blessed by an accumulation of learning that makes them superior to those who lived when the world was young.[106] Developments in contemporary science worked to strengthen the modern claim, which came to be asserted most forcefully in the English context in the "Battle of the Books" of the 1680s and '90s, while supporters of antiquity stressed the moral and aesthetic superiority of the ancients. As Joseph Levine has argued, this quarrel "was not simply about science or literature, philosophy or rhetoric, erudition or imitation, ...[but] always and everywhere about history, about the meaning and use of the past ... the method of apprehending it ... and [its] authority in the present."[107]

Given the prestige of the early Church in the minds of both Protestants and Catholics, the "modern" interrogation of the role of the past in the present was bound to challenge entrenched positions despite solid resistance on the part of both groups to "novelty" and innovation. In intramural disputes among Catholics, ultramontane defenses of the authority of the Church's magisterium, which in the view of their proponents included not only the writings of the Fathers and the decisions of councils, but the decrees of popes, and were thus more congenial to the idea of doctrinal development, competed with the Gallican "documentary" view that located the teaching authority of the Church in its ancient tradition, a "deposit" that was given and unchanging.[108] In the context of

---

[106] Francis Bacon, *Novum Organum*, Bk. I, sect. 84; summarized in Carl L. Becker, *The Heavenly City of the Eighteenth-Century Philosophers* (New Haven: Yale University Press, 1960), 132. The developments in philosophical method inaugurated by Descartes also helped to undermine the prestige of antiquity, but on different grounds.

[107] Joseph Levine, "Ancients and Moderns Reconsidered," *Eighteenth-Century Studies* 15 (1981): 84. See also idem, *Between the Ancients and the Moderns: Baroque Culture in Restoration England* (New Haven: Yale University Press, 1999), viii. The literature on the quarrel of the ancients and the moderns is enormous. For a recent survey of its French context, see *La Querelle des Anciens et des Modernes: XVIIe-XVIIIe Siècles*, Anne-Marie LeCoq and Marc Fumaroli, eds. (Paris: Gallimard, 2001).

[108] See Bruno Neveu, "L'Érudition ecclésiastique du xviie siècle et la nostalgie de l'Antiquité chrétienne," in idem, *Érudition et religion*, 341-42; and Marc Fumaroli, "Temps de croissance et temps de corruption: les deux antiquités dans l'érudition jésuite française du

the Catholic polemic against Protestants, however, the Gallican opinion
continued to hold sway. In contrast, already by the 1670s, some Reformed
and Anglican polemicists were beginning to explore the consequences of
the moderns' arguments for their own interests. In 1670, Edward Hyde,
Earl of Clarendon, for example, relying perhaps on earlier Reformed
challenges to the reliability of the Church fathers considered as witnesses
to tradition while reflecting a new and more global skepticism about the
usefulness of the past for present-day religious belief and practice,
constructed the following pyrrhonistic defense of the doctrine of *sola
scriptura* against Catholic claims for the infallibility of church tradition:

> [W]e are so totally ignorant of all that was originally
> done from that time that deserves the name of antiquity,
> that we know nothing of what was done in ancient times,
> but by the testimony of those men who lived so many
> hundred, nay thousand years after the persons lived, or
> the things were done of which they give us the
> account.... [Therefore] antiquity will be as blind a guide
> to us in matters of practice relating to religion, otherwise
> than as that antiquity is manifest to us in the Bible.[109]

As I have indicated, however, it was not the negative assertion that the
past was unknowable, but the positive claim for the superiority of the
modern age that proved especially useful for Protestants in combating the
Catholic charge of variation. One good example of this development in its
early stages occurs in Gilbert Burnet's *History of the Reformation of the
Church of England*, first published in 1679.[110] Let us concentrate on his
use of the word "progress," which had not yet definitively acquired its
modern meaning of "advancement to better and better conditions," or
"continuous improvement." In the preface to Volume I, Burnet
summarized events that occurred during the reign of Henry VIII in the
following manner:

> The grounds of the new covenant between God and man
> in Christ were also truly stated, and the terms on which
> salvation was to be hoped for were faithfully opened
> according to the New Testament. And this being in the

---

xviie siècle," *Dix-Septième Siècle* 33 (1981): 149-68.

[109] Edward Hyde, Earl of Clarendon, "Of the Reverence Due to Antiquity," in *Essays Moral
and Entertaining, on the Various Faculties and Passions* (London, 1815), 1: 78-79. For an
example of earlier Reformed arguments concerning the unreliability of the Fathers, see Jean
Daillé, *Du vrai emploi des Saints Pères*, published in 1631.

[110] Burnet's *History* was actually published in three installments: Volume 1 in 1679, Volume
2 in 1681, and Volume 3 in 1714. An abridged edition of the first two volumes was
published in 1682.

strict notion of the word, the Gospel, and the glad
tidings preached through our blessed Lord and Saviour,
it must be confessed that there was a great *progress*
made when the nation was well-instructed about it,
though there was still an alloy of other corruptions,
embasing the purity of the faith. And indeed in the whole
progress of these changes, the king's design seemed to
have been to terrify the court of Rome, and cudgel the
pope into a compliance with what he desired: for in his
heart he continued addicted to some of the most
extravagant opinions of that Church, such as
transubstantiation, and the other corruptions in the Mass,
so that he was to his life's end more papist than
protestant.[111]

In referring to "the whole *progress* of these changes," Burnet was clearly
giving the word a predominantly neutral meaning, one consistent with the
contemporary usage that identified it with onward movement in space, or
with the process of action, events, or narrative. Deployed in this fashion,
the word "progress," while perhaps implying a certain degree of
advancement, could equally well be applied to schism or error, as the
Catholics did in talking about "the *progress* of schism."[112] Jockeying for
position here, however—as Burnet's reference to "the great *progress*
made" indicates—is a modern conception of the term, and one that is

---

[111] Burnet, *The History of the Reformation of the Church of England* (London, 1880), 1: xvi
(my emphasis).

[112] The *Oxford English Dictionary* lists the most common seventeenth-century uses of the
word "progress" as follows: 1. onward march, journeying, traveling, travel; a journey, an
expedition (here, the title of Bunyan's *The Pilgrim's Progress from This World to That Which
Is to Come* of 1678 is given as an example); 2. A state journey made by a royal or noble
personage, or by a church dignitary; a visit of state; 3. Onward movement in space; course,
way (here, an example from *Paradise Lost* is given: "For see the Morn ... begins her rosie
progress smiling"); 4. Forward movement in space (as opposed to rest or regress); going
forward, advance (examples from 1656 and 1669 are given); 4b., fig. Going on to a further
and higher stage, or to further and higher stages successively; advance, advancement;
growth, development, continuous increase (usually in a good sense), advance to better and
better conditions, continuous improvement (here, two examples are given, but neither
constitutes an aggressively positive use of the term. The first is taken from Knolles, *History
of the Turks,* written in 1603 and reprinted in 1638, and reads as follows: "If you consider
the beginning, *progresse,* and perpetuall felicitie of this the Othoman Empire." The second is
taken from a 1686 edition of Chardin's *Travels in Persia*, and reads: "Having made no
further *progress* in their business." It is important to note, however, that the *OED* does not
include the following example from Bacon's *Novum Organum*, I, Aphorism 31 [1620]: "It is
vain to expect any great *progress* in the sciences by the superinducing or engrafting new
matters upon old.") For some typical Catholic uses of "the *progress* of schism/heresy," see
Perry, *From Theology to History*, 9. My thanks to Richard Strier for the conversation that
directed me to the *OED*.

especially striking because it occurs in the context of references to Catholic "corruptions" and to the "purity" of the faith that would usually entail an appeal to antiquity, in the form of the assertion that Protestant reforms constituted a return to the pristine doctrine and practice of the early Church.

In a later work, the *Censure of M. de Meaux's History of the Variations*, published in 1689, Burnet would prove far more decisive in identifying the Reformation with "progress" in the modern sense. Before turning to that work, however, I want to look briefly at an ancillary development in Reformed polemics, one that emphasized the healthy consequences of disagreement and aimed to justify the "variations" of the Reformers by invoking the "national genius" of their churches. An example of this kind of argumentation occurs in the preface to *Mr. Claude's Answer to Mr. de Meaux* (1687). Here, the translator was concerned to answer the Anglican objection that Mr. Claude's work better represented the opinions of the French Reformed Church than those of the Church of England.[113] While granting the superiority of the latter, he went on to insist that the two churches were in agreement about matters of consequence, and so, he asked, "what can it signify, if in some few others of less consideration, and more remote from the main business, there seem a small disparity? Mens judgments must have some room left to exercise freely in, and diversity of opinion in circumstantials, like Divisions in Musick, may very well be admitted, without breaking the main Cords, or doing the harmony any prejudice at all.... [Considering this,] we must make allowances for the Genius of Claude's particular Church."[114] In comparing "diversity of opinion in circumstantials" to "Divisions in Musick," this writer has gone beyond traditional discussions of *adiaphora*, which reluctantly granted the possibility of difference of opinion about doctrines and practices deemed unnecessary to salvation, to open a space for a positive view of such disagreements. Moreover, this purpose is equally well served by his attribution of "diversity of opinion" between the Church of England and the French Reformed Church to differences in national character, a strategy that reflects in turn the increasingly positive view of national particularism that had come to mark the European political scene and would effectively undermine the attractions of Catholic universalist rhetoric that had proved so compelling to converts like Perth.

To return to Gilbert Burnet and his *Censure of Mr. de Meaux's History of the Variations.* In this work, Burnet continued to assert that it was the Catholics rather than the Protestants who had varied, and to attack

---

[113] For an excellent discussion of the relations between the Church of England and the continental Reformed Churches in the earlier part of the century, see Milton, *Catholic and Reformed*, 377-528.
[114] Claude, *Mr. Claude's Answer*, translator's preface, 23.

Catholic claims to infallibility on those grounds. At the same time, however, he argued more decisively than before that the Protestant reforms were justified, not because they looked back to a pristine antiquity, but because they reflected the open-ended process of improvement implied in the "modern" claim that human beings grow in knowledge. These two competing visions are juxtaposed rather uncomfortably in the following passage:

> [M. de Meaux] has called [his book] the History of Our Variations, but the truer title had been the History of the Progress of the Reformation. If all that he has said were true, it will amount to no more than this, which we grant, without his being at so much pains to prove it, which is, that neither were our Reformers *Inspired*, nor our *Sinods infallible*. But after all, it gives no small provocation to Humane Nature, to see a man that is of a Church, whose history is one continued thread of variations, and that in so many essential points, from what itself was in Primitive time, keep such a stir with a few inconsiderable changes, that have been made among the Reformed. If all was not at first discovered, the Changes that the Reformers made, was a Progress and not a variation; but after that their Confessions were once formed, we all know that they have perhaps stuck to them perhaps with too much stiffness; so that it were a much easier thing, to show that they ought to have varied, than to prove that they have done it. In short, we are but men, and ought not to be ashamed to own that we grow in knowledge, and that we no sooner discover errors, than we forsake them.[115]

Despite the evident tensions in Burnet's argument expressed in the accusation that the Catholics have varied, the claim that the Reformation ought to be conceived of as part of an ongoing process of human improvement, supported as it is by the further suggestion that the Reformers have perhaps not varied *enough*, is clearly left in possession of the rhetorical field.

Burnet's *Censure* was not the only work appearing in 1689 to express such opinions. Reviewing an "*écrit*" entitled "A Political Examination of the Affairs of England," the Huguenot man of letters and member of a distinguished Genevan Reformed family, Jean Tronchin du Breuil,

---

[115] Burnet, *A Censure,* 22-3 (emphasis in original).

summarized its argument regarding the impossibility of re-establishing Catholicism in Britain as follows:

> [The author] says first that in matters of religion, it is much easier to proceed from credulity to knowledge, and from the constraint of liberty, than to regress (*rétrograder*). Even the people were struck by the number of gross abuses; and enlightened individuals (*gens éclairés*) had even less difficulty perceiving the yoke that burdened them and delivering themselves from it. ... Thus, whatever the court of Rome had gained by time, skill, and force, it lost in one fell swoop, by the simple effect of examination and enlightenment (*examen et éclaircissement*), no matter what efforts it made to stop this process; because even though it is not easy at any time for people to open their eyes once they have been closed by the prejudices of birth and custom, it is even more difficult to close them, once they have been opened by the light of understanding (*lumière de discernement*).[116]

It is difficult not to be struck by what might be called the "enlightened" rhetoric of this passage. Certainly, the references to "abuses" and to the burdensome "yoke" of Catholicism are as old as the Reformation itself, but the language of intellectual emancipation is new, especially insofar as it is linked to a violent repudiation of the claims of custom and tradition that had grounded the argument of prescription, for example, and to a strong sense of the inexorably forward direction of human intellectual development.

---

[116] Jean Tronchin du Breuil, *Lettres sur les matières de ce temps* (Amsterdam, 1689), 2: 24. This work has been attributed to Pierre Bayle, and to Pierre Jurieu. Tronchin du Breuil's authorship, however, is attested by Antoine-Alexandre Barbier, *Dictionnaire des Ouvrages Anonymes* (Hildesheim: Olms, 1963 [1872-79]), 2: 1304; E. Haag and E. Haag, *La France protestante ou vies des protestants français qui se sont fait un nom dans l'histoire* (Paris, 1859), 9: 428; and by Elisabeth Labrousse, *Pierre Bayle*, 1: 223, n. 68. The name of the author of the "*écrit*" is not given.

In an earlier work, *Dialogues sur les matières du temps concernant la religion* (Amsterdam, 1683), Tronchin du Breuil had placed similar opinions in the mouth of a Huguenot interlocutor: "One can proceed, [argues this character,] from error to truth, from a confused sort of knowledge to a distinct one, from ignorance to learning; but one can never go back [*rétrograder*] without betraying one's intelligence [*lumières*] and condemning oneself, no matter what pretext one invokes to justify one's behavior" (111). These remarks must provide one of the earliest examples of the "enlightened" opinion that the rejection of past errors amounts to a moral duty. It might also be suggested that the "enlightened" view, in turn, constitutes a secular analog of the thomistic imperative to inform the conscience in questions of religious truth.

The arguments I have outlined are significant in the present context because they show that by the end of the 1680s, some mainstream Protestants had formulated conceptions of religious authority and religious truth which were predicated on the rejection of certain basic assumptions that they had once shared with Catholics, and that had therefore helped to make the claims of militant Catholicism persuasive. In doing so, many such individuals had been impelled by outrage over Louis XIV's revocation of the Edict of Nantes in 1685. By promulgating the Edict of Fontainebleau, which revoked the Edict of Nantes, Louis had claimed to be acting in the cause of Catholic truth, and for many churchmen in France his aggressive policy against the Huguenots provided reassuring evidence, as Geoffrey Adams puts it, "that God had selected a sovereign ... who was ready to use all the powers of the secular sword to effect the undivided commitment of his subjects to the Catholic faith."[117] At the same time, however, there now existed, as I have explained, an articulate body of international opinion that was prepared to repudiate violence in the cause of religion. As Jonathan Israel has recently reiterated, this broad transformation in elite habits of thought had been accentuated by the many new learned journals committed to the "ideals of toleration and intellectual objectivity" that had begun to circulate internationally and to challenge before a wide audience the accepted notion that "there existed a universally known, accepted, and venerated consensus of truth."[118] These periodicals, whose contributors and audience included not only religious skeptics, but those committed to the preservation of religion, proved, as Israel acknowledges, "one of the most powerful agents shaping and propagating the 'moderate, Christian Enlightenment.'"[119] Protestant responses to the Edict of Fontainebleau reflect this changing intellectual climate, to which developments in their own polemical theology had contributed indirectly since the 1630s: Many of them spoke out against the Revocation not only because it was directed against their coreligionists, but because they had come to question the objectivist conception of religious truth and therefore to reject the justification of religious persecution that it entailed. Or, like Claude, whose arguments, as I have mentioned, were intended to stave off the impending Revocation, they had begun to resist the claim that religious belief and practice have a necessary impact on public order.[120] But Louis XIV's mistreatment of the Huguenots

---

[117] Adams, *The Huguenots and French Opinion,* 30.

[118] See Israel, *Radical Enlightenment,* 150-51.

[119] Israel, *Radical Enlightenment,* 151.

[120] For the few examples of French Catholic opposition to the Revocation, see Adams, *The Huguenots and French Opinion,* 25-30. Among the opinions cited by Adams are those of Fontenelle, a nominal Catholic, d'Aguesseau, whose Jansenist inclinations are well known, and Vauban. Only Fontenelle's argument is genuinely relativistic; d'Aguesseau and Vauban, on the other hand, oppose the Revocation on political, economic, and general humanitarian

could also be used in a more traditional polemical manner against the Catholics. In a vociferous exchange with the Catholic controversialist Varillas,. Gilbert Burnet, for example, refused to grant Louis the dignity of a crusader on behalf of religious truth. In a transparent reference to the French king, Burnet argued that princes are moved to persecute when age prevents their attaining personal glory on the battlefield. When they are older, he contended, "the same desire for military glory, joined with a superstitious disposition of mind ... leads them to violate edicts solemnly sworn, and confirmed more than once in the most authentic manner."[121] And he not only went on to claim that Louis's persecution of his Huguenot subjects stemmed from passion rather than religious conviction, but to argue that the atrocities committed by the king's troops against innocent Protestants provided clear evidence that Catholicism could not be true. In his *Censure of M. de Meaux's History of the Variations*, for instance, he proclaimed triumphantly that any cause that had recourse to such methods must of necessity be very weak. None of the great bishop's arguments, he contended, has been "successful enough to save his church the infamy of the dragoons." Moreover, he argued further that none of the so-called corruptions of the Protestants, which Catholic polemicists always brought to bear against the truth of the Reformers, could be compared to the actions of certain modern bishops, who engage princes "on to an infamous violation of edicts, and to an unheard of cruelty, [and make] panegyrics upon it."[122] Finally, in Burnet's view, the complicity of eminent churchmen like Bossuet in Louis's barbaric treatment of the Huguenots meant that they were willing to sanction a degree of royal control over religious policy in France that contradicted the traditional Catholic position on the relation of the temporal and spiritual authorities, an inconsistency that considerably weakened their own attack on Protestant "variations."[123]

In the intellectual and cultural context of the 1680s then, the cause of Catholic uniformity became increasingly identified with the vicious policies entailed by Louis XIV's Revocation of the Edict of Nantes, a circumstance which made the militant Church increasingly vulnerable to both innovative and time-honored attacks on the legitimacy of its claims, and on the broad-based assumptions that had sustained them. Taken

---

grounds. Among the eminent Catholics who did speak out against the treatment of the Huguenots were Queen Christina of Sweden and Ernst v. Hessen-Rheinfels. See Kratz, *Landgraf Ernst von Hessen-Rheinfels und die deutschen Jesuiten*, 55-56. For the papacy's tepid response to the Revocation, see below.

[121] Burnet, *Critique du neuvieme livre de M. Varillas où il traite des revolutions arrivées en Angleterre en matière de religion*, n. tr. (Amsterdam, 1686), 2.

[122] Burnet, *A Censure*, 21-22.

[123] Burnet, *A Censure*, 35. In criticizing the French bishops, and especially Bossuet, for what amounted to an Erastian position, Burnet also has in mind the Gallican Articles of 1682. For the long-term effect of the latter on the interests of James, see below.

together, Claude's arguments outlining the limits on the believer's obligations to religious authority, whether they implied a commitment to a secularized justification of religious intolerance that placed paramount importance on public order rather than true belief, or looked forward to a more fully articulated conception of religious liberty, worked to undermine the Catholic conviction, hitherto held by many mainstream Protestants, that the health of the temporal realm depended on its adherence to religious truth. In the Catholic view, this truth could be identified with demonstrative certainty because it exhibited the marks of unity, antiquity, and continuity. To this argument, which had proved consistently compelling to many non-Catholics because they shared the unitary conception of truth that underlay it, Protestant polemic had begun to offer increasingly credible alternatives. By arguing that religious truth was qualitatively different from other kinds, Chillingworth and Claude, among others, had either exempted it from the necessity of demonstration on the grounds that it was susceptible only to a moral certainty, or shown that the marks of human truth could not be applied to it. By the late 1680s, the charge that the marks of truth were irrelevant when it came to religion was considerably strengthened not only by the relativizing trend exemplified both in the earlier work of Chillingworth and in arguments that valorized national difference, but by significant changes in cultural preconceptions regarding the nature of truth in general. Given the claim that men grow in knowledge, it became far easier for Protestants like Burnet and Tronchin du Breuil to demur to the charge of variation by arguing that even religious truth should not be conceived of in monolithic fashion, as a "deposit" that was given and unchanging, but rather as a product, still incompletely defined, of the ongoing process of human improvement. In this climate, the Revocation could only prove further destructive to the Catholic cause, as outrage over the treatment of the Huguenots endowed even outmoded arguments against the militant Church with a new and corrosive power.

Needless to say, attacks on the cause of religious uniformity met valiant resistance from both sides of the confessional fence. As Mark Goldie has shown, many Anglicans, for example, continued to espouse a justification of religious intolerance that placed paramount importance on the truth of religious belief.[124] But converts to Catholicism like Perth and King James were particularly concerned to defend themselves against what they considered to be the destruction of everything that had given their lives meaning. To such individuals, Bossuet's eloquent defense of Catholic

---

[124] See Goldie, "The Theory of Religious Intolerance." On the persistence of confessional intolerance in France and the Empire, see for example Elisabeth Labrousse, "Calvinism in France," and Etienne François, "De l'uniformité à la tolérance: confession et société urbaine en Allemagne, 1650-1800," *Annales, E.S.C.* 37, no. 4 (July-August 1982): 783-800.

truth, which appealed to their need for religious certainty and to the cultural values that enabled them to make sense of their world, offered a port in a storm. They would soon be set adrift, however, when Bossuet himself was constrained to argue that the cause of Catholic universalism was perhaps best served not by the Gallican vision of Catholic unity in diversity, in which absolute monarchs protected and advanced the cause of true religion, but by a compromise of a far more radical kind. That compromise, in the form of Bossuet's defense of James's declaration, constituted an acknowledgment that adherence to Catholic truth was perhaps not always the best means of securing the political peace of a kingdom, and thus dealt a death blow to the conviction that the conversion of heretical kings would result in the reconstitution of a Catholic Europe. It amounted, therefore, not only to a tacit recognition that the bond between the religious and the secular realms could be broken, but also to a more global repudiation of the principle of universality that had enabled Catholicism to define itself against the emerging nationalist, pragmatic, and subjectivist outlook that it identified with the fragmentation of Christendom.

V. Bossuet's defense of King James's declaration

To understand the significance of James's 1693 declaration, it is perhaps best to compare it with a similar statement that he had issued the previous year, just prior to the invasion of Britain, the outcome of which would be decided by the battle of La Hogue.[125] As John Miller has pointed out, this proclamation, written by Melfort, could hardly be said to reflect a willingness on James's part to grant serious concessions in matters of religion. While it included, in Miller's words, "general assurances that James would protect the Church of England and promote liberty of conscience," there was "no promise to observe the laws or redress grievances."[126] Moreover, it was accompanied by an extensive list of those to be exempted from any general pardon upon the return of James,

---

[125] For a brief history of James's abortive attempts to regain his kingdom, see Eveline Cruickshanks, "Attempts to Restore the Stuarts, 1689-96," in Cruickshanks and Corp, eds., *The Stuart Court in Exile*, 1-15.

[126] Miller, *James II*, 237. This declaration also justifies James's recourse to French support, protests vehemently against the charge of abdication, attacks the new principles of succession, challenges William as a usurper, warns loyal subjects not to support him, asserts the indisputable title of the prince of Wales, and demands that magistrates immediately proclaim their loyalty. (See Clarke, *Life of James II*, 2: 479ff.) For a brief comparison of the 1692 and 1693 declarations, see Franck Lessay, "Les déclarations de Jacques II en exil," in *L'autre exil: Les Jacobites en France au début du xviiie siècle: Actes du colloque "La Cour des Stuarts à Saint-Germain-en Laye au temps de Louis XIV"* (Languedoc, 1993), 46-49. For an excellent analysis of the political implications of the 1693 declaration and its consequences for the Catholic party at Saint-Germain, see D. Szechi, "The Jacobite Revolution Settlement, 1689-1698," *The English Historical Review* 108 (1993): 610-28.

including some of the most important Tory churchmen, as well as Bishops Burnet and Tillotson. The provision relating to the protection of the Church of England reads as follows:

> And we hereby further declare and promise, that we will protect and maintain the Church of England as it is now by law established, in all *their* rights, priviledges and possessions, and that upon vacancies of Bishopricks and other dignities or benefices, care shall be taken to have them filled with the most worthy of their own communion.[127]

There is no mention of the Test.

George Hilton Jones has argued provocatively that the use of the possessive adjective "their" reinforces the uncompromising character of this document. That is because it appears to encourage an interpretation that would undermine the collective claims of the Anglican Church, which James conceived of, not as a true Church, "but as a group of privileged individuals for convenience called a Church." In other words, if the Church of England is not thought of as a real body, its collective rights and privileges are called into doubt, and only the personal rights of its members are assured. Moreover, Jones concludes, the proscription of clerics like Burnet and Tillotson would have helped to insure that little effective resistance to oppressive royal policies could be mounted from within the Anglican communion upon the king's return.[128]

James's 1693 declaration differs significantly in tone and content from its 1692 counterpart. Referring constantly to the king's "loveing subjects," it expresses his willingness "to lay aside all thoughts of animosity and resentment at what is past ... [and promises] our free pardon and indempnity to all ... of what degree or quality soever, who shall not by land or sea oppose us."[129] It further promises that upon his return, James will redress all grievances, summon parliament "with all speed" and assent to bills securing the frequent calling of that body in the future, and guaranteeing free elections, impartial trials, and ratification of laws "made under the present usurpation." The provisions relating to matters of religion read as follows:

> We likewise declare upon our Royal word, that we will protect and defend the Church of England, as it is now established by law, and secure to the members of it all

[127] Cited in Clarke, *The Life of James II*, 2: 487 (my emphasis).
[128] Jones, *The Mainstream of Jacobitism*, 24.
[129] Cited in Clarke, *Life of James II*, 2: 503.

> the Churches, Universities, Colleges, and Scools,
> together with their immunities, rights, and priviledges.
>
> We also declare we will with all earnestness
> recommend to ... Parliament such an impartial libertie of
> conscience as they shall think necessary for the
> happiness of the Nations.
>
> We further declare we will not dispense with, or
> violate the Test, and as for the dispensing power in other
> matters we leave it to be explained and limited by ...
> Parliament.[130]

The wording of this section of the declaration was the result of a tug of war between James's more liberal supporters and the English Catholic divines at Saint Germain to whom it was submitted for approval. As the ambiguous phrase "members of it" indicates, the latter had managed to insure that a distinction was maintained between the protection of a heresy and the collective privileges of its institutions and the securing of the king's subjects as individuals in the free exercise of their religion.[131] At the same time, this minor victory, which only succeeded in alienating James's Anglican supporters, was eclipsed by the success of the liberal faction in persuading the king to agree—much against his will—to include the promise not to dispense with the Test. They accomplished this by turning to several French clerics and doctors of the Sorbonne, including Bossuet, whose sanction of the declaration *in toto* on 12 February allowed James to consent to its publication and distribution in Britain, where it proved equally disappointing to Catholics, and provoked bitter commentary on the subject of the king's hypocrisy among his enemies.[132] In distancing himself from this futile document, James himself contended

---

[130] Clarke, *Life of James*, 2: 503. The full contents of the declaration also included promises to re-establish the Act of Settlement in Ireland and to abolish the hearth tax, an act already accomplished by parliament since the Revolution. See Jones, *The Mainstream of Jacobitism*, 33.

[131] In his *Memoirs*, James sums up the position of the English Catholic divines in a manner that indicates his implicit approval:

> They said: the king could not promis to protect and defend a Religion
> he believed erroneous.... But they agreed that the king might promise
> to secure and protect his subjects of the Church of England as by law
> established in the free and full exercise of their religion...[,] it being a
> quite different case to promis to maintain the Religion itself, or to
> maintain the professors of it in their possessions, benefices etc.

Summarized in Clarke, *Life of James II*, 2: 508-509.

[132] Pamphleteers proclaimed that while James had promised not to dispense with the Test, he had not repudiated the right to do so: Of the declaration, one writer asserted that "here is indeed no more than a simple promise not to make use of that power to dispense with the Test, which he has an undoubted Right to still." ("An Answer to the Late King James' Last Declaration," 32.)

later that the French clerics had been deceived by proponents of the declaration who had failed to show them the provision relating specifically to the Test. But this explanation does not hold water in the case of Bossuet, who, unlike the other French doctors, never publicly repudiated his sanction of the declaration or the defense that he subsequently wrote at the request of James.[133]

To understand fully the genesis of the declaration and the defense, it is essential to recall first and foremost that all the major players in this drama were committed to what they called the "long-term" interests of Catholicism, though these seem curiously vague and allowed for significant differences in how they were to be defined. In this light, let us examine the actions of two of the other protagonists, Louis XIV, who had supported the liberal faction at Saint Germain and encouraged Bossuet to placate James by writing the defense, and the pope, Innocent XII. It was Louis whom James regarded as responsible for having imposed the declaration on him in the first place, and for having insisted upon its rapid circulation in Britain.

> [W]hat hurryd the king on too fast in this affair, [he recalled] was first the little probability or hopes he had of prevailing with His Most Christian Majesty to undertake anything in his favour after such losses, and so signal a defeat at sea; which made him listen more readily to any propositions which came from his own people, despairing in a manner now of being restored in any other way than by their consent and procurement.[134]

In other words, Louis was tired of throwing good money after bad. Though the French king, reluctant to abandon a royal house linked to him by ties of blood, had made every effort during 1692 and 1693 to persuade Catholic princes to rally to James's cause,[135] the defeat at La Hogue had been costly, and Louis was reluctant to underwrite another such endeavor unless substantial British support for James could be guaranteed. Securing that support was the aim of the ill-fated declaration.

While Innocent XII's reception of James's declaration will be taken up in more detail below, it is important to note here that like Innocent XI, his predecessor but one, who detested James's high-handed attitude toward the

---

[133] F. Cabrol, basing his claim on Clarke's *Life of James*, cites Bossuet as having admitted orally that he made a mistake in writing the defense of the declaration, but that he "did not think it necessary to produce a written retraction, since the affair was completely closed." See "Bossuet, ses relations avec l'Angleterre," 561.

[134] Clarke, *Life of James*, 2: 506.

[135] See Claude Nordmann, "Louis XIV and the Jacobites," 82, 86.

papacy after 1685 and regarded it as a blatant imitation of that of Louis
XIV, with whom he was at loggerheads over the issues of the Gallican
Articles of 1682, the *régale,* and the failure of the French king to support
an international crusade against the Turks, Innocent XII had no liking for
the house of Stuart, and refused to identify James's fate with the cause of
Catholicism.[136] In 1693, then, the unfortunate James would feel the effects
of the very real tensions that had marked relations between the French
king and the Holy See for almost a generation, and that could not be
alleviated by a rhetoric of Catholic unity and universality, no matter how
powerful.

Because James's declaration had reached Britain at the end of April, his
insistence three weeks later on securing papal approval could only serve to
assuage the pangs of his own conscience. From the French point of view,
however, the public consequences of James's request could prove
disastrous, and so his communication with Rome required careful
management. Louis and his advisors, who appear to have been quite aware
that the declaration was unacceptably heterodox in content, saw danger on
two fronts should it become public at the papal court: first, they feared
that cardinals loyal to the House of Austria would make use of it further to
tarnish Louis's image among European Catholics; and second, they
foresaw that the pope would be compelled to repudiate it. As a result, they
hoped to keep it as quiet as possible, a strategy that is revealed quite
clearly in the correspondence among Bossuet, Louis, and Cardinal de
Forbin-Janson, the French ambassador to the papal court.

At James's insistence, Bossuet wrote to Cardinal Janson on 22 May
1693. This letter, which included a summary of the provisions of James's
declaration relating to religion and Bossuet's defense of them, also
informed the cardinal that he had discussed this matter with Louis and that
the king had "approved [his] opinion."[137] In addition, he requested that his
defense be shown to Pope Innocent XII. Janson responded by
complimenting Bossuet on "the beauty and solidity" of his reasoning,
while betraying at the same time a certain hesitancy about the impact this

[136] Innocent XI had objected to James's having married Mary Beatrice without papal
approval, and to the king's attempt to bully him into making his Jesuit adviser Edward Petre
a bishop or cardinal. He also doubted the wisdom of James's religious policy, fearing that
unless the king exhibited more moderation, the English Catholics would lose everything. See
Godfrey Anstruther, "Cardinal Howard and the English Court," 322-59; John Miller, *Popery
and Politics,* 229-38; and Frank McLynn, *The Jacobites* (London: Routledge and Kegan
Paul, 1985), 175. The dispute between Innocent XI and Louis XIV over the Gallican articles
and the *régale,* the compromise reached on these issues by Innocent XII and the French king,
and their relevance to the declaration will be discussed below. On relations between Louis
and the papacy in the 1660s, see Paul Sonnino, *Louis XIV's View of the Papacy (1661-1667)*
(Berkeley: University of California Press, 1966).
[137] Bossuet to Cardinal de Forbin-Janson, 23 May 1693, in Gaquère, *Vers l'unité chrétienne,*
117.

document might produce in Rome.[138] In an official "mémoire" of 16 June addressed to Louis, the cardinal explained his reservations in more detail.

> We have concluded, that great difficulties will arise if we communicate this matter to the pope directly because, however zealously he may wish to see the king of England re-established, he will think it necessary to discuss [the declaration] with his ministers, and with other cardinals and theologians, either because he does not have enough knowledge about it, or because his natural timidity leads him to believe that he cannot make a decision on his own in such an important affair, and this will produce annoying consequences.

And he went on to argue that it would be best to keep quiet about the declaration until a successful invasion of Britain by James made superfluous all objections to the means he had employed to achieve it.

> [W]hen God has given his blessing to this enterprise, [the cardinal continued] ...all these phantoms will vanish, and when all impediments to the king of England's restoration have been overcome, this court will not stand in his way; and as far as the delicate consciences of the king and the English Catholics are concerned, they will be fully satisfied by the arguments of M. de Meaux and those of the doctors that agree with him.[139]

In the meantime, it appears that James had also written to Cardinal Howard, urging him to discuss the declaration and Bossuet's defense of it with the pope. As a result, Cardinal Janson took it upon himself to inform His Holiness of the contents of the declaration "under the seal of confession." In this conversation, he emphasized the long-term advantages to the Church should James be restored and the consequent necessity of doing nothing to hinder the success of a possible invasion. Though we don't know what Innocent really thought about these arguments, it appears that the "long-term" interests of Catholicism won out, since it was ultimately decided that while under no circumstances could the papal court give formal approval to the declaration, it could be tolerated, and that therefore the best tactic was to make no official statement of any kind.[140]

---

[138] Cardinal Janson to Bossuet, n. d., in *Correspondance de Bossuet*, 5: 388.

[139] Cardinal Janson to Louis XIV, 16 June 1693, in *Correspondance de Bossuet*, 5: 529-30.

[140] Cardinal Janson to Louis XIV, 30 June 1693 and 7 July 1693, in *Correspondance de*

The origins of this *politique* decision lay in the ongoing relations between the papacy and Louis XIV. From January to August, 1693, Louis and Innocent were attempting to reach a satisfactory compromise on the issues of the extension of the king's right to administer the temporalities and spiritualities of vacant episcopal sees (the *régale*) to his entire realm, and the papal ratification of the appointments of bishops who had subscribed to the Gallican articles of 1682, suspended by Innocent XI in that year. Indeed, so hostile had relations been between the French king and Innocent XI as a result of these disputes that, though the latter could not help but be pleased at the return of so many Protestants to the Roman fold, he had manifested little public interest in the Revocation, refusing, against the king's hopes, to compromise on the *régale,* and expressing only symbolic approval of Louis's defense of Catholic uniformity.[141]

By 1693, however, both the papacy and Louis were ready to give ground. Progress had been made during the tenure of Innocent's predecessor, Alexander VIII, and Innocent XII, according to Pierre Blet a flexible man who preferred negotiating tacit agreements to hurling fulminations, and evidently cared less about the issues at stake than had Innocent XI, had begun his papacy by communicating to the king his desire to accommodate their differences.[142] Louis also wanted to reach an agreement, both in order to thwart his international opponents, who were capitalizing on his alienation from the papacy, and to avoid the domestic charge that ill fortune in war and poor harvests at home provided evidence of God's displeasure at his attitude toward Rome. In the first weeks of August, 1693, he wrote to Cardinal Janson that it was important to profit from the advantage he had incurred from a recent victory over William of Orange: deploying the Gallican rhetoric of Catholic unity in which faithful princes gallantly defend the cause of true religion to suggest that his own interests and those of the papacy coincided, Louis reminded Janson that it was necessary to take advantage of the present circumstances, and "terminate our differences to the mutual satisfaction of the Holy See and of myself, in order to cease giving my enemies and, I might very well say, those of His Holiness an opportunity to contravene an agreement that is so necessary to the well-being of our religion."[143]

Bossuet, 5: 532-34.

[141] Pierre Blet, "Les papes et la Révocation," in *La Révocation de l'Édit de Nantes,* 266-74.

[142] See Pierre Blet, *Les assemblées du clergé et Louis XIV de 1670 à 1693* (Rome: Università gregoriana, 1972), 592. Innocent XII later expressed his fundamental sympathy with the Revocation after the Peace of Ryswick in 1697, when the principality of Orange had been restored to William of Orange, now king of England. On this occasion, he urged Louis to prevent that territory from serving as a haven for Protestants fleeing France. When on 23 November of that year the French king issued an edict forbidding his newly converted subjects to enter the principality, Innocent sent him a letter praising his "royal piety." See Blet, "Les papes et la Révocation," 276.

[143] Cited in Blet, *Les assemblées du clergé,* 568.

As I have suggested, this background indicates that the policies of Innocent XII and Louis XIV regarding James's declaration were in part the product of ongoing negotiations between them that dictated a prudent silence on both sides regarding James. In order to avoid creating a situation in which Innocent would have felt compelled to publicize the contents of the declaration, Janson, acting on Louis's behalf against the wishes of James, took care that the pope did not see Bossuet's defense, which made very clear the declaration's heterodox dimensions. Even more evident here, however, is Innocent's flexible stance toward Louis, encouraged, significantly, in this case by his ambivalence toward James. In tolerating the declaration, and feigning ignorance of its very existence, Innocent protected Louis by avoiding any action that would further sully the image of the French king among European Catholics, and redound to the benefit of his enemies. The ongoing negotiations concerning the *régale* and the status of the Gallican articles and of the bishops who had subscribed to them reflected the same compromising attitude on the part of Innocent, who ultimately, maintains Blet, gave much more than he got.[144] Most important to note here, however, is the significance for James of Innocent's tacit approval of the declaration. As I have suggested, Innocent appeared willing to justify his silence by invoking the "long-term" interests of Catholicism. In the short run, however, he had effectively consigned the English Catholics to the status of an oppressed religious minority, while placing James in a position where he could not serve the cause of true religion. If I am correct in suggesting that Innocent's apparent indifference to these consequences of the declaration stemmed in part from a legacy of papal resentment at James previous "Gallican" highhandedness, then we are confronted with two historical ironies: first, that Innocent's abandonment of the English Catholics was partially motivated by an outmoded commitment to the plenitude of papal power; and second, though paradoxically, that James's fate in this case was at the same time the product of papal compromise with another Gallican prince.

On 14 July, a printed copy of the declaration appeared in Rome and aroused little comment. Breathing a sigh of relief, Janson concluded that this was because he and Cardinal Howard had managed things so carefully. Writing to Janson on 22 July, Louis XIV, who had previously undercut James by arguing that since the declaration had already been published in England, it was useless to consult the papal court about it at all, commended the cardinal's handling of the affair. In the absence of any official statement from the papal court regarding the declaration, he himself would inform James that the pope had approved it, and he warned

---

[144] Blet, *Les assemblées du clergé*, 592. For Blet's entire discussion of these negotiations, see 530-581.

Janson "not to take any further action in this matter, nor to communicate to anyone the memorandum of the Bishop of Meaux, which will only give rise to new difficulties that are capable of undermining any good effects that this declaration may have produced."[145]

Despite Louis's reference to the possible "good effects" of the declaration and the rash claims of some of James's supporters that he would be restored within six weeks of its publication, no rising ensued in Britain, and plans for an invasion were cancelled. James, who later complained of the papal court's failure to take a position on the declaration, became further convinced of the futility of such concessions, and was determined to make no more.[146] "All the frute the King reaped from this declaration," he wrote later, "was blame from his friends, contempt from his enemies, and repentance in himself."[147]

Had Gilbert Burnet been privy to the negotiations between Louis XIV and Innocent XII, he would have been pleased to note the contradictions in papal policy, as well as the damaging consequences for the Catholic cause that were implicit in Bossuet's defense, even though the bishop, like the pope, had claimed to have at heart the interests of the Church in the long run. To understand the significance of these consequences, it is necessary to turn first to Bossuet's summary of the contents of James's declaration and to his analysis of the king's predicament. This declaration, he explained, consists of two parts:

> The first is that His Majesty promises to protect and defend the Anglican Church, as it is presently established by law, and that he guarantees its members all their churches, universities, colleges, and schools, with their immunities and privileges. The second, that the said Majesty promises that he will not violate the Test oath, nor dispense from it.[148]

Proceeding to a pragmatic defense of these policies, Bossuet went on to argue that neither amounted to a violation of James's conscience. On the contrary, he maintained, it is appropriate, and even "very good" for the king to implement the provisions of the declaration both because his own

---

[145] Louis XIV to Cardinal Janson, 9 July 1693 and 22 July 1693, in *Correspondance de Bossuet*, 5: 535-56.
[146] See Miller, *James II*, 238. In his 1696 declaration, prepared before another proposed invasion that ended only in confusion, James refused to include a promise not to dispense with the Test Acts.
[147] Clarke, *Life of James*, 2: 511.
[148] Bossuet, "Preuves du sentiment de M. l'évêque de Meaux sur la déclaration du roi d'Angleterre," in Gaquère, *Vers l'unité chrétienne*, 118. All subsequent references to this text will be cited internally.

power is limited and because this course of action will restore public peace. In the case of the Test Acts in particular, he reminded the English Catholics that "the Protestants are the masters" (121), and argued further that because Catholics constitute such a small portion of the population of the kingdom, they would be making an unreasonable demand of their king and sacrificing the long-term interests of Catholicism in Britain by asking him to dispense them from it:

> As far as the second article of the king's declaration, which relates to the Test, is concerned, it only obliges His Majesty to exclude from public office those who refuse to take a certain oath: now this should not cause any difficulty, because it is perfectly possible to live in a decent christian manner without being eligible for public offices.
>
> Now if it seems hard to the Catholics to be excluded from these, they should be mindful of their situation, and remember also that they compose only a small portion of the kingdom of England; which obliges them not to demand impossible conditions of their king, but on the contrary, to sacrifice all opportunities for advancement to the more genuine advantage of having a king of their own religion. (121)

And this acknowledgment of the extensive limitations on the king's power justifies the defense of the declaration more generally:

> Those who are negotiating with the king of England on this occasion, do not ask that he approve of the Anglican Church.... They only ask for a legal protection, that is to say an external protection, one that is appropriate for a king who has no power over the consciences [of his subjects] (*qui ne peut rien sur les consciences*); and everyone agrees that this sort of protection is legitimate and permitted. (119)

It is important to note that Bossuet's position here differs significantly from that of the British Catholic divines at Saint-Germain, and in a manner that further emphasizes the weakness of James. While they had insisted that the declaration be worded in such a way as to preclude royal protection of the collective privileges of the Church of England while assuring only the personal rights of its members, Bossuet's distinction between the king's approval of the Anglican Church and the legal or external protection he may afford it allows for no such interpretation. Indeed, in Bossuet's argument the tables are turned on James, in that he may exercise his personal right to withhold approval from the Church of England while remaining obliged to guarantee its collective privileges under the law. In this respect, it may be suggested that the terms of the declaration, as James himself suspected, limited royal authority in matters of religion so decisively as to reduce him implicitly to a subject, a concern that I will return to presently.

To support further his claim that James will not act against his conscience by adhering to the terms of the declaration, Bossuet—in an astonishing maneuver, whose effect depends on an unspoken reference to the Revocation of the Edict of Nantes—turns to the implementation of that Edict by Henri IV and his successors as an example of a royal policy dictated by the tacit recognition that the power of the monarchy to enforce religious conformity was limited:

> The kings of France, by the Edict of Nantes, gave a kind of protection to the Reformed Protestants, by guaranteeing that they would not be insulted by those who wished to disturb them in their worship, and by according them certain privileges, which they ordered their officials to maintain. No one thought that their consciences were involved in these concessions insofar as they were judged necessary to preserve public peace, because it was that peace and not the supposedly reformed religion that was the reason for granting them. One can say exactly the same thing about the king of England; and if he accords greater advantages to his Protestant subjects, it is their position in the kingdom and the need for public peace that demand it. (119-20)

It is perhaps superfluous to point out that Bossuet's comparison between the policies of Henri IV and Louis XIII on the one hand, and those imposed on King James, on the other, is misleading, to say the least. In proclaiming the Edict of Nantes, as Bossuet must have been well aware, Henri IV had demanded nothing from his Catholic subjects that was contrary to their religion; rather, he had merely guaranteed limited freedom of worship to members of the Reformed religion and declared them eligible for public offices.[149] Louis XIII, moreover, while not

---

[149] On the provisions of the Edict of Nantes, see Labrousse, "Calvinism in France," 295-97. Here it is noted that the Edict did not put the Reformed religion on an equal footing with the Roman Church. "It re-established Catholicism in those few places where its practice had been discontinued and it provided everywhere for the rebuilding of Catholic churches which had been destroyed, the reopening of monasteries and convents, and above all, the restoration of property to Catholic clergy. A tight, unbroken network of parishes again covered the kingdom and all were obliged to pay tithes to the Roman Church, while its

challenging the Edict in its entirety, had begun to implement policies that eroded the privileges it had granted to his Protestant subjects.[150] In contrast, James, by agreeing to the terms of the declaration, would exclude his Catholic subjects from the public realm unless they agreed to sign an oath repudiating a primary constituent doctrine of their faith.

Moreover, by invoking the strong position in the kingdom of James's Protestant subjects as a justification for the concessions to be granted to them, Bossuet implicitly reiterated his emphasis on the minority status of British Catholics, thereby appearing to establish grounds for a comparison between them and the Huguenots. Any Catholic who read Bossuet's defense carefully would have been profoundly shocked by this implicit parallel, first of all because the case of British Recusants had traditionally been deployed by Catholic polemicists to show that the Huguenots in France did not deserve emancipation as long as British Protestants appeared to be attempting to extirpate Catholicism.[151] Bossuet, in contrast, appeared to be arguing that a minority religion, whether Catholic or Protestant, and thus true or false, must expect to endure oppression. Furthermore, in other contexts, the parallel between Catholics and Protestants could have profoundly subversive implications. As Bernard Cottret has shown, analogies between the predicaments of French Huguenots and British Recusants were extremely rare even in Protestant circles after the revocation of the Edict of Nantes, when new and radical arguments in favor of religious liberty were beginning to emerge, especially among the French Reformed diaspora. That is because, in the opinion of conservative believers in both confessions, such comparisons appeared to signal a relativizing trend of the kind epitomized by Locke's comment that everyone is orthodox to himself, and to elevate the idea of human solidarity above the cause of religious truth.[152] Thus, despite his enthusiastic support for the Revocation and his often reiterated commitment in the defense of the declaration to the long-term interests of

religious festivals were compulsory days of idleness for everybody" (295).

[150] On the gradual undermining of the provisions of the Edict of Nantes prior to 1661, see Jean Orcibal, *Louis XIV et les Protestants* (Paris: J. Vrin, 1951), and the sources cited in n. 9, above.

[151] Adams, *The Huguenots and French Opinion*, 11. Bossuet himself had previously pursued a similar line of argument against the minister Pierre Jurieu, arguing that the horrors visited upon the Huguenots by the dragonnades of the late 1680s couldn't hold a candle to similar Protestant excesses. See Adams, 19.

[152] Bernard Cottret, "Révocation et prodromes de la tolérance: le parallèle des protestants français et des catholiques d'Angleterre," *Bulletin de la société de l'histoire du protestantisme français* 126 (Oct.-Dec. 1980): 559-66. In this essay, Cottret analyzes an anonymous tract of 1687 entitled "Parallèle des Loix Pénales De France contre les Protestans avec les loix Pénales d'Angleterre contre ceux de la Religion Rom.," and concludes that the ideas it contains were "marginal" and even "visionary" (566). It should be noted that Bossuet's defense of James's declaration does not go so far as to sanction the penal laws against British Catholics. See also Pierre Blet, "Les papes et la révocation," 278.

Catholicism, Bossuet appeared to be justifying concessions to the British Protestant majority on the basis of an argument which undermined the unitary conception of religious truth that had provided a significant part of the rationale for maintaining confessional uniformity in the first place.

To understand fully the shocking about-face implicit in Bossuet's argument, it is necessary to turn once again to Louis XIV, and to the massive propaganda campaign in favor of the Revocation engaged in by men of letters in France. Geoffrey Adams has explained that even before 1685, the French Academy, in close association with the court, had actively participated in the campaign against the Huguenots, granting prizes for essays on their monarch's zeal for the true faith. A significant theme of such works was Louis's superiority to all previous French monarchs, exemplified by the Revocation itself, that "single stroke of statesmanship" which had enabled him to achieve the domestic peace and order that had consistently eluded his predecessors.[153] Bossuet had of course been an active participant in this campaign, but always as a spokesman for religious truth. If Louis surpassed his predecessors in glory, he had argued, it was not merely because he was more powerful than they, but rather because, by revoking the Edict of Nantes, he had destroyed heresy, and in so doing had returned the realm to its proper condition of spiritual unity. Waxing eloquent in his funeral oration for Chancellor Le Tellier of 1686, for example, he had reminded his audience that not even the Church fathers, in the heroic days of early Christianity, had witnessed such a "sudden dissolution of an inveterate heresy, the return to the fold of so many lost sheep that our churches are too small to hold them and finally the defection of false pastors who are ready to abandon those they have misled without even waiting for the order to do so."[154]

In contrast, Bossuet's argument that the Edict of Nantes can serve as a precedent for concessions to British Protestants that will legitimize oppression of the British Catholics, serves primarily to glorify Louis, and in so doing suggests that religious policy is entirely a function of royal power. As I have indicated, this interpretation depends on an unspoken reference to the Revocation. In other words, if the previous kings of France, in a moment of weakness, were forced to grant a measure of liberty of conscience to their subjects who professed the Reformed religion, the consolidation of monarchical power by Louis XIV has made possible a change of policy. In either case, however, the primary consideration in the formulation of policy, whether Bossuet intended that such a conclusion be drawn or not, appears to be the extent of royal power

---

[153] Adams, *The Huguenots and French Public Opinion*, 19-20.
[154] Bossuet, "Oraison funèbre de Michel Le Tellier," cited in Adams, *The Huguenots and French Public Opinion*, 23. (Adams's translation.)

and not religious unity or truth.[155]

In composing his defense of James's declaration, Bossuet had attempted to serve Louis's interests well, especially insofar as he may have hoped that his arguments would diminish James's resistance to the terms of the declaration and encourage his wholehearted participation in a new invasion of Britain that would result, in turn, in the humiliation of Louis's archenemy, William III. While it is true that Bossuet may have thought that the defeat of William would serve the long-term interests of Catholicism, and was thus convinced in this case that Louis's policies coincided with those interests, it is not at all clear that the defense supported the cause of Catholic universalism as it had been expressed in Bossuet's own rhetoric, in which Catholic kings defend religious truth by protecting the Church against her enemies.[156] It might of course be argued

---

[155] It is interesting to note in this context that in his memorandum to Louis XIV, Cardinal Janson followed up his argument that a successful invasion by James would dissipate objection to the declaration by reiterating Bossuet's implicit contrast between Louis and the previous kings of France:

> Our French Catholics, had no scruples about the edicts and declarations that Your Majesty's predecessors granted to the heretics of the kingdom, because these declarations did not involve an adherence to the principles of heresy, but merely a promise of protection, which concerned only the externals of religion.

Correspondance de Bossuet, 5: 530.

Another issue here, of course, is whether the Edict of Nantes was revocable in the first place. Huguenots, of course, argued that it was not, while Catholics replied in turn that it lacked legitimacy because, like all similar edicts of pacification, it had been exacted from the monarchy under duress, and its provisions had never been obeyed anyway. For an example of this kind of argumentation, see Bernard Meynier, S.J., *Explication de l'Edict de Nantes par les autres Edicts de Pacification, Declarations, et Arrests de Reglement* (Paris, 1686). The preamble to the Edict of Fontainebleau had justified the revocation of the Edict of Nantes precisely on the grounds that the latter had been merely an interim measure. See Adams, *The Huguenots and French Opinion*, 8.

[156] Throughout his career, Bossuet had proved willing to employ a variety of strategies in the cause of Catholicism, and on occasion these conflicted with one another. For example, at the same time that he was justifying the Revocation to Protestants at home and abroad, and composing his most eloquent polemics, he was also participating in ecumenical exchanges with Leibniz as well as with representatives of the Anglican Church. And in earlier years, of course, he had committed himself to rational argument and persuasion as opposed to persecution, especially when the interests of Versailles had demanded it. But these potentially contradictory strategies were never so at odds with one another as were his support of the Revocation, on the one hand, and his attempt to persuade James to adopt the Edict of Nantes as a model of policy on the other. Nor had he ever previously abandoned his objectivist conception of religious truth. (On the ecumenical exchange between Bossuet and Leibniz, see for example Jacques LeBrun, "Bossuet devant Leibniz," in *Leibniz (1646-1716): Aspects de l'homme et de l'oeuvre* (Paris: CNRS, 1968), 79-96. This correspondence is printed in *Oeuvres de Leibniz*, ed. A. Foucher de Careil (Paris, 1869), 2, *passim*. On Bossuet's negotiations with Anglicans, see Edmond Préclin, *L'Union des Églises Anglicane et Gallicane*, 1-6. On Bossuet's brand of ecumenicism, which he identified with the return of all wandering brethren to the Catholic Church, see Jean Deprun, "Classicisme et baroquisme

that Bossuet's commitment to Louis's interests in the defense was consistent with the role he had previously played in intramural disputes among Catholics regarding the location of authority in the Church and the proper relations between popes and kings. In the 1680s, Bossuet had been the best of episcopal and conciliar Gallicans, arguing that "indefectibility" was a property of the succession of popes from Peter to Innocent XI considered as a "moral person," and not of any individual pope, a position that allowed opposition to a given pope in the name of the Holy See considered as the embodiment of Catholic unity. Moreover, he had also been an effective framer of the Gallican claims of the monarchy, arguing in 1682 for the complete power of the crown in temporalities, and even supporting the *régale* against some of his fellow bishops, who regarded it as an illegitimate encroachment on the freedom of the French Church, on the grounds that it was not a matter of faith, and transgressed only on certain "secondary" or "adventitious" rights of the episcopacy.[157] But the defense goes beyond Gallicanism, whether episcopal or royal, insofar as it sacrifices the cause of religious truth to the exigencies of political power. Here it is important to recall the vision of Christian unity that was expressed in Bossuet's pastoral and polemical works, and that was equally characteristic of his ecclesiology. According to that vision, the power of kings serves the cause of Catholic truth, and as protectors and defenders of the faith, they forge the unity "that makes the Church so beautiful." "Let us admit, [he wrote,] that in the midst of the many enemies, the many heretics, the many unbelievers, the many rebels who surround us, we owe much to those princes who protect us from their insults; and [let us remember that] the hands which we lift up to heaven unarmed, are fortunately sustained by their power."[158]

While this image of Christian unity was certainly inflected by Gallicanism, it was also typical of the Catholic polemic of the later seventeenth century as a whole, which had attracted James and other princely converts because it appeared to provide a powerful rationale for absolute monarchy. Keeping it in mind, let us return to James, and explore the consequences for absolutism of Bossuet's defense of the declaration. In effect, by subscribing to the declaration, James had been forced to acquiesce in elevating the authority of parliament above that of the king, especially when it came to religious policy. James himself complained bitterly about the "difficult concessions regarding royal authority" that were being demanded of him, and his nonjuring supporters in Britain were even more outspoken. These concessions, they argued,

---

religieux: la controverse Bossuet-Leibniz," in *Journées Bossuet: la prédication au xviie siècle*, Thérèse Goyet and Jean-Pierre Collinet, eds. (Paris: A.G. Nizet, 1980), 361-73.
[157] See Martimort, *Le gallicanisme de Bossuet*, 556-57, 461-62, 433.
[158] Bossuet, *Sermon sur l'Unité de l'Église*, 608, 607.

had been wrested from [him] by men, the greatest part of which ... neither loved the King nor kingship itself, and who thought [James's return] a good occasion to sap the foundations of the monarchy, either by keeping it in their power to elect whom they pleased, who would still be subject to the conditions they thought fit to impose, or if the king return'd to foreclose him from exerting his power and punishing their delinquency.

And one nonjuring minister urged the king

not to make any further engagements to the Republicans; whose designes ... in the bottom were to destroy the Monarchy, or at least make the King of England no more than a Duke of Venice; that should he come in upon the foot of the Declaration, both he and all his loyal subjects would be ruined, and that in the meantime the pardoning claus in it, made the loyal men run great hazards, the Judges having declared, they had their pardons in their pockets let them act as they would in the meantime.[159]

The reasons for this resistance become especially clear when we look at Bossuet's explication of the promises regarding religion that the king was being asked to make. Again addressing the issue of greatest concern to James, he argued that the king's conscience would not be wounded in implementing these promises "because the protection and defense that he [guarantees] the Anglican Protestant Church concerns only externals, and only obliges His Majesty to leave this supposed church in the external state in which he finds it, without disturbing it or permitting that it be disturbed" (119).

To support this claim, he made the following general argument:

In order to decide this question in principle, a strong distinction must be drawn between the protection that one might give to a false church by embracing its evil opinions, and a merely external one, meant to preserve tranquility. The first sort of protection is wrong because it is based on adherence to falsehood; but the second is

---

[159] Clarke, *Life of James II*, 2: 514-15. The first part of the citation is taken from Clarke's summary of what James had to say about the opinions of these supporters in his *Memoirs*; the second quotes James directly. On James's Whig supporters, see Mark Goldie, "John Locke's Circle and James II," *The Historical Journal* 35, no. 3 (1992): 557-86.

> very good, because it is based on the love of peace, and
> its object is a very good and necessary thing, the
> preservation of public order. (119)

In the present context, it is important to note both the explicit and implicit contents of this passage. First, by arguing that the king ought to protect the Anglican Church in order to preserve public tranquility, Bossuet, in contrast to his previous practice, is espousing a theory of religious intolerance that aims to justify the regulation of religious behavior, not in the interests of religious truth or unity, but on the secular gounds that civil order demands it. Second, this political objective requires that he place limitations on the king's public behavior as opposed to his private convictions. Therefore, although Bossuet himself is by no means indifferent to the content of the king's beliefs, he appears in this context to have been drawn toward the camp of those whose arguments in favor of the regulation of religious practice depended on the claim that private religious opinions were indeed a matter of indifference to the secular authority, whose only business, on the contrary, was the supervision of public behavior. This view, in turn, depends on the defense of religious intolerance identified with Hobbes which, unlike the augustinian/ scholastic position, separates intellect from will in the conduct of the conscience by arguing that constraining the external actions of subjects has no impact on their inward beliefs. Most significantly, however, and far more disquieting for supporters of the monarchy, the distinction between private convictions and public behavior imposed on James by Bossuet's argument makes the king's conscience, rather than the subject's, the target of regulation, thereby appearing to reduce him to a private person, and implicitly acknowledging parliamentary supremacy in matters of religion.

This is not to say, of course, that the conflict between public duty and private belief had never arisen for any previous British monarch. In an eloquent essay, Kevin Sharpe has discussed the personal anguish experienced by James I, for example, when he found it necessary to impose the Oath of Allegiance. While James aggressively defended the Oath in a famous written exchange with Cardinal Robert Bellarmine that took place before a European-wide public, the measure presented several serious difficulties for the king. As Sharpe explains, the Oath separated the civil obedience of his Catholic subjects from their conscience, and so implied a larger distinction between the civic and the religious that James was reluctant to recognize. Moreover, insofar as acquiescence in this distinction violated James's beliefs, it established a disjunction between his personal and public consciences, which "should have accorded with each other and with those of his subjects." The king himself acknowledged this in a speech in the Lords: As far as his policy toward the papists is concerned, he admitted, "I must put a difference betwixt mine own private profession of mine own salvation and my politic government of the realm for the weal and quietness thereof." Not only, then, did the Oath of Allegiance depend on a secularized theory of religious intolerance that justified the regulation of religion in the name of public order, and therefore appeared to call into question the fundamentally religious nature of the realm, but, as Sharpe concludes, it undermined the identity of the king as a thoroughly public person, in whose case no barrier ought to exist between public and private selves.[160]

The consequences for royal authority of the enforced separation between the king's public and private consciences are of course nowhere more evident than in the case of Charles I, whose advisors maintained in 1641, for example, that he could consent to the attainder of the Earl of Strafford in the name of public duty, even though he had promised the Earl that no harm would come to him in the royal service. In following this advice with great reluctance, Charles complained that it was "a bad exchange to wound a man's own conscience, thereby to salve state sores." Though persuaded by the arguments of his advisors in this particular case, he bitterly resented the terms of the choice imposed on him, and was later reported to have prayed that God "never suffer me for any reason of state to go against my Reason of Conscience." As Patricia Crawford has explained, Charles regretted more than his unkindness to Strafford, for it was clear that in assenting to the Earl's execution, he had "conced[ed] a difference between the private person and the public office of the king," one that would ultimately "allow ... Parliament to wage a war to rescue him from his evil counsellors."[161]

As the fate of Charles makes especially clear, the separation of "the king's two bodies" that called the nature and extent of royal authority into question by permitting opposition to a particular king in the name of the monarchy had acquired a solid, if controversial position in British political thinking well before the accession of James II. It goes without saying, however, that such subversive interpretations of this doctrine were not characteristic of Gallican political theory, to which partisans of absolutism like James had consistently looked to provide a sanction of their own claims.[162] In this context, then, the significance of Bossuet's defense of

---

[160] Kevin Sharpe, "Private Conscience and Public Duty in the Writings of James VI and I," in John Morrill, *et al.*, eds., *Public Duty and Private Conscience*, 82, 86-87. For a discussion of James's controversy with Bellarmine, see Patterson, *James VI and I and the Reunion of Christendom*, ch. 3.

[161] Patricia Crawford, "Public Duty, Conscience, and Women in Early Modern England," in Morrill, *et al.* eds., *Public Duty and Private Conscience*, 61. and Keith Thomas, "Cases of Conscience in Seventeenth-Century England," 33. Thomas notes that Charles was forced into a similar dilemma when he agreed, under pressure, to abandon episcopacy in 1646.

[162] It can be argued, however, that when Gallican theorists applied the doctrine of the two royal bodies to the papacy, they did so in order to justify opposition to the policies of a

James's declaration lies in its tacit repudiation of the traditional Gallican position on the nature of royal authority, especially insofar as it is reflected in arguments about the public nature of the king's conscience and his duties regarding the protection of true religion. To understand this, we need only compare it briefly with the treatise on which Bossuet was engaged at the time of the declaration, the *Politique tirée des propres paroles de l'Ecriture sainte*.[163] Here, Bossuet contends in typical augustinian fashion that it is the prince's duty to exterminate all false religions in the state, and with eloquent intensity he invokes the example of the good kings of the Old Testament, "who pulverized the idols that their subjects had adored:" "Asa, Ezechias, and Josias, [he proclaimed] ... destroyed the temples and altars [of these idols]; they broke the vessels employed in their sacrilegious rites; they destroyed their sacred forests; they killed their priests and prophets; and they purged the earth of all these impurities" (228).

But the prince's obligations to true religion do not end here. As a "public personage" (243), he must embody devotion to truth, and "draw his people toward religion" (231) by manifesting his personal piety in public practice. King Josias in particular, he claimed, not only overthrew idols "throughout the kingdom of Israel," but "renewed the alliance of the whole Israelitish people with God, standing erect on the steps of the temple, in the sight of all his subjects, who swore solemnly after him to walk in the ways of the Lord" (231).[164] Moreover, he argued, this commitment to true religion must be absolute, and, invoking the example of Jehu, he excoriated those "*politique*" rulers of the Old Testament (243) who justified the protection of false cults in the name of public order. Thus, he explained,

> Jehu massacred the priests of Baal, broke his statue, and set his temple afire. And, so that he would appear to be fulfilling all his religious duties, he took the holy man Jonadab, son of Rechab, into his own chariot, so that he could witness his conduct. 'Come, he said, and see how zealous I am in the cause of the Lord.' But he departed not from the sins of Jeroboam, nor from the golden calves that he had erected at Bethel and at Dan. Reason of state would not permit it.

particular pope in the name of the legitimate authority of the Chair of Peter.
[163] See n. 49 above. Bossuet began the *Politique* in 1677 and continued working on it until his death in 1704 (Introduction, xii). All further references to the *Politique* will be cited internally.
[164] Bossuet follows Augustine exactly in his choice of Josias as a model ruler. See Ernest W. Nelson, "The Theory of Persecution," in George Lincoln Burr, ed., *Persecution and Liberty: Essays in Honor of George Lincoln Burr* (New York: Century, 1931), 7.

> Such is the religion of a *politique* ruler. He does not
> fear to be zealous in those matters that do not wound his
> ambition, and he even appears to want to please good
> men: but a false politics prevents him from achieving
> genuine piety. (243)

If we apply this argument to James, it is impossible not to conclude that
in following the terms of the declaration he will be guilty of a far greater
crime than Jehu. For that king, as Bossuet acknowledged, at least
committed himself publicly to the cause of true religion, while James,
pressed like Jehu by considerations of reason of state, has agreed not
merely to the tacit sanction of a false cult, but rather to its public
protection. In addition, because James's profession of his Catholic beliefs
is consigned by the terms of the declaration to the private sphere, it is
impossible for him to fulfill his primary duty as a ruler, at least as that
duty is delineated in the *Politique*. In other words, because his personal
piety cannot be reflected in public practice, he will no longer embody the
public conscience of the realm, or personify its condition of religious
unity. Therefore, when viewed from the perspective of the *Politique*, the
declaration not only prohibits James from performing his proper function
as a monarch, but effectively forces him into sin. James himself was
clearly aware of these implications. Begging his spiritual advisor, Rancé
of la Trappe, to advise him what course to take, he wrote the following:

> [I suppose that] it is not reasonable to believe that those
> who are demanding my return would ask me to do
> anything against my conscience, even though they can
> demand many difficult concessions from me regarding
> royal authority; and it seems to me that it will be a great
> advantage for the Church to have a Catholic king in
> England. I beg you to convey frankly to me your opinion
> about this matter, because no man who desires to be a
> good Christian should do anything by which he might
> gain the whole world, but lose his own soul.[165]

But while the consequences of Bossuet's defense were serious enough

---

[165] James II, *Copie fidelle des lettres que le St. Roy d'Angleterre a ecrittes au Rd. Pere Dom
Armand Jean Ancien Abbé de La Trappe*, in *Miscellanies of the Philobiblon Society* London,
1872-76), 14: 21 (19 September 1693). The date of this letter shows clearly that James's
conscience had not been assuaged by Bossuet's defense of the declaration. On James's
relations with Rancé, see A. J. Krailsheimer, *Armand-Jean de Rancé, Abbot of la Trappe:
His Influence in the Cloister and the World* (Oxford: Oxford University Press, 1974), esp.
265-69. Krailsheimer speculates that it was most probably through Perth that James first
heard of La Trappe (266).

in James's particular case, they also had important theoretical repercussions. For, in sanctioning the split between the public and private consciences of James imposed by the declaration, Bossuet effectively acknowledged that the public profession of true religion by a monarch did not necessarily guarantee political unity and stability in a kingdom. Given Bossuet's oft-reiterated commitment to the long-term interests of Catholicism, it is difficult not to draw the ironic conclusion that these interests were scarcely well served by short-term concessions that so thoroughly undermined a large portion of the rationale for Catholic militancy.

It might of course be argued that the casuistical distinction between the long- and short-term interests of Catholicism was nothing new. In the British context, as Alexandra Walsham has explained, it had been used by some Catholic writers to justify occasional conformity, especially on the part of elites, whose economic and social survival was essential "to preserve the resilience of a healthy and wealthy Catholic body" that would prove useful to the Church should it be returned to its former condition of grandeur.[166] Other clergymen, however, repudiated this stance, refusing to regard the long-term interests of Catholicism as an acceptable justification for complicity with falsehood in the present. "Compromising in the interval 'til time serve our turn,' protested Cardinal Allen in 1581, was no way to either 'deliver our soules, or ever recover the Realme to the unity of Gods Church againe.'"[167] Walsham goes on to argue that the disagreements among clergymen regarding the proper behavior to be enjoined on the faithful not only reflected genuine differences of opinion regarding the morality of occasional conformity, but also concern for the public image of the Catholic community. That was because accounts of stubborn recusancy, as opposed to reports of flexible co-operation with the demands of the authorities, were thought to serve the cause of Catholic truth by "reanimat[ing] ... a flagging faith" and "unnerv[ing] the adversary."[168] Thus, according to Walsham, the figure of the stalwart

---

[166] Alexandra Walsham, *Church Papists: Catholicism, Conformity and Confessional Polemic in Early Modern England* (Rochester, NY: Boydell Press, 1993), 70. It is interesting to note that for the casuists whom Walsham is discussing, Jehu provides a model of behavior: in their version of Jehu's story, his continued adherence to the false cult of Baal served as a cover for his real policy—the eventual destruction of all idolatrous priests (56). See also Peter Holmes, *Resistance and Compromise*, 108.

[167] Walsham, *Church Papists*, 36-37. Arnold Pritchard notes that Allen was not consistently so militant. At the same time, however, he warns against taking ostensibly loyalist or compromising statements on Allen's part too seriously, and criticizes Peter Holmes for ignoring the contexts of such statements. See Arnold Pritchard, *Catholic Loyalism in Elizabethan England* (Chapel Hill, NC: University of North Carolina Press, 1979), 10-36, 153-55.

[168] Walsham, *Church Papists,* 47.

recusant, whether or not he or she represented the dominant ethos of British Catholicism, fulfilled an important polemical function, while the occasional conformer, on the other hand, most probably represented the pragmatic behavior of individuals subject to the demands of the authorities and to the necessity of communicating with their neighbors on a daily basis.

It is certainly possible to approach the contradictions of Bossuet's position from a similar perspective. From this point of view, the bishop's great polemical writings, printed, reprinted, and circulated throughout Europe, would serve to sustain the public image of militant Catholicism, while the defense of the declaration, on the other hand, would represent the kind of quiet compromise dictated by the exigencies of international politics. Thus, the split between public profession and private belief enjoined on James by the defense, while thoroughly alien to the spirit of the *Politique*, for example, would not indicate any thoroughgoing incoherence in Bossuet's thinking, but rather a kind of casuistical temporising, a strategic retreat from militancy imposed on Bossuet by the peculiarities of the British national context. For James in turn, according to this view, the defense leaves room for mental reservation, because adherence to the long-term interests of Catholicism effectively implies a less than complete commitment to the religious policies that he promises to implement in the declaration.

But this analysis is too generous, for when we remember that the defense itself implicitly glorifies Louis for the consolidation of monarchical power represented by the Revocation, while reminding James that he must compromise the cause of religious truth because "the Protestants are the masters," it is difficult not to conclude that Bossuet has committed himself to the proposition that might makes right, and thus to the kind of relativism—at least so far as religion is concerned—that has given casuistry a bad name. This move toward relativism on Bossuet's part is also evident from a last, brief look at the separation between James's public and private consciences imposed on him by the defense. As I have indicated, the distinction between the king's private beliefs and his public behavior appeared to reduce him to a subject, an implication of Bossuet's argument that becomes especially clear if we turn, for example, to Hobbes's discussion of the location of the public conscience under civil government. In *Leviathan*, Hobbes had argued that in the "condition of meer nature" people have no choice but to act as their consciences dictate because no rule other than private reason exists to determine action. In a commonwealth, however, "the measure of Good and Evil actions ... is the Civill Law; and the Judge the Legislator, who is alwayes the

Representative of the Commonwealth."[169]

Under civil government, in other words, private consciences must yield
to the public conscience of the law, which is embodied in the legislator.
Now insofar as James's private conscience, like that of a subject, must
submit to regulation that prevents any expression of its decisions in public
action, it appears—at least according to the terms of Hobbes's
argument—that he cannot embody the public conscience and therefore, by
implication, that he cannot be the legislator, having been replaced in that
position by Parliament, whose claim to be entitled to control the king's
public behavior depends in turn on its appropriation of sovereign authority
in religious matters. Thus, even if we were to persist in seeing Bossuet's
defense of the declaration as a form of casuistical temporizing, we would
still have to conclude that it does significant damage to the cause of royal
absolutism, which most seventeenth-century Catholics had defended, not
only on the grounds that it was the form of government most suited to
maintaining stability and unity in a state, but also that it reflected God's
ordering of the universe as a whole. Therefore, its arguments were
nothing if not coherent. Moreover, they sought transcendent justification.
In contrast, Bossuet's defense reflects a kind of *ad hoc* pragmatism that
appeared to adjust a divinely sanctioned political theory to local
circumstances, and further, to make the Church's support of Catholic truth
contingent on the power of the secular authorities to impose adherence to
it.

In examining Bossuet's defense of James's 1693 declaration and its
contexts, I have sought to provide an example of the disarray in which
articulate Catholic universalism found itself at the end of the seventeenth
century. This state of affairs was reflected in the recourse of all parties in
the affair to the pie-in-the-sky rhetoric of the "long-term" interests of
Catholicism, which consigned an effective defense of the Catholic cause to
a distant and misty future, and served to only to dignify incoherent
policies in the present. Indeed, given the intellectual, cultural, and
political developments that I have described, it was difficult to know
exactly where Catholic interests lay and just how to secure the future of
the universal Church. The easiest way, of course, was to identify Catholic
interests with one's own, as did James and Louis XIV, with very different
consequences. Innocent XII, however, appears to have had a far more
confused sense of how to proceed: if the cause of papal power coincided
with the interests of the Church as a whole, how was it advanced by
undermining James and endangering the salvation of his subjects on the
one hand, while compromising with Louis in the name of an appearance of

[169] Thomas Hobbes, *Leviathan*, Richard Tuck, ed. (Cambridge: Cambridge University Press,
1991), 223 (ch. 29).

Church unity on the other? As far as Bossuet is concerned, it can only be said that he too identified Louis's interests with the cause of Catholicism, but that he did the job of defending them too well, insofar as he abandoned the Gallican vision of Church unity to espouse an Erastian one.

In delineating the longer-term intellectual, cultural, and political contexts of James's declaration and Bossuet's defense, I have argued that the decline of Catholic universalism was in significant part the product of developments in religious controversy, of intramural disputes within Catholicism, and of the unintended consequences of a notorious attempt to impose religious uniformity. From a broader perspective, I am suggesting that the climate of opinion that made Catholic universalist claims ever more difficult to sustain cannot be fully understood without paying attention to the religious factors that contributed to it. That is to say that the dramatic change in elite mentalities that characterized the 1680s and the decades following is a phenomenon of complex origins whose continuity with the past should not be underestimated. I have especially in mind here the impact of religious controversy, which in various forms, both oral and written, had reached a broad European public since the mid-sixteenth-century and helped to destabilize the notion of a universal religious truth in the first place. In this essay, I have traced the development of the Protestant polemic of the 1680s back to the 1630s, and it would not be difficult to show how, even prior to that time, arguments elaborated by the mainstream confessions to defend the truth of their respective faiths helped to generate ways of thinking about religion that would prove corrosive of belief, and thus constitute an essential precondition for the intellectual upheavals of the turn of the eighteenth century.[170]

It is true, however, that the partisans of Catholic universalism of the 1690s found themselves in a new and uncomfortable world, where it seemed necessary to repudiate intransigent militancy in favor of a policy of subservience to the secular authorities that would supposedly protect the interests of Catholicism "in the long run." For true believers like Perth, James's declaration, tacitly supported by the papacy, and actively defended by militant Catholicism's most articulate spokesman, signaled a moment of crisis and disillusionment because it was clear to them which choice had been made. As Perth himself wrote to James from Rome during the negotiations preceding the declaration, "religion is gone and a wicked policy set up in its place."[171]

---

[170] Elsewhere, I have shown how Catholic arguments defending the Church's claim to possess the *notae*, or marks of the true Church, encouraged a rationalistic approach to religious truth. See Susan Rosa, "Catholic Polemic and the Rise of Cultural Rationalism: An Example from the Empire," *Journal of the History of Ideas* 57 (1996): 87-107.

[171] Perth to James, cited in Miller, *James II*, 238.

Adversaries or Allies?
Occasional Thoughts on the Masham-Astell Exchange[1]

Jacqueline Broad
Monash University

Abstract

Against the backdrop of the English reception of Locke's *Essay*, scholars have identified a little-known philosophical dispute between two seventeenth-century women writers: Mary Astell (1666-1731) and Damaris Cudworth Masham (1659-1708). On the basis of their brief but heated exchange, Astell and Masham are typically regarded as philosophical adversaries: Astell a disciple of the occasionalist John Norris, and Masham a devout Lockean. But in this paper, I argue that although there are many respects in which Astell and Masham are radically opposed, the two women also have a surprising amount in common. Rather than interpret their ideas solely in relation to the "canonical" philosophies of the time—Lockean empiricism and Malebranchean occasionalism—I examine the ways in which Astell and Masham are influenced by the metaphysical theories of the Cambridge Platonists, Ralph Cudworth and Henry More. On this basis, I argue that a remarkably similar theological approach underlies the metaphysical and feminist arguments of Astell and Masham.

I. Introduction

For historians of philosophy, the late-seventeenth century is renowned for its great philosophical antagonisms. During this time, no publication was greeted with greater criticism and controversy than John Locke's *Essay Concerning Human Understanding* of 1690. More recently, against the backdrop of the English reception of Locke's *Essay,* scholars have identified a rare occurrence in the history of philosophy: a heated philosophical dispute between two women. In 1696 and 1705, Mary Astell (1666-1731) and Damaris Cudworth Masham (1659-1708) exchanged

[1] This paper was originally derived from chapters 4 and 5 of my book, *Women Philosophers of the Seventeenth Century* (Cambridge: Cambridge University Press, 2003). I presented an earlier version of the paper at a symposium on "Women Philosophers in the Seventeenth and Eighteenth Centuries" at the Pacific Division of the American Philosophical Association meeting in Seattle, 29 March 2002. I am extremely grateful to Sarah Hutton and Catherine Wilson for their comments on that occasion, and to the organizers of the symposium, Eileen O'Neill and Bill Uzgalis. I would also like to express my gratitude to the Australian Research Council: this paper was revised while I was a research associate for the ARC-funded Mindful Things project in the Philosophy Department at Monash University in 2002. In addition, I would like to thank Jeremy Aarons, Karen Green, Rae Langton, and audience members at a La Trobe University staff seminar in May 2001. Special thanks to James Buickerood for his many excellent suggestions and comments on several aspects of this paper.

opposing views about the love of God. Their exchange was far more anonymous than the famous Locke-Stillingfleet and Leibniz-Clarke debates—neither woman named the other in print, and it is only recently that commentators have started to examine their conflict in detail.[2] But the tone of the dispute was no less bitter or acerbic than its masculine counterparts. Astell, in particular, took great offence at Masham's remarks, despite the fact that the latter's insults were not explicitly directed at her.[3]

In her day, Mary Astell was highly acclaimed as the author of *A Serious Proposal to the Ladies* (1694), a popular feminist treatise calling for the higher education of women. She is now best known as one of the earliest feminists to employ Cartesian ideas in defense of female reasoning abilities.[4] But prior to her *Proposal,* from 1693 to 1694, Astell was engaged in a more conservative enterprise: a correspondence with the "English Malebranche", John Norris. In these letters, published as *Letters Concerning the Love of God* in 1695, Norris defends the thesis that one ought to love and desire God alone, and Astell gives her qualified assent to this view. Astell's anonymous part in the correspondence was highly praised by her English peers, and her letters also won the admiration of Leibniz.[5]

But in 1696 an anonymous work, titled *A Discourse Concerning the Love of God,* issued a scathing reply to the *Letters* and to Norris's

---

[2] On the Astell-Masham exchange, see Richard Acworth, *The Philosophy of John Norris of Bemerton* (1657-1712) (New York: Georg Olms Verlag, 1979), 172-80, 237-38; Sarah Hutton, "Damaris Cudworth, Lady Masham: Between Platonism and Enlightenment," *British Journal for the History of Philosophy* 1 (1993): 34-37; Ruth Perry, *The Celebrated Mary Astell: An Early English Feminist* (Chicago: University of Chicago Press, 1986), 73-82, 87-97; Patricia Springborg, "Astell, Masham, and Locke: Religion and Politics," in Hilda L. Smith, ed., *Women Writers and the Early Modern British Political Tradition* (Cambridge: Cambridge University Press, 1998), 105-25; Patricia Springborg, "Introduction" to Mary Astell, *A Serious Proposal to the Ladies, Parts I and II* (London: Pickering & Chatto, 1997), xiv-xix; and E. Derek Taylor, "Mary Astell's Ironic Assault on John Locke's Theory of Matter," *Journal of the History of Ideas* 62:3 (2001): 505-22. For the earliest historical account, see George Ballard, *Memoirs of Several Ladies of Great Britain (who have been celebrated for their writings or skill in the learned languages, arts and sciences),* with an introduction by Ruth Perry (Detroit: Wayne State University Press, 1985), 332-8. On the similarities between Masham and Astell, see Margaret Atherton, "Cartesian Reason and Gendered Reason," in Louise M. Antony and Charlotte Witt, eds., *A Mind of One's Own: Feminist Essays on Reason and Objectivity* (Boulder and Oxford: Westview Press, 1993).
[3] I am indebted to James G. Buickerood, "What Is It With Damaris, Lady Masham? The Historiography of One Early Modern Woman Philosopher" (forthcoming), for bringing this point to my attention.
[4] On Astell's feminist arguments, see my *Women Philosophers of the Seventeenth Century*, chapters 4 and 5.
[5] C. I. Gerhardt, ed., *Die Philosophischen Schriften von Gottfried Wilhelm Leibniz* (Berlin: Georg Olms Hildesheim, 1960), vol. III, 199.

Practical Discourses of 1693. The *Discourse* was written by Damaris Masham, a close friend of John Locke's,[6] and the daughter of the distinguished Cambridge Platonist, Ralph Cudworth. Norris had previously expressed an admiration for Masham's "extraordinary Genius".[7] In 1688, he dedicated his *Theory and Regulation of Love* to her, referring to the "Esteem, wherewith your Ladyship honour'd my former writings".[8] Then in 1689, in *Reflections upon the Conduct of Human Life*, Norris compliments Masham for being "so much a *Mistress*" of the works of Descartes and Malebranche.[9] Of his own philosophy, Norris says that "the more your *Ladyship considers*, the more you will be convinc'd both of the *Truth* of what I have *Discours'd*, and of the *Reasonableness* of what I *design*".[10] But by 1696, Masham had become more sympathetic to the empiricist views of Locke, a permanent resident in her home from 1691. Far from finding Norris's views "reasonable", in her *Discourse* Masham attacks Norris for espousing an impractical or "unserviceable" moral theory, rather than one based on common sense.[11] It is obvious, she says, that creatures are designed for a sociable life, and they can no more love and desire God alone than fishes can fly in the air.[12] Masham also targets Astell's part in the correspondence, dismissing her as a "young Writer,

---

[6] Masham met Locke in London in about 1681 and they began to write to one another shortly thereafter. The bulk of their correspondence is dated from 1683 to 1689, Locke's period of exile abroad. Upon his return, Locke lived with the Masham family at Oates from 1691 until his death in 1704. On Masham's indebtedness to Locke and the Cambridge Platonists, see Hutton, "Damaris Cudworth, Lady Masham," 29-54.

[7] John Norris, *The Theory and Regulation of Love. A Moral Essay. In Two Parts. To which are added Letters Philosophical and Moral between the Author and Dr Henry More* (Oxford: Henry Clements, 1688), "The Epistle Dedicatory," n. pag.

[8] Norris, *Theory and Regulation*, "Epistle."

[9] John Norris, *Reflections upon the Conduct of Human Life: With reference to the Study of Learning and Knowledge. In a Letter to the Excellent Lady, the Lady Masham* (London: S. Manship, 1690), 62.

[10] Norris, *Reflections*, 160.

[11] Commentators have speculated that there were also personal differences between Norris and Masham: in 1692, Norris was accused of breaking the wax seal on one of Locke's letters to Masham; and Masham apparently became offended when Norris failed to omit a mistaken reference to her "blindness" in the first edition of his *Reflections*. In a letter to Jean Le Clerc (18 June 1703), Masham says that her eyes are "not strong enough to hold out well for all the use I have, or would Willingly make of them: altho they never were in any either Apparant, or Invisible Likelihood, that I know of, of leaveing me in the Dark; as Mr Norris long ago perswaded many that they had done, by a Printed Letter to me to Console me for being Blind" (Universiteitsbibliotheek, Amsterdam [UvA], MS J.58ᵛ). For further details on relations between Locke, Norris, and Masham, see Charlotte Johnston, "Locke's *Examination of Malebranche* and John Norris," *Journal of the History of Ideas* 19 (1958): 551-8.

[12] Damaris Masham, *A Discourse Concerning the Love of God* (London: Awnsham and John Churchil, 1696), 82-83.

whose Judgment may, perhaps, be Byassed by the Affectation of Novelty".[13]

In their subsequent replies, both Astell and Norris mistake Masham's work for the work of Locke.[14] Their misattribution is understandable given that Masham's arguments are steeped in the empiricist philosophy of Locke's *Essay*.[15] Masham has been described as a "bluestocking admirer" of Locke,[16] someone who "sat loyally" at Locke's feet as a pupil,[17] and "a clear and ardent exponent" of Locke's ideas.[18] As a consequence of their brief exchange, Astell and Masham are typically regarded as philosophical adversaries: Astell a disciple of Norris, Masham a devout Lockean. Commenting on the differences between the two women, Ruth Perry says that "All of this was predictable: that Masham's position would be as sensible and down-to-earth as Astell's was abstract and idealist, that Masham would focus on life-on-earth while Astell stressed preparation for the hereafter. Like seconds in the duel between Locke's empiricism and Norris's idealism, their exchange is a fascinating reprise of that debate".[19] Patricia Springborg likewise observes that in this exchange "Astell proved to be the spiritual daughter of Ralph Cudworth and Masham the Platonist consort of Locke".[20]

There are, to be sure, many fundamental differences between Astell and Masham due to their respective allegiances to Norris and Locke. Astell was a fierce and persistent critic of Locke in all her subsequent writings; and Masham's *Discourse is* heavily indebted to Locke's *Essay*. Nevertheless, in this paper, I argue that Astell and Masham also have a surprising amount in common. The similarities are apparent, I believe, if we look at each writer independently of her so-called "mentor". In recent times, scholars have started to question the ways in which we incorporate

---

[13] Masham, *Discourse*, 78.

[14] Their replies can be found in John Norris, *Practical Discourses upon several Divine Subjects* Vol. IV (London: S. Manship, 1698); and Mary Astell, *The Christian Religion, As Profess'd by a Daughter Of The Church of England. In a Letter to the Right Honourable, T.L. C.I.* (London: R. Wilkin, 1705).

[15] Locke himself formulates objections to occasionalism following Norris's attack on his *Essay*, and there are similarities between Locke's criticisms and those of Masham. Locke's critiques of Norris can be found in the posthumously published *Examination of Malebranche* (1706) and "Remarks Upon some of Mr. Norris's Books," in *A Collection of Several Pieces of Mr. John Locke* (1720).

[16] Irvin Ehrenpreis, "Letters of Advice to Young Spinsters," in *The Lady of Letters in the Eighteenth Century* (Los Angeles: 1969), 14.

[17] Benjamin Rand, ed., *The Correspondence of John Locke and Edward Clarke* (1927; rpt., New York: Plainview, 1975), 14.

[18] Ada Wallas, *Before the Bluestockings* (London: G. Allen and Unwin, 1929), 95.

[19] Perry, *The Celebrated Mary Astell*, 97.

[20] Springborg, "Introduction" to Astell, *Proposal*, xv.

women thinkers of the past into the philosophical canon.[21] One common method of inclusion is to show that women participated in the great intellectual debates of their time, and that they were perceptive critics of their famous male contemporaries. To some extent, this is a plausible approach: women such as Astell and Masham were not writing in an intellectual vacuum—they were well acquainted with the contemporary literature, and, for the most part, the only way they could engage in philosophy was through the guidance and mentorship of men. But it is also agreed that the "add women and stir" method is somewhat limited. First, with this approach there is the danger that women's philosophy will not be appraised in its proper historical context. Sarah Hutton has observed that if we interpret their ideas only in relation to dominant philosophical trends, then we may overlook the profound influence of lesser-known figures.[22] We might also ignore the importance of those areas that no longer conform to modern standards of philosophy, such as moral theology or natural philosophy. Scholars ought to be cautious, therefore, about assimilating the views of women thinkers to the "canonical" philosophies of their time. Second, there is the problem that if we interpret women's writings as that of "surrogate men" or "men in petticoats" (as Mary Astell remarked in 1705),[23] then we may lose sight of the subtle divergences in *women's* thought. Yet these divergences are often crucial for establishing a place for women in the history of philosophy: some of the most original and modern contributions from early women writers, for example, are their derivations of *feminist* ideas from the philosophies of their male contemporaries. To put it simply, it is now well established that these women were the interlocutors of influential male philosophers; it is time, one might argue, to appraise women's philosophy on its own terms, and to focus on lines of development in their writings, independently of the male-dominated traditions.

In the following discussion, I take a middle path. I begin by examining the differences between Mary Astell and Damaris Masham in light of their respective allegiances to John Norris and John Locke. But then I focus on a somewhat subtle, but no less significant, philosophical influence on their work: I emphasize that both women are indebted to the Cambridge-

---

[21] Here I am thinking of Sarah Hutton, "Damaris Cudworth, Lady Masham," and "Like Father Like Daughter? The Moral Philosophy of Damaris Cudworth, Lady Masham," presented at the South Eastern meeting of the American Philosophical Association in Atlanta, 28-30 December 1996; as well as Eileen O'Neill, "Disappearing Ink: Early Modern Women Philosophers and their Fate in History," in Janet A. Kourany, ed., *Philosophy in a Feminist Voice: Critiques and Reconstructions* (Princeton: Princeton University Press, 1998), 39-43.

[22] Hutton, "Like Father Like Daughter?"

[23] Mary Astell, *The Christian Religion, As Profess'd by a Daughter of The Church of England. In a Letter to the Right Honourable, T.L. C.I.* (London: R. Wilkin, 1705), 293.

Platonist tradition. The Cambridge Platonists were a group of philosopher-theologians associated with the University of Cambridge in the mid-seventeenth century.[24] Masham spent her formative years in the company of the Platonists at Christ's College, Cambridge; and her letters to Locke demonstrate a strong familiarity with the doctrines of her father, Ralph Cudworth, and his colleagues, Henry More and John Smith. Astell, on the other hand, was partly educated by her uncle Ralph, a former student of Emmanuel College in the heyday of Cambridge Platonism; and her early writings also demonstrate a sympathy for the views of Henry More. Although there is no univocal "Cambridge" position, the members of this group are united in their theological purpose: the Cambridge philosophers tend to accept or dismiss a philosophical viewpoint solely in order to affirm the existence of a providential God, the spiritual world, and immaterial souls. From this tradition, I argue, Masham and Astell each inherit a distinctive conception of God's relationship to the created world, and a critical stance toward occasionalism. Finally, I demonstrate that, unlike Locke and Norris, both Masham and Astell are champions of women's education, and they argue that women ought to improve their rationality to become useful members of society. In these respects, I maintain, they can be regarded as intellectual allies, rather than mere "seconds in the duel" between Norris's occasionalism and Lockean empiricism.

II. Background: The Astell-Masham exchange

The primary difference between Astell and Masham lies in their opinions about Norris's theory of love. Although Norris has been called a "Cambridge Platonist", this label is somewhat inappropriate given that he was first and foremost an Oxford-trained advocate of Nicolas Malebranche's philosophy.[25] The Malebranchean theory of causation, known as *occasionalism*, is an unorthodox blend of Cartesianism and Augustinian theology, according to which there is no genuine interaction between the soul and body. The Cambridge Platonists, on the other hand, claim that there is a "vital congruity" between the soul and body that enables the two substances to interact. Toward this end, they adapt the ancient Platonic doctrine of a "World Soul", the theory that an incorporeal

---

[24] The central figures in this group are Ralph Cudworth (1617-1688), Henry More (1614-1687), John Smith (1618-1652), Nathanael Culverwell (*c.*1618-*c.*1651), and Benjamin Whichcote (1609-1683).
[25] On Norris's philosophy, see Acworth, *The Philosophy of John Norris*; Charles McCracken, *Malebranche and British Philosophy* (Oxford: Clarendon Press, 1983), 156-79; and Flora Isabel MacKinnon, *The Philosophy of John Norris* (Baltimore: Psychological Review Publications, 1910).

"spirit of nature" (or "plastic nature") pervades the material world. The Platonists and occasionalists also have significantly different conceptions of God's causal role in his creation: the occasionalists maintain that God plays a *direct* causal role in the created world, whereas the Cambridge Platonists hold that God acts *indirectly* through a spiritual intermediary. The Malebrancheans, moreover, believe that God ought to be the sole object of our desire, whereas the Platonists reject such an extreme position. Although Norris was initially supportive of the Cambridge-Platonist theories, from 1688 he was an avowed occasionalist. The *Practical Discourses* (1693 and 1698) and *Letters Concerning the Love of God* are clear expressions of Norris's break with Platonism. To call Astell "the spiritual daughter of Ralph Cudworth"[26] is therefore misleading: if Astell were a supporter of Norris's occasionalism, then this would *distance* her from Cudworth's theology and metaphysics.

Norris, like his mentor Malebranche, acknowledges that if matter consists only in extension, figure, and motion, then it is inconceivable how it could cause any effect in a thinking substance. Material things, Norris maintains, are completely without power or force, and all bodies are utterly disconnected from souls. Instead, there is a perfectly harmonious *correlation* between souls and bodies, orchestrated by God. Norris defends this view in an essay titled "A Discourse Concerning the Measure of Divine Love, with the Natural and Moral Grounds upon which it stands", in the third volume of his *Practical Discourses* (1693).[27] It is a common belief, he says, that bodies have some inherent qualities that are analogous to our sensations. But there is no more reason to suppose that "there is such a Quality as Heat, resembling what you feel in Fire, then you have to conclude *Pain* to be in a *Needle*".[28] There is nothing conceivable in bodies but magnitude, figure, and motion, so they cannot possibly have any other essential qualities. This view is held by many seventeenth-century thinkers, including Galileo, Descartes, Boyle, and Locke. But these men are mistaken, Norris says, in supposing that material objects still have the power to cause our sensations in some way, because "the very same Reasons which prove that Bodies have not any Qualities in them like our Sensations, do also prove that they do neither produce Sensations in us".[29] If bodies are mere magnitude, figure, and motion, then they cannot produce "sentiments of the mind". This is because there is no proportion or affinity between the cause and the effect: a material thing cannot

---

[26] Springborg, "Introduction" to Astell, *Proposal*, xv.

[27] John Norris, *Practical Discourses Upon several Divine Subjects*, Vol. III (London: S. Manship, 1693), 1-83.

[28] Norris, *Practical Discourses*, III: 25.

[29] Norris, *Practical Discourses*, III: 32.

"produce an Effect more Noble and Excellent and of an Order so very much higher than it self".[30] Furthermore, he says, bodies affect each other through impact and resistance.[31] But the body cannot move the soul in the same way, since the soul is penetrable: "And therefore since Spirits make no resistance against Bodies, it is not possible that Bodies should have any Action, or make any Impression upon Spirits."[32]

Norris believes instead that we must look to forces outside of bodies to explain apparent causal relations between the body and soul. Only a being of infinite wisdom and power could produce all things by the immediate efficacy of will. Hence Norris claims that God must be the only causal agent, and the only efficient cause of all sensations is divine intervention. Material things, on the other hand, are merely the *occasions* for that intervention. When the sun shines in my eyes, it is God who gives me the sensations of heat and light. "'Tis not the most delicate Fruit, or the richest Perfume, that delights either our Tast or our Smell," he says, "but 'tis God alone that raises Pleasure in us by the Occasion of these Bodies."[33] Similarly, when I will my leg to kick, my volition is merely the occasion for God to intervene and make my leg move. Even if the material world did not exist, according to Norris, we could still have the sensations we currently have. God could, if he so pleased, raise in my soul the sensation of burning without the presence of fire.

Norris uses this theory of causation to argue that God must be the sole object of our love. He maintains that we love only that which brings us pleasure, and because God is the only truly causally efficacious being, only he can be the cause of our pleasure. Consequently, God alone is deserving of our love. No causally inefficacious being could be "a fit or reasonable object of love" if it never really causes our pleasure.

Mary Astell agrees with Norris that we ought to love and desire God alone.[34] But she believes that this claim holds up *whether or not*

---

[30] Norris, *Practical Discourses*, III: 28.

[31] Norris markedly differs from Malebranche on this point. Malebranche's occasionalism is just as much a theory about body-body relations as soul-body interaction (see Steven Nadler, *Malebranche and Ideas* [Oxford: Oxford University Press, 1992], 4). For Norris, however, occasionalism applies *only* to soul-body relations, and not to body-body relations; one body can be the efficient cause of motion in another body through impact. On Norris's position, see John Norris, *An Essay Towards the Theory of the Ideal or Intelligible World ... Part II* (London: S. Manship, 1704), 223-24, 231-33; Norris, *Practical Discourses*, III: 34-35; and McCracken, *Malebranche and British Philosophy*, 172, n. 52.

[32] Norris, *Practical Discourses*, III: 34.

[33] Norris, *Practical Discourses*, III: 55.

[34] More specifically, Astell agrees with Norris's claim that creatures deserve only a love of *benevolence*, a disinterested love motivated by altruism and charity. God, on the other hand, merits a love of *desire*. The creatures could never satisfy our desires, she says, so it is irrational to desire them as our good. An absolutely perfect being, on the other hand, could

occasionalism is true. Even if bodies were able to affect souls, she says, God would still be the only deserved object of our love, because all our good is brought about solely by his will. She points out that "If a bountiful Person gives me Money to provide my self Necessaries, my Gratitude surely is not due to the Money but to the kind Hand that bestowed it".[35]

By contrast, Damaris Masham rejects Norris's theory on the grounds that it opposes the "everyday experience" of human beings.[36] Following Locke, Masham denies that we have any innate moral principles; all our moral ideas are derived from either sensation or reflection on the mind's activities. Hence no human being is born with the notion that "we ought to love and desire God alone"; it is not a self-evident truth. Human beings must "know many other Truths before we come to know this; which is a Proposition containing many complex ideas in it"; and we are not capable of framing such propositions "till we have been long acquainted with pleasing Sensations".[37] To attain the idea of "love", for example, we must first experience the sensation of pleasure in our interactions with other creatures. We come to love our children or our friends, Masham says, because their being is a pleasure to us.[38] In this way, we learn that love is "that Disposition, or Act of the Mind, we find in our selves towards any thing we are pleas'd with".[39] So in Masham's view, we can love God only *after* we have loved other people: "if we lov'd not the Creatures, it is not conceiveable how we should love God."[40]

Masham is also critical of Astell's support for Norris's Malebranchean views. Masham says that

> how unserviceable or injurious soever it [i.e. Malebranche's theory] really is to Piety, it has yet been

want nothing that we could wish for him, so he does not need our charity; we can only desire him as our good. Masham, however, believes that creatures can be loved with *both* a love of desire *and* a love of benevolence.

[35] Mary Astell and John Norris, *Letters Concerning the Love of God, Between the Author of the Proposal to the Ladies and Mr. John Norris: Wherein his late Discourse, shewing That it ought to be intire and exclusive of all other Loves, is further cleared and justified* (London: J. Norris, 1695), 282.

[36] Masham, *Discourse*, 29.

[37] Masham, *Discourse*, 66.

[38] Masham, *Discourse*, 18. Locke also claims that "the Being and Welfare of a Man's Children or Friends, producing constant Delight in him, he is said constantly to *love* them", in John Locke, *An Essay Concerning Human Understanding*, edited by Peter H. Nidditch (Oxford: Clarendon Press, 1979), II.xx.5, 230.

[39] Masham, *Discourse*, 18. Here she echoes Locke's definition in the *Essay* that "our Ideas of Love and Hatred, are but the Dispositions of the Mind, in respect of Pleasure and Pain in general, however caused in us"; see Locke, *Essay*, II.xx.4-5, 230.

[40] Masham, *Discourse*, 62.

> Seriously and Zealously pretended to be of great Use to Religion; And that not only by a young Writer, whose Judgment may, perhaps, be thought Byassed by the Affectation of Novelty; But also it is made the very Ground of Christianity, by a Man of establish'd Character in the World of Philosophical Science.[41]

Here Mary Astell is undoubtedly "the young Writer" in question: in "The Preface" to the *Letters*, Norris refers to Astell as a "young Gentlewoman";[42] and it is extremely unlikely that Masham is referring to anyone else. From this, we can infer that Masham's attack on Norris's moral theory is also implicitly directed at Astell.

Nevertheless, in a forthcoming paper, James Buickerood points out that other supposed references to Astell in the *Discourse* are not so well founded.[43] In the "Preface" to the *Letters*, for example, Astell modestly describes her own writings as "crude Rapsodies".[44] Then in the *Discourse*, Masham's observes that "Pompous Rhapsodies of the Soul's debasing her self, when she descends to set the least part of her Affections upon any thing but her Creator ... are plainly but a complementing God with the contempt of his Works".[45] These "rhapsodies", according to Masham, are "only allowable as the unpremeditated Raptures of Devout Minds, and not the Productions of Philosophical Disquisition".[46] Commentators typically interpret these remarks as references to Astell's letters; and Astell herself takes the same view. But, as Buickerood observes, there is no compelling evidence that Masham's remarks were deliberately aimed at Astell: the only connection between the two writers is their shared use of the word "rhapsodies"—a perfectly common word at the time.

Commentators also suggest that Masham is critical of Astell's proposal for a female academy. In the first part of the *Proposal*, Astell says that she proposes to "erect a Monastery, or if you will (to avoid giving offence to the scrupulous and injudicious, by names which tho' innocent in themselves, have been abus'd by superstitious Practices,) we will call it a Religious Retirement". This "Retirement", Astell says, will offer women a "convenient and blissful recess from the noise and hurry of the world".[47]

---

[41] Masham, *Discourse*, 78.
[42] Astell and Norris, *Letters*, sig. A3^r.
[43] James G. Buickerood, "What Is It With Damaris, Lady Masham? The Historiography of One Early Modern Woman Philosopher," forthcoming.
[44] Astell and Norris, *Letters*, sig. b4^v.
[45] Masham, *Discourse*, 27.
[46] *Ibid.*
[47] Mary Astell, *A Serious Proposal to the Ladies, Parts I and II*, edited by Patricia Springborg, new edition (London: Pickering & Chatto, 1997), 18.

In the *Discourse,* Masham says that Malebranche's enthusiasm "can End in nothing but Monasteries, and Hermitages; with all those Sottish and Wicked Superstitions which have accompanied them where-ever they have been in use".[48] She concedes that retirement is sometimes useful for "Those who live always in the hurry of the World",[49] but

> As for Monasteries, and Religious Houses, (as they are call'd) all who are acquainted with them, know that they are nothing less than what is pretended; And serve only to draw in Discontented, Devout People, with an imaginary Happiness. For there is constantly as much Pride, Malice, and Faction, within those Walls, as without them; And ... very often as much licentiousness.[50]

For Masham, it is more reasonable to assume that God created human beings to enjoy a sociable, rather than a monastic life. It is possible that Masham here regards Astell's *Proposal* as an expression of Malebranchean monasticism.[51] But there is no compelling evidence that Masham has Astell explicitly in mind in the above passages. As James Buickerood points out, Masham's comments are explicitly aimed at *Malebranche's* proposals for monasteries, not Astell's.[52] Hence Masham's "criticisms of Astell" in the *Discourse* may not be as extensive or as scathing as scholars have thought.

It is undeniable, however, that Masham's Lockean views on morality set her at odds with Astell. Like Locke, Masham believes that our idea of love originates with our sensations. On these grounds, Masham claims that we must love the creatures before we can love God, else we can have no idea of love. She dismisses Astell and Norris's claim that we must love

---

[48] Masham, *Discourse*, 120. Masham's comment is preceded by the claim that Norris's opinions are in danger of "introducing, especially amongst those whose Imaginations are stronger than their Reason, a Devout way of talking". Astell also felt herself implicated in this remark.

[49] Masham, *Discourse,* 125.

[50] *Ibid.*

[51] There is evidence that Masham had a copy of the *Proposal* in her library when writing the *Discourse.* Locke's journal for 22 December 1694 reads:
To Oates,
Delivered to my Lady Masham
Mrs Astels Proposal to ye Ladies
Mr Norris's letters.
(Bodleian Library, University of Oxford, Lockc MS f. 10, f. 251).

[52] Buickerood, "What Is It With Damaris, Lady Masham?"

and desire God alone, and she rejects a life devoted solely to contemplation.

In her response, *The Christian Religion* (1705), Astell attacks Masham's Lockean definition of love, pointing out that this confounds "the notion of Love with the sentiment of Pleasure, by making Love to consist barely in the act of the Mind toward that which pleases".[53] But equating love with pleasure poses a problem for moral agency: since we cannot help being pleased with that which pleases, then this "love" "is no more in our power than the motion of our Pulse".[54] For this reason, Astell says, it is far better to define love as an intellectual endeavor of the soul toward good. She also takes up Masham's assertion that every human's experience confutes the view that no creature is a good to us. Astell says that she will allow this point "just so much and no more than they will allow me, That the daily sense and experience of Mankind disproves what a great Philosopher asserts when he tells us, That *Flame* is not *Hot and Light*, nor *Snow White and Cold*, nor *Manna White and Sweet*".[55] If all philosophical explanations must be answerable to common sense (as Masham suggests), then by the same light Locke's theory of secondary qualities is highly questionable. Overall, Astell apparently finds nothing in the *Discourse* to make her revise her opinions about the love of God and his creatures.

These are the views, then, that have led commentators to regard Astell and Masham as philosophical opponents. Their debate might not have been as extensive or as antagonistic as some scholars suggest, but the two women do occupy different moral positions. I now demonstrate, however, that in the early stages of their exchange, the two women agree in one key respect: they both oppose any theory that denies interaction between souls and bodies.

III. Astell's objections to Norris

Masham is simply wrong to regard Astell as the unquestioning disciple of Norris. Although Astell's early letters are not directed against Norris's occasionalism, there are lines of dissent throughout their correspondence. In her first letter, Astell expresses a difficulty she found when reading volume three of Norris's *Practical Discourses*.[56] She points out that if God is the only true cause of all our sensations, then he is also the only true cause of our *pain*. Yet we do not love that which causes us pain, and thus

---

[53] Astell, *Christian Religion*, 131-32.
[54] Astell, *Christian Religion*, 136.
[55] Astell, *Christian Religion*, 131.
[56] Although Astell does not name Norris's "A Discourse Concerning the Measure of Divine Love", her comments indicate that she is referring to this essay in particular.

"if the Author of our Pleasure be upon that account the only Object of our Love, then by the same reason the Author of our Pain *can't* be the Object of our Love".[57] In other words, Norris's argument leads to the paradox that the cause of our sensations is both the object of our *love* and of our *aversion*. To avoid the inconsistency, Astell suggests that "that which Causes Pain does us Good as well as that which Causes Pleasure",[58] and that we ought to love God because he alone does us good, not merely because he is the author of our pleasure.

In his reply, Norris concedes that we must love God in spite of, not because he causes our pain, and that pain comes from God "only indirectly and by Accident".[59] But Astell dismisses this explanation, saying that "though Pain considered abstractedly is not a Good, yet it may be so circumstantiated, and always is when GOD inflicts it as to be a Good". We ought to love God because, in his infinite wisdom, he "designed Pain as well as Pleasure in order to our Happiness".[60] We must love him even though he inflicts pain, because he intends for painful sensations, like our pleasurable ones, to contribute to our overall good.

Here the basis of Astell's criticism of Norris is her conception of God. Like the Cambridge Platonists, Astell advocates an *intellectualist* theology according to which God's wisdom and benevolence are capable of overriding his omnipotence. An intellectualist, according to John Henry, maintains that God "had no choice but to create the world in accordance with the moral demands placed upon Him by His own goodness and in accordance with the essential relationships inherent in the nature of things". [61] While Norris's theory emphasizes God's *causal power*, Astell maintains that God's omnipotence is constrained by his *wisdom and goodness*. A supremely rational and perfectly benevolent being, she says, could only cause pain in order to bring about good. In the *Proposal*, she adheres to the same idea: "GOD being Infinitely Wise," she says, "all his Judgments must be Infallible, and being Infinitely Good he can will nothing but what is best, nor prescribe any thing that is not for our Advantage".[62] In *The Christian Religion*, she says that God always does what is "best and most becoming His Perfections, and cannot act but

---

[57] Astell to Norris, 21 September 1693; in Astell and Norris, *Letters*, 5.

[58] Astell and Norris, *Letters*, 6.

[59] Norris to Astell, 13 October 1693; *Letters*, 17.

[60] Astell to Norris, 31 October 1693; *Letters*, 33, 34.

[61] John Henry, "Henry More Versus Robert Boyle: The Spirit of Nature and the Nature of Providence," in Sarah Hutton, ed., *Henry More (1614-1687): Tercentenary Studies* (Dordrecht: Kluwer Academic Publishers, 1990), 62.

[62] Astell, *Proposal II*, 153.

according to the essential Nature and Reason of things".[63] There are no random or arbitrary features, such as pain, in God's universe.

Astell's notion of divine wisdom and goodness is responsible for her eventual rejection of Norris's occasionalist metaphysics. In her final letter, Astell attacks the central premise of Norris's philosophy: the view that God is the only efficient cause of our sensations. She objects "First, That this Theory renders a great Part of GOD's Workmanship Vain and Useless" and "secondly, That it does not well comport with his Majesty".[64] For the first, Astell argues that if external objects are not able to produce our sensations, then these objects cannot serve any relevant purpose. Yet, if this is so, then Norris's theory is contrary to the idea that an infinitely wise being creates nothing in vain: it would be unnecessary for God to give us the inclination to believe that material things cause our sensations when he himself causes them.

> That this Theory renders a great Part of *GOD's* Workmanship vain and useless, it may be thus argued. Allowing that Sensation is only in the Soul, that there is nothing in Body but Magnitude, Figure and Motion, and that being without Thought itself it is not able to produce it in us, and therefore those Sensations, whether Pleasure or Pain, which we feel at the Presence of Bodies, must be produced by some higher Cause than they; yet if the Objects of our Senses have no natural Efficiency towards the producing of those Sensations which we feel at their Presence, if they Serve no further than as positive and arbitrary Conditions to determine the Action of the true and proper Cause, if they have nothing in their own Nature to qualifie them to be instrumental to the Production of such and such Sensations, but that if *GOD* should so please (the Nature of the things notwithstanding) we might as well feel Cold at the presence of fire as of water, and heat at the Application of Water or any other Creature, and since *GOD* may as well excite Sensations in our Souls without these positive Conditions as with them, to what end do they serve? And then what becomes of that acknowledged Truth that *GOD* does nothing in vain, when such Variety of Objects

---

[63] Astell, *Christian Religion*, 95.
[64] Astell to Norris, 14 August 1694; in Astell and Norris, *Letters*, 278. This letter and Norris's reply are included as "Two Letters by way of Review" in an appendix to the *Letters*.

as our Senses are exercised about are wholly unnecessary?[65]

An infinitely wise being, Astell suggests, would not permit such superfluous features in his design. Norris's idea of a God who could make us feel cold at the presence of fire offends Astell's belief in a supremely rational deity.

Astell's second objection is that Norris's theory does not comport well with God's majesty. She implies that it would be beneath a perfect being to be constantly intervening in earthly events, when he could simply create an instrument to enact his will. Instead Astell asks

> Why therefore may there not be a *sensible Congruity* between those Powers of the Soul that are employed in Sensation, and those Objects which occasion it? Analogous to that vital Congruity which your Friend Dr. *More (Immortality of the Soul, B. II. Chap. 14. S. 8.)* will have to be between some certain Modifications of Matter, and the plastick Part of the Soul, which Notion he illustrates by that Pleasure which the preceptive Part of the Soul (as he calls it) is affected with by good Musick or delicious Viands, as I do this of *sensible* by his of *vital Congruity*, and methinks thay are so symbolical that if the one be admitted the other may. For as the Soul forsakes her Body when this vital Congruity fails, so when this sensible Congruity is wanting, as in the Case of Blindness, Deafness, or the Palsie, &c. the Soul has no Sensation of Colours, Sounds, Heat and the like, so that although Bodies make the same Impression that they used to do on her Body, yet whilst it is under this Indisposition, she has not that Sentiment of Pleasure or Pain which used to accompany that Impression, and therefore though there be no such thing as Sensation in Bodies, yet why may there not be a *Congruity* in them by their Presence to draw forth such

---

[65] Astell and Norris, *Letters*, 278-80. This objection anticipates John Locke in his "Remarks Upon some of Mr. Norris's Books, Wherein he asserts F. Malebranche's Opinion of Our Seeing all things in God", in *A Collection of Several Pieces of Mr. John Locke*, 2nd ed. (London: R. Francklin, 1739). Locke's essay was written in 1693 and first published in 1720. He observes that "if the perception of colours and sounds depended on nothing but the presence of the object affording an *occasional cause* to God Almighty to exhibit to the mind, the Ideas of figures, colours and sounds; all that nice and curious structure of those organs is wholly in vain" (48).

> Sensations in the Soul? Especially since in the next
> place, it seems more agreeable to the Majesty of GOD,
> and that Order he has established in the World, to say
> that he produces our Sensations *mediately* by his Servant
> Nature, than to affirm that he does it *immediately* by his
> own Almighty Power.[66]

Astell implies that there is a natural efficacy in bodies to produce
sensations in the soul. She accepts Norris's claim that sensory qualities do
not reside in the material objects themselves. But against Norris, she
suggests that there is something in the body, a "sensible congruity," that
promotes its interaction with the soul and enables the body to cause
sensations. In so far as material bodies are connected to, or have a
correspondence with, certain plastical powers in the soul, they do "really
better our condition", they do "contribute to our happiness or Misery",
and they do "in some sense produce our Pleasure or Pain".[67] God's
"servant nature", according to Astell, acts as a causal agent in the natural
world, making material things "necessary Instruments", rather than mere
"occasions".[68]

Astell's theory of a sensible congruity between "certain Modifications
of Matter, and the plastick Part of the Soul" owes its origins to the
Cambridge-Platonist doctrine of "plastic nature" or "the spirit of nature".
The Cambridge school, namely More and Cudworth, were devoted to
stemming the rise of "Hobbist atheism" by using a blend of Cartesian and
Platonist principles to affirm the reality of the immaterial world. The
Cambridge men, like Astell, believe that "it seems not so agreeable to
Reason ... that Nature as a Distinct thing from the Deity should be quite
Superceded or made to Signifie Nothing, God himself doing all things
Immediately".[69] Instead, they strike a balance between mechanistic and
occasionalist-style philosophies. They argue that there is a spiritual
intermediary between spirit and matter, giving material things life and
activity, when they would otherwise be dead and passive. In *The*

[66] Astell to Norris, 14 August 1694; in Astell and Norris, *Letters,* 280-82.
[67] *Letters,* 284.
[68] Norris objects by saying that "even Instruments belong to the Order of efficient Causes,
though they are less principal ones, and 'tis most certain that GOD has no need of any, since
his Will is efficacious itself" (Norris to Astell, 21 September 1694; *Letters,* 306-307). This
counterobjection is not very strong, because one might still ask: if God has no need of
material objects, and "his Will is efficacious itself", then why do such objects even exist?
[69] Ralph Cudworth, *The True Intellectual System of the Universe: The First Part; Wherein,
All the Reason and Philosophy Of Atheism is Confuted; And Its Impossibility Demonstrated,*
facsimile reprint of 1678 edition (Stuttgart-Bad Cannstatt: Friedrich Frommann Verlag,
1964), 150.

Immortality of the Soul (1659), Henry More calls this intermediary the "spirit of nature",

> A substance incorporeal, but without Sense and Animadversion, pervading the whole Matter of the Universe, and exercising a plastical power therein according to the sundry predispositions and occasions in the parts it works upon, raising such *Phaenomena* in the World, by directing the parts of the Matter and their Motion, as cannot be resolved into mere Mechanical powers.[70]

More claims that the union between soul and body cannot be explained in mechanical terms, but only in terms of a "vital congruity" between the plastic part of the soul and the body.[71]

In her challenge to Norris, Astell refers to a passage in *The Immortality of the Soul* where More claims that this congruity is "chiefly in the *Soul* it self", but that it can also be in matter. More says that

> it is termed *Vital* because it makes the *Matter* a *congruous* Subject for the Soul to reside in, and exercise the functions of life. For that which has no *life* it self, may tie to it that which has. As some men are said to be tied by the teeth, or tied by the ear, when they are detained by the pleasure they are struck with from good Musick or delicious Viands.... Now as we see that the *Perceptive* part of the Soul is thus vitally affected with that which has no life in it, so it is reasonable that the *Plastick* part thereof may be so too; That there may be an Harmony betwixt Matter thus and thus modified, and that Power that we call *Plastick*, that is utterly devoid of all Perception. And in this alone consists that which we call *Vital Congruity* in the prepared Matter, either to be organized, or already shaped into the perfect form of an Animal.[72]

---

[70] Henry More, *The Immortality of the Soul; So farre forth as it is demonstrable from the Knowledge of Nature and the Light of Reason,* facsimile reprint of 1659 edition (Bristol: Thoemmes Press, 1997), 450.

[71] Mary Astell was not the only woman philosopher to take an interest in More's theory. On Anne Conway's treatment of vital congruity, see Sarah Hutton "Anne Conway Critique d'Henry More: L'Esprit et la Matiere," *Archives de Philosophie* 58 (1995): 371-84.

[72] More, *Immortality of the Soul*, 263-64.

In the same chapter, More calls the spirit of nature the *"Inferiour Soul of the World"*,[73] and says that matter enjoys a vital congruity with this part of the soul. Likewise, in an earlier letter to Norris (31 October 1693), Astell explains her theory of sensation with reference to the "inferior" and "superior" parts of the soul.[74] The inferior part, she says, corresponds to sensible objects, it feels sensations of pain, colour, and so on; whereas the superior or intellectual part, comprised of the understanding and will, is capable of knowing abstract truths.[75]

In sum, there are significant differences between Astell's metaphysical views and those of Norris in the *Letters*. Astell advocates a theory of causation that reaffirms the body's interaction with the soul. She believes that material beings are capable of a sympathetic relationship with the soul and are necessary, not arbitrary features of the created world. In these respects, Astell has a closer affinity with the Cambridge Platonists, rather than Norris.[76] There are, moreover, strong similarities between Astell's objections to occasionalism and those of Damaris Masham.

IV. Masham's objections to Norris and Leibniz

First, Masham arrives independently at Astell's own objection that Norris's theory "renders a great Part of GOD's Workmanship Vain and

---

[73] More, *Immortality of the Soul*, 266.

[74] Although Astell borrows this notion from Norris's *Christian Blessedness*, she takes the distinction more literally than he intended. In a letter dated 13 November 1693, Norris claims that he cannot form a "clear Idea of any such Parts", and he only meant for the distinction to be a figure of speech (*Letters*, 60).

[75] Astell to Norris, 31 October 1693; *Letters*, 37.

[76] In his recent article, "Mary Astell's Ironic Assault on John Locke," E. Derek Taylor reminds us that Astell does not completely abandon occasionalism in her later work. Taylor observes that in one section of the *Christian Religion*, Astell refers to God as "the true Efficient Cause of all our Good, of all our pleasing sensations" (*Christian Religion*, 141). Then in another passage, Astell appeals to "the efficacy of the Divine Will" to explain relations between the mind and body (*Christian Religion*, 337). Taylor also suggests that Astell echoes the terminology of Norris's response to her final objections in the *Letters*. According to Taylor, Astell's reference to "the Powers of GOD giving you divers modifications" (*Christian Religion*, 141) is a clear reference to Norris's claim that only God has the power to give our spirits "new Modifications" (*Letters*, 289). It is reasonable to conclude, therefore, that Astell was probably persuaded by Norris's rejoinder.

I do not deny that Astell appears to recant her objections to Norris in the *Christian Religion*. My claims in this paper primarily relate to Astell's views in the *Letters* and the *Proposal*, Parts I and II. But I do think that Astell harbors *some* ambivalence to Norris's ideas in that later work. In one passage in the *Christian Religion*, she says "neither do I comprehend the Vital Union between my Soul and Body, nor how and in what manner they are joyn'd, tho' I am sure that it is so" (*Christian Religion*, 51). We must not forget, moreover, that Astell herself introduces the terminology of "modifications" in the "Two Letters by way of Review" (*Letters*, 280), and so it is not obvious that she is deliberately echoing Norris's letter in the aforementioned passage.

Useless".[77] In the *Discourse*, Masham argues that if material beings are causally inefficacious, and if it is God himself who represents the idea of material things to our souls, then our sensory organs must be completely superfluous. Masham accuses Norris of detracting "from the Wisdom of God, in framing his Creatures like the Idols of the Heathen, that have Eyes, and see not; Ears, and hear not, &c."[78] If we believe that creatures are the occasional, rather than the efficient causes of our sensations, then

> the Wisdom of God cannot herein be equally admired, because it is not equally conspicuous. For if God immediately exhibits to me all my Idea's, and that I do not truly see with my Eyes, and hear with my Ears; then all that Wonderful Exactness and curious Workmanship, in framing the Organs of Sense, seems superfluous and vain; Which is no small reflection upon infinite Wisdom.[79]

This is also the foundation of Masham's objection to Leibniz's theory of pre-established harmony, as presented in his "New System" of 1695. On the question of soul-body interaction, Leibniz says that he can find no intelligible way of explaining how the body transmits or communicates anything to the soul, or vice versa. Instead he claims that there is a "perfect agreement" or an "adaptation of the soul to the body". He believes that God created the soul so that everything must arise in it from its own inner nature, with a perfect conformity to the things outside it. The soul and the body follow their own separate laws, without corporeal laws being affected by the soul and "without bodies finding windows through which to exert their influence over souls".[80]

Masham engaged in a correspondence with Leibniz from early 1704 until 1705. In one letter to Leibniz, Masham comments on his theory of concomitance, saying that

> such an inference as this from our Ignorance, I remember Father Malbranche (or some other assertor of

---

[77] Astell to Norris, 14 August 1694; Astell and Norris, *Letters*, 278. Here I am being charitable to Masham by assuming that she lighted upon this objection herself: she may have been influenced by Astell's criticisms in the "Appendix" and simply not acknowledged the debt.

[78] Masham, *Discourse*, 29-31.

[79] Masham, *Discourse*, 31-32.

[80] Leibniz to Masham, May 1704; in *Leibniz's New System and Associated Contemporary Texts*, trans. and ed. R. S. Woolhouse and Richard Francks (Oxford: Clarendon Press, 1997), 206.

> his Hypothesis) would make in behalf of Occasional
> Causes: to which Hypothesis, amongst other exceptions,
> I think there is one, which I cannot (without your help)
> see, but that yours is alike Liable to and that is from the
> Organization of the Body; wherin all that Nice Curiositie
> that is discoverable seeming useless; becomes
> Superfluous, and Lost labour.[81]

By "some other assertor", Masham obviously meant John Norris. She rejects Leibniz's system of pre-established harmony for the same reason she rejects Norris's occasionalism: it makes sensory organs and other material bodies superfluous and redundant.

There is evidence that Masham's criticisms of occasionalism and pre-established harmony are influenced by her father's theological principles. One of Cudworth's main theses in *The True Intellectual System* is that God presides over everything. Cudworth opposes those mechanical theories that render God an "idle Spectator" in his creation, thus making "his Wisdom altogether Useless and Insignificant, as being a thing wholly Inclosed and shut up within his own breast, and not at all acting abroad upon any thing without him".[82] But he also challenges the view that God does everything "Immediately and Miraculously".[83] The theory of plastic nature is essential to Cudworth's system, because it strikes a medium: it is "a living Stamp or Signature of Divine Wisdom" in the created world, and yet it does not require God to exert a "sollicitous Care or Distractious Providence".[84]

In another letter to Leibniz, Masham defends Cudworth's theory of plastic nature. From 1703 to 1706, Jean Le Clerc published selections from *The True Intellectual System* in his new journal, *Bibliothèque Choisie*.[85] Cudworth's views were greeted with controversy. As each issue of the periodical appeared, the French scholar Pierre Bayle (1647-1706) published his own highly critical response to Cudworth's philosophy.[86]

---

[81] Masham to Leibniz, 3 June 1704; in *Leibniz's New System*, 209.

[82] Cudworth, *True Intellectual System,* 148.

[83] Cudworth, *True Intellectual System*, 150.

[84] Cudworth, *True Intellectual System*, 150, 155.

[85] For further details see Rosalie Colie, *Light and the Enlightenment: A Study of the Cambridge Platonists and the Dutch Arminians* (Cambridge: Cambridge University Press, 1957), 117-44, and Susan Rosa, "Ralph Cudworth and the *République des Lettres*: The Controversy about Plastick Nature and the Reputation of Pierre Bayle," *Studies in Eighteenth-Century Culture* 23 (1994): 147-60.

[86] These rejoinders were published in Henri Basnage de Beauval's *Histoire des Ouvrages des Savants* and in Bayle's *Continuations des pensées diverses sur la comète*.

Plastic nature or "plastic powers" are the executors of God's grand design, his causal instruments in the natural world. These incorporeal spirits have the formative power to determine the organization, growth, vitality, and movement of living things. But while plastical powers within the universe act like minds in that they are purposeful, they are also unconscious and nondeliberative in their activities.[87] Against this view, Bayle claims that Cudworth's theory of an insensible plastic nature implies that matter might conceivably exist and act by itself, independently of God.[88] Bayle suggests that the doctrine is atheistic in tendency, because it makes it unnecessary to suppose that wherever purpose is exhibited, God must be at work; in short, it appears to make God superfluous.

Masham defends her father's theory in a letter to Leibniz, dated 20 October 1705. Masham criticizes Bayle for saying that God cannot make an unconscious agent act for wise ends unless God himself is giving perpetual direction to material causes (i.e., unless occasionalism is true). Masham says

> my Fathers Hypothesis is methinks sufficiently secur'd from *the Retorsion of Atheists*, without being *in the same case* with any one which makes God the immediate Efficient Cause of all the Effects of Nature. Since my Father dos not therein assert (as Mr Bayle says he dos) That *God has been able to give to Creatures a Facultie of Produceing Excellent Works (viz such as is the Organization of Plants and Animals) seperate from all Knowledge* &c.: but onely a Facultie of Executeing instrumentally his Ideas or Designs, in the Production of such *Excellent Works*: so that (*according to him) there is* (differently from what Mr Bayle asserts of his Hypothesis) *an inseparable union betwixt the Power of Produceing Excellent Works, and the Idea of theire Essence, and manner of Produceing them*: and it seems to me that there can be no pretence to the *Retorsion of Atheists* unless it were asserted, That God had been able to give to Creatures a Facultie of Produceing *excellent works*; the Ideas whereof never were in any

---

[87] Masham says that plastic natures can be likened to "habits" in humans, such as "those of singing and danceing: which shall oftentimes direct the motions of body, or voice without any consideration of what the next note, or motion should be" (Masham to Leibniz, 20 October 1705; in Gerhardt, ed., *Die Philosophischen Schriften*, vol. III, 372). Here she echoes Cudworth, *True Intellectual System*, 157.

[88] Colie, *Light and the Enlightenment*, 138.

understanding: But my Father is so far from asserting
any such thing as this, that he holds the Operations of
the Plastick Nature to be *essentially and necessarilie
Dependent* on the ideas in the Divine Intellect.[89]

In short, God gives creatures a faculty of executing his "ideas"
instrumentally. These ideas or essences must have existed prior to the
existence of the creatures, and, moreover, they must have existed in a
mind. From this we can conclude that plastic nature is essentially and
necessarily dependent on the ideas in the divine mind: the plastical powers
could never be autonomous.[90] Matter does not have the power to act
independently of God; it has "onely a Pow'r to Execute the Ideas of a
Perfect Mind; if there were no *Mind* in the universe; this Pow'r in the
Matter must Lye for ever Dormant and unproductive, of any such
Excellent Work as is spoken of".[91]

From Masham's remarks, it is unclear whether or not she holds
Cudworth's theory as her own. Nevertheless, her argument does depend
upon a presupposition that underlies her earlier objections to Norris and
Leibniz. In her defence of Cudworth's doctrine of plastic nature, Masham
once again makes the divine mind or *divine wisdom* a fundamental premise
in her argument.[92] Like Astell, Masham's aim is to promote the wisdom of
God against the imputations of occasionalism, and to affirm the harmony
and order he has established in the world.[93] In defending her father's
theory of plastic nature, Masham emphasizes the connections, relations,
and interactions between matter and spirit. Material things, she suggests,
could never be radically separate or detached from spirits and God.

Finally, Masham also shares Astell's belief that Norris's theory does
not comport well with God's majesty. Astell implies that it would be
beneath a perfect being to be constantly intervening in earthly events, as
Norris believes he does. Similarly, Masham says that it is "unworthy of,
and mis-becoming the Majesty of the great God, who is of Purer Eyes
than to behold iniquity, to be as it were at the beck of his sinful Creatures,

---

[89] Masham to Leibniz, 20 October 1705; in Gerhardt, ed., *Die Philosophischen Schriften*,
vol. III, 370-71.
[90] Cudworth writes that "if there had been no *Perfect Mind* or *Intellect* in the World, there
could no more have been any *Plastick Nature* in it, then there could be *an Image in the Glass*
without a *Face*" (*True Intellectual System,* 172).
[91] Masham to Leibniz, 20 October 1705; in Gerhardt, ed., *Die Philosophischen Schriften*,
vol. III, 371.
[92] For this point, I am indebted to Hutton's "Like Father Like Daughter?"
[93] In *Occasional Thoughts*, Masham's intellectualism is more explicit. She says that the
divine will is "one steady, uniform, unchangeable result of infinite Wisdom and
Benevolence, extending to and including All his Works" (69).

to excite in them Sentiments of Delight and Pleasure, whenever they are dispos'd to transgress against his Laws".[94] Masham rejects Norris's theory because it forces God to be "a partner in our wickedness".[95] On Norris's view, every act that carries our desires toward the creature is sinful, or "a kind of Spiritual Adultery".[96] An unacceptable consequence of this theory is that God *intended* human beings to have such sinful desires.

In sum, if Masham had paid closer attention to Astell's early writings, she would have detected many affinities with her own. In Norris's occasionalist philosophy, bodies are incapable of affecting the soul. Both Masham and Astell, however, object to any view of matter that suggests that a supremely rational God has rendered it causally ineffective or purposeless. They are both, moreover, motivated by an intellectualist aim: to promote the goodness and wisdom of God against the imputations of occasionalism, and to affirm the rational order that he has established in the world. These same theological principles are employed in Astell and Masham's feminist arguments for women's education.

V. Their feminist views

In seventeenth-century England, the "intellectual deficiency" and "innate irrationality" of women were cited as reasons for their exclusion from universities. A woman's worth was defined primarily in terms of her body or her physical being. In the *Proposal*, Astell is principally concerned with opposing the stereotypical view that women are mere material objects, or beings possessed of a limited intellect. She calls on women to consider the welfare of their "true selves", their *minds*, and rails against the "unthinking mechanical way of living, when like Machins we are condemn'd every day to repeat the impertinencies of the day before".[97] She encourages her female readers to break with tradition and history, and to rely on their own introspective capacities to acquire knowledge. In other words, Astell's objective in the *Proposal* is the same as that of the *Letters*: to reaffirm the worth of a part of God's creation that has been rendered purposeless, by reaffirming its connection with the spiritual-intellectual realm. The same principle that leads Astell to reject an utter separation between spirit and matter—the idea that *God creates nothing in vain*—also leads her to reject the view that women are not fully rational. In the second part of the *Proposal*, Astell says that "GOD does nothing in vain, he gives no Power or Faculty which he has not allotted to some proportionate use, if therefore he has given to Mankind a Rational

---

[94] Masham, *Discourse*, 102.
[95] *Ibid.*
[96] Masham, *Discourse*, 115.
[97] Astell, *Proposal I*, 32.

Mind, every individual Understanding ought to be employ'd in somewhat worthy of it".[98] The author of our being would not allow any superfluities in his supremely intelligent design; thus, "If GOD had not intended that Women shou'd use their Reason, He wou'd not have given them any, for He does nothing in vain".[99] She warns that when a woman is taught that her duty is to serve men, or to live a life devoted solely to the body, she is taught to disregard her obligations to God. Instead Astell stresses that women must be educated so that their rationality is exercised toward higher virtues, and not neglected as vain and useless. "For unless we have very strange Notions of the Divine Wisdom," she says, we must admit that "Our Powers and Faculties were not given us for nothing".[100] Even when propounding Cartesian method in the second *Proposal*, Astell's examples of self-evident principles are a significant indication of these beliefs. "If it be farther demanded what these Principles are?" she says, "no body I suppose will deny us one, which is, *That we ought as much as we can to endeavour the Perfecting of our Beings, and that we be as happy as possibly we may.*"[101] She emphasizes that women must use their rational faculties to move closer toward perfection and God, "the Supream and Universal Reason":[102]

> For since GOD has given Women as well as Men
> intelligent Souls, why should they be forbidden to
> improve them? Since he has not denied us the faculty of
> Thinking, why shou'd we not (at least in gratitude to
> him) employ our Thoughts on himself their noblest
> Object, and not unworthily bestow them on Trifles and
> Gaities and secular Affairs? Being the Soul was created
> for the contemplation of Truth as well as for the fruition
> of Good, is it not as cruel and unjust to preclude Women
> from the knowledge of one, as well as from the
> enjoyment of the other?[103]

"A desire to advance and perfect its Being," she says, "is planted by GOD in all Rational Natures, to excite them hereby to every worthy and becoming Action."[104] A supremely rational God would not have given

---

[98] Astell, *Proposal I*, 118-19.
[99] Astell, *Christian Religion*, 6.
[100] Astell, *Proposal II*, 149.
[101] Astell, *Proposal II*, 82-3.
[102] Astell, *Christian Religion*, 13.
[103] Astell, *Proposal I*, 22.
[104] Astell, *Proposal I*, 12.

women this desire unless he required them to act on it. Therefore women must be educated to use their reason to raise themselves toward perfection.

Masham premises her feminist arguments on similar presuppositions. Masham's only published feminist work, *Occasional Thoughts in Reference to a Vertuous or Christian Life*, was first written in about 1703, and was revised and corrected for publication after Locke's death. Ruth Perry believes that Masham partly rewrote the work in response to some of Astell's points in *The Christian Religion*.[105] But Perry's reasons for saying this are unclear. There is actually more evidence that Masham was *positively* inspired by the second part of Astell's *Proposal* (1697). In this work, Astell claims that women will find knowledge useful, not just for their souls, but for the management of their families and relations with their neighbors. The education of children, Astell says, should "be laid by the Mother, for Fathers find other business, they will not be confin'd to such a laborious work, they have not such opportunities of observing a Childs Temper, nor are the greatest part of 'em like to do much good, since Precepts contradicted by Example seldom prove Effectual".[106] The idea that the improvement of women's reason will benefit the education of children is taken up by Masham in the latter half of *Occasional Thoughts*. The foundation of Masham's feminism, like Astell's, is the belief that a supremely wise and benevolent God would not have endowed women with reason, if he did not intend for them to exercise their rational faculties toward perfection. Masham points out that

> no one is Born into the World to live idly; enjoying the Fruit and Benefit of other Peoples Labours, without contributing reciprocally some way or other, to the good of the Community answerably to that Station wherein God ... has plac'd them; who has evidently intended Humane kind of Society and mutual Communion, as Members of the same Body, useful every one each to other in their respective places.[107]

Women, she says, must be educated for the sake of order and harmony in society; because mothers, after all, are the early educators of men, and if mothers are not educated, then the education of men will suffer too.

These views bear a notable resemblance to Plato's claims about the education of women in Book V of *The Republic*. Plato argues that women must be educated so that they might become the best they can possibly be.

---

[105] Perry, *The Celebrated Mary Astell*, 96.
[106] Astell, *Proposal II*, 149-50.
[107] Masham, *Occasional Thoughts*, 179-80.

The natures of men and women, he says, do not differ in any crucial respects when it comes to the capacity to learn; men and women, therefore, must have a common education. Plato justifies this view with appeal to the State. To attain the highest good for the State, female citizens must be permitted to attain the highest good suitable to their natures. In this way, the State—like "a body and all its members"—will achieve harmony, unity, and concord. But Masham takes these Platonist ideas further when she argues that a woman's education is also for the *individual's* benefit.[108] Masham says that it is essential that women be educated for the sake of their own spiritual welfare. She emphasizes that "Women have Souls to be sav'd as well as Men".[109] They are endowed by God with rational abilities which enable them to understand the principles behind their religious beliefs. But, she says, "be Nature ever so kind to them in this respect, yet through want of cultivating the Tallents she bestows upon those of the Female Sex, her Bounty is usually lost upon them; and Girls, betwixt silly Fathers and ignorant Mothers, are generally so brought up, that traditionary Opinions are to them, all their lives long, instead of Reason".[110] Women must be taught that "their Duty is not grounded upon the uncertain and variable Opinion of Men, but the unchangeable nature of things".[111] Masham believes that "chastity" in particular is an overrated virtue because it gives the impression that a woman's moral duty consists in regulating her body alone. As part of the educational process, she says, women must be taught to value and cherish their minds as well as their bodies.

VI. Concluding remarks

At the end of the seventeenth century, Mary Astell and Damaris Masham were engaged in a dispute about the love of God. Masham attacks Norris and Astell's theory that God alone ought to be sole object of our love. She dismisses their moral views on Lockean grounds as an affront to common sense. Several years later, Astell responds to Masham in equally hostile terms, and criticizes Masham's definition of love as consisting in nothing but the bare sentiment of pleasure. As a consequence of their brief exchange, commentators have regarded these women as opponents, or "seconds in the duel" between Norris's occasionalism and Locke's empiricism. But this common interpretation obscures significant similarities between the two women. If one looks beyond the canonical

---

[108] On the limitations of Plato's feminism, see Julia Annas, "Plato's *Republic* and Feminism," *Philosophy* 51 (1976): 307-21.
[109] Masham, *Occasional Thoughts,* 166.
[110] Masham, *Occasional Thoughts* 162-63.
[111] Masham, *Occasional Thoughts,* 17.

philosophers of the time, and to the influence of Cambridge Platonism, it is possible to detect a common theological outlook in the works of Astell and Masham. This theology brings the two writers closer together in terms of their metaphysics and their feminism. In Norris's occasionalist philosophy, matter is causally impotent and incapable of affecting the mind. Astell and Masham, however, object to any view of matter that suggests that a supremely rational God has rendered it causally ineffective or purposeless. Their objections to Norris depend upon a teleological presupposition: that God has designed a harmonious order, where each part is suited to its end, and where there is no waste or "lost labour". In his infinite wisdom, according to Astell and Masham, God would not have created material things if they did not serve some purpose. Likewise, a supremely wise being would not have endowed *women* with a rational faculty, if he had not wished them to use it. In both cases, the writers regard created things as purposeful and there for the sake of some greater goal. Their theological beliefs lead to a re-establishing of connections between the material and intellectual worlds: to be purposeful, material things must have a sympathetic interaction with the intellectual realm; and, similarly, *women* must be more than mere bodies to fulfill their divine purpose. In these respects, at least, it is possible to regard Astell and Masham as allies, rather than adversaries.

Belief and Animal Spirits in Hume's *Treatise*[1]

Marina Frasca-Spada
Cambridge University

Abstract

The terminology Hume uses for his descriptions of the sentiments characterizing belief—the "force," "vivacity" and "steadiness" of conception—is derived from the contemporary physiology of animal spirits and brain traces in the style of Malebranche. This essay shows how studying the ways those terms were used within Malebranchean physiology provides a key to Hume's usage: in particular I suggest that, as in the accounts of the motions of animal spirits, so too in Hume's descriptions of belief there is a crucial difference between "force" and "vivacity," which refer to intensity, and "steadiness," which is connected with repeated experience and custom. I then show how Hume's phenomenological descriptions of belief in terms of force and vivacity are substantiated with vignettes from common life and sociability, and are intended simply to account for the sentimental raw materials of belief on which experience and custom exercise their stabilizing and calibrating action.

> *The brain contains ten thousand cells,*
> *in each some active fancy dwells.*
> —Matthew Prior

The aim of this essay is to explore Hume's view that belief is a particular manner of conceiving what is believed—the difference between an idea we believe in and one which is merely entertained lies in their "force," or "vivacity," or "steadiness." This theory is commonly regarded as problematic, indeed as "beyond redemption," to use Jonathan Bennett's typically brisk assessment.[2] To mention only the most obvious difficulties, how can Hume account, on the basis of such a theory, for our ability to hold calm beliefs, or even beliefs of which we are hardly aware at all?

I first present Hume's view that belief is a particular force, liveliness and steadiness of conception, and explore the similarities and connections between belief and impressions, which are also characterized by a special force and liveliness. I then consider the possible roles in Hume's investigations of the human mind of the Malebranchean physiology of animal spirits and brain traces. The force and liveliness terminology is the typical idiom of this brand of animal economy. But in the pages of the

---

[1] I am grateful to Nick Jardine, Andrea Branchi, Susan James, Peter Kail, Peter Lipton, Emilio Mazza, Sandy Stewart, and the participants in the conference "Hume Studies in Britain 2" (Edinburgh, September 2002) for their generous advice and encouragement.
[2] Jonathan Bennett, *Locke, Berkeley, Hume: Central Themes* (Oxford: Clarendon Press, 1971), 294.

Treatise it is divorced from its original application to bodily events, and is used instead in the service of Hume's attempted phenomenological descriptions of belief as a sentiment. The question then is: how successful was Hume in transforming the physiological idiom into a language for the narration of feeling and experience? And what is the role of this narration within his theory of belief?

I. Force, vivacity and steadiness

For a start, what exactly does Hume mean when he talks about the force, vivacity, liveliness, steadiness, etc. of belief? These terms do not, in fact, all mean even the same *sort* of thing. They are easily split into three groups with not much in common, namely one including force, strength, and vigor; a second vivacity, liveliness, vividness and brightness; and finally steadiness, solidity and firmness.[3] Consider the following passage:

> an opinion or belief is nothing but an idea, that is
> different from a fiction, not in the nature, or the order of
> its parts, but in the *manner* of its being conceiv'd. But
> when I wou'd explain this *manner*, I scarce find any
> word that fully answers the case, but am oblig'd to have
> recourse to every one's feeling, in order to give him a
> perfect notion of this operation of the mind. An idea
> assented to *feels* different from a fictitious idea, that the
> fancy alone presents to us: And this different feeling I
> endeavour to explain by calling it a superior *force*, or
> *vivacity*, or *solidity*, or *firmness*, or *steadiness*.[4]

So belief is not a distinct perception, but an act of the mind or mode of presentation of a perception. When we conceive an idea there is also, in our mind, a second-order internal "act" or "feeling" having to do with whether the idea in question is believed or merely entertained; and this feeling is characterized as superior force, vivacity, solidity, and so on. Hume suggests that with "this variety of terms, which may seem so "unphilosophical" he is no more than pointing out to his reader a certain quality of believed ideas. And indeed the groups "force" and "vivacity," as they are used for the first introduction of belief in the *Treatise*, seem to suggest that belief is some sort of intensity of the believed idea. This also

---

[3] See the analysis of these terms in the excellent article by Stephen Everson, "The Difference between Feeling and Thinking," *Mind* 97 (1988): 401–13.

[4] David Hume, *A Treatise of Human Nature*, ed. L. A. Selby-Bigge. 2nd ed., revised and variant readings by P. H. Nidditch (Oxford: Clarendon Press, 1978), 629. All citations from the *Treatise* are from this edition; they will appear in the text as follows: (T629).

is the most plausible reading of the comparison Hume suggests between belief and the intensity of a color:

> When you wou'd any way vary the idea of a particular object, you can only increase or diminish its force and vivacity. If you make any other change on it, it represents a different object or impression. The case is the same as in colours. A particular shade of any colour may acquire a new degree of liveliness and brightness without any further variation. But when you produce any other variation, 'tis no longer the same shade or colour. (T96)

Here the "shade or colour" corresponds to the mental content, the object or impression copied by the idea; and belief has nothing to do with that. Belief is not a mental content, it is the "force and vivacity," or "degree of liveliness and brightness" of that content—its intensity. This is the Humean theory of belief that Bennett regarded as hopeless. As I mentioned at the outset, even the obvious fact that we do routinely hold beliefs to which we pay hardly any attention is enough to create problems for it. And as well as believing unremarkable and boring ideas we also entertain, without believing them, ideas which are very lively indeed: as Kames pointed out at the time in his response to the *Treatise*, "poetry and painting produce lively ideas, but they seldom produce belief"—in fact, "can any man doubt ... that poetry makes a stronger impression than history?"[5] In other words, we are also able to distinguish between holding calm beliefs, and merely entertaining lively ideas. How does Hume account for this flexibility of the mind in interpreting the force and vivacity of ideas sometimes as belief, and sometimes as mere vividness of imagination? Finally, to borrow again from Bennett's philosophical prose, I can easily both believe that the Sahara is warm and entertain the thought that it is extremely hot.[6] How does Hume account for the mind's ability to distinguish between calm, absent-minded beliefs and exciting figments of the imagination?

It may seem tempting to answer the questions above by admitting that Hume did not think things through. But that would, I think, be hasty: Hume was well aware of these difficulties. Issues such as the different impacts on readers' feelings of historical works and poetical fictions, the ways in which writers exploited such differences to make their works

---

[5] Henry Home, Lord Kames, *Essays on the Principle of Morality and Natural Religion* (Edinburgh, 1751), 222–23; but see the whole of his Essay I, "Of Belief," in Part 2, 221–30.
[6] Bennett, *Locke, Berkeley, Hume*, 294; see the comments on this in Everson, "Difference," 402–403.

more attractive or more persuasive, and the causes and consequences of possible confusions on the readers' part, were topical and hotly debated by his contemporaries.[7] Moreover, as I mentioned, Kames made it sure that he would not forget about them. The tormented page of the Appendix that I have quoted above is, in fact, part of his attempt to respond to Kames's strictures. This response we are now to examine carefully. As we shall see, it is crucially important that the third group of terms—'steadiness,' 'solidity' and 'firmness'—does not invite an interpretation in terms of intensity. Before focusing on steadiness, however, I propose to explore in more detail Hume's uses of the force and liveliness groups of terms, and the relations that such uses reveal between belief and sense impressions.

II. Force, vivacity, and the world out there

In Book 1 of the *Treatise* 'force' and 'vivacity' appear in connection with the distinctions between impressions and ideas, between ideas of the memory and of the imagination, and between believed and merely entertained ideas.[8] This is how Hume introduces impressions and ideas in page 1 of the *Treatise*:

> the difference betwixt these consists in the degrees of force and liveliness, with which they strike upon the mind, and make their way into thought or consciousness. Those perceptions, which enter with most force and violence, we may name *impressions*.... By *ideas* I mean the faint images of these in thinking and reasoning. (T1)

'Force,' 'liveliness' and 'violence' are indeed so typical, and so often repeated by Hume in connection with impressions, that many readers regard them as defining the only or main difference between impressions themselves and the ideas that reproduce them in thought. Similarly, ideas of memory "are much more lively and strong than those of the imagination ... the former faculty paints its object in more distinct colours, than any which are employ'd by the latter." Ideas of memory "flow in upon the mind in a forcible manner," while those of the imagination are "faint and languid" (T9). It is important, however, to note that in the cases both of impressions *versus* ideas and of ideas of memory *versus* ideas of

---

[7] See my "Quixotic Confusions and Hume's Imagination," in Peter Kail and Marina Frasca-Spada, eds. *Impressions of Hume* (Oxford: Oxford University Press, forthcoming).
[8] In Book 2 they are of course crucial for the descriptions of the passions. It may be worth remembering that in the treatment of passions there appears a problem corresponding to that of calm beliefs, namely that of calm passions which are, however, strong enough to prevail over violent passions (T417–19): see the interesting discussion of Jane L. McIntyre, "Hume's Passions: Direct and Indirect," *Hume Studies* 26 (2000): 77–86.

the imagination, force and liveliness, however important, are by no means all there is to the distinction. As well as being more lively than the corresponding ideas, impressions are the originals from which those ideas are copied; they are nonrepresentational, while ideas do represent former impressions; and they are innate, while ideas are acquired through experience. Similarly, the main feature of memory is not the force and liveliness of its ideas, but rather that, contrary to the imagination, as well as the ideas themselves it also preserves "their order and position" (T9–10). Evidently "force" and "liveliness" are used as the phenomenological markers, convenient because readily available to introspection, of those perceptions which, were Hume prepared to talk in Lockean or in commonsense realist terms, he would describe as taking place in the presence of something out there, or as being caused by a real object and mirroring it. So the key to making sense of them, and hence of belief, is to be found as close as Hume's frame of reference will allow us to go to the world out there—that is, in sense impressions.[9]

Hume is explicit in stating a fundamental connection between belief and impressions. For example he says that "the objects of conviction and assurance ... approach nearer to the impressions, which are immediately present to us" (T624–25). Moreover, they have a similarly powerful practical impact:

> Wherever we can make an idea approach the impressions in force and vivacity, it will likewise imitate them in its influence on the mind; and *vice versa*, where it imitates them in that influence ... this must proceed from its approaching them in force and vivacity. Belief, therefore, since it causes an idea to imitate the effects of the impression, must make it resemble them in these qualities, and is nothing but *a more vivid and intense conception of any idea*. This ... may give us a notion after what manner our reasonings from causation are able to operate on the will and the passions. (T119–20)

---

[9] I have presented in detail my view that Hume's sense impressions are non-intentional and that they are the objects of our experience in "Hume on Sense Impressions and Objects," in Michael Heidelberger and Friedrich Stadler, eds., *History of Philosophy of Science: New Trends and Perspectives*, Vienna Circle Institute Yearbook (Dordrecht, Boston and London: Kluwer Academic Publishers, 2001), 13–24. For a classic discussion with a very different emphasis see Barry Stroud, *Hume* (London: Routledge and Kegan Paul, 1977), 27–33. See also Cass Weller, "Why Hume is a Direct Realist," *Archiv für Geschichte der Philosophie* 83, no. 3 (2001): 258–85.

So a believed idea is able to operate on the will and the passions in virtue of its similarity to sense impressions in terms of "vividness" and "intensity" of conception.[10] In certain pages Hume even seems to suggest that the force and liveliness of impressions actually *is* belief:

> the *belief* or *assent*, which always attends the memory and senses, is nothing but the vivacity of those perceptions they present ... To believe is in this case to feel an immediate impression of the senses, or a repetition of that impression in the memory. 'Tis merely the force and liveliness of the perception, which constitutes the first act of judgment, and lays the foundation of that reasoning, which we build upon it, when we trace the relation of cause and effect. (T86)

Here the "force and liveliness" of sense impressions is the first actuation of reason in judgement, being the starting point of all causal reasoning—conversely, "all probable reasoning is nothing but a species of sensation" (T102).[11] As soon as I have an impression of the "cause," I expect its usual "effect," that is, I conceive it in a strong and lively manner. My expectation is the basic act of "probable reasoning," and consists of the force and vivacity that the impression of the first event lends to the idea of the second which is associated with it in my mind. Whatever Hume means by "force" and "vivacity", they can—crucially—be transferred from one perception to another:

> *when any impression becomes present to us, it not only transports the mind to such ideas as are related to it, but likewise communicates to them a share of its force and vivacity.*... when the mind is once enliven'd by a present impression, it proceeds to form a more lively idea of the related objects, by a natural transition of the disposition from the one to the other. The change of the objects is so easy, that the mind is scarce sensible of it, but applies

---

[10] See Everson, "Difference," esp. 407–408 (strangely underestimated by Stroud, *Hume*, 74). Everson in fact finds that the connection between impressions and beliefs is so close that there is a danger of not being able to differentiate between them at all—for his solution see idem, "Difference," 410–13.

[11] This close connection between sense impressions and belief is a long-term conviction of Hume's. See Part 3 of *Dialogues concerning Natural Religion*, ed. Norman Kemp Smith (Edinburgh: Thomas Nelson and Sons, 1947), 154, where Cleanthes observes: "Consider, anatomise the eye; survey its structure and contrivance; and tell me, from your own feeling, if the idea of a contriver does not immediately flow in upon you with a force like that of sensation."

> itself to the conception of the related idea with all the
> force and vivacity it acquir'd from the present
> impression. (T98–99)

So the present impression is the provider of the liveliness and strength of conception which is the concrete sensational (or sentimental) material of belief. In this sense it is necessary—"absolutely requisite," to use Hume's terms—for belief to occur: "belief is a more vivid and intense conception of an idea, proceeding from its relation to a present impression" (T103).

III. Belief and the animal spirits

Focusing on force and liveliness, as I have done so far, highlights the similarities and connections between (sense) impressions and believed ideas. But there are also very remarkable differences. In particular, while belief is one of the major topics in Book 1 of the *Treatise*, impressions, after being introduced in the first few pages, are hardly discussed at all. Impressions of reflections, or passions, are the subject of Book 2. Sense impressions are deliberately left out because they constitute, according to Hume, a topic for natural philosophers and anatomists—as he puts it, "the examination of our sensations belongs more to anatomists and natural philosophers than to moral" (T8). To Hume the "science of human nature" or "science of man" was, as he called it, an "anatomy of the mind" which, however, did not include natural philosophy and anatomy proper.

But many of Hume's contemporaries saw things differently. For Nicolas Malebranche the "science de l'homme" has as its main focus the soul. In his *La Recherche de la vérité* of 1674–75 the physiological accounts of sense impressions and thought processes are omnipresent and of fundamental importance. Malebranche's detailed descriptions of the workings of the body are aimed at accounting for the ways in which the soul is bound and conditioned by its dependence on the body; and in his pages the explanations of mental or passional states are in mechanistic terms of flow or agitation of animal spirits, brain fibres, impressions and traces on the brain's substance, and so on. The fundamental importance of Malebranche's work for eighteenth-century British culture has recently begun to be recognized. In *Thinking Matter* John Yolton has reconstructed in detail the reception of Malebranchean physiology in the works of metaphysicians and moral philosophers, natural philosophers and medics. He also points out that it was massively present in the pages of Chambers's *Cyclopaedia*.[12] Here, as well as having entries specifically

---

[12] John W. Yolton, *Thinking Matter: Materialism in Eighteenth-Century Britain* (Oxford: Blackwell, 1984), "The Physiology of Thinking and Acting," 152–89, esp. 162–72; Yolton

devoted to them, spirits and brain traces appear, often accompanied by
open references to Malebranche and quotations from his *Recherche*, in
such other entries as "Brain," "Circulation (of spirits)," "Passion,"
"Habit," "Memory," "Error," "Imagination"—the entry on the
imagination being, in fact, a near-literal translation of a section of
Malebranche's *Recherche*.[13]

Chambers's assessment of the theory of animal spirits is revealingly
cautious:

> The existence of animal spirits is controverted: but the
> infinite use they are of in animal oeconomy and the
> exceedingly lame account we should have of any of the
> animal functions without them, will still keep the
> greatest part of the world on their side. And in effect,
> the learned Boerhaave has gone a good way towards a
> demonstration of their reality.[14]

On one point this qualified endorsement of the theory of animal spirits
leaves us in no doubt: they play major roles in the "science of human
nature" as it was practiced in early eighteenth-century Britain. "Moral
physiology," to use John Sutton's apt name for it,[15] was a very important
element of the eighteenth-century culture of sensibility: by the time Hume
was writing his *Treatise* animal spirits, brain traces and imaginary
dissections of the brain were popular enough to make their appearance in
works addressing wide readerships. As well as in the *Cyclopaedia* they are

considers, among others, the works of Bernard de Mandeville, George Cheyne, John
Jackson, Benjamin Martin, Samuel Colliber and Isaac Watts. See also the seminal discussions
by Robert F. Anderson, *Hume's First Principles* (Lincoln: University of Nebraska Press,
1966), esp. ch. 13, "Material Foundations of Knowledge," 111–32; and by John P. Wright,
The Sceptical Realism of David Hume (Manchester: Manchester University Press, 1983).
Useful materials can also be found in Charles J. McCracken, *Malebranche and British
Philosophy* (Oxford: Clarendon Press, 1983); and Stuart Brown, "The Critical Reception of
Malebranche, from His Own Time to the End of the Eighteenth Century," in Steven Nadler,
ed., *The Cambridge Companion to Malebranche* (Cambridge: Cambridge University Press,
2000), 262–87.
[13] As noted by Wright, *Sceptical Realism*, 189 and 235, n. 4. The relevant section of the
Recherche is Book 2, Part 1, ch. 1.
[14] Ephraim Chambers, *Cyclopaedia* (London, 1738), "Spirit." For a similar attitude see
Bernard Mandeville's *Treatise of the Hypochondriack and Hysterical Passions* (London,
1711), where the existence of the animal spirits is unambiguously stated, but in a dialogue
and in response to a sceptical query by one of the characters.
[15] John Sutton, *Philosophy and Memory Traces. Descartes to Connectionism* (Cambridge:
Cambridge University Press, 1998), for example 46–49 and, specifically on Malebranche,
195–97.

to be found, for example, in Addison's essays in *The Spectator*.[16] They were routinely evoked even in novels and poems, where, as another recent reader, Ann van Sant, has put it, physiological language "provided a means of imagining and explaining interior experience."[17] Now, it is well known that Hume regarded Malebranche's *Recherche* as a work of major importance and as an antecedent to his own investigations.[18] He was also familiar with a number of other, more recent works in which animal spirits and brain traces made their appearance—Addison's and Chambers's, for example.[19] It is tempting to think that the avoidance of physiological accounts in his pages is an oddity calling for an explanation!

[16] In *The Spectator* see, for example, no. 275 for an imaginary dissection of a beau's brain, and no. 417 for the animal spirits.

[17] Ann J. van Sant, *Eighteenth-Century Sensibility and the Novel: The Senses in Social Context* (Cambridge: Cambridge University Press, 1993), 11–12. The animal spirits are also to be found in, for instance, *Tom Jones*, *Tristram Shandy* (see, e.g., Book 1, chs. 1–2), and Henry Brooke's long philosophical poem on *Universal Beauty* of 1735. On the importance of physiology for the literature of sensibility see G. J. Barker-Benfield, *The Culture of Sensibility: Sex and Society in Eighteenth-Century Britain* (Chicago and London: Chicago University Press, 1992), ch. 1, "Sensibility and the Nervous System" (esp. 15–23); G. S. Rousseau, "Nerves, Spirits, and Fibres: Towards Defining the Origins of Sensibility," *Blue Guitar* 2 (1976): 125–53; and Robert F. Brissenden, *Virtue in Distress: Studies in the Novel of Sentiment from Richardson to de Sade* (New York: Harper and Row, 1974), 37–48. Also Christopher Lawrence, "The Nervous System and Society in the Scottish Enlightenment," in Barry Barnes and Steven Shapin, eds., *Natural Order: Historical Studies of Scientific Culture* (London: Sage, 1979), 19–39. Among the intellectual pursuits whose physiology was the object of much attention there was, of course, reading itself: see Adrian Johns, "The Physiology of Reading in Restoration England," in James Raven *et al.*, eds., *The Practice and Representation of Reading in England* (Cambridge: Cambridge University Press, 1996), 138–61; and idem, "The physiology of reading," in Marina Frasca-Spada and Nick Jardine, eds. *Books and the Sciences in History* (Cambridge: Cambridge University Press, 2000), 291–314.

[18] On Hume and Malebranche see C. W. Doxee, "Hume's Relation to Malebranche," *Philosophical Review* 25 (1916): 692–710; Ralph W. Church, "Malebranche and Hume," *Revue internationale de philosophie* 1 (1938): 143–61; and, more recently: Peter Jones, *Hume's Sentiments. Their Ciceronian and French Context* (Edinburgh: The University Press, 1982); Wright, *Sceptical Realism*; Luigi Turco, *Lo scetticismo morale di David Hume* (Bologna: Editrice CLUEB, 1984), 55–56; John P. Wright, "Hume's Criticism of Malebranche's Theory of Causation: a Lesson in the Historiography of Philosophy," in Stuart Brown, ed., *Nicolas Malebranche, His Philosophical Critics and Successors* (Assen/Maastricht: Van Gorcum, 1991), 116–30; G. Gori, "Da Malebranche a Hume: modelli della mente umana, immaginazione, giudizi naturali. Un percorso storiografico," in Antonio Santucci, ed., *Filosofia e cultura nel settecento britannico, vol. 1—Fonti e connessioni continentali; John Toland e il deismo* (Bologna: Il Mulino, 2000), 113–34; and, with more emphasis on Malebranche than on Hume, Steven Nadler, "Malebranche on causation," in Nadler, ed., *Cambridge Companion to Malebranche*, 112–38 (the comparison with Hume is in 133–36).

[19] No. 412 of *The Spectator* is cited in Book 2 of the *Treatise* (T284). On Hume as a reader of Chambers's *Cyclopaedia* see James Force, "Hume's Interest in Newton and Science," *Hume Studies* 14 (1988): 166–216.

IV. The animal spirits in Hume's *Treatise*

In fact, on one occasion Hume does offer a detailed explanation of a mental phenomenon in terms of animal spirits and brain traces. The issue is our tendency to confuse ideas that are associated. Hume's presentation is cautious: he announces that the importance and consequence of this tendency is such that it is worth, just for once, to pause briefly to examine its causes; but, he warns, "we must distinguish exactly betwixt the phaenomenon itself, and the causes, which I shall assign for it.... The phaenomenon may be real, tho' my explanation be chimerical" (T60). He then proceeds to introduce his own "imaginary dissection of the brain," an impeccably well informed rehearsal of the common animal spirits story. Confusion, he says, arises due to the uncertainty of the spirits' movement:

> whenever [the mind] dispatches the spirits into that region of the brain, in which the idea is plac'd; these spirits always excite the idea, when they run precisely into the proper traces, and rummage that cell, which belongs to the idea. But as their motion is seldom direct, and naturally turns a little to the one side or the other; for this reason the animal spirits, falling into the contiguous traces, present other related ideas in lieu of that which the mind desir'd at first to survey. This change we are not always sensible of; but continuing still the same train of thought, make use of the related idea, which is presented to us, and employ it in our reasoning, as if it were the same with what we demanded. This is the cause of many mistakes and sophisms in philosophy (T60–61).[20]

This phenomenon is ideally illustrated, he concludes, by "the figures of poets and orators"—should metaphysicians regard such examples as "below their dignity," they may find equally good ones in their own "discourses" when they fall victims of the common human tendency "to use words for ideas, and to talk instead of thinking in their reasonings" (T61–62). Much could be said of this page's background. Very briefly, it belongs to Hume's intervention on one of the most topical questions of contemporary natural philosophy, that is, the conceivability and existence of a vacuum. So here he is confronting, and disagreeing with, the sacred

---

[20] Cf. Nicolas Malebranche, *Recherche de la vérité*, Book 2, Part 2, ch. 2 (in *The Search after Truth*, trans. and ed. Thomas M. Lennon and Paul J. Olscamp [Cambridge: Cambridge University Press, 1977], 134–35). Also Chambers, *s.v.* "Trace" and "Error."

monsters of his time: Newton, Locke, Samuel Clarke. His reference, in discussing this issue, to such literary frivolities as rhetorical figures is a piece of cheerfully deliberate breaching behavior, crowned as it is by the wicked poke about the metaphysicians' own confusions of closely related mental items, words and ideas—a case in point being, in his view, precisely that of a vacuum, a mere word which is all too often mistaken for an idea. This is the frame of reference within which Hume introduced his tentative physiological explanation—a mechanistic and Cartesian one which was familiar to all his readers and eminently respectable, and hence, if presented with due caution, ideally suited to lend both additional polemical edge and natural-philosophical respectability to his highly unconventional treatment of empty space.

It has been noticed that, as in the passage above, on practically every occasion that Hume mentions animal spirits and brain traces it is in connection with errors and the mechanism underlying them.[21] In this he is following closely Malebranche's own lead: the "search after truth" which gives Malebranche's work its title is an experience of endless frustration, with more than half of his massive book being devoted to classifying and minutely accounting for the different errors to which our senses, imagination, understanding, inclination, and passions are prone.[22] But even when he does mention the animal spirits Hume gives to his own accounts of errors a very different spin. Consider an example of Malebranche's physiological talk, as rendered into English by Chambers:

> It may be observed, that the fibres of the brain are more
> agitated by the impression of objects, **which it perceives
> by sensation,** than by the course of the animal spirits;
> and for this reason the soul is more affected with
> objects, which it perceives by sensation, and which it
> looks on as present, and capable of giving it pleasure or

---

[21] Turco, *Lo scetticismo*, 64 n. 18. The only occurrence of the animal spirits in Hume's *Treatise* not in direct connection with errors is T98–99. On error see also T122–23: "belief not only gives vigour to the imagination, but ... a vigorous and strong imagination is of all talents the most proper to procure belief and authority. 'Tis difficult for us to withhold our assent from what is painted out to us in all the colours of eloquence; and the vivacity produc'd by the fancy is in many cases greater than that which arises from custom and experience. We are hurried away by the lively imagination of our author or companion; and even he himself is often a victim to his own fire and genius."

[22] Histories of errors were in vogue toward the end of the seventeenth century. For example, Pierre Bayle's first idea for what was to become his *Dictionnaire historique et critique* took precisely the shape of a dictionary of errors. See Anthony Grafton, *The Footnote. A Curious History* (Cambridge, MA: Harvard University Press, 1997), 192–95. While Bayle's project was historical and aimed at producing an alphabetical classification, Malebranche's attempt at a rational classification and explanation of errors in terms of mechanical natural philosophy and animal economy is evidently "philosophical."

pain, than by those perceived by *imagination*, which it
judges to be distant.—And yet it sometimes happens, that
in persons, whose animal spirits are extremely agitated
by fasting, waking, **drinking,** a fever, or some violent
passion, these spirits move the inward fibres of the brain
as forcibly as outward objects do; so that those persons
perceive things by sensation, which they should only
perceive by *imagination*; **[and they think they see
objects before their eyes, which are only in their
imaginations.]** for *imagination* and *sensation* only differ
from each other, as the greater from the less.[23]

So, according to Malebranche, between something sensed and something
merely imagined there is only a difference in degree; and if our spirits are
in an altered state the boundary between them may be unclear. Hume too
acknowledges that altered bodily states can turn force and vivacity into
bad indicators of the difference between impressions and ideas—"in sleep,
in a fever, in madness, or in any very violent emotions of the soul, our
ideas may approach to our impressions" (T2), as he puts it at the
beginning of the *Treatise*. His account of the phenomenon is very
Malebranchean:

When the imagination, from any extraordinary ferment
of the blood and spirits, acquires such a vivacity as
disorders all its powers and faculties, there is no means
of distinguishing betwixt truth and falshood; but every
loose fiction or idea, having the same influence as the
impressions of the memory, or the conclusions of the
judgment, is receiv'd on the same footing, and operates
with equal force on the passions.... Every chimera of the
brain is as vivid and intense as any of those inferences,
which we formerly dignify'd with the name of

---

[23] Chambers, *Cyclopaedia*, "Imagination." The only alterations by Chambers are two small
additions (in bold in the text) and a cut (in bold and square brackets). Cf. Lennon and
Olscamp's translation in Malebranche, *Search*, Book 2, Section 1, ch. 1, i, 88: "it should be
noted that the fibers of the brain are agitated much more by the impressions of objects than
by the flow of spirits. And this is why the soul is much more influenced by external objects
that it judges as present and capable of making it feel pleasure and pain than it is by the flow
of animal spirits. However, it sometimes happens that persons whose animal spirits are
highly agitated by fasting, vigil, a high fever, or some violent passion have the internal fibers
of their brains set in motion as forcefully as by external objects. Because of this such people
sense what they should only *imagine*, and they think they see objects before their eyes, which
are only in their imaginations. This shows that with regard to what occurs in the body, the
senses and the imagination differ only in degree, as I have just suggested."

conclusions concerning matters of fact, and sometimes as
the present impressions of the senses. (T123)

It is evident that, while Malebranche had offered a whole causal
explanation of the phenomenon in detailed physiological terms, in Hume's
text all physiological underpinnings are carefully left in the background. A
passing mention of the "extraordinary ferment of the blood and spirits"—
this is as bodily as his language will go—then he glibly moves on to the
phenomenological oddity of ideas conceived at such times and the
impossibility of distinguishing truth from falsehood, thus introducing the
impact on action of "every loose fiction or idea" and of the vivid chimeras
of the brain.[24]

And yet, while pursuing his own kind of "science of human nature"
devoid of natural philosophy and anatomy, Hume still cast his attempted
phenomenological descriptions of experience in the idiom of the animal
spirits and brain traces physiology, transposing that theory into his own
explorations of experience. Take the case of "impression" itself. In
Malebranche and in Chambers, an impression is a mechanical interaction
between an object and "the surface of the fibres of our nerves"—the
resulting "agitation" of the fibres is then "communicated to the brain"
where it engraves a "trace," that is, a "mark" or, again, an
"impression."[25] On the other hand, Hume famously wrote that by
"impression" he did not intend "to express the manner, in which our
lively perceptions are produced in the soul, but merely the perceptions
themselves" (T2). Similarly, Malebranche's "force," "agitation" and
"excitement" of the animal spirits are turned by Hume into the force and
liveliness of impressions; and what in Malebranche was the effortless
passage of the animal spirits through the oft-used brain fibres of very
deeply engraved traces[26] is transformed by Hume into the ease with which
the mind transfers vivacity from one perception to those habitually
associated with it.

---

[24] For other cases in which the animal spirits appear very discreetly see T98 (it connects "the
spirits [being ...] elevated" to the "vigour and vivacity" of an operation of the mind) and T99
("any new object naturally gives a new direction to the spirits"), both in connection with the
transference of vivacity from an impression or idea to such ideas as are related to it; T185
(acts of the mind which are "forc'd and unnatural" correspond to ideas which are "faint and
obscure" because "the posture of the mind is uneasy; and the spirits being diverted from their
natural course, are not govern'd in their movements by the same laws, at least not to the
same degree, as when they flow in their usual channel"); in the Appendix T630–31; and they
are mentioned in T28, T135 (in connection with their materiality), 203, 211, 230, 269, 275
(origin of impressions), 290, etc.
[25] Chambers, *Cyclopaedia*, "Imagination" and "Trace;" and Malebranche, *Recherche*, Book
2, Part 1, ch. 1, 87–88.
[26] *Recherche*, Book 2, Part 1, ch. 5, 106.

There are occasions when a physiological residue of Hume's transposition almost surfaces in his text. For example, in commenting on the fashion among contemporary "poets" of borrowing names and events from history for their fictional stories, he suggests that in this way they "procure a more easy reception for the whole, and cause it to make a deeper impression on the fancy and affections." The historical name or event "bestows a force and vivacity" on the fictional materials which in the poem or story are united, and hence, however contingently, associated with it. And this is how he puts it:

> The vividness of the first conception diffuses itself along the relations, and is convey'd, as by so many pipes or canals, to every idea that has any communication with the primary one. (T122)

Here the mechanistic physiological model suddenly pops up in the middle of the discourse on the phenomenology of belief, with the transference of belief among ideas being described as if belief were a fluid, in terms of diffusion and with the image of the conveyance of vividness as if through pipes and canals.[27]

V. The steadiness of belief

The question with which I started this essay was: how successful is Hume in his attempt to transform the idiom of mechanistic physiology into a language for the description of feeling? If all there is to Hume's theory of belief were the use of "force" and "liveliness" to refer to sentimental intensity, clearly not much. But it is not, and for two reasons. The first is that, when talking about belief, Hume's descriptions of what experience feels like in terms of physiological-language-turned-phenomenological are often accompanied by vivid illustrations from everyday life and experience which, in a very typically Humean version of the Scottish moralist style, lend to his discussion the required phenomenological subtlety and insight. This emerges with clarity, for instance, in connection with the phenomenology of memory. Malebranche explains carefully the workings of memory as the result of the differential strength of the action of animal spirits on the substance of the brain, then concludes in passing that by following his mechanistic model "one will have the pleasure of discovering the causes of all these surprising effects of the memory, of which Saint Augustine speaks with so much admiration in the tenth book

---

[27] In my interpretation the use of the animal spirits story in the *Treatise* does not, *pace* Wright, commit Hume to realism; in fact it need not even be regarded as a clue to any such commitment. For his attitude to animal spirits is so noncommittal that it boils down to a mere reference to, without actual endorsement of, a current theory.

of his *Confessions*."[28] Hume, by contrast, never offers causal explanations, but rather he chooses to illustrate those surprising effects in a series of vignettes. So we find a man trying to remind another of a shared "scene of action," and the sudden change of feel when remembrance finally clicks (T628). And we are told of the painter enlivening his recollection of a certain passion before painting it by observing someone actuated by it, and of liars becoming convinced of their own lies by dint of repeating them (T85–86). Also, in the discussion of general terms, we find that "to explain the ultimate causes of our mental actions is impossible;" but that the way general terms work is similar to another of memory's characteristics, namely the ability of a single word to conjure up a whole run of long-forgotten verses (T23). All these cases are very Malebranchean—they are the sorts of phenomena Malebranche was trying to account for with his physiological discussions. Instead of offering hypothetical natural-philosophical causal explanations of them, Hume prefers to capture them with his peculiar combination of introspective descriptions of sentiments and lively sketches of sociability. We know that the anatomist of the mind who wrote the *Treatise* did not wish to be a painter; but he did address his readers' understanding by means of a certain amount of drawing.[29]

The second reason why there is more to Hume's theory of belief than a description of sentimental intensity has to do with the third group of terms he uses to characterize belief, that which includes "steadiness," "solidity" and "firmness".

In his elegant discussion of Hume's theory of belief John Passmore observed that in the *Treatise* we find, in fact, no less than three different theories, which are presented early on and coexist, somewhat uneasily, to the very end. The first of these theories regards belief as a more vivid and intense way of conceiving an idea; the second connects this believed idea with a present impression, thus rooting belief in experience; while the third regards belief as arising "only from causation" (T107), that is, as the result of probable reasoning, thus highlighting the element of reasonableness of certain beliefs above others. These three theories, Passmore suggests, mark a trend, albeit not a consistent one, "from the doctrine that all beliefs are on the same footing to the doctrine that some

---

[28] *Recherche*, Book 2, Part 1, ch. 5, 107.

[29] It would be interesting to compare Hume's use of description and illustration in this case, with the combination of explanation and sentimental description and illustration in his historical writing. On anatomy, painting and drawing in Hume see M. A. Stewart's splendid "Two Species of Philosophy: The Historical Significance of the First *Enquiry*," in Peter Millican, ed., *Reading Hume on Human Understanding: Essays on the First "Enquiry"* (Oxford: Clarendon Press, 2002), 67–95.

beliefs are much more rational than others."[30] What I have been discussing so far are Hume's first and second theories of belief. To make sense of steadiness it is necessary to go for a brief venture into the third.

According to this third Humean theory of belief, it is not even strictly speaking the case that belief is one and the same as liveliness. In Hume's own words:

> the great difference in their feeling [of poetical enthusiasm, and a serious conviction] proceeds in some measure from reflexion and *general* rules.... A like reflexion on *general rules* keeps us from augmenting our belief upon every increase of the force and vivacity of our ideas. Where an opinion admits of no doubt, or opposite probability, we attribute to it a full conviction; tho' the want of resemblance, or contiguity, may render its force inferior to that of other opinions. (T631–32)[31]

Hume never offered a full discussion of the pragmatic logic of his "reflexion and general rules." He observed that a sceptic would relish how all our attempts to correct our natural gullibility and to rank our beliefs must be guided by something which is as "unphilosophical" as the general rules, and so similar, in its actual working, to prejudice itself. Passmore's conclusion is in a tone of regret for Hume's carelessness and apparent lack of serious engagement with this issue. The tasks of exploring the meaning of Hume's attitude or of trying to reconstruct its reasons are beyond the scope of my discussion. I would only like to suggest that Hume's hidden reference to the physiology of animal spirits and brain traces may provide us with a clue to belief as steadiness and to the workings of the general rules. Consider another of Hume's vignettes, that which presents us the two readers of the same book, one of whom believes it to be a romance, and the other a true history:

---

[30] John Passmore, *Hume's Intentions*, 3rd ed. (London: Duckworth, 1980), 61–63; the quotation is from 61.

[31] On T632 and the meaning and use of the "general rules" see Thomas K. Hearn, Jr., "'General Rules' in Hume's *Treatise*," *Journal of the History of Philosophy* 8 (1970): 405–22; W. H. Walsh, "Hume's Concept of Truth," in Godfrey Vesey, ed., *Reason and Reality*, Royal Institute of Philosophy Lectures, vol. 5, 1970–1971 (London: Macmillan, 1972), 99–116; and Marie A. Martin, "The Rational Warrant for Hume's General Rules," *Journal of the History of Philosophy* 31 (1993): 245–57. Also of interest the observations in John Laird, *Hume's Philosophy of Human Nature* (London: Methuen, 1932), 91–92; André-Louis Leroy, *David Hume* (Paris: Presses Universitaires de France, 1953), 69–72; Lewis White Beck, "A Prussian Hume and a Scottish Kant," in *Essays on Kant and Hume* (New Haven: Yale University Press, 1978), 111–29, esp. 122ff.; and Annette C. Baier, *A Progress of Sentiments: Reflections on Hume's "Treatise"* (Cambridge, MA: Harvard University Press, 1991), ch. 3, 54–77.

> they plainly receive the same ideas, and in the same
> order; nor does the incredulity of the one, and the belief
> of the other hinder them from putting the very same
> sense upon their author. His words produce the same
> ideas in both; tho' his testimony has not the same
> influence on them. The latter has a more lively
> conception of all the incidents. (T97–98).

These two readers embody the difference between entertaining a lively idea, and assenting to it. It is clear that the difference between them lies with the distinction between the liveliness of the ideas—which is obviously the same for both readers—and the liveliness of our conceiving those ideas, which constitutes the difference between the readers' responses— suspended disbelief, in one case, and actual belief in the other. On the same basis, while "a poetical description may have a more sensible effect on the fancy, than an historical narration" by setting "the object before us in more lively colours" or by collecting "more of those circumstances, that form a compleat image or picture," it is still the case that "the ideas it presents are different to the feeling from those, which arise from the memory and the judgment": for all the "seeming vehemence of thought and sentiments" which derives from the liveliness of the contents, there is still "something weak and imperfect" in the conception (T631). Now, this distinction makes very good sense if we regard the two sorts of liveliness as corresponding, respectively, to a forceful movement of the animal spirits, and to their steady and easy flow in the more deeply engraved traces in the brain: as Hume puts it on a different occasion, it is the "ferment of the spirits" as opposed to "their orderly motion" (T423).[32] The steady and orderly motion of the animal spirits, we know from Malebranche, Chambers and the others, occurs when they move along the particularly deep and large traces opened up by frequent use. My suggestion is that we regard that orderly motion as corresponding to belief as steadiness, solidity and firmness of conception. If so, it will lead us straight to repeated experience and to custom as the root of all stabilizing and calibrating factors of belief, including "reflexion and general rules."[33]

---

[32] I am grateful to Peter Kail for suggesting this point. Apart from a couple of appearances of firmness in the text of the *Treatise* (T97, 105, 106 together with "solidity," "force" and "vivacity" and with "vigour," 116) the steadiness group is typical of the Appendix. In fact, the parts of the Appendix on belief are a translation of the force and vivacity materials in the text into the frame of reference of steadiness. For example, in the text we find that beliefs approach impressions because of the "*vivid and intense conception*" (T119–20), while in the Appendix this is because they "strikes us, as something real and solid" (T627).

[33] It is interesting to remember that in connection with religious belief Hume seems to think that liveliness and vivacity of conception are far from desirable qualities, so that one of the

So tracing Hume's terminology back to Malebranchean animal economy provides the key for us to interpret its variety. Force and vivacity are features of individual perceptions as such. Steadiness, solidity and firmness, by contrast, depend on repetition and custom, thus linking those individual perceptions to a wider range of experiences; and as such they only belong to individual perceptions insofar as these are members of a class of oft-repeated experiences. The special feeling typical of a believed idea does not depend exclusively on its sentimental intensity, but also on the way in which that idea fits in with the rest of our experience.

VI. Conclusion

I started this essay by asking how successful was Hume in transforming the physiological idiom of force, vivacity and steadiness into a language for the narration of feeling and experience, and what is the role of this narration within his theory of belief. My answer to the first question is a qualified yes: quite successful. But Hume's theory of belief is, contrary to appearances, very complex. First there is an attempted phenomenological description of believing in the typical Humean introspective style—it is in this connection that Hume uses the 'force' and 'vivacity' terminology borrowed from animal economy. Second, the phenomenological description is substantiated and specified by vignettes derived from common experience and sociality. Taken together, these two combine to produce a surprisingly subtle and insightful picture. The third element of Hume's theory of belief has to do with steadiness and the mechanisms of stabilization and calibration of belief, that is, with reflection and general rules. The basis for these mechanisms is custom. This is probably the aspect which Hume regarded as the least interesting of his work on belief—so for example, when presenting the "Rules by which to judge causes and effects," he flippantly declares that "here is all the LOGIC I think proper to employ in my reasoning; and perhaps even this was not very necessary, but might have been supply'd by the natural principles of our understanding" (T175). The fact that Hume did not devote much effort to this logic does not, however, diminish the significance of its presence.[34] Hume's theory of belief is not simply that believed ideas are strong and lively; the strength and liveliness of believed ideas is no more than the raw sentimental material of belief.

It is evident that animal spirits are of only historical interest. And yet, I think that they do help us to make better sense of a book that is still as lively as Hume's *Treatise*. Hume and his contemporaries assigned the

---

great advantages of ancient polytheistic religions is precisely that they are believed less forcibly—see for instance in *The Natural History of Religion*.

[34] As pointed out by Baier, *Progress of Sentiments*, 56–57.

investigations of perceptions, passions and understanding to the "science of man" or "the science human nature." This intellectual enterprise, which has played such an important part in the genealogy of present-day philosophy, had at the time close links on the one hand with natural history and animal economy or physiology, and on the other with logic and metaphysics. Being a typical expression of this "science of human nature," Hume's theory of belief is rooted in the natural inquiries as well as in the moral-philosophical discourse of the time. Moreover, the "science of man" as a learned pursuit was on a continuum with the less highbrow forms of interest in human nature which made up the eighteenth-century culture of feeling. A difficult, bulky book such as Hume's *Treatise of Human Nature* was at one extreme of a wide range of writings which included, at the other extreme, sentimental novels and poetry, and in the mid-range brief and elegant essays and moralizing writings.[35] It is well known that the *Treatise* was an uncompromisingly "anatomical" work that hardly contained any "painting" to address the taste and feelings of contemporary "conversable" readers. But it still belongs to that culture insofar as it was those same readers' understanding that its author was trying to address. So the way Hume presented and justified his views was drastically different from anything a philosopher would now do when addressing a readership of philosophers. In particular, the illustrations and vignettes peppering his pages on belief are not decorative optionals or mere presentation devices: they actually add to the argument or fine-tune it in crucial ways. Exploring Hume's treatment of belief by reconstructing the cultural idiom in which it was cast may have strange and contrasting effects. On the one hand, this operation is likely to make Hume's work appear more alien. But on the other it also uncovers in that work a way of doing philosophy that is well worth redeeming.

---

[35] See my "The Science and Conversation of Human Nature," in William Clark, Jan Golinski and Simon Schaffer, eds., *The Sciences in Enlightened Europe* (Chicago: University of Chicago Press, 1999), 218-45, and "Quixotic Confusions and Hume's Imagination."

1946 Lectures on David Hume's Philosophy
W. V. Quine
Edited By James G. Buickerood

Of the old timers, I feel most congenial to Hume.
—W. V. Quine[1]

Editorial introduction

Quine's name and philosophical views are not infrequently linked with
Hume's. It cannot be said, however, that Quine himself discussed Hume's
philosophy in any great detail in the works he published in his lifetime.
Thus there has been a gap in our view of Quine's understanding and
appreciation of an important predecessor of at least one dimension of his
philosophical perspective. The following text fills that gap to a degree.

In 1946 Harvard remained on the academic schedule it had followed
during the Second World War of three terms of equal duration per year
with fall, spring and summer terms. Before that year and before his leave
from the university for naval service, Quine had been asked to teach a
course in the history of philosophy, but until his return from the U.S.
Navy had been successful at fending off such requests. For the Summer
1946 term he finally relented and chose to teach a course on Hume,
Philosophy 14c, which was to meet at 10:00 a.m. on Mondays,
Wednesdays and Fridays. He began preparation during the winter of 1945-
1946. Twenty-five students were enrolled in the course, of whom twelve
were undergraduates and thirteen were graduate students.[2] Quine was not
at that time, and remained, fundamentally unenthusiastic about teaching
the course, as he recorded in *The Time of My Life*:

> I tried to make a virtue of the necessity. The critical
> knowledge of Hume that I would need for my course
> would mesh with my own philosophical thinking,
> providing enrichment and perspective. The course,
> moreover, once given, could be readily given again.
> Rationalize as I might, however, preparation dragged. I

---

[1] W. V. Quine, in an interview with the semiannual serial, *Veery* 3 (1993): 21.
[2] W. V. Quine, *The Time of My Life: An Autobiography* (Cambridge, MA: M.I.T. Press,
1985), 190. Class meeting days and times are listed on the first numbered card in the primary
portion of the manuscript. The enrolled students' degree status was entered on Quine's class
roster.

dawdled. It was a struggle to keep ahead. By the end of
the course my lecture notes were full and ready for a
repeat performance in another year, but I could not bear
to offer the course again. Determining what Hume
thought and imparting it to students was less appealing
than determining the truth and imparting that.

The conclusion of that summer term, concluded Quine, left "the ordeal of
Hume forever behind me."[3]

Still, at the conclusion of the 1946 lectures, Quine did give some
thought to the approach he might take were he to teach Hume again in
future. "If give course again," reads an unnumbered card included with
the lecture notes, "stress untenability of Hume's doctrine 'whatever is
different is separable,' or 'whole is nothing but sum of its parts,' used in
his argument on cause; how this doctrine would invalidate his own theory
of relations (no possible basis for contiguity and succession), and his
theory e.g. of time (*Treatise* 1.2.3)."

Description of the manuscript

The bulk of the manuscript of these lectures now in the possession of
the Quine estate was discovered by Douglas Boynton Quine soon after W.
V. Quine's death in December 2000. This primary portion consists of five
hundred thirty-nine 3 x 5 index cards, five hundred eight of which Quine
numbered in the sequence used to compose the text of the lectures. Thirty-
one additional cards in this portion are unnumbered; these cards contain
tables and supplementary materials described below.

In the summer of 2002, Douglas Quine and Roger F. Gibson, Jr.
discovered an additional three cards and the typed class roster for the
course in which the lectures were given in Quine's Emerson Hall office.
Two of this portion's cards are in Quine's handwriting; the third is the
printed text of the final examination given students in the course. At this
time, Quine and Gibson also discovered an integral part of these lectures:
W. V. Quine's annotated copy of Hume's *Treatise*, without which it
would be very difficult, indeed impossible, to follow the detailed analyses
comprising parts of these lectures.

This copy of the *Treatise* is undoubtedly the one Quine read and
annotated in preparation for and during the course of his lectures.[4]

---

[3] Quine, *Time*, 194.

[4] Quine's copy is a 1946 reprint of David Hume, *A Treatise of Human Nature*, ed. L. A.
Selby-Bigge (Oxford: Clarendon Press, 1888). This is the edition to which all subsequent
Treatise page references owe. In addition to this text, Quine penciled a card identifying
editions of Hume's works that he used to be the *Dialogues* and first *Enquiry* as found in
Edwin A. Burtt, ed., *The English Philosophers from Bacon to Mill* (New York: Random

Throughout this text, but especially in Book 1, Quine wrote, mostly in pencil (sometimes in red pencil), marginal comments that are reflected in the lectures, constructed a table laying out Hume's classification of impressions referred to in the lectures (and included below, 234), and assigned certain arguments, paragraphs and passages of Hume's text numbers in distinct series. The latter two sorts of marginalia prove crucial to understanding Quine's lectures, and so are reproduced here in the exact locations Quine read and referred to them during his lectures. The numerals written in the manuscript corresponding to these numbered parts of Hume's text are rendered in this edition in bold type, reproducing the emphasis Quine's hand lent them on his note cards.

The two handwritten cards in the supplementary portion of the manuscript contain lists of texts and secondary sources Quine used or intended to use in the course of his lectures. The list of Hume's texts on one of these cards—*Treatise*; first *Enquiry*; *Dialogues concerning Natural Religion*—is repeated with more bibliographic specificity on a card at the opening of the series constituting the first portion of the manuscript as I have noted. The present edition refers to those versions of these texts Quine evidently used in this course as identified here. The remainder of that card is taken up with Quine's reading recommendation for that term's reading period: Church's, Kemp Smith's and Laird's books on Hume referred to in notes to the text below. The second handwritten card simply lists the titles of these three works in addition to H. H. Price's *Hume on Our Knowledge of the External World*, C. W. Hendel's *Studies*, and T. H. Green's edition of Hume's *Works*.[5] The printed card in this portion contains the final examination for this course:

PHILOSOPHY 14c
HUME

Synopsize and discuss Hume's views regarding four of the following six topics. Indicate also the principal observations made by Church, Laird, or Smith, insofar as they relate to any of the chosen topics.

1. Abstract ideas.
2. Space and time.

House, 1939). The *Dialogues*, he correctly noted, are also to be found in Charles W. Hendel, Jr., *Hume Selections* (New York: Charles Scribner's Sons, 1927).

[5] H. H. Price, *Hume's Theory of the External World* (Oxford: Clarendon Press, 1940); Charles W. Hendel, Jr., *Studies in the Philosophy of David Hume* (Princeton: Princeton University Press, 1925). The Green and Grose edition of Hume that Quine used is identified in n. 33 below.

3. Cause.
4. External objects
5. Pride and love
6. The artificial virtues.

Final. August, 1946.

Quine's handwriting is on the whole legible. There are places however where the penciling is too faint to make out. In some of these instances, I have been able to reconstruct what Quine wrote with a degree of confidence; in others—amounting to no more than about a dozen words—I have failed. Yet I believe that in no case of failure is the substance of the lectures appreciably diminished. Rather, so far as one can tell, the unreadable material is exclusively parenthetical, consisting, it appears, of one or another kind of self direction, such as a reminder to cover a point in fact covered in the text, or a reminder to cover something in fact presented subsequently in the lectures.

The primary portion of the manuscript includes, in addition to the text proper, preparatory and supplementary notes pertinent to Quine's study of Hume and to his presentation of that material to his students.

One card at the beginning of this portion bears the title: "W. V. Quine's 1946 Lectures on David Hume's Philosophy." The succeeding card lists the days and times of class meetings and the principal readings for the lectures as identified above, though with some more bibliographical specificity that will be reflected in editorial notes and interpolated quotations below. Twenty-three cards are densely covered with tables correlating pages of Hume's *Treatise* and references to that work in R. W. Church's *Hume's Theory of the Understanding* (1935), J. Laird's *Hume's Philosophy of Human Nature* (1932), and N. Kemp Smith's *Philosophy of David Hume* (1941), books to which Quine referred in the course of the term. Page references from the "*Treatise* to Church, Laird, Smith" cover three of these cards; page references in "Church to *Treatise*" cover three more. The tables detailing page references in "Laird to *Treatise*" take up ten cards; and seven cards are devoted to references in "Smith to *Treatise*."

The contents of the remaining unnumbered cards in this portion are:
1) A note on what Quine wished to focus should he repeat the course, quoted in full above (172).
2) "Order of battle, 5th – 9th weeks.
    Fifth week: Physical objects; identity.
                   Minds.
                   Mop up Book 1.
    Sixth week: First lecture: last two sections of *Enquiry*."
Nothing further is entered here; Quine left this projected plan

uncompleted.

3) After mentioning Selby-Bigge's editions of Hume's *Treatise* and "*Inquiry*," Quine wrote that he intended to "End up course with lectures explaining Kant's attempted answer to Hume and its shortcomings."

The remaining three cards contain abbreviated citations of or allusions to philosophical works pertinent to his interest in Hume that Quine consulted himself or recommended to students. The first three of these works are not mentioned expressly in the lectures. Identified and completed, these citations are:

4) J. N. Findlay, "Morality by Convention," *Mind* 54 (1944): 142-69.

5) "Hume, Causality: See" G. H. von Wright, *The Logical Problem of Induction* (Helsinki: Edidit Societas Philosophica, distribuit Akateeminen Kirjakauppa, 1941).
C. D. Broad, "Hr. von Wright on the Logic of Induction (II)," *Mind* 53 (1944): 97-119.

6) "Constitution system: Locke: vol. I, p. 279; vol. II, p. 28." That is, Locke, *Essay* 2.12.1, and 3.4.16, on the names of simple ideas and the constitution of complex by simple ideas.[6]

Editorial principles

This edition of Quine's lectures on Hume attempts to keep editorial intrusion to a minimum. In addition to the real merits of this principle in general, I have judged it particularly suitable in this case inasmuch as the potential readership of this text falls into at least three overlapping yet certainly distinct classes: students of Quine's thought; students of Hume; and philosophers and scholars focused mainly on the issues addressed here by both writers. The respective interests and backgrounds of members of these classes may very well differ from one another in ways that are likely to mitigate against the ready usefulness of any elaborately introduced and robustly annotated text.

The following constitutes the entirety of the lecture notes written by Quine the course he taught on Hume's philosophy in the summer of 1946 with some few exceptions and qualifications. Occasionally Quine evidently forgot that he had covered a point in a previous lecture and so repeated that point on a later date (e.g., on 190, below). Such repetitions and indications of them have been omitted. Neither can I see any useful purpose in including the twenty-three cards of cross references of pages in Hume's *Treatise* with pages in Church's, Laird's and Kemp Smith's works on Hume. All other unnumbered supplementary cards have been omitted from the text proper, though the complete contents of each of them have

---

[6] The edition of Locke that Quine used is identified below, n. 11.

been included or at least described in the introduction or footnotes to the text with sufficient indication of the source. Finally, the lectures in places contain notes set off by asterisks, some of which are clearly reminders to Quine himself to cover or to repeat either some substantive point, take attendance, or announce some course-specific information such as student paper submission dates, or indications that he had done so. With some obvious exceptions, signaled by parenthetical asides integrated within the text absenting Quine's asterisks, these sorts of Quine's notes have been omitted, as have all crossings out.

This edition makes no attempt to disguise or otherwise mitigate the character of the following text as lectures, but I have decided some changes from the handwritten notes to be advantageous for publication. While Quine's handwriting is for the most part clear, its legibility does vary through the course of the manuscript, in places becoming rather difficult to make out. Doubtless, despite all efforts, some deciphering will prove erroneous. Again, though I have as a rule worked to keep editorial intrusion and overt textual interpretation at a minimum, a number of types of intervention seemed desirable in the interest of clarity and readability.

All editorial interpolations—additions and some sorts of corrections—in the text and in the footnotes are included within angle brackets.

Original spelling has been retained, with a very few exceptions. Straightforward spelling errors, few as they are, have been silently corrected. Other spelling irregularities have been decided in favor of Quine's clear preference in his published work, where I have identified these.

I have not made sentence fragments and other irregular sentences conform to accepted grammatical standards in those cases where I judged their meaning sufficiently clear or where the lack of clarity is intrinsically interesting. Common, informal verbal contractions such as 'isn't,' 'can't,' and 'doesn't' have been left to stand as originally written.

Quine used or mentioned a few foreign words; these words are italicized. The meaning of Quine's very occasional colloquial German abbreviations has been silently rendered in English.

Unconventional contractions, verbal, numerical and other symbolic abbreviations have been expanded into English. Verbal abbreviations are very numerous and not altogether consistent or systematic, and so are subject to interpretation. Among very many others appear 'hp' for which I have rendered 'hypothesis;' I have interpreted 'H' as 'Hume;' 'a/c' as 'account;' 'dipl' to be 'diplomatic;' 'thy' as 'theory;' 'phps' as 'perhaps;' 'difft' to be 'different;' 'q'n' as 'question;' 'thot' as 'thought;' 'psg' to mean 'passage;' 'vble' as 'variable;' 'prpns' as 'perceptions;' 'exx' to mean 'examples;' 'cspdg' as 'corresponding;' 'expce' as 'experience.'

Symbolic abbreviations and the shorthand use of symbols pose other interpretative challenges. Some symbolic expressions are strictly formal and have thus been rendered here as written. Other uses of mathematical and logical symbols pretty clearly constitute a species of shorthand Quine used, not intended to be interpreted strictly, and so not reproduced here. Numerals in English sentences, as for instance, in 'more than 1 kind,' have been rendered here in English; in this case, as 'more than one kind.'

The equals sign ('=') has sometimes been interpreted as 'equals'; in other places as 'as,' or 'that is,' depending upon the immediate context of its occurrence and readability while retaining Quine's meaning. In other cases, such as its parenthetical appearance clearly indicating synonymity of the word following the sign with the word immediately antecedent to the parenthesis, the sign has simply been deleted, as the parenthetical construction clearly enough implies some degree of synonymity or equivalence of terms.

The plus sign ('+') following page numbers in a text quoted or referred to has been rendered as 'f.' or 'ff.' where it has indicated pages of a text referred to or quoted in the manuscript. In a few instances the plus sign is used to signify something of the order of 'and successors,' as in 'Kant + +'; such uses have been expanded in just this way.

Though each new paragraph is Quine's own, I have not retained all of his paragraph breaks, for a great many of them were clearly created as visual aids merely. In some parts of the manuscript, each sentence is indented as if it were a distinct paragraph. To reproduce this feature would work against the intelligibility and readability of the text.

Quotations from and references to identifiable sources (Quine often provided incomplete but sufficient indication of their source) have been identified, where necessary, but have in no case been altered from the manuscript version in the body of this text, even if inaccurate. Notes have been added with the correct citation in those cases where Quine's information is clearly erroneous, and with full bibliographical information in all cases possible.

Some quotations from Hume and from Locke are not written out in the manuscript but are clearly indicated there as having been read during the lectures. Quine tended to adopt such shortcuts more frequently as the term went on. These quotations have been added on the evidence provided by Quine's annotated copy of the *Treatise* and from a copy of the edition of Locke that it is clear Quine used. These additions are included as per the above editorial stipulation within angle brackets. It has rarely been possible to be certain as to precisely how much of a passage Quine quoted or intended to read in such cases; these sorts of notes to himself read something like: 'Read p. 608, foot,' indicating that the passage to be read lay on what I estimate to be the final quarter of the identified page. Yet it is clear enough from those (usually early in the course) passages that he did trouble to write out in his notes that while the cited page number and, e.g., 'foot' correctly identifies the location of the beginning of the passage quoted, he often continued his quotation well within the succeeding page. Thus in an attempt to achieve completeness without pretense to utter fidelity to an event that cannot now be recaptured, I have perhaps quoted rather more of the cited source than Quine actually read in 1946.

Again on the basis of the principle of keeping editorial intrusion to a minimum, I have supplied notes merely with bibliographic and other immediately pertinent information to texts Quine mentioned in his lectures. If Quine referred to or quoted a text, the exact location of the passage and the edition from which it is quoted is provided if possible or practicable. If Quine failed to identify a textual source for a position to which he alludes, I have attempted to supply this; in some cases I have failed. There is quite a number of names—some more familiar to some readers than others—mentioned in the text for which I have supplied some little information. To do any more would make this text unwieldy and inconsistent with what I take the spirit of the lectures to have been. Such omissions will in many cases be readily enough rectified by readers with some acquaintance with early modern and with classic analytic philosophy in any event.

All book titles have been regularized in italic form. Quine usually accurately underlined them in his manuscript, but in some cases, such as the titles of Plato's and Aristotle's works, failed to do so. Minor punctuation irregularities in citations of texts, especially of Locke's *Essay* and Hume's *Treatise*, have been silently rendered consistent.

Quine's forms of citation of Locke's *Essay* and Hume's *Treatise* have been changed from the older conventions of, e.g., 'Bk. II, Ch. VII, §3,' and 'Bk. I, Pt. II, §2,' respectively, to the less cumbersome Arabic numeral system now common, reading '2.7.3,' and '1.2.2.'

All manuscript underlining for emphasis and titles has been represented with the use of italics. In cases where Quine carefully indicated his (rather than his subject text's) emphasis within a quotation by using a series of subscripted points rather than lines, the emphasis has been signaled by underlining within the quoted text (e.g., below, 191).

Quine included some asterisked footnotes in his manuscript. These are here numbered in the same sequence as editorial footnotes, but Quine's own notes are not contained within angle brackets.

Now and again Quine wrote what to the reader can seem enigmatic directions to himself to explain or illustrate a point or thesis, presumably extemporaneously, since no part of this manuscript contains such expository material. These directions are included within the body of the text where they originally appear. For the majority of these, I have attempted no reconstruction of such illustrations or explanations, even where the tack Quine is likely to have taken seems clear to me.

Acknowledgments

The publication of these lectures is made possible by the generosity and assistance of Douglas Boynton Quine and the estate of W. V. Quine. I am grateful to Dr. Quine not only for the opportunity to publish this manuscript, but for his further aid in deciphering W. V. Quine's handwriting and otherwise interpreting the text. I am very grateful also to Roger F. Gibson, Jr. who, after arranging communication with Dr. Quine, helped in discussing many points of the deciphering and interpretation of the text. His extensive understanding of Quine's work has been invaluable in the preparation of this edition. I am as well indebted to Ernest Lepore for his timely aid and encouragement. Finally, my grateful thanks go to Patricia Alexander Buickerood as always for her technical and other sorts of assistance with this project. While the admission may be customary and formulaic, it is notwithstanding worth saying that the responsibility for errors is solely my own.

W. V. Quine's 1946 Lectures on David Hume's Philosophy

David Hume was a Scotchman. Born Edinburgh 1711; died 1776. The house of Hume, also spelled Home, belonged to the Scotch nobility. Moderate means. David Hume studied at Edinburgh and then returned to the family country-seat in Berwickshire to study and meditate. At the age of twenty three he worked for a few months in a business office in Bristol; then gave it up and settled down in France to write his *Treatise*, which came out in 1739 (when Hume was twenty eight). By this time he had returned to his father's house and was continuing his philosophical writings; *Essays* came out in 1741. By this time he had begun to aspire to a chair at Edinburgh, but was disappointed. In 1746 and again 1748 he traveled in Europe as a diplomatic secretary. This was period also of *Enquiry concerning Human Understanding*. Then returned to Scotland and continued his writing. Besides *Inquiry concerning Principles of Morals* and *Dialogues concerning Natural Religion*, his writing now took a political turn: *Political Discourses* (1751). And from 1753 on, *History of England*, finished 1761. But philosophy wasn't neglected; *Natural History of Religion*, "Of the Passions," "Of Tragedy," "Of the Standard of Taste" (1757). 1763-1769, posts in Paris and London as diplomatic secretary again. Then retired to Edinburgh on his pension and royalties.

So Hume's career as thinker and writer occupies three fields: philosophy, political economy, history. Hume was of some importance as an historian. His history was a considerable success. And even those who criticize it as tendentious are ready to admit that it was distinguished for its time and an important milestone in historiography. But Hume's greatness is in philosophy. And, within philosophy, his greatness is in theory of knowledge. Hume's philosophical writings treat of ethics and religion as well as theory of knowledge, but the theory of knowledge is the keystone of the structure.

Historically the theory of knowledge begins as a quest for certainty. Mathematics is the shining example of a science in which we can be certain of our conclusions. If this virtue were shared by the other sciences, notably physics and the rest of the natural sciences, there would have been little speculation over the theory of knowledge. Philosophers worry about theory of knowledge because the human understanding is in *trouble*; and its trouble is the uncertainty of knowledge about the world. Investigators in physics and other empirical sciences are aware that they are engaged in framing hypotheses which can never be fully proved, can never achieve anything beyond a respectable degree of probability short of certainty. Physics traffics in opinions.

There is a degree of uniformity in the *opinions* of all concerned, in the matter of physics, which may well be envied by the philosophers who, each in his peculiar way, are out for certainty. It happens that we can often be more *certain* that something is highly *probable* than that something is certain. But this circumstance does not do away with the philosophical urge to find a bed-rock of certainty somewhere beneath the probabilities of natural science. And the motives for this quest are two-fold.

(1) Uncertainty is an *unsatisfactory* end-point. So if we can't aspire to certainty in natural science itself, we want to penetrate back to underlying principles of natural science, broader and more fundamental, for which certainty *can* be claimed.

(2) Further, it is argued that if there are not some such underlying certain principles, the so-called merely probable laws of science cease even to be probable; for, we can't say for *certain* that they are probable; they become merely probably probable; and it is not certain that they are probably probable, so they are merely probably probably probable; until finally every probability is modified by an infinite series of probabilities, which amounts to not being probable at all.

Briefly: there can be no probability without some certainty on which to base the probabilities.

I should say that I can't quite subscribe to this reasoning, for it overlooks the possibility of what in mathematics is called a convergent product. Thus, suppose the probability of a particular law of physics is 3/4. I.e., there are three chances out of four that the law is true. (We never know probabilities of laws numerically this way, but let's go on for the sake of argument.) Now suppose our law is only probably probable, but that this second-order probability is 15/16. (I.e., there are fifteen chances out of sixteen that the probability of the law was 3/4.) And suppose, it is only probably probably probable, but that the third-order probability is 35/36. And that the fourth is 63/64; and the fifth is 99/100; and, in general,

$$\text{the nth is } \frac{4n^2-1}{4n^2}.$$

Then the net probability is not vitiated by all these qualifications to complete indifference or toss-up (1/2), as might be expected. It reduces rather to

$$\lim_{n \to \infty} \pi \frac{4n^2-1}{4n^2} = \frac{2}{\pi} = \text{about } \frac{7}{11},$$

which isn't much worse than the original 3/4.

But there isn't much comfort in this alternative, for it would be pretty hard to persuade ourselves that it held. Especially that it *certainly* held. So there remains sufficient motive for seeking certainty in the underpinnings of natural science: not merely in order to have something better than the probability of natural science, but in order even to make science safe for probability itself.

This quest for certainty goes back to Plato, and nobody knows how far beyond. The probability problem that we have just now been considering cannot, of course, be read into Plato. Nevertheless he regarded the science of nature as of an *inferior grade of knowledge*, and he was in search of basic principles, to which certainty might attach, *behind* the science of nature. Mathematics, then as now, was the prototype of certainty. Proofs in geometry and theory of number were accomplished by analyzing the concepts and finding basic relationships which, clearly and obviously and with full certainty, held among them. There were the *axioms*, self-evident truths—evident as soon as one clearly understands the concepts involved. And the other truths of geometry or theory of number followed from such axioms by successions of obvious steps of necessary inference. If we could only get a comparably clear understanding of other concepts, outside mathematics, we might hope for equally indubitable knowledge regarding them; mathematics merely happened to be that part of the job that was already pretty well in hand.

This analysis of concepts was *dialectic*, conducted typically through the Socratic procedure of cross-questioning. Viewed by Plato primarily as an analysis of *forms*; hence the word *Idea*, which originally meant *form* or *shape*, reminding us that geometry was the prototype of necessary reasoning. Plato was under no illusion that dialectic offered a royal road to factual knowledge about the world. Dialectic was an extension of mathematical certainty beyond the bounds of mathematics, but it was no substitute for the observation and guesswork of natural science. Physics remained a lower-grade accomplishment, incapable of being elevated to the level of genuine knowledge. But the ultimate realities *underlying* physical phenomena (*viz.* the *ideas*, for Plato) could be known with all the certainty of mathematics itself. Philosophy was a generalization of mathematics.

Hopefulness over the prospects of gaining fundamental certainties about reality had its ups and downs. Before Plato there were the Sophists, and after Aristotle there were the Skeptics; both groups represented a low in hopefulness, and both groups pointed to the inconsistencies of philosophers—inconsistencies between philosophies and inconsistencies within philosophies—to justify their defeatism. But hope springs eternal. Or *perennial* would be more accurate; it keeps coming back. Aristotle shared with Plato the hopeful view that the basic truths of objective reality could be known with certainty, through an intellectual apprehension of essences. And this was the tradition that dominated the Middle Ages. I'm not prepared to formulate this as a sharp issue; I think of it as a matter of degree: a very great deal about God and reality and the general nature of things was believed to be accessible to the human mind, with complete certainty, through the simple expedient of taking thought.

And thus we come down to the seventeenth century and Descartes, who, like the Sophists and the Skeptics of antiquity, was moved to attack the methodological complacency of the metaphysicians. Like the Sophists and Skeptics, Descartes was disturbed by the fact that the sweeping certainties of the metaphysicians were neither as convincing, taken separately, nor as compatible, taken together, as might reasonably be required. But Descartes was a mild man, and a man with a will to believe. He did not emulate the Sophists and Skeptics by abandoning himself and metaphysics to a nihilism of doubt and defeatism. His purpose was quite the opposite: to buttress metaphysics by performing a more conscientious and painstaking dialectic than ever had been known before. He hoped in this way to arrive at certainty in so genuine a sense that there could no longer be disagreements and inconsistencies in metaphysics, nor any future justification for the counsels of skepticism and despair. It is one of the great ironies of the history of thought[7] that this new focusing of attention on method, for which Descartes's motive was the strengthening of metaphysical certainty, should have brought on—step by step through Locke and Berkeley to Hume—a golden age of metaphysical skepticism.

What I have said of Plato, that his ideal of certainty in philosophy was inspired by mathematics, is yet more clearly true of Descartes. Descartes was a great mathematician, and the founder of analytical geometry. He was familiar with the way in which the most abstruse and surprising mathematical relationships can be broken down into a series of short steps each of which is self-evident on the basis of a mere understanding of the concepts concerned. In short, as Descartes says, *certain* knowledge resolves into *intuition* and *deduction*. Intuition, or contemplation of the basic concepts of a mathematical theorem, gives us knowledge of the self-evident truths or *axioms* which are needed; and then deduction leads us from these axioms to the theorem itself, step by step. Such is the nature, Descartes says, of *all* certain knowledge; but his inspiration is mathematics. So Descartes's method for reconstituting philosophy on a solid basis was to make a clean sweep of everything by provisional doubt, and then begin anew with self-evident axioms gained by intuition. "The things which we conceive very clearly and distinctly," he said, "are all true." And this virtue attached, he found, to his first axiom: "I think, therefore I am." "I see very clearly," he wrote, "that to think it is

---

[7] Others: Berkeley's anti-hyloism for spiritual supremacy; Malebranche, Cordemoy, etc. against causality for glory of God. ⟨See, e.g., George Berkeley (1685-1753), *A Treatise concerning the Principles of Human Knowledge* (1710); Nicolas Malebranche (1638-1715), *Recherche de la vérité* (1674); and Géraud de Cordemoy (1626-1684), *Le Discernement de l'âme et du corps* (1666).⟩

184 W. V. Quine

necessary to be."[8] So here was a first axiom, furnished by intuition.

Descartes's next principle was the existence of God. Evidently he regarded this as a case of deduction rather than intuition, since he offered a *proof*—the so-called ontological proof; yet there is no attempt to indicate axioms from which the deduction proceeded, much less any rules of deduction. The so-called proof, however, was this: *I find* (perhaps by introspection; maybe this is an axiom furnished by intuition) *that I have an idea of a perfect being. But non-existence is an imperfection* (perhaps intuition again: apprehension of part of the essence of the concept of perfection: or, as we should now say, grasping part of the meaning of a term). *Therefore the perfect being of which I have an idea exists.* This proof is not original; goes back to Anselm.

Both of these arguments are bad, as you all know. The "cogito ergo sum" depends on a prejudicial phrasing, "I think," subject and predicate, imputing an attribute (thinking) to a substance, a mind. He assumed his "I am" in his "I think;" circular. Couldn't get it from mere assumption that thinking was going on. When he wrote "I see very clearly that to think it is necessary to be," he was quite right. To do anything it is necessary to be. In fact, even not to do anything it is necessary to be. Everything *is*. Necessarily, everything *is*. *I*, if such there be, *am*—*cogito* or *non cogito*. If Descartes felt that it was immediately obvious to intuition that *I think*—imputing thinking to an object which is I—he might as well have felt it immediately obvious to intuition that *I am*—*without* any deduction, without any dependence on I think. If on the other hand he felt the thinking was more obvious than the being, all he was justified in accepting at the start was "Thinking is taking place." From this he might fairly plausibly argue "Thought *is*," but not "*I am*."

The fault with the ontological argument is a misconception of existence. Non-existence isn't an imperfection, in the sense that non-existent beings are not perfect. Rather, there *are* no non-existent beings, perfect or otherwise. Everything exists, and so on one point Descartes is trivially right: any perfect being exists. Perhaps the real trouble is in the prejudicial phrase "I have an idea of a perfect being," i.e., "There is a perfect being of which I have an idea." Of course the latter implies existence, by assuming it; same would hold of a unicorn, *if* there were a unicorn of which I have an idea. But when I truly say "I have an idea of a unicorn," I say it not in that sense but in the sense "I have a unicornuine idea," and from this there follows no unicorn. The same holds for God. And the fact that perfection implies existence is no help—in the sense that every perfect

[8] ⟨René Descartes, *Descartes: Selections*, ed. Ralph M. Eaton (New York: Charles Scribner's Sons, 1927), 30.⟩

being exists; indeed unicornuinity implies existence in exactly the same way.

It may very well be that, as Descartes says, "The things which we conceive very clearly and distinctly are true." But, as he himself added, "there is some difficulty in ascertaining which are those that we distinctly conceive." And in particular he overestimated the distinctness with which he conceived his "cogito ergo sum" and his ontological proof of God.

Descartes went on thus, using his method of affirming that which by his fallible standards was clear and distinct, until he had spun out a whole system of philosophy scarcely more rigorous and restrained than the mistrusted systems of his predecessors. God, once misproved to exist, served as a bulwark to Descartes's method of continuing to infer truth from clarity and distinctness; for God, being perfect and therefore good, would not deceive us—at least not in so ruthless a way as to allow us clear and distinct conception of falsehoods.

This is pretty lame, and I think that from the point of view of Descartes's actual motivation it puts the cart before the horse. God being the cart, and clarity and distinctness the horse. Because it is evident from Descartes's *Discourse on Method* that the one principle of which he was basically convinced, prior to any theological inferences, was that clearness of ideas is a guarantee of truth. "The things which we conceive very clearly and distinctly are true." And this was doubtless a generalization of Descartes's experience with mathematics, and with the intuiting of mathematical axioms. I venture to say that Descartes became convinced of the validity of this precept inductively, through his mathematical experience, and afterward cast about for a reason *why* the things we conceive clearly should be true. Why should the self-evidence of mathematical axioms be a guarantee of their *truth*, rather than merely a compulsion to belief—possibly mistaken belief—on our part? And similarly for any other self-evident truth? And the explanation which Descartes concocted, after the fact, was that God is too good to make falsehoods appear to us as self-evident truths. Descartes's theory was that we have innate ideas, implanted by God, and that we have only to reflect clearly upon them in order to see them in their true relations. (As we do, e.g., in reducing a theorem of geometry to its first beginnings.) And God wouldn't have implanted these ideas in us otherwise than as they should be.

Leibniz, writing at the end of the same century (seventeenth), made a more devious and refined use of God in connection with certainties about the world. Since God is good, he must have made the world as good as it logically can be. If anything were better it would have to be at the expense of something else's being worse, through *necessary* incompatibilities. And by the apprehension of clear and distinct ideas it is theoretically possible to determine such relationships of *necessary* incompatibility. It is likewise theoretically possible to determine in this way what is good, what is better than what else. So that, if the human mind were up to such complex reasoning, it could determine—purely by taking thought, and without recourse to observation and experiment—all the facts about the world. Reminiscent of Plato's Idea of the Good, as the idea whose apprehension is the all-inclusive form of knowledge. Knowing what is good, what is best all things considered, is for Leibniz knowing what is the case.[9] Actually infinitely complex, therefore impossible for us; so we fall back on methods of probability as a second best.

Here we have a clearer awareness, than in Descartes, of the difference between truths of fact and truths of reason; not as a difference in reality (all is in a sense necessary, since the optimity of the world follows necessarily from the necessary goodness of God), but as a difference in method of knowing. *Ratio cognoscendi vs. Ratio essendi*. But Leibniz followed Descartes in his trust in the contemplation of clear and distinct ideas, innately implanted in us as a means of our penetrating far into reality by the pure light of reason. If he was more rigorous than Descartes, the difference is one of detail.

Descartes's focusing of attention on the methodology of knowing did not restrain him, nor various of his successors such as Leibniz, from flights of undisciplined metaphysical fancy. Yet it did have an important restraining effect elsewhere in later philosophy. As Eaton says, "It sets the fashion for philosophizing outward from the inner world of self-consciousness."[10] This is Descartes's step toward Locke and Hume.

John Locke, toward the end of the same century (seventeenth), faced the methodological issue with complete directness by turning his attention squarely to the human understanding itself, its mode of operating, and its potentialities. The purpose of Locke's great work, *Essay concerning Human Understanding* (1689), was "to inquire into the original, certainty, and extent of human knowledge, together with the grounds and degrees of belief, opinion, and assent." Book 1 of this essay is devoted to arguing that there are no innate ideas.[11] Ideas implanted by God, and to be trusted for their veracity because of the goodness of God, had been[12] a crutch for Descartes. This notion of innate ideas was indeed much older than

---

[9] ⟨See, e.g., G. W. Leibniz (1646-1716), "Discourse on Metaphysics" (1686), and *Monadology* (1714).⟩

[10] ⟨Eaton, "Introduction," in *Descartes*, xxx.⟩

[11] ⟨John Locke, *The Works of John Locke*, ed. J. A. St. John (London: Henry G. Bohn, 1843). This edition was reissued in two vols.in 1854, 1872, 1882 and 1892. Quine clearly used one of the two-volume issues, but which one is unknown. The pagination of each issue from 1854 through 1892, remained identical, so this passage (*Essay* 1.1.2) is to be found at 1: 128.⟩

[12] ⟨A⟩s we have seen ⟨above, 185.⟩

Descartes, and a part of the long tradition. It appeared in Plato in an extravagant form as the doctrine of *reminiscence*, which appears for example in the *Meno* and *Phaedo*: the doctrine that so-called learning is only a matter of bringing out into the open what we have latently known all along. This is the *radical* doctrine of innate ideas: *all* ideas are innate, and all education is *literally* education: *educing* what is already present within us. The doctrine of reminiscence must have seemed particularly apt as applied to mathematics: all manner of surprising things about circles and triangles could be brought out of an ignorant, untrained mind by the right sort of step-by-step questioning. You can extract the most abstruse theorem from an untrained mind by going back to self-evident fundamentals and asking leading questions, step by step, until the proof is complete.

This appeal of the example of mathematical method, which must have tempted Plato into his doctrine of reminiscence, surely operated equally to encourage Descartes in his belief in innate ideas. But Locke made a clean sweep of the whole theory of innate ideas. I believe more good than harm has come to subsequent philosophy from Locke's ignorance of mathematics; the hypnotic effect of contemplating the miracle of mathematical certainty was a danger to which Locke was immune. Locke viewed the mechanism of learning and understanding with a candid eye and saw that knowledge comes from outside, from experience; and that there was no natural place for innate ideas in the mental economy. And though Locke's throwing over the tradition of innate ideas was no doubt psychologically dependent on his not having the mathematical bent of Plato, Descartes, or his own contemporary Leibniz, the result was beneficial even for purposes of an eventual clearer understanding of the nature of mathematical knowledge itself.

Locke's repudiation of innate ideas was the beginning of *empiricism*: the doctrine that knowledge stems from experience. If there are no innate ideas, and innate knowledge of truths concerning them, everything we know must come to us through our senses. The mind begins as a blank tablet, upon which sense experience writes. In sweeping away innate ideas, Locke swept away cherished certainties and prepared the way for skepticism. It is not obvious why innateness should be so bound up with certainty. Couldn't we have innate *wrong* ideas as well as acquiring wrong ideas—if there are to be innate ideas? Would it be much more heinous of God to deceive us in the one way than in the other? The reason Locke's repudiation of innate ideas prepared the way for skepticism is simply this: he brought the knowing process out into the open, where common sense could be brought to bear on it. If knowledge is to be traced to sensations, let's trace it. We know our sensations pretty well, can enumerate them more or less, and thus have a working basis for detailed analysis of knowledge. The mysteries of innate ideas afforded dark places where wishful thinking could flourish; and this Locke cleared away.

—*To here June 19*

Towards end of last meeting, suggested not evident why innateness of idea should be so bound up with certainty, and antithetical to skepticism. Different, indeed, later with Kant. In Kant, in the eighteenth century, innate ideas reappear in a form which *does* account for the certainty of innate knowledge regarding them. Kant's notion is that the structural limitations of the mind compel all experience to conform to certain structural norms in order that it be experience-able at all. But there was no comparable treatment of innate ideas by Locke's predecessors. But with Descartes and the others of Locke's predecessors, the connection of innate ideas with certainty seems to be essentially negative: merely that explicit examination of the knowing process was thwarted. But Locke, with his *tabula rasa*, laid the knowing process open to critical examination and thus prepared the way for skepticism. Yet Locke, like Descartes, was only a way-station in the movement toward skepticism. The end isn't reached until the next century, in Hume. It is characteristic of Locke to stop short of radical conclusions which his own observations bring within easy reach. There are several examples, as we shall see.

Locke's most central idea is the idea of *idea* itself. According to Locke our first ideas are direct sense-impressions. Further ideas are formed from these by combination—either through perceiving them in combination, or through combining them in the imagination. Locke showed a persistent tendency to mentalize, or subjectivize, the things which in the Aristotelian tradition had been spoken of as real essences. "The essences of the ... species of things are nothing else but these abstract ideas" (3.3.12). "All the great business of genera and species, and their essences, amounts to no more but this: That men making abstract ideas, and settling them in their minds with names annexed to them, do thereby enable themselves to consider things, and discourse of them as it were in bundles, for the easier and readier improvement and communication of their knowledge; which would advance but slowly were their words and thoughts confined only to particulars" (3.4.end.).[13]

An incidental consequence of Locke's attitude on essences was that in biology he saw no reason to believe in the immutability of animal and vegetable species, such as had been supposed from Aristotle onward (3.6.14ff.). This is a question of fact, not to be decided *a priori*; but the doctrine of the subjectivity of essence was calculated to make the mind more receptive to the fact of instability of biological species. Even given

---

[13] ⟨This citation is incorrect; it should be 3.3.20.⟩

the Aristotelian view that there was something more to species (biological and otherwise) than arbitrary or conventional grouping or degrees of resemblance, it would have been logically *possible* that heredity was not species-closed. But the thought was more tempting when species were pried loose, by Locke, from absolutism. So Locke paved the way for Darwin.

Locke's doctrine of subjectivity of essence, subversive of tradition though it was, is one example of Locke's stopping short of yet more radical conclusions which he has brought within easy reach. For, there are many passages which strongly suggest that instead of stopping with subjective *ideas*, he might just as well have thrown these over in turn and stopped with sheer *words*. We find "name" and "idea" running parallel in passage after passage, as if "name" might serve the purpose alone. "By the same way that they [people] come by the general name and idea of man, they easily advance to more general names and notions" (3.3.8). Again: "To be a man, or of the species man, and to have a right to the name man, is the same thing" (3.3.12). [In response to a question on "simplicity" or "epistemological priority," sketched my whole double-aspect theory of idealism and realism.[14]] Again: "Between the nominal essence and the name there is so near a connexion, that the name of any sort of thing cannot be attributed to any particular being but what has this essence, whereby it answers that abstract idea whereof the name is the sign" (3.3.16). Again: "The names of simple ideas, and those only, are incapable of being defined" (3.4.7). Here an awareness that other names *could* be defined—hence no need, we might suppose, of presupposing anything else (so-called ideas) to mirror them. Why not keep just the simple ideas (sense impressions), with their names; and then let *defined names* alone do the work of so-called complex ideas? Again: "Though therefore it be the mind that makes the collection, it is the name which is as it were the knot that ties them fast together. What a vast variety of different ideas does the word triumphus hold together, and deliver to us as one species! Had this name been never made, or quite lost, we might, no doubt, have had descriptions of what passed in that solemnity; but yet, I think, that which holds those different parts together, in the unity of one complex idea, is that very word annexed to it; without which the several parts of that would no more be thought to make one thing, than any other show, which having never been made but once, had never been united into one complex idea, under one denomination. How much, therefore, in mixed modes, the unity necessary to any essence depends on the mind, and how much the continuation and fixing of that unity depends on the

---

[14] ⟨Possibly Quine reviewed the sorts of considerations he later published in, e.g., "On What There Is," *Review of Metaphysics* 2 (1948): 21-38.⟩

name in common use annexed to it, I leave to be considered by those who look upon essences and species as real established things in nature" (3.5.10). And in summary: "The consideration then of ideas and words, as the great instruments of knowledge, makes no despicable part of their contemplation who would take a view of human knowledge in the whole extent of it: and perhaps, if they were distinctly weighed and duly considered, they would afford us another sort of logic and critic than what we have hitherto been acquainted with."[15] Yet Locke never took the step of throwing the complex ideas overboard and letting names do their work for them. This was left for Tooke.

Tooke's doctrine of abbreviations: a single word is introduced in place of a complex of words; and there is no need to suppose a corresponding single idea introduced as a complex of ideas. For Tooke there *is* no *combining* of ideas. There are the simple ideas (corresponding to sense perceptions), there are the names for them, and there are the abbreviations of complexes of such names.[16] Tooke writes: "I consider the *whole* of Mr. Locke's essay as a philosophical account of ... abbreviations in language" (p. 24).[17]

—June 21

Tooke suggests that if Locke had said "word" wherever he said "idea," the essay would have been clearer and more correct. "Perhaps it was for mankind a lucky mistake (for it was a mistake) which Mr. Locke made when he called his book, An Essay on Human *Understanding*. For some part of the inestimable benefit of that book has, merely on account of its title, reached to many thousands more than, I fear, it would have done, had he called it (what it is merely) a *Grammatical* Essay, or a Treatise on *Words*, or on *Language*. The human *mind*, or the human *understanding*,

---

[15] ⟨Locke, *Essay* 2.21.4.⟩

[16] ⟨Quine here inserted a card reading: "How many haven't had *any* history modern philosophy (Descartes and successors)? Read it (Weber, Windelband, Russell, Cushman, etc.), Descartes through Hume (including Leibniz, Locke, Berkeley) right away. Maybe it will illuminate your notes." The works referred to are: Alfred Weber, *A History of Philosophy*, trans. Frank Thilly (New York: Charles Scribner's Sons, 1896); Wilhelm Windelband, *A History of Philosophy; with Especial Reference to the Formation and Development of its Problems and Conceptions*, trans. James H. Tufts. 2nd edition (New York: Macmillan, 1901); Bertrand Russell, *A History of Western Philosophy* (New York: Simon and Schuster, 1945); and Herbert Cushman, *A Beginner's History of Philosophy*. 2 vols. (Boston: Houghton Mifflin, 1910-1911).⟩

[17] ⟨John Horne Tooke, Ἔπεα πτερόεντα; or, *The Diversions of Purley*. 2 vols. (Philadelphia: William Duane, 1806-1807), 1. This is the edition Quine appears to be using—very possibly the copy given him by B. F. Skinner. See Quine, *Time*, 110. Elsewhere (e.g. in *Theories and Things* [Cambridge, MA: Harvard University Press, 1981], 212), Quine quotes from what he identifies as a Boston, 1806 edition; I have located no such edition.⟩

appears to be a grand and noble theme; and all men, even the most insufficient, conceive that to be a proper object for their contemplation: whilst inquiries into the nature of *language* (through which alone they can obtain any knowledge beyond the beasts) are fallen into such extreme disrepute and contempt, that even those who 'neither have the accent of christian, pagan, or man,' nor can speak so many words together with as much propriety as Balaam's ass did, do yet imagine *words* to be infinitely beneath the concern of their exalted understanding" (24f.-n.).[18]

Tooke's repudiation of complex ideas should not be thought of as a theory that discourse calls for no mental activity; nor that adoption of complex definitions ("abbreviations") involves no thought. I think the point is rather that the bringing in of intermediary unexplained *units*, "ideas," is a poor way to clarify the process which connects stimulation with discourse. Obscures rather than explains; like the substantial forms of Toletus and the other mediævals, against which Descartes inveighed;[19] or like the *vertu dormitif* in Molière. Tooke has been followed (unknowingly?) by modern scientific linguists and by the behaviorists in psychology.

One more relevant passage from Locke: "This whole mystery of genera and species, which make such a noise in the schools, and are with justice so little regarded outside of them, is nothing else but abstract ideas, more or less comprehensive, with <u>names annexed</u> to them" (3.3.9). Might have been less noise still if these so-called abstract ideas, which make their share of noise in Locke's own discourses, were abandoned in turn in favor of the "names annexed to them." But this step remained for Tooke.

Vigorously though Locke objected to the doctrine of innate ideas, a remnant of that doctrine, or of the spirit underlying it, remained in his philosophy: Locke accepted unquestioningly the point of view that ideas come first and language after; and that language is a tool for expressing ideas which are already there to be expressed, and are there whether or not attaining expression. Hume, actually, is like Locke on this point; and so is Berkeley. Neither of them followed Tooke's course. Tooke was the pioneer in this particular form of nominalism; and Tooke wrote later—shortly after Hume's death.

But there were also other important places where Locke stopped short of more radical conclusions which he had brought within easy reach; and on these other points Berkeley or Hume did follow through. One notable case is Locke's theory of matter, and of primary and secondary qualities.

---

[18] ⟨I.e., 24-25, n. (m).⟩

[19] ⟨Franciscus Toletus (1532-1596), Spanish Jesuit, professor of philosophy at Collegio Romano. See, e.g., his *Commentaria una cum quaestionibus in VIII libros De physica auscultatione* (Venice, 1600.⟩

Actually Locke distinguishes three sorts of qualities in bodies:

> Primary qualities: "bulk, figure, number, situation, and motion or rest of their solid parts."

> Secondary qualities: "the power that is in any body, by reason of its insensible primary qualities, to operate after a peculiar manner on any of our senses, and thereby produce in us the different ideas of several colors, sounds, smells, tastes, etc."

> Powers ordinarily so-called: "the power that is in any body, by reason of the particular constitution of its primary qualities, to make such a change in the bulk, figure, texture, and motion of another body, as to make it operate on our senses differently from what it did before. Thus the sun has a power to make wax white, and fire to make lead fluid" (2.8.23).

Both second and third are powers, but second mistakenly not regarded so.

This point of view is close to that of Democritus and the other atomists. According to Democritus (420 B.C.), matter is made up of atoms which differ only in shape and size, not in substance. What we take to be differences in color, taste, etc. are just blurred ways of grasping differences in textures of atomic makeup. Though old as Democritus, this is also the point of view of modern physics (nineteenth century)—due in part surely to Locke himself. An ideal of physics: reduce everything to mass in motion. Explain all in terms of impact of billiard balls. Theory of chemical elements seemed to be a deviation from Democritus, for here were qualitative differences between atoms. But the ideal remained Democritan: absolute and irreducible difference between substances of atoms was felt unreasonable, and *explanatory* value would have inhered in a theory which made pseudo-atoms of these, composed of smaller *real* atoms in different combinations, so that qualitative differences again reduced to bulk, shape, motion.

Mendeléeff's periodic table hinted, in fact, that such an explanation might be possible.[20] In twentieth century, borne out conclusively. Differences of so-called atoms are differences of constitution from protons, electrons, etc. And we now know that elements can be transmuted: natural breakdowns from radium through uranium to lead; and artificially—even to creating a new element, Pl. We aren't back to Democritus, for there remains difference between a few kinds of sub- (or real) atoms (electrons, protons, neutrons, positrons). And current physics has departed in far more fundamental and bewildering ways: relativity of space and time; discontinuity;[21] indeterminacy; transmutability of energy

---

[20] ⟨Dimitri Mendeleev (1834-1907), Russian chemist, most prominent of a number of nearly cotemporaneous discoverers of periodic law.⟩

[21] Minimal quanta of energy.

and matter. But this is because we can't help it. We'd prefer the other kind of theory still, if it worked (and didn't have to be forced by excess complication). There is something fairly fundamental in our preference for explaining all properties in terms of what Locke calls primary; and it was to this preference that Locke gave voice. Yet all the qualities, primary and secondary, are conveyed to us by our senses. Why the distinction? Why the premium on qualities of the kind conveyable by the pressure component of the sense of touch? (As opposed to wet-dry, hot-cold, and non-touch.)

—To here June 23 ⟨i.e. June 24⟩

Locke says why he thinks the secondary qualities aren't in the objects: "Let us consider the red and white colors in porphyry: hinder light from striking on it, and its colors vanish…. Can any one think any real alterations are made in the porphyry by the presence or absence of light?" (2.8.19) "Pound an almond, and the clear white color will be altered into a dirty one, and the sweet taste into an oily one. What real alteration can the beating of the pestle make in any body, but an alteration of the texture of it?" (2.8.20) *Hume* cites further reasons, in describing this philosophy (1.4.4): "A man in a malady feels a disagreeable taste in meats, which before pleased him the most…. That seems bitter to one, which is sweet to another…. Colors reflected from the clouds change according to the distance of the clouds, and according to the angle they make with the eye and luminous body. Fire also communicates the sensation of pleasure at one distance, and that of pain at another."

The question isn't quite dispelled. Shape and size also change with our point of view. (Illustrate.) And motion. (Train.) We say the ellipse isn't in the penny, etc. O.K., say the changing color isn't in the porphyry, but some standard optimum-condition color *is* (analogous to optimum-condition circularity of penny). Point seems to be that we have *another* perhaps more *basic* sense which fixes those optimum-condition shapes: touch. Not so with color etc. A reason why this sense is felt to be basic was advanced by late L. J. Henderson[22]—fanciful but interesting: The sense which communicates the primary qualities is the most dependable sense, because the oldest: prenatal. In womb, the foetus senses no sound nor color etc.; nor even temperature, wet-dry; nor, ordinarily, pain; just resistance (kicking). And it is this particular part of the sense of touch that conveys the *primary* qualities. Locke's view that color and various other qualities were subjective, and not inherent in the objects, was not new with him. As remarked, it goes back to Democritus; and it occurs also in

---

[22] ⟨Lawrence J. Henderson (1878-1942), a physiologist and sociologist, and a founder and Senior Fellow of Harvard's Society of Fellows. See Quine, *Time*, 108-109.⟩

seventeenth century in Hobbes and Descartes. But the distinguishing out of primary qualities, and exempting them from this subjectivity, was vital for Locke for a special reason: it was only thus that he was able to preserve his belief in the existence of material substance at all.

Prior to Locke, the traditional belief in material substance throve. Substance was one thing, attribute another; and matter was a substance whose *existence* did not *depend* on the sensible qualities. Matter was a substance *having* the qualities, insofar as they were really objective qualities of matter, or *causing* them, insofar as they were subjective; and so long as this point of view persisted, a shift of one or another of the supposed qualities of matter from objective to subjective status in no way jeopardized belief in matter as such. But Locke changed this underlying situation by coming forward with a new, more skeptical doctrine of *substance*: "There is an ... idea which would be of general use for mankind to have, as it is of general talk, as if they had it; and that is the idea of substance, which we neither have nor can have by sensation or reflection.... We have no such clear idea at all, and therefore signify nothing by the word substance, but only an uncertain supposition of we know not what, i.e., of something whereof we have no particular distinct positive idea, which we take to be the substratum or support of those ideas we know" (1.4.18).

Then on material substance, in particular, or *body*: "The primary ideas which we have peculiar to body, as contradistinguished to spirit, are the cohesion of solid and consequently separable parts, and a power of communicating motion by impulse. These, I think, are the original ideas proper and peculiar to body" (2.23.17). Locke is hesitant over the point, but seems to see that there is no clear alternative to recognizing that the idea of substance is no more than the idea of the aggregate of constituent properties; the substance is nothing over and above, or rather *under and below*, its properties. This is the only view consistent with Locke's empiricism—his insistence that all ideas (in particular that of substance or body) are ideas of sense or compounds of these. Body—so far at least as we have any idea of it—cannot go beyond the sensible qualities. And this is why it is so vital to Locke, if body (matter) is to be admitted at all, that there be *primary* qualities—qualities inherent in the matter and not merely in us. For the idea of matter is merely the idea of *these* qualities; and if *these* disappear—if all qualities become secondary—matter itself vanishes and there is just sensation, which is not sensation *of* anything at all.

And this is exactly what happens in the philosophy of George Berkeley, Bishop of Cloyne. Berkeley, who was two generations after Locke and a generation older than Hume, took the radical next step which Locke had declined to take: he reasoned that *all* properties were secondary, in that they were all sensory and there was no justification for giving one sense priority over another; and accordingly, agreeing in effect with Locke that matter was no more than the sum of its primary qualities, he concluded that there was no matter at all. Thus Berkeley concluded (*Principles of Human Knowledge*, section 8) that the words *sensible thing* and *idea* are synonymous; there is nothing outside, over and above our ideas themselves—over sense perceptions and the compounds formed in the mind of the ideas yielded by sense perception. Hume goes along with Berkeley in this, and goes him one better: same for spirit.

These considerations reveal a second way in which Locke failed to draw the radical consequences of his reflections; failed to make a natural next step for which he had prepared the way.

The first instance was his failure to abandon complex ideas in favor of words; this he left for Tooke. The second instance was his failure to abandon substance; this step he left for Berkeley and Hume.

There is also a third important instance: *causality*. Locke writes: "In the notice that our senses take of the vicissitude of things, we cannot but observe that several particular, both qualities and substances, begin to exist; and that they receive this their existence from the due application and operation of some other being. From this observation we get our ideas of cause and effect. That which produces any simple or complex idea we denote by the general name, cause; and that which is produced, effect" (2.26.1).

Just what is this "producing" that we observe? All that sense impressions can convey is invariable concomitance or succession. [expand.] By Locke's own empiricist standards, there should be no additional idea of causality as "production." A case could be made out against it, in his own terms, as strong e.g. as Locke's own case against innate ideas, real essences, etc. Failure to repudiate causality, in the sense of necessary connection over and above observed concomitance, was a striking case of Locke's tendency to stop short of the more radical and distasteful conclusions. And Locke was stubborn on this one. In defense of causality he came out with arguments typical of the old metaphysical dialectic that Locke usually was so critical of. One of his arguments is far worse than typical; incredibly bad. "Whatever is produced without any cause, is produced by *nothing*; or in other words, has nothing for its cause. But nothing can never be a cause, no more than it can be something, or equal to two right angles." Quoted by Hume, with proper scorn, 1.3.3. Sheer play on words; reminiscent of Lewis Carroll;[23] hard to imagine Locke taking it seriously; a case, surely, of his frantically trying to evade the natural consequences of his point of view. It was left to Hume to face these consequences; they even passed Berkeley. But the consequent

---

[23] ⟨See below, 213-14.⟩

skeptical theory of causality, which denies all justification for any idea of causality beyond observed uniform concomitance devoid of any guarantee for the future, is the keynote of Hume's theory of knowledge (or non-knowledge).

—To here June 26

(*Treatise* 1.1.1) What Locke called ideas are called by Hume *perceptions*, and divided into *impressions* and *ideas*. Impressions are our actual sense experiences as they come; ideas include memories of these, also objects of the imagination, also all other ideas in the ordinary present day sense of the term (whatever that is). In Locke's time as well as Hume's, I suppose "idea" had as part of its connotation the characteristic of being copied or otherwise derived, somehow, from something more real or fundamental: physical objects, for Locke, the causes of simple ideas in sensation. I suppose Hume's change of terminology reflects his added skepticism regarding those physical objects. He prefers to think of the sense experiences themselves as the fundamental things, and leave the question of external objects open for further debate. Therefore no longer appropriate to call the content of sensation *idea*, insofar as idea connotes being derived or copied from something *more* fundamental. Therefore the word *impression* instead. "Impressions are compleat in themselves" (p. 458). Unlike Locke: *two-fold* form: exact copies one of other; different only in intensity.

For Locke, same idea—now in sense, now in memory and imagination. Locke speaks of essences, Hume of events or types of events? Distinction between impressions and ideas: vivacity. But Kemp-Smith pp. 210f[24] and 2 ½ ⟨"in sleep, in a fever, in madness, or in any very violent emotions of soul, our ideas may approach to our impressions: As on the other hand it sometimes happens, that our impressions are so faint and low, that we cannot distinguish them from our ideas" (*Treatise*, 2)⟩. Or can we defend Hume by saying that it *is* a matter of degree with marginal cases and no further arbiter? Therefore not a case of confusion (in sense of error) so much as indeterminacy, settled by systematization?

Besides into impressions and ideas, perceptions are cross-classified into Simple and Complex. (Following Locke.) 3

Impressions		
Ideas		
	Simple	Complex

---

[24] ⟨Norman Kemp Smith, *The Philosophy of David Hume: A Critical Study of its Origins and Central Doctrines* (London: Macmillan, 1941), 210ff.⟩

⟨"There is another division of our perceptions, which it will be convenient to observe, and which extends itself both to our impressions and ideas. This division is into SIMPLE and COMPLEX. Simple perceptions or impressions and ideas are such as admit of no distinction nor separation. The complex are the contrary to these, and may be distinguished into parts. Tho' a particular colour, taste, and smell are qualities all united together in this apple, 'tis easy to perceive they are not the same, but are at least distinguishable from each other" (*Treatise*, 2)⟩.

How to construe "admit of no distinction nor separation"? Turns out in discussion of extension that (in case of color) must be minimally extended. Elsewhere **8 1/2** scarlet seems simple. ⟨"To give a child an idea of scarlet or orange, of sweet or bitter, I present the objects, or in other words, convey to him these impressions" (*Treatise*, 5).⟩ And explicitly on p. 637: "Blue and green are different simple ideas."

Among the simples, one-to-one correspondence between impressions and ideas. **4**

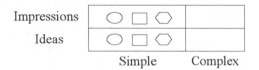

Simple   Complex

⟨"After the most accurate examination, of which I am capable, I venture to affirm, that the rule here holds without any exception, and that every simple idea has a simple impression, which resembles it; and every simple impression a correspondent idea" (*Treatise*, 3).⟩ But subject to exception later.

Not so with complex. **5**

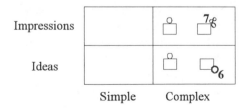

Simple   Complex

⟨"I must make use of the distinction of perceptions into *simple and complex*, to limit this general decision, *that all our ideas and impressions are resembling*. I observe, that many of our complex ideas never had impressions, that corresponded to them, and that many of our complex impressions never are exactly copied in ideas" (*Treatise*, 3).)[25]

Exceptions to correspondence between simples: **10** —serious; from Descartes, *Rules*[26]—**11**

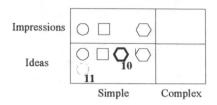

<("Suppose therefore a person to have enjoyed his sight for thirty years, and to have become perfectly well acquainted with colours of all kinds, excepting one particular shade of blue, for instance, which it never has been his fortune to meet with. Let all the different shades of that colour, except that single one, be plac'd before him, descending gradually from the deepest to the lightest; 'tis plain, that he will perceive a blank, where that shade is wanting, and will be sensible, that there is a greater distance in that place betwixt the contiguous colours, than in any other. Now I ask, whether 'tis possible for him, from his own imagination, to supply this deficiency, and raise up to himself the idea of that particular shade, tho' it had never been conveyed to him by his senses? I believe there are few but will be of opinion that he can; and this may serve as a proof, that the simple ideas are not always derived from the correspondent impressions; tho' the instance is so particular and singular, that 'tis scarce worth our observing, and does not merit that for it alone we should alter our general maxim" (*Treatise*, 6). 11: "But besides this exception, it may not be amiss to remark on this head, that the principle of the priority of impressions to ideas must be understood with another limitation, *viz.* that as our ideas are images of our impressions, so we can form secondary ideas, which are images of the primary; as appears from this very reasoning concerning them. This is not, properly speaking, an exception to the rule so much as an explanation of it. Ideas produce the images of themselves in new ideas; but as the first ideas are supposed to be derived from impressions, it still remains true, that all our simple ideas proceed either mediately or

---

[25] (The bold numerals **6** and **7** in this illustration signify the following passages in *Treatise*, 3, as indicated in Quine's annotated copy. **6**: "I can imagine to myself such a city as the *New Jerusalem*, whose pavement is gold and walls are rubies, tho' I never saw any such." **7**: "I have seen *Paris*; but shall I affirm I can form such an idea of that city, as will perfectly represent all its streets and houses in their real and just proportions?")

[26] (Descartes, *Rules for the Direction of the Mind*, rule 14.)

immediately from their correspondent impressions" (*Treatise*, 6f.).⟩

[A student observes in re **10**: since the interpolated simple idea isn't faint as compared with any corresponding impression, it should *be* an impression!]

—To here June 28

Impressions cause the ideas. **8** ⟨"*That all our simple ideas in their first appearance are deriv'd from simple impressions, which are correspondent to them, and which they exactly represent*" (*Treatise*, 4).⟩ Like Locke: "all ideas come from the senses" (but different in terminology "impression"). As Hume himself says, equivalent to denying the existence of innate ideas. **12** ⟨"the present question concerning the precedency of our impressions or ideas, is the same with what has made so much noise in other terms, when it has been disputed whether there be any *innate ideas*, or whether all ideas be derived from sensation and reflexion" (*Treatise*, 7).⟩ Like Locke even to the pineapple: **9** ⟨"We cannot form to ourselves a just idea of the taste of a pine-apple, without having actually tasted it" (*Treatise*, 5).⟩ But unlike Locke: cause of impressions unknown. (Except insofar as impression of "reflection" rather than of "sensation" which is the next distinction.)

(*Treatise* 1.1.2) Causation of ideas and of impressions of reflexion.[27]

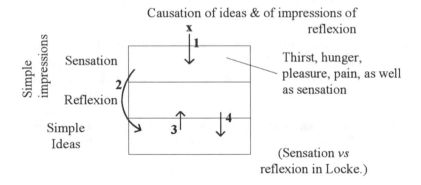

Causation of ideas & of impressions of reflexion

x

1

Simple impressions

Sensation

2

Reflexion

Thirst, hunger, pleasure, pain, as well as sensation

Simple Ideas

3

4

(Sensation *vs* reflexion in Locke.)

[27] ⟨The bold numerals **1** through **4** in this illustration signify the following assertions in *Treatise*, 7f., as numbered in Quine's copy of the book: **1**: "An impression first strikes upon the senses, and makes us perceive heat or cold, thirst or hunger, pleasure or pain of some kind or other." **2**: "Of this impression there is a copy taken by the mind, which remains after the impression ceases; and this we call an idea." **3**: "This idea of pleasure or pain, when it returns upon the soul, produces new impressions of desire and aversion, hope and fear, which may properly be called impressions of reflexion, because derived from it." **4**: "These again are copied by the memory and imagination, and become ideas."⟩

Church (*Hume's Theory of the Understanding*, 21): "Since impressions of reflection are subsequent in time to those of sensation, and therefore 'secondary' and derivative, why should they not be called ideas?" For, Hume seems to have limited "idea" previously to the derivative or copy. The answer, as Church says, is in Hume, p. 458: Because impressions of reflection are "original facts and realities, complete in themselves, and implying no reference to other passions, volitions, and actions."[28] In what sense "original facts and realities, complete in themselves"? Irreducible characteristic? Perhaps a qualitative difference: The compelling quality of emotions, so different from memory and imagination, so forceful and involuntary, like sensations. Really perhaps: an internal sensation (James-Lange: "hope" – "fear").[29] But also they are not representative (supports Smith's point, read ⟨above⟩ that vivacity isn't really it[30])—whereas ideas (insofar as *simple*!) *are*. (Except when got by interpolation.)

(*Treatise* 1.1.3) New division of ideas into Memory and Imagination:

	Impressions:	vivid	Constrained	Simples:
Ideas	Memory:	medium		Exactly alike except for vivacity
	Inspiration:	faint	Free	

But Hume is vague: memory an idea? p. 8: "somewhat intermediate betwixt an impression and an idea." And p. 84 he even speaks of "impressions of memory." But basically yes; and should be, by criterion of non-originality (*sufficient* condition). Though imagination ("perfect ideas"—p. 8) have distinction of freedom of combinability. Simple ideas can be recombined in imagination in all ways. "Wherever the imagination perceives a difference among ideas, it can easily produce a separation" (p. 10).

(*Treatise* 1.1.4) But this "freedom" of imagination (separability and *recombining*) is not capricious, but guided by gentle forces:

Resemblance,

---

[28] ⟨Ralph W. Church, *Hume's Theory of the Understanding* (London: George Allen and Unwin, 1935), 21.⟩

[29] ⟨The James-Lange theory of emotion entails that emotion consists of the patient's perception of his or her bodily changes as they occur. See William James (1842-1910), "What is an Emotion?," *Mind* 9 (1884): 188-205; idem, *The Principles of Psychology*. 2 vols. (New York: Henry Holt, 1890); 2: 442-85; and Carl G. Lange (1834-1900), *Über Gemüthsbewegungen* (Leipzig: T. Thomas, 1887).⟩

[30] ⟨See above, 196, on Smith, *Philosophy of David Hume*, 210ff.⟩

Contiguity,
Cause and effect.

Cause-and-effect (and the others) can be mediate (e.g. fourth cousin), but then becomes correspondingly weak in its influence on the imagination. 1 ⟨"That we may understand the full extent of these relations, we must consider, that two objects are connected together in the imagination, not only when the one is immediately resembling, contiguous to, or the cause of the other, but also when there is interposed betwixt them a third object, which bears to both of them any of these relations. This may be carried on to a great length; tho' at the same time we may observe, that each remove considerably weakens the relation. Cousins in the fourth degree are connected by *causation*, if I may be allowed to use that term; but not so closely as brothers, much less as child and parent. In general we may observe, that all the relations of blood depend upon cause and effect, and are esteemed near or remote, according to the number of connecting causes interpos'd betwixt the persons" (*Treatise*, 11f.).⟩

Aristotle was the pioneer in association of ideas; and resemblance, contiguity, and *contrast* were the principles (*On Memory and Reminiscence*[31]). No clear reason for dropping *contrast*; absorbed into resemblance? Causality is an addition—but an ephemeral one, as we shall see. Word "association" came with Locke; pejorative. Causes of association "are mostly unknown, and must be resolved into *original* qualities of human nature, which I pretend not to explain" (p. 13). Like Newton's gravity (Laird says Hume says[32]). 2 ⟨"Here is a kind of ATTRACTION, which in the mental world will be found to have as extraordinary effects as in the natural, and to shew itself in as many and as various forms" (*Treatise*, 12f.).⟩ And "There is a certain regular mechanism, which is susceptible of as accurate a disquisition, as the laws of motion, optics, hydrostatics, or any part of natural philosophy" (Hume, end of *Dissertation on the Passions*[33]). Complex ideas issue from above forces of association, and are classifiable into: Relations, Modes, Substances.

(*Treatise* 1.1.5 (on relations) and 7) Let's consider relations first from a logical point of view, before examining Hume. And attributes, before considering Hume on abstract ideas. Begin with *predicate*. Simplest kind is an intransitive verb. *One-place predicate*. More generally, whatever you can say about an object is a one-place predicate. Best represented as a

---

[31] ⟨451b19-20.⟩

[32] ⟨John Laird, *Hume's Philosophy of Human Nature* (London: Methuen, 1932), 37.⟩

[33] ⟨Hume, "A Dissertation on the Passions," in *The Philosophical Works*, ed. Thomas Hill Green and Thomas Hodge Grose. New ed. 4 vols. (London: Longmans, Green, 1882-1886), 4: 166.⟩

matrix in one variable. Now an *attribute* is an abstract entity associated with a one-place predicate. Class? Could be; depends on point of view; classes differ from attributes only in "principle of extensionality." Classes (or attributes) come, indeed, to outrun predicates, according to classical mathematics; so not *definable* as "abstract entities associated with one-place predicates," besides vagueness thereof. But this is how we get at them from language (or, as nominalist supposes, how we project them from language). "Universals." These, if we think of them as ideas, are the clearest case of Hume's "abstract ideas." Or, if we don't, the ideas *of* them are the abstract ideas.

Now besides one-place predicates, we may consider two-place. Simplest kind is transitive verb. More generally, whatever you can say (truly or falsely) about two objects. Best represented as a matrix in two variables. Just as attributes are abstract entities associated with one-place predicates, so *relations* are abstract entities associated with two-place predicates. Extensionally—just as attributes may be thought of as classes—so relations as classes of ordered pairs; or, double-barreled classes. Just as abstract as classes, but Hume doesn't treat them under abstract ideas, nor like them. Let's first consider Hume's treatment of abstract ideas. (section 7).

(*Treatise* 1.1.7 (order changed)[34]) Hume is a nominalist. He does not believe in universals. Section 7 is about the ideas, and hence perhaps not about the universals themselves, and indeed Hume therefore has little to say clearly on the point of nominalism properly so-called. His thesis in section 7 is rather that there are no abstract ideas except in the sense of concrete ideas used abstractly (with help of language). "No impression can become present to the mind, without being determined in its degrees both of quantity and quality" (p. 19), and ideas are copies of these impressions; an abstract idea is "a contradiction in terms" (p. 19). Perhaps the one place where he commits himself on universals as distinct from their ideas is on foot p. 19, where he simply *affirms* nominalism as "generally received in philosophy." "'Tis a principle generally received in philosophy, that everything in nature is individual, and that 'tis utterly absurd to suppose a triangle really existent, which has no precise proportion of sides and angles." So he takes nominalism for granted, and uses it to prove his conclusion about no abstract ideas, which he infers thus (foot p. 19f.): "If this therefore be absurd in *fact and reality*, it must also be absurd *in idea*; since nothing of which we can form a clear and distinct idea is absurd and impossible." Latter principle is a vestige of rationalism used often by Hume: "Nothing of which we can form a clear

---

[34] ⟨Presumably the note refers to the sequence of arguments 1-3 identified in the succeeding paragraph.⟩

and distinct idea is absurd and impossible." "Anything that we can clearly
conceive is possible." So Hume uses this principle to infer that there are
no abstract ideas from ontological nominalism: Argument 3.

Not his only argument for the claim that there are no abstract ideas.
Another already mentioned:[35] Argument 2.

And his last argument of all is foot p. 18ff.: abstraction doesn't imply a
separation, because can't separate the precise length of a line from the line
(what kind of thing remains?). And what is not distinguishable is not
different. (Essentially same as Argument 2: can't have line without its
length.) Argument 2 is that the abstract idea itself would be indeterminate,
therefore impossible; Argument 1 is that the *remainder* after abstracting
away the abstract idea would be indeterminate, therefore impossible. The
doctrine is Berkeley's. And like Berkeley, Hume says that what purport to
be abstract ideas are particular ones which have "become general in their
representation."

How it works:

(1) Association by resemblance: present perception induces memory
of past similars.

(2) Association by contiguity: general *name* learned in application to
various of those similars.

(3) Through this compound route, name evokes complex idea of
several appropriate similars, as needed. ("Readiness of the
imagination to supply others as needed" thus explained; this is the
element of generality.)

Note that "similarity in a special respect" is needed here. Suppose first
idea raised by word "apple" is a particular green apple seen an hour
earlier; *suitable* resemblant is a red apple, but not a green leaf. Our past
associations by resemblance must be sorted, so that only those are in
"readiness" which resemble the given one in the same *respects* as others
do in connection with which the word had been learned by contiguity.
⟨"when a globe of white marble is presented, we receive only the
impression of a white colour dispos'd in a certain form, nor are we able to
separate and distinguish the colour from the form. But observing
afterwards a globe of black marble and a cube of white, and comparing
them with our former object, we find two separate resemblances, in what
formerly seem'd, and really is, perfectly inseparable.... When we wou'd
consider only the figure of the globe of white marble, we form in reality
an idea both of the figure and colour, but tacitly carry our eye to its
resemblance with the globe of black marble; And in the same manner,
when we wou'd consider its colour only, we turn our view to its
resemblance with the cube of white marble" (*Treatise*, 25).⟩ So a case not

[35] ⟨Above, previous paragraph, referring to the passage quoted from *Treatise*, 19.⟩

merely of resemblance but of overlapping resemblance-*systems*. Hume's analysis of this is wanting. But no criticism of his point of view. (Possible approach: word-habit is readiness to bring forth just such particular ideas as resemble *all* the contiguity-named ideas *more closely* than some of them resemble each other.

—To here July 1

In short, a general term has as its "meaning," or anyway behavioral content, the particular "readiness" or "power" or habit which we have of producing right concrete instances in idea. It has no abstraction as additional meaning. Hume defensibly declines to "explain" the existence of such habits. Way the mind works; observation says so. But he gives analogues (pp. 22ff.).

Hume's attitude on abstract ideas throws new light on his notion of simple ideas and impressions, and brings contradictions. Colors would be abstract ideas. Can't have green without a shape. Yet we saw (p. 637, cited above, ⟨197⟩) "Blue and green are different simple ideas." Maybe a simple idea should *really* be fixed in color and minimal (in view of his remarks on geometry) in size.

Determinacy of ideas in all details is basis of Hume and Berkeley's nominalism. Has since been objected (by W. E. Johnson, Laird, *et al.*[36]) that Berkeley and Hume's basic assumption of determinacy of impressions and ideas is wrong. But Moncrieff (here)[37] points out that Hume would say in cases of indeterminacy that we aren't having the idea at all; *merely* using the word—which indeed we do. As to impressions themselves, question of determinacy depends on what we mean by an impression. Construe impression as something which we can note more or less carefully—as if we were immediately to forget and falsify a detail or delete a minimum-sized (i.e., simple) part? Then Hume is sustained. Construe as whole locus of vacillation—then Laird etc. are sustained.

(*Treatise* 1.1.5) Hume treats relations quite differently.[38] What difference does he feel? Relations not so clearly understood in those days. If abstract idea (attribute idea) gives way to ideas of instances, then idea of relation should give way perhaps to ideas of ordered pairs; but too sophisticated. Problem was double: problem of things being connected with others not themselves, unlike attribute; *and* the problem of the abstractness of the connection. It is former that seems to occupy Hume to exclusion of latter. Basically, Hume's notion of relation is *association* of

[36] ⟨W. E. Johnson, *Logic. Part I* (Cambridge: Cambridge University Press, 1921), xxix; Laird, *Hume's Philosophy of Human Nature*, 58.⟩
[37] ⟨I.e., Bruse Moncrieff, a graduate student attending this course.⟩
[38] Doesn't reject (like abstract idea), but admits (Relations, Modes, Substances: section 4).

ideas (by resemblance, contiguity, and causation)—an irreducible connection, yet doesn't quite claim to account for "philosophical" relations. Thus,

Relation:

Common language: connection of ideas for association as above.

Philosophical: any circumstance in which we care to compare.

[Logical extreme nowadays: any class of ordered pairs.]

Seven sources of relation in philosophical sense:

1. Resemblance*: This relation needed for all comparison.
2. Identity: (persistence through time) "common to every being whose existence has any duration."
3. Space and time: a species comprising many (distant, above, after, etc.)
4. Quantity or number: a species comprising many.
5. Degree of a quality: a species comprising many.
6. Contrariety.
7. Cause and effect.

Only example of contrariety is existence *vs.* non-existence. 1 ⟨"no two ideas are in themselves contrary, except those of existence and non-existence" (*Treatise*, 15).⟩ And later (p. 66) Hume says there *is* no idea of existence, really, except the idea of the object in question itself. So not much left of contrariety! So he needn't have worried about "exception" (paragraph 6, p. 15). Cause and effect to be examined later.

All these relations obviously, as described (pp. 14f.), turn on contiguity and/or resemblance, which for Hume are the basis. Except "distant" under paragraph 3, Space and Time. Maybe it is for this kind of thing that Hume vaguely thought contrariety needed. Cf. his general neglect of negation. He is logically unclear.[39] Question arises about resemblance: how can simple ideas resemble without *something* in common, and therefore not simple? Hume went into this as an after-thought: p. 637.

Just what is Hume's thesis about relations? That all relations (philosophical sense, therefore corresponding to all matrices in two variables) are of one of the seven kinds? And that all these reduce to resemblance and contiguity (and cause; eliminable);

plus logical negation (supply);

plus other logical connectives (?);

plus non-relational particulars (simple impressions and their copies and compounds)?

I.e., that all two-place predicates are translatable into these terms, insofar as significant? *No.* Would be tough to establish this. He doesn't claim it;

---

[39] See last paragraph of section ⟨5⟩ on p. 15: seems to allow negation as a matter of course.

philosophical relations come in as a grudging, irreducible concession. "Hume's theory of Relations."[40] Important in any case that there *are* primitive relations (resemblance and contiguity), irreducible to the ontology of impressions and ideas. Do we have ideas *of* them? And are they abstract, or at least subject to Hume's criticism of abstract ideas? I leave this to you to ponder.[41]

—To here July 3

(*Treatise* 1.1.6) Difference between mode and substance is difference between river and the water that passes through it. Other example of mode: a dance. Not to be confused with abstract idea; another *kind* of distinction. Thus "river," "dance," etc. are abstract *too*; but *each* river or dance is a mode. Similarly for substance. "We have no idea of substance, distinct from that of a collection of particular qualities" (p. 116, end first paragraph). [One of the natural conclusions which Locke stopped short of. Repudiation of the substratum.] [Even Locke's example of gold, malleability, *aqua regia*.] For, only the particular qualities can come through the senses. Similarly for modes. But are they really collections of qualities? Can he mean this? For qualities are gone with abstract ideas; and anyway, is collection thereof a higher abstraction still? Maybe he says more nearly what he means middle p. 16, beginning paragraph two: "Idea of substance as well as that of mode is nothing but a collection of simple ideas, united by the imagination." Now we know: simple ideas, not qualities; and collection is merely combination in a complex idea, which *is* the imagination's business. Idea of a piece of gold (a substance) is just our total complex impression of it, or rather its copy in an idea. Similarly for our idea of any particular mode, e.g. a river or a particular procession.

(*Treatise* 1.2.3) Hume's theory of space (extension) is in the long paragraph on p. 34. It is the idea of visual points (colored minima) occurring together. Therefore idea of visually complex impressions in general (general in the sense of abstracted from them, *selon* ⟨i.e., according to⟩ theory of abstract ideas; see last sentence of paragraph). Visually simple impressions can't give it, for they have only color and feel; too small for shape, which is reserved to complex impressions. It is the idea of any complex of simples together as for contiguity-association. Finally (concrete content) it is the idea of any extended object (used representatively, with words, in the manner of abstract ideas). An abstract

[40] ⟨Possibly an allusion to Ralph W. Church, "Hume's Theory of Philosophical Relations," *Philosophical Review* 50 (1941): 353-67.⟩
[41] ⟨At this point Quine evidently announced a paper assignment and topics. (Much of this line is only imperfectly discernable.) He required a one thousand word essay on "Ideas of relations in Hume."⟩

idea boils down to a *word*, with a "readiness" to bring forth, in connection with it, any of many relevant concrete ideas. And in the present instance it is the word "extension" and a readiness to bring forth any idea of an extended object (which equals a congeries of contiguous minimum color-points or touch-points).

The treatment of time (p. 35) is analogous except that here it is succession instead of contiguity. But there is a difference. Space-points may be qualitatively alike (purple), yet several are better than one and suffice to give extension. Whereas time-points consecutive and qualitatively alike are no good; there must be *change*. Feels, probably, there is a real difference: numerical difference of space points is capable of being sensed, when thus contiguous, even if there is nothing else. But numerical difference of moments is not. When we *do* sense duration of an unchanging presentation it is because of other changes in background—e.g. internal senses; and then it is the *latter* that gives idea of time.

Extension, or space, comes from contiguity; time from succession. But these are relations. Are they then ideas of relations? No. Hume is pretty explicit in the case of extension: idea not of the contiguity itself but of the complex (in any given concrete case) which *exhibits* the contiguity within it. Presumably so also with time. But there we must recognize complex impressions which are successions, not just configurations. The hearing of a song is as good a *single* complex impression as the seeing of a painting. This is O.K., but worth recognizing clearly. Now a new difference between extension and time, for Hume, has to do with the bounds of the complex impressions which are the concrete embodiments of the respective abstract ideas of extension and time. In the case of space, the concrete complex impressions may, I suppose, be anything up to content of whole visual field at any one time; no more. (Though it is not very clear just how far to carry Hume's subjectiveness. Sometimes, e.g., he even seems to allow the *same* simple idea to be tangible and visual—as if construction of external objects were under way.) But what limit for time?—In the extreme, time would become a single concrete life-long complex impression. For Locke, like Hume, extension and duration (or time) were from contiguity and succession. But, unlike Hume, they were ideas of reflexion; reflecting on arrangement of sensations, or on train of sensations. Hume has no place for such reflexion—which is a source of general difficulty for him—because of his doctrine that all ideas (practically) must copy impressions. He does have impressions of reflexion, but these are limited to passions, emotions, desires and aversions. "None of which," (as he says foot p. 33) "I believe, will ever be asserted to be the model, from which the idea of space is derived." So he is driven to his theory of ideas of space and time as abstract ideas having complex impressions as their concretions.

(*Treatise* 1.2.1) Let's look back now to Hume's negative argument for *finitude*. In section 1, argues our ideas of space and time not infinitely divisible. Might distinguish two senses of divisibility of an idea (e.g. of an extended particular):

(1) division into simples of which it is a complex idea,

(2) an ultimate relation between one *simple* "big" idea and various *simple* "small" ones.

In either case, infinite divisibility of ideas (or of corresponding impressions) not to be hoped for, because it would presuppose infinitely small extensions as impressions (whether constituent or related), which is in any case absurd. But, which of (1) and (2) is Hume? Apparently (1); see the phrase "*simple and* indivisible," p. 27, line 7. Conflicts with notion (in places previously cited) that a color is simple. But this conflicted *also* with abstractness of color, which was likewise documented.[42] Still, as we see, requiring simples to be minimal in extent is *not* essential to his present conclusion that ideas are not infinitely divisible; this would hold under either sense.

But then a final remark undermines the whole: "This however is certain, that we can form ideas, which shall be no greater than the smallest atom of the animal spirits of an insect a thousand times less than a mite" (p. 28). How? Not copies of simple impressions! And not compounds having other *smaller* ones as *parts* (if this is Hume's sense of part). By some indirect derivation? *How*, then? And, if so, couldn't we go on without end in like fashion? Or *should* he have said: no idea, but way of using words? There is a great unsolved problem of the status of indirect scientific constructs like electrons etc. And his mite-particle is one such. Maybe they should be tied into the system without presupposing ideas in any *image*-sense (for which Hume has a predilection), but by some derivative constructions regarding use of words and not insisting on ideas at all (spirit of Tooke; might have been carried further and applied to all complex ideas, as Tooke wanted). This is no solution, but only a hint of a program. Remains to see what the verbal constructions are like, what ones are acceptable to an empiricist in Hume's spirit.

—To here July 5

(*Treatise* 1.2, *passim*)

(Re indirect scientific constants. Electron; mite-particle; geometric point.)

Key: contextual definition. Cf. Russell, descriptions.[43]

---

[42] ⟨Above, 196-97 and 204, respectively.⟩
[43] ⟨Bertrand Russell (1872-1970), "On Denoting," *Mind* 14 (1905): 479-93; idem, "Philosophy of Logical Atomism," *Monist* 28 (1918): 495-527; *Introduction to Mathematical*

Appealing to operational criteria.

Such is modern empiricism.

Some inkling pp. 47f., talking of indirect "correction" of size-comparisons.[44]

Carnap, *Aufbau*.[45] (But presupposes a logic which presupposes universals.)

If such a construction program were put into effect, question of infinitely divisible space would become: are there smaller and smaller entities, without end, even in this realm of contextually defined pseudo-objects or constructions? Might still say no (modern physics); criteria of most remote sorts peter out finally. Then Hume's condemnation of space as unempirical remains valid. Could still *explain* classical geometry as a fiction convenient in reasoning but having no genuine content. But this is an *acceptance* of Hume's allegation, coupled with a pragmatic *use* of geometry, as a short-cut, in full knowledge of its strict absurdity. Jeffreys has a chapter on physical geometry (mensuration) in *Scientific Inference*.[46] Same really needed for arithmetic. Hume doesn't face the question: what is our idea of a trillion? Really have a trillion parts each of which is a copy of a simple impression?

Contextual: 'There are three things x such that Fx' for

'$\exists x \, \exists y \, \exists z \, [Fx \, . \, Fy \, . \, Fz \, . \, x \neq y \, . \, x \neq z \, . \, y \neq z \, .$

$\~\exists w \, [Fw \, . \, w \neq x \, . \, w \neq y \, . \, w \neq z]]$'.

And similarly for all numbers. The ideal of empiricist construction might be formulated thus:

Assume: statement connectives; quantification; identity; indefinitely many *empirical* predicates, one or many places. (Problem: which are empirical?) Express all other *entire* sentences in this language, or reject.

—⟨T⟩o here July 8

What I developed last time can be summarized as a contrast between three senses of empiricist "construction:"

    (1) Naïve (Hume): construction of ideas from constituent ideas (and constituent *spatially*—making cramps).

    (2) Sophisticated: construction of terms from constituent words

Philosophy (London: George Allen and Unwin, 1919); idem and Alfred North Whitehead *Principia Mathematica*. 3 vols. (Cambridge: Cambridge University Press, 1910-1913), 1: 66ff.⟩

[44] Cf. also Berkeley, *New Theory of Vision* ⟨sections 52-78⟩.

[45] ⟨Rudolf Carnap (1891-1970), *Der logische Aufbau der Welt* (Berlin: Weltkreis-Verlag, 1928).⟩

[46] ⟨Harold Jeffreys, *Scientific Inference* (Cambridge: Cambridge University Press, 1931), 107-30.⟩

(which may indeed have ideas connected, but this thought becomes less essential and important now).

(3) Hyper-sophisticated: construction of *contexts* from constituent words. This carries us much farther than (2), yet is certainly no less admissible. An important discovery. Russell.[47]

This contrast applies not only to the construction of mathematical ideas (number, geometrical elements, etc.), but also physical objects, electrons, everything. But the immediate question that led us to these considerations was that of the infinite divisibility of space.

Hume's arguments to the contrary turned on his naïve conception of construction: an idea of an infinitely divisible object in space would have to be made up of infinitely many component ideas, and this is impossible. The issue would have to be reconsidered under the sophisticated version of construction: can we define geometrical language *in context* in such a way that

(a) all full statements containing them boil down to empirically acceptable vocabulary (empirical predicates and logical connectives, etc.),

(b) the propositions of infinite divisibility become true?

Actually there is an equal problem, not recognized by Hume, in the infinite divisibility of numbers themselves—and even in the infinite generability of whole numbers.[48] In *all* these problems, the answer—even for the sophisticated notion of construction—is very likely *no*.

This set of problems involves difficulties a proper consideration of which would take us too far from Hume. In part the problem depends on how *much* in the way of auxiliary logical signs we accept. If we accept the whole machinery of modern logic (not just the signs enumerated last time), we can indeed get infinite extent and divisibility of number system. And by devious methods involving appeal to Descartes's analytical geometry we can perhaps hook in the infinitely divisible conception of geometry. *But* this logic entails assumption of abstract objects, contrary to Hume's nominalism—and contrary, I think, to whole Humean spirit (whereas the sophisticated form of construction as such is not). Toeing the mark—using only the mild logical auxiliaries hitherto listed, which do not violate nominalism—I expect the answer is *no* all along the line, so that the negative conclusion given by Hume's own naïve conception of construction comes to be sustained.

I've spoken earlier of how Descartes's thought, and indeed Plato's, was influenced by the impressive certainty of mathematical reasoning.[49] Hume

---

[47] ⟨See n. 43 above.⟩
[48] Former reduces to latter, by taking fractions as pairs.
[49] ⟨Above, 183-84 and 182, respectively.⟩

has seen fit not merely to question this certainty, but to repudiate a conclusion of the mathematicians themselves: infinite divisibility of space. On p. 71, Hume remarks that geometry is inexact and lacking in demonstrative certainty because "it depends on appearances." More particularly, because it depends on shapes, which are complex ideas whose properties reduce to spatial relations *between* simpler ones. And there are external relations, concerning which we cannot gain the *certainty* which we can have over *internal* relations. This contrast between external and internal relations begins on p. 69. *Resemblance* is an *internal* relation, in the sense that "it is invariable so long as the resembling ideas remain the same." Similarly for *contrariety*, *proportion in quantity or number*, and *degrees in any quality*. Not so for *identity* (as duration), *relations of time and place*, or *causation*.

Seems arbitrary. Survival of old distinction between essence (property) and accident? Why aren't the space-relations of three spots as *intrinsic* to the complex idea of the three spots, as the proportion 3/2 between it and the idea of two of the spots?

Hume isn't good at logical abstractions. Much better in his conclusions than in the logical underpinnings which he sometimes gives them. He has found trouble in geometry, in the nonsense of infinitely divisible space; he has found no trouble in arithmetic; therefore he supposes a theory of internal *vs.* external relations which regards external ones as objects of only fallible knowledge, and rests geometry on them, while regarding internal ones as objects of certain knowledge, and resting arithmetic on them (proportions of quantity and number). Actually, as already remarked, maybe he should have felt trouble also in arithmetic—over infinite divisibility, and infinite extensibility.

Of the exactness and certainty of arithmetic he says (p. 71): "There remain ... algebra and arithmetic as the only sciences, in which we can carry on a chain of reasoning to any degree of intricacy, and yet preserve a perfect exactness and certainty. We are possest of a precise standard, by which we can judge of the equality and proportion of numbers; and according as they correspond or not to that standard, we determine their relations, without any possibility of error." The basic method is pairing off units, for equality. In more complex cases we "proceed in a more *artificial* manner" (p. 70)

Compare this with Descartes's "intuition and deduction." *Internal* relations, such as one-to-one correspondence of given units, can be *intuited* with complete certainty. The more artificial manner is step-by-step deduction, where each step is in turn intuited certainly. Not so with geometry. But Hume was a little uneasy about his cavalier treatment of geometry. Top p. 72 he tries to concede that geometry works out pretty dependably in *practice*, but he does not make it clear why it should.

By the time of the *Enquiry*, his repentance was complete: he granted geometry, along with arithmetic, absolute certainty. (Section 4, part 1, beginning): "All the objects of human reason or enquiry may naturally be divided into two kinds, to wit, *relations of ideas* and *matters of fact*. Of the first kind are the sciences of geometry, algebra, and arithmetic; and in short, every affirmation which is either intuitively or demonstratively certain."[50] He has got away from his old division of relations into internal and external, with its prejudice to geometry. The new division is reminiscent of it, but the phrasing suggests more clearly the following point of view:

(a) what we can know by considering and comparing the content of ideas, without which they wouldn't *be* those ideas, *vs.*

(b) what we may suppose or observe about the way impressions do or will succeed one another.

A copy of Leibniz's truths of reason *vs.* truths of fact; but brings us close to modern (Kant and successors) *analytic vs. synthetic*.[51]

To get this distinction in modern form, useful to switch again (à la Tooke) to talking about words and meaning—relations instead of ideas. And then we get theory of mathematical truth as with modern logical positivists *et al.*: true because this is the way the words are properly used; otherwise their meaning would be altered. Same for logical truth itself, and easier to see there: 'p ⊃ p' because this is the way we use 'if'. [Illustrate by telling about Levy-Bruhl.[52]] But difficulty: drawing line. Which principles e.g. of physics etc.? Some, reasonably. And then there is still, as before, the question (though abandoned in *Enquiry*) of infinite divisibility: *can* the words of such a geometry make sense for an empiricist? Doubtful, as already remarked, even under a sophisticated (but nominalistic) construction.

—*July 10*

I explained view that logical truths are true by virtue of meanings of (i.e., way we resolve to use) signs; therefore certain. Same doctrine holds for mathematics. In fact, mathematics reduces to logic; but this is a strong logic incompatible with nominalism. Still, even failing such reduction, certainty of mathematics can be attributed to same source: true by virtue of how we use signs. This, as seen, is close to Hume as of *Enquiry*. But

[50] ⟨The text of the *Enquiry concerning Human Understanding* that Quine appears most often to have cited is included in Burtt, ed., *The English Philosophers*, 585-689. This passage, with some variation in spelling, is on 598.⟩

[51] ⟨See. e.g., G. W. Leibniz, *Monadology* (1714), sections 33ff.; and Immanuel Kant (1724-1804), *Critique of Pure Reason*, "Introduction," section 4 (A6/B10 – A10/B14).⟩

[52] ⟨Allusion unidentified with confidence, but cf. Quine, *Word and Object* (Cambridge, MA: M.I.T. Press, 1960), 59n.; and idem, *Ways of Paradox and Other Essays*. Rev. ed. (Cambridge, MA: Harvard University Press, 1976), 109.⟩

there is still a question *what* mathematics is certain? With infinitely divisible space or not? Because it might be (and probably is, given nominalism) that *no* meaningful use of signs could embody *such* principles.

Hume's advance in *Enquiry* is *good*, insofar as recognizing that geometry *and* algebra can be demonstrative because dependent on sheer meanings. But he should continue (as empiricist) to be critical of possibilities of meaningfulness. Perhaps he was in a hopeless quandary because lacking sophisticated idea of construction of ideas; sensed that anything in the way of a critical attitude toward meaningfulness carried him too far, given the poverty of the naïve method of construction; so that at the period of the *Enquiry* he abandoned this side pretty completely, at least for mathematics, and adopted an attitude of submissive acceptance. But the problem is still alive, and worth reconsidering now from the point of view of an enlightened empiricism—empiricistic and nominalistic as before, but armed with the sophisticated conception of construction. But we shall not.

(*Treatise* 1.3.3) Then we come to the most celebrated and iconoclastic of Hume's doctrines: the doctrine of causality. The doctrine, in its negative part, amounts to this: there is no possible logical basis for belief in causal law and scientific prediction. There is no more than a logically unjustifiable habit of mind, or faith in so-called scientific method. Our naïve view of cause: necessary connections, in nature, between events. Things have to be thus and so when others are thus and so. And indeed every event has antecedents of this kind rendering it inevitable. Philosophers long before Hume found trouble justifying what we so naïvely assume on this subject.

Certainly the arguments in favor of causality which Hume attacks were indefensible. Hobbes's (p. 80) was best of a bad lot: appeal to "Principle of Sufficient Reason," which figured so prominently also in Leibniz: no reason why something should happen in one moment rather than another if causality not granted. But Principle of Sufficient Reason is, in effect, assumption of causality itself. *Petitio principii.* Samuel Clarke's (p. 80): (1) cause must precede effect, (2) anything uncaused would have to be its own cause, therefore (3) anything uncaused would have to precede itself. First assumption doubtful, though Hume doesn't object to it.[53] (Actually it may be asked how an immediate cause *can* precede effect; *actio in*

[53] ⟨See, e.g., Thomas Hobbes (1588-1679), *Liberty and Necessity*, in *The English Works of Thomas Hobbes of Malmesbury*, ed. Sir William Molesworth. 11 vols. (London: J. Bohn, 1839-1845), 4: 276; and idem, *Elements of Philosophy*, in *English Works*, 7: 85. See also *The Leibniz-Clarke Correspondence*, ed. H. G. Alexander (New York: Philosophical Library, 1956), throughout.⟩

distans; and therefore how *any* cause can.) But Hume doesn't need to, for
he can rightly attack second premiss: *petitio principii*. Locke's argument
(p. 81) for causality—whatever is produced without any cause is produced
by *nothing*, has nothing for its cause—is a sophistry (and indeed
elementary linguistic confusion) reminiscent of Lewis Carroll, *Through
Looking Glass*, pp. 139-140.[54]

There *were* indeed philosophers before Hume who repudiated
causality—and with as much ulterior purpose as those who defended it.
Thus Malebranche and other followers of Descartes repudiated
causality—so far as matter upon matter—for the glory of God. (Hume
cites, pp. 158ff.). But Hume's argument is without ulterior purpose; and,
not stopping with matter, it repudiates cause—in the naïve sense of
necessary connections between matters of fact—altogether.

First thing for Hume to examine is this alleged necessity itself. He
argues that there is no necessity but constant conjunction (p. 88), because
there is no further connection that the senses could give us. No such
"necessity" can be *real* necessity in the sense of necessary truths of reason
(mathematics), because of conceivability of break of connection (p. 89).
The appeal here to conceivability of the opposite is a vestige of the
rationalist tradition. A poor criterion, because hard to decide what we are
imagining and what we are merely verbalizing without imagining.
Through Looking Glass, pp. 100-101.[55] Modern survival of the principle:
contradictions are meaningless (i.e., can't be clearly conceived).
Wittgenstein *et al.*[56] See especially p. 95: "What is absurd is
unintelligible." Difficulties: (1) no test of meaningfulness; (2) indirect
proof. But Hume's argument remains that the so-called necessity in
supposed causal connections is no more than constant conjunction; and this
is important.

Now constant conjunction is observed only in present and memory; yet
it leads us to expect *same in future*; *this* is apparently bound up somehow
with our feeling of a necessary connection. To account for this, Hume
inquires into nature of expectation, therefore *belief*. P. 94: Belief consists
in entertaining an idea *as realized in existence*. But existence is not a
predicate; an idea of a horse or unicorn is no different from the idea of

---

[54] ⟨Lewis Carroll, *Through the Looking-Glass, and What Alice Found There* (London and
New York: Macmillan and Co., 1895). This is pretty clearly the edition Quine used. This
passage, where Alice claims to see "nothing" on the road to the White King's astonishment
and envy, is in chapter 7, "The Lion and the Unicorn." Cf. above, 195.⟩
[55] ⟨Carroll, *Through the Looking-Glass*, chapter 5: "Wool and Water," where the White
Queen claims to believe sometimes as many as six impossible things before breakfast in
response to Alice's assertion that one cannot believe impossible things.⟩
[56] ⟨E.g. Ludwig Wittgenstein (1889-1951), *Tractatus Logico-Philosophicus*, trans. D. F.
Pears and B. F. McGuinness (London: Routledge and Kegan Paul, 1961), 4.461.⟩

same as existing. (Or of God; cf. my remarks on Anselm's ontological proof of God, *à propos* Descartes.[57]) So difference between believing and not must lie in manner of entertaining the idea, not in the idea itself.

Hume's solution is same as in his distinction between memory, imagination, and impression: *vivacity*. So, definition of belief (p. 96): *a lively idea related to or associated with a present impression*. Particularly suited to belief in a constant conjunction continuing: present reappearance of A, lively idea of B as expected. More *general* version of same theory, of belief as vivacity simply, occurred way back on p. 86, before the theory was argued: "the *belief* or *assent*, which always attends the memory and senses, is nothing but the vivacity of those perceptions they present; and ... this alone distinguishes them from the imagination." Certainly fits, if the distinction between memory and imagination itself is right; for, the big difference between the two is that we *believe* memory. And there are minor empirical corroborations which Hume also notes, notably (p. 117): "I have often heard in conversation, after talking of a person, that is in any way celebrated, that one who has no acquaintance with him, will say, *I have never seen such-a-one, but almost fancy I have; so often have I heard talk of him.*" In particular, then, the belief accompanying so-called necessary connection—rather, accompanying the experience of past constant conjunction—is the extra *vividness* with which a new encounter of A leads us to imagine the conjoined B *by association*. Association by constant conjunction is based *always* on resemblance no less than contiguity. For, it is based on "repetition"—but there is no perfect repetition; only resemblance among succeeding quasi-instances of the quasi-repeated: All expectation of one object because of another is by *custom* (p. 102).

—To here July 12

So the "necessity of connection" is just the constant conjunction; and the expectation engendered is accounted for by association. Whence then our *idea* itself of necessary connection in this sense? For Hume it is an idea copied from an *impression of reflection*—internal sensation of compulsion *to associate* (foot p. 165). Observed *constant conjunction* invokes this impression, since it strongly compels us to associate (by resemblance plus association)—see p. 156. The "necessity" we feel is *subjective*—necessity on our part to associate or expect; and *it is this* that we *sense* internally when we sense the impression of reflection which is the prototype of the idea of necessary connection. And so expectation by so-called scientific method *is a species of sensation* (p. 103).

[57] ⟨Above, 184-85.⟩

An interesting confirmation of this theory of Hume's comes from contemporary psychiatry: in the neurotic phenomenon of *indecision*. A person whose troubles or mental discomforts are too much to be conveniently borne usually protects himself by repressing his feelings *in general*, so that there results an apathy and a dull depression, taking the place of the grief he is fleeing from. Emotions generally—impressions of reflexion, in Hume's phrase—are less *vivid*, converging in a dull neutral. And what happens to belief? Pros and cons become about equal and there is indecision—as there should be by Hume's theory, if the sense of necessary connection is an impression of reflexion!

Now *cause*, provisionally taken as a basic type of association-relation along with resemblance and contiguity, comes now for Hume to *reduce* to these latter; nothing additional. Definition appears top p. 170: ⟨"We may define a CAUSE to be 'An object precedent and contiguous to another, and where all the objects resembling the former are plac'd in like relations of precedency and contiguity to those objects, that resemble the latter.'"⟩ Thus:

(type A)	(type B)	
o	' –	horizontal = contiguity (or succession)
	–	
o	–	
	=	
o	–	
	–	
o	–	Then, granted the *whole columns*
o	–	horizontal *also* = cause-effect.
o	–	
	=	
o	–	
	–	
o	–	
	–	(Note there may be extras of type B.)
o	–	

No doubt "resemblance" in Hume's definition is too vague, for it could allow resemblance in unlike respects. Suitable refinement would probably be like what I suggested in connection with Hume's theory of abstract ideas. Thus: If $a_1, a_2, \ldots a_n$ are respectively contiguous to (or similarly succeeded by) $b_1, b_2, \ldots, b_n$; and everything that resembles all of $a_1, \ldots, a_n$ more than some of $a_1, \ldots a_n$ resemble each other is included among $a_1, a_2, \ldots, a_n$; and similarly for $b_1, b_2, \ldots, b_n$. Trouble here is that we cover only full correlation; no allowance for there being extra b's with other causes.

Maybe "respect of resemblance" is fundamental and must be developed more fully, in connection with an improved theory of abstract ideas. And then certain respects (as relevant to science) to exclusion of others. This is a live problem still today. Also might allow for concomitant variations. A misgiving that might from a *too* empiricistic view arise in connection with *any* such definition of cause is its reference to absent (past and *future*) pairs of resemblants. Hume notes this and so proposes an alternative (p. 170, middle): ⟨"'CAUSE is an object precedent and contiguous to another, and so united with it, that the idea of the one determines the mind to form the idea of the other, and the impression of the one to form a more lively idea of the other.'"⟩ Odd—determining cause by introspection. Almost "cause if I think it's a cause." The previous approach suits our usual attitudes better: never *know* it's a cause (past, present, future), but *conjecture* from samples.

Problems of cause and prediction can be separated:

(1) Cause—as a necessary connection, in some irreducible sense, *vs.* mere concomitance (constant conjunction).

Hume has elected the latter. But

(2) Prediction might still be hoped for: observations of past *constant conjunctions* giving us *grounds* for rightly expecting continuation of same (without thought of necessary connection in any further, irreducible sense).

Hume has explained our prediction psychologically: "Why we expect," in terms of association. But question remains: is it in *fact*, apart from our psychological vagaries, more likely than otherwise that the conjunction will continue? Is our psychological propensity *just*? This is the problem of prediction, or *induction*—a central problem of philosophy. Hume's answer is *no*.

—To here July 15

Uniformity of nature p. 89: ⟨"If reason determin'd us, it wou'd proceed upon the principle, *that instances, of which we have had no experience, must resemble those, of which we have had experience, and that the course of nature continues always uniformly the same.*"⟩—the traditional principle by which to try to justify induction, prediction) is sheer postulate. P. 90: ⟨"probability is founded on the presumption of a resemblance betwixt those objects, of which we have had experience, and those, of which we have had none; and therefore 'tis impossible this presumption can arise from probability."⟩ Reappears p. 104. In a sense it has a ground, *viz.*, observed always true; but this would be circular as argument for induction. In effect: induction proved true by induction. (p. 91 and again p. 105.) It works, yes; or has; but that is irrelevant, unless we *assume* causality in order to infer from this past success that the success will continue. Hume's negative doctrine is inevitable, I think, in any thoroughgoing empiricism; and it does not depend on the more extreme or questionable features of his particular underlying system of elements and psychology.

This is not to say that we cannot develop refined techniques of induction. Modern statistical theory. Essence of explanation of why we can do this is on p. 105: we use induction to establish induction. And we thus inductively arrive at a science of statistical method. Hume uses this principle to counter the objection entertained p. 107, *viz.* that ⟨if "belief is nothing but a more forcible and vivid conception of an idea; it shou'd follow, that that action of the mind may not only be deriv'd from the relation of cause and effect, but also from those of contiguity and resemblance."⟩ Actually, as Hume points out by various examples, we often *do* believe or expect because of such "accidental" associations. E.g., p. 113, *credulity* as over-sensitivity to resemblance; p. 114, *impiety* as over-dependence on resemblance. Such was Locke's *derogatory* use of "association." And note "extravagance," p. 120. But better thinkers *don't*; because better thinkers are the ones who have done a more thorough job of *applying induction to induction*—i.e., empirically arriving at scientific method. Thus, for Hume the *primitive* form of induction is *simple induction*: sheer accumulation of instances (top p. 131). Simple conditioning, as observed and measured in experiments on rats (Skinner)[58]. Last section of the part, pp. 176-78, makes the animal point. Accounted for very well by Hume's mechanism of vividness through association by contiguity and resemblance. This much is all at the unreflective stage (p. 133; we might say "*unreasoned*"?).

But *contrariety* drives us farther (p. 133; p. 150). Contrariety makes us give up one hypothesis, and we shift to a second best, which we yet don't believe strongly enough (not vivid) because too few instances. So we try to get *more* for it, by experiment (manufacture of impressions) (p. 138). Sometimes (as recognized p. 104, foot) a *single* experiment may decide us—but this is because of indirect implication *via rules of scientific method*, together with other more specific *scientific beliefs*, already established *and knit together (for greater vividness) in a system of "physical objects"* (p. 108).

These general rules of scientific method are *themselves* established by induction, or derived from general principles (e.g. uniformity of nature) so established. They include all the refinements of statistical method.

---

[58] ⟨B. F. Skinner (1904-1990) published a series of papers involving experimentation on rats from 1930, some of which formed the basis of his *The Behavior of Organisms; an Experimental Analysis* (New York: D. Appleton-Century Co., 1938). Skinner was a Junior Fellow with Quine at Harvard in the 1930s.⟩

Familiar ones, less refined than some, are *Mill's methods*—the now classical ways of discovering causal connections (though Mill was ninety-five years younger than Hume):

   (a) Method of agreement: if given event accompanies a, b, c, d, ... and a, e, f, g, ..., then *a* is the cause.—See Hume, paragraph 5, p. 174!

   (b) Method of difference: if given event accompanies a, b, c, d, ... and not b, c, d, ..., then *a* is the cause. —See Hume, paragraph 6, p. 174!

   (c) Method of concomitant variations: Same as paragraph 7, p. 174![59]

Hume doesn't say why these are right; *impossible* to *defend*. But he says why *believed*. In each case [observe], association by contiguity and resemblance. And the rules are believed *by induction* because they work, or because derived from principles (uniformity of nature etc.) which induction establishes—ultimately by sheer undeliberated conditioning. In this way we may, by scientific method, be led to so-called beliefs which *don't* correspond to greater vividness (p. 141) in any immediately perceived sense of impression-of-reflexion "necessity." Perhaps an extension of "belief," definitionally extended through rules of scientific method (which ultimately rest on beliefs in the direct sense).

—To here July 17

Hume's point of view on scientific method is startlingly summed up p. 149: ⟨"all reasonings are nothing but the effects of custom; and custom has no influence, but by inlivening the imagination, and giving us a strong conception of any object."⟩ And the best summary of the central argument is in bottom paragraph p. 166. ⟨"Before we are reconcil'd to this doctrine, how often must we repeat to ourselves, *that* the simple view of any two objects or actions, however related, can never give us any idea of power, or of a connexion betwixt them: *that* this idea arises from the repetition of their union: *that* the repetition neither discovers nor causes any thing in the objects, but has an influence only on the mind, by that customary transition it produces: *that* this customary transition is, therefore, the same with the power and necessity; which are consequently qualities of perceptions, not of objects, and are internally felt by the soul, and not perceived externally in bodies?"⟩ So probability is wholly subjective. The only things we can *know*, apart from immediate perceptions, would seem to be the demonstrative sciences of arithmetic and algebra (plus, as seen in *Enquiry*, geometry). But now in a curious argument, pp. 180-82, he repudiates even these things! For, we can err in calculation; we check, but

---

[59] ⟨John Stuart Mill (1806-1873), *A System of Logic, Ratiocinative and Inductive* 3.8.1-6.⟩

this can err; we check the check, and so on in infinity; probabilities on probabilities, reducing to nothing.

This is precisely the argument which, as I pointed out in the first lecture, fails to allow for possibility of convergent product.[60] And this is just the case where we'd expect a convergent product, the superimposed probability being larger each time. Still, Hume has a point—if *none* of the probabilities are (except subjectively) any good *at all*, which is his position. A check of figures is at once an empirical judgment which can go wrong; we cannot get beyond *causal*, non-arithmetical support here. At best, trusting memory (which is itself of the nature of causal inference, though Hume doesn't cover this point very well in his analysis of causality). We are driven to "animal faith" all along the line. Hume doesn't say we *shouldn't* trust our scientific methods. Merely that this is ultimate. Vain to ask for a more ultimate justification of anything than that *these methods themselves* support the thing in question. "Meaningless" to ask, as modern logical positivists phrase it.

After cause, the next great skeptical thesis in Hume concerns physical objects. But in rejecting our assurance of physical objects, unlike the case of cause, he was preceded by Berkeley. I've already touched on this—how Berkeley took the step for which Locke with his hesitating empiricism had prepared the way.[61] What Locke said of the subjectivity of the secondary qualities, Berkeley said of the so-called primary qualities as well; so that there was no longer any empirical evidence for physical *objects* at all, except insofar as conceived as bundles of sense impressions (or constructs in some more devious sense—say by modern contextual definition). I remarked that various of Descartes's followers had in part anticipated Hume in denying causality, *viz.* among material objects, and that they had done so with an ulterior theological purpose.[62] The same was true of Berkeley's denial of all matter: it secured God's position as cause of our impressions, since impressions could no longer be attributed to the efficacy of matter. This seems a bit transparent, since any *problem* in accounting for impressions which is occasioned by abandoning matter is insofar an argument *against* abandoning matter, and evidence *for* it. However this may be, *Hume's* skepticism with regard to material objects, like his skepticism with regard to cause, was altogether disinterested (see p. 409). Not skepticism to bolster belief, but skepticism as such.

Hume's negative arguments are essentially Berkeley's, and need not detain us. The essential point is that there is nothing but experience to go on, and experience gives us only the appearances, not an additional reality

[60] ⟨Above, 182-83.⟩
[61] ⟨Above, 194-96.⟩
[62] ⟨Above, 214.⟩

behind them. Here, as in causality, Hume doesn't proclaim the *opposite* belief. In causality he is in *favor* of believing in predictions, etc., but it is animal faith, and vain to ask for ultimate evidence. Similarly as to bodies: ⟨"Thus the sceptic still continues to reason and believe, even tho' he asserts, that he cannot defend his reason by reason; and by the same rule he must assent to the principle concerning the existence of body, tho' he cannot pretend by any arguments of philosophy to maintain its veracity. Nature has not left this to his choice, and has doubtless esteem'd it an affair of too great importance to be trusted to our uncertain reasonings and speculations. We may well ask, *What causes induce us to believe in the existence of body?* but 'tis in vain to ask, *Whether there be body or not?* That is a point, which we must take for granted in all our reasonings" (p. 187).⟩ So the treatment of bodies, like that of cause, divides into two parts: (a) the negative part, arguing that there is no ultimate evidence for necessary connection (or physical objects), and (b) the positive part, explaining the derivation of our ideas of necessary connections (or of physical objects). So let's turn to latter.

Purpose of hypothesis of external, continued existences is mentioned foot p. 198: simplifies our system of impressions, gives more coherence. Reduces multiplicity of entities. Particularly (as anticipated p. 108) it simplifies the causal network. Here is a *purpose*, then, but Hume must still say, in terms of his psychology, what the *mechanics* of arriving at ideas of *external continued existences* are. He says the "continued" is prior to the "external" (p. 199). His reasoning, as appears from succeeding pages, is this:

1. Successive resembling impressions are welded into a so-called *enduring* single object. Even others not successive are welded to it under certain conditions.

2. This *identification* among temporally different impressions encounters difficulties when thought of as identity of the impressions themselves, so we "externalize"—i.e., we say the enduring object is something other than the impressions.

On 1: Why are *successive* wholly resembling impressions to be viewed differently *at all*—hence giving an *enduring* object instead of one momentary one? Because synchronous with changing *backgrounds*, foot p. 200f.: "time, in strict sense, implies succession, and when we apply its idea to any unchangeable object, 'tis only by a fiction of the imagination, by which the unchangeable object is suppos'd to participate of the changes of the co-existent objects." Seems a little roundabout on Hume's part—saying it is a fiction of participation in change, instead of letting time in the first place rest on any changes of the co-existent objects themselves, without fiction. But a detail; let pass. Further on 1: the welding of such impressions into an enduring object leads Hume to some curious remarks on *identity*: for identity enters as relating these welded impressions, insofar as each is thought of *as* the fused object itself. Hume asks (p. 200) whence the idea of identity.

There ensues a confusion, similar to the confusions infesting identity right down to Wittgenstein. (a) "In that proposition, "*an object is the same with itself*, if the idea express'd by the word, *object*, were no ways distinguish'd from that meant by *itself*; we really shou'd mean nothing." But that's as it *should* be; we are not supposed to mean anything here, except a logical truth; it *should* be trivial. This doesn't mean identity itself is trivial, though Hume seems to think so—see p. 201: "We cannot, in any propriety of speech, say, that an object is the same with itself, unless we mean, that the object existent at one time is the same with itself existent at another." *Of course we can*. We can even say: "The first complex impression I ever had containing blue was also the second I ever had containing yellow." Same fallacy appears more strikingly in Wittgenstein: [explain].[63]

Hume, in the former passage (p. 200) in which he complains of triviality of "an object is the same with itself" where identity is properly construed, apparently felt this wasn't quite a convincing objection, for he added another: that furthermore the proposition would not "contain a subject and a predicate, which however are implied in this affirmation." Three rebuttals:

 (i) *petitio principii*; *why* implied?
 (ii) can't it have a subject and predicate which however happen to be the same?
 (iii) (the *real* one) a statement of identity ordinarily has two *different* terms (call them subject and predicate if you will), not to be confused with the designated objects (which are one).

—To here July 19

The true purpose of the identity concept, not appreciated by Hume and others, is as a means to linearizing statements which would otherwise run something like this:

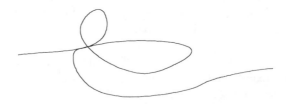

---

[63] ⟨Possibly Wittgenstein, *Tractatus*, 5.5303; cf. Quine, *Word and Object*, 117.⟩

We hark back, in the linear rendering, by saying "itself," "the former," "the same," it, etc. And often it is necessary to point out only afterward, as in afterthought or because there wasn't room for full provision in the running statement, that such-and-such further terms belong back at the same point.

Moreover, *descriptions* give rise to identities which are not even products of sheer meanings. E.g., Morning Star and Evening Star; but not necessarily just physical objects; also (cited before) "the first complex impression I have had containing blue that was also the second I ever had containing yellow." Hume's naïve sense of construction, forcing him to seek ideas as straight composition of copies of simple impressions, makes him less willing to accept this real notion of identity—perhaps—than if he knew about contextual definitions.

But not whole story, for it was one of the logical signs which *I assumed* in speaking of contextual definitions, and Hume would still be entitled to ask *whence*. *Not* contextually defined. He might ask same of logical negation (which he seems to assume uncritically) and of quantification (which he didn't fully know about). But all these are legitimate questions. Actually identity *can* be defined, if we really have a catalogue of *all* our basic empirical predicates. [Explain.] This is probably the right way to handle the whole thing, if the catalogue can be supposed given. Question remains of explaining negation, quantification, conjunction; maybe we *have* to take these without further comment.

Anyway, let's see now what Hume does about accounting for idea of identity. His course is already determined by the line on p. 201 previously quoted: "We cannot, in any propriety of speech, say, that an object is the same with itself, unless we mean, that the object existent at one time is the same with itself existent at another." Not quite as though Hume makes identity consciously *mean* "duration," i.e, recurrence with full similarity (especially successively), but rather that this is the *source*, and that identity thus derived is confusedly taken as sameness out-and-out, i.e., identity properly so-called. Mechanism is this:

(1) Suppose our *total* impressions, background and visceral and all, stay the same (or exactly repetitive) for a time. This *is* identity *sensu stricto*, for no time has passed!—by meaning of "time." So here identity is *properly* applicable.

(2) Suppose next the background alone changes, giving us a measure of time. If a particular impression still stays unchanging (or exactly repetitive), the case is enough like (1) so that we *confuse* it with (1) and *impute* identity.

—To here July 22

(3) Next natural shift—recurrence after interruption—still enough like situation (2) so that we repeat the practice also here, other things

being equal. But this is the weakest stage of the three; we decline to identify here when in conflict with systematic inferences based more on (2) and causal reasoning—concluding then mere resemblance rather than identity.

The source of the *idea* of identity is evidently an impression of reflexion: the sense of the *uninterrupted progress of thought*. See p. 256: "it must be the uninterrupted progress of the thought, which constitutes the identity." And, as Hume eloquently describes on pp. 255-61, this breaks down into association by resemblance, contiguity, and causation—as indeed it should. This fits our conception of physical objects well: unite the contiguous as parts of the object; the resemblant as stages of the objects; and cut off the contiguous beyond where resemblance (i.e, duration in time) reinforces it. And depend on causation (as seen) to decide interrupted cases. Hume points out how continuity operates strongly. It should, involving resemblance and contiguity. Strong enough to identify stages of river as *same* river despite even the known (inferred) change in substance.

In choosing this example perhaps he had Heracleitus in mind—who urged the fallacy of identifying, just as Hume does, and used the river as his example: can't step into same twice. This effecting of strictly improper but natural identifications among our sense data, says Hume, is the extent of the vulgar view; no dichotomy yet between objects and impressions. Latter is made philosophically, when paradoxes arise; e.g., subjectivity of impressions (pushing one eye, etc.) without changes in "object" according to causal network. Interruption *vs.* continuance. And thus we have our physical objects. Thus attributing *interruption* to perceptions, *continuance* to objects (p. 215).

Modern empiricism could, compatibly with Hume's *basic* orientation, depart from his view of physical objects in a radical way: Don't attribute "enduring object" to *fallacious* identification of impressions; instead, get identity as *I* have explained; then externalize "enduring" object from the start as the object of this identity. Then what Hume analyzes as source of idea of *identity* (*viz.* uninterrupted progress of thought) is to be viewed rather as source of uniting as *manifestations of* one object. Identity of *this* object (or any) with self *of course* holds, and is explained in our new way. All of Hume's observations about the rôle of contiguity, resemblance, and causation, and especially continuity, come now to figure in the explanation of how we form *things*, not identity. "Principle of individuation" becomes not a criterion for identity but a criterion for thinghood. Identification ceases to be a fallacy. Heracleitus becomes wrong: we *can* step into the same *river* twice, but in so doing we are not stepping into the same material substance; *river* is one kind of thing (a mode), *substance* another; *impression* a third. River and substance are two ways of combining events (physical point-events or impression-events) into things. *Both* valid; things can overlap. The explicit accounting for the several external objects (over and above the above general characterization of our ways of limiting them) should proceed by some kind of logical construction *from* (not confusion *with*) impressions.

Russell undertook to sketch such a scheme in *Our Knowledge of the External World*. Begin with so-called *perspectives*, *viz.* whole fields of momentary experience, between which we can recognize part-similarities for correlation. Imagine many different perspectives (corresponding to different minds or "points of view") simultaneously. Class of all the parts of all these corresponding to one given constituent impression of one of them is a *momentary-state-of-a-physical-object*. Can correlate such states in turn by taking neighboring sets of perspectives in time, and get *thing* in its temporal entirety—with adjustments based on causal laws (and complicating the definition) where there are questions of "right" identification after interruption.[64] One fault: intersubjectivity of starting point. Carnap tries to re-do it avoiding this; also being more rigorous all along the line.[65]

—To here July 24

But another fault remains still with Carnap: assumption of a logical apparatus that provides classes, classes of classes, etc.—anti-nominalistic. The desirable would be to get along without such machinery, by subtle use of contextual definition—not available to Hume (and not accomplished yet). Contextual definition would explain all new predicates, of kinds applicable to so-called physical objects, in application to variables or contents referring to so-called physical objects. But these whole contexts would be explained ultimately, as wholes, as abbreviations of long expressions made from our primitive vocabulary. (Probably impossible.) Identity, then—as a small detail—would be then extended also to physical objects, by a parallel to my basic definition of identity as applied to perceptions. The "vulgar" view would not enter as a stage; but Hume was unconvincing here anyway. Remains a general problem on the score of psychology *vs.* epistemology. Maybe Hume is nearer the truth genetically; but ours would be an account of how it *might as well be*—an account of how firmly we *can* reconstitute the world. If the proposed modern construction is impossible (as it may very well be) then from an empirical view there is *only* the genetic account: psychology of meaningless verbal behavior.

We now leave physical objects and turn to minds. Hume's attack on the

---

[64] ⟨Russell, *Our Knowledge of the External World as a Field for Scientific Method in Philosophy* (London: George Allen and Unwin, 1926), 94ff.⟩
[65] ⟨Carnap, *Aufbau.*⟩

belief in mental substance is like that on necessary connection and on physical substance: *no corresponding impression* (p. 233). It's his old argument on substance, as of early pages: most we can have is abstract idea embodying (and concretized by) the several observed states *of* the alleged substance. But the alleged mind in particular *self*, is peculiar in that it is not a substance in which the perceived qualities are supposed to inhere, but rather in which the perceptions themselves occur. Hume's usual form of argument is still available, though (p. 251): "If any impression gives rise to the idea of self, that impression must continue invariably the same, thro' the whole course of our lives; since self is suppos'd to exist after that manner [substance]. But there is no impression constant and invariable." So, just as there is properly no justifiable physical object but the sum-total of the impressions "of the object," so, Hume holds, there is properly no mind but the sum-total of *all* perceptions "by the mind." P. 253: "They are the successive perceptions only, that constitute the mind." There is no receptacle, no theater. The mind is the life, the sum total of experiences. In this, as in cause, Hume out-Berkeleyed Berkeley. Hume applied to the mind the same destructive considerations that Berkeley had applied to body.

As in the uniting principle of physical objects (or as Hume says, the basis of identity), so with the self, causality is the most important. More important even than memory, for we forget experiences, but still consider that they were *ours*. Continuity (reducing to resemblance and contiguity) and causality (reducing to same) are the main bases. Here, as with physical objects, we should speak perhaps of constitution rather than of a seemingly spurious "identification" of the distinct. But in either case we have a subversion of popular beliefs, insofar as the latter seem to involve something unchanging and "simple"—which is lacking either way.

Magnitude of the step can best be brought out by this sort of supposition: You have your choice: you and someone else are simultaneously going to be changed into two quite different people, different places, different appearances, different memories. One of the new incarnations is going to be ugly, hated, miserable; other is going to have everything good. Do you care which? By present doctrine you shouldn't!—for it means nothing to say it is you rather than he. No continuity or causation (nor even memory, which, however, Hume says, isn't the main thing anyway top p. 262). Popular feeling is that there is something *further* which could be said to be you or not. Hume says: find a justification in experience for *such* a conception.

Book 1 of *Treatise* is commonly considered most important part of Hume. *Enquiry* covers largely the same ground. Smoother, and in some respects more correct; because written years later; but less detailed and on the whole less provocative. Provides, however, a good *review* of book 1 of *Treatise*, as well as new matter here and there. And a good piece of literature. Its one hundred fifty pages divide into twelve sections, of which the first seven go over the arguments of the *Treatise* with regard to impressions and ideas, association, belief, causality. Apart from condensation and omission, the main novelty of these sections is the point already touched on in class regarding mathematical certainty:[66] beginning section 4, he relents toward geometry, as compared with his attitude in *Treatise*, and accords it the same good will that he previously had reserved for arithmetic and algebra. It is here that he introduces his contrast between *relations of ideas* and *matters of fact*—according certainty to mathematics on the ground that it concerns merely the relations of ideas and is therefore under our control—a point of view toward mathematics which, essentially, had been shared by Locke.

—To here July 26

I had recurred to Hume's remarks in the *Enquiry* on mathematical knowledge. How he relents toward geometry. The significant shift in the *Enquiry,* as regards philosophy of mathematics, is to the conception of *relations of ideas vs. matters of fact*. Former are under our control and afford certainty. It's not altogether clear how this notion fits with the rest of Hume's doctrine. Can't contrast ideas with matters of fact in the sense of mind *vs.* external world, for no external world is assumed. Only possible contrast is between complex ideas (voluntary combinations in imagination) and impressions (as they come, involuntarily). But this isn't a clear contrast between mathematical and empirical science, because voluntary compounding occurs in both; and ultimate dependence on simple impressions is required equally in both. The answer is suggested early in section 7: difference merely of precision. If we could develop other, non-mathematical ideas with more precision, perhaps much of the same certainty could be hoped for in other fields as in mathematics. And there is no reason why mathematics should have a monopoly of certainty. Mathematics has done better than other branches just because of (a) accident of having attained precision, or (b) easier topics for precision. This *is* mathematics; any additions to the realm of comparable precision would be *called* mathematics too.

This view harks back to Leibniz's program of a *universal characteristic*: analyze all our concepts precisely in terms of clear and distinct ideas; then, when a problem arises, *calculemus*.[67] This is probably right. It doesn't say we can know everything; what relates to the succession of impressions remains unknowable until experience reveals it.

---

[66] ⟨Above, 211-12.⟩

[67] ⟨E.g., G. W. Leibniz, "On the General Characteristic," in idem, *Philosophical Papers and Letters*, ed. Leroy M. Loemker. 2nd ed. (Dordrecht: D. Reidel, 1969), 221-28.⟩

Leibniz himself recognized this distinction, in his distinction between truths of reason and truths of fact. What can be known with certainty (given precision enough in our ideas) is that which proceeds from their mere manner of composition—or, from the more elastic point of view of Tooke and of modern "logical construction:" that which proceeds logically from mere definition of terms. This version in terms of definition isn't accepted by Hume himself. He distinguishes, on next to last page of *Enquiry*, between statements true by definition (*"where there is no property, there can be no injustice"*—because injustice is defined as violation of property) and the certainties of mathematics (*"the square of the hypotenuse is equal to the squares of the other two sides"*).[68] But given more intricate conceptions of definition than Hume knew, perhaps those others (mathematics) reduce also to "analytic"—following from definition of terms. Surely so if for Hume they follow from relations of our ideas—if the definitions exhaust the ideas, embodying all connections not matters of fact. Even logical truth, not worried about by Hume, is on same footing. Only we finally get to a point where appeal strictly to *definition* seems hardly feasible—but still our certainties at that level may be in same spirit, *viz.* analytic in the sense of following from the ways we see fit to *use* our terms (badly called "implicit definition").

A few other scattered points in sections 1 through 7 worthy of notice: One remark, end second page of section 2 (immediately after middle of section 2), capable of giving Hume's opponents a sense of indignation, and rightly: ⟨"when we analyze our thoughts or ideas, however compounded or sublime, we always find that they resolve themselves into such simple ideas as were copied from a precedent feeling or sentiment. Even those ideas, which, at first view, seem the most wide of this origin, are found, upon a nearer scrutiny, to be derived from it."⟩ (p. 594). Perfectly easy to find plenty of ideas without corresponding impressions: resemblance etc., cause, existence, substance, probably identity, etc. Hume's normal approach is the other way around—*objecting* to an idea, rejecting or revising it, *because* it has no corresponding set of impressions. E.g., less than two pages farther on (end of section): ⟨"When we entertain … any suspicion that a philosophical term is employed without any meaning or idea (as is but too frequent), we need but inquire, *from what impression is that supposed idea derived?* And if it be impossible to assign any, this will serve to confirm our suspicion."⟩ (pp. 595-96). This is the *inquisition* of which Reid spoke, as quoted by one of

---

[68] ⟨Burtt, ed., *The English Philosophers*, 688. All references to Hume's *Enquiry* are to this text, unless otherwise noted.⟩

the commentators.[69] This pair of passages, two pages apart, a beautiful case of circularity. Actually of course the first passage is the one at fault; Hume's doctrine of ideas copying impressions has no *such* basis, but is his ultimate standard of meaningfulness: his empiricism.

Mid next section (3), surprising remark: "I do not find that any philosopher has attempted to enumerate or class all the principles of association." Seems to overlook Aristotle, who speaks of this subject in terms of principles of *recollection*, in *On Memory and Reminiscence*; as I mentioned before, he is in two-thirds agreement with Hume: resemblance, contiguity, *contrast* (instead of causality).[70]

On last page of section 4 [p. 617] an interesting analogy is drawn by Hume between his doctrine of induction and "pre-established harmony." The allusion is to Leibniz. Leibniz, like Hume, was in trouble over relations. Though Hume was less ready to recognize his trouble. And Leibniz's trouble was for a different reason: not because he wanted his ultimate realities to be simple impressions, but because he wanted them to be simple souls. But the result was the same: no mechanism for connecting them. Leibniz faced it out (unlike Hume with his simple impressions). The problem was: how can souls act on one another, or perceive one another (in particular perceive matter, which after all is a congeries of small souls)? Answer: they can't! Hence no causation or interaction among souls for Leibniz; but they are so created as to go on parallel, like watches synchronized. So this idea of preëstablished harmony is one of the famous ways of dealing with problem of cause or interaction.[71] Another is *occasionalism*, discussed by Hume near end of part 1 of section 7. Doctrine of Malebranche and other followers of Descartes. This is the doctrine mentioned earlier, whereby God is sole cause, and the so-called causes in nature are *occasions* for God to intervene. Thus different from preëstablished harmony.[72]

Since cause is so central to Hume, well to know of these celebrated alternatives. But in particular Hume's cited analogy between preëstablished harmony and his own doctrine of induction puts latter in an interesting light: as if:

—To here July 29

---

[69] ⟨Laird, *Hume's Philosophy*, 25-26. Laird refers to Reid's comment in *An Inquiry into the Human Mind on the Principles of Common Sense*, section 8. See Reid (1710-1796), *Inquiry*, in *The Works of Thomas Reid, D. D.*, ed. Sir William Hamilton. 7th ed. 2 vols. (Edinburgh: Maclachlan and Stewart; London: Longman, Grccn, *et al.*, 1872), 1:144.⟩

[70] ⟨Above, 201.⟩

[71] ⟨E.g., G. W. Leibniz, "Discourse on Metaphysics," and "Correspondence with Arnauld," in idem, *Philosophical Texts*, trans. Richard Francks and R. S. Woolhouse (Oxford: Oxford University Press, 1998).⟩

[72] ⟨Above, n. 7, and 220.⟩

(1) Nature *in fact* goes on in its normal causal ways, but we can't *know* it in any direct sense. (Does Hume believe it does? *Sure*; it's human nature to *believe* it!)

(2) Meanwhile man goes on *believing* in these causal connections, without any access for proper knowledge, because of a *parallel* mechanism in the *mind*, so-called custom! God has preëstablished this harmony between each mind and nature (and therefore, by transitivity, also between the minds!) Quite unexpectedly Leibnizian.

Apart from the points I have touched on, the *Enquiry* in sections 1-7 and also 9 and 12 is mainly a repetition, in rephrased and condensed form, of book 1 of *Treatise*.

Section 8 repeats in effect pp. 399-412 of *Treatise* and adds more. It constitutes a fine little twenty-page essay on freedom of the will. This is a great traditional problem of philosophy. If the events of the world are determined by causal laws, how is the will free to change things? And, if not, how can there be praise and blame, ethics, reward, religion? Hume begins by arguing in support of causal laws, including human actions along with other phenomena. This may seem strange in view of Hume's skepticism over causality, but it needn't. Hume believes in the regularities of nature and counsels us all to, but says they can't be established in any more ultimate terms. It is our nature to believe in them, and he goes on from there. No call to draw line in this respect between objects and persons. And he cites many instances to show that it is common sense to believe in causality among actions, or uniformity of nature including human nature. The unyielding quality of jailer and executioner are as causal as the unyielding quality of the prison walls and the axe; and as predictable. But there is still freedom of the will, in the sense of "*a power of acting or not acting, according to the determinations of the will.*" This fits with determinism; merely that the will is a link in the causal chain. But is determined by earlier links—as indeed is presumed popularly by predictions of action, by psychology of motives, by threat and incentive. Hume goes into the details of such causes of will in *Treatise*, pp. 413-18, and especially book 3. Will consider briefly later.[73]

But, continuing now with section 8 of *Enquiry*: as Hume points out in an interesting footnote, there is a special reason why people are tempted to think the causal chain itself may lapse in human actions: frequent sense of indifference, indecision, *not* being motivated or caused. Yet when we *do* act, we are caused—even if trivially. Here we are feeling as caused

[73] ⟨Below, 243.⟩

things, not as observers of external caused things. Latter method always sustains determinacy, even when directed to ourselves; and former doesn't count—for a caused stone doesn't feel at all. But there is also *another* reason for wanting to think of the will as not only free (in the sense of an effective part of causal chain) but undetermined. This other reason is justification of praise and blame: for how can we praise or blame constrained volitions? Why doesn't all blame go back to God as first cause (if our actions *are* caused) and not to us? This raises the problem of evil: Why isn't God guilty? Hume mentions the optimistic solution: Polyanna, Leibniz, Émile Coué, and Mrs. Eddy. Mrs. Eddy's solution is that there is no evil. Leibniz's is that there is evil, but no more than logically necessary compatibly with greater goods; best of all *possible* worlds. The latter exonerates God, but doesn't explain still why *man* is to be blamed. (Mrs. Eddy's removes the whole problem, but is implausible.)[74]

Hume's answer is that praise and blame are instinctive and ultimate like induction. Mechanism of it—or of our moral standards—is subject of *Treatise*, book 3. Even if we know intellectually that a crime is part of a good whole (he goes on to say in *Enquiry*) we instinctively react against it—as we react with pain against the pulling of a tooth for our general good. Hume leaves it at this. One wonders incidentally how serious he is about his hypothesis that everything is right with regard to the whole.

This was a ticklish religious point which he didn't need to face in this particular connection. But we begin to see what he felt about it on turning to section 11, where he quotes his imaginary friend personifying Epicurus. For his friend argues, and very well, against theological arguments concerning the nature of this world of experience—arguments seeking to picture it as better than it is. Hume's supposititious friend begins by considering the *teleological argument* for existence of God—the argument from design. There is so much system and pattern in the world, surely it couldn't have come about by blind chance. This is the most popular argument down to present day. Another argument, considered earlier, was the *ontological*: existence follows from the definition of God. I have already criticized this; and we saw earlier that Hume rejected it.[75] And

---

[74] ⟨See, e.g., G. W. Leibniz, *Theodicy* (1706). Émile Coué (1857-1926) was a French psychotherapist whose views were fashionable in the 1920s. His pertinent works include *La Maîtrise de soi-même par l'autosuggestion consciente*. Nouv. ed. (Nancy: L'auteur; Paris: Oliven, 1923); and *Self Mastery Through Conscious Autosuggestion* (New York: American Library Service, 1922). Mary Baker Eddy (1821-1910), founder of the Christian Science movement, articulated her doctrine that there is no evil in *Science and Health with Key to the Scriptures* (Boston: Christian Scientist Publishing Co., 1875).⟩

[75] ⟨Above, 184-85 and 214, respectively.⟩

recurs in *Dialogues*.[76]

A third well-known one is the *cosmological*—that of first cause. Everything must have a cause, therefore the totality of events in the world must as a whole have a first cause. It is defined as God. This is really a part of the teleological argument, in that the latter also takes God as cause, but argues further that this cause, God, must be intelligent and purposeful in view of the evidence of design in the world. Actually the cosmological argument itself has a conspicuous flaw. By the same reasoning that the totality of the world must have a cause (*viz.* that anything has a cause), we could ask in turn for the cause of God. If it is a satisfactory answer to say that God is self-caused, or eternal and therefore uncaused, why not say this of the world itself in the first place?

The teleological argument, or argument from design, is free from this defect. It is—as Hume recognizes—a purely empirical argument, like any argument in natural science. We see that, in general, where there are marks of intricate organization there is a designing mind behind the thing. (Or do we? Surely most cases of intricate organization, from snow crystals to living animals, are not man made; to suppose design is to beg the question.) But suppose we do; this is, if justifiable at all, an empirical generalization. And existence of God is inferred from it as an empirical conjecture.

In the section, 11, under consideration, Hume stresses this empirical character, but declines to say whether he feels it is a *bad* empirical argument, *bad* science. Discussion of this topic is not needed for the point he is going to make regarding optimism. He reserves appraisal of the teleological argument to *Dialogues concerning Natural Religion*, sheltering himself, there as in section 11, behind a fictitious anonymity. In section 11, for sake of argument, the teleological argument is accepted. And it is agreed that the Creator would have indeed to be ingenious and able—really inconceivably so—to produce so remarkable a world. But then how do people argue for optimism—that it is the best of all possible worlds, or that there are better things to come, rewards for the just, etc.? On the ground that so good a Deity, and so powerful a one, would not find it in him to leave all the imperfections and injustices which we seem to find in the world; he must have made adjustments, of a kind that it is not given us to see, but only to infer from God's attributes. And how did we infer God's attributes? From the nature of the observed world which he designed. How, then, are we warranted in arguing that God's attributes are really such as to lead him to make the world *better* than we observe

---

[76] ⟨Possibly Quine had in mind Hume, *Dialogues concerning Natural Religion*, part 9, in Burtt, ed., *The English Philosophers*, 734f.⟩

it?—Here is the main point of section 11.

It is remarkable enough that God was able to make as ingenious a world as this one as we know it; and perhaps it is remarkable that God was benevolent enough to put as much good in the world as we can actually observe in it—though this point is more tenuous. But what ground for inferring that God is even more skillful and even more benevolent than needed for those already incredible achievements—and hence concluding that the world is really even better than it looks? The net content of such an argument is that, because the world looks as good as it does, it must be even better than it looks; and such reasoning is quite lacking in empirical basis, direct or indirect.

—To here July 31

The general tenor of section 11 is that it is a lost cause to try to establish religious tenets by reasoned argument, *a priori* or *inductive*. Section 10 on miracles takes the same line. It is the nature of a miracle to be—other things being equal—incredible; and we have *real* evidence for believing it only if the evidence in favor is so strong that it would be just as much of a miracle for that evidence to exist *without* the alleged miracle as with it. This doesn't in fact happen; testimony can be wrong unmiraculously—especially remote testimony, remote from us and/or from the fact reported.

All of this may be viewed as argument against religion. Actually it is argument against both *deductive* and *naturalistic arguments* for religion. It is argument that the only way to religion is a third, independent one: *faith*. And there are plenty of theologians who are in full agreement with Hume on this point. Hume says of divinity and theology, at very end of *Enquiry*: "its best and most solid foundation is *faith* and divine revelation."[77]

It is especially noteworthy in Hume's case that he is not being any rougher on religion than on science!—for science also rests ultimately on *faith* in inductive principles incapable of non-inductive substantiation. Faith which, in the latter case, has a mechanism consisting in *custom*; but this is no justification; anything has *some* mechanism. Pinning things on faith doesn't mean *rejection* by Hume. He is all in favor of induction, and admits to it; it is even his method in the empirical psychology that constitutes much of the *Treatise*.

So it doesn't mean rejection of religion. Does *he* accept it on faith just as he does induction? Could. Of course not quite free to say he doesn't. But he doesn't close his eyes to the fact that there *is* conflict between science and religion, anyway a natural religion that talks about miracles or

[77] ⟨In Burtt, ed., *The English Philosophers*, 689.⟩

otherwise makes counter-scientific statements about the world. Such was the religion of his day, and the fundamentalism of today, and much even of more moderated religions. There is such conflict, and, insofar, it is a conflict between faiths; not between faith and reason, or between faith and science, but between faith and faith; for scientific method itself goes back to faith of its own kind, in the form of acquiescence in the mechanism of custom.

So it is a small miracle, as Hume says (end section 10), when we allow religious faith to supervene over scientific faith in cases of conflict. Which is *right* it is, presumably, impossible to say except *from a scientific point of view* or *from a religious point of view*. We may prefer the one, insist on it, despise those who deviate from it in favor of the other; but there is no higher court. Such is Hume's skepticism.

As applied to science it is the doctrine of *positivism*: it is vain to seek certainty behind science (the problem I spoke of at the beginning of the course), vain to seek a foundation for science beyond science itself. Summed up at end of *Enquiry*: ⟨"While we cannot give a satisfactory reason, why we believe, after a thousand experiments, that a stone will fall, or fire burn; can we ever satisfy ourselves concerning any determination, which we may form, with regard to the origin of worlds, and the situation of nature, from, and to eternity?"⟩ [*Enquiry* pp. 687-88; cf. p. 689.]

Book 2 of *Treatise*: When Hume divided the impressions into those of sensation and those of reflection in book. 1, he had little to say of latter; reserved to book. 2. Now he elaborates his classification, insofar as concerns impressions of reflection, as follows:[78]

ideas	impressions			
	original *(sensation)*	secondary *(reflection)*		
		emotions *(calm)*	passions *(violent)*	
		[sense of beauty and deformity]	direct *(from pain or pleasure alone)*	indirect *(from same in conjunction with other qualities)*

Takes up the psychology of origins of impressions of reflection. Omits that of impressions of sensation because not mental enough for him;

---

[78] ⟨This tabular classification is written on Quine's copy of Hume's *Treatise*, 275; i.e. at the opening of Book 2.⟩

physical and physiological, insofar as there is anything to be said of origins.

Part 1 of book 2 devoted to one pair of impressions of reflection: passions of pride and humility. Opposites, but paired: same *object*: self. Since pride differs from humility, *causes* differ; therefore cause is not *object*. (Also: if cause were self, pride and humility would be perpetual.) Relation to *object* is not of effect to cause, but a kind of association: 'turning our view to.' Foot p. 278: "the productive principle.... ⟨e⟩xcites the passion, connected with it; and that passion, when excited, turns our view to another idea, which is that of self.... the one produces ... [the passion], and the other is produc'd by it. The first idea ... represents the *cause*, the second the *object* of the passion." The pointing to self is "not only by a natural but also by an original property" (p. 280); i.e., ultimate, no further resolution; we merely observe that it always happens—like association of ideas.

It *isn't* a *case* of old association of ideas; is it a sign of omission from earlier account thereof? This is not *association in imagination*, but evocation of an idea by an impression; but no excuse, because same is true of the regular association. Commonly: *impression* evokes an *idea* in *imagination* by resemblance, contiguity, etc. Here we evidently have, in pride → self, *another* ultimate principle of association, along with contiguity and resemblance? Similarly for humility. And similarly for many others, e.g. (Hume says) hunger → idea of food. Something different, all this, from what Hume calls association of ideas. More forceful and less controllable, perhaps. ("Association" was a "gentle force.") It is an additional, irreducible factor in Hume's dynamics of perceptions, *besides* association.

Now to *causes*, as against *objects*, of pride and humility.

Causes: valuable and/or undesirable *qualities*.

Subjects: that in which those causative qualities inhere (own mind, body, possessions, etc.).

So object is *self*, i.e. total train of perceptions; causes are qualities, i.e. abstract ideas. No such things really, but we can easily see what Hume means: review his account of cause:

(instances of quality a)	(instances of pride)
a_1	p_1
a_2	p_2
.	.
.	.
.	.
a_n	p_n

By his literal terminology, each *instance* of the quality *a* causes pride, and they are *similar* to one another. The *respect of similarity* is quality *a*, if we admit qualities for the moment; and Hume *loosely* says now the *quality* is the cause. Not really even as loose as it looks, for Hume, because to speak of an abstract idea is *really* (he holds) to speak of any one of its instances. But it does mean that the causes coalesce with the subjects! Add to this a further complication in that the subjects aren't perceptions but extended objects (or self)? But for Hume these *are* same, and it is rather the so-called identity of an extended object with itself that he repudiates.

But, phrasing causes of pride and humility in terms of *qualities*, as Hume does, next note that not *all* qualities cause pride and humility. Only those which cause *pleasure* and/or *pain*, which are *sensations* (p. 285). And not all these, always, but only when inhering in a subject 'part of ourselves or nearly related.'

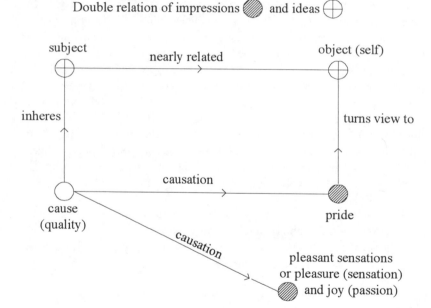

Double relation of impressions ◉ and ideas ⊕

Now what of this relation between subject and object of pride? Sometimes *very* near: sheer identity. As where cause is virtue (vice for humility parallel), or beauty of own person (deformity for humility parallel). Or external: object is property, or a blood-relation, or a product of own workmanship, or native land, or a man whom the object physically resembles. Closer the relation, stronger or more likely the pride. Note that, from point of view of a rigorous formulation, no sharp line between case where object is identical with subject and case where not. For should we say the cause (quality) is elegance and the subject possessions, or the cause (quality) is wealth and the subject self? Or again: cause (quality) is refinement and beauty of city, etc., and subject is Boston, or subject is self (as object) and quality is that of being Bostonian? Any quality of an object related to *s* (self) *is* another quality of *s*, unless we have a standard of intrinsic *vs.* extrinsic—which Hume tacitly assumes. Common sense to assume it, but how formulate? Oh well.[79]

How would it be in terms of sheer impressions and ideas, rather than qualities and enduring physical objects? [Re-doing above diagram.] Let's give special license to "self," otherwise can't do much.

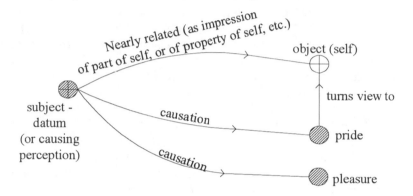

How *close* this relation between subject and object of pride? Section 6:

   I. Closer than for joy. (Because joy is easier, having only a subject and not also an object to enliven.)

   II. Oligopoly on the subject. (Otherwise, perhaps, the *self* isn't limned so clearly; weaken association of ideas.) Hume seems to put insufficient emphasis on superiority — *invidious* comparisons — which is so much of the essence of pride. For his system it is rather incidental—merely a means to *accentuating* the *self-association* by method of differences or contrast from other persons.

—To here August 2

---

[79] ⟨On a separate unnumbered card Quine included a précis of a twenty-minute presentation on Hume's doctrine of double relations given by a graduate student in the course, Robert Yost: "In theory of passions, Hume's 'double relation' seems to have two meanings: (1) p. 284, where he summarizes his basic principles, doubleness is: (a) passions related by similar affective tone, (b) causes of them related by inherence in same subject; (2) elsewhere, e.g., p. 289, where e.g. pride is made to involve doubleness, it is in (a) as before. (b) inherence of cause in subject closely related to self (to which passion 'points'). Not clear how pride can partake of (1). Strength of pride is attributed to doubleness—hence presumably (2); but (2) is not in his basic principles. Or does (1) equal (2) finally?"⟩

Last time, began considering respects in which relation between subject and object of pride (or humility) must be close. Saw two:

I. Closer than for joy.

II. Such that the subject (or other things having same quality, i.e. cause) bears the relation to few if any persons other than the self.

Hume mentions three more:

III. Other people must enjoy the subject.

IV. Connection must be firm and lasting.

V. Connection gains by fitting general laws—i.e. by falling under an already conceived type which usually fits I - IV. (Rank, etc.)

Both IV and V are familiar factors in strengthening an association. But how does III work? Due to *sympathy*. Other person's enjoyment of object enhances our own, for we *sympathize* and thus imbibe part of his pleasure to add to our own; thus one of the components of the pride-complex (*viz.* causing pleasure) is increased, increasing whole.

What *is* sympathy? How does it work? Manifestations of feelings in others are, for us, associated with the feelings themselves, because of past contiguity between such feelings and similar outward manifestations observed in our own bodies. So the feelings are vividly associated, therefore present in imagination (standard association theory of Hume). But then a special added event: *they are turned into impressions and felt* (p. 317). Here is a turning of the tables: impressions copying ideas. (But not in the first place, of course.) A mysterious transmutation. Hume had indeed provided for causing of impressions of reflection by ideas; but didn't lead us to expect it to be a copying. Just an ultimate phenomenon that Hume observes; no question of explanation needed. Seems to happen primarily or exclusively with passions; thus (p. 353) "Every lively idea is agreeable [odd], but especially that of a passion, because such an idea becomes a kind of a passion, and gives a more sensible agitation to the mind, than any other image or conception." Fits pretty well with rest of Hume's psychology. Difference between idea and impression is only vivacity. If idea of a passion becomes more lively, e.g. through association (by past uniform contiguity, or cause) with outward manifestations in another person, perhaps the increased liveliness of the idea will be enough to push it over into the impression category—just a matter of degree.

Why only passions, and not also sensations? Two possible answers why *not*, plus a third answer: that it *can* happen also to sensations.

1) Perhaps the manifestations of passions in others are a much better association than anything we can find for sensations. People don't manifest latter. Nearest they can come is describe in words. If anyone were artist enough with words maybe he could bring it off—and give us sensation of taste of a boiled potato by sheer

description. But writers aren't that good.

2) (better) *Resistance* to letting an idea of a sensation get vivid to the point of being an impression, because of our systematization of impressions of sense into a physical world. There is no comparable systematization of passions, so no such resistance. And this brings us to—

3) Sometimes, if people don't set as much store by systematization as we do, an idea of sensation *does* make the grade and become an impression! So-called hallucination, and insanity—disorganization of the systematization of impressions. Happens also in dreams. Sleep is a relaxation of our pursuit of system; a normal periodical insanity.

Hume should have allowed for copying of ideas into impressions *generally*, and at the beginning. Departing thus from doctrine of impressions of sensation always being caused outside; but not dangerously—because he can still say that the *first* event in any set of qualitatively like impression events *is* caused from outside; though another of the set *may* be caused from inside by copying the copy. This would rub out the main line dividing impressions of sensation from impressions of reflection, but so much the better. And it would make a virtue of what Hume, in book 1, felt to be a slight imperfection—the question of hallucinations as seeming to blur his conception of impressions *vs*. ideas.

So *sympathy* is the contagion of another's passion—through our associating so vividly to his manifestations as to bring the idea of the passion up to impression strength. But we can also get the effect without help of another's *manifestations*; but only seeing a causal *situation*. Example on p. 385, foot: man asleep, in danger of being trampled. No reason why this association by causality shouldn't also vivify idea to the point of impression of sorrow, if seeing another's manifestations can do it. Sympathy is needed, we have seen, in explaining pride and humility; *viz.*, to explain why these are increased when other people enjoy (and/or suffer from) the *subject*.

Hume also makes much further use of sympathy. He uses it to explain the gregariousness of the human animal, p. 363: ⟨"In all creatures, that prey not upon others, and are not agitated with violent passions, there appears a remarkable desire of company, which associates them together, without any advantages they can ever propose to reap from their union. This is still more conspicuous in man, as being the creature of the universe, who has the most ardent desire of society, and is fitted for it by the most advantages.... A perfect solitude is, perhaps, the greatest punishment we can suffer. Every pleasure languishes when enjoy'd a-part from company, and every pain becomes more cruel and intolerable."⟩

Something wrong here: why pain more cruel alone? Why not less, since unaccentuated by sympathy with pain in others (supposing a generally unpleasant situation, not just a pain in the one person)? Recalls also the old statement p. 353, where he was also discussing gregariousness: "Every lively idea is agreeable." There is something in this; grief is more agreeable than depression, apathy. There is an agreeable quality to tragedy, because of vividness, despite disagreeableness of the content of the ideas. Maybe liveliness is itself, other things being equal, pleasant rather than neutral, and maybe this is ultimate; such is Hume's notion.

Hume uses sympathy also as basis for some queer ideas on aesthetics: Back on pp. 298ff. his basic views on beauty appear: the instances of beauty are those visual qualities which cause pleasure. (Or: those perceptions, having visual qualities such that all perceptions having these visual qualities cause pleasure.) Similarly for deformity, in relation to pain.

—To here August 5

This much seems all right. But *how* does beauty give pleasure? E.g. functional beauty: comfort, convenience. But not *this* pleasure to *me*, if not mine—unless by *sympathy* (p. 364). Similarly personal beauty, largely health and vigor. Again by sympathy; indeed a case of functionality. Also there are other standards of beauty than functionality. Typically, *balance*. This he explains (p. 364) again by sympathy: conveys ideas of fall, harm, pain. What we would call *em*pathy, not sympathy, not sharing feelings of owner of the beautiful or ugly object, but imagining feelings of *being* the object. (Likewise for personal beauty as health-functionality.) But this distinction needless here; Hume's account covers all such cases under sympathy. Present case is type of man in fall; idea of pain is vivified to impression not by seeing manifestations of the feeling, but by seeing causes calculated to bring it about (trampling, toppling). But this is far-fetched. If we can vivify the idea of painful fall to an impression of pain by looking at a lop-sided design, we surely ought to be able to get an *impression* of the taste of a boiled potato from a very middling verbal description. And what then of the beauty of balance—giving impression of pleasure of *not* toppling? But this is an impression that we don't even get from *real* non-toppling. Hume's sympathy is getting badly overworked.

Main topic of part 2 (of book 2) is love and hatred. Hume's theory is that these are like pride and humility, but that the *object* is other than self. All the rest stands: subject, cause (quality), causing of pleasure, relation of subject and object.

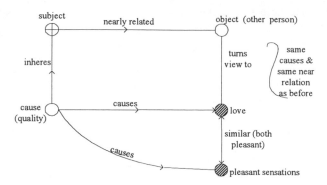

This link between pleasure (or pleasant sensations) and pride should also be drawn into the old diagram. It is what makes for the *double relation* that Hume so often refers to (e.g. p. 333): "of ideas [subject] to the object of the passion, and sensations [pleasant] to the passion itself." So, Hume says, pride, humility, love, hatred form a square:

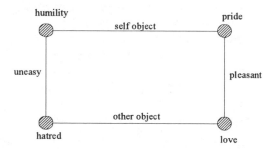

Then there is *this* connection, also, between love and pride: love of a near relation (admiration, etc.) induces also pride, since the 'turning view to object' goes on easily to self. And the 'near relation' of subject to object is a fairly near relation to self. Hume says easier in this direction than opposite, because near relation etc. reminds us of (or 'turns view to') self more easily than *vice versa*. This is because mind passes more easily from remote to near than *vice versa*; likewise it passes more easily from less important to more important; perhaps because latter is intrinsically more vivid and therefore takes less associative power to make it vivid enough for awareness. "Whatever has the greatest influence is most taken notice of; and whatever is most taken notice of, presents itself most readily to the imagination" (p. 342).

Since love (and hatred) can vary as to object, a new consideration arises not operative in pride (and humility): love can transfer to a different object closely related to the first, since the needed *near relation* between subject and object will often hold almost as nearly to the new, related object.

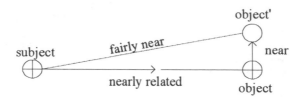

And, since attention goes more easily to the near or important than to the far and unimportant, this transfer (*directing the view* onward to new object) should be easier from less to great than *vice versa*. Yet, says Hume, the reverse is the case: more easily love son on account of loving father; servant on account of master; etc., than *vice versa*. Reason is lame: p. 344: love of an important person is *ipso facto* the greater, so there is more of it to spread to lesser connections than *vice versa*. Why wouldn't (contrary to Hume) pride, for the same reason, diffuse itself into love?

Love and hatred carry with them another pair of passions: *benevolence* and *anger*. These are "originally" conjoined to love and hatred; no further explanation; ultimate. He includes various further descriptive details of love and hatred, mostly quite plausibly: That the reason we love more for deliberate benefits than for accidental ones, because evidence of a *lasting* disposition in the person to be beneficial. Item IV of the five features of the "narrow relation" as described for pride (and carried over for love). That we love relatives or old friends more than strangers because of durability; same IV again. And other points, of less philosophical than psychological interest.

Sympathy comes in again, as basis for our love of the rich and powerful; gives reasons to believe this more central than expectation of benefits. And sympathy operates directly, of course, to explain passion of *pity*. Indeed, same thing? No, a passion added to the sympathetically contrasted impression of sorrow. For, the same sympathetically imbibed impression can be accompanied by a passion opposite to pity, *viz. malice*. Like love and hate, pity and malice have subject and object; same structure; only the associated sensations are unpleasant. But in the case of malice, while the associated sensations are unpleasant, the quality of the passion itself is *pleasant*. Why this? And *envy* is in a like and opposite state: sensations pleasant, passion unpleasant. Essentially, explains them in terms of pride and humility, by a new principle of *relativity*: magnitude or strength or vividness of an impression is increased by contrast.

Hume's example: warm and cool hand, put in same water; water feels cool and warm respectively. Another example he might have cited: after-images, opposite to original. How does this explain malice? Our own pleasures seem *more* pleasant in contrast to the bad lot of the object of malice. Thence the pleasure investing malice. Increase in pride. And envy? Our own pleasures seem less pleasant (or pains greater) in contrast to the happy lot of the object of envy. Thence the pain investing envy. Increase in humility. Sometimes we get malice and envy, sometimes pity or sympathetic joy. Both opposite forces are at work; what decides? Their relative strength in the given case. Sympathy can be increased by vividness—sight of the suffering, extremeness of it, etc.; and the opposite—the factor of contrast with our state—can be increased by closeness of parallelism, facilitating the comparison and contrast.

—To here August 7

Review division,[80] for there is yet a further one: direct-indirect. Foregoing—pride, humility, love, hatred, pity, malice, envy, etc., were indirect: depended on relations over and above pain and pleasure-giving. Direct: desire, aversion; grief, joy; hope, fear. And the *will*: "*the internal impression we feel ... when we knowingly give rise to any new motion of our body, or new perception of our mind*" (p. 399). *Internal* impression. Sensation or reflection? Latter, presumably; emotion or passion (calm or violent)? He hedges: "and tho', properly speaking, it be not comprehended among the passions" (p. 399). This is subjunctive; not a flat denial. And on p. 438 he comes out with the affirmative: volition is a passion, and indeed a direct passion. And certainly volition is will, especially in view of foregoing definition of will.

Next he argues the freedom (or efficacy) of will *and* the fact that the will is caused—as already seen in *Enquiry*.[81] And goes on to consider in detail *how* the will is caused. On this subject his important thesis is that man is *not* a rational animal in the sense of being guided primarily by reason; on the contrary, (1) "reason alone can never be a motive to any action of the will," and (2) "it can never oppose passion in the direction of the will" (p. 413). Reason never enters except occasional or an engineering basis—finding means. "Reason is, and ought only to be the slave of the passions" (p. 415). Passion, he argues, is "original," copying nothing in nature; therefore irrelevant to reason, and incapable of contradicting it—except in the case of a misconception of fact causing a passion. Only in this, and in engineering, is the reason relevant. We *think* reason guides actions more than it really does, because we confuse calm

[80] ⟨Above, 234.⟩
[81] As on ⟨230-31 above.⟩

desires with reason. So study of causes of will becomes first a study of causes of direct passions generally. Hume begins with the violent and what turns a calm passion (or emotion?) into a violent one.

Passions readily unite; the stronger gaining added strength from the force of the weaker. "⟨A⟩ny *attendant emotion is easily converted into the predominant.*" Opposition and uncertainty increase passions. Ultimate observation? No explanation. "*Puts spirits in agitation.*" *Custom* has an *ultimate* tendency, other things being equal, to make us (a) do things more easily, (b) incline to things (cf. nostalgia). Contrary to uncertainty, spirits subside. *Surprise*, contrariwise, by force of uncertainty, augments passions generally, including unpleasant ones. Also surprise is *cœteris paribus* pleasant. (Because increased vividness is pleasant? And surprise is a sudden [ultimate] attraction of attention?) Another force that strengthens passions is *imagination*. For, passion depends on the contemplation of the subject in idea (impressions of reflection, caused by ideas of subject), so naturally vivified by increase of this component. Hume doesn't avail himself of this obvious explanation, but asks merely if the effect of imagination on passions proceeds from the principle "*any attendant emotion is easily converted into the predominant*" (p. 424). In particular then contiguity in space and time, on the part of the subject, are a force for strengthening passions. For, these strengthen imagination. Ultimately, laws of association. How about "absence makes the heart grow fonder?" Hume would have a pat explanation here too: uncertainty. But looks like contradiction. Maybe explanation is: uncertainty on anything tends to heighten *all* present passions on whatever subject; but increased clarity of knowledge or imagination of the subject heightens particular passion toward that subject. This would be consistent, but there is some question how fully it fits experience.

Then (pp. 438ff.) to main lines again: *all passions are founded on pain and pleasure.* Their subjects are always goods and evils (construed, as Hume does, hedonistically). Mind has *original* tendency to seek pleasure and avoid pain.

	GOOD	EVIL
Direct passion from certain or probable	JOY	SORROW
Direct passion from uncertain	HOPE	FEAR
Direct passion from good or evil apart from *expecting* (respectively)	DESIRE	AVERSION

These latter directly actuate the WILL.

Book II ends with a rather appendicial little section on curiosity, or love of truth. Says the search for truth is essentially the same, in its motivational structure, with *hunting*. The *chase*. This point of view is reflected interestingly in Portuguese: the word for research is *pesquisa*. Not hunting, exactly, but what it does suggest is *fishing*: *pesca*. Same in Spanish. (My Portuguese etymologist proposes an unrelated etymology, but I should like to suppose he is wrong.) Why like hunting? Pleasure consists in the action, attention, difficulty, uncertainty—yet at the same time there must be an *idea* of utility, though it be only token. Why pleasant? Uncertainty makes for more forcefulness of feelings generally; discovery makes for increased vividness of an idea; latter (said Hume earlier) is *cæteris paribus* pleasant; and pleasantness augmented by general agitating effect of previous or concurrent uncertainty. And maybe (Hume says little of all this) utility is needed in order that the uncertainty be serious and thus effective as agitating spirits and enlivening passions. Queer he doesn't mention pride as a factor.

Turning in book 3 to Moral distinctions—virtue *vs.* vice—Hume asks whether these are based on reason or passions. We know what his answer will be, having seen the corresponding answer to the question of the determinant of the will. Passions. In this he contradicts much of the tradition, including Locke, who comes in for anonymous mention p. 463: ⟨"There has been an opinion very industriously propagated by certain philosophers, that morality is susceptible of demonstration; and tho' no one has ever been able to advance a single step in those demonstrations; yet 'tis taken for granted, that this science may be brought to an equal certainty with geometry or algebra."⟩ Locke had asserted (*Essay*, 1.3) that moral rules are capable of strict demonstration, but never got around to it, despite pressure e.g. of Molyneux: ⟨"Writing to ... ⟨Locke⟩ on the subject of the Essay in general ... Molyneux observes: 'One thing I must needs insist on to you, which is, that you would think of obliging the world with a treatise of morals, drawn up according to the hints you frequently give in your Essay, of their being demonstrable according to the mathematical method....' To which Locke replies, 'Though by the view I had of moral ideas, while I was considering that subject, I thought I saw that morality might be demonstratively made out; yet whether I am able so to make it out is another question.... to show my readiness to obey your commands, I shall not decline the first leisure I can get, to employ some thoughts that way....' With this half-promise Mr. Molyneux was not content, but in a letter written shortly after again urges the philosopher to set about a system of ethics. 'There remains only,' he says, 'that I again put you in mind of ... Practica, or ethics: you cannot imagine what an earnest desire and expectation I have raised in those that are acquainted with your writings, by the hopes I have given them, from your promise of endeavour⟨i⟩ing something on that subject. Good sir, let me renew my requests to you therein; for believe me, sir, ⟨'twill⟩ be one of the most useful and glorious undertakings that can employ you....' Locke,

however, after further solicitation from his friend, finally excused himself
... for not entering upon the undertaking.")[82]

But Hume argues it can't be done. Roughly his argument is that he sees
no way it could be done. He breaks this argument into two parts:

> (1) Distinction between good and evil belongs to actions of mind in
>   relation to external objects—obviously: willed action in world
>   situations. But (p. 465) he is at a loss to find such a relation.

Lamely put—but of the essence of his really soundest arguments all down
the line: necessary connection, substance, rational willing: that there *is*
nothing that anyone can show, just declamation.

> (2) Even if there were such relations, and the distinction between
>   good and evil were thus drawn by reason, how could good gain its
>   *obligatory* character? This would still have to be irrational.

His point in brief is that *should* has to be irrational, because reason can
only push it back: *should in order that*. But why *should* the latter in turn
be achieved? Reason can only say: *in order that*. Infinite regress. We have
to cut the series: an ultimate *duty* not dictated by reason must be the end of
the line. Point of view regarding will, book 2, is exactly the same: reason
can answer why do you *want* to do this? only by saying "Because it will
bring that about." Why do you want that brought about? Same old regress.
We must cut the sequence, saying "Just because I want to;" "just because
I like it." Sheer taste, finally, that which reason serves as an engineer.
And similarly for right and wrong: non-rational moral sense, finally,
which reason serves as engineer.

Case is parallel even in Hume's doctrine of cause and induction.
Scientific method can answer "Why is such-and-such a method of inquiry
or statistics sound?" Because it has always worked;" or, "Follows from
such and such general principle—uniformity of nature, etc.—which is
attested by experience." Asked how past experience can give us any
assurance that this method will continue to work, or that the uniformity of
nature will continue, scientific method can only say: "Generally things
long observed to work have continued." Same question can be asked
again. We must cut the series, saying "I've become used to expecting this
sort of thing." Sheer custom. Reason in science goes back to *custom*,
which is ultimate. Reason in volition goes back to *taste*. Reason in ethics
goes back to *moral sense*.

This attitude of irrationalism regarding the basis of will and virtue,
Hume seems to have got from Francis Hutcheson; and Kemp Smith argues
pretty convincingly that this part of the *Treatise* was done before Book 1.
He argues that Book 1, Hume's significant and revolutionary theory of

---

[82] ⟨Locke, *Works*, 1: 155, 156 n.⟩

knowledge, came as an extension of Hutcheson's theory of value: theory that all value depends finally on feeling, not reason.[83] Now what is this moral sense? "To have the sense of virtue, is nothing but to *feel* a satisfaction of a particular kind from the contemplation of a character" (p. 471). It is a form of pleasure. Good music, Hume says, affords one kind of pleasure, and is called *harmonious*; good wine affords a second kind, and is called *savory*; and good character affords a third kind, and is called *virtuous*. Three kinds of pleasure among many. Actually, even music may afford more than one kind of pleasure, being both harmonious and lively; and wine may afford more than one kind, being both savory and intoxicating; and likewise a character may afford more than one kind, being both virtuous and amusing, or picturesque, romantic, etc. So he must single out what pleasure it is in particular which is produced by contemplation of a character insofar as it is *virtuous*. Can't single it out except by pointing to things characteristic of it: the peculiar kind which makes us *praise*; and vice *condemn*.

When we praise or blame, we refer only to *motives*, not *actions* (p. 477). Therefore those aspects of character which admit of *virtue* (and *vice*)—which excite that *kind* of pleasure (and pain) in us—are *motives*. Therefore "*no action can be virtuous ... unless there be ... some motive to produce it, distinct from the sense of its morality*" (p. 479). Why distinct? Otherwise circularity: sense of its morality is sense of the morality of the motive. If the motive *makes* the action moral, the morality can't underlie the motive.

—To here August (9)

This last quotation was from p. 479—beginning part 2. But now, to see the mechanism of the moral sense at its clearest, let's skip to part 3; afterward returning to part 2, which, dealing with "artificial" virtues, is less direct. Saw that the traits of character that can be called *virtuous* or *vicious* (a) give pleasure or pain, but also (b) have to do with *motives*. *Actions* are relevant to moral judgments only as evidence of motives (p. 575). Examples of virtues (p. 578): meekness, beneficence, charity, generosity, clemency, moderation. The *actions* issuing from such virtues are such as to give us pleasure; but the special meaning of *virtue* is that it is the possession of *motives for* such actions; such motives, evincing an enduring disposition, serve to make us value the person's character as a lasting source of these benefits. The pleasures coming from the actions

---

[83] ⟨Kemp Smith, *The Philosophy of David Hume*, 12-51. Francis Hutcheson (1694-1746), *An Inquiry into the Original of Our Ideas of Beauty and Virtue* (London, 1725); and *An Essay on the Nature and Conduct of the Passions, with Illustrations on the Moral Sense* (London, 1728).⟩

themselves are of two kinds: *direct* (e.g. generosity and clemency work to our gain when directed on us) and *sympathetic*: pleasure from the pleasure which these bestow on other people when directed on them. Our pleasure is greater, of course, when we are the direct beneficiary; and greater, through sympathy, when beneficiary other than self is near, or loved; and greater when agent has power to *act* on his motives than when he hasn't. But the *virtue* is the *same*; and insofar as our pleasure is to be classified as *moral sense*—approbation—*it* is the same. But this is only because of the meaning of "virtue:" general traits of character: *that part* of our valuing of a person which corresponds to rules of motivation of his actions. (Such is trend of pp. 581-85.) Differences of pleasure in other respects are just non-moral; moral sense is, by the mere meaning of the word, marked off in a more inclusive sense.

—To here August 12

Case is same (as Hume says, p. 582) with *beauty*: the functionality which often underlies beauty gives more pleasure when we are the direct beneficiary, or someone with whom we have strong sympathy, than otherwise; indeed the pleasure afforded by the beautiful object is, insofar, greater; but the object is said to be equally beautiful regardless—as if what we call *sense of beauty* were, by the usage of the word, limited to *that part* of our pleasure which remains common under such changes of direct beneficiaries. Except, of course—which Hume omits to mention—the identity of the beneficiary *in relation to agent* (not in relation to me as judge of virtue). Thus a man is the more magnanimous for helping someone who has injured him.

Sense of beauty and sense of virtue are alike in this abstracting from special circumstances. The residue rests on recognition of *causal efficacy* by general rules, and not counting in special additional circumstances such as identity of beneficiary (friend or foe) or actual applicability (whether people are *allowed* to sit in the functionally beautiful armchair; whether the virtuous man is able to execute his good purposes [p. 585]). All that is said of virtue of course applies equally and oppositely to vice: vicious motives lead to actions giving pain, either by direct action or sympathetically by giving pain to someone else. But, insofar as vicious, considered in abstraction from identity of victim (except in relation to agent—e.g. matricide). Also, pain and pleasure must here be taken algebraically: lessening of pain counts as pleasure, and makes for virtuousness of a motive; and *vice versa*.

And now Hume takes up the question of *pride and humility* from the moral standpoint; previously his concern had been merely with them as passions, respectively pleasant and unpleasant, but without regard to right and wrong. Now why is humility a virtue—or, let us say, pride a vice? I.e., why does pride (on the part of others) lead to actions painful to us or others? Because, as Hume stressed in discussing passions, our impressions are relative: heightened by contrast, diminished by lack of contrast. (After-image.) Manifestation of pride by another lowers, by contrast, our self-esteem; he leads our attention to the alleged good points of himself, and by contrast our own good points are less vivid to us. So *we* suffer pain of humility. (Not *only* by contrast, but also because our pride depended also on few people *sharing* the thing that caused our pride; one of Hume's old four points on the near relation between subject and object of pride.) Pride in others is vicious, because painful to us, because conducive to humility in us, which is a painful *passion*. But two moral precepts come out of this analysis: (1) Pride, when backed up by genuine possession of the qualities of which one is proud, is less vicious, because our humility-pain may be partly offset by *love* of the person for those qualities, or *sympathy* with his being so fortunate. But not entirely; still room for envy. (2) Pride *concealed* is no vice at all, because what we don't know won't hurt us. So the only humility which is a virtue, by *these* particular considerations, is that to which we are enjoined by good breeding.

So far, a virtue is a pattern of motivation which, in others, causes pleasure in us; algebraically; directly or sympathetically; and a vice, pain. But, Hume points out (pp. 587-90 and 606-614), even this is broader than customary usage, which distinguishes between moral virtues and *natural abilities*: prudence, temperance, frugality, industry, assiduity, enterprize, dexterity. This subsidiary distinction can be drawn in this way, mainly: the natural abilities give pleasure directly to him who has them; and to us by sympathy with him; while the moral virtues give pleasure directly to others than him who has them—and thus to us directly or by sympathy with them. But this is not quite coincident with the common classification, because e.g. assiduity or dexterity on the part of another may be *also directly* to our benefit. And there is one so-called natural ability, *wit*, which *primarily and directly* gives pleasure to others than him who has the ability. Hume's main conclusion is that the division between moral virtues and natural abilities is a fuzzy and inessential one. As to "good or ill desert of virtue or vice" (p. 591), the mechanism is via love and hatred. Hume's treatment of the latter passions provided that virtue is a cause of love and vice of hatred (because of causing pleasure and pain); and that wanting to confer pleasure on object of love and pain on object of hatred is "original" with those passions.

Having done with virtues and vices of the basic kind for Hume, called "natural," let's turn back to part 2 to consider others which present additional problem. The prototype is the virtue of *justice*, as Hume calls it, or *equity*—in the special sense of respect for property. What *virtuous motive* for an honest act? Public interest? Too remote. Benefit of individual object of the act? No, because honesty differs from generosity and benevolence. Solution: no "natural" motive for equity, no simple passion. Equity is one of the *artificial* virtues, couched in social custom, learned from our fellows. An imposed norm. Natural only in that a society is a natural phenomenon; artificial in that it is not instinctive, but taught to us.

Following in its main lines the social contract theory of Thomas Hobbes (a century before Hume), and Locke, he accounts for the morality of honesty as an institution developed by society for mutual benefit—protection of the property of each. So it is a case of engineering: reason enters as a means, to serve the general end of security of property. The means devised is "a convention enter'd into by all the members of the society" (p. 489). So, "*'tis only from the selfishness and confin'd generosity of men, along with the scanty provision nature has made for his wants, that justice derives its origin*" (p. 495). Among people benevolently disposed to one another, or in plenty, or both, justice is no virtue.

How do the senses of virtue and vice come to attach to these artificial or conventional norms? Here Hume invokes (p. 499) a general statement on virtue and vice: "every thing, which gives uneasiness in human actions, upon the general survey, is call'd Vice, and whatever produces satisfaction, in the same manner, is denominated Virtue." We sense the uneasiness, in the case of injustice, by *sympathy*. Including sympathy in other people's estimate of us. And this latter is the channel through which the *artifice* works: making people's awareness more lively by indoctrination.

Idea of justice is inseparable from that of *property*. Inculcation of the ideal of justice is in order *that property be stable*, for everyone's average gain. When idea of property first developed in pre-history, idea probably was that everyone keep what was already in his physical possession. Because *custom makes us fond of things*; harder to relinquish than not to have had; therefore greater average happiness by this rule. For continuing administration of property institution, four main principles:

Occupation: first possession (discovery of island).

Prescription: long possession (whereat former claims lapse).

—To here August 14

Accession: adjuncts possession property ⊃ property.

Succession: primogeniture, etc.

All these are cases of natural association of ideas. But what is (physical) possession (presupposed throughout)? Cause-effect; power to use, alter, destroy. Important refinement of property institution is *transfer by consent*. Basis of commerce. Reason: ecology; division of labor. Utility of this desire is multiplied by trading in *futures*, so as to distribute advantages not only of ecology and division of labor but also of *seasons*. And this needs a new auxiliary institution: *promise*. So, three artificially devised relations to reduce conflicts of self-seeking for collective benefit:

(1) *ownership* (property), having its legal symbol in a *title*;
(2) *transfer*, having its legal symbol in a *deed*;
(3) *promise*, having its legal symbol in a *note*. *Money* is an alternative method.

What is a promise? Not a *willing to pay*, for it doesn't immediately precede the paying. Nor a *desire* to pay in the future, for we can promise while explicitly desiring the opposite. Nor a *resolution*, for this would carry no obligation—no morality of complying. He says it is a sheer fiction, *as if* 'willing an obligation' (p. 519). Willing obligation is temporally all right, since obligation does come right after. But absurd as real obligation, like willing a taste; for natural morality is decided by feeling. A fiction. So *fidelity*, like *justice*, is an artificial virtue arising through social convention as a prop for the institution of property. Or, to restate it in the jargon used a century later by Marx, these are bourgeois virtues.

These forces operate in both cases:

(1) Reason shows us the advantage, to us and everyone, of general honesty (*justice* in sense of respect for property; *fidelity* in the sense of respect for property).
(2) *Sympathy* with welfare of others makes us esteem these virtues also in ourselves, or in others not affecting our welfare.
(3) "Artifices of politicians" and "education" reinforce those motives by inculcating general rules, accentuating peoples' awareness.
(4) Resulting praise and blame strengthen our attitude again, through sympathy of attitudes.

Artificial on the score of (3). And this is essential, (a) because sympathy alone, with public in general, would be too weak to offset own interests; (b) because general rules would dissolve in favor of sympathy for special individuals (natural virtue of humanity). But the general rules are necessary to avoid chaos.

Actually the artifice of indoctrination, even, is insufficient, so we resort also to *government*: enforcement. This is (Hume says) a mechanism of substituting *present* evils (punishment) for the remote evils of deteriorating society—thus offsetting the tendency to discount remote goods and evils (the basic psychological law that the proximate is most vivid). There is a perhaps more essential need for government, or police, which Hume doesn't consider: even if we could take into consideration with full vividness all the remote social consequences of *our* act of dishonesty, including what little effect this *one* deviation might have on the deterioration of other peoples' honesty, it would commonly turn out that the harm to us, both direct and through sympathy with others, would be less than the gain. Like burning theater. Yet to each man's *greater* advantage for *everyone* to stay in line. So contribute to the police force.

This consideration opposes the view that everyone would be moral if he could see all consequences; on the contrary, consequences themselves have to be adjusted to this end, and law and punishment are needed no matter how shrewd the people.

Out of this device there arises a *third* artificial virtue, along with *justice* (or honesty toward property) and *fidelity* (or honesty toward promises); *viz.*, *loyalty* to the state. Because, *insofar* as government is needed for social ends just noted, and continues to serve those ends, general loyalty to it is in the public interest. But here again, as in the other two artificial virtues, education (or propaganda) and *policing* are needed—and for the same reasons. Note that there is *no* policing for *natural* virtues! So these three virtues (justice [to property], fidelity [to promises], loyalty [to state]) all go back to maintenance of property. A fourth artificial virtue is, in Hume's analysis, separate from the property concept *viz.* *chastity in women*; but similar to the other three in being an artificial virtue inculcated for the good of society. The particular good in this case is care of the young, which connects with Hume's theory (in the *Passions*[84]) of love of relations. This force, love of relations, toward making a man care for his children, is weakened if he is not sure they are his own. He might also have mentioned a connection with property, under succession (e.g. primogeniture)—this having a basis in an association of ideas (son to father) which is weakened if the blood relationship is in doubt.

Keynote of Hume's doctrine in theory of knowledge and ethics alike: Vain to seek a rational foundation. Ultimately we can only describe psychological behavior, not justify it. The basic tenet underlying all this can be phrased in Kant's words thus: *no synthetic a priori judgments are possible*. Kant's words, but not Kant's doctrine; Hume's doctrine, which Kant opposed. Doctrine that, apart from reports of immediate experience itself, the only judgments which are certain are those which follow merely from the meanings of the terms and have no factual content. For *there are no necessary connections between matters of fact*. This view was essentially present already in Locke's rejection of innate ideas; but it was left to Hume to take it in full seriousness and ruthlessly draw the consequences: the consequence that there is no rational basis for prediction, even probable prediction; no rational basis for scientific law, even probable law; and no rational basis for right and wrong.

Hume in turn didn't see the fundamental maxim clearly in terms of a distinction between analytic and synthetic. Unclear on the dependence on *meanings* of what he called "relations of ideas," as opposed to "matters of fact," in *Enquiry*. But it fits his point of view. All that is certain (apart

---

[84] ⟨Hume, "Dissertation on the Passions," in *The Philosophical Works*, 4: 156-57.⟩

from isolated immediate experience) is *analytic*. And this is the creed likewise of the empiricists of today. And it was in denying precisely this that Kant undertook to save science and ethics. Kant tried to provide for *a priori* (i.e., certain apart from experience) *synthetic* (i.e., non-analytic) judgments. This he did by his elaborate doctrine (which there is certainly no time for here) to the following effect: the mind imposes a certain general *mold* on experience, not merely by compounding ideas, but by sifting or conditioning the train of possible *impressions themselves*. The mind is *susceptible* only to *impressions* that conform to certain preconceived conditions or patterns; and the mind can *know*, by reflecting on itself, what those conditions are; and therefore the mind can know *something* about the course of any possible train of future impressions themselves; so there *are some* necessary connections among the *impressions*, knowable in advance; and so *not* all certain knowledge in advance of experience is analytic. And in this way, in particular, knowledge of *causality* or *uniformity of nature* was to be provided for; Hume's skepticism in this regard thus overcome, and science saved. A ridiculously obscure and difficult theory as set forth by Kant, and largely indefensible in its details; but ingenious in its general conception. However, its basic shortcoming is suggested in Kant's own words: his program was to show how *a priori* synthetic knowledge is *possible*. Not to show that we in fact have it, but how we might construct a *myth* coherently according to which man would have such knowledge if the myth were true. And clearly he can't do more.

So there has remained the Humean point of view, down into modern empiricism. In fact it develops into two divergent modern trends: modern *constructive empiricism*, and *pragmatism*. By no means exhaustive of Hume-inspired trends; nevertheless affords an illuminating contrast.

Constructive empiricism: explain all meaningful scientific discourse by contextual definition on the basis finally of reference to direct experience.

Pragmatism: abandon such a project as impossible, and say that our discourse is merely variously conditioned by experience without being wholly reducible to empirical terms. Abandon, therefore, empirical criticism of concepts; instead, judge any form of discourse in terms of its *utility*—this utility being measured within empirical science by ordinary empirical methods. Just as Hume didn't undertake to translate references to physical objects into discourse about experience (as a constructive empiricist would), but said it was psychologically a mere confusion, or false identification. But no hint that it lacks utility.

What is common to the Humean tradition, whether constructive empiricism or pragmatism or something else, is the negative: no metaphysical truth behind experience. While it is a skepticism, it is not a doctrine of despair and inactivity. The same old drive to science and induction exists, and is applauded; but it is a natural drive, its methodology is ultimate and irreducible to deductive logic, and the effort to find a formulation below and beyond science itself is vain and doomed to failure. Skepticism as a counsel of despair and inaction exists in Hume only with regard to this latter point. Indeed, Hume points out quite eloquently that skepticism in this sense, far from being antithetical to science, is decidedly in the scientific spirit. *Enquiry*, foot p. 608: ⟨"Nothing ... can be more contrary than such a philosophy to the supine indolence of the mind, its rash arrogance, its lofty pretensions, and its superstitious credulity. Every passion is now mortified by it, except the love of truth; and that passion never is, nor can be, carried to too high a degree. It is surprising, therefore, that this philosophy, which, in almost every instance, must be harmless and innocent, should be the subject of so much groundless reproach and obloquy. But, perhaps, the very circumstance which renders it so innocent is what chiefly exposes it to the public hatred and resentment. By flattering no irregular passion, it gains few partisans: By opposing so many vices and follies, it raises to itself abundance of enemies, who stigmatize it as libertine, profane, and irreligious."⟩[85]

---

[85] ⟨Hume, *Enquiry*, in Burtt, ed., *The English Philosophers*, 608.⟩

Abraham Trembley and His Polyps, 1744: The Unique Biology of Hydra and Trembley's Correspondence with Martin Folkes[1]

Howard M. Lenhoff and Sylvia G. Lenhoff

University of Mississippi, Oxford

Abstract

The young Genevan, Abraham Trembley (1710-1784), while a tutor to the sons of Count Bentinck in Holland, engaged in studies of the freshwater hydra or "polyp," studies that produced dramatic results. The discovery of regeneration, grafting and asexual reproduction or "budding" in animals brought him international repute. Whereas most attention has been focused on the regeneration studies, our paper emphasizes the special excellence and significance of his experiments proving that animal reproduction could take place without gametes. Instrumental in bringing Trembley's work from the Continent to England was Martin Folkes, President of the Royal Society. Folkes guided Trembley's admission to membership in the Society and the award of its Copley Medal to him. The intense and excited correspondence between Folkes and Trembley portrays Folkes far differently than do either the early negative histories or the recent revisionist studies of the Society, which ignore Folkes's relationship with Trembley and focus heavily on Folkes's contemporary detractors. We explain Trembley's good fortune in selecting the hydra as his major research animal and touch upon reactions to his findings. Finally we consider Trembley's superb *Mémoires* and his legacy to science.

I. Introduction

Martin Folkes, president of Britain's Royal Society, wrote excitedly from London on November 1, 1744 to Abraham Trembley, a young Swiss working as a tutor in Holland. Trembley recently had been honored with

[1] We thank the Trembley family of Geneva, especially the late Jean Gustave Trembley, for permission to use their collection of the correspondence between Martin Folkes and Abraham Trembley; the Royal Society of London for access to the original letters of Abraham Trembley to Martin Folkes (MSG 250); the British Library for access to the Egerton Collection; the Biology Department and staff of the library at the University of Mississippi for their help and support; and Jesus College of Oxford University for hosting HML as a Senior Research Fellow while carrying out some of this research. We especially thank Dr. Quynh Giao Tonnu, who as an undergraduate at the University of California, Irvine, translated the letters of Folkes and Trembley from French into English and who helped organize the letters and translations for scholarly study.

We dedicate this paper to the memory of our mentors, Dorothy Stimson and W. Farnsworth Loomis. Dr. Stimson was that special scholar who would have laughed at her student's celebrating the importance of Martin Folkes, a Royal Society president she had somehow managed to omit completely from her major history of the Society. And to Dr. Loomis, "Farnie," brilliant adventurer in science old and new, our deep appreciation for having introduced us to Trembley, his "polyps" and the remarkable *Mémoires*.

membership in the Society and then with its prestigious Copley Medal for
the most important scientific discovery of the year:

> These are new wonders that unfold continuously. They
> are infinitely instructive in what they teach us about the
> imperfection of our knowledge. How mistaken we have
> been till now in taking rules which perhaps concern only
> a very small part of creation for general laws which we
> could apply to all the operations of nature. May God
> preserve you, my dear Sir, to extend further and further
> these beautiful discoveries.[2]

Those few lines from Folkes's letter offer a glimpse into what Karl Ernst
von Baer, a pioneer figure in modern embryology in the nineteenth
century, was to call "the beginning of a new era" in the life sciences.[3]

   Trembley's studies on the "polyps" (the freshwater cnidarian, hydra)
created great excitement. His discoveries of animal regeneration,[4]
grafting[5] and asexual reproduction by budding not only played havoc with
long accepted views of nature, but also engendered serious questioning in
matters of religion and philosophy. Of more enduring import, however,
was the role of Trembley and his polyps in moving the study of natural
history from its focus on collecting and classification to one of careful
observation and experimentation.

   In that drama, several elements have been little noted. To begin, though
Trembley's experiments on regeneration most often hold center stage, his
discovery of animal asexual reproduction by budding has special
significance. We focus on this discovery. Next is the role of Martin Folkes
in bringing Trembley and his polyps to international prominence. We find
that this Royal Society figure has been given short shrift or worse in
various accounts and his association with Trembley ignored. Then we
explore the "gift of chance" afforded by Trembley's stumbling upon the
hydra, a "living gastrula," as his primary research organism. Finally,
after offering a few reflections on Trembley's relative anonymity today
among present-day scientists and historians, we describe what may be his
major conceptual legacy.

---

[2] Archives of the Trembley family in Geneva, Switzerland.
[3] Quoted by John R. Baker, *Abraham Trembley of Geneva, Scientist and Philosopher 1710-
1784* (London: Edward Arnold, 1952).
[4] See Howard M. Lenhoff and Sylvia G. Lenhoff, "Abraham Trembley and the Discovery of
Regeneration," in *A History of Regeneration Research: Milestones in the Evolution of a
Science*, ed. Charles E. Dinsmore (Cambridge: Cambridge University Press, 1991), 47-66.
[5] See H. M. Lenhoff and S. G. Lenhoff, "Tissue Grafting in Animals: Its Discovery in 1742
by Abraham Trembley as He Experimented with Hydra," *Biological Bulletin* 166 (1984): 1-
10.

II. Biographical snapshot of Trembley

Oxford scientist Dr. John R. Baker was Trembley's biographer *par excellence*, and one need look no further for a rich, comprehensive and balanced account of Trembley's life.[6] In brief, Trembley (1710-1784) came of a prominent Genevan family of French Huguenot origin, which in the period of Trembley's youth was of limited means. With his relative Charles Bonnet, Trembley grew up in a time of cultural flowering in his native city. At the Geneva Academy he studied mathematics, successfully defending his thesis on the subject of the infinitesimal calculus. To seek work and avoid dependence on his family, however, and drawn perhaps by the impressive Dutch intellectual climate of the time, he moved to Holland. Living in Leiden temporarily, he came to be friends with such academic leaders as 'sGravesande, Albinus and Allamand. By 1736 he was employed at The Hague as tutor in residence in the household of Count William Bentinck. There Trembley was responsible for the upbringing of the Count's two young sons. It was during his near decade at the Bentinck mansion of Sorgvliet, educating the boys and introducing them to the study of nature, that he made his most striking discoveries, those that were to earn him the sobriquet "father of experimental zoology."[7] In 1744 Trembley published his *Mémoires, pour servir à l'histoire d'un genre de polypes d'eau douce, à bras en forme de cornes*, a beautifully illustrated treatise detailing the meticulous observations and ingenious experiments that led to his tradition-shattering findings on the lower organisms.[8]

The Bonnet connection brought him into touch with the great scientist, René-Antoine Ferchault de Réaumur, who carried word of Trembley's findings to the French King, court and Academy and with whom he remained in active correspondence until Réaumur's death in 1757.[9] John Baker commented that

> Réaumur, Trembley and Bonnet form a distinctive trio in XVIIIth-century biology. They were in continuous touch by correspondence, and Trembley and Bonnet were intimate friends. The two younger men owed almost everything to the French naturalist at the outset of their careers, and neither of them achieved distinction over so

[6] Baker, *Abraham Trembley*.
[7] J. Schiller, "Queries, Answers and Unsolved Problems in Eighteenth-Century Biology," *History of Science* 12 (1974): 184-199.
[8] Leyden: Verbeek.
[9] Maurice Trembley, ed., *Correspondance inédite entre Réaumur et Abraham Trembley*. Introduction par Émile Guyénot (Genève: Georg, 1943).

wide a field as he. Trembley, however, was the greatest
of the three as an observer: his discoveries, though far
less diverse, were more important than any made by
Réaumur in biology. Bonnet started in the matter-of fact
style of the two, but passed on to philosophical biology
and speculation.[10]

Trembley's British connection stemmed through the Bentincks to
Martin Folkes of the Royal Society and a life-altering relationship with the
second Duke of Richmond. After leaving the Bentincks in 1747,
Trembley's scientific work diminished, with his time increasingly
dominated by politics, diplomacy, education, moral philosophy and
religion. Through the Duke, he participated in the peace negotiations
leading to the Treaty of Aix-la-Chapelle, and the Duke, upon his
deathbed, charged Trembley with the education of his fifteen-year-old son.
For four years Trembley led the young Richmond on the traditional Grand
Tour of the Continent, meeting with major Enlightenment figures along
the way.

   At the completion of the Tour, Trembley was endowed handsomely by
the King of England and the Duke, enabling him to return to Geneva,
where at the age of forty-six he married, fathered five children and
dedicated much of his remaining years to their care and upbringing—from
the cradle—and to their education, writing seven volumes on the subject.

III. Trembley's discovery and proof that polyps reproduce asexually by budding without involving gametes

Trembley achieved his greatest fame for discoveries in a field we know
today as developmental biology. He is recognized primarily for his
discovery of regeneration of an animal from an amputated piece of that
animal, an important contribution in itself. The notoriety of that discovery
in the eighteenth century, however, often was linked to the idea of
regeneration as an alternative form of reproduction that did not involve
copulation and gametes. That was a naïve interpretation, because
regeneration from an amputated piece of an animal is not a normal means
of reproduction. Furthermore, it is relatively easy to demonstrate
regeneration. A simple snip of a scissors or a slice by a razor is the major
technical skill required, followed by a brief period of observation.

   To prove experimentally that hydra reproduce asexually by budding
without the involvement of gametes, however, was far more difficult. His
work to establish and verify the newly discovered phenomenon of asexual
budding embodies Trembley's approach to scientific investigation that was

---

[10] Baker, *Abraham Trembley*, 24.

to excite the interest and admiration of a number of men in positions of scientific leadership, including Martin Folkes, and to earn Trembley's admission to the Royal Society and award of its Copley Medal as well as membership in the French Academy.

Beyond reflecting his virtuosity as a careful and perceptive observer, the studies of budding show Trembley not satisfied until he had tested even the most compelling observations with experiments, and at a time when many practitioners of natural history were preoccupied with description and classification, Trembley's emphasis on life processes stands out. Intent on securing "the clearest proofs" by encouraging others to repeat his experiments, Trembley in his correspondence and in his *Mémoires*, spells out in great detail his "considerations" and "precautions," what modern investigators would call their materials and methods. "Insofar as I am able," Trembley writes in his first Memoir,[11] "I shall bring the reader into my study, have him follow my observations, and demonstrate before his eyes the methods I used to make them." "It is not enough to say ... that one has seen such and such a thing. This amounts to saying nothing unless at the same time the observer indicates how it was seen, and unless he puts his readers in a position to evaluate the manner in which the reported facts were observed" (2).

In his third Memoir, Trembley described his reasoning and procedures as he carried out those classic experiments. First, both Trembley and Réaumur considered that the process of budding in hydra, first observed by Leeuwenhoek (1704) and "an anonymous gentleman" (1704), might be explained by the possibility that "eggs or little polyps had been simply deposited and fastened on the [outside surface of the polyp's] skin where they remain attached while they grow" (99). Although not known in the eighteenth century, there is indeed a sea anemone, *Epiactus prolifera,* which reproduces in that way.[12] That is, larvae from fertilized eggs implant on the surface of the side of the sea anemone and give the appearance of being buds as they develop into small sea anemones; these eventually leave the surface of parent anemone and settle nearby.

For his proof of asexual reproduction by budding in an animal, Trembley believed he must prove conclusively that the bud grew out of the parent hydra, and that it was a continuation of it with linked body cavities, which Trembley called "stomachs." He writes: "After carefully scrutinizing a young Polyp through a magnifying glass, however, and especially after following its development, the observer can scarcely doubt

---

[11] All English translations from Trembley's *Mémoires* are taken from S. G. Lenhoff and H. M. Lenhoff, *Hydra and the Birth of Experimental Biology—1744: Abraham Trembley's Mémoires Concerning the Polyps* (Palo Alto, CA: Boxwood, 1986).

[12] D. F. Dunn, "Reproduction of the Externally Brooding Sea Anemone *Epiactis prolifera* Verrill, 1869," *Biological Bulletin* 148 (1975): 199-218.

any longer that the mother puts forth the young out of her own body.... It can be seen distinctly that the excrescence which is the beginning of a new polyp is nothing other than a continuation of the mother's skin which has swollen and risen in that spot. The observer can even discern that the excrescence already forms within it a small tubular cavity which communicates with the tube shaped by the mother's skin, or in other words, with her stomach" (99).

But even such clear observation was not sufficient evidence. Trembley felt compelled to continue further, that he needed to determine definitively "the nature of the union between the young polyps and their mothers" (99). Did "the stomachs of the offspring communicate with those of the mothers" or not? His first experiment to elucidate the nature of the connection "consisted of attempting to open a polyp in such a way that I could distinctly see the connecting passage, presuming one existed"(100).

For this experiment, he placed a budding hydra in a few drops of water in the palm of his hand. Then he "cut off about half of the young polyp's body with a scissors, opening its stomach to view. At the upper end of the portion still attached to the mother there was now an opening through which I could look by using a magnifying glass. It seemed to me that the stomach of the young polyp did indeed connect with that of the mother" (100). Such evidence supported the concept that the bud had developed asexually from an evagination of the side of the parent hydra's body column, and not from a fertilized egg implanted there.

Concerned that he still might be "deceiving" himself, he carried out a modified experiment using better lighting, and again he saw an opening connecting the bud's stomach with that of its mother. Ever so cautious, Trembley posed mechanisms that would support the view that buds did *not* develop asexually, and he devised experiments to disprove those alternative mechanisms, such as one supposing the involvement of a transparent membrane. He wrote: "It was still possible, however, that at the place where the two polyps joined there could be a skin [that is, a transparent membrane] which did not impede the passage of light but which nevertheless separated the ... stomachs" of the parent hydra from that of an implanted bud which might have originated from a fertilized egg (100).

> With this aim in mind, I cut the remaining cylindrical portion of the mother lengthwise and removed the half opposite that from which the young one projected. This operation exposed the area on the lining of the mother's stomach where the hole connecting it to the stomach of the young one ought to be. Then I saw it quite distinctly (Plate 8, Fig. 5, *t*), and looking through it with a magnifying glass, I observed the opening (Fig. 5, *o*) at

the end of the remaining portion of the young polyp. Next, reversing the position of the two sections of polyps prepared in this way, I looked through the opening on the young polyp (Fig. 6, *e*) and very clearly saw light through the connecting passage (Fig. 6, *i*). In order to have no remaining qualms on the matter, I placed these portions of polyps into a small shallow glass and, through a magnifying glass, observed them again very attentively. Positioning them in the glass as I had already done in my hand, I saw the connecting opening that I was seeking so clearly that I no longer had the least reason to question its existence. (100-101; see Figure 1.)

Nonetheless, still not entirely convinced that a transparent membrane was not present, he sought absolute experimental proof that the cavity ("stomach") of the bud and that of the parent were connected and not separated by such a transparent membrane. To do so he fed only the parent hydra and observed the colored contents of the food being digested in "her" body cavity being transferred to the cavities of the attached buds. He writes, "After the mother has eaten ... one sees the bodies of the young Polyps that are attached to her swell, filling up with food as though they had taken it themselves through their own mouths.... Even a cursory look affords one every reason to believe that the food has passed from the stomach of the mother into theirs through the connecting opening between them" (101).

Trembley then confirmed those findings with even more experiments involving colored food. "I have repeated this experiment very often with all the variations to which it lends itself." Finally he was satisfied: "Having witnessed the facts I have just reported, I could no longer harbor the least doubt in the world that a communicating opening existed between a mother Polyp and her young one. It was clear that the skin of the young Polyp was absolutely nothing more than a continuation of that of its mother, and that the Polyps, like many plants, genuinely multiply by giving off shoots" (102).

Thus, through these series of experiments and related ones, Trembley proved conclusively that the small hydra attached to the side of the larger parental hydra was truly a bud that developed along the side of the body column of the parent by a specific developmental evagination, and that it was not a fertilized gamete which embedded there and grew, as Trembley, Réaumur and others had considered possible and as is the case with the progeny of *Epiactus prolifera*.

Referring to this original line of experimentation using food of different colors to elucidate developmental and physiological processes,

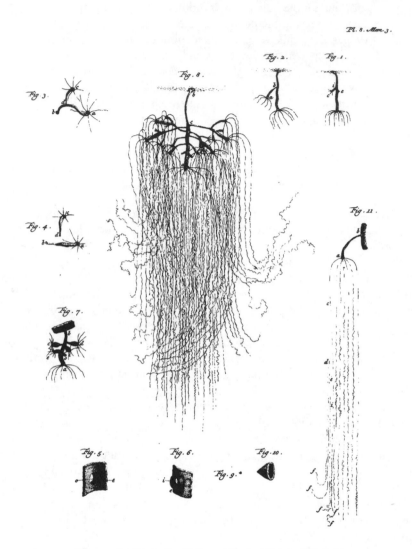

Figure 1. Plate 8 of Trembley's Third *Mémoire*

Fig. 5 shows the inner surface of a piece of skin taken from a polyp on which a young polyp is growing. The connected opening between the mother and the offspring is seen at *t*, and *o* is the opening at the end of the remaining portion of the offspring after its anterior half has been removed.

Fig. 6 depicts the same specimen as Fig. 5, but as it appears on the outside. The remaining portion of the offspring is at *e*; *i* indicates the opening communicating between the mother and her young.

Fig. 9 represents a bud severed from its mother "natural size," and Fig. 10 shows it as seen under a microscope.

Baker credits Trembley with being the first zoologist to have used the technique of vital staining (68-70). Baker also summed up the rigor and logic of Trembley's experimentation when he wrote, "Today we accept asexual reproduction in animals as a matter of course, and we may be apt to overlook the fact that very critical researches were required to establish its reality.... The first serious student of budding in animals was Trembley, and he exposed the facts so convincingly that they have never been questioned" (90).

IV. How Trembley's discoveries became known in the eighteenth century

Word of Trembley's discoveries traveled first to France. Encouraged by his cousin, Charles Bonnet, who had discovered parthenogenesis using aphids, Trembley early in his researches had initiated a correspondence with Réaumur. Impressed by Trembley's startling findings, Réaumur announced them to the Paris Academy of Sciences and described them in the preface to the sixth and final volume of his *History of the Insects* (1742).[13] Their correspondence lasted until Réaumur's death seventeen years later.[14]

News quickly spread from France and Holland to Great Britain, primarily through a series of letters to the Royal Society of London, some never mentioning the little known Trembley. Among those letters was one from Georges-Louis Leclerc, comte de Buffon, the prominent French naturalist in his "first, and perhaps ... only contribution ... to the Royal Society" of London.[15] Within a short time there followed another seven reports of Trembley's discoveries in volume 42 (1744) of the *Philosophical Transactions*, the volume covering presentations made to the Society during 1742 and 1743. Most of those letters were addressed to Martin Folkes, president of the Royal Society between 1741 and 1752. Folkes initiated a voluminous correspondence with Trembley, repeating many of Trembley's experiments and describing them in a well-illustrated article in the *Philosophical Transactions* (1744), dated March 24, 1743. We shall discuss the critical role of Folkes and his correspondence with Trembley below.

The last reference to Trembley's experiments to appear in volume 42 of the *Philosophical Transactions* is a letter written to Folkes, on May 23/June 4, 1743, by the second Duke of Richmond (1744), the man who

---

[13] René-Antoine Ferchault de Réaumur, *Mémoires pour servir à l'histoire des insectes*. 6 vols. (Paris: Imprimerie Royale, 1742).
[14] See Maurice Trembley, ed., *Correspondance*.
[15] Harcourt Brown, "Madame Geoffrin and Martin Folkes: Six New Letters," *Modern Language Quarterly* 1 (1940): 215-41.

later, on his death bed, was to hire Trembley to raise his eldest son.[16] The second Duke was brother-in-law to Charles Bentinck, brother of Count William Bentinck, Trembley's employer, and he had learned of Trembley's research during family visits to Holland.

Another member of the Royal Society, Henry Baker—author of a number of books on the microscope, subsequent awardee of the Copley Medal, and son-in-law of Daniel Defoe—was also a beneficiary of Trembley's generosity in sharing information. Baker hastily in 1743, a year before Trembley's *Mémoires* appeared, published his own book on Trembley's and his own discoveries.[17]

Trembley was not only elected a fellow of the Royal Society in 1743, but also was then awarded its coveted Copley Medal. His major opus, *Mémoires, pour servir à l'histoire dun genre de polypes d'eau douce, à bras en forme de cornes,* was published in 1744.[18]

Thus, in a few years Trembley became well known in British scientific circles. A key role in getting the hitherto obscure young tutor from Geneva admitted to membership in the Royal Society and to receive its prestigious Copley Medal was played by Martin Folkes.

V. Martin Folkes and the Royal Society

The Martin Folkes who emerges in correspondence with Abraham Trembley is a markedly different figure from the man who comes to us in the histories of the Royal Society. Why has his reputation suffered in the earliest portrayals on down to contemporary revisionist writings about the period, and how might we understand the neglect of his important role regarding those "beautiful discoveries" on Trembley's polyps?

First, to quote David Miller, writing in 1989: "The image we have of the Royal Society in the eighteenth century, as presented in the standard survey histories, is of an institution in the doldrums."[19] Again Miller: "Writing on the history of the Royal Society has definite humps in the late

---

[16] Duke of Richmond, Lennox and Aubigne, Part of a letter from his Grace the Duke of Richmond, Lennox and Aubigne, F.R.S. to M. Folkes, Esq; Pr.R.S. *Philosophical Transactions* 42 (1744): 510-13.

[17] Henry Baker, *An Attempt towards a Natural History of the Polype: In a Letter to Martin Folkes, Esq.* (London: R. Dodsley, 1743).

[18] Trembley's opus was translated into German in 1775 by J. A. E. Goeze as *Des Herrn Trembley Abhandlungen zur Geschichte einer Polypenart des süssen wassers: mit hörner förmigen Armen* (Quedlinburg: C. A. Reussner, 1775); into Russian in 1937 by I. I. Kanaev as *Memuary k istorii odnogo roda presnovodnykh polipov s rukami v forme rogov* (Moscow: Narkomedrav SSSR, Gosudarstvennoe izd-vo biologischeskoi i meditsinskoi literatury, 1937); and into English in 1986 by S. G. Lenhoff and H. M. Lenhoff in *Hydra*.

[19] David P. Miller, "'Into the Valley of Darkness': Reflections on the Royal Society in the Eighteenth Century," *History of Science* 27 (1989): 155-66.

Table 1. Folkes – Trembley Correspondence, 1742/43

Folkes to Trembley	*Trembley to Folkes*
1) January 14	
2) March 11	
	1) March 12
3) March 25	
	2) April 5
4) April 7	
5) April 9	
	3) April 12
6) April 19	
	4) April 23
	5) April 28
7) May 2	
	6) May 3
	7) May 17
8) May 20	
	8) May 31
9) June 1	
	9) June 7
10) June 8	
11) June 26	
	10) July 2
12) July 14	
	11) August 13
13) September 28	
	12) November 1
14) November 14	
	13) November 27
15) November 30	
	14) December 6
16) December 21	

TABLE 2. Chronology of Letters from Folkes to Trembley, 1744-1747

1744	*1745*	*1746*	*1747*
17) April 2	27) September 14	29) January 24	34) December 10
18) May 4	28) December 12	30) February 13	
19) May 19		31) July (no date)	
20) June 18		32) July 16	
21) June 28		33) September 16	
22) August 4			
23) October 1			
24) October 26			
25) November 1			
26) November 2			

seventeenth and early nineteenth centuries, with a trough in the eighteenth century." Martin Folkes, for one, appears to have fallen into that trough and has not yet been fully extricated from it.

In addition to Miller, a number of contemporary scholars have been doing yeoman's work in reevaluating eighteenth-century science, more particularly the role of the Royal Society in it. In 1996 Richard Sorrenson labeled as a "misperception" the long-held and persistent view among scholars "that the Royal Society was in decline during the eighteenth century."[20]

In 1999 G. S. Rousseau and David B. Haycock[21] stated their intent "to continue the important work of these scholars [Miller and Sorrenson] by examining a previously overlooked figure in the history of the Royal Society mid-century: its president, the natural philosopher and antiquarian Martin Folkes 1690-1754, and to re-examine the infamous attack upon his presidency by John Hill." Rousseau and Haycock offer the most authoritative available account of Folkes's life and his Royal Society presidency, giving important major emphasis to documenting the various attacks upon Folkes and the "cabal" against him.[22] Only in one sentence, however do they mention any connection between Folkes and Trembley, pointing out that, "When news of M. Abraham Trembley's discovery of the fresh-water polypus reached England, Folkes made his own studies in microscopy, which were published in *Philosophical Transactions.*"[23] David Miller makes an interesting side comment on J. L. Heilbron's 1983 evaluation of Folkes: "Heilbron partially resuscitates the presidency of Martin Folkes, which is usually seen ... as an antiquarian-dominated nadir, on the grounds that experimentation at the Society revived somewhat with the popularity of electricity."[24]

What we may be lacking in these valuable newer analyses of the Royal Society and of Folkes's role in it is an appreciation of the importance of the burgeoning sophistication developing then in biological studies, those on the lower organisms in particular.

Marie Boas Hall captured succinctly the historic aversion of many intellectuals to studies like those on the polyps: "It was above all the apparent triviality of the study of the very small, the serious contemplation of insects and nematode worms ... that struck all these early eighteenth-

---

[20] Richard Sorrenson, "Towards a History of the Royal Society in the Eighteenth Century," *Notes and Records of the Royal Society of London* 50 (1996): 29-46.
[21] G. S. Rousseau and David B. Haycock, "Voices Calling for the Reform of the Royal Society in the Mid-Eighteenth Century—Martin Folkes, John Hill and William Stukely," *History of Science* 37 (1999): 377-406.
[22] David B Haycock, "'The Cabals of a Few Designing Members': The Presidency of Martin Folkes, PRS and the Society's First Charter," *Antiquaries Journal* 80 (2000): 273-84.
[23] Rousseau and Haycock, "Voices Calling," 381.
[24] Miller, "'Into the Valley,'" n. 12.

century satirists."[25] Perhaps we moderns as well find it difficult to recognize experimentation on the lowly polyp and nematodes as having equal importance with the study of "the celestial Bodies." (Interestingly, there seemed no problem that the 2002 Nobel Prize in Medicine was awarded to three scientists who studied one species of nematode.)

The correspondence between Folkes and Trembley revolving around those "beautiful discoveries" on the polyp should provide a more balanced view of both Martin Folkes and the significance of the work in natural history of the time as it was evolving into experimental zoology. The correspondence from Trembley to Folkes is in the archives of the Royal Society, and we have had the good fortune to see the Folkes letters through the kindness of the Trembley family granting us access to family archives.[26] The dates of those letters are listed in Tables 1 and 2.[27]

The Folkes we find in these documents is a leader who recognizes good research, greatly appreciates the newness and importance of discoveries on life processes, is sharp enough to learn to experiment usefully on those processes and to make original observations and raise important questions about them. As he guided Trembley to recognition in Britain he showed administrative and political ability in his handling of the Royal Society, maneuvering to get members caught up in the excitement of the discoveries by witnessing them themselves. It was not hyperbole for Trembley to speak of Folkes playing in Britain a similar role regarding the polyps to that played by Réaumur on the Continent (Trembley to Folkes, April 12, 1743). This Folkes managed, despite serious problems caused by the long-standing needs for reform of the Royal Society, the mockery and carping of "the skeptics," the cabals of the pro and con antiquarian groups, and the preference of many members for emphasis on the physical sciences.

VI. Martin Folkes, Trembley and the polyps

On notification of his election to membership in the Royal Society, Trembley wrote its president, Martin Folkes: "I will never forget, Sir, that I owe this honor to your kindness to me more than anything else" (June 7, 1743). Indeed, though the list of Trembley's champions came to be a distinguished one, including Bonnet, Réaumur, the Bentincks and the Duke of Richmond, Folkes early on was fascinated by sketchy reports of

---

[25] Marie Boas Hall, *Promoting Experimental Learning: Experiment and the Royal Society 1660-1727* (Cambridge: Cambridge: University Press, 1990).

[26] The source of the Trembley/Folkes correspondence is indicated in n. 1 above.

[27] Table 1 lists the Trembley/Folkes letters between January 1742 and December 1743. Table 2 lists only the letters from Folkes to Trembley between 1744 and 1747. Trembley's letters to Folkes during that period are not available in the archives of the Royal Society. No attempt was made in these tables to account for the slight differences in the calendars of the so-called Old System and New System.

the remarkable properties of the "polypus" and sought out its young researcher when he was still an obscure tutor in the Bentinck household in Holland.

At ease in the fashionable international world of savants and salons, Folkes prevailed upon his friend, Madame Geoffrin, a celebrated hostess of the *philosophes* in Paris, to get him further information on the new discoveries and the man behind them. She responded that Paris is awash in gossip about who deserved title to first discovery, "Mr. Bonet," or a Mr. Tremblet" of Holland. Then from a visit to Réaumur's study, she learned that the French *savant* shortly would be publishing news of Trembley's findings on regeneration in the Preface to his sixth volume on the "Insects."

Folkes proceeded to solicit a copy of this material from Réaumur and also to obtain via the Bentincks a report from Trembley himself. On receipt of that report Folkes wrote Trembley on January 14, 1742/43 to offer "a thousand thanks" for "such a satisfying account" and warm congratulations on "this beautiful observation" and to entreat the young researcher to supply him with polyps and their food for conducting some experiments. He had read Trembley's report at the Royal Society meeting, but by repeating Trembley's experiments himself and having other Society members witness and repeat them as well, he would seek to convince those who still harbored doubts about these "new insights into one of the greatest mysteries of nature." Folkes also expressed to Trembley his reverence for the Divine in the "smallest works" of nature, "which men of another time could not appreciate," as well as his "mistrust" of "the general School rules, that I feel are not at all solid."

A lasting friendship was to develop between the young Swiss tutor and the Englishman twenty years his senior who had been prominent in the affairs of the Royal Society for more than a generation. Congenial personalities emerge in their correspondence; Trembley's biographer terms him a "lovable man," and the *Dictionary of National Biography* offers Folkes as "a man of extensive knowledge ... described as upright, modest, and affable."[28] But beyond this rapport of manners, that very first letter of Folkes to Trembley touches directly on several strongly shared enthusiasms: Both leaned on the Newtonian tradition, on empiricism and experimentation in the study of nature, with an accompanying distrust of grand theory; both valued the rich possibilities for discovery in a doctrine-free and theory-free study of the smallest of God's creatures.

In Folkes's case, the linkage to Isaac Newton was more than philosophical. Before becoming President of the Royal Society in 1741, Folkes had afforded the Society frequent service as vice president,

---

[28] Warwick W. Wroth, "Martin Folkes," in *Dictionary of National Biography* 8: 361-362.

beginning in 1722-23 under Newton. On Newton's becoming too ill to attend to his duties at the Society, he had Folkes assume his duties there. Hans Sloane, however, was chosen over Folkes to succeed Newton, and Folkes did not become President until Sloane retired. During those intervening years that included additional stints as vice president, Folkes is cited primarily in the older literature as the Fellow of the Society suggesting in 1736 that in lieu of the small Copley monetary award of the past, "a medal or other honorary prize should be bestowed on the person whose experiment should be best approved, by which means he apprehended a laudable emulation might be excited among men of genius to try their invention, whom, in all probability, may never be moved for the sake of lucre."[29]

Characterized in the histories as "an antiquary" and a Royal Society "President to whom scientific research made but a slight appeal," Folkes in his correspondence with Abraham Trembley belies this portrait.[30] Their letters during the year after Folkes initiated their relationship with the hope that Trembley "would be willing to trust me with some of these animals" reveal quite a different story (January 14, 1742/43).

By March 1743, Trembley had managed to get polyps in a healthy condition to Folkes. The Englishman responded happily the day following their arrival:

> I had with me 20 gentlemen of the Royal Society to see
> them at my house this morning. All that I have done was
> to convince them that the polyps were really animals,
> and it has been a true satisfaction for me that no one
> doubted that. We watched them with a magnifying glass,
> where we particularly admired the structure of their
> arms.

Folkes continued with observations the group made on the bodies of the polyps and their feeding behavior. He pledged to continue to follow Trembley's lead in these studies, expressing the hope that Trembley would "not find me unworthy of this present you have given me." (March 11, 1743). He begins in this letter to urge Trembley to publish "your beautiful book" that he "awaits with impatience." Folkes repeats his admiration for Trembley's approach: "I wish we could have here more people who would apply themselves to Natural History in the same manner you have approached it." He concludes with a request that Trembley send a small

---

[29] *The Record of the Royal Society of London for the Promotion of Natural Knowledge.* 4th ed. (Edinburgh Morrison and Gibb for the Royal Society, 1940), 112-13.
[30] Henry Lyons, *The Royal Society 1660-1940: A History of its Administration under its Charters* (Cambridge: Cambridge University Press, 1944), 180 and 161.

additional container of polyps for Royal Society study in the event he cannot find them locally though he "will search for them incessantly."

After Trembley forwards elaborate instructions for the care, feeding and carrying out of regeneration and budding experiments on the requested shipment of animals, Folkes writes from London on March 25, 1743 that

> It is with joy that I have been in a position to convince the most skeptical .... In addition to the Society, I have shown the polyps to more than 150 people, many of whom I had never even met, but who had come to my house ... and it is with pleasure that I saw none of them leaving unsatisfied.

In this letter Folkes not merely describes the results of his repeating Trembley's experiments, he also questions Trembley's indication that the gut of the polyp "is a *caecum* that has no natural opening at all on the bottom."[31]

By April Folkes is writing about several sessions of the Royal Society where "the assembly was populous" and he had reported on the polyps and presented demonstrations with them (April 7, 1743). Two days later he writes again to thank Trembley for correcting him on several errors he has made for "being new at this," and sends several pages detailing additional observations he has made on the polyps' feeding behavior and budding (April 9, 1743).

Letters that follow show Folkes continuing to experiment with the polyps, to report on them to the Royal Society and to generate interest and activity there. He translates Trembley's newer findings for the Society, encourages the search for specimens of the animals and their prey in Britain, and experimentation on them by other Fellows. He appears to be doing some battle at the Society on one hand with those favoring emphasis primarily on astronomical research and on the other with members more interested in the amassing of collections of various kinds. Folkes praises Trembley's experimentalism and concern with processes, hoping that his young correspondent will lead researchers "onto a better path than that of the ordinary [biological] collectors" who are "too devoted to looking at descriptive details" instead of "the real marvels" afforded by study of animal behavior, feeding and reproduction. In such study of small creatures, Folkes asserts, we find the perfect work "of the great Creator no less than in the great machines of the Universe, the celestial Bodies" (April 9, 1743).

---

[31] Later observations and histological evidence by many workers demonstrate that Folkes was correct.

From Trembley's side came words of appreciation for all Folkes was doing to convince the skeptics of the accuracy of his findings on the polyps (April 5, 1743). Continuing to encourage Trembley to publish and to carry out experiments on several other creatures, Folkes worries that Trembley get the help of "suitable people" and good equipment and offers to send Trembley special microscope mountings if they would be useful to him. They write as colleagues, sharing data on their work as well as information on mutual acquaintances and on other matters, scientific and political as well. By the time of a letter postmarked April 28, 1743, Trembley writes of the possibility of war between England and France, and offers to serve as neutral go-between in order for the correspondence between Folkes, the Society and Réaumur and the French Academy to continue. It is a role he indeed later came to play.

By May Folkes has got a number of other Fellows carrying out experiments to the extent that some of them get in his way and diminish his stock of polyps. Yet he has several new findings to report and about which to question Trembley. He is sending Trembley "a small, newly invented microscope, produced here, perhaps its only merit being that it is quite portable. I beg of you to accept it from me" (May 2, 1743).

Writing from The Hague, "which is in all its [spring] splendor," and where the Bentincks also had a home, Trembley is eager to return to Sorgvliet and his research. He seeks to comfort Folkes in his battles with the skeptics and writes, "If those who persist in their skepticism do not dare to observe the polyps, it is useless to try and persuade them" (May 17, 1743).

Folkes takes but one paragraph in his letter to Trembley of May 20, 1743, to express what gives him "the greatest of pleasure in the world," Trembley's election to the Royal Society "in a very full meeting." He then goes on for several pages to recount his and Henry Baker's new findings with the polyps. Trembley, in his letter of May 31, 1743, comments on some of their findings:

> I have never seen as you have, Sir, those young polyps that remained so long without arms and then grow them later. I have further never seen the [amputated] horns become offspring as you have told me Mr. Baker has observed. These are two new facts for me. I would be infinitely obliged to you Sir, if you would continue to observe them and to inform me of what you are seeing. All these facts are very interesting.[32]

---

[32] Trembley is correct. There is no evidence to date that amputated arms of a hydra regenerate.

Trembley has encouraged Folkes to repeat even his most difficult and delicate experiments, those of "reversal," of turning the polyps inside out. Folkes fears his "clumsiness," but if Trembley will advise him closely, he will try (June 1, 1743).

A new subject related to the polyps is generating great controversy, that of the "coral flowers." Folkes decides (as had Trembley) that Count Marsigli whose view that the corals were plants had long been dominant "let his imagination flow too much." (June 8, 1743). The controversy is to continue well into the future.

Their correspondence over the summer months of 1743 (Folkes to Trembley, June 1, 8, 26, July 14, and Trembley to Folkes, June 7, July 2 and August 13), shows them sharing back and forth specimens of other small creatures. On July 2 (Trembley to Folkes) there is a lengthy discussion of the tufted polyp and methods for studying it. Trembley asks Folkes to send some of his English green polyps. He says it is important to try regeneration experiments on a variety of animals.

The men communicate further, though it seems more lightheartedly, over the skeptics and now the satirists. On July 14, 1743 Folkes writes that "At Cambridge our polyps have been a little ridiculed." He makes light of the mockery as coming from "Gentlemen devoted only to poetry and classical knowledge."

September brings exciting news. Near the end of a long letter describing continuing studies and concerns, and the remark that "we are here, in general, only in the cradle of this science," Folkes announces that on November 30 he will have the honor of naming Trembley the recipient of the Copley Medal for that year (September 28, 1743).

Into the ensuing fall and winter the letters yield further deliberations on the corals or "sea polyps" and other organisms and much discussion of the preparation of Trembley's forthcoming *Mémoires*. (Folkes to Trembley, November 14, November 30, and December 21 1743, and Trembley to Folkes, November 1, November 27, and December 6, 1743).

The men were to continue their correspondence and relationship for years, but we will take leave of them with Folkes's letter to Trembley of December 21, 1743, in which he compliments Trembley on his latest experiments and remarks that "This [discovery] indeed shows us that we are still very far from knowing the secret maneuvers of Nature."

Reviewing these excerpts from the correspondence between Trembley and Folkes, is it possible to believe that either Trembley or Folkes was a man "to whom scientific research made but a slight appeal"?[33]

[33] Lyons, *The Royal Society*, 161.

VII. Reaction to Trembley's discoveries

Most of the early attention given to Trembley revolved around his discovery of regeneration. In 1712, Réaumur described the regeneration on crayfish of appendages that had been amputated.[34] Réaumur's work went largely unnoticed, perhaps because he did no more than confirm scientifically what the common folk and fishermen had reported since the times of Aristotle, Pliny, and Augustine.

Trembley's discovery, however, was more remarkable, and far more controversial and unsettling, for he demonstrated the generation of an entire animal from a small piece of that animal, a process that required neither gametes nor copulation. This finding, and particularly his proof of asexual reproduction by budding, called into question the accepted wisdom among his contemporaries on how animals reproduce.

The scientific world was somewhat prepared for Trembley's discovery of regeneration, because Charles Bonnet, in 1740 studying aphids, had just described parthenogenesis for the first time.[35] In the parthogenesis Bonnet described, however, eggs were involved. Trembley's findings in regeneration gained more credence when others confirmed it in a number of different animals.

Even though Trembley's evidence for regeneration of complete animals from a small part of one was overwhelming, some of his contemporaries continued to harbor doubts about it because the regeneration experiments had been carried out with an animal that few had ever heard of and even fewer had seen. Was it truly an animal or rather a plant, or perhaps a "zoophyte," Leibniz's predicted missing link between the plant and animal kingdoms?[36] Voltaire sarcastically referred to the green hydra as a vegetable: "This production called a polyp is much more like a carrot or an asparagus than an animal." Others, like Goldsmith, mocked Trembley's discoveries.[37] At that time biologists had not agreed that sea anemones and other "sea flowers" were animals. It was not until 1756 that Ellis's work, stimulated by Trembley's discoveries, proved that all members of the phylum Cnidaria were part of the animal kingdom.[38]

---

[34] D. M. Skinner and J. S. Cook, "New Limbs for Old: Some Highlights in the History of Regeneration in Crustacea," in C. E. Dinsmore, ed. *History of Regeneration Research*.

[35] Virginia P. Dawson, *Nature's Enigma: The Problem of the Polyp in the Letters of Bonnet, Trembley and Réaumur* (Philadelphia: American Philosophical Society, 1987).

[36] R. Josephson, "Old and New Perspectives on the Behavior of Hydra," in H. M. Lenhoff and P. Tardent, eds., *From Trembley's Polyps to New Directions in Research in Hydra: Proceedings of a Symposium Honoring Abraham Trembley (1710-1784)*, *Archives des Sciences* 38, no. 3 (1985): 347-58, esp. 348-51. Also published separately as "Exemplar" of Societé, de Physique et d'Historie Naturelle (Geneva: Georg, 1985).

[37] See Baker, *Abraham Trembley*, 45-46.

[38] H. M. Lenhoff and S. G. Lenhoff, "How the Animal Nature of Marine Cnidarians was Recognized and the Nematocyst Discovered," in *Biology of Nematocysts*, ed. David A. Hessinger and H. M. Lenhoff (San Diego: Academic Press, 1988), 1-16.

When Charles Bonnet published his findings showing that pieces of earthworms regenerate, more naturalists became convinced that Trembley's findings were valid.[39] Late in the century, Spallanzani widened the list of animals that regenerate lost parts to include amphibians.[40]

VIII. Theoretical and philosophical reactions to Trembley's discoveries

If Trembley, in his studies at Sorgvliet, was quietly comfortable in pursuing ideas that might seem outlandish, reactions to his findings often were neither calm nor benign. Theological and philosophical questions that were hotly debated have been treated thoroughly in the literature. The next paragraphs summarize some of those questions briefly.

Trembley's discoveries did not fit well with the views of a large group of naturalists, the preformationists. According to their theory of embryonic development, a miniature embryo is present in the egg or sperm, and the embryo develops by the growth of those smaller preexisting parts. This view was promoted by such distinguished scientists as Swammerdam and Bonnet.

Trembley's data, however, appeared to support the rival theory of epigenesis, the view that the organism develops gradually from material that was not preformed. To further confuse the picture, materialists like La Mettrie, who believed in the "animal machine," used Trembley's discovery to support their views.[41] They asked, for example, if an animal were cut into ten pieces and each became a new individual, what did that signify about the original animal soul and its material nature?

Trembley himself appears to have avoided becoming involved in these arguments about preformation, epigenesis, the animal machine, and the Chain of Being. Only one speculative piece of writing from his later years suggests that despite the support his discoveries seemed to lend to theories of epigenesis, he leaned toward a kind of preformationist approach.[42] These sorts of philosophical questions do not seem to have interested him much; he was far more concerned with his findings and with experimental methodology. He harbored a profound distaste for theories in general. We refer those interested in further exploring these debates to a fine book by

---

[39] Charles Bonnet, "An abstract of some new observations upon insects communicated in a letter to Sir Hans Sloane, Bart late President of the Royal Society, etc." Trans. from French by P. H. Z. Esq; F. R. S., *Philosophical Transactions* 42 (1744): 458-88.
[40] C. E. Dinsmore, "Lazzaro Spallanzani: Concepts of Generation and Regeneration," in idem, ed., *A History of Regeneration Research*, 67-89.
[41] Aram Vartanian, "Trembley's Polyp, La Mettrie, and Eighteenth-Century French Materialism," *Journal of the History of Ideas* 11 (1950): 259-86.
[42] See Baker, *Abraham Trembley*, 185.

Virginia Dawson, *Nature's Enigma*,[43] as well as to the writings of Vartanian[44] and Charles Bodemer.[45]

IX. Biological factors accounting for Trembley's rise to fame: developmental properties of hydra as gastrula

It was fortuitous that hydra were among the first creatures that Trembley observed in the waters from the ditches and ponds of Sorgvliet and then used in most of his research. Hydra are one of the few members of the phylum Cnidaria which live in fresh water; most cnidarians, such as the sea anemones and jellyfish, are marine. Cnidarians stopped their embryonic development at a stage equivalent to the diploblastic (two-cell layered) gastrula of vertebrate and other embryos, with hydra being one of the model examples of a "living gastrula." Think of a ball with two layers of cells surrounding a cavity. Hydra could be said to resemble an elongated diploblastic gastrula with its "mouth," equivalent to the vertebrate gastrula's point of opening, called the blastopore. A major difference between the hydra and an elongated gastrula is that the hydra's mouth is surrounded by a ringlet of tentacles.[46] The gastrula stage, or tissue stage of embryonic development, is considered to be relatively malleable with a high degree of plasticity compared to the next level of embryonic development. That level consists of relatively complex organs formed in embryos as they became triploblastic (three-cell layered) with the development of the third cell embryonic cell layer, the mesoderm. It is possible to remove parts of the gastrula without harming development significantly. Cells of the vertebrate gastrula, for example, are considered to be virtually stem cells, that is their embryonic fate is not yet determined. Such could also be said of the cells of regenerating hydra. The process of budding can be thought of as the outpocketing of areas of the gastrula's two-layered wall.

In essence, then, the hydra can be considered a living early embryo in which it is possible to investigate with relative ease some developmental and cellular phenomena, such as regeneration, budding and grafting. In fact it is this rationale that has attracted a number of present day scientists to using hydra in their researches. Hydras and gastrulas are made up of epithelial tissues, that is, two layers of cells both attached to an acellular material called basement membranes in vertebrates, mesolamella in hydra,

---

[43] See Dawson, *Nature's Enigma*.

[44] Aram Vartanian, *Diderot and Descartes: A Study of Scientific Naturalism in the Enlightenment* (Princeton: Princeton University Press, 1963).

[45] Charles W. Bodemer, "Regeneration and the Decline of Preformationism in Eighteenth-Century Embryology," *Bulletin of the History of Medicine* 38 (1964): 20-31.

[46] For illustrations demonstrating the embryonic homologies between the gastrula and hydra, see H. M. Lenhoff, "Ethel Browne, Hans Spemann, and the Discovery of the Organizer Phenomenon," *Biological Bulletin* 181 (1991): 72-80.

and mesoglea in other cnidarians. The chemical composition of the mesolamella of hydra has been found to be nearly the same as the composition of the basement membrane of vertebrates—or is it the other way around?[47]

In 1744 Trembley made most of the major discoveries possible with the existing tools of the day on the development of hydra, except for one. We refer to the classic experiments of Ethel Browne (Harvey) in 1907 showing that when a piece of the mouth region of a hydra is grafted to the body wall of another hydra, a new hydra is induced to develop there. Those experiments, worthy of a Nobel Prize, were also made possible because of the gastrula-like diploblastic structure of hydra.[48]

If Trembley had investigated most other freshwater organisms, he would not have discovered budding, regeneration and grafting, nor would he have been able to turn an animal inside out. It was this serendipity of his encountering the freshwater "polyp" which allowed Trembley to make his startling discoveries in such a short time, rocketing the unknown tutor to prominence among scholars and the public in the eighteenth century.

X. Biological factors accounting for Trembley's descent into obscurity

So how to account for Trembley's return to general obscurity in later generations? Again it may be the special nature of Trembley's research animal that offers us clues. One explanation is offered by eminent contemporary cell biologist, Joseph Gall: "Indeed, just because regeneration and asexual reproduction are such fundamental biological process, one imagines that they are self-evident facts that did not have to discovered by a single individual who performed real experiments."[49]

A second key to the puzzle may lie in the extremely long interval between Trembley's findings and the ability of later researchers to approach the distinctive characteristics of Trembley's gastrula-like polyps and press his studies further to reveal the "secret maneuvers of Nature" entailed in the developmental and cellular phenomena of budding, regeneration and grafting.[50]

Early twentieth-century Nobel laureate Thomas Hunt Morgan is reported as saying "in a lighter moment, that since he had been unable to solve the problem of regeneration ... he had decided to try something easier such as the problem of heredity."[51] Only in recent years have we

---

[47] B. Barzansky, H. M. Lenhoff and H. Bode, "Hydra Mesoglea: Similarity of its Amino Acid and Neutral Sugar Composition to that of Vertebrate Basal Lamina," *Comparative Biochemical Physiology* 50B (1975): 419-24.

[48] See H. M. Lenhoff, "Ethel Browne."

[49] Joseph G. Gall, "Foreword," in *Hydra*.

[50] Folkes's letter to Trembley of December 21, 1743.

[51] John Tyler Bonner, *Morphogenesis: An Essay on Development* (Princeton: Princeton

acquired the extraordinary array of tools of molecular biology allowing current investigators to approach an understanding of the chemistry of surfaces of hydra cells and of its mesolamella, and the identification of genes controlling some aspects of hydra's morphogenesis.[52] Louis Wolpert, noted contemporary developmental biologist, has said: "The trouble with Trembley was that he was two hundred years ahead of his time."[53]

XI. Trembley's legacy:
a paradigm of pragmatic experimental investigation and reporting

Trembley left no theory that would explain the phenomena he discovered. We think that was all to the good, because few such theories of that time had much lasting value. But he did leave in his *Mémoires* a legacy, a model for pragmatic biological discovery and for objective reporting of experimental findings so that they could be repeated by others. The organization of these *Mémoires* bears a remarkable resemblance to the design of research publications by today's biologists. Trembley had the unique gifts of being a perceptive observer, of skill in carrying out experimental research and ability to explain logically in fine clear language, the thought processes behind his experimental methodology.

XII. The *Mémoires* as an eighteenth-century monograph

Trembley's *Mémoires* are in many ways characteristic of a large genre of mid-eighteenth-century writings on natural history and on "small creatures" in particular. Similar works were produced during this period, for example, by the other two members of the Bonnet-Trembley-Réaumur trio: Réaumur's multivolume *Mémoires* on the insects, appearing over the years from 1732-1742, and Bonnet's *Insectologie* in 1745. Books of the period on "the Insects" are the work of both professional scientists and amateurs, of academics and virtuosi. Some are pietistic in the vein of the Abbé Pluche, others iconoclastic like La Mettrie's; some enshrine the lofty theoretical debate of university faculties, whereas others exude the humbler air of the country doctor or parson during his free time examining the beauty of God's handiwork as expressed in His minute creatures. Some are multivolume and range over a wide array of subjects,

University Press, 1952), 3.
[52] H. Shimizu, X. Zhang, J. Zhang, A. Leontovich, K. Fei, L. Yan and M. P. Sarras, Jr., "Epithelial Morphogenesis in Hydra Requires de novo Expression of Extracellular Matrix Components and Matrix Metalloproteinases," *Development* 129 (2002): 1521-32.
[53] From discussion in a conference symposium on regeneration held at the annual meeting of the American Society of Zoologists, December 30, 1988, San Francisco, California.

Buffon's running in encyclopedia style to forty-four quarto volumes, Réaumur's to six, and Bonnet's to eight.

Trembley may have modeled his *Mémoires* on Réaumur's classic in various elements of design and format. The *Mémoires* of both men also are similar in an insistent emphasis on careful reporting of observations and experiments, as contrasted with the heavy theoretical speculation that was still rampant in many of the treatises on natural history popular throughout the Enlightenment even while those treatises included material from the rigorous scientific inquiry that some of their authors were beginning to pursue. Regarding the heated philosophic and religious arguments of the time fueled by Trembley's discoveries, there is little to be had from exploring his *Mémoires*. Instead we find eighteenth-century thinking in a format that is the general rule today for reporting research results.

XIII. Structure of the *Mémoires* as a model for reporting biological discoveries

Trembley organized the *Mémoires* in a methodical, topical manner. Memoir I is essentially an "introduction" to the reader of the three species of hydra he found, with a general description of their form and movements and some observations on the structure of the animal's parts. It is noteworthy that detailed material on structure is reserved for the relevant sections on function. In Memoir II Trembley deals with "materials and methods" of the animal husbandry entailed, how to collect the polyp, feed and maintain it, with some observations on color and functional morphology that are related to its feeding. Memoir III is a "results" section, dedicated entirely to one of the most notable attributes Trembley has discovered in the animal, that is its "amazing reproduction" by asexual means. The first sixty-six pages of Memoir IV complete the "methods" and "results" as Trembley presents all the other "operations" he has carried out on the polyp. These include sectioning the animal in almost every manner conceivable; the making of monsters; and the famous inversion experiment in which Trembley details his procedures for deftly turning the tiny creatures inside out, the experiment which inadvertently led to the first experimental grafts of animal tissue.

The closing eighteen pages of Memoir IV, which are set off from the experimental material, are very much analogous to the "discussion" section of a modern scientific paper. Here Trembley discusses the relationship of his polyps to the "polyps of sea" or cuttlefish, and other presumably polyp-like creatures, presenting a "literature search" on the subject. The search is instructive regarding the progress of zoological studies to that time. Trembley dutifully incorporates references to the ancients, Aelian, Aristotle, Augustine, Massarius, Pliny, wryly remarking, "I believe one may be allowed to doubt the accuracy" of some of their assertions. Elsewhere he demurs from judging the degree to which the ancients' views should be heeded, since such judgments require knowledge of the specific observations on which their views were based and how they carried out these observations. "Such details," he says with profound understatement, "are not found in the works of any of these writers." From the ancients Trembley leaps centuries to Swammerdam, to Réaumur and to other contemporaries such as the English minister, Mr. Hughes, who have demonstrable factual information to impart.

In his final pages of discussion on the question of characteristics distinguishing animals from plants, Trembley permits himself to hold forth at some length on the perils of general rules, of hypothesizing on the basis of insufficient facts, and on the importance of drawing limited conclusions. Polyps, he says, do not constitute some newly hypothesized class of "Zoophytes" or "Animal-Plants," as he himself had once suggested;[54] they should be looked upon instead as simple animals. He urges philosophers to drop the preconceptions that blind them so that they can pay attention to the facts before their eyes, just as children do. He argues that had men not been held back by suppositions that one or another thing was "impossible," natural history would be far more advanced and regeneration among animals, for example, would have been discovered long since. (Disarmingly, Trembley admits that his own supposition of this kind, that pieces of an animal could not become complete animals, contributed significantly to his discovery of regeneration.) He ends this final "discussion" section and the *Mémoires* with a plea for expanding careful observation and experiment and not mixing our own notions with what we learn from close examination of nature itself.

XIV. Conclusion

The authors hope that their bio-historical exploration of Abraham Trembley's "Beautiful Discoveries" and Martin Folkes's role in promoting them will assist scholars who are revisiting the science of the eighteenth century. Trembley's letters to Folkes in the archives of the Royal Society and his correspondence with the Bentinck family and Lady Portland in the Egerton Collection of the British Library are both readily available. They are treasures as yet hardly mined. Perhaps their value as well as a fuller appreciation of the richness of the beginnings in the eighteenth century of experimental zoological science awaits increased collaboration between biologists and scholars of history.[55]

[54] See Maurice Trembley, ed., *Correspondance*, 61.
[55] One such treasure we read was a letter of the Egerton collection written by Trembley to Count Bentinck. In it Trembley records with drawings the division of the single cell diatom, *Synedra*, into two cells. John Baker, who describes this letter in his autobiography of

Should readers find some of our arguments and conclusions problematic, we stand with Monsieur Trembley, who wrote in one of those engaging letters to Folkes on August 13, 1743:

> I believe it is good that a number of people push their skepticism to the extreme. This has caused excitement and more people are aware of the subject of these gentlemen's disbelief. A little passion does no harm.

Trembley states that Trembley was "the first human being to witness cell-division," but at a time one hundred years before cells were described. Baker, *Abraham Trembley*, 156.

The Work of the Fool: Enlightenment Encounters with Folly, Laughter and Truth

Dorinda Outram
University of Rochester

Abstract

The focus of this paper is a debate between university professors and a court Fool staged in 1737 by Friedrich Wilhelm I of Prussia. What is reason, and what is folly, asked the Fool, and then, what is truth? I examine the thirty-seven theses put forward by the Fool for the public debate at Frankfurt-Oder, as well as some contemporary accounts of the event. Then I put the debate in the context of contemporary controversies such as those sparked by Spinoza on the nature of truth. I offer this as a contribution to a wider project about the difficult search for usable definitions of truth in the Enlightenment, a period in which notions of scientific truth were sharpened.

> *To speak truth with a smile, no rule forbids*
> —Horace, *Satires*, I.1.24-25

> *For it is written, I will destroy the wisdom of the wise, and*
> *will bring to nothing the understanding of the prudent.*
> *Hath not God made foolish the wisdom of this world?*
> —I Corinthians 19

In spite of the work of Robert Darnton, Roger Chartier, and many other cultural historians, it is still very easy to think of the Enlightenment as in the end crucially shaped by the work of the great philosophers and critics, by Locke, Spinoza, Voltaire, Hume, and Kant. In this paper I want to argue that philosophical work also happened at the level of practice and performance, through actions which were not centrally concerned with texts or with formal philosophical systems, but which nonetheless exteriorized some problems central to the Enlightenment.[1] This paper also invites readers to ask about the values that we invoke when we write about the fool and the joker. A challenge for historians is to find a way of writing about such figures that neither becomes in its turn fool-ish, jokey

---

[1] This project is also at the heart of my "Masks, Truth and Nostalgia: Enlightenment Problems and our Responses," *Figurationen,* Erste Jahrgang 2000, Heft 2: 93-107. It is a pleasure to acknowledge the support, encouragement, and generous discussions of foolishness and Fool-ishness of PD Martin Gierl, Stephen J. Kunitz, M.D. and William T. Lewek, M.D.

and anecdotal; or one which extinguishes the light figures of fools with an avalanche of academic analysis. Such a method of course only succeeds in exactly replaying the conflict between the fool and the scholar, between academic knowledge and the deeper truths of contradiction, doubleness and irony which are the subject of this paper. I hope I can write about the contexts and actions of Enlightenment fools and jokers so that their values are brought to the surface, and can be demonstrated as being as much, and at the same time, paths to truth as they are exhibitions of jokes and mockery.

Truth definition preoccupied the Enlightenment. It was a central problem for Wolff, Thomasius, and Crusius, not to mention Rousseau and Hume and many others. Debates over the supremacy of theological truths based on divine revelation *versus* philosophical truth based on reason loomed large. The extent of this concern was such as to imply that far from being easily recognizable, truth was a slippery customer. The problem of truth seemed for many both ineluctable and irresolvable. Rousseau's comments in his first *Discours* betray the intractability of the problem, even for one who believed in the indivisibility of truth:

> Par combien d'erreurs, mille fois plus dangereuses que la vérité n'est utile, ne faut-il point passer pour arriver à elle? Le désavantage est visible; car le faux est susceptible d'une infinité de combinaisons; mais la verité n'a qu'une manière d'être. Qui est-ce d'ailleurs, qui la cherche bien sincèrement? Même avec la meilleure volonté, à quelles marques est-on sûr de la reconnoître?[2]

II

This paper examines and contextualizes one such performance of the relation between truth and folly. This was a debate staged in 1737 at Frankfurt-an-der-Oder between an assembly of professors from the local university who were required to argue on the side of reason, and Salomon Morgenstern, the intimate and buffoon of King Friedrich Wilhelm I of Prussia, the proponent of the claims of foolishness, It is important to note that Morgenstern was not a fool of the medieval kind. He was not, that is, in motley, on the royal payroll, and without other life outside his calling. Morgenstern was a fool of a new kind, a composite person, who combined the functions of Professor of History and Geography at the University of Halle, with that of frequently making available his fooling to Friedrich Wilhelm I. The theses advanced in this debate by Morgenstern were

---

[2] Jean-Jacques Rousseau, *Discours sur les sciences et les arts* (1751), in *Oeuvres complètes*, ed. Bernard Gagnebin (Paris: Gallimard, 1964), 18.

printed in 1737, with a second edition in 1739, under the title *Vernunfftige Gedanken über Narren und Narrheit.* The content of this pamphlet will form the basis of discussion later in the paper of the relationship between foolishness, and contemporary obsessions by philosophers and theologians with defining the nature of truth.

The debate of 1737 was a deliberately staged performance. Every staging, even the staging of foolishness, is demonstrative. It brings to the surface and demonstrates through character, plot and action, the existence of an enclosed universe that both carries and exhibits its own meanings. This is true whether the performance is devised in a way that leaves the boundary between play and audience untouched, or whether, like Ludwig Tieck's 1797 play *Der gestiefelte Kater,* that boundary is questioned at every turn.[3] One of the scenes in this play shows a mock debate, under the chairmanship of an irascible monarch, between the court scholar, who is a historian, and the court fool. It is tempting to see this as referring to the actual debate that took place in 1737 in Frankfurt-an-der-Oder. Here, a royal impressario, Friedrich Wilhelm I, pitted his fool against the professoriat of the local university

Public debates were not in themselves an unusual form of encounter for an age that delighted in public competitions between musical virtuosi or chess champions, in which academic theses were defended in public, and which knew itself to be the heir to the great theological debates of the Reformation. What makes the Frankfurt debate unusual was its deliberate staging by a monarch, the response of the Frankfurt professoriat, and the use of the court fool in a public setting well beyond the boundaries of court life. What makes this debate important and interesting, as well as being unusual, is its revelation of a turning point in the relationship of *levitas* and *gravitas,* between seriousness and mockery. The fool's contribution to the debate proceeded on the assumption that in the end these two qualities may not be such opposites after all. Whether the professors could tolerate this version of truth and truth finding was another matter.

Just as public disputation was in itself not an unusual event, and had long historical roots, so did the fool-ishness that was in play in the Frankfurt debate. What went on here was not just wild japes and meaningless riddling ridicule. It had longer roots than that, in the

---

[3] Ludwig Tieck, *Der gestiefelte Kater,* trans. and ed. Gerald Gillespie. Edinburgh Bilingual Library, 8 (Edinburgh: Edinburgh University Press, 1974), 88-89 (Act 2), has an enraged monarch fling his sceptre at a court scholar's head, as a check to his pretensions, and then yells "What presumption is this! The Fool pleases me, me, his King, and when he is to my taste, how can you dare say that the man is absurd? You are Court Scholar and he is Court Fool ... where is the big difference between you?"

quodlibet debates of medieval universities, in which deliberately ridiculous theses were maintained. These roots can also be found even in the work of a devoted scholar like Erasmus. At one point in his *Adages,* he discusses the small figurines called Sileni because they represented the god Silenus, drinking companion of Bacchus, and buffoon to the gods.[4] These images could be opened to reveal totally different images in their interior. Erasmus uses the figures, as he does again in his *Praise of Folly,* as bases for his discussion of the disjunctions and contradictions between exterior appearance and interior reality. He uses the *Sileni* as basis for a more general argument that any given object might therefore need many ways rather than one way to define and understand it. He points out how easy it was, in the same way, to mistake Socrates for a buffoon, because of his ugly, peasant-like exterior, his unbroken flow of humor, and his frequent statements that that there was only one thing to know, which was that he knew nothing. Such irony is one of the marks of fool-ish discourse Erasmus goes on to point out that there might be more real and native wisdom in one single ordinary man, who in the world's judgment is an ignoramus and a simple-minded fool, than in many pompous theologians, or in professors three or four times over, who are stuffed with their favorite Aristotle, and swollen with a plethora of doctoral definitions, conclusions and propositions.

In describing the figures of Silenus, Erasmus also shows how human affairs themselves are inherently mysterious. It is difficult to find truth when our experience is characterized by disconnection between outer experience and inner reality. Worse, inner reality is itself characterized by contradiction. Two hundred years later we find a Prussian monarch, whether knowing of their ancestry or not, sustaining many of these observations. In doing so he was also implicitly combating the new Enlightenment idea that truth was unitary and transparent, unlike the *Silenus* figurines, which had to be opened before their meaning was revealed. Also in play for the monarch was the Enlightenment project of creating a universal human subject characterized by the use of reason.

We have several different sources for our knowledge of the 1737 debate. The first account is from the pen of a most reluctant participant in it. Johann Jacob Moser, famous as one of the founders of German public law, and holder of a chair in the law faculty at Frankfurt-Oder, discusses

---

[4] This account of the *Sileni* relies on the analysis in William Barker, *The Adages of Erasmus* (Toronto: University of Toronto Press, 2001), 243-47. Erasmus also extensively discusses the *Sileni* in his *Praise of Folly:* Desiderius Erasmus, *Praise of Folly and Letter to Martin Dorp, 1515*, trans. Betty Radice (London: Penguin, 1971), 67, 68, 85, 86, 103, 235.

the experience in his autobiography.[5] For many reasons, this is hardly to be read as a neutral account. By the spring of 1737 Moser was already in dispute with the Prussian education bureaucracy, and rumors of hostility between him and the rest of the moribund law faculty at Frankfurt–Oder had come to the ears of a monarch bent on the revival of the institution. When Moser was summoned to the debate, he was at dinner in his own home. He held the summons responsible for the severe illness he suffered a short time later.

Moser's reaction was so deep that he went to Morgenstern, who had accompanied the king to Frankfurt, and begged to be allowed to excuse himself from the debate, or at the very least, to be allowed to make a serious and not a comic speech. In the end, Moser was excused from speaking, but had to attend the debate, where the king mockingly clapped at his entrance, and took the opportunity of the hiatus caused by Morgenstern's late arrival to interrogate him on the difficult situation in the University. This situation was of more than local significance. The Frankfurt faculty, like many others in the German lands, had the duty not only of teaching law, but also of delivering legal opinions. A slothful or inept Faculty meant a clogged legal system, and so a potential injury to royal government and prestige. The Frankfurt situation, in other words, was far more important than official irritation at a few underachieving professors. Moser had been appointed to deal with this situation. The debate the king was staging was another attempt to do so, though Moser missed its significance, and perceived in it only a threat to his own *gravitas*.

Friedrich Wilhelm attempted to discipline and humiliate the Frankfurt Professors by forcing them into a public contestation with his Fool. The monarch personally orchestrated the debate. No wonder the king chose such a drastic method of shaking up the Frankfurt faculty and publicly demonstrating their inability to turn a witty phrase, let alone a legal opinion. While his partiality for inventive and hurtful humor undoubtedly came into play, the king had another reason for wanting to achieve faculty

---

[5] Moser, *Lebens-Geschichte Johann Jakob Mosers, von ihme selbst beschrieben* (n. p., 1768); see also Mack Walker, *Johann Jacob Moser and the Holy Roman Empire of the German Nation* (Chapel Hill: University of North Carolina Press, 1981); Moser's autobiography reached a third edition printed in four parts in Frankfurt-Main, 1777-1783. References are to this edition. My account here relies heavily on these two sources. Compared to Mack's account, however, I place considerably more emphasis on Morgenstern and the theses he maintained, and interpret the debate as part of a culture of foolishness, rather than as an episode in Moser's individual biography. Reinhard Rurup, *Johann Jacob (sic) Moser: Pietismus und Reform* (Wiesbaden: Franz Steiner Verlag, 1965), 68, treats the debate with Morgenstern in a footnote.

reform even by unorthodox means if necessary. The eighteenth century saw a wave of new universities created in the German lands, and also at older institutions such as Frankfurt-Oder, some enforced vitality. In the year of the Frankfurt debate, the new University at Göttingen was to open its doors under the patronage of the Elector of Hannover, who concurrently ruled England as George II. The Prussian monarchy had already revitalized Halle. Würtemburg had founded the Carlsakademie that was to be the *alma mater* of Georges Cuvier and Friedrich Schiller. These universities were in heavy competition with each other for students and for star professors. Economic advantages were expected from them, as was the production of loyal bureaucrats and clergy. In this context, it is little wonder that Friedrich Wilhelm became interested in what was going on in Frankfurt.

Accounts of the conversation between the king and Moser are no less interesting. Moser entered it in despair. As he writes in his autobiography: "I became so depressed, that I broke out involuntarily: this is an unhappy day for the university." The king teased him about the foolishness of academic life. He strongly expressed the opinion that mother wit was preferable to university learning, just as Erasmus had in his essay on the *Sileni,* and also did in the *Praise of Folly.* Moser began to reply to the king's serious concerns about the law faculty. Thinking that he had dazzled the king with his legal knowledge and suggestions for university reform, Moser then made the mistake of coming back to the starting point of the conversation. He asked again to be allowed to deliver a serious speech on foolishness, suggesting the classical biblical texts such as "The fool saith in his heart there is no God" (Psalm 14:1; Ps. 53:1). At this the king exploded in exasperation, and accused Moser of hypocrisy in religion. He yelled at Moser: "So what? Everybody's a fool about something. I'm a fool for a soldier, somebody else is a fool for pious vanity, somebody else is a fool about something else. It's just a joke and we can have it."[6] But Moser couldn't.

Then, appositely, after this royal declaration about the universality of foolishness, the king's buffoon, Morgenstern, appeared, dressed in an extraordinary costume. A long blue velvet coat with red lapels, and a red vest, embroidered with silver hares, the animal emblem of foolishness, drew the eyes of the audience. In a parody of contemporary fashion, an enormous wig hung down to his waist. In place of the aristocratic sword he hung a fox's tail. On his hat he had pinned a hare's scalp. The costume had many functions. Its mockery of the elite was clear. So was its mobilization of ancient symbols against the professoriat. The costume

---

[6] Moser, *Lebens-Geschichte,* 1: 170-74; Walker, *Johann Jacob Moser,* 86-95.

made him an iconic object, covered with symbols of foolishness and low cunning, a being who literally appropriated to himself symbols which were animal instead of rational, which were drawn from everyday proverbs rather than learned discourses.

Let us pause for a moment and discuss Moser's reaction. Moser was in any case a difficult man to invite. He had compromised his career with his previous employer, Karl-Alexander, Grand-Duke of Würtemburg, by refusing his invitation to attend a masked ball to open the Carnival season. He had no liking for games with identity that could be played with masks. He had had the experience before of being, by audience and professors alike, laughed out of another public disputation, at Tübingen in 1720. Moser himself described the opponent who triggered round after round of laughter against him as "a hare's cousin." In the Prussian case, he was manifesting a severe reaction against such aggressive levity. He was signaling his dislike of staged games and public performance, of the artificial and the contradictory. He would not have liked a Silenus figure. But why, all this being said, was Moser's reaction so extreme as to account, at least in his own mind, for the onset of a serious illness? Why did he not see the debate as a lighthearted exercise that could also offer him a way of possibly regaining the favor of the monarch?[7]

What seems to be at stake for Moser was the enforced confrontation between the apparent levity of the Fool with the *gravitas* of the *Lehrstand*. He begs Friedrich Wilhelm to be allowed to make a serious rather than a comic speech, and clearly dreads being in the same space as that composite being which is Morgenstern, who is both a Fool and a Professor. To have been forced into the intimate encounter of public debate with a Fool was bad enough. To be faced with a Fool who was also a Professor, was even worse, because Morgenstern's dual role implied that there was really no sharp or necessary division between the two roles. The staging of the debate also implied that the academic forms of reasoning normally used in such public disputations were not separate and superior forms of truth-discovery, but existed on the same level as the ridicule, riddles, paradoxes, witticisms, irony, folk adages and proverbs, insults, and contradictions characteristic of the interventions of fools. The debate was a confrontation between fools' wisdom and professors' knowledge.

---

[7] Walker, *Johann Jacob Moser*, 26, 81; it is a pleasure to acknowledge my debt to Walker's account of the debate. For Morgenstern's costume, see Walker, 92-93, although my account offers some different interpretations.

For the conduct of the debate we turn to our second source.[8] This is a manuscript letter bound in with the Göttingen University Library copy of Morgenstern's pamphlet mentioned at the beginning of this paper. The letter, dated November 1737, would appear to be an eyewitness account of the staging of the debate. There is no indication of its writer or its recipient, but the language and spelling indicate a writer of Swabian origin. The writer is clearly in the printing trade ("wir fahren mit dem Druck fleissig fort ... Hier nebst folgen wieder vier Aushangerbogen"), and probably concerned with the printing of Morgenstern's pamphlet. The writer is explicit about the King's personal intervention in the debate. He had "den ganzen actum allerhoechst selber dirigiret." Friedrich Wilhelm, who appeared to be enjoying himself, could hardly have made clearer the importance he attached to the debate. The professors, previously personally invited by soldiers bearing the royal command ("wurden durch unteroffizieren dazu eingeladen."), debated Morgenstern's theses before a noisy audience of university students. The king orchestrated their responses. Every time a thesis was debated

> geben Ihro Maejestaet mit Pfeiffen und Hande klatschen ein Zeichen an die anweisender studiosus ihr Vergnugnen zu aussern, welches auf hervorargung des koeniglichen Stabes unterbrochen werden musste; und so verfuhr man bis zum Ende aller Desen (Thesen).

Naturally the outcome of the debate was not in doubt. The anonymous letter writer continues:

> Ihro Maejestaet machtet hiernechst dem Herrn Defensore (Morgenstern) eine gnadige Reverence und erhoben sich von dannen. Herr Magister Morgenstern danckete mit einem Schnaltzer und Pfiff ihnen hinten nach, denen die studierenden Jugend folgeten. Abends darauf brachte diese Ihro Maejestaet eine serenata(m), [*sic*] welche aller gnadigst geruherten nach volbrachte Music, die ganze Schar hoch schreien und wetzen zu lassen: auch nachdem das, es lebe das ganze koenigliche Haus hoch, item das Pereat, etc., vorueber, musste das es lebe der Herr Vizekanzler Morgenstern hoch erfolgen, womit diese Freude beschlossen wurde. Dergleichen Ehre and hohe Gnade ist noch keiner Universitaet in Deutschland

---

[8] With gratitude I acknowledge the assistance of PD Martin Gierl and Professor Emeritus Wilhelm Braun with the reading of the unusually difficult handwriting of this letter

widerfahren. Dieser wird Franckfurt in ihren Annalibus
voraus haben.

These extraordinary events were followed by the publication of our
third source of knowledge of the debate. This was Morgenstern's
pamphlet, printed in Frankfurt-Oder in 1737, and reprinted two years later
in Schwabach.[9] His pamphlet records the theses on reason and folly that
he successfully defended in the Frankfurt debate. It was titled *Vernunfftige
Gedanken über Narrheit und Narren* (*Rational Thoughts on Fools and
Foolishness*), in a way that recalled Christian Wolff's habit of beginning
his writings with the phrase *Vernunfftige Gedanken*. Wolff had been
banished from Prussia in 1723 and forced to give up his chair at Halle,
due to his project for transferring the methods of mathematics to theology.
He was invited to return by Friedrich William's son, Friedrich II, in 1740.
Wolff was exactly an example of the abstract philosophical approaches
both to practical and to spiritual life which the king who had strong Pietist
sympathies, so much disliked. Morgenstern, as his mouthpiece, not only
echoed the royal opinions, but made them more visible and compelling
through performance.

The body of the pamphlet contains thirty-eight theses. Of these, eleven
(21-32) are directed specifically against the pretensions of the
Gelehrtenstand to superior wisdom. (We have no record of the counter-
arguments advanced by Morgenstern's unfortunate opponents).
Morgenstern sustains the thesis, already contained in the monarch's abuse
of Moser, that while all the major *Stände*, that is the farmers, the soldiers,
and the courtiers, are prone to their own particular forms of folly, the
Gelehrtenstand has no rival in its foolishness. This was a position of
course not lost on his audience. Morgenstern (theses 1-6) defines as a fool
someone who has ideas that are out of touch with reality, or who uses
inappropriate means to gain ends which may be in themselves perfectly
rational. (Here the modern reader hears echoes of the satire directed in
1726 by Jonathan Swift against the professors of the floating island of
Laputa.) Morgenstern does not relate foolishness to mental illness or pure
stupidity, in ways that became increasingly common after the mid-century.
"Foolishness," in Morgenstern's theses is in fact a complex term. It may
refer to the specific arsenal of ways of thinking and rhetorical moves
which the buffoon uses, which may be powerfully derogatory in the
original sense of the word, and may also be powerful engines for the

[9] The two copies of Morgenstern's pamphlet known to me are the 1737 version in the Stadts-
und-Universitäts Bibliothek, Göttingen (call number 8 Satir II 540), and the 1739 copy held
in Cambridge University Library (call number 7180.d.263). There are no textual differences
between the editions.

discovery of truth. But it may also mean the very detachment from reality, or foolish self-satisfaction, that it was Morgenstern's job to satirize.

He then sustains in thesis 7 the commonplace found since antiquity, that foolishness is universal. "Diese haben die Alten schon so wohl volkommen erkennet, als nachdrucklich ausgedruckt: stultorum plena sunt omnia! Die ganze Welt ist voller Narren/Vom Hirten an bis auf den Pfarren!" Here Morgenstern mixes an adage that originates in Cicero's letter *Familiares* (*To his Friends*: 9.22.4) with a satirical popular verse. This mixing of references is very characteristic of fool-ish discourse. Fools' reason does not include the scrupulous weighing of different sources and their division into different genres that professorial knowledge did. The next point to be made is that Morgenstern's theses on the universality of foolishness, though hardly original, contradicted the characteristic argument of the Enlightenment that on the contrary, it is the universality of the capacity for reason that defines the human race.

Morgenstern proceeded with his attack in his eleventh thesis. If fools are so frequently encountered, and foolishness is to be encountered in every *Stand*, then it is not surprising that "Demnach ist ein Klüger nichts anders, als der seinen Trieb zur Narrheit überwindet." Cleverness is the result of a perpetual struggle with its opposite, foolishness. Its origin is dialogic, not singular. And rather than being an inherent property of the "clever," it is one which even they can only maintain by struggle. Intellect, like life, is inextricably linked with its opposite. Cleverness can tip over into foolishness, happiness into misery. As Morgenstern sustained in thesis 11: "Daraus ist ohne Hererey abzunehmen, wie das Klug seyn kein Handwerk: sondern das solches bey jedem Menschen mit Narrheit, wie das Glück mit Unglück immer vermischet." Morgenstern knows, as a Fool, that knowledge arises from contradiction. Like and unlike are bound together in the same person, just as they are in the *Sileni* figures. That is another part of what fool-ishness teaches: the way that knowledge is gained by holding opposites present to each other. Morgenstern's theses are like the *Sileni* whose external appearance is contradictory to their content. He uses the external appearance of an academic disputation not to allow the display of academic erudition, but to disparage the professoriat, and to call into doubt their distinctive knowledge claims. There is one final contradiction here, and it is an important one. It lies in Morgenstern's own position. Morgenstern was essentially given the responsibility of disciplining through ridicule and humiliation. But he himself was manipulated by the monarch. This contradictory position closes the circle in contradiction. Not only did the Fool utter contradictions, but he embodies them.

The view that reason and folly are inextricably bound up with each other, is at odds with the position that truth was essentially self-consistent. The philosopher Christian Crusius was shortly after to echo Morgenstern in arguing that the common assumption that truth could not be contradictory was in fact false.[10] On the other hand, Wolff for example maintained, against Crusius, that "*Es kann etwas nicht zugleich sein und auch nicht sein.*"[11] Morgenstern's theses may thus be read as part of the continuing warfare against Wolff even after his exile from Prussia. Is it any coincidence that Friedrich II recalled Wolff immediately after his accession in 1740, only three years after the debate at Frankfurt-Oder? And may we not be able to see the history of attitudes to contradiction and its relation to truth, both by philosophers and others, as an indication of important changes in categories of what counted as acceptable experience?

There is a final point. Could the Frankfurt debate have happened anywhere else than in the German lands of the early eighteenth century? Perhaps not. The smallness of the courts of most of the German states, where intermediary bodies were absent or severely weakened, meant the monarchs were closer up to every decision than were those of the great monarchies of France or Austria. Monarchs had personal interests, and pursued them. Subjects (like Moser) could have, whether they appreciated it or not, very close encounters to the source of power. Issues that would have been decided in Versailles by complex infighting between court factions, were decided in Berlin by direct monarchial or ministerial order. That the Prussian monarch should take a direct personal interest in the affairs of the university of Frankfurt-Oder, and decide to reorder things there by an inventive application of his own sense of humor, was therefore not surprising.

III

Let us now put this debate in the tradition of the mockery of scholars and by scholars. Professors who were offended by the debate with a fool, in fact had hardly a leg to stand on. Ridicule in this period was one of the main ways in which scholars made their opponents impossible to take seriously, whatever the intrinsic value of their arguments.[12] That Morgenstern was a professor as a well as court fool meant he could speak

---

[10] Crusius, *Dissertatio philosophica de usu et limitatibus principii rationis determinantis vulgo sufficientis* (Leipzig: Langenheim, 1743); *Ausführliche Abhandlung von dem rechten Gebrauche und der Einschränkung des sogenannten Satzes von Zureichenden oder besser Determinirenden Grunde*, trans. Christian Friedrich Krause (Leipzig: Langenheim, 1766), 2, 8-10 (par. 1-3).

[11] Christian Wolff, *Vernünfftige Gedanken von Gott, der Welt und der Seele des Menschen, auch allen Dingen überhaupt* (1751; rpt., Hildesheim: Olms, 1983), 6-9, 16-18; Cap. II: 10, 12-15.

[12] Carl Friedrich Floegel, *Geschichte der Komischen Literatur* (Liegnitz & Leipzig, David Siegert,1784), I: v; Wolfgang Martens, "Von Thomasius bis Lichtenberg: zur Gelehrtensatire der Aufklärung," *Lessing Yearbook* 10 (1978): 17-34.

from both inside and outside the profession. While he might be foolish as professor, as a Fool he was professorial. His double role in this contest deepened the irony that could be extracted from his arguments and made his ridicule hard to shrug off. The ridiculing of scholars by satirists outside the scholarly community was in fact commonplace in the Enlightenment. Swift's scathing portrait of the scientists on Laputa's floating island, themselves precisely unable to calibrate ends or means, or remain in touch with reality, was just as Morgenstern defined foolishness. England had seen already half century at least of ridicule of the *virtuosi* of the Restoration. Charles II and his Fool, Thomas Killigrew, mocked the fellows of the Royal Society of London and the professors of Gresham College. The monarch and the Fool mocked in particular Robert Boyle's and William Petty's experiments with atmospheric pressure and their experiments with underwater navigation.[13]

Nor did the ridicule just come from outside the scholarly community. So widespread was ridicule of one scholar by another, that self-appointed guardians of the Republic of Letters issued many vain exhortations to their brethren to abstain from *ad hominem* arguments, and aggressive ridicule.[14] Ridicule was a device for establishing dominance, and an effective one at that.[15] If intensive ridicule was worth using, however, something serious must be at stake. Attacks by ridicule were paradoxical: they aimed to take away seriousness from opponents and leave it for the ridiculer. Yet ridicule concentrated around important ideas.

The intensity of this struggle, the deadly seriousness of ridicule, came also from the fact that in the eighteenth century the right to devote concentrated attention to objects of science and learning was not easily accorded. The laughter of Swift against the professors of Laputa was paralleled by the real-life laughter that greeted Linnaeus's scientific work, or Charles II's jokes at the expense of Boyle and Petty.[16] No wonder

---

[13] Walter Houghton, "The English *Virtuosi* of the Seventeenth Century," *Journal of the History of Ideas* 3 (1941): 51-73; R. H. Syfret, "Some Early Reactions to the Royal Society," *Notes and Records of the Royal Society of London,* 7 (1950): 207-58. Sometimes inventors working outside the universities even mocked themselves, fully relishing how their own roles oscillated between wise (for their technical knowledge), and foolish (because of the unpredictability of their results). See Herbert Breger, "Narrische Weisheit und Weise Narrheit in Erfindungen des Barock," *Aesthetik und Kommunikation: Beiträge zur politischen Erziehung* 45-46 (1981): 114-22.

[14] Martens, "Von Thomasius bis Lichtenberg."

[15] Floegel, *Geschichte der Komischen Literatur.*

[16] Dorinda Outram, *The Enlightenment* (Cambridge: Cambridge University Press, 1995), 50-51; Lorraine Daston, *Eine kurze Geschichte der wissenschaftlichen Aufmerksamkeit* (Munich: Carl Friedrich von Siemens Stiftung, 2001); Simon Schaffer, "Wallification: Thomas Hobbes on School Divinity and Experimental Pneumatics," *Studies in the History and Philosophy of Science* 19 (1988): 275-98.

Moser and other professors had objected to being forced into debate with the Fool. Ridicule was the unwanted, dialogic, companion of the emergence of science and scholarship as self-standing occupations with their own ways of thinking. Ridicule was a powerful enemy of organized learning because it so effectively invited the questioning of its formality and protocols. Levity drops out of scholarly life when discipline formation comes in. The use of foolishness was directly contrary to the divisions of academic labor which were already emerging in this period.

Foolishness and truth could be in very direct relationship to each other, unbuffered by the use of specialized language, or academic decorum. Friedrich I, King in Prussia and father of Friedrich Wilhelm I, had recognized this very clearly. After the death of his official Fool, Pussman, a struggle broke out between the king and the Berlin clergy, who objected to the king's wish that Pussman be buried in consecrated ground. Friedrich won, with the comment that "Pussman war ein Prediger der Wahrheit, und hat meiner selbst nicht geschont, verdient folglich mitten in der Kirche zu liegen, wo nichts als lauter Wahrheit gepredigt werden soll."[17] The Fool as a preacher of truth comes, as the King's comment makes clear, very close to the idea of *Narrenfreiheit*. This word refers to the fool's freedom to say anything he wants to anyone he pleases. It is obviously a concept which is part of the complex history of who may say what to whom, and where. It is also a subversive idea, having to do with the truths that can be brought to light if the normal patterns of deference and civility in society are no longer maintained.[18]

IV

There is a link between *Narrenfreiheit* and the *Philosophenfreiheit*.[19] Philosophers' freedom and fools' freedom are each subversive, the former because it involves the idea that philosophers can say what they want without acknowledging the superior claims of theology, the latter because it claims that fools may at any time say what they want to say, and to whomever they want to say it. Seventeenth- and eighteenth-century fools in the German lands worked within a culture of ridicule and fool-ishness, often venturing into a no-man's land lying between current conflict between the truths of revelation and scripture on the one hand, and the

---

[17] Carl Friedrich Floegel, *Geschichte der Hofnarren* (Leipzig: Siegert, 1789), 218.

[18] W. E. Knowles Middelton, "What did Charles II call the Fellows of the Royal Society?", *Notes and Records of the Royal Society of London* 32 (1997-8): 13-16, quotes Pepys, *Diary*, 13 Feb 1667/8 on Tom Killigrew who "may with privilege revile or jeere anybody, the greatest person, without offense, by the privilege of his place."

[19] Jonathan Israel, *Radical Enlightenment: Philosophy and the Making of Modernity, 1650-1750*. (Oxford: Oxford University Press, 2001).

truths of human reason on the other. Fools' truth became the third form of truth. What defined fools' truth as different was not only *Narrenfreiheit*, and not only particularly foolish ways of proceeding, speaking and performing. In a hierarchical world abounding in conflicts over superiority and inferiority, such as that between philosophers and theologians, fools humor was leveling. For Friedrich I, for example, fools' truth was as good as theological truth, and his fool who by definition reached the truth he preached by nonrational ways, deserved to lie among the educated men who dedicated themselves to the profession of theology. In the same way, Tieck's monarch sees the fool and scholar (a historian) as equal. Let us leave the last world with Salomon Morgenstern, who in his final thesis pointed out the fact that foolishness is universal leads to the conclusion that all men are in this respect equal:

> Die Narrheit ist in der Welt nothwendig und unentbehrlich ... beynahe alle Freude entstehet von, durch, über und bey Narren! Ein Narr macht durch närrischen Vortrag dessen was ein Narr gethan, einen Narr frohlich.... hat die Natur die Anstheilung der Narrheit allgemein gemacht; und jedem seinen bescheidenen Theil gegeben. Denen Vornehmen wachst daher die Gelegenheit zu dass sie Menschen zu seyn sich erinnern; und die Geringern ziehen daraus den Trost dass andere durch den Stand nicht eben zugleich über die allgemeinen Menschlichen Schwachheiten erhoben.

The social order is undermined by the foolishness common to men. Only the king is not leveled. He can stop and start the performance of foolishness at will. The presumption of the universality of folly leaves all subjects equal beneath him, without the protections of privilege. Through the staging of folly, the king begins the modernization of the social order long before the Jacobins made all equal because equally subject to the Terror. That Morgenstern, the king's buffoon, the manipulated manipulator, was essential to sustain the disciplinary staging of foolishness leads us straight back into the contradictions of truth.

Eighteenth-Century Spanish Political Economy: Epistemology and Decline[1]

Jorge Cañizares-Esguerra
State University of New York, Buffalo

Abstract

The main preoccupation of eighteenth-century Spanish political economy was the identification of the causes of national decline. The discipline developed in full awareness that European discourse scathingly critical of things Spanish had already framed the debate. Spanish intellectuals dismissed foreign observations, claiming that they alone were capable of being objective on the subject. Patriotism, however, narrowed the choices available to political economists to theories that explained decline in terms of luxury and emasculation. Many intellectuals found the virile and humanist culture of the Spanish Renaissance (*Siglo de Oro*) an alternative to the new French forms of courtly and public sociability introduced by the Bourbons. But traditional theories regarding the negative effects of luxury on national prosperity had to confront the record left behind by some *Arbitristas*. As eighteenth-century Spanish political economists realized that traditional paradigms could further damage the economy, they engaged in endless debates over the causes of economic decline, the identification of which became a patriotic crusade. Two clear positions emerged from this debate. The first was that the causes of decline were already well known, and advised immediate reform along the lines suggested by the much-maligned foreign observers. The second advocated historical research, on the view that previous shallow theorizing had led Spain astray, causing more economic damage than stability. Advocates of this second position maintained that instead of speculative theorizing in political economy, careful archival research into the historical processes of decline was necessary. Political economy in Spain developed along these two mutually exclusive tracks.

After traveling through the sprawling territories of the Spanish empire, Zacharie de Pazzi de Bonneville, also known as *le philosophe La Douceur*, concluded in 1771 that "there is no nation more brutish [*abruti*], ignorant, savage, and barbarous than Spain." In Paris in 1777, Joseph La Porte reached similar conclusions in his *Le voyageur françois* (1766–1795) a massive compilation of travel narratives presented as letters by a roving, fictional observer to a *salonnière* back home. For La Porte, Spain was a

[1] The author wishes to thank Antonio Feros and John H. Elliott for their kind invitation to present an earlier version of this paper in Spanish at the seminar *La evolución histórica de la España moderna: éxitos y fracasos* that took place in Soria, Spain in July 2001, generously financed by the Fundación Duques de Soria. Sharp criticism by two anonymous reviewers of the original paper in Spanish forced me to clarify my arguments. Antonio Feros also offered pointed commentary and bibliographical help as I composed a new draft in English. Thanks to Jeffrey Speicher for helping me smooth some wrinkles in the translation. Finally, the members of the Workshop on Early Modern Studies at the University of Chicago read and commented this paper and helped me rethink my conclusions.

land of superstitious folk, still practicing sciences inherited from the Moors, namely, "judicial astrology, cabala, and other Arab inanities." Spaniards, he further argued, had boundless admiration for Aristotle, "whose senseless and tenebrous philosophy" they blindly followed. Finally in 1781 the Abbé Raynal maintained, in the same melodramatic tone that characterizes so many of the pages of his *Histoire philosophique des deux Indes*, that "never has a nation been as enslaved to its prejudices as Spain. In no other place has irrationality [*le déraison*] proven as dogmatic, as close, and as subtle." References to the backwardness and ignorance of Spain extracted from the pages of scores of eighteenth-century travelers and authors would most likely fill a thick volume. The European Enlightenment had no patience with Spain, for it stood for all the things the literati most hated.[2]

These criticisms, many of which were broadcast not only by overzealous ideologues but also by important and scholarly figures such as the baron of Montesquieu, left a lasting mark on the soul of the Spanish Enlightenment. The state and local intellectuals spent considerable amounts of energy seeking to deny the charges leveled by foreigners, particularly the French. There is no better example of how anxiously Spaniards sought to refute these negative images than the cultural and scientific policies undertaken by the crown. To counter the views of the French Minim Louis Feuillée, who in the wake of expeditions to Peru and the Caribbean early in the century maintained that the New World remained largely unknown owing to Spain's lack of scientific curiosity, and to rebuff Carl Linnaeus, who complained that Spain had done nothing to improve the knowledge of plants, the crown poured millions into building botanical gardens and outfitting countless natural history expeditions to the colonies. Although this project did not yield concrete economic returns, it was so massive that by the end of the century Alexander von Humboldt could not contain his surprise. Enlightened botanists such as Antonio José Cavanilles used the generous policies of the crown to name new plant species after prominent local men in order to remind the European public of the accomplishments of the Spanish literati.[3]

[2] Zacharie de Pazzi Bonneville, *De l'Amérique et des américains* (Berlin: Samuel Pitra, 1771), 61; Joseph de La Porte, *Le voyageur françois*, 42 vol. (Paris: Cellot, 1768-95), 16: 94; Raynal is cited by Manfred Tietz, "l'Espagne el *l'Histoire des deux Indes* de l'abbe Raynal," in *Lectures de Raynal: L'Histoire des deux Indes en Europe et en Amérique au XVIIIe siècle*, ed. Hans-Jurgen Lüsebrink and Manfred Tietz (Oxford: Voltaire Foundation, 1991), 100.
[3] To what degree most eighteenth-century Spanish scientific policies were shaped by patriotic agendas is something that merits further research. See for example the works of Jean-Pierre Clément, "De los nombres de plantas," in *Ciencia y contexto histórico en las expediciones ilustradas a América*, ed. Fermín del Pino (Madrid: Consejo de Investigaciones Científicas,

Neither criticism of Spain's alleged backwardness, nor patriotic responses to foreign scorn were new to the eighteenth century. There was, however, one novel development. Whereas in the past censure had been focused on the alleged idolatrous and superstitious nature of Spanish Catholicism and on the brutality and greed exhibited by conquistadors and troops in America and Holland, by the mid seventeenth-century European intellectuals found themselves grappling with the reality of Spanish "decline." [4] Travelers and observers began to hammer out a narrative of a nation in precipitous freefall, creating a cautionary morality tale of a country that had gone from riches to rags, squandering opportunities at every turn. This master narrative maintained that the spread of aristocratic values among the laboring population, the irrational rejection of the new sciences and technologies developed in the rest of Europe during the Scientific Revolution, and the building of a fiscally irresponsible, overstretched empire had condemned Spain to chronic state of depopulation and vagrancy. [5]

Yet in all these neat narratives of decline, causes and effects were difficult to sort out. Was vagrancy, for example, an innate trait of the local population caused by the North African climate of Castile as many

1988), 141-71; and Fermín del Pino and Angel Guirao, "Las expediciones ilustradas y el estado español", *Revista de Indias* 47 (1987): 380-83. On how patriotism shaped most other areas of intellectual production, see Cañizares-Esguerra, *How to Write the History of the New World. Histories, Epistemologies, and Identities in the Eighteenth-Century Atlantic World* (Stanford: Stanford University Press, 2001), ch. 3. On Linnaeus's views of Spain and the ensuing debate, see Ricardo Pascual, *El botánico José Quer (1695-1764): Primer apologista de la ciencia española* (Valencia: Cátedra e Instituto de Historia de la Medicina, 1970). On the views of Feuillée see his "Epitre" in *Journal des observations physiques, mathématiques et botaniques.... sur les côtes orientales de la Amérique Méridionale et aux Indes Occidentales* (Paris: Pierre Giffart, 1714). For a succinct and illuminating study of the development and failure of Spain's investment in botanical research, see Francisco. J. Puerto Sarmiento, *La ilusión quebrada: Botánica, sanidad y política científica en la España Ilustrada* (Barcelona: Edicones del Serbal, 1988).

[4] J. N. Hillgarth, *The Mirror of Spain, 1500-1700. The Formation of a Myth* (Ann Arbor: University of Michigan Press, 2000). On the Spanish "Black Legend," see Julián Juderías, *La leyenda negra: Estudios acerca del concepto de España en el extranjero.* 9th ed. (Barcelona: Araluce, 1943); Ricardo García Carcel, *La leyenda negra. Historia y opinion* (Madrid: Alianza, 1981); Charles Gibson ed., *The Black Legend. Anti-Spanish Attitudes in the Old World and New* (New York: Knopf, 1971); William S. Maltby, *The Black Legend in England: The Development of Anti-Spanish Sentiment, 1558-1660* (Durham, NC: Duke University Press, 1971); and Benjamin Schmidt, *Innocence Abroad. The Dutch Imagination and the New World. 1570-1670* (Cambridge: Cambridge University Press, 2001).

[5] On travelers to Spain, see Alfred Morel-Fatio, "Comment la France a connu et compris l'Espagne depuis le moyen âge jusqu' à nos jours," in *Etudes sur L'Espagne.* Première série (Paris, F. Vieweg, 1888), 1-114; Jean Sarrailh, "Voyageurs français au XVIIIe siècle. De l'abbé de Vayrac à l'abbé Delaporte," *Bulletin Hispanique* 36 (1934), no. 1; Francisco Aguilar Piñal, "Relatos de viajes de extranjeros por la España del siglo XVIII. Estudios realizados hasta el presente," *Boletín del Centro de Estudios del Siglo XVIII,* 4-5 (1977): 203-208; José María Díez Borque, *La vida Española en el Siglo de Oro según los extranjeros* (Barcelona: Ediciones del Serbal, 1990).

alleged? Or was it rather the product of the spread of aristocratic values among populations long locked in a crusading campaign against Islam? Was vagrancy actually caused by the massive arrival of cheaper foreign goods and textiles that since the late sixteenth century had forced local manufacturing out of business? By the same token, was the disproportionate growth of the clergy caused by the search for alternative forms of employment? Or was the swollen clerical state the reason for the poorly performing economy in the first place, for the clergy had promoted a culture of profligate ritual excess, ignorance, and lack of entrepreneurship?

Early modern debates over the cause of national decline began first in Spain. In the early seventeenth century the country witnessed an explosion of "*arbitrista*" literature that sought to explain why Spain had rapidly lost ground to other European powers. The remedies for decline formulated by some *arbitristas*, however, proved ultimately detrimental. Like other European intellectuals bent on explaining the rise and fall of empire, many *arbitristas* blamed courtly emasculation for the current plight of the nation. Not surprisingly they pressed for a return to Christian piety and advised renewed military campaigns to bring the warrior out of the effete courtier. To pay for these wars and avoid unwanted "luxury," they promoted the taxation of "sumptuary" items. These recipes, to be sure, only worsened the fiscal deficit and further slowed down the economy.[6] No wonder these *arbitristas* became figures of ridicule and scorn in seventeenth-century Spanish theater.[7] Eighteenth-century literature cautioned repeatedly against the example of the *arbitristas*, whose misguided theories had further compounded the crisis. Thus, it was the patriotic responsibility of the intellectual to identify the cause of decline accurately. But for all the realization that many *arbitristas* had done more harm than good, Spanish intellectuals remained wedded to traditional discourses. It was difficult for new paradigms to spread.

Since the Renaissance traditional discourses had held that decline was caused by the loss of civic virtues. Theories of the decline of Rome were emblematic of this approach. Self-indulgent and decadent elites, it was argued, had left the defense of the Roman Empire in the hands of professionals. As commerce and territory grew, and as citizens became

---

[6] J. H. Elliott, "Self-Perception and Decline in Early Seventeenth-Century Spain," in *Spain and Its World 1500-1700. Selected Essays* (New Haven: Yale University Press, 1989), 241-61; Luis Perdices Blas, *La economía política de la decadencia de Castilla en el siglo XVII: Investigaciones de los arbitristas sobre la naturaleza y causa de la riqueza de las naciones* (Madrid: Sintesis, 1996). *Arbitristas* were a variegated group, most holding very dissimilar, even opposing ideas. I have thus hedged my assertions about *arbitrismo* with qualifiers such as "many" and "some."

[7] Jean Vilar, *Literatura y economía. La figura satírica del arbitrista en el Siglo de Oro* (Madrid: Revista de Occidente, 1973).

merchants or, worse, idle, effete courtiers, Romans turned over the affairs of the state to mercenaries and emperors. Soon Romans caved in, unable to take power away from emperors and cowardly surrendering to the barbarian onslaught.[8]

This discourse of decline through emasculation, however, came in for criticism as the eighteenth-century commercial revolution unfolded. As absolute monarchies consolidated and as mercantilism and new cultures of sociability and consumption came of age, a new discourse of "commercial humanism" replaced the theories of decline induced by trade and luxury. The views of Bernard Mandeville and Adam Smith typified this transformation. In *The Fable of the Bees* (1714) Mandeville argued that private "vices" were in fact public virtues; luxury and the pursuit of wealth benefited society as whole. Adam Smith's doctrine of the "invisible hand" also held that self interest became civically virtuous by means of the law of unintended consequences, a form of indirect providence. Theories of checks and balances of power helped scholars to account for decline. Lack of parliaments, not excessive commerce, caused nations to decline.[9] In Spain, patriotic epistemology and the opposition to new forms of sociability and consumption slowed down the spread of the discourse of commercial humanism.

Patriotic epistemology and the critique of new forms of sociability

It is plausible to argue that a fundamental feature of the Spanish Enlightenment was the tension that obtained between rejection of scornful foreign visions of Spain and the need to accept the reality of decadence while identifying its causes.[10] The critique of foreign views was a central

---

[8] J. G. A. Pocock, *The Machiavellian Moment: Florentine Political Thought and the Atlantic Republican Tradition* (Princeton: Princeton University Press, 1975).

[9] Idem, *Virtue, Commerce, and History* (Cambridge: Cambridge University Press, 1985); Thomas Horne, *The Social Thought of Bernard Mandeville: Virtue and Commerce in Early Eighteenth Century England* (New York: Columbia University Press, 1978); Richard Olson, *The Emergence of the Social Sciences 1642-1792* (New York: Twayne, 1993), chs. 9 and 11; Istvan Hont and Michael Ignatieff, eds., *Wealth and Virtue: The Shaping of Political Economy in the Scottish Enlightenment* (Cambridge: Cambridge University Press, 1983); Albert O. Hirshman, *The Passions and the Interests: Political Arguments for Capitalism before its Triumph* (Princeton: Princeton University Press, 1977); and Emma Rothschild, *Economic Sentiments: Adam Smith, Condorcet and the Enlightenment* (Cambridge, MA: Harvard University Press, 2001).

[10] For other important characterizations of the Spanish Enlightenment, see Richard Herr, *The Eighteenth-Century Revolution in Spain* (Princeton: Princeton University Press, 1958); Jean Sarrailh, *La España Ilustrada de la segunda mitad del siglo XVIII* (México: Fondo de Cultura Económica, 1957); Francisco Sánchez-Blanco Parody, *Europa y el pensamiento español del siglo XVIII* (Madrid: Alianza, 1991); Concepción Castro, *Campomanes: estado y reformismo ilustrado* (Madrid: Alianza, 1996); Manuel Sellés, José Luis Peset and Antonio Lafuente, eds., *Carlos III y la ciencia de la Ilustración* (Madrid: Alianza, 1989); Antonio Mestre, *Mayans y la España de la Ilustracion* (Madrid: Espasa Calpe, 1990).

concern of the age. Foreigners were dismissed because they were thought to pass judgment on a nation they barely knew. Spanish intellectuals characterized the foreign observer as shallow and ignorant, lacking in the linguistic and cultural tools needed to make sense of the country they purportedly sought to interpret. The views of the Valencian Juan Bautista Muñoz typify this attitude. Immediately after a member of the entourage of the papal nuncio in Madrid, the former professor of mathematics at the Sapienza in Rome, Cesareo Giuseppe Pozzi, published *Saggio de educazione claustrale per li giovani* (*Essay on the Education of the Cloistered Youth*), 1778, Muñoz wrote a scathing critique, for the Italian had ridiculed local customs of clerical training. Muñoz castigated Pozzi for the philosophical and theological views underpinning the latter's educational proposals. More important, Muñoz set out to prove that the erudite Benedictine was in fact a fraud, who had lifted most of his entries on pedagogy from fashionable French texts on the assumption that Spanish audiences were too benighted to notice. A foreigner like Pozzi felt entitled upon arrival to pontificate on matters he barely understood simply because he held Spaniards in contempt. Pozzi, Muñoz argued, typified the European intellectual who "without any knowledge of Spanish learned traditions, having most likely read a few of our books we ourselves dismiss, pigeonhole us as ignorant, as defilers of good taste."[11] Muñoz was not alone. In 1782 the powerful ambassador in Rome and leading patron of the Spanish Enlightenment, José Nicolás de Azara, reviewing Henry Swinburne's *Travels through Spain, in the years 1775 and 1776* (1779) also offered a broader critic of foreign travelers. "Swinburne," Azara mockingly remarked, "should be praised for his sharp observational powers, for after having spent two, three days [in Spain] he already knew that all roads were terrible, hostels even worse, and the whole country a hellhole where stupidity runs rampant."[12]

The condemnation of ignorant foreign observers reached a climax in the wake of the publication of the article "Espagne" in the *Encyclopédie méthodique* (1783) by Nicolas Masson de Morvilliers. An author more given to rhetorical flourishes than to serious scholarship, Morvilliers caused an uproar after he argued that Spain had contributed nothing to the

---

[11] "de sin tener conocimiento de la literatura española, sin haber quizás leído más que algún libro despreciado por nosotros mismos, nos imponen a todos la nota de ignorantes y corrompedores del buen gusto." Juan Bautista Muñoz, *Juicio del tratado de la educación del M. R. P. D. Cesareo Pozzi* (Madrid: Joachim Ibarra, 1778), 8.

[12] "Swinburne debes ser felicitado por su perpicaz penetración que, a los dos o trés días de haber entrado ... ya había descubierto que todos los caminos eran malos, las posadas peores, el país parecido al infierno, donde reina la estupidez." Letter by José Nicolás de Azara (Roma, June 6, 1782) included in Azara's prologue to Guillermo Bowles's *Introducción a la historia natural y a la geografía física de España*. 2ⁿᵈ ed. (Madrid: Imprenta Real, 1782); cited in Jean Sarrailh, *La España Ilustrada*, 322, n. 134.

store of knowledge in the last millennium. In *Oración apologética por la España y su mérito literario* (*Apologetic Peroration for Spain and its Literary Merit*), 1786, Juan Pablo Forner denounced these views as typical of the French, whose liking for grand philosophical systems such as Descartes's made them fond of sweeping and outlandish statements. Morvilliers stood for those foreign observers "who after having simply perused our annals, having never read our books, clueless of the state of our higher education, ignorant of our language, prefer not to draw upon the proper sources of instruction but on what comes easier, namely, fiction. Thus, at the expense of our sad peninsula, they spin off fantastic novels and fables as absurd as the stories retailed by our early writers of books of chivalry."[13]

For all their rejection of foreign scorn, Muñoz, Azara, and Forner were perfectly aware that Spain had lost ground to rival powers. These authors spent their lives identifying the origins of decline and seeking solutions. Yet they also thought that Spaniards, or expatriates who had made Spain their home, were better prepared than foreigners to tackle this difficult intellectual problem.[14] This patriotic epistemological discourse lies at the core of the Spanish Enlightenment and gives the period its peculiar texture. This discourse surfaces repeatedly throughout the century. In fact it helps explain the work of one of the leading intellectuals of the age: José Cadalso.

Cadalso's *Cartas marruecas* (*Moroccan Letters*), 1793, is paradoxically a work that privileges the views of a foreign observer. Using fictional letters penned by a Middle Eastern traveler, a conceit introduced by Montesquieu in *Lettres Persanes*, Cadalso uses the Moroccan Gazel to discuss the dilemmas and problems of contemporary Spanish society. It would appear that by making Gazel central to his narrative, Cadalso, unlike Azara, Muñoz, and Forner, was not interested in discrediting foreign reporters. But Cadalso held fast to patriotic views of epistemology. Cadalso made Gazel credible precisely because the latter was always ready

---

[13] "hombres que apenas han saludado nuestros anales, que jamás han visto uno de nuestros libros, que ignoran el estado de nuestras escuelas, que carecen del conocimiento de nuestro idioma ... [que] en vez de acudir a tomar en las Fuentes la instrucción debida ... echan mano, por más cómoda, de la ficción y texen a costa de la triste Península novelas y fábulas tan absurdas como pudieran nuestros antiguos Escritores de caballerías" Juan Pablo Forner, *Oración Apologética por la España y su mérito literario* (Madrid: Imprenta Real, 1786), 10-11.

[14] The views of long-term residents and foreign scholars who spent their lives studying Spain were welcome. See for example the cases of the Irish Ricardo Ward and Guillermo Bowles and the French Count Francisco de Cobarrús whose writings were well received and even acclaimed. The Scottish historian William Robertson, who never set foot in Spain, was made honorary member of the Royal Academy of History, although eventually his views proved controversial. On Ward, Bowles, and Cobarrús, see Sarrailh, *La España Ilustrada*, 323-28. On Robertson, see Cañizares-Esguerra, *How to Write the History of the New World*, 171-74.

to listen and to learn from Spaniards. Throughout the text, Gazel appears as eager to be taught and be educated by Nuño Núñez, a deeply learned Spanish man well acquainted with the sources of national history. Moreover Gazel speaks fluent Spanish and embraces Spanish sartorial fashions. Ultimately it is Núñez's voice that Gazel parrots. Núñez (representing Cadalso in the text) uses Gazel to vent his criticisms of Spain.[15]

Cadalso was a fierce proponent of patriotic epistemology. In fact his *Cartas* were first conceived to address the criticisms of Spain leveled by a foreign observer: Montesquieu. In *Lettres Persanes*, Montesquieu had found the honor and *gravitas* of the Spanish people as inflated and ridiculous, the cause of Spanish stagnation. Such a culture of exaggerated honor seemed to value idleness over manual labor. Cadalso was at a loss to explain why a man as learned as Montesquieu had dared to offer such sweeping and shallow generalizations of a nation he barely knew. Cadalso could not understand why Montesquieu had chosen to speak "without any knowledge of our history, religion, laws, mores, and nature." When Cadalso first read Montesquieu's letter no. 78 he became so enraged that he spent several years (1768-1771) writing a defense of Spanish nation: *Defensa de la nación española (Defense of the Spanish Nation)*.[16]

This defense, to be sure, not only called into question the credibility of foreign observers, it also sought to offer an alternative account of the origins of national decline. Cadalso dismissed Montesquieu's views outright as he argued that Spain's problems were not found in the culture of Castilian honor but in an aging stagnant economy, with its shallow job market and lack of avenues of social mobility. Cadalso insisted that this stagnation started with the reign of Philip II, that "prejudicial king" (*un rey perjudicial*) whose rule created the conditions that made the vagrancy and culture of idleness in Spain possible. According to Cadalso, Philip II's stubborn and fiscally ruinous defense of an overstretched empire was to blame for the crisis of productivity that engulfed Spain in the seventeenth century.

Cadalso's ferocious epistemological patriotism forced him to fall back on traditional *arbitrista* paradigms. As he set out to oppose Montesquieu, Cadalso defended the culture of Spanish honor and *gravitas*. Cadalso's political economy assumed honor and manliness to be the engine of Spanish history: when scarce, the nation declined; when abundant, it

[15] A characterization of Gazel as a traveler can be found in José Cadalso, *Cartas marruecas*, ed. Manuel Camarero (Madrid, Editorial Castalia, 1985), letters 1 and 2.
[16] "sin el menor conocimiento de su historia, religión, leyes, costumbres y naturaleza," José de Cadalso, *Defensa de la nación española contra la Carta Persiana LXXVII de Montesquieu (texto inédito)*, ed. Guy Mercadier (Toulouse: Institut d'Etudes Hispaniques, Hispano-Americaines et Luso-Bresiliennes, Université de Toulouse, 1979), 4.

prospered. Cadalso understood the Spanish past as cyclical, with periods of growth followed by decline. Phoenicians, Romans, and Visigoths, he argued, had at different times dominated Spain. These virile invaders encountered a bountiful land and flourished. Soon, however, prosperity turned into decline and manliness into emasculation. New waves of virile invaders displaced earlier arrivals that had turned weak and effete: Phoenicians fell to the Romans, who gave in to the Visigoths, who in turn surrendered to the Moors. According to Cadalso, the *Reconquista* was part of this cyclical pattern of conquest, expansion, and decline. The effeminate Moors were defeated by the more rugged Christian troops, who embarked in a new cycle of prosperity-cum-expansion. This cycle reached its apogee in the Renaissance. Yet the arrival of Philip II brought prosperity to a halt and set off once again an age of "absolute decline in the sciences, the arts, the military, commerce, agriculture, and population growth."[17] Under the Habsburgs traditional Spanish honor and virility became a mockery of themselves as the nation came to be led by buffoons and the mentally ill.

Like some *arbitristas*, Cadalso identified luxury induced by commerce as a threat. However, unlike these *arbitristas*, Cadalso did not seek to enhance the nation's virility by taxing it to death or by promoting new military campaigns. His theory of decline rather led him to oppose the new forms of sociability sponsored by the Bourbons. Cadalso detested the Francophile character of Spain's new public sphere, which he found decadent and fake. In his efforts to castigate this culture he contributed to the creation of a new literary figure: the *petrimetre*, a shallow and effete character who aped French fashions and who was given to vacuous and affected conversations. In *Los eruditos a la violeta* (1770) and *Cartas marruecas* (1793), Cadalso presented a ferocious critique of the new civilization of sociability and consumption that seemed to be eating away at the virile soul of the Spanish nation.[18]

In an effort to halt the spread of shallow new foreign forms of sociability, intellectuals chastised the moral corruption they seemed to be inducing. Clearly Cadalso was not the first to make this connection. Diego de Torres Villarroel had already maintained that the new forms of sociability were manifestations of corruption and symptoms of decline. An

---

[17] "de la decadencia total de las ciencias, artes, milicias, comercio, agricultura y población" Cadalso, *Defensa*, 10.

[18] Some authors did not react angrily to the views of Montesquieu, who after all used his *Lettres Persanes* to ridicule French mores rather than Spain's. These authors agreed wholeheartedly with Montesquieu and suggested that positions like Cadalso's avoided coming to grips with the real problems of the nation. See, for example, Antonio de Capmany (also known as Pedro Fernández), "Comentarios sobre el doctor festivo y maestro de los Eruditos a la Violeta, para desengaño de los españoles que leen poco y malo" [1773], in Julián Marías, *La España posible en tiempo de Carlos III*. 2nd ed. (Madrid: Planeta, 1988), 130-52.

author whose distinct and powerful voice has yet to be understood, Torrres Villaroel turned to Francisco Quevedo, the seventeenth-century writer who masterfully deployed irony to defend Spain against foreign scorn, for inspiration. In *Visiones y visitas* (*Visions and Errands*), 1743, Torres de Villarroel follows Quevedo through a fictional tour of Madrid only to find the capital sunk in decadence. His pen portraits of dissolute and ignorant courtiers, gluttonous priests, swindling doctors, and writers and *petrimetres* engaged in vacuous banter in the pursuit of fleeting fame, are all literary jewels. They also reveal a deep hostility toward the new forms of public sociability embedded in the rising culture of *tertulias,* salons, academies, and cafes of mid-eighteenth-century Spain.[19]

This critique of the shallow, new culture of literary sociability went hand in hand with a positive evaluation of the Renaissance as a golden age. Cadalso, again, exemplifies this trend. He turned to the Spanish Renaissance to help him deflect Montesquieu's criticism of the accomplishments of the Spanish mind. Montesquieu had argued that Spain's intellectual production did not go beyond books of chivalry and boring scholastic tomes. Cadalso replied to these charges by insisting that early modern Spain had been a nation intellectually more precocious than France, churning out books of rhetoric, navigation, cartography, poetry, mathematics, and theology.[20] The revival or invention of the Spanish Renaissance as a patriotic strategy to counter foreign charges of Spanish ignorance and backwardness occupied the energies of scores of eighteenth-century intellectuals. Thus, a central objective of the Spanish Academy created by the Bourbons in 1712 consisted, in the words of a leading advocate of neoclassical reform in drama, Juán de Iriarte, in "drafting apologetic defenses of the national language to counter the slanders of foreigners. Some rob us of our national pride, confusing us with Africans or Asians. Others cannot find among us more than one or two good authors and maintain that our science is limited to a couple of sonnets and a handful of syllogisms. [The Academy] needs to praise the great luminaries of our fatherland by reissuing their works and resurrecting their names."[21] These initiatives proved remarkably successful. Hundreds of

---

[19] Torres Villaroel, *Visiones y visitas de Torres con Don Francisco de Quevedo por la corte*, ed. Sebold Russell (Madrid: Espasa-Calpe, 1966). A similar sensibility is to be found in the light comedy of Ramón de la Cruz, *Sainetes*, ed. Francisco Lafarga (Madrid: Cátedra, 1990).
[20] Cadalso, *Los eruditos a la violeta* [1772], ed. Nigel Glendinning (Salamanca: Anaya, 1967), 167.
[21] "Componer apologías de la lengua patria en vindicación de las calumnias extranjeras, que hasta nacionalidad le niegan, haciéndole africana o asiática algunos, circunscribiendo otros a uno o dos el número de nuestros buenos autores, y afirmando que toda la ciencia de España se reduce a dos coplas y cuatro silogismos.... [El rol de la Academia consiste] en hacer elogio de los grandes y esclarecidos varones de nuestra patria resucitando sus memorias y sus

early-modern manuscripts and books by well- and little-known authors
were either reissued or published for the first time in the eighteenth
century.

For Cadalso and many others, the visions, styles, and sensibilities of
the Spanish Renaissance stood for the "authentic," a means to oppose
fashionable new intellectual currents that were foreign, effete, shallow,
and fake. According to these intellectuals the way to address the problem
of decline involved first and foremost the implementation of new cultural
policies. As Antonio Mestre has repeatedly shown, the most representative
figure of this type of approach was Gregorio Mayans y Siscar. With the
support of Dutch and German printers and scholars, Mayans y Siscar
invented a new period in historiography, namely, the *Siglo de Oro*, a
gilded age whose exacting, elegant, and profoundly "authentic"
scholarship he urged his countrymen to imitate. Many were inspired by
this vision.[22] The very category of "*siglo de oro*," a label now used to
refer to a period in the literature of the seventeenth century, was first
coined in the Spanish Enlightenment to describe the intellectual
accomplishments of the sixteenth century.[23]

Epistemology and Spanish decline

In addition to concerns over the rise of new forms of sociability and
consumption, discourses on decadence were framed by debates over
whether the causes of decline were known and over how fast to enact
reforms. Many scholars, however, concluded that it was the very
obsession with finding causes that accounted for Spain's decline in the first
place. In the following pages I demonstrate how these concerns help make
sense of key eighteenth-century Spanish texts on political economy.

The views of Manuel Antonio de Gándara on the causes of decline were
typical of the debates of his age. In *Apuntes sobre el bien y el mal de
España* (*Notes on the Strength and Ills of Spain*), 1759, Gándara showed
that at least twenty-seven contradictory models could be cited to explain
Spanish decline. So many models, however, obscured rather than clarified
the real causes of decadence. Facing so many narrative of decline,
Gándara argued, authorities could not spring into action to enact much-

---

nombres." Juan de Iriarte cited in Emilio Cotarelo y Mori, *Iriarte y su época* (Madrid:
Estudio Tipográfico "Sucesores de Rivadeneyra," 1897), 16.

[22] Antonio Mestre, *Mayans y la España de la Ilustración*; François Lopez, *Juan Pablo
Forner et la crise de la conscience espagnole au XVIIIIe siècle* (Bordeaux: Bibliothèque de
l'Ecole des hautes études hispaniques, 1976).

[23] François Lopez, "Comment l'Espagne eclairée inventa le Siècle d'Or," in *Hommage des
hispanistes Français a Noël Salomon* (Barcelona: Editorial Laia, 1979), 517-25; Antonio
Juárez Medina, *Las reediciones de obras de erudición de los siglos XVI y XVII durante el
siglo XVIII español* (Frankfurt am Main: Lang, 1988).

needed reforms.[24] Gándara thought that political economy should investigate how all these seemingly unrelated models were in fact connected. Many *arbitristas* and early eighteenth-century authors such as Gerónimo de Uztariz (author of *Theórica, y práctica de comercio y de marina* [1724, 1742]), he complained, had correctly identified the symptoms yet had failed to discover the root cause of all Spanish ills, namely, the policy of allowing unchecked foreign imports while actively thwarting local manufacturing. The inability of most *arbitristas* and previous political economists to pinpoint *the* cause of all symptoms had in itself become a problem for the economy. By seeking to treat the symptoms as opposed to the actual disease, these intellectuals had further wounded the body politic.[25]

León de Arroyal begged to differ. In his *Cartas económico-políticas* (*Letters on Political Economy*), 1790s, Arroyal took issue with writers such as Gándara. According to Arroyal there was more than one cause to blame. The causes of decadence, he argued, were multiple, interlocking and yet to be fully identified (e.g., the cumbersome and archaic structure of the state; the many regulations choking both commerce and the treasury; the culture of litigation undermining the implementation of the law; and the absence of checks and balances limiting centripetal, authoritarian monarchical forces as well as centrifugal, aristocratic ones). For Arroyal the task at hand was the opposite of that urged by Gándara. Political economists should seek to discover the causes through empirically and historically disciplined research. "Until the causes of Spanish decadence are discovered," he insisted, "all efforts to halt its devastating manifestations will prove in vain."[26]

Narratives of decline seemed to have oscillated between the two alternatives sketched by Gándara and Arroyal. On the one hand stood those who sought to create a deductive science in which all symptoms of decline were accounted for with a single all-encompassing theory. On the other hand stood the likes of Arroyal who understood political economy as a historical science and who were fearful that hasty theorizing could compound the crisis by introducing misguided reforms. There was, however, a third position, first sketched by Melchor Gaspar de Jovellanos, one of the leading figures of the Spanish Enlightenment.

---

[24] Miguel Antonio de Gándara, *Apuntes sobre el bien y el mal de España* [1759], ed. Jacinta Macías Delgado (Madrid: Instituto de Estudios Fiscales, 1988), 53-81.

[25] Gándara, *Apuntes*, 86.

[26] "Mientras no se descubra [la causa de la decadencia española] será vano cualquier esfuerzo que se haga para contener sus funestos efectos." León de Arroyal, *Cartas económico-políticas (con la segunda parte inédita)* [1790s], ed. José Caso González (Oviedo, Universidad de Oviedo, 1971), 9.

Jovellanos has been the focus of much sustained scholarly attention, yet scholars have failed to notice that the treatise in which Jovellanos laid out his program of liberal reform, the *Informe sobre la ley agraria* (*Study on Agrarian Law*), 1794, was organized around similar epistemological concerns as those that informed the writings of Gándara and Arroyal. [27] Like Arroyal, Jovellanos thought that when it came to finding the cause(s) of decline much prudence was needed and advised intellectuals to weigh models "with great care and circumspection so as not to put forth irresponsible theories on subjects in which errors have proven to have such a generalized and pernicious influence."[28] Yet for all his calls to prudence, Jovellanos sought to identify a single cause to account for all the ills of the nation.

Paradoxically, Jovellanos identified *the* cause of decline in the very hectic search for causes. Like Gándara, Jovellanos insisted that previous legislative efforts at reforming Spanish agriculture had in fact contributed to making things worse. In fact the desperate search for explanatory models to understand decline had led to the issuing of many contradictory laws. Reform for Jovellanos consisted in getting rid of these laws, for they acted as "hurdles in the path to progress."[29] Jovellanos understood political economy to be a discipline charged not with designing ways to stimulate the economy but with removing obstacles. Such inclinations led him to embrace Adam Smith's doctrine of *laissez-faire*. The state for Jovellanos was an instrument of negative intervention, entirely devoted to eradicating traditional entitlements and clearing up the tangle of old legislation. By insisting that the cause of decline was the poorly informed search for causes, Jovellanos sought to reduce the role of state intervention and reform to promoting education and building new infrastructure.

Juan Sempere y Guarinos was another leading eighteenth-century political economist who found wayward epistemological approaches to be the sole cause of Spanish decline. In *Historia del luxo* (*History of Luxury*), 1788, Sempere set out to prove that the continuous attempts on the part of intellectuals to find luxury as the cause of decline was at the root of most problems. The fundamental problems of the nation, according to Sampere, consisted "in coming up repeatedly with false and inexact ideas on the most crucial points of legislation and politics; in getting effects and causes often confused; and [finally] in attributing to one [event] causes that

---

[27] On Jovellanos, see Javier Varela, *Jovellanos* (Madrid: Alianza, 1988).
[28] "con gran detenimiento y circunspección para no aventurar el descubrimiento de la verdad en una materia en que los errores son de tan general y perniciosa influencia." Melchor Gaspar de Jovellanos, "Informe sobre la ley agraria," in *Obras sociales y políticas*, ed. Patricio Peñalver Simó (Madrid: Publicaciones Españlas, 1962), 95.
[29] "el problema no tanto estriba en presentarle estímulos [a la agricultura] como en remover los estorbos que retardan su progreso." Jovellanos, "Informe sobre la ley agraria," 104.

belong to a very different one. From these factors stem our tendency to issue not only useless laws but also laws that often have the very opposite effect than the one legislators originally intended them to have."[30]

Sempere argued that the many laws introduced by the Habsburgs to curtail sumptuary consumption had destroyed national manufacturing. Seeking to eradicate the alleged moral decadence caused by luxury, lawmakers had passed laws that severely damaged local industries, promoted unemployment, vagrancy and prostitution, and ultimately contributed to weakening the moral fiber of the nation. Moral philosophers had long blamed luxury for developments that in reality had completely different causes. Sempere, for example, sought to prove that the reported loosening of paternal authority and loss of female decorum among leading Spanish households had not been caused by profligate consumption that led to pampering elite children, as moralists had long held, but by the introduction of the *mayorazgo*, an institution that handed down the family patrimony to the first son, allocating inheritances regardless of the moral behavior of the children.[31] Thus, Sempere laid the blame for the decadence of Spain squarely at the feet of the elites, whose ignorance had blinded them into enacting "immoral and stupid" policies.[32]

Political economy in the Affair Masson de Morvilliers

To shed light on the nature of the Spanish Enlightenment, many authors have focused on the Spanish debate triggered by the publication of Masson de Morvilliers's 1783 *Encyclopédie Méthodique* article, "Espagne." Morvilliers's disparaging views of Spain generated a groundswell of indignation and alternative views of how to reply his criticisms. Richard Herr in his magisterial *The Eighteenth-Century Revolution in Spain* (1958) maintained that these debates were emblematic of growing political and ideological tensions in the Iberian Peninsula in the wake of the French Revolution. Despite the various reforms introduced in the eighteenth century, particularly by Charles III, Spain had remained solidly united behind the monarch. The French Revolution and the arrival of a new king,

---

[30] "qual es el de formarse generalmente ideas falsas, e inexactas, acerca de los más importantes puntos de la legislación, y la política; confundirse frequentemente las causas con los efectos; atribuirse a unas los que lo son de otras muy diferentes: de donde proviene el promulgarse leyes, no solamente inútiles, sino muchas veces contrarias al objeto, y a las intenciones de los mismos legisladores que las expidieron." Juan Sempere y Guarinos, *Historia del luxo y de las leyes suntuarias de España.* 2 vols. (Madrid: Imprenta real, 1788), 1:8.

[31] Sempere y Guarinos, *Historia del luxo*, 2: 176-218.

[32] Juan Sempre y Guarinos, *Consideraciones sobre las causas de la grandeza y de la decadencia de la monarquía española*, ed. Juan Rico Giménez (Alicante: Instituto de Cultura "Juan Gil-Albert," 1998), 158 (quotation), 79; 118-23, 157-58, 179-80 (for examples of elite ignorance of political economy).

Charles IV, changed the political landscape from consensus to growing polarization. Two parties, conservatives and liberals, emerged along rigid ideological lines. Herr used the Morvilliers affair to explore this tension. To typify the conservative side of the debate Herr turned to the writings of Juan Pablo Forner, an intellectual who, according to Herr, mindlessly defended Spain while upholding traditional Christian values. In Herr's narrative, the writings of Luis Cañuelo, the editor of the daily *El censor* (*The Censor*) typified the liberal side of the debate. Cañuelo shared many of Morvilliers's dismal views of Spain while urging immediate reform.[33]

This interpretation of the affair was challenged in 1967 by José Antonio Maravall. Forner, Maravall argued, was a protoromantic, a patriot well acquainted with the idioms of the Enlightenment, not a conservative critic of secular modernity. Drawing on Maravall's insights and on the works of Antonio Mestre on Gregorio Mayans, whose scholarship Forner sought to emulate, the French Hispanist François Lopez also presented Forner as a modern. According to Lopez, Forner followed in the footsteps of Mayans and sought to recover the intellectual and religious traditions of Spanish humanism. His attack on Morvilliers and those who thought that Spain needed radical reforms was therefore no endorsement of ultramontane conservative ideologies.[34]

For all the virtues in Maravall and Lopez's approach, I want to explore the debate from a different perspective. At the core of the controversy that followed the publication of Morvilliers's "Espagne," I argue, lay two views of political economy: one that advocated careful empirical historical research; another that sought all-encompassing interpretations derived from first principles. These views, thus, were rooted in different epistemologies.

[33] Richard Herr, *The Eighteenth-Century Revolution in Spain*, 219-30 and *passim*. This interpretation of the affair Morvilliers actually first originated in the mid nineteenth century with Marcelino Menéndez Pelayo. Menéndez Pelayo set out to denounce contemporary Spanish liberals as shallow Franco-Anglophiles, heirs to those who have taken Morvillier's side in the debate. Forner, on the other hand appeared as an authentic Spanish intellectual. Emilio Cotarelo y Mori, a leading *fin-de-siècle* scholar, simply inverted the heroes in Menéndez Pelayo's account, helping to perpetuate this Manichean narrative. See Marcelino Menéndez y Pelayo "Mr. Masson, redivivo," *Revista Europea* (30 de julio, 1876), 8, no. 127 and "Mr. Masson, redimuerto," in *Revista Europea* (24 de septiembre, 1876), 8, no. 135, reproduced in *La polémica de la ciencia española*, ed. Ernesto y Enrique García Camarero (Madrid: Editorial Alianza, 1970), 209-30, 239-68; Cotarelo, *Iriarte y su época*, 312-22.

[34] José Antonio Maravall, "El sentimiento de nación en el siglo XVIII: La obra de Forner" [1967], in *Estudios de la historia del pensamiento español S.XVIII*, ed. Ma. Carmen Iglesias (Madrid: Biblioteca Mondadori, 1991), 42-60; Lopez, *Juan Pablo Forner*. On Forner see also see Francisco Sánchez-Blanco, *El absolutismo y las luces en el reinado de Carlos III* (Marcial Pons: Madrid, 2002).

Forner sought to reply to Morvilliers, avoiding the path taken by previous patriotic defenses. Antonio José de Cavanilles and Carlo Denina, for example, had already answered the charges leveled by the French. Both replies, however, consisted in compiling lists of prominent authors. This was a well-established genre. Patriots had long confronted European derision of the alleged Spanish intellectual backwardness by assembling bio-bibliographies. Nicolás Antonio's *Bibliotheca hispana nova* [1696] and *Bibliotheca hispana vetus* [1696] typified the genre. Antonio's were lengthy reference treatises listing old and new manuscripts and books by accomplished Spanish authors. As European mockery grew over the course of the eighteenth century, this type of patriotic reference book multiplied. The political economist Juan Sempere Guarinos, who had identified the cause of Spanish decline in the secular tendency of the elites to misdiagnose the true causes of decline, also turned to the genre of bio-bibliography to demonstrate to Europeans that Spaniards had made great intellectual strides under the Bourbons.[35] Juan Francisco Masdeu, Francisco Xavier Lampillas, and Juan Andrés, Spanish Jesuits in exile in the papal states who were confronted daily with charges by local intellectuals that Spanish bad taste had stunted the development of Italian literary traditions from Roman times to the early modern period, compiled lengthy bio-bibliographies from antiquity to the present, demonstrating the richness and variety of Spain's literary history.[36]

Forner chose a different line of defense. In *Oración apologética por la España* (*Apologetic Peroration for Spain*), 1786, he sought to demonstrate that Spanish and French intellectual traditions had developed on the basis of radically different epistemologies. Turning the tables on the European critics, Forner insisted that Spanish traditions were empirical, skeptical, and pragmatic. The French, on the other hand, were given to systematic, deductive, and ultimately speculative thought, most of it useless. Forner set Morvilliers firmly within Cartesian intellectual styles. Like Descartes, Morvilliers demonstrated an unrestrained liking for sweeping generalization, all-encompassing explanatory models, and ridiculous theories. French critics of the Spanish nation were all like Descartes and Morvilliers, engaged in endless speculative debates about the ultimate structure of things, from gravitation to the nature of magnetic and electric fluids. Forner pitted this style against the skeptical traditions of the

---

[35] Juan Sempere y Guarinos, *Ensayo de una biblioteca española de los mejores escritores del reynado de Carlos III*. 6 vols. (Madrid: Imprenta Real, 1785-89).

[36] Juan Francisco Masdeu, *Historia crítica de España y de la cultura española*, 20 vols. (Madrid: Sancha, 1783-1805); Francisco Xavier Lampillas, *Ensayo histórico-apologético de la literatura española contra las opiniones preocupadas de algunos escritores modernos italianos*. 7 vols (Zaragoza: Blas Miedes, 1782-89); Juan Andrés, *Origen, progresos y estado actual de toda la literatura*. 10 vols. (Madrid: Sancha, 1784-1806).

Spanish Renaissance. Spaniards like Juan Luis Vives, he argued, understood that seeking to pinpoint the real causes of physical phenomena was pointless and thus turned to the study of ethics and the science of jurisprudence. Scholasticism, Forner insisted, was an Arab invention that first spread to France, not Spain. It was when Spain betrayed its true skeptical self by embracing scholasticism that the nation began to decline.[37]

Forner championed a view of Spain as the cradle of the skeptical humanism that the likes of Vives and Francis Bacon had espoused. In *Discurso sobre la historia de España* (*Discourse on the History of Spain*), 1796, Forner laid out an agenda for the discipline of political economy along the epistemological lines he had championed in *Oracion apologética*. Like any other history of Spain written in the eighteenth century, Forner sought to explain the causes of the nation's decline. But unlike his contemporaries, Forner thought that many details and factors remained to be elucidated through historical research. Forner, for example, went over the factors adduced by Raynal to account for Spain's decline, including among others, the expulsion of Jews and Moriscos, hikes in taxation to finance chronic fiscal deficits by an overstretched empire, and persecution of new forms of knowledge. All these factors, Forner argued, were plausible but also tinged by ideological commitments that assumed that religious freedom, *laissez-faire*, and entrepreneurship caused growth. Raynal's commitment to ideology made him pick and choose the evidence. Forner had no time for this type of approach, for it was both reductive and dangerous. These models sought to put the "blame of decline on only one cause" and explained all symptoms deductively.[38] Such commitment to theories and ideologies promoted reforms whose effects were unpredictable: "either good or bad, useful or pernicious, wise or foolish."[39] The epistemological alternative to Raynal's narrative of Spanish decline according to Forner was meticulous empirical research. Forner urged intellectuals to visit archives and write empirically informed monographs on the causes of decline.

Forner practiced what he preached. In the very book where he castigated ideologically informed theories of decline, Forner put forth a history of Spanish historiography. It rattled expectations and most likely irritated the king, for Forner claimed that the best scholarship had been

---

[37] Forner, *Oración apologética por la España, passim.*
[38] "al modo de los que forman sistemas [muchos] echaron el peso que ocasionó la ruina sobre un solo defecto, y de él fueron derivando la serie de males que se atropellan después para enflaquecer y debilitar la monarquía." Juan Pablo Forner, *Discurso sobre el modo de escribir y mejorar la historia de España. Informe fiscal* [1796], ed. François Lopez (Barcelona: Editorial Labor, 1973), 165.
[39] "buenas y malas, útiles y perniciosas, sabias y desconcertadas." Forner, *Discurso sobre el modo de escribir historia de España*, 166.

produced under the Habsburgs, not the Bourbons. Quality had considerably declined under the latter. When it came to the history of historiography, narratives of early modern decline under Habsburg rule did not hold up to empirical scrutiny.

Forner's epistemology alarmed the editors of *El censor (The Censor)*.[40] Thrice shut down by the crown, this weekly came out irregularly between 1781 and 1787. Aimed at poking fun at all sorts of collective behavior, the weekly had in fact a very serious intent. It sought to reform a Spanish culture corrupted by superstition and ignorance. The weekly, for example, took it upon itself to ridicule *villancicos*, for the lyrics of Spanish Christmas carols reportedly promoted immorality rather than virtue.[41] The weekly, to be sure, made fun of the new francophile cultures of sociability and consumption. However, it forcefully denounced those who blamed luxury as the cause of decline. *El censor* repeatedly ran articles sanctioning commerce and trade as virtuous.[42] The weekly was the voice of a sector of the local intelligentsia who saw most foreign criticisms of Spain as reasonable and who wanted civic republican values to spread among the elites.

El censor often ran articles by foreign travelers identifying the chief cause of Spanish decline as the excessive concentration of land in a few hands and the absence of a free market of land rents.[43] Although the editors seemed to have believed that the true cause of decline lay in the lack of civic republican traditions among the elites, they did not dismiss foreign views out of hand. On the contrary, editors welcomed foreign critiques as the only way to identify and correct the problems of the nation.[44] *El censor* had no patience with patriotic apologies for things Spanish and derided the genre of compiling bio-bibliographies, for they lulled the nation into believing that there was no need to change anything in light of such an alleged record of unparalleled intellectual accomplishments.[45]

El censor harshly criticized Forner's *Discurso apologético* for having handed the enemies of reform a subterfuge to delay implementing

---

[40] It is not entirely clear whether the editor was Luis Cañuelo. See José Miguel Caso González, "Estudio," in *El Censor Obra Periódica comenzada a publicar en 1781 y terminada en 1787*, ed. José Miguel Caso González (Oviedo: Universidad de Oviedo. Instituto Feijoo de Estudios del siglo XVIII, 1898). On *El Censor* and the project it represented, see Sánchez-Blanco, *El absolutismo y las luces*.

[41] discursos 84-85 (December 22 and December 29, 1785).

[42] discurso 54 (January 1, 1784); discursos 124-127 (September 28 to October 19, 1786).

[43] discurso 22 (July 5, 1781); discurso 52 (December 18, 1783).

[44] discurso 53 (December 25, 1783); discurso 65 (March 18, 1784).

[45] discurso 59 (February 5, 1784); discurso 79 (November 17, 1785); discurso 81 (December 1, 1785).

change.[46] For the weekly, Forner's epistemology sanctioned political paralysis and ultimately conservative agendas. In the process of articulating a critique of Forner, *El censor* offered an alternative view of political economy. If Forner construed the discipline as a branch of history, *El censor* took it to be a branch of medicine. The metaphor of the body had long been applied to the study of society. Hobbes, for example, compared a well-regulated hierarchical polity to the harmoniously well-integrated operation of the parts of the body.[47] But *El censor* took this analogy one step further.

The Spanish body politic, the weekly argued, was ill. Sick bodies may have many symptoms, but these symptoms are all manifestations of a single disease. The medical metaphor allowed the weekly to articulate a view of political economy as a deductive science. Decline, like disease, should be explained by monocausal theories. It was the task of the critic to be the physician of the body politic, rooting out the cause of the malaise immediately. Delaying therapy was not an option.[48]

The debate sparked by the publication of Masson de Morvilliers's article suggests that political economy in Spain developed along two rather different paths. Fearful of a record of reforms that in the past had caused more harm than good and incensed by the mocking criticism of the French, writers like Forner insisted that political economy needed to avoid becoming Cartesian. Instead of seeking to bring disparate social phenomena into a single narrative of decline though deductive logic, these writers turned political economy into a historical discipline. Another group begged to differ. For them the historicism of Forner was simply a plot by conservatives to avoid reform. Drawing on the metaphor of the body politic this group presented political economy as a deductive science meant to inform immediate social reform.

Conclusion

Eighteenth-century Spanish authors maintained an ambiguous and paradoxical relationship with foreigners. The Valencian Gregorio Mayans y Siscar found in Dutch and German editors and printers the support he

---

[46] discurso 120 (August 31, 1786); discurso 165 (August 5, 1787).
[47] See Thomas Hobbes, *Leviathan. Or the Matter, Forme and Power of a Commonwealth Ecclesiasticall and Civil*, ed. Michael Oakeshott (New York: Collier Books, 1962), 19. On bodily metaphors of the polity in Spain, see Francisco Rico, *El pequeño mundo del hombre. Varia fortuna de una idea en las letras españolas* (Madrid: Editorial Castalia, 1970). For studies of the metaphor in general, see Leonard Barkan, *Nature's Work of Art: The Human Body as Image of the World* (New Haven: Yale University Press, 1975); and Emma Spary, "Political, Natural, and Bodily Economies," in Nicholas. Jardine, James A Secord, and Emma C. Spary, eds., *Cultures of Natural History* (Cambridge: Cambridge University Press, 1996), 178-96.
[48] discurso 157 (June 14, 1787).

needed to make known to the world the contribution to scholarship of the Spanish Renaissance and to popularize the concept of a Spanish Golden Age. Cadalso, on the other hand, chastised foreign observers as shallow and unreliable while at the same time maintaining that Spain had historically been reinvigorated by cycles of foreign interventions. Yet one would be tempted to characterize the Spanish Enlightenment as "nationalistic" or even narrowly provincial, bent on denouncing foreign critics of things Spanish, for intellectuals were obsessed with setting the record straight and defending the nation. Their patriotism, however, was of a "cosmopolitan" kind. Intellectuals dismissed foreigners precisely because the latter sought to present Spain as marginally "European." Eighteenth-century authors furiously sought to assert their Europeanness, and in the process invented the Spanish Golden Age.

The evidence presented in this paper shows that these authors were right. The debates over causation in political economy demonstrate the "Europeanness" of Spanish discourse. The ideas held by Forner, for example, anticipated Edmund Burke's in almost every respect. Like Forner, Burke linked his epistemological critique of French *philosophes* to conservative theories of change and reform. Like Forner, Burke privileged historical and empirical research as the appropriate foundation of the human sciences and dismissed as politically dangerous French speculative theories and systems. Clearly Forner and Burke belonged in the same cultural world.

Progress, Cyclicality, and Decline: Competing Philosophies of History in Pre-Revolutionary French Historical Writing

Andrew Smith
University of Western Ontario

Abstract

No single theory of time dominated the historical writing of pre-Revolutionary France; *contra* J. B. Bury's view, neither the idea of progress nor any other metahistorical narrative enjoyed a hegemonic influence over French historians in the eighteenth century. Instead, the historical literature of this era reflected the fierce rivalry between several philosophies of history. Competition between various metahistorical narratives served to accelerate the development of intellectual rigor in historical studies, helping to transform history from a topic to a discipline.

The historical writing of pre-Revolutionary France reflected contemporary debates over various theories of time; neither the idea of progress nor any other metahistorical narrative exerted a dominant influence over historians.[1] Instead, the historical literature of this period was shaped by intense competition among several philosophies of history. The period since the Renaissance had witnessed the accelerated development of secular historical writing, a phenomenon termed by F. Smith Fussner "the historical revolution."[2] While the same period also saw thinkers advance notions of general progress and improvement (the most famous being Condorcet), it would be a mistake to maintain that progressivist ideas underlay all or even most works of history produced in *ancien régime* Europe. In *The Idea of Progress* J. B. Bury argued that after the early eighteenth-century debate over the relative accomplishments

---

[1] The degenerative, cyclical and permanentist world views were competing secular metahistorical paradigms at this time. While the degenerative view saw history as a continuous process of decline from an early Golden Age, cyclicalism saw history as a long series of patterns. Permanentism stresses the element of constancy in history, especially in terms of human nature. Henry Vyverberg, *Historical Pessimism in the French Enlightenment* (Cambridge, MA.: Harvard University Press, 1958), argues that these last two conceptions of history were dominant in eighteenth-century French thought. In my view, he overstates his case, committing the mirror image of Bury's error; both Bury and Vyverberg obscure the sheer complexity of eighteenth-century French historical thought.

[2] Fussner, *The Historical Revolution: English Historical Writing and Thought, 1580-1640* (London: Routledge and Kegan Paul, 1962). Other standard works on the growth of the discipline of history include J. B. Black, *The Art of History: A Study of Four Great Historians of the Eighteenth Century* (New York: F. S. Crofts, 1926); Herbert Butterfield, *The Origins of History* (London: Methuen, 1981); and Ernst Breisach, *Historiography: Ancient, Medieval, and Modern* (Chicago: University of Chicago Press, 1983).

of ancient and modern peoples was resolved in favor of the moderns, the idea of progress became the dominant theory of history.[3] While nearly eighty years old, Bury's work remains of immense value to the student of intellectual history. In its essentials, Bury's definition of the idea of progress as the belief that "civilization has moved, is moving, and will move in a desirable direction"[4] remains the one used by students of notions of progress.[5] Nevertheless, Bury's work was very much a product of its time and sound criticisms of particular of Bury's assertions have accumulated in the decades since its publication. For instance, while Bury followed Comte in maintaining that the idea of progress was essentially unknown in the ancient world, more recent scholarship has demonstrated the existence of progressivism in Greek and Roman times.[6]

Another important historiographical debate Bury initiated revolves around the possible religious origins of the idea of progress. According to Bury, the idea of progress, a secular yet eschatological theory of history, served as a replacement for the Christian view of history as expressed by Saint Augustine. While the similarities between Bury's discussion of the continuities between Enlightenment and Christian thought and Carl L. Becker's argument in *The Heavenly City of the Eighteenth Century Philosophers* are obvious, it was rejected by later students such as W. Warren Wagar.[7]

In addition to these rather particular criticisms of Bury, broader methodological objections to his approach to intellectual history have also been advanced in recent decades. Bury's piece is a classic example of the "Great Man" approach to intellectual history denominated "textualist" by Quentin Skinner, a tradition which is still reflected in many undergraduate "Great Books" courses.[8] In tracing the development of the idea of

[3] J. B. Bury, *The Idea of Progress; An Inquiry into its Origin and Growth,* 3rd ed. Introduction by Charles A. Beard (1920; rpt. New York: Dover, 1955).
[4] Bury, *Idea of Progress*, 2.
[5] For instance, this is the definition used by Sidney Pollard, *The Idea of Progress: History and Society* (London: Watts, 1968), Charles L. Van Doren, *Idea of Progress* (New York: Praeger, 1967), and even the authors of popular works, such as Michael Creal *et al.*, *The Idea of Progress:The Origins of Modern Optimism* (Toronto: Macmillan, 1970).
[6] Ludwig Edelstein, *The Idea of Progress in Classical Antiquity* (Baltimore: The Johns Hopkins University Press, 1967). See also E. R. Dodds, *The Ancient Concept of Progress and Other Essays on Greek Literature and Belief* (Oxford: Clarendon Press, 1973).
[7] W. Warren Wagar, *The Idea of Progress since the Renaissance* (New York: Wiley, 1969).
[8] Quentin Skinner, *The Foundations of Modern Political Thought* (Cambridge: Cambridge University Press, 1978). Bury is not a perfect representative of the textualist way of doing intellectual history insofar that he occasionally stops his narrative to examine the social, political, and technological contexts of the various positions in question. For instance, he prefaces his discussion of the intellectual developments of the nineteenth century by mentioning the creation of the British railway system (329). That being said, Bury's overall approach toward intellectual history is textualist in that he focuses on the writings of famous thinkers rather than on sermons, school texts and other more popular media. Other important

progress, Bury presents the reader with a succession of great political thinkers and philosophers: Plato, Aristotle, Polybius, Descartes, Fontenelle, Voltaire, and finally Comte. The ideas advanced by each thinker are treated in chronological sequence in the process of tracing the gradual emergence of the idea of progress. Bury's approach contrasts with the current trend in intellectual history, which involves the examination of demotic or popular ideas and the wider cultural context in which a particular great thinker operated.[9]

Bury maintains that while the doctrine of progress had roots in the classical and Christian writings that were part of the common heritage of every European country, progressivism emerged first in France and later spread to other countries, including England. Or as Bury put it, "the idea of Progress could not help crossing the Channel."[10] While Bury's analysis of the evolution of the idea of progress in the British and German national environments contained many interesting observations, it was nevertheless distorted by his assumption of French origins.[11] On a related note, the causal link Bury drew between the development of Cartesianism and the idea of progress is questionable. While Cartesianism may have accelerated the emergence of the doctrine of progress by emphasizing the power of

---

works dealing with the idea of progress (and opposing theories of history) that fall squarely in the textualist tradition include Jeffrey Paul von Arx, *Progress and Pessimism: Religion, Politics, and History in Late Nineteenth-Century Britain* (Cambridge, MA: Harvard University Press, 1985); Robert Nisbet, *History of the Idea of Progress* (New York: Basic Books, 1980). Because they focus on high thought, these approaches contrast somewhat with that taken by David Spadafora in *The Idea of Progress in Eighteenth-Century Britain* (New Haven: Yale University Press, 1990), and even more so with the general approach taken in the following works of intellectual history: Arnold Burgen, Peter McLaughlin, and Jürgen Mittelstrab, eds., *The Idea of Progress* (New York: W. de Gruyter, 1997); Raymond Gastil, *Progress: Critical Thinking about Historical Change* (Westport, CT: Praeger, 1993); and Peter J. Bowler, *The Invention of Progress: the Victorians and the Past* (Oxford: Blackwell, 1989). While source considerations and other factors have led me to base the present work mostly on elitist sources of the type relied on by Bury, I am mindful of the limitations of this approach.

[9] One of the most influential examples of the demotic approach to history of ideas is Richard Ashcraft, *Revolutionary Politics and Locke's Two Treatises of Government* (Princeton: Princeton University Press, 1986). Ashcraft uses such sources as sermons and pamphlets to place Locke's ideas in context.

[10] Bury, *Idea of Progress*, 217.

[11] However Bury's decision to treat the evolution of the idea of progress after the eighteenth century in separate sections devoted to British, French, and German developments anticipates in many ways the current trend in Enlightenment studies. This trend is inclined to deny that there was single phenomenon called "the Enlightenment" rather than many national enlightenments (e.g., the Scottish Enlightenment, the francophone Enlightenment, the Protestant Enlightenment, and even the Lausanais Enlightenment.) For an analysis of this historiographic development and why we should avoid using the term "the Enlightenment" in the singular, see Pocock, *Barbarism and Religion*, vol. 1. *The Enlightenments of Edward Gibbon, 1737-1764* (Cambridge: Cambridge University Press, 1999), 5-7, 55-56, and *passim*.

reason and the immutability of natural laws, Bury's assertion that Cartesianism was the chief midwife of progressivism is implausible.[12] At most, Cartesianism can be said to have had a mixed effect on the idea of progress.[13] It has been argued convincingly that the anti-empirical element in Cartesianism inhibited historical research, and it was historical research that stimulated the idea of progress by forcing comparisons between different periods.[14]

In his 1990 study of *The Idea of Progress in Eighteenth-Century Britain*, David Spadafora contests Bury's claim that the idea of progress was imported from France.[15] On the basis of extensive research on the English and Scottish Enlightenments and their social and religious contexts, Spadafora concludes that "the development of the idea of progress in Britain took place in a fundamentally independent way" and was not imported from the Continent. Since French intellectual history is outside the purview of his work, Spadafora neither challenges nor affirms Bury's assertion that the idea of progress was both strongly developed and pervasive in eighteenth-century France. In the view of the present author, Bury went too far in emphasizing the extent to which French thinkers between the *Querelle* and the Revolution embraced progressivist ideas.[16] While pre-Revolutionary French proponents of the idea of progress have and continue to attract substantial attention, we should be cautious in seeing them as representative of French Enlightenment thought as a whole. To adopt this view is to ignore the sophistication and complexity of historical thinking in this period. The number of prominent French thinkers who perpetuated neoclassical notions of degeneracy and cyclicality undermines the thesis that progress was the dominant view of time in pre-Revolutionary France. Moreover, by mid-century, Voltaire, Rousseau, and other thinkers adapted the older theories of degeneration by

---

[12] Bury, *Idea of Progress*, 65.

[13] R. G. Collingwood concluded that the "general tendency of the Cartesian school was sharply anti-historical." *The Idea of History* (New York: Oxford University Press, 1956), 63. While Collingwood does see the Bollandists who did so much for the development of history as partially influenced by Descartes, he argues that the general thrust of Cartesianism (especially the doctrine of innate ideas) as anti-historical. When John Locke attacked this doctrine he indirectly contributed to the growth of historical study and the idea of progress (even though other elements of his philosophy were anti-historical in tendency). The idea that Cartesianism inhibited the development of history is echoed by Joseph M. Levine in his study of the eighteenth-century English historical thought, *The Battle of the Books: History and Literature in the Augustan Age* (Ithaca, NY: Cornell University Press, 1991).

[14] See R. G. Collingwood's brilliant argument in a chapter programmatically titled "Progress as Created by Historical Thinking" in *The Idea of History*. Any extended discussion of the effects of Cartesianism on the development of progressivism must take seriously Emile Faguèt's conclusion that the Enlightenment chilled historical study between 1760 and 1815.

[15] Spadafora, *Idea of Progress*, 381-85.

[16] For details of the *Querelle* between the Ancients and the Moderns that raged around 1700, see below.

changing the period that should be seen as the peak. It is significant that they continued to accept the underlying paradigms of cyclicality and degeneration.

Just as importantly, we must be careful to avoid lumping all "progress thinkers" together in a way that obscures the many subtle variations on the idea of progress that are possible (significantly, the idea is referred to in the singular in the title of Bury's work). Just as the French Enlightenment was distinct from the English and Scottish Enlightenments, the ideas of progress prevailing in France differed from those widespread in Britain. In 1967, Charles Van Doren established a useful typology of "progress authors" that uses several criteria for the purposes of classification.[17] For instance, proponents of the idea of progress can be divided into those who believe progress is potentially indefinite and those who think that it will reach a terminal point after which conditions will plateau.[18] Another line of demarcation established by Van Doren of equal relevance to this study lies between those who see progress as inevitable and those who consider it contingent on agents making the right decisions. One way of organizing progressivist thinkers that did not occur to Van Doren involves distinguishing between those who see progress as the directed product of human reason and those who see it as a blind or spontaneous phenomenon similar to Darwinian evolution. While French thinkers placed great emphasis on reason and conscious choice in articulating causal explanations for progress, Scottish Enlightenment figures such as David Hume tended to see progress as occurring not as the result of a growing commitment to rationality but rather as the unintended result of individual actions.[19] These quite different conceptions of progress would be bequeathed to the generations that would struggle to make sense of the turbulent post-1789 world.

A sampling of historical writing in pre-Revolutionary France reveals the tension between competing views of history. In the aftermath of the *Querelle* of the Ancients and Moderns, some French thinkers held the discipline of history in contempt, an attitude engendered by the

---

[17] Charles Van Doren, *The Idea of Progress*, 14.

[18] Karl Marx is a nineteenth-century example of someone who thought along these lines.

[19] The role of "unintended consequences" in Hume's theories of progress and spontaneous (or unplanned) order are detailed in Ronald Hamowy, *The Scottish Enlightenment and the Theory of Spontaneous Order* (Carbondale, IL: Southern Illinois University Press, 1987). See also John Dwyer, *Age of the Passions: An Interpretation of Adam Smith and Scottish Enlightenment Culture* (East Linton, Scotland: Tuckwell Press, 1998.). The influence of this form of the idea of progress on later thinkers is explored in Norbert Waszek, *The Scottish Enlightenment and Hegel's Account of "Civil Society"* (Boston: Kluwer, 1988). A prominent modern adherent of this idea of progress who acknowledges his intellectual debts to the Scottish Enlightenment is F. A. Hayek, *Knowledge, Evolution, and Society* (London: Adam Smith Institute, 1983).

neoclassical roots of post-Renaissance humanist historiography.[20] In his
Reflections on History, d'Alembert flatly stated that "history is the lowest
form of knowledge."[21] The aspersions d'Alembert cast on historical study
were intimately related to his belief that great progress had occurred in
recent centuries in the fields of fine art and literature; while chronicles
filled with useless facts and might have been fine for monks in the Middle
Ages, the development of *belles lettres* and philosophical publications in
the vernacular has rendered historical writing obsolete. However, in other
writings, d'Alembert did talk about reforming history, hoping to preserve
historical writing by transforming it into "philosophical history."[22]
Philosophical history differed from its nonphilosophical or *érudit*
predecessors (for instance, the detailed Bollandist records of martyrs) in
several key ways. Firstly, matters of style were of primary importance;
philosophical history was designed to be a positive pleasure to read, not a
turgid recital of facts. It was unconcerned with recording and transmitting
details for their own sake. Instead, particular facts were important only
insofar they could be used to illustrate broader themes of universal
importance. *Philosophe* historiography contained a strongly moralistic and
judgmental element as well as a prescriptive one; the historian's role was
seen as making both moral evaluations related to the past and policy
prescriptions for the future.[23] Of course, *philosophe* historiography was
not a static entity and evolved in the direction of greater scholarly rigor
and sophistication in the use of sources. Several researchers who have
looked at historical writing in the eighteenth century see the fusion or
convergence of two quite different traditions as the major historiographic
development of the period. In other words, the synthesis of the erudite
antiquarianism typified by the Benedictines and *Académie des Inscriptions*

---

[20] Mark Hulliung, *The Autocritique of Enlightenment: Rousseau and the Philosophes*
(Cambridge, MA: Harvard University Press, 1994), 41.
[21] Jean Lerond d'Alembert, "Mémoires et réflexions sur Christine, reine de Suède," in
Œuvres de d'Alembert. 5 vols. (Paris: Belin, 1821-1822), 2:119.
[22] For an excellent discussion of d'Alembert's opinions on this subject and on the politics of
scholarship in France and mid-century, see Pocock, *The Enlightenments of Edward Gibbon*,
Chapter 8. Gibbon wrote "Essai sur l'étude de la littérature" in response to what he
perceived as d'Alembert's unfair attacks on erudition. A similar debate raged in England at
this time between the defenders and opponents of the Society of Antiquaries, but Gibbon's
interest in this topic seems to have emerged while he was living on the Continent.
[23] Denys Hay sees the moralizing philosophical historians of the eighteenth century to have
played a crucial role in the long transition from medieval annalism to modern analytical
historical writing. See Hay, *Annalists and Historians: Western Historiography from the
Eighth to the Eighteenth Centuries* (London: Methuen, 1977). Unfortunately, Hay devotes
relatively little space to the eighteenth century, the period in which he sees the fusion two
separate traditions in the works of Hume and the later historical writings of Voltaire to
produce the modern historical tradition. Hay's thesis seems closely akin to that commonly
associated with Eduard Fueter, *Geschichte der neureren historiographie* (München: R.
Oldenbourg, 1911).

and the lightly researched philosophical histories that were written for popular consumption helped lay the foundations of modern historiography.[24] It is important to keep in mind that this synthesis was the product of period of intellectual fermentation in which different interpretations of history were in intense competition. Perhaps if this debate had been less vigorous, the pressure to combine the best elements of the two traditions in effort to produce persuasive works of history would have been less strong.[25]

The best way to grasp the nature of the contest between different views of history in eighteenth-century France is to examine specific writers and historical debates; this is the function of the following pages. The author does not pretend to offer a comprehensive treatment of eighteenth-century French historical thought and some methodological problems with his focus on a few elite thinkers will be raised at the end of the paper.

While Bury freely admits that Montesquieu (1689-1755) should not be classified as a proponent of the idea of progress, he argues that his influential if unsystematic writings indirectly helped to prepare the ground for progressivism.[26] After reading Montesquieu's moderately famous *Considerations on the Causes of the Greatness of the Romans and their Decline* and his even more popular *The Spirit of the Laws,* it is hard to come to the same conclusion. [27] While the cyclicalist historical paradigm underlying the first work is indicated by its title, the historical theory contained in *The Spirit of the Laws* was more complex because cyclical ideas were combined with assertions of the belief that the human condition

---

[24] This idea was first articulated by Arnaldo Momigliano, *Studies in Historiography* (London: Weidenfeld and Nicolson, 1966), and is supported by the research of Hay, *Annalists and Historians*, esp. chapter 8; and Daniel Roche, *France in the Enlightenment*, trans. Arthur Goldhammer (Cambridge, MA: Harvard University Press, 1998), chapter 3. Roche argues that neither the *Académie des Inscriptions* nor the Benedictines were methodologically removed from the type of history "written by men of letters" (101). Roche sees a visit Voltaire paid to Dom Calmet in order to consult his library while researching the *Essai sur les moeurs* as symbolic of a rapprochement between the two approaches.

[25] It is a truism that debate can be a powerful stimulus to intellectual rigor; it is the dialogue between two or more worldviews that transforms a subject into a discipline. For a study of how intellectual debate forced the evolution of historical writing in a different context, see Joseph Levine, *The Battle of the Books*.

[26] See also Gilbert Chinard, "Montesquieu's Historical Pessimism," in *Studies in the History of Culture*. 2nd ed. (Freeport, NY: Books for Libraries, 1969), 161-72. Chinard wrote this article in response to a 1915 work by Gustave Lanson in which Montesquieu was presented as a proponent of the idea of progress. Chinard commented that while Lanson saw Montesquieu as sharing his century's prevailing belief in progress, Montesquieu's historical theory was unrepresentative and quotes Condorcet's criticisms of Montesquieu to this effect. Chinard's view of Montesquieu's philosophy of history is shared by Henry Vyverberg, *Historical pessimism.*

[27] Montesquieu, *Considérations sur les causes de la grandeur des Romains et de leur décadence*, trans. David Lowenthal (New York: Free Press, 1965); and *idem, The Spirit of the Laws*, trans. Anne M. Cohler *et al.* (Cambridge: Cambridge University Press, 1989).

is essentially static.[28] Montesquieu's views on the subject of commercial society were just as ambiguous. While he argued that "commerce cures destructive prejudices," he also stated that "the laws of commerce perfect mores for the same reason that these same laws ruin mores."[29] He conceded that commercial interaction between countries leads to peace, but while "the spirit of commerce unites nations, it does not unite individuals in the same ways," the growth of commerce can corrode the bonds of society.[30] Montesquieu argued that this is true on both an interpersonal level and on a more abstract constitutional one, holding that the participation of the English nobility in commerce was the root cause of the decay of monarchical authority in that country.[31] He also maintained that the commercial prosperity of nations and cities is cyclical, observing that "commerce is subject to great revolutions" and shifting lines of trade.[32] Montesquieu gave Tyre, Venice, and "Colchis" (an area of commercial greatness in ancient times that was in the eighteenth century "a vast forest") as examples of cities that went into economic decline after a fleeting period of commercial supremacy.[33] He also stressed the impermanence of commercial greatness by arguing that the causes of commercial revolutions are manifold: "commerce, sometimes destroyed by conquerors, sometimes hampered by monarchs, wanders across the earth, [and] flees" from impediments to more hospitable locations.[34]

While Montesquieu's writings were informed by a cyclicalist understanding of history, Rousseau advanced a theory of outright degeneration in his *Discourse on the Sciences and the Arts* and the *Discours sur l'origine d'inégalité*. In October 1749 the *Académie de Dijon* had posed the following question for an essay competition: "has the

---

[28] The relation between different conceptions of human nature as either fixed or culturally malleable and theories of history is explored in Maurice Mandelbaum, *History, Man, and Reason: A Study in Nineteenth-Century Thought* (Baltimore: The Johns Hopkins University Press, 1971), a work that provides considerable insight into eighteenth-century developments. The more one thinks about the relationship between the human nature question and historical thought, the more one questions the link Bury draws between Cartesianism and progressivism. After all, the doctrine of innate ideas and the belief that the thinker can use introspection to understand humanity in general leads naturally into the permanentist belief that human nature is uniform over time and space.

[29] Montesquieu, *Spirit*, 338.

[30] Montesquieu, *Spirit*, 339.

[31] Montesquieu, *Spirit*, 350.

[32] Montesquieu, *Spirit*, 354.

[33] Montesquieu, *Spirit*, 341, 358.

[34] Montesquieu, *Spirit*, 358. The diffusion of this idea in French society is indicated by a passage in de Volney's 1789 work *Les Ruines des empires*, in which the author observes the decline of ancient cities like Palmyra and speculates that London and Paris may one day lie silent and in ruins. See Bury, *Idea of Progress*, 199.

restoration of the sciences and the arts tended to purify morals?"[35] While
on his way to visit Diderot in prison, Rousseau read of the competition
through an announcement the *Académie* had placed in the *Mercure de
France*. Seeing lights around him, Rousseau had an epiphany as ideas
flooded his mind; his prize-winning response to the question was a strong
negative. He argued that "our souls have been corrupted in proportion to
the advancement of Sciences and Arts to perfection."[36] Rousseau did not
dispute that substantial changes had occurred in European society since the
Middle Ages; "the Peoples of that Part of the World which is today so
enlightened lived, a few centuries ago, in conditions worse than
ignorance."[37] He merely questioned whether this intellectual progress had
been desirable; before the revival of arts and letters, "our morals were
rustic but natural."[38] Rousseau blamed "Sciences, Arts, and Letters" for
undermining men's desire for liberty, making "them love their slavery and
turn[ing] them into what is called civilized peoples."[39] Rousseau extended
his analysis beyond Europe to examine the pernicious effects of learning in
the ancient and non-Western worlds; looking at China, he argued that if
respect for learning makes a nation morally great, why is China, a nation
ruled by scholars, proverbial for moral corruption of all sorts?[40] And
while Sparta lacked the learning of Athens, this "happy ignorance" only
improved the moral character of the community.[41]

Rousseau's essay generated responses ranging from angry criticism to
outright agreement. Falling somewhere in between, the Abbé Raynal did
not challenge Rousseau's main thesis and even poked fun at some of
Rousseau's other critics, arguing that many were "ill-humored at seeing
luxury attacked so vigorously." Echoing Montesquieu, Raynal suggested
that while luxury is rightly restricted in a small republic, it should not be
forbidden in a large state the size of France. Raynal also asked why
Rousseau had not identified the period at which the onset of decadence in
Europe had began, a point on which Rousseau has remained rather vague.
"He should have indicated his starting point, in designating the epoch of
decadence." Raynal's core criticism was that while Rousseau had

---

[35] This question is not entirely dissimilar from the question that had been posed the year
before by the *Académie de Soissons* on "causes des progress de la décadence du goût dans les
sciences at les arts." See Turgot, *Oeuvres de Turgot et documents le concernant*, ed. Gustave
Schelle (Paris: F. Alcan, 1913-1923), 1: 30.
[36] Jean-Jacques Rousseau, *Discourse on the Sciences and Arts: (First Discourse) and
Polemics*, ed. Roger D. Masters and Christopher Kelly; trans. Judith R. Bush, Roger D.
Masters and Christopher Kelly (Hanover, NH: University Press of New England for
Dartmouth College, 1992), 7.
[37] Rousseau, *Discourse*, 4.
[38] Rousseau, *Discourse*, 6.
[39] Rousseau, *Discourse*, 5.
[40] Rousseau, *Discourse*, 8.
[41] Rousseau, *Discourse,* 9.

identified a problem, he had not outlined any solutions; he asked "what practical conclusions can be reached from the thesis which the author upholds." Raynal considered and then discarded a number of state-based solutions (such as sumptuary laws), arguing that change must take place at the level of the individual conscience. [42]

In 1753 the *Académie de Dijon* held another essay competition. This time, the question was "what is the origin of inequality among men, and is it authorized by natural laws?" In his essay (which did not win the first prize) Rousseau argued that while men had originally been equal, the unfortunate development of laws, language, and private property had resulted in the growth of inequality.

The standard view is that Rousseau's ideas (especially his historical concepts and rejection of the idea of progress) were antithetical to the main body of the French Enlightenment. Maurice Cranston states that the 1750 *Discours on the Sciences and the Arts* constituted "a sustained attack on everything the Enlightenment stood for, and everything the Encyclopedia was intended to promote."[43] However, there are a number of reasons for supposing that this position is an exaggeration resting on an oversimplified view of the French intellectual landscape. The question posed by the *Académie de Dijon* in 1749 suggests that its members thought that the idea of progress was debatable, or at the very least, non-axiomatic. The fact that Rousseau won a prize in the first competition hardly confirms the view that he was a figure whose ideas ran entirely against the grain. Moreover, a careful re-examination of those thinkers alleged to have strong progressivists suggests that their historical theories were not as dissimilar to Rousseau's as has been suggested.

In depicting the French origins of the idea of progress, Bury assigned a prominent role to Anne-Robert Jacques Turgot (1727-1781) and the discourse he delivered in 1750 at the Sorbonne at the age of twenty-three entitled *"Philosophical Review of the Successive Advances of the Human Mind."*[44] Strangely, both Bury and Turgot's first biographer, Condorcet, neglect to mention Turgot's 1748 essay on "The Causes of the Progress and Decline of the Sciences and the Arts."[45] To be fair to Bury,

---

[42] Raynal, "Observations on the Discourse which was awarded the first prize at Dijon," in Rousseau, *Discourse*, 23.

[43] Cranston, introduction to Jean-Jacques Rousseau, *Discours sur l'origine et les fondements de l'inégalité parmi les hommes*, trans. and ed. by Maurice Cranston (New York: Penguin, 1984), 24.

[44] Turgot, *Oeuvres*, 1: 214. Over a year earlier, Turgot had delivered a *discours* that combined progressivist and religious themes entitled *Discours sur les avantages que l'établissant du christianisme a procué au genre humain. Prononcé en latin, 3 juillet, 1750* (*Oeuvres*, 1:194-214). The existence of this earlier work supports the thesis adumbrated by Carl Becker regarding the religious origins of the idea of progress.

[45] According to Gustave Schelle, Condorcet published "Vie de Turgot" in 1786. (Introduction, Turgot, *Oeuvres*, 1: 2.) The essay is in *Oeuvres*, 1: 116-42.

progressivist ideas did play a leading role in the *Philosophical Review*, but these ideas are by no means unalloyed. While Turgot saw the development of writing as one of the great advances in human history, he recognized that it had drawbacks as well as benefits, since writing slowed the process of innovation by which languages perfect themselves.[46] Similarly, the growth of the territory ruled by Rome was the cause of the ultimate destruction of its constitution; "les lois de Rome, faits pour govener un ville, succumbèrent sous le poids de monde entier."[47] Like many contemporaries, Turgot saw the reign of Augustus as the very peak of Roman civilization. The contemporaries of Augustus had reached the highest possible level of artistic attainment, and while the moderns had outstripped the Romans in the scientific and technological spheres, in "la poésie, la peinture, la musique, ont un point fixe ... les grands homes du siècle d'Augustus y arrivèrent et sont encore nos modèles."[48] After Augustus, little of value was created, and Rome entered into a period of "decadence générale où tout se précipite." Turgot blamed the fall of Rome on tyranny, luxury, and the proliferation of writers in the provinces who corrupted the pure Latin of Rome. However, the fall of Rome was counterweighted by the rise of Christianity, so the last centuries of the Empire did not see complete retrogression in every sphere.

Of course, no matter how one interprets Turgot's historical philosophy, it would be imprudent to assume that he represented his time as a whole. He was unusual in many ways; intellectually brilliant, his 1748 Bachelor of Theology thesis was described by a bishop as the best undergraduate thesis he had ever heard. Turgot was an advanced linguist who impressed other native francophones with his ability to translate directly from English to German. Furthermore, he had an uncanny ability for prediction; as early as 1750, Turgot had forecasted the eventual political independence of the colonies in the New World.[49] Turgot's father

---

[46] Turgot, *Oeuvres*, 1: 223. "Les langues se perfectionnent toujours avec les temps, quand elles ne sont pas fixées par des écrits qui eleviennent un règle pour juger de leur pureté." Turgot seems to have mixed feelings about whether linguistic evolution was progress or degenerations; in his section entitled "Examen de quelques raisons qu'on donne de la decadence des sciences et du gout." Turgot mourns a species of linguistic decadence, namely, the fact that the original meaning of metaphors becomes forgotten over time. (Turgot, *Philosophical Review*, in *Oeuvres*, 1:126.) Turgot did see progress as entirely dependent on the existence of language; without being able to record knowledge achieved in the past, humanity would be unable to progress, since men would be too busy reinventing what had already been developed and then lost. See Pierre Juliard, *Philosophies of Language in Eighteenth-Century France.* (The Hague: Mouton, 1970), chapter 5.
[47] Turgot, *Oeuvres*, 224.
[48] Turgot, *Oeuvres*, 277.
[49] See *Philosophical Review of the Successive Advances of the Human Mind*, in *Turgot on Progress, Sociology and Economics: A Philosophical Review of the Successive Advances of the Human Mind, On Universal History and Reflections on the Formation and the*

had been an *intendant* and the scion of a great Norman family that had served royal authority for several generations and Turgot also had a brilliant career in officialdom, filling such important offices as a *maître des requêtes*, *intendant* of Limoges, and finally *Comptrôleur Général des Finances*. [50] Serving in Limoges between 1761 and 1774, he saw firsthand a *généralité* that was clearly failing economically. By the time of Turgot's tenure in office, Limoges had retrogressed agriculturally and commercially from a seventeenth-century peak and symptoms of the decline from earlier prosperity were abundant. For instance, while Limoges had been an important wine exporting region in the seventeenth-century, Bourdeaux producers had since displaced Limogian vintages in many markets, leading to the abandonment of viticulture. [51] Turgot discussed the similar decline in the region's cattle-raising business; in his letters to his superiors in Paris, he argued that while "at one time, oxen were reared in these regions and sold for Slaughter in Paris," Limoges this was no longer the case and that the share of the *generalité* in the national tax burden should therefore be reduced. [52] Interestingly, he does not suggest practical measures to reverse this decline; the French state simply had to accommodate itself to the region's decay.

Despite the challenges Turgot faced in attempting to implement an ambitious body of reforms relating to the *corvée*, military conscription, taxation, transport, and the grain trade, he found time to write extensively, producing works dealing with monetary theory and economic history as well as mines and quarries. [53] Today, Turgot's best-known works are his *Philosophical Review of the Successive Advances of the Human Mind* that has been discussed above, the *Universal History*, and his *Reflections on the Formation and Distribution of Wealth*. [54] Turgot did express some progressivist and semi-progressivist ideas in his published works but this does not mean that his overall view of history was purely or even essentially progressivist. Rather, it was nuanced, sceptical, and tentative. Turgot's usual attitude toward a given period seems to have been an eagerness to point out the ways in which it combined retrogression in one field with advancement in another. Even in the *Philosophical Review*, he sounded a note of caution that echoes cyclical theories of history, stating that "progress, although inevitable, is intermingled with frequent periods

Distribution of Wealth, trans. and ed. Ronald L. Meek (Cambridge: Cambridge University Press, 1973), 47 for this prediction.

[50] Douglas Dakin, *Turgot and the Ancien Régime in France* (London: Methuen, 1939).

[51] Dakin, *Turgot and the Ancien Régime*, 43.

[52] Turgot quoted in Dakin, *Turgot and the Ancien Régime*, 42.

[53] See introduction by Meek in *Turgot on Progress*.

[54] While those who heard Turgot deliver *Philosophical Review* reacted favorably, this work, on which Bury relies heavily in his depiction of Turgot as a progressivist thinker, was not printed until many years later. See Brumfitt, *Voltaire Historian*, 126.

of decline."[55] Turgot pointed to the many countertrends that can sometimes nullify the progress that has been made in another field, referring to history as a "complex of different events, sometimes favourable, sometimes adverse, which because they act in opposite ways must in the long run nullify one another."[56] Moreover, the way in which Turgot positioned his discussion of particular economic themes in his essentially chronological *Reflections on the Formation and Distribution of Wealth* also undermined the idea of progress.[57] In a discussion of the origins of agriculture and landholding clearly influenced by Locke, Turgot stated that while at first there was enough land for everyone, a shortage eventually resulted from increased population. Unable to establish their own farms, some latecomers were obliged to take paid work on the farms of others, a practice that promoted the growth of inequality and the concentration of wealth.[58] At this point in Turgot's discussion of the rise of civil society, the modern reader assumes that Turgot's chronological narrative is at an end, because he has reached the development of the system of wage labor. Somewhat jarringly, Turgot continued his story by discussing the subsequent establishment of slave societies "by violent men," showing how classical slavery only gradually softened, evolving into serfdom and then the successive forms of feudalism.[59] Thus, the reader is left with the impression that things have come full circle and that we have now returned to something approximating the relatively happy state that obtained before the introduction of slavery. (Turgot did not mention the Roman Conquest of Gaul, but this may have been in his mind.) Far from transmitting a view of history as linear progress, this passage reflected a somewhat more complex if not cyclical conception of the past.

Mark Salber Phillips has identified a trend in the historical writing of the eighteenth century away from the traditional narrow focus on high politics (biographies of rulers and the like) towards more interest in socio-economic developments.[60] The increased attention paid to change in everyday life over the centuries arguably reflected a greater awareness of technological, economic, and social evolution. Voltaire's long career as a

---

[55] Turgot, *Philosophical Review*, in *Turgot on Progress*, 88.
[56] Turgot, *Philosophical Review*, 44.
[57] Turgot, *On the Formation and the Distribution of Wealth*, in *Turgot on Progress*, 110-82.
[58] Turgot, *Formation and the Distribution of Wealth*, 125.
[59] Turgot, *Formation and the Distribution of Wealth*, 124-125.
[60] See Mark Salber Phillips. "Reconsiderations of History and Antiquarianism: Arnaldo Momigliano and the Historiography of Eighteenth-Century Britain," *Journal of the History of Ideas,* 57 (1996): 297-316. While Phillips focuses on English and Scottish developments, the trend he identifies in these countries does seem to have had French parallels.

historian helps to illustrate this phenomenon.[61] In his early histories, such as his 1731 *History of Charles XII,*[62] there was little or no attention paid to changes in everyday life. Historicism (in the sense of the word as used by Friedrich Meinecke) was lightly developed in this work as well as in those historical works by Voltaire that had been commissioned by rulers.[63] For instance, Voltaire's highly partisan *Histoire du Parlement de Paris* did not develop the theme of progress to any real extent, perhaps because it was a rush job produced in conjunction with the royal campaign against that institution.[64]

The historical works by Voltaire in which consciousness of social change was most evident are *Le Siècle de Louis XIV*[65] and the *Essai sur les mœurs et l'esprit des nations et sure les principaux faits de l'histoire depuis Charlemange jusqu'à Louis XIII.*[66] In the *Siècle,* Voltaire moved beyond the political history to discuss developments in other fields, especially literature and the arts. However, Voltaire's interest in social history did not seem to have been grounded in a belief in progress. Those who see Voltaire as a believer in linear progress should consider a 1738 letter outlining the plan of this work in which Voltaire stated that one of his motives for writing a history of France under Louis XIV was to illustrate the extent to which France has declined since his reign.[67] Voltaire's adoption of a thematic rather than a chronological structure in this work allowed him to treat progress and regression in various fields separately but in a way that drove home a deeply pessimistic message. Voltaire compared the artistic achievements of the age of Louis XIV with

[61] The only real book-length study of Voltaire *qua* historian is J. H. Brumfitt, *Voltaire Historian* (Oxford: University Press, 1958).

[62] Voltaire, *History of Charles XII with a life of Voltaire by Lord Brougham, and Critical Notices by Lord Macaulay and Thomas Carlyle,* ed. O. W. Wight (New York: Hund and Houghton, 1864)

[63] Friedrich Meinecke, *Historicism: The Rise of a New Historical Outlook,* trans. J. E. Anderson (London: Routledge and Kegan Paul, 1972). Meinecke's use of the term "historicism" is clearly very different from Karl Popper's definition of "historicism" as the belief that history is governed by directional laws (e.g., the law of proletarianization). In this context "historicism" means an awareness of how life in other periods varies from one's own.

[64] Brumfitt, *Voltaire Historian.* For information on the struggles between the forces of the Crown and the Parlement de Paris, see John Rogister, *Louis XV and the Parlement of Paris, 1737-1755* (Cambridge: Cambridge University Press, 1995).

[65] Voltaire worked on this history for nearly twenty years before it was published in 1751. All pages references are to *Histoire du siècle de Louis XIV,* ed. Gustave Masson and G. W. Prothero (Cambridge: Cambridge University Press, 1881).

[66] While chapters of this work appeared in the *Mercure de France* in the 1740s, the first complete edition appeared in 1756. The edition cited here is *Essai sur les moeurs et l'esprit des nations, et sur les principaux faits de l'histoire depuis Charlemagne jusqu' à Louis XIII.* Introduction, bibliographie, relevé de variantes, notes et index par René Pomeau (Paris: Garnier, 1963).

[67] Cited in Brumfitt, *Voltaire Historian,* 49.

the two other great periods of human history (ancient Greece and Rome).[68] According to Voltaire, the artistic mediocrity of the Age of Louis XV became clear once a comparison of the artistic brilliance of Molière and Racine is considered. To be fair to those who would emphasize the progressivist elements of his thought, Voltaire did concede that France has become more prosperous since the reign of Louis XIV. However, he also strongly defended the economic policies of Colbert as having laid the basis for future prosperity; the obvious implication is that current prosperity is due to past policies and that France's current leadership will eventually lead to decline in the economic field. Two things are striking about Voltaire's depiction of the reign of Louis XIV as the golden age of French civilization. First, since Voltaire is widely seen as an apostle of religious toleration, his remarkable effort to downplay the Revocation of the Edicts of Nantes deserves notice. The mildness of Voltaire's criticisms of this policy (which mostly related to the national economic interest) was censured by many of his contemporaries.[69] Another significant point is that the era that Voltaire depicted as the peak of French history was precisely the period in which saw the *Querelle* between the Ancients and the Moderns.[70] In other words, the era which the Moderns glorified (the late seventeenth century) in the course of advancing the idea of progress is the same period Voltaire presented as the high-water mark of French history.[71] There is a tremendous irony here that Bury and others did not detect; for while Bury presented the *Querelle* as laying the foundation for the widespread acceptance of progressivism, part of the mixed legacy of the *Querelle* may have been to lend credence to a newer form of cyclicalism that saw the day of the *Querelle* as the peak.

---

[68] See the first chapter of Brumfitt, *Voltaire Historian*.

[69] Brumfitt, *Voltaire Historian*, 58.

[70] The need to flatter appears to have played a role in the development of the idea of progress. The adulation of Louis XIV was led to the presentation of the King as not just as the equal of Augustus but as perhaps his superior. This theme was then extended to cover their respective nations and time-periods, leading to the view that the moderns were superior to the ancients. Charles Perrault (1628-1703) made this comparison in *Le Siècle de Louis le Grand* (1687) and in *La Parallèle des Anciens et des Modernes* (1688). See Jacques Barchilon and Peter Flinders, *Charles Perrault* (Boston: Twayne, 1981).

[71] Often the glorification of the period involved the glorification of the reigning monarch as well. Changes in the way in which the King and his conquest were portrayed were linked to the evolving ways in which people compared modern times with the ancient world. For instance, while comparing the Sun King with Augustus was common throughout the reign, at first the young Louis was complimented by assertions that he approach the great Augustus in grandeur, by the end of the reign, Louis was seen as equalling and even surpassing even Augustus.

While Voltaire did not title the *Essai sur les mœurs* a history, it was nothing less than a history of the world in two volumes.[72] Covering thousands of years and every inhabited continent, Voltaire presented the reader with a mass of fact and commentary. While this sprawling text disproves the notion that Voltaire had evolved a systematic view of the past, some aspects of this work did have a direct bearing on the idea of progress. If we accept that emphasizing racial categories lends credence to permanentist views of history, Voltaire's stress on the sheer physiological differences between different human races takes on significance for the historian of the idea of progress.[73] According to Voltaire, "il n'est permis qu'à un aveugle de douter que les Blancs, les Nègres, les Albinos, les Hottentots, les Lapons, les Chinois, les Américains, soient des races entièrement différentes."[74] Like his contemporary Buffon, Voltaire perceived racial characteristics as essentially immutable over time, an idea he supported with the observation that when Africans are brought to cold climates, their children remain African in appearance. That being said, Voltaire was not a crude racist in the sense of believing that all Europeans are superior to all members of other races. In fact, Voltaire compared the savages of other continents to "our savages" (namely the European peasantry) quite favourably. "Il faut convenir surtout que les peoples du Canada et les Cafres, qu'il nous a plu d'appeler sauvages, sont infiniment supérieurs aus nôtres."[75] Comparing the rustics of Europe to the tribesmen on North America and Africa, Voltaire commented while the latter are free, "nos sauvages n'ont pas même d'idée de la liberté." Voltaire even used geological events to impress the reader with the non-progressive and occasionally catastrophically regressive element of history. He pointed out

---

[72] This work had been dedicated to one Mme du Châtelet, who shared d'Alembert's dislike of history. For du Châtelet's dislike of history, see René Pomeau's introduction to the *Essai sur les mœurs*.

[73] Clearly, permanentism with its stress on the immutability of characteristics and the essential sameness of people over time (if not from country to country) runs contrary to the basic thrust of historicism, which involves stressing the differences between people living in different periods (see n. 42). Voltaire's ideas anticipated the nineteenth-century notion of polygenesis. Excellent information on the European origins of the polygenesis thesis can be found in Stephen Jay Gould, *The Mismeasure of Man*. 2nd ed. (New York: Norton, 1996), 62-104; and in Nicholas Hudson, "From 'Nation' to 'Race': The Origin of Racial Classification in Eighteenth-Century Thought," *Eighteenth-Century Studies* 29 (1996): 247-64.

[74] Voltaire, *Essai sur les mœurs*, 6. To contextualize Voltaire's views on race, see Emmanuel Chukwudi Eze, ed. *Race and the Enlightenment: A Reader* (Cambridge, MA: Blackwell, 1997). The only real problem with this excellent work is that the editor refers to "the Enlightenment" in the singular even though the current trend stresses the existence of many separate but interconnected enlightenments in Europe. My point in examining Voltaire's views on race is not to judge him for failing to conform to modern standards; rather, it is to relate his position in the eighteenth-century debates on race to his philosophy of history.

[75] Voltaire, *Essai sur les mœurs*, 23.

that while many places on land were formerly under water, examples of the reverse process are also legion. "J'ai vu, il y a quarante ans, les cloches de dix-huit villages près du Mordick, qui s'élevaient encore au-dessus de ses inundations, et qui ont cede depuis à l'effort des vagues."[76] It is true that there are progressivist elements in the *Essai sur les mœurs*, but these are balanced by the presentation of scenarios and facts that leave an impression of regression or cyclicality. Rather than struggling to find an overall pattern in the mass of contradictory ideas that Voltaire presented, one is tempted to conclude that he did not see a general directional movement, progressive or otherwise, running through history. Voltaire's sense that history lacked a broad pattern of the sort described by Hegel and Vico was reinforced by his ideas on historical causation; in addition to highlighting the role of chance in history, Voltaire stressed poly-causality, enumerating multiple factors ranging from long-term economic trends to the personal characteristics of great men.[77] For instance, in the *Dialogue entre un Brachmane et un Jésuite,* the decision by a Brahman in India to begin walking with one foot instead of another, began a complicated sequence of events that resulted in the death of Henry of Navarre.[78]

It is significant that in the entry dealing with the *Querelle* between the ancients and the moderns that appeared in the later editions of the *Dictionnaire philosophique,* Voltaire spoke about the *Querelle* as an ongoing phenomenon, observing that the great struggle "des moderns et des anciens n'est pas encore vidé, il est sur le bureau depuis l'âge d'argent qui succéda à l'âge d'or." Voltaire also remarked that "les hommes ont toujours prétendu que le bon vieux temps valait beaucoup mieux que le temps présent."[79] In other words, Voltaire recognized that the idea of progress did not yet enjoy uncontested hegemony. The chief proponent of the modern view Voltaire cites is Fontenelle; for Voltaire, the representative ancient is "the chevalier Temple."[80] Voltaire's concluding

---

[76] Voltaire, *Essai sur les mœurs*, 4.

[77] Brumfitt, *Voltaire Historian*, 127.

[78] Brumfitt, *Voltaire Historian,* 122. Voltaire's apparently strong belief in the role of chance in history does conflict, however, with his theism.

[79] "Anciens et modernes," in Voltaire, *Dictionnaire philosophique*, in *Œuvres de Voltaire*, ed. Adrien-Jean-Quentin Beuchot. 72 vols. (Paris: Werdet et Lequien fils, 1829-40), 26: 343.

[80] "Even though the chevalier Temple, who has made it his business to disparage all the moderns, claims that in architecture they have nothing comparable to the temples of Greece and Rome: but, for all that he is English, he must agree that the Church of St. Peter is incomparably more beautiful than the Capitol was." Even though Voltaire was unusual in that he had travelled to England, the fact that Voltaire cites a participant in the English Battle of the Books instead of a French *querellist* suggests that the English debate was not a mere echo of the French one but rather an integral part of a transnational dialogue. Other

statement suggests that he was in general but not total agreement with the moderns; "There are therefore spheres in which the moderns are far superior to the ancients, and others, very few, in number, in which we are their inferiors. It is to this that the whole dispute is reduced."[81]

After examining the works written by and for a comparatively small elite, the student of eighteenth-century French historical thought is still left wondering how far these differing conceptions of history reached those lower down the social scale. Luckily, Daniel Roche has discovered the diary a peasant named Pierre Bordier kept between 1741 and 1781 that helps answer this question.[82] As one would expect from someone closely tied to the land, Bordier thought about time in a cyclical rather than a linear way. Indeed, Bordier extended this pattern beyond the annual cycle to cover longer period and appears to have been fascinated with a quasi-mystic book entitled *Prophèties perpétuelles* that deals with cyclical structures of history.[83] Bordier tried to relate these ideas to his own careful records of local crop conditions, concluding that the thesis that major crop crises would occur every twenty-eight years was tolerably accurate.

While his most famous work, the *Esquisse d'un tableau historique des progrès de l'esprit humain*,[84] was written after 1789 and therefore technically falls outside the scope of this survey, the historical ideas of the marquis de Condorcet (1743-1794) deserve to be examined if for no other reason to present a contrast with those eighteenth-century French thinkers who had a more sceptical view of progress. This work was written between July 1793 and March 1794, and it is standard for commentators to point out the irony of a proponent of progress who is about to be devoured by the Revolution he had supported. Condorcet had earlier submitted a proposal to the Assembly for the establishment of a comprehensive system of national education. This plan had not been approved, and Condorcet continued to lobby for national education. After reading the *Tableau historique* it becomes clear why Condorcet was so intensely interested in popular education; in his theory, general social progress is almost entirely dependent on the improvement of the intellect and the diffusion of ideas.[85] Condorcet divided human history into precisely ten eras; the penultimate era was tellingly titled the period "from

individuals that Voltaire mentions in this entry include Lucretius, Horace, Nestor, Kepler, and Newton.

[81] Voltaire, *Philosophical Dictionary*.

[82] Daniel Roche, *France in the Enlightenment*, 91-92.

[83] According to Roche, this work was attributed to Pythagoras, Joseph the Just, and Daniel the Prophet.

[84] Antoine-Nicolas de Condorcet, *Sketch for a Historical Picture of the Progress of the Human Mind*, trans. June Barraclough. 2nd ed. (Westport, CT: Greenwood Press, 1979).

[85] Condorcet, *Sketch*, 183.

Descartes to the Founding of the French Republic."[86] In advancing his idea of progress, Condorcet adumbrated a theory of historical causation that veered close to what would today be called "intellectual determinism." For Condorcet, ideas were the real motive power behind social change, with factors like climate (Montesquieu's suggestion) or chance playing only a minor role. Like Gibbon, Condorcet attributed the fall of the Roman Empire to the growth of Christianity; "the triumph of Christianity was the signal for the complete decadence of philosophy and the sciences."[87] Moreover, for Condorcet, it was great minds, the rare innovators, who were most responsible for humanity's progress or stagnation. We ought to celebrate the "certain men of genius" who are "humanity's eternal benefactors" such as the anonymous inventor of writing. [88]

The contrast between Condorcet's thinking and the version of the idea of progress advanced by the Scottish Enlightenment thinkers is striking.[89] In his *History of England*, David Hume stressed that progress is often the result of either chance or the unintended consequences of self-interested individual actions rather than wise choices.[90] Hume saw feudalism as declining because luxury loving barons commuted feudal tenures into money rents not as the result of conscious dissatisfaction with the system. Hume argued that property rights emerged only gradually and had nothing to do with the development of abstract notions of justice. The real reason for property rights was that insecure feudal overlords had once demanded allodial land grants from the king.[91] Likewise, Parliament's emergence was a function of the increasing power of the aristocracy, not the result of the diffusion of new theories of political rights. In the works of Hume and the other Scottish Enlightenment thinkers, a sort of unseen hand transmuted actions with silly motivations into sources of progress; despite blindness to the future on the part of selfish individuals, progress manages to occur. For instance, while Hume saw the Puritans as "absurd" in their doctrines, he also argued that they had indirectly helped to create the modern British constitution.[92]

---

[86] Condorcet, *Sketch*, 125.

[87] Condorcet, *Sketch*, 72.

[88] Condorcet, *Sketch*, 7.

[89] For this observation, I am partially indebted to Gladys Bryson, *Man and Society: The Scottish Inquiry of the Eighteenth Century* (Princeton: Princeton University Press, 1945), and Spadafora, *Idea of Progress*, 310-15.

[90] David Spadafora sees this idea as closely linked to the Smithian notion of the invisible hand: *Idea of Progress*, 310.

[91] David Hume, *The History of England from the Invasion of Julius Caesar to the Revolution in 1688* (London: Longman, Green, *et al.*, 1864), "Appendix II," 1: 446.

[92] Hume's comments on social and economic progress are generally contained in the Appendices of the *History*, see Appendices I and II in vol. I, and Appendix III in vol. 3.

So while both Hume and Condorcet can be described in general terms
as proponents of the idea of progress (to use Bury's simplistic
terminology), their accounts of how progress occurs were radically
different. The economic, philosopher, and intellectual historian F. A.
Hayek distinguished "rational constructivist" views of society from the
evolutionary perspective he shared. According to Hayek, the rational
constructivists (particularly Comte and the twentieth-century advocates of
social engineering and centrally planned economies) credited human
reason with a greater ability to understand society and direct social
evolution than was really justified. Hayek argued that the rational
constructivists were wrong to see purposeful reason as underlying past
social developments.[93] Faced with the hen-and-egg question of whether
reason created civilization or civilization created reason, a follower of
Condorcet would likely answer that, of course, reason preceded
civilization.[94] Hayek took the opposite view, one which was anticipated by
the great contemporary opponent of "politics in the abstract," Edmund
Burke. Burke, of course, upheld the traditional institutions that had been
produced by hundreds of years of blind evolution as superior to anything
reason could erect.

One outcome of the eighteenth-century debates over the existence,
degree, and causation of progress was the development of two very
different views of society, one seeing social institutions as the product of
human design and therefore amenable to redesign, the other stressing that
social order is the product of blind evolution and the actions of countless
self-interested individuals. The nineteenth and the twentieth centuries saw
the struggle between these two very different views of how progress
comes about. On the one hand were the advocates of progress through
planning and the conscious engineering of society. On the other sat the
defenders of tradition and an unplanned economic order as the foundation
of all progress. The roots of this fundamental disagreement lie in the
Enlightenments of the eighteenth century; arguably, this debate is the most
important outgrowth of the metahistorical debates of the eighteenth
century.

[93] F. A. Hayek developed these ideas in *The Fatal Conceit: the Errors of Socialism* (Chicago:
University of Chicago Press, 1989), and in *The Counter Revolution of Science: Studies on the
Abuse of Reason.* (Glencoe, IL: Free Press, 1952). Hayek condemns the *Ecole polytechnique*
as one the earlier breeding grounds of rational constructivism. What Hayek calls "rational
constructivism" is similar to what Michael Oakeshott terms "rationalism." See Oakshott,
Rationalism in Politics and Other Essays (New York: Basic Books, 1962).
[94] Hayek does not go so far as to stand this argument on its head by arguing that civilization
preceded reason. He does, however, assert that they coevolved.

"The Most Hidden Conditions of Men of the First Rank": The Pantheist Current in Eighteenth-Century Germany "Uncovered" by the Spinoza Controversy

John H. Zammito
Rice University

Abstract

Conventionally the Spinoza "renaissance" has been connected with the Pantheism Controversy *circa* 1785. What concerns me is not the "renaissance" *after* 1785, but the one already in place and unexpectedly *uncovered* in 1785. My claim is that a great deal of this productive clarification of positions had taken place already, starting in the 1750s, though it only came to light in the 1780s. I offer two thick descriptions. The first is a cultural-historical description of the impulses animating Lessing and Mendelssohn to their pathbreaking project of "vindicating" Spinoza in the early 1750s. The second is a brief intellectual-historical sketch of the metaphysical and scientific impulses galvanizing in the young Johann Gottfried Herder a new vitalist sense of Nature.

> ...*eine Explosion, welche die geheimsten Verhältnisse würdiger Männer aufdeckte und zur Sprache brachte. Verhältnisse, die, ihnen selbst unbewußt, in einer sonst höchst aufgeklärten Gesellschaft schlummerten. Der Riß war so gewaltsam, daß wir darüber, bei eintretenden Zufälligkeiten, einen unserer würdigsten Männer, Mendelssohn, verloren.*
>
> — Goethe[1]

I. Introduction

In his autobiography, J. W. v. Goethe made the well-known observation cited in the epigraph above with reference to the Pantheism Controversy. His language poses the historical issue of this essay. The revelation explosively made public, i.e. brought into discourse, the most hidden conditions (or connections or relations—all of which senses are active in the German term [*Verhältnisse*]) of leading thinkers. That is, they had been unaware that they *shared* this interest—though each of them, Goethe implies, cultivated it in privacy. A bond was exposed that had not been explicit among them. For Goethe this was ironic for an epoch, the Enlightenment, which prided itself on bringing things to light and which elsewhere had succeeded very well in illuminating such shared premises. And we should note, finally, the violence of the image: this was an

---

[1] *Dichtung und Wahrheit* I (Leipzig, 1977), 690.

explosion whose destructive path [*Riβ*; literally, "fissure"] could indeed cost someone (Mendelssohn) his life.

The Pantheism Controversy, a long tradition of interpretation has maintained, inaugurated the first affirmative public treatment of Spinoza in the high culture of modernity, a Spinoza "renaissance."[2] In Winfried Schröder's words, "there is no question ... that only in the Spinoza renaissance of the 1780s did authors take up the productive clarification of positions [*Auseinandersetzung*] vis a vis the philosopher..."[3] My claim is that a great deal of this productive clarification of positions had taken place already, starting in the 1750s, though it only came to light in the 1780s. What concerns me is not the "renaissance" *after* 1785, but the one already in place and unexpectedly *uncovered* in 1785. "The simultaneity of Goethe's turn to Spinoza with Lessing's and Herder's veneration for Spinoza illuminates the timeliness and necessity of Goethe's Spinozism: Goethe's path to Spinoza is the path of the [entire] German Spinoza Renaissance."[4] What was that path? My concern will be to ask how and why Spinoza could become a constructive—if still clandestine—element in the most innovative thought of the period after 1750. What Jacobi exposed in the mid-1780s clearly had a considerable gestation period, but unlike a lot of valuable recent work on this question, I propose to concentrate on the period after 1750, the *Hochaufklärung*, not the *Frühaufklärung*.[5]

In the same conversation which led Goethe to his observation, Lessing had characterized Spinoza, not without irony, as a "dead dog."[6] How had the dog come back to life? Throughout the growing literature on Spinozism in eighteenth-century Germany there are acknowledgments that

---

[2] Hermann Timm, *Gott und die Freiheit: Studien zur Religionsphilosophie der Goethezeit. Bd. I. Die Spinozarenaissance* (Frankfurt: Klostermann, 1974).

[3] Winfried Schröder, *Spinoza in der deutschen Frühaufklärung* (Würzburg: Königshausen and Neumann, 1987), 146.

[4] Martin Bollacher, *Der junge Goethe und Spinoza: Studien zur Geschichte des Spinozismus in der Epoche des Sturms und Drangs* (Tübingen: Niemeyer, 1969), 17.

[5] See, for instnace, A. W. Gulyga, *Der deutsche Materialismus am Ausgang des 18. Jahrhunderts* (Berlin: Akademie, 1966); Jean-Paul Wurtz, "Tschirnhaus und die Spinozismusbeschuldigung: die Polemik mit Christian Thomasius," *Studia Leibnitiana* 13, no.1 (1981): 61-75; Konrad Cramer, Wilhelm Jacobs and Wilhelm Schmidt-Biggemann, eds., *Spinozas Ethik und ihre frühe Wirkung* (Wolfenbüttel: Herzog August Bibliothek, 1981); Karlfried Gründer and Wilhelm Schmidt-Biggemann, eds., *Spinoza in der Frühzeit seiner religiösen Wirkung* (Heidelberg: Lambert Schneider, 1984); Stefan Winkle, *Die heimlichen Spinozisten in Altona und der Spinozastreit* (Hamburg: Verein für Hamburger Geschichte, 1988); Rüdiger Otto, *Studien zur Spinozarezeption in Deutschland im 18. Jahrhundert* (Frankfurt, etc: Peter Lang, 1994); Paolo Cristofolini, Jean-Toussaint Desanti, René Pomeau and Paul Vernière, eds., *Spinoza au XVIIIe siècle* (Paris: Méridiens Klincksieck, 1990); Hanna Delf, Julius Schoeps and Manfred Walther, eds., *Spinoza in der europäischen Geistesgeschichte* (Berlin: Hentrich, 1994).

[6] F. H. Jacobi, *Spinozabüchlein*, in Heinrich Scholtz, ed., *Die Hauptschriften zum Pantheismus Streit zwischen Jacobi und Mendelssohn* (Berlin: Reuther & Reichard, 1916).

the climate for Spinoza-reception changed significantly at mid-century, but there has been little convincing historical work explaining exactly how or why. Thus David Bell, in what is a "history of ideas" largely cut loose from context, labels the engagement of Lessing and Mendelssohn with Spinoza a "turning point," but he gives no explanation of how or why it could emerge. Without any historiographical context he protests: "it is both exaggerated and misleading to give Mendelssohn, as it were, the 'credit' for the new attitudes to Spinoza in the later eighteenth century."[7] Alexander Altmann, to cite another prominent scholar, writes: "The time for a fresh approach to Spinoza ... was propitious" when Mendelssohn published his *Philosophische Gespräche* in 1755.[8] Again, we are offered the intimation that a change in climate had emerged by mid-century, but not given enough historical context to define or explain it.

Spinoza was as important as a *figure* (Bayle's "virtuous atheist") as for his formulation of distinct philosophical claims. Indeed, I will argue here that it is the figure of Spinoza—and concretely of Spinoza as an exemplary Jew—which may well lie at the origin of the renaissance of Spinoza in the *Hochaufklärung*. But that is only one side; the other concerns itself primarily with Spinoza's ideas, and how they seemed to offer a way out of impasses of eighteenth-century discourse in the linked spheres of metaphysics, physical theory, biology and anthropology bound up in the term "hylozoism." That is, what properties could intelligibly be ascribed to matter, and how would this explain such problems as the causal relations of distinct substances, the principles of action at a distance, chemical attraction, electricity and heat, the mysteries of biological generation, and the mind-body relation?

Insofar as I am interested in *intellectual*, as contrasted with cultural, history, it is this extraordinary bundle of theoretical issues associated with hylozoism that draws my attention. The philosophical question I would like to pursue is the connection of the problem of physical influx with the idea of hylozoism, a question whose Newtonian and Lockean connection Yolton has highlighted in terms of "thinking matter" and others have discerned in the "sensorium" notion of space that figured so centrally in the Leibniz-Clarke correspondence.[9] But as a *cultural* historian I find the idea of a Berlin milieu for free thinking equally crucial. I propose to offer

---

[7] Bell, *Spinoza in Germany from 1670 to the Age of Goethe* (London: Institute of Germanic Studies, University of London, 1984), 24.

[8] Alexander Altmann, *Moses Mendelssohn: A Biographical Study* (London: Routledge and Kegan Paul, 1973), 35.

[9] John W. Yolton, *Thinking Matter: Materialism in Eighteenth-Century Britain* (Minneapolis: University of Minnesota Press, 1983); Yolton, *Locke and French Materialism* (Oxford: Clarendon Press, 1991); on the Leibniz-Clarke correspondence see most recently: Ezio Vailati, *Leibniz and Clarke: A Study of Their Correspondence* (New York: Oxford University Press, 1997).

two "thick descriptions." The first is a cultural-historical description of the impulses animating Lessing and Mendelssohn to their pathbreaking project of "vindicating" Spinoza in the early 1750s. The second is an intellectual-historical description of the impulses galvanizing the young Herder and transmitted to his new friend, Goethe, in Straßburg at the outset of the 1770s involving a new vitalist sense of Nature.

What was it in Spinoza's position that made him the most hated among the so-called "atheists" in early modern thought? The argument that it was his *esprit de système*, his mathematical and categorical style of argumentation, his apodictic claims—in short, his decisively *modern* philosophical approach—seems to have considerable merit. And here, again, Bayle's account proved authoritative. Bayle made Spinoza the "systematic atheist, and according to a method totally new [*Athée de Systême, et d'une méthode toute nouvelle*]."[10] As Bollacher argues, "What particularly irked Bayle and other enemies of Spinoza was Spinoza's will to system, the claim of his philosophy to necessity."[11] Part of the ire arose from the violation of disciplinary boundaries and disciplinary hierarchies. In the first vein, Bollacher suggests, the mathematical or geometric intrusion into metaphysics provoked resentment.[12] But in the second vein, Spinoza represented a particularly virulent repudiation of the preeminence of theology among the faculties, and especially its authority over philosophy.

In the eighteenth century, to practice philosophy in a German university—or even outside it—was always to work in the shadow of theology. The disciplinary project of philosophy in the early modern period was to liberate itself from the yoke of theology. This found literal expression in the German eighteenth century in the widespread (though brief) adoption of the term *Weltweisheit* for the discipline.[13] The obvious thrust of the term was toward secularization. The German situation, with its massive confessional investment in the institution of the university dating back to the Reformation, made the issue of this liberation of

[10] Bayle, "Spinoza," in idem, *Historical and Critical Dictionary: Selections*, tr. Richard Popkin (Indianapolis: Hackett, 1991), 288-338.
[11] Bollacher, *Goethe und Spinoza*, 28.
[12] Bollacher, *Goethe und Spinoza*, 29; on the contestation of mathematical method (*l'esprit geométrique*) in German academic philosophy, see Giorgio Tonelli, "Der Streit um die mathematische Methode in der Philosophie der ersten Hälfte des 18. Jahrhunderts und die Entstehung von Kants Schrift über die 'Deutlichkeit,'" *Archiv für Philosophie* 9 (1959): 37-66.
[13] Werner Schneiders, "Zwischen Welt und Weisheit. Zur Verweltlichung der Philosophie in der frühen Moderne," *Studia Leibnitiana* 15, no. 1 (1983): 2-18, esp. 8ff.

disciplinary philosophy from theology dangerous and protracted.[14] Nevertheless—and this was the signal achievement of Christian Wolff—a new disciplinary self-conception did crystallize for philosophy in early eighteenth-century Germany: the idea of philosophy as a "rigorous science."[15] Wolff wanted philosophy as science to constitute the primary and dominant faculty of the entire university. Wolff put a fundamental challenge to the traditional disciplinary ascendancy of theology, jurisprudence and medicine by claiming they offered merely a historical knowledge of their fields, whereas "only philosophy could raise this knowledge to the theoretical level of a knowledge of principles [*Gründewissens*]."[16]

That explains why the orthodox theologians, having won their propaganda campaign by 1700, intimidating even so powerful a figure as Leibniz into conformity, could not stop their denuciations of Spinoza and especially their witch-hunt for suspected "Spinozists" even deep into the era of Goethe and Herder.[17] School philosophy alone was not strong enough to overcome them. Nor was the new culture of the *gebildeten Stände*. Hermann Timm points out that as late as 1740, some 80 percent of literary production had to do with Christianity, faith and knowledge.[18] The energies for liberation drew rather from the newly emergent natural sciences.

II. Berlin and the affirmation of freethinking in the *Hochaufklärung*

> *On the count of toleration, there is virtually no other way the nature of our states could go than the one which Spinoza then pointed out to them, to their general loathing.*[19]

The German *Hochaufklärung* (1750-1780) has suffered scholarly neglect relative to the *Spätaufklärung* or even the *Frühaufklärung*.[20] Yet

---

[14] Notker Hammerstein, "Zur Geschichte der deutschen Universitäten im Zeitalter der Aufklärung," in *Universität und Gelehrtenstand 1400-1800*, ed. Hellmut Rössler and Günther Franz (Limburg: Starke, 1970), 145-82, esp. 146.

[15] See esp. Werner Schneiders, ed., *Christian Wolff 1679-1754* (Hamburg: Meiner, 1983).

[16] Hans Erich Bödeker, "Von der 'Magd der Theologie' zur 'Leitwissenschaft': Vorüberlegungen zu einer Geschichte der Philosophie des 18. Jahrhunderts," *Das achtzehnte Jahrhundert* 14, no. 1 (1990): 19-57, cited from 32.

[17] Bollacher, *Goethe und Spinoza*, 35.

[18] Timm, *Spinozarenaissance*, 21.

[19] Herder, *Sämtliche Werke*, ed. Berhard Suphan. 32 vols. (Berlin: Weibmann, 1877-1913), 16: 418.

[20] For the concept of *Hochaufklärung* I draw on Rolf Grimminger, "Aufklärung, Absolutismus und bürgerlichen Individuen. Über den notwendigen Zusammenhang von

there is mounting evidence that the course of *Aufklärung* took a decisive turn in Germany around the middle of the eighteenth century.[21] How can this shift in climate be discerned, especially at its very outset? Unappetizing for our current political taste as it may be, the old-fashioned connection to the reign of Frederick II of Prussia (1740-1786) may turn out to be historically more important than we would like to concede.[22] Three particular features of his new reign are central here: first, his reinstatement of Christian Wolff at the University of Halle; second, his revitalization of the Berlin Academy, especially through the recruitment of French intellectuals; third, closely related to this, his interest in fostering "freethinking" in the sphere of religion. One of his first gestures was to remove the restriction on newspaper publication in Berlin, though he hastily restored it in the wake of criticism of his Silesian conquest. Still, his name was notoriously associated with freethinking. Lessing's bitter commentary from 1769 should not divert us from reckoning a considerable novelty to Frederician Berlin.[23] By the end of his first decade of rule, his innovations had effected a shift in climate.

More generally, there is a decisive historical connection between *Hochaufklärung* and a political-cultural transformation of German society centered in the large cities. What is at issue has been called "bourgeois emancipation" but would perhaps more prudently be termed the emergence of elements of what only in the nineteenth century could securely be termed a *Bildungsbürgertum*. In the categories of Hans Erich Bödeker, there was a contest between these new "*gebildeten Stände*" and the established "*Gelehrtenstand*," in which questions of the uses of philosophical knowledge played a significant role: "the '*gebildeten Stände*' were not any longer identical at all with the traditional '*gelehrten Stand*.' ... Accordingly the traditional concept of the '*gelehrten Stände*' was devalued and confined to the guild quality of the traditional scholarly estate."[24] The uncoupling of *Bildung* from traditional *Gelehrsamkeit* is

---

Literatur, Gesellschaft und Staat in der Geschichte des 18. Jahrhunderts," in *Hanser Sozialgeschichte der deutschen Literatur vom 16. Jahrhundert bis zur Gegenwart. Bd. 3: Deutsche Aufklärung bis zur Französischen Revolution*, ed. Rolf Grimminger (Munich: Hanser, 1980), 15-99, esp. 48ff.

[21] See the volume, *Wissenschaft im Zeitalter der Aufklärung*, hg. v. Rudolf Vierhaus (Göttingen: Vandenhoeck and Ruprecht, 1985).

[22] For the older view, see e.g. Wilhelm Dilthey, "Friedrich der Große und die deutsche Aufklärung," *Gesammelte Schriften* (Leipzig and Berlin: Teubner, 1927), 3: 83-209.

[23] Lessing, Letter to Nicolai, August 25, 1979, in *Sämtliche Schriften*, ed. Karl Lachmann and Franz Muncker. 23 vols. (Stuttgart: Göschen, 1886-1924), 17: 29 [hereafter cited in the form: LM: vol: p].

[24] Bödeker, "Die 'gebildeten Stände' im späten 18. und frühen 19. Jahrhundert: Zugehörigkeit und Abgrenzungen. Mentalitäten und Handlungspotentiale," in *Bildungsbürgertum im 19. Jahrhundert. Teil IV*, ed. Jürgen Kocka (Stuttgart: Klett-Cotta, 1992), 22.

central to the *Hochaufklärung*. Something about the acquistion and management of learning was centrally in dispute here, not only at the level of the individual person but also at the social-historical level, and that was precisely the burden of the key term for the epoch, *Aufklärung*.[25]

An ideal of *Geselligkeit* came to be articulated which is of immeasurable importance for a grasp of the *Hochaufklärung*.[26] One of its most important manifestations in the early eighteenth century was the emergence of a vast number of "moral weeklies," centered above all in the cities, which offered instruction in taste and style along with—as their title suggests—a great deal of moral instruction.[27] There were dramatic shifts in the structure of reading.[28] Religious texts came to be displaced by cultural ones, Latin texts by German ones. But even more important was the shift that Rolf Engelsing has characterized as from "intensive" to "extensive" reading, i.e., from the close and repeated reading of a few texts, to the continuous assimilation of ephemeral reading material, above all in the form of periodical literature.[29] It was in this era that the periodical press took shape in Germany.[30]

The new *Bürger* needed to achieve *independence* in judgment: *Selbstdenken*. To be capable of thinking for oneself was to have achieved "maturity," *Mündigkeit*.[31] To achieve *Selbstdenken*, to become *mündig*, was a matter of *personal* knowledge, of the cultivation of individual judgment (*Urteilskraft*), which could only be successful by drawing upon *all* of one's own life experience, the physical and the emotional alongside the logical-cognitive. Emancipation meant thinking for oneself (*Selbstdenken*) and even freethinking (*Freidenken*), i.e. submission even of the most fundamental features of church and state to critical scrutiny. The terminology of *Freydenker* or *Freygeister* only became established around mid-century, displacing an older reliance on imported French terms, *libertin* and *libertinage*. Thus *Zedlers Universallexicon* (1736) had no

---

[25] Lewis White Beck dates the prominence of the term *Aufklärung* to 1750: Beck, *Early German Philosophy* (1969; rpt. Bristol: Thoemmes, 1996), 322.

[26] Wolfram Mauser, "Geselligkeit: Zu Chance und Scheitern einer sozialethischen Utopie um 1750," in *Entwicklungsschwellen im 18. Jahrhundert*, ed. Karl Eibl (Hamburg: Meiner, 1989 = *Aufklärung* 4, no. 1 (1989)), 5-36.

[27] W. Martens, *Botschaft der Tugend. Die Aufklärung im Spiegel der deutschen moralischen Wochenschriften* (Stuttgart: Metzler, 1968).

[28] Herbert G. Göpfert, ed., *Buch und Leser* (Hamburg: Hauswedell, 1977). "Reading [was a] medium of self-discovery and self-comprehension of the educated" but also "they wished to learn how to understand and interpret their world." (Bödeker, "gebildeten Stände," 37.)

[29] Rolf Engelsing, *Der Bürger als Leser: Lesegeschichte in Deutschland 1500-1800* (Stuttgart: Metzler, 1974).

[30] Paul Raabe, "Die Zeitschriften als Medium der Aufklärung," *Wolfenbütteler Studien zur Aufklärung* 1 (1974): 99ff.

[31] It is no coincidence that these are Kantian categories. See Norbert Hinske, ed., *Eklektik, Selbstdenken, Mündigkeit* (Hamburg: Meiner, 1986 = *Aufklärung* 1, no. 1 [1986]).

entries for *Freidenker* or *Freigeist* but did address their conceptual content under the French derivation *Libertiner*. By 1758, Johann Mehlig's *Historisches Kirchen- und Ketzer Lexikon* has no use for that French term, inserting instead an article on *Freydenker* in which Mehlig reports: "that is how those are called who would earlier generally have been termed libertines," which Reiner Wild takes to be a sign that the latter was "already by the midcentury an obsolete usage."[32] The next year, Trinius published the *Freydenker-Lexikon*.

One of the obviously essential features of "bourgeois emancipation" was that it was *urban*, that is, these new groups tended to be located in the larger cities, especially Hamburg and Berlin, but also Leipzig and Frankfurt am Main.[33] The growth of both Hamburg and of Berlin was striking over the course of the eighteenth century.[34] With that growth came distinct changes in the cultural milieu of those large cities. Helen Liebel has given us a vivid image of Hamburg in this era; Horst Möller has done the same for Berlin.[35] What their accounts demonstrate is the interconnection of these two cities in the revitalization of the eighteenth-century German economy in the long, slow recovery from the devastation of the Thirty Years War. Franklin Kopitzsch identifies a crucial feature of this urbanism:

> The rise of Hamburg as Germany's leading port and trading city, the rise of Brandenburg-Prussia to a european great power are inexplicable without the politics of tolerance of their leading strata. Tolerance was always limited, however: thus in Hamburg as in Brandenburg-Prussia the Jews were in an unambiguously poorer legal position than other minorities.[36]

---

[32] Reiner Wild, "Freidenker in Deutschland," *Zeitschrift für historische Forschung* 6 (1979), 253-85, citing 258.

[33] Reiner Wild, "Städtekultur, Bildungswesen und Aufklärungsgesellschaften," in *Hanser Sozialgeschichte der deutschen Literatur vom 16. Jahrhunder bis zur Gegenwart. Bd. 3: Deutsche Aufklärung bis zur Französsischen Revolution*, ed. Rolf Grimminger (Munich: Hanser, 1980), 103-32.

[34] Helga Schultz, *Berlin 1650-1800: Sozialgeschichte einer Residenz* (Berlin: Akademie, 1987), 163-320.

[35] Liebel, "Laissez-faire vs. Mercantilism: The Rise of Hamburg and The Hamburg Bourgeoisie vs. Frederick the Great in the Crisis of 1763," *Vierteljahrsschrift für Sozial und Wirtschaftsgeschichte* 52 (1965): 207-38; Möller, *Aufklärung in Preußen: Der Verleger, Publizist und Geschichtsschreiber Friedrich Nicolai* (Berlin: Colloquium, 1974 = Einzelveröffentlichungen der Historischen Kommission zu Berlin, Bd. 15).

[36] Franklin Kopitzsch, "Gotthold Ephraim Lessing und seine Zeitgenossen im Spannungsfeld von Toleranz und Intoleranz," in *Deutsche Aufklärung und Judenemanzipation*, ed. Walter Grab. Jahrbuch des Intstituts für deutsche Geschichte. Beiheft 3 (Tel Aviv:Universität Tel-Aviv, Institut f r Deutsche Geschichte, 1980), 29-85, citing 32-33.

It is this connection of the new urban culture of the *gebildeten Stände* in Berlin (and Hamburg) with the problem of social tolerance, especially regarding Jews, I would like to suggest, which offers us the best purchase on the concrete impulses behind the Spinoza renaissance launched by Lessing and Mendelssohn.

The "renaissance" of Spinoza in Germany began at the moment that the young Lessing chose to abandon his formal university studies and move to Berlin to take up a career as a freelance writer [*freier Schriftsteller*].[37] Lessing brought his commitment to tolerance with him.[38] Alexander Altmann calls it a family tradition: "Tolerance was in his blood, as it were."[39] Lessing's grandfather had written a dissertation on toleration of religious sects, and even as a schoolboy Lessing appeared to be concerned with such issues. As a university student, he was drawn to a consideration of dissenters and their fates, such that he created a mini-genre for himself, the *Rettung*, or vindication, to which he devoted a good deal of writing from the late 1740s into the early 1750s.[40]

Lessing, as a university student in Leipzig, found himself in a milieu that pursued freedom of thought and expression into its most problematic quarters. The key figure here would appear to be Lessing's friend, Christlob Mylius, with his journals, *Der Freygeist* and *Der Wahrsager*.[41] Lessing characterizes the former as follows:

> Mr. Mylius was not long in Leipzig when in the year
> 1745 he began his *Freygeist* and he continued it happily

---

[37] On the notion of the *freier Schriftsteller* see Hans J. Haferkorn, "Zur Entstehung der bürgerlich-literarischen Intelligenz und des Schriftstellers in Deutschland zwischen 1750 und 1800," in *Deutsches Bürgertum und literarische Intelligenz 1750-1800*, ed. Bernd Lutz (Stuttgart: Metzler, 1974 = *Literaturwissenschaft und Sozialwissenschaften*, 3), 113-276. On Lessing's ambition: "Seine Wunschvorstellung deckt sich mit dem Konzept eines freien Schriftstellers, der nach keiner Seite hin Konzessionen zu machen gezwungen ist. Diesen Plan glaubt er am ehesten in einer großen Stadt, in der ein urbaner Wind weht, verwirklichen zu können... So verzichtet er kurzentschlossen auf alle Stipendien und auf die Unterstützung von seiten der Eltern und begibt sich in das tollkühne Abenteuer eines freien Schriftstellerlebens nach Berlin." Gustav Stichelschmidt, *Lessing: Der Mann und sein Werk* (Dusseldorf: Droste, 1989), 56.
[38] On Lessing and tolerance, see F. Kopitzsch, "Gotthold Ephraim Lessing und seine Zeitgenossen im Spannungsfeld von Toleranz und Intoleranz," *passim*.
[39] Altmann, *Moses Mendelssohn*, 37.
[40] See, e.g, Lessing, "Gedanken über die Herrnhuter" (1750), LM: 14: 154-63.
[41] A. Altmann notes that Mylius "seems to have been a follower of Spinoza" (37). His footnote refers to a dissertation by Hans Schmoldt, *Der Spinozastreit* (Berlin, 1938), but he admits that "only the vaguest conjectures are offered" (768, n. 10). David Bell notes, without any supporting documentation, that "Lessing's friend, Christlob Mylius, who enjoyed a reputation as a freethinker, might have commended Spinoza to Lessing." Bell, *Spinoza in Germany*, 28. Winfried Schröder has cautioned us against the presumption that there were many such "follower[s] of Spinoza." Still, *interest* in Spinoza and other "free thinkers" suffices for our purposes.

for fifty two issues. The title promised much, and I
doubt that these days one could easily find a more
diffuse one.... Incidentally, as to the content of the
Freygeist, even the most ardent nitpicker could not find
the least thing there which could contribute to the harm
of Christian virtue or religion... [Nevertheless] from that
moment the title of his book became his pseudonym, and
his acquaintances have long since been used to link the
names Mylius and *Freygeist* as naturally as one
nowadays links the name Edelmann with mockers of
religion.[42]

This passage tells us a great deal. It suggests the radical flavor that the
term, and the commitment it embodied, carried at mid-century. Mylius
became notorious as a freethinker. But Lessing labors to introduce a
distinction in tone and meaning between what Mylius and freethinking
entail and what Johann Christian Edelmann had made even more notorious
in Germany, a reckless contempt for religion in general. Lessing
expressed a far more negative view of Mylius's second journal, which he
launched in Berlin in 1749: "The writing is sloppy, the morality is vulgar,
the jokes are pedestrian and the satire is offensive." Mylius appeared to
wish to make the journal over into a "scandalous chronicle of the city....
As a newcomer to Berlin without a doubt he had formed an all too grand
conception of the freedom of the press here."[43] Erich Schmidt offers the
details of the short life of this journal, whose provocations swiftly led to
government censorship.[44]

According to Schmidt, this second journal did have one redeeming
grace: "the only thing that gets taken seriously is the question of
freethinking [*Freigeisterei*]."[45] Martin Fontius has drawn our attention to a
little essay which appeared in *Der Wahrsager* in 1749, "Freigeister,
Naturalisten, Atheisten," which he suggests, "sought to open the way for
freedom of thought (*la libre pensée*)."[46] Scholarly tradition has assumed
the essay to have been written by Lessing, and it is included in at least one

---

[42] Lessing, "Vorrede [zu den] *Vermische Schriften des Hrn Christlob Mylius*" (1754), LM: 6: 399-401.
[43] *Ibid.*
[44] Erich Schmidt, *Lessing. Geschichte seines Lebens und seiner Schriften*. 2 vols. (Berlin: Weidmann, 1909), 1: 183.
[45] *Ibid.*, 183.
[46] Martin Fontius, "Littérature clandestine et pensée allemande," in *Le Matérialisme du XVIIIe siècle et la Littérature clandestine*, ed. Olivier Bloch (Paris: Vrin, 1982), 251-62, citing 252.

edition of Lessing's works.[47] The essay attempts to distinguish between the three concepts in its title, the better to come to terms with the ubiquitously negative usage of the term *Freigeist*. But rhetorically it accepts a very negative sense of the latter itself and proceeds to the question of how best to bring someone suspected of *Freigeisterei* to his senses. The essay distinguishes between a theoretical and a practical freethinker. The former is amenable to persuasion based on the stronger arguments, and one need only bring these thoughtfully to bear. There is no need for "*Strafprediger.*" Even less fruitful is such a blustering approach in regards to the practical freethinker, who, like a wayward child, thinks not at all.

> Laying down the law [*Gesetzpredigten*] will not win these people over even if you went on forever.... Whoever is not interested just in quarrelling and namecalling should conduct himself gently and on principle with his unbelieving opponents if he doesn't want to ruin everything with violence. Before all else what we need here is deeply learned men.[48]

The appeal, thus, is for a more tolerant approach to dissent, a more thoughtful approach to remonstrance, and ultimately, perhaps, even a reconsideration of the viewpoints of naturalism and even atheism (though these fall out of the author's frame).

Fontius notes that at roughly the same time Lessing was composing a play entitled *Der Freygeist* and Schmidt goes so far as to argue that the article in *Der Wahrsager* served as direct inspiration for Lessing's play.[49] The play hardly lionizes the freethinker. Rather, much as the article would suggest, the plot revolves around a thoughtful Christian pastor's gentle persuasion. If it does not actually convert the freethinker, it renders some of the more extreme postures to which the latter felt entitled by the abuse of the orthodox more problematic, and thus represents a victory of tolerance *on both sides*.[50]

---

[47] "Freigeister, Naturalisten, Atheisten," *Lessings Werke*, ed. Julius Petersen and Waldemar von Ohlshausen. 25 vols. (Berlin: Bong and Co., 1925), 24: 161-166. Given the tenor of Lessing's composition of the play *Der Freygeist* at that time, Fontius doubts that Lessing could have been the author of the essay as well.

[48] "Freigeister, Naturalisten, Atheisten," 164-65.

[49] Schmidt, *Lessing*, 184: "Dieser Artikel allein geht Lessing an, der 1749 wohl auch davon beeinflußt sein Schauspiel 'Der Freigeist' schrieb."

[50] Lessing, *Der Freygeist*, LM: 2: 49-124. For a consideration of this whole constellation, see Thomas Saine, *The Problem of Being Modern, or The German Pursuit of Enlightenment from Leibniz to the French Revolution* (Detroit: Wayne State University Press, 1997), 171-86: "The Battle Against Freethinkers" and "Lessing's Sincere Freethinker."

What is clear is that the young Lessing was in a milieu in which the notion of *Freigeisterei* was prominent, and that it was central to his personal project. As Schmidt puts it:

> Even before exposure to the dangerous atmosphere of Berlin Lessing was, in step with the "free spirit" Mylius, already enlightened enough to consider a freethinker, *esprit fort, Freigeist* something more than a puppet with which the moral weeklies like governesses keep their children full of fear of the lord.[51]

Lessing believed it was essential to break the idea of freedom of thought loose from the orthodox clerical opprobrium and popular dread it conventionally encountered. (Indeed, the first members of the public he wished to shake from these preconceptions were his smalltown pastor father and pious mother.[52]) That proved to be the distinctive character of Lessing's entire journalistic endeavor in Berlin: "the penetrating and constantly repeated call to 'thinking for oneself [*Selbstdenken*],' 'judging for oneself [*Selbsturtheilen*],' is the organizing center of all the individual efforts regarding the public even in Lessing's early years."[53] As Wolfgang Martens puts it, "The drive towards truth, seeking, thinking for oneself [*das Selbstdenken*] which can actualize itself in the form of criticism, that is Lessing's thing."[54] Stichelschmidt goes at the same point: "His ambition someday to be known as something like a German Molière he put on ice for the time. Instead the sharp intellectual wind of Berlin awakened the critic in him, whose polemical edge took the breath away even from the dwellers of this 'metropolis of intellect.'"[55]

Crucially, Schmidt points to the language Lessing put into the list of characters for the first draft of *Der Freigeist*. The freethinker, Adrast, is described as "without religion, but full of virtuous dispositions [*ohne Religion, aber voller tugendhafter Gesinnungen*]."[56] That is the starting point from which we must understand not only Lessing's notion of freethinking, but more specifically his linkage of this idea to the problem of Spinoza. At the same time Lessing composed *Der Freigeist* he worked as well on a little one-act play, *Die Juden*, in whose protagonist Schmidt

---

[51] Schmidt, *Lessing*, 143.
[52] On Lessing and his family's resistance to free-thinking (and Mylius), see Stichelschmidt, *Lessing*, 47ff., 69ff., 100ff.
[53] Wilfried Barner, "Lessing und sein Publikum in der frühen kritischen Schriften," in *Lessing in heutiger Sicht* (Breme/ Wolfenbüttel: Jacobi, 1976), 331.
[54] Wolgang Martens, "Lessing als Aufklärer: Zu Lessings Kritik an den Moralischen Wochenschriften," in *Lessing in heutiger Sicht*, 244.
[55] Stichelschmidt, *Lessing*, 64.
[56] Schmidt, *Lessing*, 143.

correctly discerns precisely the same essential feature: "ein Jude, doch 'voller tugendhafter Gesinnungen.'"[57] One important literary source was Gellert's novel, *Die Schwedische Gräfin* (1746), in which for the first time in German literature a positive image of a Jew was developed.[58] Lessing read that novel in Leipzig. Franklin Kopitzsch suggests that the situation of Jews in Leipzig may have contributed to Lessing's work as well: "It should not be overlooked that Lessing was writing in a city which was open to Jews only during the market times and even then only upon payment of a personal tax.... For so an alert an observer of contemporary affairs as the young Lessing, it can be assumed that this situation of the Jews in Leipzig could not have remained unknown."[59]

Karl Guthke has given us good reason to make the connection between Lessing's general concern with religious toleration and the specific question of the Jews in German society.[60] The entire action of *Die Juden* turns upon precisely the theme of individual versus group estimations.[61] The issue is not just doctrinal, in other words, but social. If one can be "full of virtuous dispositions" even without religion, if dissent in doctrine does not result in deviance in conduct, should this not be tolerated? Lessing's dramatic argument takes the form of an insistence that one should not infer from religious dissent to moral-social danger, i.e. no institutional or social sanctions should derive from doctrinal affiliation but only from individual comportment.

Alexander Altmann proposes that Lessing came to know the Gumpertz family in Berlin and that it was his esteem for them that led him to the idea of a play about a Jew acting the good Samaritan.[62] Gründer claims that "Mendelssohn knew that Aron Emmerich Gumpertz, who had mediated his acquaintance with Lessing, was Lessing's model for the noble Jewish traveller in the comedy."[63] While I am prepared to recognize

---

[57] Schmidt, *Lessing*, 148.

[58] Wolfgang Martens, "Zur Figur eines edlen Juden im Aufklärungsroman vor Lessing," *Begegnungen von Deutschen und Juden in der Geistesgeschichte des 18. Jahrhunderts* (Tübingen: Niemeyer, 1994), 65-77.

[59] F. Kopitzsch, "Gotthold Ephraim Lessing und seine Zeitgenossen," 38n.

[60] K. Guthke, "Lessing und das Judentum: Rezeption. Dramatik und Kritik. Krypto-Spinozismus," *Wolfenbütteler Studien zur Aufklärung* 4 (1977): 229-71; revised as: "Lessing und das Judentum, oder Spinoza *absconditus*," in Guthke, *Das Abenteuer der Literatur* (Bern/Munich: Francke, 1981), 123-43, 329-56; citation from latter version.

[61] Lessing, *Die Juden*, LM: 1: 373-411. See Wilfried Barner, "Lessings *Die Juden* im Zusammenhang seines Frühwerks," in *Humanität und Dialog: Lessing und Mendelssohn in neuer Sicht* (Detroit: Wayne State University Press, 1982= *Lessing Yearbook: Sonderheft*), 190-209.

[62] Altmann, *Moses Mendelssohn*, 40.

[63] Karlfriedrich Gründer, "Johann David Michaelis und Moses Mendelssohn," in *Begegnungen von Deutschen und Juden in der Geistesgeschichte des 18. Jahrhunderts* (Tübingen: Niemeyer, 1994), 34.

the place of Lessing's acquaintance with the Gumpertz family in the context of *Die Juden*, I think this is too reductive. A connection that brings all this in more subtly involves the court figure, Marquis d'Argens, for whom Aron Gumpertz worked as personal secretary.[64] In 1751, Lessing wrote a very interesting comment on d'Argens's most important work, the *Lettres juives* (1736-38): "The author of the *Jewish Letters* has frequently enough declared himself an enemy of religion, but never an enemy of virtue."[65] Once again we see evidence of a central theoretical crux in Lessing's approach to the whole problem.

Guthke has suggested that it was not personal experience so much as book learning that animated this piece.[66] The decisive book involved in Lessing's composition of *Die Juden*, Guthke intimates, was Pierre Bayle's *Dictionary*. That is, the figure of Spinoza could very well have served as inspiration for Lessing's little play. It is not just that the Jew of the play comes from Holland; rather, it is because the play allows no other particularity to this persona but the idea of the virtuous nonbeliever as such. Certainly Spinoza was the cardinal instantiation of this in Bayle's cultural system. We have every reason to believe that this was the most important source for Lessing's initial impression of Spinoza. Schröder observes that "we know, by and large, nothing about whether [Lessing] knew of the texts of Stosch, Wachter and the rest of the early Spinozists."[67] Even more complex is the question of Lessing's acquaintance with the clandestine Spinoza literature. Niewöhner and Nisbet have established clearly that Lessing was acquainted with it by the time of the composition of *Nathan der Weise*.[68] But the issue stands open how much of this he could have known already as he brought his university studies to an end.

What that betokens is that the intellectual work of constructing a useful reception of Spinoza remained to be commenced almost anew after mid-

[64] Altmann, *Moses Mendelssohn*, 23-25.
[65] Cited in Friedrich Niewöhner, *Veritas sive Varietas: Lessings Toleranzparabel und das Buch von den drei Betrügern* (Heideberg: Lambert Schneider, 1988), 40.
[66] Guthke, "Lessing und das Judentum."
[67] Schröder, *Spinoza*, 146. In particular, one might ask about the influence of Johann Edelmann, e.g., Walter Grossmann, "Edelmann und das 'öffentliche Schweige' des Reimarus und Lessing: Toleranz und Politik des Geistes," *Zeitschrift für Kirchengeschichte* 85 (1974): 358-68. Certainly Lessing knew of Edelmann, but there is no evidence that he ever took his ideas seriously. I agree with Bollacher: "Edelmanns Schriften waren vergessen, sein Wirken war ohne Einfluß auf die Spinozarenaissance." Bollacher, *Goethe und Spinoza*, 37.
[68] Niewöhner, *Lessings Toleranzparabel*; H. Nisbet, "*De tribus Impostoribus*: On the Genesis of Lessing's *Nathan der Weise*," *Euphorion* 73 (1979): 365-87; Nisbet, "Spinoza und die Kontroverse 'De Tribus Impostoribus,'" in *Spinoza in der Frühzeit seiner religiösen Wirkung*, ed. Karfriend Gründer and Wilhelm Schmidt-Biggemann (Heidelberg: Lambert Schneider, 1984), 227-244.

century. The decisive issue for a new Spinozism was revising Bayle.[69]
What is striking is that for a generation of young German minds starting
roughly at mid-century, Bayle's characterization of Spinoza's personal
integrity seemed, despite its ostensible generosity, to harbor still too
disparaging an assessment.[70] The new beginning lies in the reception of
Bayle's characterization of Spinoza by the young Lessing. The impulse
that drew Lessing to Spinoza was not so much the latter's particular
philosophical system but rather his paradoxical figure, especially as Bayle
had creatively fashioned it, as the "virtuous atheist." Bayle was crucial for
the young Lessing, as biographers from Danzel onward have noted; the
Dictionary "was one of the chief sources of Lessing's education."[71] In
particular, "it is impossible that he was not familiar with Bayle's article"
on Spinoza.[72] But the question of what exactly Bayle meant for Lessing is
a bit more complex. Just as Bayle is himself extraordinarily elusive, his
reception was ambivalent. On the one hand, Bayle could be read as the
advocate of toleration based on skepticism. But on the other, Bayle could
be read as the advocate of conformity out of fideism.[73] This conflict of
readings is particularly provoked by his famous biographical entry on
Spinoza. He goes to great lengths to accentuate the virtue of Spinoza's life
(against other critics who could not resist tarring that life with their
loathing for his teachings), yet only after he utters every sort of
disparagement of the teachings in such a manner as to affirm the expulsion
of Spinoza from his religious community and by extension from all social
acceptance.[74] Bayle's treatment of Spinoza—not only for its partial
vindication but even more for its remaining *vindictiveness*—took on
peculiar salience for Lessing in the context of the Berlin *Aufklärung.*

Lessing began *theorizing* religious-cultural tolerance for Germany, with
the Jews as his test case, on the basis of Bayle's famous representation of
Spinoza as a man virtuous without Christianity. And that theorizing took
place *before* his meeting with Mendelssohn and before he took up his
career in Berlin. The encounter with Moses Mendelssohn in early 1754

---

[69] "[Mendelssohn] legt darauf Gewicht, die Autorität Bayles in Fragen des Spinozismus zu
zerstören, der maßgeblich die öffentliche Meinung über Spinoza formte." Herbert Lindner,
Das Problem des Spinozismus im Schaffen Goethes und Herders (Weimar: Arion, 1960), 29.
[70] "Das durch Bayles Autorität sanktionierte Spinozabild, das mit seinem Atrheismusvorwurf
jede kritische Annäherung an das verrufene System dem Verdacht aufwiegender Blasphemie
aussetzte, bestimmte nicht nur Goethes Urteil in der 'Ephemerides,' sondern prägte auf lange
Jahrzehnte hinaus die communis opinio der 'spinozistisch' gleeihbedeutend war mit
'ungereimt' und 'gottlos.'" Bollacher, *Goethe und Spinoza*, 24-25.
[71] T. W. Danzel, *Gotthold Ephraim Lessing: Sein Leben und sein Werk* (Leipzig, 1850), 220.
[72] Bell, *Spinoza in Germany*, 27.
[73] See Gerhard Sauder, "Bayle Rezeption in der deutschen Aufklärung," *Deutsche
Vierteljahrsschrift für Literaturwissenschaft unde Geistesgeschichte: Sonderheft*, 1975, 83-
104.
[74] Bayle, "Spinoza."

proved a remarkable personal confirmation of the entire line of thought that Lessing had been pursuing. That realization defined the basis of Lessing's and Mendelssohn's immediate engagement.[75] A consideration of the context solidifies the linkage of freedom of thought, the situation of the Jews, and the figure of Spinoza. Lessing published *Die Juden* in the fourth part of his *Schriften* of 1753-55. In a preface he explained his motive for composing the text and expressed interest in how the public would respond.[76] The most important response came from the prominent Orientalist at the University of Göttingen, Johann Michaelis. In his review in the widely read *Göttingische Gelehrte Anzeigen*, Michaelis expressed doubts that a Jew of such character and distinction as Lessing created was believable:

> The unknown traveller is ... so perfectly good, so noble,
> so carefully ... educated, that it is—while not
> impossible—nevertheless really all too improbable that
> among such a people so noble a character could form
> itself in this manner... for almost the entire people must
> make its living at trade....[77]

In short, Michaelis was guilty of precisely the misjudgment the play attempted to expose and defeat.[78]

By the time of the Michaelis review, Lessing and Mendelssohn had become intimate friends. The latter was understandably unhappy with Michaelis's views, and Lessing found a way to bring all this before the public. In his new journal, *Theatralische Bibliothek*, Lessing cited extensively from Michaelis's review, then reprinted a letter Mendelssohn composed and sent to their mutual friend, Gumpertz, expressing his dissatisfaction over the review.[79] Lessing then forwarded the issue of his

[75] Altmann, *Moses Mendelssohn*, 36ff.

[76] Lessing, "Vorrede [zu] *G. E. Lessings Schriften. Dritter Teil*" (Berlin 1754), LM: 5: 267-271.

[77] Michaelis, review of *Die Juden* (June 13, 1754) cited in Karlfried Gründer, "Johann David Michaelis und Moses Mendelssohn," 34.

[78] I cannot agree with Gründer's argument that Lessing's traveller is "eine unabsichtliche Karikatur" and that from a social historical vantage "hier ist eine Reizbarkeit, für deren Bewältigung nichts zu Verfügung steht; insbesonder scheint literarischer Geplätscher nicht die richting Form dafür zu sein" (35). The play certainly was not received in that light. At a student production in Göttingen in 1777 the play sufficed to inspire Georg Lichtenberg to dedicate himself to combatting such prejudice. The reception of Michaelis itself suggests how timely and penetrating the play proved. To be sure, it is not yet mature Lessing. It pales before *Nathan der Weise*, but most scholars recognize it as a crucial precursor. More important, I suggest, it has a very important place in the emergence of a new Spinozism.

[79] Lessing, "Über das Lustspiel *die Juden*, im vierten Theile der Lessingschen Schriften," (*Theatralische Bibliothek: 1. Stück*, 1754) LM: 6: 159-66.

journal with a cover letter to Michaelis which proclaimed that the author
of the letter reprinted in the journal issue was living proof of the error of
Michaelis's judgment, for he was everything Michaelis believed
"unwahrscheinlich," indeed, he was "a second Spinoza, without the
latter's errors"!

> He really is a Jew, a person of approximately twenty
> years, who without all instruction has achieved a great
> mastery in languages, in mathematics, in philosophy, in
> poetry. I envision him as a glory of his nation, if he is
> allowed to mature by his own coreligionists, who have
> generally pursued against people of his sort an unhappy
> spirit of oppression [*unglücklicher Verfolgungsgeist*]. His
> honesty and his philosophical spirit permit me to
> consider him already a second Spinoza, fully the equal of
> the first, but for the latter's errors.[80]

That depiction tells us a great deal, not only about Mendelssohn but about
how Lessing perceived him and in what context. There is strong reason to
suspect that Spinoza was one of the earliest and most intense topics of
discussion between them.

Mendelssohn, perhaps even more than Lessing, was concerned with
the figure of Spinoza. For him it represented a far more vital personal
precedent and problem. Yirmiahu Yovel has characterized Mendelssohn's
ambition in sharp contours:

> As a German (and European) he wanted to be
> 'enlightened,' as a Jew he wanted not only to be
> europeanised, but also to prove that a Jew, measured by
> the most advanced achievements of cultivated Europe,
> could play an outstanding role and even be a prominent
> spokesman of the Enlightenment.[81]

For Mendelssohn, accordingly, Spinoza was an unavoidable forerunner as
important for his prominence as for his errors.[82] But his engagement with
Spinoza involved more than the question of the latter's personal virtue.
Far more, for Mendelssohn, steeped in rigorous Judaic studies and rapidly
assimilating the most advanced forms of contemporary European,
especially German, philosophy, it was a matter of Spinoza's doctrinal

---

[80] Lessing to Michaelis, October 16, 1754 (LM: 17: 39-41, citing 40).
[81] Y. Yovel, "Mendelssohn zwischen Spinoza und Kant," in *Spinoza in der europäischen Geistesgeschichte*, 13.
[82] Bell takes the same line: "Mendelssohn was attracted to Spinoza in the first place because here was a Jewish philosopher working in the rationalist tradition." *Spinoza in Germany*, 24.

positions. As Altmann puts it, when Lessing and Mendelssohn first began to discuss Spinoza, "it was undoubtedly Mendelssohn who introduced Lessing to a deeper understanding of philosophy in general and of Spinoza in particular."[83]

Mendelssohn wished to restore Spinoza to respectability *through* a redemption or *Rettung* of his philosophical project. The goal, however, was not to affirm Spinoza's philosophical positions but to historicize them as a necessary transition from Cartesianism to the Leibniz-Wolff system. By rendering Spinoza's philosophy obsolete one could also render it innocuous. Indeed, the idea of a historicization of Spinoza's philosophy allowed and fostered the discrimination of philosophy from theology and the prospect of a dispassionate critique of the purely philosophical arguments.

That line had been inaugurated by Christian Wolff himself in his critique of Spinoza in his *Theologia rationalis* (1737). This was simply the single most important *philosophical* consideration of Spinoza in the first half of the eighteenth century in Germany, and the basis for all the significant impulses of the Spinoza renaissance of the second half.[84] Crucially, Wolff's refutation had been translated and included in the famous translation of Spinoza's *Ethics* by the Wolffian Johann Schmidt in 1744.[85] That work, too, sought to make possible an objective philosophical dissection of Spinoza's thought. Similar in tenor and directly relevant for Mendelssohn (and Lessing) was a third publication: Philipp Joseph Pandin de Jariges's *Examen du Spinosisme et des Objections de Mr. Bayle contre ce système* (1746), published by the Berlin Academy.[86]

Mendelssohn, no less than Lessing, set out from Bayle's essay and its problems. As Bell writes, "It is thus of prime significance that Mendelssohn rejects Bayle's approach." Mendelssohn sees even Bayle as discrediting Spinoza's *thought* as immoral. His goal would be to prove that "Spinozism is reconcilable with morality." In so doing Mendelssohn would accomplish "an important advance," namely "the beginning of the process of freeing Spinoza criticism from the dubious authority of the *Dictionnaire*."[87]

The *Philosophische Gespräche* appeared anonymously in 1755. The most explicit statement of his general approach to Spinoza is in the second of the four dialogues:

---

[83] Altmann, *Moses Mendelssohn*, 37.

[84] Jean L'École, "La Critique Wolffienne du Spinozisme," *Archives de Philosophie* 46 (1983): 553-67; Cornelia Buschmann, "Wolff's 'Widerlegung' der 'Ethik' Spinozas," in *Spinoza in der europäischen Geistesgeschichte*, 126-41.

[85] Ursula Goldenbaum, "Die erste deutsche Übersetzung der Spinozaschen 'Ethik,'" in *Spinoza in der europäischen Geistesgeschichte*, 107-25.

[86] Altmann, *Moses Mendelssohn*, 35.

[87] Bell, *Spinoza in Germany*, 26.

> Philopon: The misfortune of this man has always touched me in an extraordinary way. He lived in moderation, alone and irreproachable.... In the labyrinth of his meditations, he goes astray and, out of error, maintains much that agrees very little with his innocent way of life.... How unjust is the irreconcilable hatred of scholars towards someone so unfortunate.
>
> Neophil: Of all Spinoza's adversaries, only Wolff is not subject to this reproach. This great philosopher, before he refutes Spinozism, casts it in its proper light. He shows the strongest side of it, and, precisely by this means, he has discovered its weaknesses better than anyone else....[88]

Mendelssohn had written the dialogues in response to a challenge by Lessing to emulate the Earl of Shaftesbury in composing a philosophical dialogue. He presented Lessing with the text, and the latter published it without his knowledge. Followed within a year by a second book, *Über die Empfindungen*, they established Mendelssohn as a major new voice in philosophy in Germany, a Wolffian who outshone any disciple Wolff had known in his lifetime, in the rather thoughtless words of Michaelis.[89] Ironically, Michaelis in his review of *Philosophische Gespräche* imputed the work to Lessing.[90] Mendelssohn sent him a letter clarifying the matter, but asked that his name be kept secret, and Michaelis publicly corrected his misapprehension forthwith.[91] Meanwhile, Lessing published an enthusiastic review of the text, focusing specifically on its innovative approach to Spinoza. In Lessing's view, Mendelssohn had done as much as could be done to vindicate Spinoza, both as a figure and as a thinker.[92] Indeed, as the wider reception indicated, Mendelssohn's presentation of Spinoza found a warmer reception than any remotely positive account had ever received in Germany. It was the beginning of the renaissance.[93]

---

[88] Moses Mendelssohn, "[Philosophical] Dialogues," in Mendelssohn, *Philosophical Writings*, trans. Daniel Dahlstrom (Cambridge: Cambridge University Press, 1997), 96-129, citing 106-107.

[89] Michaelis reviewed Mendelssohn's second book in *Göttingische Anzeigen* on October 9, 1755. Gründer, 36.

[90] Michaelis's review appeared in *Göttingische Anzeigen*, May 29, 1755, according to Gründer.

[91] Mendelssohn to Michaelis, Sept. 7, 1755; Michaelis in *Göttingische Anzeigen*, October 2, 1755. Gründer, 36.

[92] Lessing, [Review of] *Philosophische Gespräche* (Berliner privilegierte Zeitung, 1755), LM: 7: 13-14.

[93] Lindner ascribes a similar pathbreaking role to Mendelssohn: "Am Anfang stehen Mendelssohns 'Gespräche' (1755). Ihnen liegt ganz offenkundig die Absicht zugrunde, Spinoza ein besseres Ansehen zu verschaffen und die Schmähflut wider ihn aufzuhalten. Mit

Mendelssohn sets his "vindication" of Spinoza directly into the context of what in eighteenth-century philosophical discourse had come to be called (in terms posed by Leibniz) the "three hypotheses," i.e. the contest of metaphysical vision between occasionalism, pre-established harmony and physical influx in explaining the interaction of substances, of spirit and matter, or, most pointedly, mind and body. Mendelssohn takes for granted the superiority of the Leibnizian system, with its rigorous denial of intersubstantial causation. "As soon as one concedes this in the sense in which Leibniz took it, one is compelled to ban all physical influence of substances from nature."[94] What Mendelssohn then does is to assimilate Spinoza's separation of the *modes* of matter and intellect to the Leibnizian distinction of *substances* in pre-established harmony. He goes on:

> Spinoza even avails himself of all the evasions of the Leibnizians. He appeals, like them, to our ignorance about the inner structure of our body and finally to the fact that no one has yet demonstrated the impossibility of such a machine that could produce, in a mechanical manner, all the actions to which this or that individual body is determined.[95]

This is precisely the issue which John Yolton has documented to have run like a red thread through eighteenth-century philosophical discourse, the problem associated with Locke's conjecture about "thinking matter," or hylozoism. Of course, Mendelssohn couches it negatively: the inaccessibility of the inner structure of body allows all sorts of "evasions" through which the empirical experience of ordinary life can be reconciled with all manner of metaphysical presumptions. But the prospect lurked in this formulation, and "thinking matter" expressed it vividly, that a whole new possibility of physical monism and thus of a vindication of the widely disparaged "physical influx" model was in the offing.

The "popular philosophers" of the Berlin *Aufklärung* were attuned to the most important issues in metaphysics and natural philosophy circulating on the European level. To be philosophically awake in Germany at mid-century was to be attuned to this discourse whose vehicle was the French language but whose terms had been set by Newton and by Leibniz, and which had as much to do with natural science as with metaphysics. While some important contributions were being composed in the German language, the debate through mid-century was conducted

viel Geschick bemüht sich Mendelssohn, die Angriffe auf Spinoza als Auswüchse reiner Vorurteile zu entkräften." Lindner, 29.
[94] Mendelssohn, "Dialogues," 99.
[95] Mendelssohn, "Dialogues," 102.

primarily in the French tongue. John Yolton's *Locke and French Materialism* has shown that this francophone discourse of the Enlightenment, especially at mid-century, turned upon the "three hypotheses."

The participation of Berlin intellectuals in the French-language discourse of the European Enlightenment is something whose significance has not yet been sufficiently appreciated. Berlin was a European center; twenty percent of its population was Huguenot-French; French was an important language not only for Frederick II's court and for his Academy but for the city itself. Not only Leibniz, who wrote some of his most important work in French, but even Christian Wolff had a European reception. Figures like Merian and Formey and Sulzer linked the Berlin discourse with that of the wider Francophone Enlightenment. And of course La Mettrie and Maupertuis (and Voltaire) brought this Francophone discourse to Berlin in their very persons.

Perhaps the most famous benchmark for historians of philosophy considering the eighteenth century in Germany is the Prize Competition inaugurated by the Berlin Academy for 1762, for which Mendelssohn submitted the winning entry and Kant's text was distinguished as suitable also for publication under the Academy's imprimatur.[96] At the time of the contest, Lessing was in Breslau, in Silesia, distant from the philosophical action in Berlin but he took an interest in what was going on. In fact, it was in these years that Lessing devoted himself to a more rigorous study of philosophical texts. Among them, we have reason to believe, was Spinoza's *Ethics*. In the course of these studies, Lessing composed two brief texts, one of which clearly served as the basis for a letter to Mendelssohn and the other may well have.[97] At least one interpreter has suggested these might have served as Lessing's response to Mendelssohn's contribution to the Prize Competition.[98]

What is at stake in Lessing's brief texts is the viability of the relation of Leibniz to Spinoza which Mendelssohn had convinced him of a decade earlier in Berlin.[99] More familiar now with Spinoza, Lessing no longer

---

[96] Paul Guyer, "Mendelssohn and Kant: One Source of the Critical Philosophy," *Philosophical Topics* 19 (1991): 119-52.

[97] Lessing, "Durch Spinoza ist Leibnitz nur auf die Spur der vorherbestimmten Harmonie gekommen," LM: 14: 294-96; Lessing, "Über die Wirklichkeit der Dinge außer Gott," LM: 14: 292-93.

[98] Bell, *Spinoza in Germany*, 34.

[99] Karl Rehorn, *G. E. Lessings Stellung zur Philosophie des Spinoza* (Frankfurt/M: Diesterweg, 1877); Reinhard Schwarz, "Lessings 'Spinozismus,'" *Zeitschrift für Theologie und Kirche* 65 (1968): 271-90; Friedemann Regner, "Lessings Spinozismus," *Zeitschrift für Theologie und Kirche* 68 (1971): 351-75; Daetlev Pätzold, "Lessing und Spinoza: Zum Beginn des Pantheismus-Streits in der deutschen Literatur des 18. Jahrhunderts," in *Aufklärung, Gesellschaft, Kritik: Studien zur Philosophie der Aufklärung (I)*, ed. Manfred

found Mendelssohn's reconciliation so satisfactory. Not only were Leibniz and Spinoza incompatible; Spinoza made more metaphysical sense. Of course, Lessing still adopted the notion that the monism that he defended in Spinoza's system was a theistic one: pan*en*theist as much as pantheist. But the potential for a thoroughly immanent approach to nature was there: *Deus sive natura* involved the distinction between *natura naturans* and *natura naturata*, but it also moved powerfully toward the assimilation of these into a polarized unity. What is of interest in these slender documents from Lessing is the way in which they reflect the advanced stage of the discussion of the "three hypothesis" in metaphysics by the mid-eighteenth century, and the necessity to find a more monistic solution to the problem.

As Mendelssohn's letter in reply betokens, none of this made any sense to him; he persisted for the balance of his life in his views on the relation between Spinoza and Leibniz uttered in the *Philosophische Gespräche*. But these texts were a warning to him that Lessing had shifted ground; indeed, these texts, together with Lessing's very early "Christianity of Reason," may well have accounted for Mendelssohn's tacit concession when he was first confronted by Jacobi's report that Lessing was embroiled in Spinozism. But these also served as Mendelssohn's basis for inventing a "refined Spinozism" [*geläuterte Spinozismus*] for Lessing that would rescue him, if no longer Spinoza himself, for morality and religion.[100]

III. The new materialism in natural philosophy

The history of science has recognized a very important generational break that substantially changed the orientation of science around the middle of the century starting in Britain.[101] D'Alembert's *Preliminary Discourse to the Encyclopedia* is a particularly useful source for this, since it shows an acute awareness of the generational shift and its scientific and philosophical issues.[102] The Newtonianism that prevailed in the eighteenth century did not carry the scientific revolution forward according to the

Buhr, Wolfgang Förster (Berlin: Akademie, 1985), 298-355; Henry Allison, "Lessing's Spinozistic Exercises," in *Humanität und Dialog*, 223-33.

[100] Moses Mendelssohn, *Morgenstunden*, reprinted in Heinrich Scholtz, ed., *Die Hauptschriften zum Pantheismus Streit zwischen Jacobi und Mendelssohn*.

[101] See, for example, Robert E. Schofield, *Mechanism and Materialism: British Natural Philosophy in an Age of Reason* (Princeton: Princeton University Press, 1970). For an important revision in the interpretation of these developments see the pointed criticisms of Schofield in P. M. Heimann and J. E. McGuire, "Newtonian Forces and Lockean Powers: Concepts of Matter in 18th-Century Thought," *Historical Studies in the Physical Sciences* 8 (1971), 233-306, esp. 234-35 and *passim*.

[102] Jean D'Alembert, *Preliminary Discourse to the "Encyclopédie"* (Indianapolis: Bobbs-Merrill, 1963); see also Cassirer's use of D'Alembert's work in *Philosophy of the Enlightenment* (Princeton: Princeton University Press, 1951), 8ff.

conventional model of the "mechanization of the world picture."[103] Rather it pursued the most speculative series of "queries" (or, in fact, hypotheses) Newton felt prepared to interject into later editions of his *Opticks*, which centered around the properties that could legitimately be considered inherent in particulate matter.[104] While Newton considered inertial velocity an inherent property of bodies, he did not feel prepared to recognize any other forces, like attraction or repulsion, as inherent. Newton recognized the existence of forces, and their vital importance to physical science, but he found it impossible to recognize them as immanent properties of particulate matter. Instead he simply termed them "etherial" or "imponderable principles" of physical action. Obviously, the term "principle" is extremely vague as to the exact nature of these phenomena, i.e., as to their substantive reality and metaphysical implications. Hence his sense of matter retained a good part of the Cartesian notion of inert matter.

Still, over the course of the eighteenth century Newton's atomism led to extremely fruitful speculations about the structure of the physical world that undercut the notion of inert matter. The scientists of the eighteenth century pursued the leads Newton had offered in the *Opticks* by studying attraction and repulsion in chemical and electrical phenomena, and as they did so, they began to redefine the properties of the physical world in such a way that the Cartesian notion of inert matter, and with it the Cartesian notion of mechanical cause as the impact model of force, came to seem entirely inadequate. They recognized the necessity of the physical postulation of such forces as real elements in the explanation of natural phenomena, especially in the nascent sciences of "electricity," chemistry and biology. Already Leibniz, and, following him, Boscovich pursued these lines aggressively, both in the metaphysical and in the physical vein, articulating a theory of physical "dynamism" which, in Boscovich,

---

[103] See, e.g., E. J. Dijksterhuis, *The Mechanization of the World Picture* (Oxford: Clarendon Press, 1961); J. L. Heilbron, *Elements of Early Modern Physics* (Berkeley: University of California Press, 1982).

[104] Henry Guerlac, "Newton's Changing Reputation in the Eighteenth Century," in Raymond Rockwood, ed., *Carl Becker's Heavenly City Revisited* (1958; rpt. Hamden, CT: Archon, 1968), 3-26; A. Rupert Hall. and Marie Boas Hall, "Newton's Electric Spirit: Four Oddities," *Isis* 50 (1959): 473-77; I. Bernard Cohen and Alexandre Koyré, "Newton's Electric and Elastic Spirit," *Isis* 51 (1960), 337; J. E. McGuire, "Force, Active Principles, and Newton's Invisible Realm," *Ambix* 15 (1968): 187-208; idem, "Transmutation and Immutability: Newton's Doctrine of Physical Qualities," *Ambix* 14 (1967): 69-95; idem, "The Origins of Newton's Doctrine of Essential Qualities," *Centaurus* 12 (1968): 233-60; idem, "Atoms and the 'Analogy of Nature': Newton's Third Rule of Philosophizing," *Studies in History and Philosophy of Science* 1 (1970): 3-58; Max Jammer, *Concepts of Force: A Study in the Foundations of Dynamics* (Cambridge: Harvard University Press, 1957), 158-87; Mary B. Hesse, *Forces and Fields: The Concept of Action at a Distance in the History of Physics* (New York: Philosophical Library, 1962), 157-88.

completely eliminated the idea of particulate matter (extended mass) and replaced it with a point center of force.

Eighteenth-century science gradually substantialized the problematic forces which experiment had revealed to be operating in the physical world: light, heat, electricity, and magnetism. In Schofield's terms, "The materialized, substantial causes are almost all imponderable, highly tenuous fluids, and most of these are partially characterized by their possession of varying forces of attraction and repulsion."[105] Schofield blamed this more naturalistic and metaphysical approach on continental influences and "religious mysticism."[106] Conversely he associated the more abstract and mechanistic approach of the earlier generation with "Augustan rationality" and with deism. Still, he did admit that there were some difficulties in carrying on scientifically in the mechanistic mode once the physical importance of forces had to be acknowledged.[107] The mechanists could not "assign magnitude or a determination of form to any of the various forces of attraction and repulsion which they used with such ingenuity in their speculations."[108] It had become impossible, scientifically or philosophically, to enforce a categorial distinction between matter and force, between "inert matter" and "active principles." And no mechanistic account could give a satisfactory explanation for the origins or the nature of "force" as such.

The crisis of the so-called "iatromechanical" approach in the biological sciences, i.e., the approach which sought to explain all biological phenomena in terms of the inert-matter, impact-theory-of-force approach of mechanical cause, is crucial. While Newtonianism came to dominance in the Dutch school of life sciences led by 'sGravesande and Boerhaave at the end of the seventeenth century, by the mid-eighteenth century that approach could no longer hold. In the school of Montpellier these issues came to a theoretical crisis, and, in the thought of men like Maupertuis, Buffon, Bordeu and Bonnet, achieved as much clarification as the preliminary state of the medical sciences allowed.[109] In a brilliant essay,

---

[105] Schofield, *Mechanism*, 95.

[106] Schofield, *Mechanism*, 99.

[107] Schofield, *Mechanism*, 94.

[108] Schofield, *Mechanism*, 100.

[109] The new science reached France by the late 1740s, where it spurred both the development of philosophical materialism in Condillac, La Mettrie, and especially Holbach, and the development of the more eclectic approach of the Encyclopedists, D'Alembert and Diderot. Diderot, who figured prominently in both the materialist and the Encyclopedist approaches (they were by no means mutually exclusive), gave literary expression to the impact of these ideas in his *D'Alembert's Dream*. See Lester Crocker, "Diderot and Eighteenth-Century French Transformationism," in Bentley Glass *et. al.*, *Forerunners of Darwin: 1745-1859* (Baltimore: Johns Hopkins University Press, 1959), 114-43. Bordeu appeared in fiction as the attending physician in Diderot's provocative little essay on the perplexities in implication of the new science, *D'Alembert's Dream*. Diderot represents a remarkable figure in this

Sergio Moravia has documented the shift in medical thought from the "iatromechanical" to the "vitalist" orientation. By focusing on Bordeu, Moravia demonstrated the perplexity and the resolution through which the school of Montpellier, and with it the emergent science of biology, passed over the course of the eighteenth century.[110]

The most sustained analysis of this new synthesis in the natural sciences is the work of Peter Hanns Reill.[111] In an extensive series of essays, Reill has offered the most comprehensive and persuasive account of the crystallization of the new scientific model of the late-eighteenth century. In an essay suggestively titled "Between Mechanism and Hermeticism," Reill demonstrates the complex strategy of the new science to avoid both the dead ends of strict mechanism and the appeal to "occult qualities" of the Neo-Platonic/Hermetic tradition, "to create a middle realm with its own inherent structure."[112] Thus, "the principles of mechanical natural philosophy which had supported Cartesian, Leibnizian, Wolffian and early Newtonian science were attacked in the name of a reanimated nature filled with matter imbued with active, vital forces."[113] Reill sees how centrally a metaphysical commitment—mind-body dualism—figured in the

---

whole matter, for he seemed at once at home with the utter materialists, and yet attuned to aspects which one would normally associate with the more *vitalist* currents of the age. His insertion of the redoubtable Dr. Bordeu into his text suggests he was quite aware of the importance of Bordeu's conjectures. See H. Dieckmann, "Théophile Bordeu und Diderots *Rêve de D'Alembert*," *Romanische Forschungen* 52 (1938): 55-122.

[110] Sergio Moravia, "From Homme Machine to Homme Sensible: Changing Eighteenth-century Models of Man's Image," *Journal of the History of Ideas* 39 (1978): 45-60.

[111] See Peter Hanns Reill's essays: "Science and the Science of History in the Spätaufklärung," in *Aufklärung und Geschichte*, ed. H. E. Boedeker, George Iggers, Jonathan Knudsen and Peter H. Reill (Göttingen: Vandenhoeck and Ruprecht, 1986); "*Bildung, Urtyp* and Polarity: Goethe and Eighteenth-Century Physiology," *Goethe Yearbook* 3 (1986), 139-48; "Anti-Mechanism, Vitalism and their Political Implications in Late Enlightened Scientific Thought," *Francia* 16, no. 2 (1989): 195-212; "Buffon and Historical Thought in Germany and Great Britain," in *Buffon 88: Actes du Collque international pour le bicentenaire de la mort de Buffon*, ed. Jean Gayon, *et al.* (Paris: Vrin, 1992), 667-79; "Die Historisierung von Natur und Mensch. Der Zusammenhang von Naturwissenschaften und historischem Denken im Entstehungsprozeß der modernen Naturwissenschaften," in *Geschichtsdiskurs: Bd. 2: Anfänge modernen historischen Denkens* (Hamburg: Fischer, 1994), 48-61); "Science and the Construction of the Cultural Sciences in Late Enlightenment Germany: The Case of Wilhelm von Humboldt," *History and Theory* 33, no. 3 (1994): 345-366; "Anthropology, Nature and History in the Late Enlightenment: The Case of Friedrich Schiller," in *Schiller als Historiker*, ed. Otto Dann, Norbert Oellers and Ernst Osterkamp (Stuttgart: Metzler, 1995), 243-65; "Analogy, Comparison, and Active Living Forces: Late Enlightenment Responses to the Skeptical Critique of Causal Analysis," in Johann van der Zande and Richard Popkin, eds., *The Skeptical Tradition around 1800* (Dordrecht: Kluwer, 1998), 203-11.

[112] P. H. Reill, "Between Mechanism and Hermeticism: Nature and Science in the Late Enlightenment," in Rudolf Vierhaus, ed., *Frühe Neuzeit—Frühe Moderne?* (Göttingen: Vandenhoeck & Ruprecht, 1992), 393-421, citing 401.

[113] Reill, "Between Mechanism and Hermeticism," 400.

mechanistic model, and how the new science had to challenge its premises. "The new mid-eighteenth century alternative to mechanism denied both of the principal characteristics of matter ascribed to it by the mechanists, namely its inert nature and its aggregative composition."[114] Since "none of the postulated active forces could be seen directly, nor could they be [directly] measured," Reill notes, "a new form of reasoning was demanded," a kind of semiotics: "comparative, functional analysis and analogical reasoning."[115] The scientists of the second half of the eighteenth century had "a strong commitment to close observation," and their real contributions in physics came not in theory but in experimentation: they "designed elaborate experiments and instruments to register what was not immediately perceptible."[116]

Reill points to the paradoxical role of Hermann Boerhaave in this revolution. Though "a convinced Newtonian mechanist," Reill points out, "Boerhaave introduced the Trojan horse of substantialized forces."[117] Boerhaave's two most famous students, La Mettrie and Haller, each in paradoxical ways carried the revisionist impulse to a breakthrough around mid-century.[118] La Mettrie was as notorious in the middle of the eighteenth century for materialism as Spinoza had been for the prior century. But his materialism carried within it a great deal of the scientific novelty of the age.[119] Haller simply was the most important pioneer in physiology of his generation, yet his religious and philosophical orientation was very traditional. The nasty exchange between the two figures exposed the crisis of metaphysical and theological commitments that natural scientific developments were occasioning. La Mettrie recognized that Haller's own science was enmeshed in the new breakthroughs but that his personal religious commitments could not accommodate their implications. Callously, he exposed Haller's discomfort by dedicating the anonymous and scandalous *L'Homme Machine* to him.[120] Haller spent the balance of

[114] Reill, "Between Mechanism and Hermeticism," 402.
[115] Reill, "Between Mechanism and Hermeticism," 405-406.
[116] Reill, "Between Mechanism and Hermeticism," 416.
[117] Reill, "Between Mechanism and Hermeticism," 409.
[118] Here I part company sharply from Wim Klever, "Hermann Boerhaave (1668-1738) oder Spinozismus als rein mechanische Wissenschaft des Menschen," in *Spinoza in der europäischen Geistesgeschichte*, 75-93. Klever is correct in his description of Boerhaave's mechanism but fundamentally misguided about the persistence of this mechanism in the later eighteenth century. Holbach is, in this light, retrograde, not exemplary relative to the developments in natural philosophy. La Mettrie, by contrast, is far more in step with these developments.
[119] Aram Vartanian, *La Mettrie's L'homme Machine: A Study in the Origins of an Idea* (Princeton: Princeton University Press, 1960).
[120] Raymond de Saussure, "Haller and La Mettrie," *Journal of the History of Medicine* 4 (1949): 431-49.

his career mending metaphysical fences between his pioneering physiology and the materialism it so largely presaged.[121]

This tortured role as scientific inspiration and theological-metaphysical obstacle makes Haller a crucial figure in the transition to the new science in Germany. The new generation of biologists learned a great deal from the pioneering work in comparative physiology done by Haller, and in particular from his controversial account of "irritability" and "sensitivity."[122] A parallel and crucial controversy emerged in the sphere of theories of biological generation. Haller, in part for religious reasons, clung to the increasingly indefensible theory of "preformation," using his enormous prominence in Germany to squelch the superior epigenetic theories of C. F. Wolff and force the latter off to the remoteness of St. Petersburg.[123]

The struggle with Haller among the young scientists was a struggle to create metaphysical space for the new materialism.[124] Despite Haller, the whole movement was towards "vitalism." Scientists were finding "vitalism" a necessary element in their *physical* theorizing. In the search for a new theoretical language, antiquated terms frequently served to describe the most novel experiments. Scientists, embarrassed at the metaphysical baggage their borrowed terms carried with them, sought to find a clearer and more appropriate language without sacrificing the richness and determinacy of their experimental and theoretical results. Thus, Stahl proposed the antiquated language of "animism" to help characterize the elements in experimental phenomena for which the "iatromechanical" approach had no lexicon. Unquestionably he wanted with this language to reintroduce into natural science a considerable

---

[121] Richard Toellner, "Hallers Abwehr von Animismus und Materialismus," *Sudhoffs Archiv* 51 (1967): 130-44.

[122] G. Rudolph, "Hallers Lehre von der Irritabilität und Sensibilität," in K. E. Rothschuh, ed., *Von Boerhaave bis Berger* (Stuttgart, 1964); Shirley Roe, *Matter, Life and Generation: Eighteenth-Century Embryology and the Haller-Wolff Debate* (Cambridge: Cambridge University Press, 1981); A. Vartanian, "Trembley's Polyp, La Mettrie and Eighteenth-Century French Materialism," *Journal of the History of Ideas* 11 (1950): 259-86; Thomas S. Hall, *Ideas of Life and Matter: Studies in the History of General Physiology 600 BC - 1900 AD.* 2 vols. (Chicago: University of Chicago Press, 1969), 1: 351-407; 2: *passim*; idem, "On Biological Analogs of Newtonian Paradigms," *Philosophy of Science* 35 (1968): 6-27; J. Schiller, "Queries, Answers and Unsolved Problems in Eighteenth-Century Biology," *History of Science* 12 (1974): 184-99; P. Ritterbush, *Overtures to Biology: The Speculations of Eighteenth-Century Naturalists* (New Haven: Yale University Press, 1964).

[123] Roe, *Matter, Life and Generation.*

[124] The struggle with Haller's positions is salient in the writings of all the key figures of the new science (and the new Spinozism) of the later eighteenth century. This is particularly the case with Herder; see Simon Richter, "Medizinistischer und ästhetischer Diskurs im 18. Jahrhundert: Herder und Haller über Reiz," *Lessing Yearbook* 25 (1993): 83-95. See also John Neubauer, "The Freedom of the Machine: On Mechanism, Materialism, and the Young Schiller," *Eighteenth-Century Studies* 15 (1981/82): 275-90.

amount of traditional metaphysics, an enterprise for which few of his younger contemporaries in the biological sciences felt any enthusiasm.[125] Yet they took up his language, *faute de mieux*. That suggests the desperation of their search for resources.

What needs to be introduced into this context is the idea of Spinoza's metaphysics as a theoretical resource for the articulation of a more subtle and dynamic materialism. I am particularly concerned to bring these developments in the natural sciences in Germany after the middle of the eighteenth century into consideration with reference to Johann Gottfried Herder. Herder has long enough been seen as a rhapsodizer, a poet or a mystic. I would like to retrieve Herder as a significant figure in the emergence of natural philosophy in Germany. Herder pursued rigorous philosophical studies over the entire span of his career. As Marion Heinz rightly stresses, there is a "continual sequence of systematically developed sketches and texts on fundamental problems of epistemology and metaphysics in Herder's work."[126] To be sure, he developed no *system*, but that was precisely because he believed that the penchant to system was the great error of German philosophizing. "Nothing makes me sicker than the arch-error of the Germans, to build systems, so please let me be with my philoso*phizing art* of speaking: I am contemplating some few such contributions, but I have no taste for [system] building."[127] That did not mean he was an "unsystematic" thinker.[128] The difference between the "spirit of system" and the "systematic spirit" was articulated brilliantly at mid-century by Jean d'Alembert, and it describes Herder very aptly.[129]

Herder sought to explain the fundamental, unanalyzable concepts of space, time and force in a more lucid and defensible form than German school metaphysics had hitherto achieved. That entailed, as Heinz spells out precisely, a "double structure of spiritualization of nature and naturalization of spirit."[130]

---

[125] H. Metzger, *Newton, Stahl, Boerhaave et la Doctrine Chimique* (Paris, 1930); L. S. King, "Stahl and Hoffmann: A Study in Eighteenth-Century Animism," *Journal of the History of Medicine* 19 (1964): 118-30; idem, "Basic Concepts of Eighteenth-Century Animism," *American Journal of Psychiatry* 124 (1967): 797-802; L. R. Rather, "G. E. Stahl's Psychological Physiology," *Bulletin of the History of Medicine* 35 (1961): 37-49; L. J. Rather and J. B. Frerichs, "The Leibniz-Stahl Controversy," *Clio Medica* 3 (1968): 21-40; 5 (1970): 53-67.

[126] Heinz, *Sensualistischer Idealismus* (Hamburg: Meiner, 1994), xvi.

[127] Herder to Scheffner, 31 Oct. 1767. *Briefe I*, 92.

[128] Heinz (*Sensualistische Idealismus*, xiv) strongly objects to this widespread charge against Herder, and she is right.

[129] Jean D'Alembert, *Preliminary Discourse to the "Encyclopedia" of Diderot* (Chicago: University of Chicago Press, 1995), 94-95; Ernst Cassirer, *Philosophy of the Enlightenment*, 8.

[130] Heinz, xix. Kondylis, *Die Aufklärung im Rahmen des neuzeitlichen Rationalismus* (Stuttgart: Klett-Cotta, 1981), 622, argues that Herder was never quite comfortable, for

> What characterizes the sketches of the year 1769 is
> Herder's effort to make conceivable the unity of body
> and soul of every existent through the unification of
> powers [*Kräfte*] which Kant had divided between the
> immaterial and the material monads, the power of
> representation on the one hand, and the forces of
> attraction and repulsion on the other.[131]

In his last year in Riga Herder devoted himself to an intense study of
Leibniz's *Nouveaux essais* along with some of his earlier essays, and to
the study of Spinoza in a Leibnizian context.[132] Beate Dreike has noted
that the most important features of Herder's engagement with Leibniz
were his acceptance of the theory of dynamism and his rejection of the
idea that substances could not interact.[133] Wolfgang Pross agrees: "The
main point of Herder's criticism is the incommunicability of the monads,
which already in Diderot's article [in the *Encyclopédie*] had been
identified as the critical point of the entire system."[134] In short, Herder
sought to revise Leibnizian dynamism from a transcendent to an immanent
monadology. In this he was following in the footsteps of Kant, but he was
also carrying the argument even further than Kant then had taken it, and,
of course, in a direction Kant explicitly repudiated after the "critical
turn."[135] He sought to ground both the physical and the moral world, both
nature and spirit, in attractive and repulsive forces which were
unanalyzable but actual, efficient causes.[136] He read Leibniz through
Spinoza and Spinoza through Leibniz to find a philosophical mode for
articulating his consistently naturalist insight.

---

religious reasons, to abandon dualism. His endeavor was to *spiritualize* matter, but not to go
all the way to a full monism. This ambivalence is important to note, and it is *this* that might
warrant the charge that Herder was "unsystematic." However, one could mount a variant of
the same charge, in the inverse direction, against Kant's posture of "rational faith" in the
critical philosophy. There is a case to be made that as a complement to "religion within the
limits of pure reason" Kant was careful to conceive "pure reason within the limits of
religion."

[131] Heinz, *Sensualistischer Idealismus*, xix, xxii.

[132] Heinz, *Sensualistischer Idealismus*, xxi; Regine Otto, Herder auf dem Weg zu Spinoza,"
Weimarer Beiträge 10 (1978): 165-177.

[133] Beate Dreike, *Herders Naturaffassung in ihrer Beeinflussung durch Leibniz' Philosophie*
(Wiesbaden: Steiner, 1973 = *Studia Leibnitiana. Supplementa*, 10).

[134] Wolfgang Proß, "Commentary" on "Wolff, Baumgarten und Leibniz," in *Herder und die
Anthropologie der Aufklärung* (Darmstadt: Wissenschaftliche Buchgesellschaft, 1987), 863.

[135] It was in this context that Kant's *Allgemeine Naturgeschichte* exerted its maximal
influence on Herder, but one should not ignore such lesser essays as Kant's "Physical
Monadology." That Kant abandoned these endeavors almost at the same moment that Herder
took them up is a historical irony, not a philosophical verdict.

[136] Pross, "Commentary" on "Wolf, Baumgarten und Leibniz," 851.

As Herbert Lindner correctly surmises, Herder's "transformation of Spinozism was initiated by Leibniz's philosophy."[137] If Leibniz was important for Herder (and Goethe), it was because he dynamized the natural order. "The fixed substance of Spinoza was transcended by the admixture of the Leibnizian principle of force."[138] Force and dynamism were essential for the new natural philosophy, but it was equally essential that these be seen as immanent in nature.

> By rendering the 'active side' of Leibniz in a materialistic manner and introducing it into their vision of nature, Goethe and Herder were able to overcome the mechanistic tendencies of Spinozism. Nature could now be seen in constant movement and development. The events of nature took on a process character.[139]

But Leibniz in his turn robbed the material world of all metaphysical reality, whereas for Herder and Goethe, Lindner rightly observes, "Nature had the most exalted reality."[140] Thus Herder complains against such idealistic metaphysics:

> It is simply madness [to think] that we are merely self-reflecting pure spirits, philosophical atoms in ourselves: we are sensual creatures, who must enjoy nature sensually or not at all. Sensual impressions, forces, drives are the strongest things we have, as they are the earliest and the freshest [*frühesten und jugendlichsten*].[141]

This insistence on the actual world in Herder (and in Goethe) is important. It brings them both far closer to the viewpoint of "physical influx" than Leibniz was at all prepared to go. But it also shows how the project of a theory of "physical influx," of "hylozoism," needed to appropriate Spinoza. While Herder always placed Spinoza in the company of Leibniz and Shaftesbury, it was clear that Spinoza took pride of place in that triad. That was because Spinoza put a monistic approach to Nature at the center of his thought. It made Spinoza a viable resource for the new vitalism, even as it prepared the way for Idealism and Romanticism. It was the philosophical soul of the Spinoza renaissance. To be sure, this Spino*zism* stands in considerable tension with the formulations of Spinoza

---

[137] Lindner, *Problem des Spinozismus*, 89.
[138] Lindner, *Problem des Spinozismus*, 92.
[139] Lindner, *Problem des Spinozismus*, 93.
[140] Lindner, *Problem des Spinozismus*, 90-91.
[141] Herder, *Sämtliche Werke*, Suphan 8: 358.

himself, for whom the monism of substance did not entail the interaction of modes; nonetheless, the filiation was explicit and fructifying.[142]

Herder was convinced that insufficient attention had been paid to the physicality, indeed, the animality of man: "We are at once animal spirits [*Tierartiger Geister*].... The whole foundation of our soul is [composed of] obscure ideas, the liveliest, the most, the mass, out of which the soul prepares its finer [ideas], the most powerful drives of our lives."[143] Herder insisted that man always be situated in nature: anthropology was part of the philosophy of nature. This insistence on the actual world in Herder brings him far closer to the viewpoint of "physical influx" than Leibniz was at all prepared to go.[144] But it also shows how the project of a theory of "physical influx," of "hylozoism," needed to appropriate Spinoza.

The question of Spinoza emerged for Herder out of his struggles to think his way through the relation of philosophy and "anthropology" in the years after his passage out of the tutelage of Immanuel Kant. It was the stimulus of the problems of "vitalist materialism"—specifically the writings of Diderot and Robinet—that informed his reading of Leibniz and Spinoza and carried him in a direction significantly different from Kant's.[145] Moreover, it is essential to see Herder's "empirical psychology"—the correlate of this metaphysical vitalism—shaped by the reception of Leibniz by the French thinkers Condillac and Diderot.[146] A philosopher of lesser rank, whom Herder nonetheless read and cited frequently, the Marquis d'Argens, in *Philosophie de bon sens* (1763) made the essential point: "Whatever the theologians will bring forward in order to find philosophical grounds to insist that matter cannot think and cannot have any moving force, will only be an empty grab-bag of words."[147] Herder himself makes reference, crucially, to "Maupertuis' ladder," i.e. to the idea of the great chain of being, especially in the immanent and genetic sense of that notion as Maupertuis, Buffon and Diderot were

---

[142] For a careful exposition of Spinoza's own doctrine, see James Collins, *Spinoza on Nature* (Carbondale and Edwardsville, IL: Southern Illinois University Press, 1984).

[143] Herder, *Viertes Kritisches Wäldchen*, DKV: 2: 275. This conviction was the basis of Herder's dispute with Mendelssohn in the letters concerning the *Bestimmung des Menschen*.

[144] "In the second half of the eighteenth century Leibniz was readily simplified in a monistic manner—and not just by Herder—to be set against the two-substance dualism of Wolff." Helmut Pfotenauer, *Literarische Anthropologie* (Stuttgart: Metzler, 1987), 13.

[145] Wolfgang Proß, "Herder und die Anthropologie seiner Zeit," in Proß, ed., *Herder und die Anthropologie der Aufklärung*, 1128-1216.

[146] That is, Condillac's dissertation on the monad, submitted to the Berlin Academy for the contest of 1747 and published together with the winning entry for that prize contest shortly thereater Condillac, *Les Monades*, ed. Laurence Bongie (Oxford: Voltaire Foundation, 1980); and Diderot, "Leibnizianisme," in the *Encyclopédie*. On the influence of these thinkers on Herder's Leibniz reception see Proß, "Herder und die Anthropologie seiner Zeit," 1138-42.

[147] Cited in Proß, "Herder und die Anthropologie seiner Zeit," 1162.

developing it over the 1750s.[148] Thus it was hylozoism, the need to see matter and spirit in continuity, that carried Herder decisively to Spinoza.

The earliest mention of Spinoza in Herder's writings is in his essay "Wie die Philosophie zum Besten des Volks allgemeiner und nützlicher werden kann" of 1765.[149] But that was only a mention, probably an echo from Kant's lectures, not a token of textual familiarity. Still, the context suggests that Herder was already situating Spinoza, as Mendelssohn had proposed, within the philosophical dynamic of the "three hypotheses." Lindner suggests that Mendelssohn's *Philosophische Gespräche* may very well have been the first source for Herder's engagement with Spinoza.[150] He affirms Willi Vollrath's argument that Herder began seriously to work through Spinoza's ideas in 1769.[151] There is evidence of this engagement in the "Grundsätzen der Philosophie" of 1769.[152] This meditation picks up directly on the lines of speculation that Mendelssohn had introduced, but in a far more favorable manner. Indeed, without any knowledge of them, Herder replicated the philosophical line of thought that Lessing's brief texts had worked out only a few years earlier for his correspondence with Mendelssohn.[153]

As Hermann Timm has argued, "The impulse is commonly shared. All are caught up in a general concept of power, force or life."[154] In his *Erziehung des Menschengeschlechts*, for example, "Lessing formulated an analogy between biological science, psychological pedagogy and traditional theology of development [*Bildungstheologie*], with the

---

[148] Herder, *Journal meiner Reise*, DKV: 9: 19.

[149] Herder, "Wie die Philosophie," in Ulrich Gaier, ed., *Johann Gottfried Herder: Frühe Schriften 1764-1772* (Frankfurt: Deutsche Klassiker Verlag, 1985 = *Johann Gottfried Herder: Werke in zehn Bänden,* Bd. 1), 101-34.

[150] "Herder was familiar with Mendelssohn's Gespräche. It is entirely possible that they served as his first exposure to Spinoza as such. But Herder at the same time took a critical view of them." Lindner, *Problem des Spinozismus*, 29n.

[151] Willi Vollrath, *Die Auseinandersetzung Herders mit Spinoza* (Gießen, 1911); Regine Otto, "Herders Weg zu Spinoza."

[152] "Spinoza believed that everything existed in God. He ... only assumed One Center, he called it God and World. One can therefore term him with equal justice an idealist as an atheist; he never was this latter... Thus God belongs to the world, as the world to God. He is the principle: Everything is therefore contingency insofar as it has its ground in God, but also necessary in so far as it belongs necessarily to the Thought of God." See Herder, *Sämtliche Werke*, Suphan 32: 228.

[153] Lessing, "Über die Wirklichkeit der Dinge ausser Gott," LM: 14: 292-93, and "Durch Spinoza ist Leibniz nur auf die Spur der vorherbestimmten Harmonie gekommen," LM: 14: 294-96. See Henry Allison, "Lessing's Spinozistic Exercises," *Lessing Yearbook: Supplement: Humanität und Dialog* (1982), 223-33.

[154] "There is a generalized schematic antithesis, through which the traditional conceptual dichotomies from every domain are called up, from contemporary psychology through the theology of incarnation and crucifixion all the way to presocratic oppositional metaphors. Everywhere one seeks contradictory oppositions, in order to place oneself between them." Timm, *Spinozarenaissance*, 228.

speculative consequence of a cyclical self-confirmation of the highest being."[155] Herder elaborated the idea into an "axiom of a general ontology of life."[156] One found this dynamic polarity, Herder wrote,

> spread throughout the whole world order. Everywhere two forces set against one another which nonetheless must work together and in which only by the combined and appropriate influence of both emerges the higher reality of a wise order, development, organization, life. All life arose in such a manner from death, out of the death of lesser forces, all wholes of order and of design from light and shadow, out of diverging, mutually opposing forces, where the higher positive law, which limits and transcends both, alone inaugurates and harmonizes *cosmos*, world, design, whole, highest good, communal happiness. Mathematics, physics, chemistry, physiology of living beings all seem to me to provide evidence for this everywhere. In man, it seems to me, this contrariety is consequently only the most blatant perhaps because he is the most spiritual, developed being of our world, the convergence and center of our creation.[157]

This ubiquitous vitalism was fully developed by the mid-1770s. Herder wrote these lines in "Über die dem Menschen angeborene Lüge" which can be dated to those years. Herder's clearest treatment of Spinoza in this early period is offered in the final, 1778, version of *Vom Erkennen und Empfinden der menschlichen Seele*.[158] It would only find full literary expression in Herder's masterworks of the 1780s.

What I wish to suggest is that Herder's vitalist-materialist assimilation of Spinoza, as the Lessing reference suggests and as a consideration of the early thoughts of Goethe on nature would confirm, characterized the entire Spinoza renaissance. The congruity in the reception of Spinoza at this

---

[155] Timm, *Spinozarenaissance*, 278.
[156] Timm, *Spinozarenaissance*, 285.
[157] Herder, *Sämtliche Werke*, Suphan 9, 536-40.
[158] "Die Hinwendung des jungen Herder zu Spinoza is von bemerkenswerter Kontinuität, welche auch in der Bückeburger Zeit, die unter dem Zeichen einer teilweisen Wiederannäherung an Hamann, einem weitgehenden Offenbarugsglauben und mystischen Neigungen stand, nich unterbrochen wurde. Die Wurzeln der großen Spinozaschrift 'Gott. Einige Gespräche von J. G. Herder' reichen zurück in die Frühzeit, und die revolutionäre Umwertung der Person Spinozas und des Spinozismus, die etwa mit dem Aufbruch von Riga anhebt, steigert sich bis zur Spinoza-Apotheose in der 3. Fassung der Akademieschrift 'Vom Erkennen und Empfinden der menschlichen Seele', die 1778 im Druck erschien, aber schon in Bückeburg in Angriff genommen worden war." Bollacher, *Goethe und Spinoza*, 143.

historical moment is striking. It is situated, metaphysically, in the problem of the "three hypotheses," and more specifically in a monist resolution of that problem: hylozoism as a reformulation of "physical influx." The assimilation of Spinoza to Leibniz in this fashion, I submit, was most successfully achieved by the young Herder. It made Spinoza a viable resource for the new vitalism. That was the philosophical soul of the Spinoza renaissance that burst upon the public in 1786 but had been germinating for decades.

Review Essay

J. G. A. Pocock
The Johns Hopkins University

Jorge Cañizares-Esguerra, *How to Write the History of the New World: Histories, Epistemologies, and Identities in the Eighteenth-Century Atlantic World* (Stanford, CA: Stanford University Press, 2001). Pp. xx + 450. ISBN 0-8047-4693-1 (pbk.) $24.95.

"Enlightenment" is now a term imperiled, not by attenuation or disintegration of its meaning, but by the multitude and richness of the meanings it has collected and the phenomena it has usefully come to describe. It is doubted whether we can continue to write of "The Enlightenment" as a unitary or universal historical process, and those who passionately defend this usage generally do so in the name of some specific description of "enlightenment" to which they wish to give priority, whether to defend or attack it. To say, as their adversaries do, that this was not "The Enlightenment" (and that nothing was) is not to say that the "enlightenment" they are describing did not exist, has not been accurately described, or did not have the significance they ascribe to it. It is only to say that other "enlightenments" were going on and need attention, now or at some other moment.

Jorge Cañizares-Esguerra concludes his fascinating study of the diversities of historiography in the age to which the term in question is applied with a chapter headed "Whose Enlightenment was it anyway?" Perhaps the query should have been "Why are we talking about Enlightenment in the first place?" but the rephrasing does not diminish the usability of the term, or the very considerable value of Cañizares's enterprise. He is writing about a cultural area—Spain and Spanish America—into which it has been held that Enlightenment did not penetrate, and which was indeed resistant to 'Enlightenment' in several of its accepted senses. It is his intention to show that some of those most hostile to Enlightenment in these senses, and to the culture promoting Enlightenment so defined, achieved historiographical, methodological and philosophical results more "enlightened" than did their adversaries. These scholars were clerics and creoles practicing a baroque erudition in a baroque culture. /Were they therefore Enlightened, what do we mean by the term, and do we even have to answer the question?

The Enlightenment which provides the thesis to Cañizares's antithesis is one of the most illustrious denoted by the term: the French and Scottish philosophical historians who had organized "the history of civil society" and "les progrès de l'esprit humain" into a sequence of stages determined by the workings of the human mind under specified historical conditions. When the attention of some of them was brought to the societies of pre-Columbian America, they chose to relegate all, as nearly as possible, to the hunter-gatherer condition known as "savagery," and they went so far as to doubt and deny early Spanish accounts of the cities and empires of Mexico and Peru, on the grounds that their peoples had not attained the conditions—arable agriculture, ferrous metallurgy, wheeled traffic, money and letters—necessary to the establishment of civilization as this Enlightenment understood it. Of these conditions it is the last—letters—which is the crucial theme of Cañizares's book. The French and Scottish *philosophes* (if we can agree upon this epithet) were bitterly condemnatory of the ferocities of the Conquest; but instead of denouncing the sixteenth-century Spaniards as barbarians who had destroyed an empire, they chose to present them as barbarians in a deeper sense, self-glorifying or self-deceived in describing what they overthrew as more glorious and less "savage" than it had been. This came to be fiercely resented by the creole and partly Amerindian heirs of the conquistadors, who resorted to the strategy, not unknown in the history of settler nationalisms, of deriving part of their history, legitimacy and identity from the indigenous cultures they had displaced. It was therefore matter of dispute among creoles, *philosophes* and *peninsulares* whether the Mexica, Inca and as they reappeared Maya, had possessed a civilization and in particular whether their writings, pictograms and inscriptions could be deciphered and shown to possess meanings—especially those that could be assembled into a narrative historiography.

The *philosophes* denied all this. For Cañizares's purposes they consist of three names: Cornelius de Pauw, William Robertson and Guillaume-Thomas Raynal (behind whom we must detect the team of authors including Diderot—if Diderot may be imagined as a team player—brought together to complete the *Histoire des Deux Indes*). Cañizares treats them under a common rubric; he sees them as *philosophes* so confident of the "new way of reading" they had devised, a way of reading historical evidence in search of the laws of the human mind and its progress or development in history, that they were prepared to criticize and disregard any historical narrative that did not fit these laws; an opportunity that must open before any critic who comes to know a text better than did its author. In Central and Andean America they came up against data that did not fit their laws, and ended by denying both that Amerindians had been capable of cities and empires, and that Spaniards were to be believed when they narrated meeting with such phenomena. It is a classic case of the *esprit de système* to which the Enlightenments returned in the process of becoming revolutionary; the erection of *méthode* into a *système* which permits the philosopher to know better than the evidence before him.

In this there is of course much truth; yet I think Cañizares's case could have been enriched if he had admitted some more differentiation between his *philosophes*. Edward Gibbon, who knew this world well, was cautious about de Pauw, deeply admired Robertson, and thought Raynal an ill-mannered mountebank. It is the second figure of the three he singles out for us, and I am not quite happy when Cañizares—as he sometimes does—presents this formidable man as something of a lightweight, easily flattered and (this is the issue) interested in history only in so far as it presents the laws of the progress of society. There are two ways in which a treatment of Robertson may deepen our understanding of this part of the story Cañizares has to tell.

Robertson had made his name with a great essay on the history of western Europe since the fall of Rome. This did not entail stadial history—or an exclusive concentration on the laws of progress—for the reason that European history was thought to contain no savage stage, having since earliest times been settled by waves of shepherd peoples moving out of Eurasia. When he came to apply the stadial theses of his friends Adam Smith and Adam Ferguson to America, he was operating with a system of Old World history Eurasiocentric rather than Eurocentric, which explained human history all across the historically familiar continent, but failed to make sense in the New World. The two stadia which explained everything were the domestication of hoofed mammals, facilitating the shepherd stage, and their subsequent yoking to a heavy plough, facilitating agriculture and appropriation, law and commerce, urbanization and empire. Neither of these could be discerned in the Americas, and it was easy first to relegate all Americans to the hunter-gatherer condition, second to affirm that peoples in this condition could not possibly have erected such cities as the Spaniards described.

In an ideal world of the Strange Multiplicity,[1] there were two steps which should now have been taken. One—within the range of possibilities Cañizares is here considering—was the invention of new laws of progress which would explain the creation of cities in pre-Columbian economies and cultures; the other—with which he does not need to concern himself here—was a reconsideration of hunter-gatherer culture, aimed at asking whether it indeed remained entrapped in the all but pre-conscious condition called savagery. Neither step was of course taken, and it is doubtful whether anyone so much as proposed either. It is easy to affirm

---

[1] James Tully, *Strange Multiplicity: Constitutionalism in an Age of Diversity* (Cambridge: Cambridge University Press, 1995).

all manner of motives, hegemonic and imperialist, why this did not happen; but it can be added that neither would have been at all easy. It is the former possibility explored, indirectly, in *How to Write the History of the New World*. To see how it arises we must return to the second way of treating William Robertson that Cañizares might have taken up.

It would be a simplification to describe Enlightened historiography, as it functioned in northwestern Europe, as the reduction of reading to discovering the laws of the mind. Here I wish to invoke Arnaldo Momigliano's account of Gibbon's success in reconciling "philosophy" with "erudition," and ways in which I have tried to elaborate his thesis.[2] The gist of the matter—well known to Adam Smith, who was well known to Robertson—is that "philosophic" or "conjectural" history supplied a "natural" history of how the mind would have operated if left to itself, but had to coexist, in a relation of mutual criticism, with a "civil" history of how it actually had operated in a diversity of circumstances both material and contingent, supplied by the narratives of former historians and by the cumulative descriptions of past states of government, society, economy and culture, built up since the Renaissance by antiquarians, *érudits* and philologists. The great Enlightened historians, of whom Robertson was held to be one, were those who knew how to play each against the other: philosophy against erudition, nature against contingency, what could not have happened against what could not have happened otherwise. They set their faces against philosophers who thought they knew better than the evidence: Gibbon despised Voltaire for refusing to acknowledge the inscription of Singanfu, Robertson criticized Voltaire, as Gibbon criticized Raynal, for refusing to give their evidence in footnotes.

Enlightenment was a neoclassical culture, and was therefore in constant dialogue with the humanism whose critical techniques its historians were trying to surpass. It is of great importance, and Cañizares most valuably reminds us, that *les lumières* were surrounded by colleagues whose methods of exegesis remained what we call baroque; biblical and neoplatonist, allegorical and cabbalist, interested in the ideograms and pictograms they supposed in order to decipher scripts from China to Peru. But while philosophers and philologists were tracing the history of the human mind from the scripts of Egypt to those of China, the Jesuits and *académiciens* were learning to read Chinese and constructing the history of both empire and steppe from the writings of their own historians. The erudition of Enlightenment was of course classical and neoclassical, and

[2] Arnaldo Momigliano, "Gibbon's Contribution to Historical Method," in *idem, Contributo alla Storia degli Studi Classici* (Rome: Edizione di storia e letterature, 1955), ch. 8; J. G. A. Pocock, *Barbarism and Religion* (Cambridge: Cambridge University Press, 1999), vol. 1: *The Enlightenments of Edward Gibbon*, chs. 6-9; vol. 2, *Narratives of Civil Government*, chs. 16, 20, 21, 24.

may be termed European and therefore Eurocentric; but as it ventured eastward, into Arabic, Chinese and later Sanskrit sources, it encountered texts it could read and narratives it could at least believe it understood. This was what did not happen in the Americas; Cañizares's book inquires whether this vast incomprehension of the Mexican and Andean pasts could have been overcome or diminished.

Robertson gave up early, and all I have to add to Cañizares's account of why he did so is that he was not impelled by the philosophic over-confidence of de Pauw or Raynal; it may have been his command of European erudition that convinced him there was nothing to be found in Mesoamerican scripts. Stewart Brown's edition of *William Robertson and the Expansion of Empire*[3] does not appear in Cañizares's bibliography, but contains little that is relevant to his subject. This is a Spanish and Spanish-American story, and we learn to see Robertson as a distant stranger—he never traveled—in a fierce and often petty world of conflict between creoles and *peninsulares*, advocates of French Enlightenment and Spanish or Spanish-American patriots, of which he can have understood little even after he found himself savagely attacked by Francisco Clavijero—a member, to complicate the story, of a large party of Jesuits exiled after their Society's dissolution to rustication in Italy and Spain. They employed their learning in the intellectual politics of the Academy of History—a body rather unique in its period, set up to exploit the unorganized riches of the Spanish archives—and sought to defend either the royal government of the sixteenth century or (less certainly) the conquistadors against the charges of genocide leveled by the *leyenda negra*, and (very seldom indeed) to attend to the endeavors of creoles—engaged in building a vigorous intellectual culture—to construct a history which might, as intended by some but by no means all, contain a pre-Conquest narrative in some way continuous with the creole.

The scene is further complicated by the presence of some—Campomanes, for some time the Academy's director, is one of them—who genuinely endorsed the Enlightenment narrative known to us all, and wished to import and impose it on what they considered an intolerably backward society. This whets the appetite for more about Spanish Enlightened historiography. Neither Robertson nor any of the northern historians had much to say about Spain in their accounts of European progress; Robertson tended to join Raynal in depicting Castilians, at least, as unreconstructed Visigoths in a state of arrested development; and one wonders if there was a counternarrative of Celtiberians, Carthaginians, Romans, Visigoths and Arabs, such as

---

[3] Stewart J. Brown, ed., *William Robertson and the Expansion of Empire* (Cambridge: Cambridge University Press, 1997).

eighteenth-century historiography was certainly capable of constructing. In baroque historiography, there seems to have existed a choice between an exclusive (possibly Castilian) emphasis on the Visigothic origins of the kingdom, and the vision of an ideal and eternal Hispania to whose history all people since the Noachides and the Trojans had contributed.[4] We learn from Cañizares the enticing detail that some of the Academy insisted that medieval Arab culture was Spanish and part of Spanish history; is this a *thèse patriote* or a *thèse des lumières*, and should one even ask what the Holy Office thought about it? We are too far from Amerindian history to demand that Cañizares should explore this subject, and the history of a settler society seldom depends on a reconstruction of that of the homeland; he takes us instead through a bitter and barren history, in which some outstanding scholars appear but spend too much time preventing the publication of one another's works.

The scene returns to America for the concluding actions of the story. We are introduced to a creole culture, largely clerical as the country-born elites, of both Spanish and Amerindian descent, find other paths to advancement closed against them.[5] This culture was both patriot and baroque—the two terms converge to become one—and the meaning of the latter is that its intellectual skills and world view were of the seventeenth century far more than of the eighteenth. Surviving into the latter age, however, they merged with the patriot instincts of a settler community desiring its own culture and history to produce a serious assault on the problem of deciphering ancient *inscriptions et belles-lettres* and extracting a coherent narrative of pre-Conquest history. These sources of information were pictographic and ideographic, and the perception of time they employed, if brilliantly organized, was far removed from the Christian. It was a consequence that deciphering them was a problem for the puzzle-solving, not the narrative, mind, and called for all the Renaissance intellect's powers of visualizing and pictorializing patterns of symbolic resemblance. This is a book which Frances Yates would have vastly enjoyed; the present reviewer, a slave to the narrative linearity of script and print, has as a rule not the faintest idea what was going on.

And here perhaps is the problem. By "whose Enlightenment was it anyway?", Cañizares points to the paradox that it was the magical and cabbalist baroque mind, not the critical and universalist Enlightenment, that achieved the Enlightened objective of breaking through to the

---

[4] Maria José Hidalgo de la Vega, "Ancient History in Spanish Historiography," in Gudmundur Hálfdanarson and Anne Katherine Isaacs, eds., *Nations and Nationalities in Historical Perspective* (Pisa: PLUS, 2001), 133-46.

[5] Here Cañizares acknowledges his debt to D. A. Brading, *The First Americans: the Spanish Monarchy, Creole Patriots, and the Liberal State, 1492-1867* (Cambridge: Cambridge University Press, 1991).

inscribed consciousness of a wholly discontinuous culture—if indeed this was an Enlightened and not a Romantic objective; the study must conclude with Humboldt, who knew who Herder was. But there is no turning baroque minds into postmodern; they were as neoclassical as their *philosophe* opponents, and were looking for a narrative history, in which Maya, Toltec or Inca might play Etruscans to their Romans or Romans to their Goths (and since many of them were still thinking in terms of sacred history, the figure could be pressed further). The question is whether the techniques of baroque decipherment were going to give them anything so linear. If the Maya or Mexican past was irredeemably esoteric, it was pagan without being civic; hence of course Manco Capac and (to everyone's credit) Mama Ocello, the Peruvian equivalents of the classical-Enlightened legislator. But they supplied neither the Solon, the Confucius nor the Muhammad needed for a classical-Enlightened history, and Quetzalcoatl remained bizarre beyond the possibility of allegory. At the end of this brilliant and massively learned study of a historically important branch of Enlightenment, one is left wondering whether Enlightenment in this setting had a Revolutionary or a Romantic future. The next inquiry might be into whether the Romantic and Liberal intellect was closer to the baroque, or farther from it; the answer might very well be ambivalent.

Book Reviews

Joseph M. Levine, *The Autonomy of History: Truth and Method from Erasmus to Gibbon* (Chicago: University of Chicago Press, 1999). Pp. xviii + 249. ISBN 0-226-47541. $27.50.

Students of the eighteenth century are greatly indebted to Joseph M. Levine, not least for his work on scholarly milieux and the interpretative impetus that he has rewardingly drawn from close study of the great occasions of scholarly controversy, most notably, the *querelle* and the "Battle of the Books." His new collection of essays traces the emergence of historical self-consciousness between the Renaissance and the late, immediately prehistoricist, experience of Enlightenment. For Levine, the "long eighteenth century" has been stretching backward for some time, and the coherence of a scholarly project which began with *Humanism and Historiography* in 1996, with its roots in the analysis of fifteenth-century transformations in thought, is becoming more apparent as he takes his analysis forward to the opening of the nineteenth century.

As a direct result of these quietly profound inquiries into the historicity of what he calls "ordinary history," Levine was asking students of the history of history to practice reflexivity long before that term became fashionable; it is one of the many virtues of his work that her rarely, if ever, descends into the language of academic fashion. Indeed, *The Autonomy of History* asks basic questions about method in a way that suggests that the problems of method wrestled with by Erasmus and Thomas More are still pertinent in a post-historicist universe. This is, then, a continuous survey of intellectual history over *la longue durée*. It is one, however, undertaken in the classical style that, to use a favored, if contentious, word of Levine's, "emerged" as historicism developed (another contentious concept); it is only problematically related to the New History and its promotion of *la longue durée* as a profitable mode of analysis. What is more, Levine has major concerns with the nature and the practice of the New History, it whatever form it might present itself, and this is a tension that is apparent in his ready use of historical development as a given in the history of historiography; he assumes, rather than establishes, the cogency and the superiority of historicism, whose contested history is notable by its absence in this study of its supposed prehistory.

This is not to say that historicism is not more cogent or even, perhaps, superior to its rivals, but it is to argue that more needs to be done if such assumptions are to work when historicism is the chosen mode for studying its own history. Levine situates himself squarely within the tradition of historical reflection identified by R. G. Collingwood, whose philosophical program he seeks to substantiate by an appeal to the history of history, but, surely, more needs to be done in order to accept that program than to say, as Levine does in his introduction, that he finds it the most persuasive of all currently available philosophies of history? Levine's division of academic labor between history and philosophy is not so easy to instantiate as he implies, and a project to substantiate Collingwoodian history would still need to be more philosophical in orientation than Levine assumes it to be. He berates Quentin Skinner for being too philosophical in his discussion of historical technique, but it is equally possible to state that Levine needs to be more philosophical if his history is to persuade the sceptical, let alone the consciously postmodern, reader.

There is, naturally, much to commend in this study, not least its persuasive purchase on related subjects over a long period of time, its elegant combination of historical generalization and detailed analysis, and its deployment of an amazingly disparate cast of characters. from the great names in historical writing to probably deservedly obscure controversialists of long defunct polemic. There is also an invaluable sense of a personal history in the book, as an intelligence that grew and matured in earlier decades comfortably draws on older scholarship of the sort that younger historians would now all to easily and damagingly ignore. The somewhat elderly provenance of much of the secondary literature alluded to in the chronologically earlier sections of the book is suggestive; there is a passion for intellectual continuity in Levine, and it is one that he practices in his own work. Even Burkhardtian typology is rescued in the essay on More, and this small instance speaks volumes about the hidden continuities between German and American intellectual history that Levine nowhere explicitly addresses in the text, but which he often tacitly sanctions in his expositions of texts and debates.

In short, one can begin to reconstruct (and locate in time) Levine's historicist frame of mind from study of his books, but, how typical is his intelligence, and if it is typical, what is it that it typifies? *Au fond*, it typifies a passion for coherence, in which narratives emerge, and developments can be gauged; in which philosophies triumph, and methods justify themselves over epochs, that is historically, rather than immediately, that is philosophically: it is to praise Vico against Descartes. It is History that necessarily emerges as the victor in the attempt to maker sense of ourselves, and rival modes of interpretation, philosophical and religious, lose out to its disciplinary superiority in Levine's not entirely disinterested reckoning. In this sense, the ironic Gibbonian lament that theologians describe truth in its pure form, whilst historians are left merely to chronicle its debased particularities, is a supreme historicist parable in the argument of *The Autonomy of History*.

This is, of course, to study Levine's essays as a contribution to method, but that is precisely because he offers them to this end in his fascinatingly pregnant preface, which really needs to be opened up and expanded. Ultimately, one rather doubts that the assembled essays provide anything like as coherent a study as Levine thinks they do, and one has chronological doubts about this, as well as more directly interpretative ones. One is left to conclude when closing this volume that history is no more autonomous than is philosophy; as Bernard Williams has recently argued, philosophy needs to be more historically minded than it has tended to be: likewise, historians need to be more philosophically adventurous than they have hitherto tended to be. This was, after all, true of much historical thought in the eighteenth century. Curiously, by excluding Voltaire and the *philosophes* from his story, as well as scanting the contribution made by the historians who flourished in the atmosphere of the Scottish Enlightenment, Levine is disablingly foreshortening an account of historical practice in the eighteenth century in favor of a historicist teleology; can historicism combine with such teleological readings of its own assumed past and remain historicist? This is but one of the fascinating paradoxes that litter Levine's interesting intervention in the intellectual history of intellectual history.

Brian Young
University of Sussex

Barbara J. Shapiro, *A Culture of Fact. England, 1550-1720*. (Ithaca, N. Y.: Cornell University Press, 2000). Pp. x + 284. ISBN 0-8014-3686-9. $45.00.

Historians have not had an easy time characterizing the period between the Renaissance and Enlightenment. The great blocks of history that lie between these two periods, unfortunately, have been trapped under the rather oxymoronic heading of "early modern history." Is there a more accurate way to categorize this disparate and conflicting age? In her new synthetic work, Barbara Shapiro offers a possible response to the dilemma of defining the period that lasted roughly from 1550 to 1720. She suggests that it was marked by a fascination with and a reliance on the concept of fact. From law to history and literature, and from geography, to politics, religion and, of course, natural philosophy, the world of the learned depended on the "matter of fact."

With a hint of Cartesianism, Shapiro begins with what she knows best. To define the idea of fact, she starts in the realm of law—the subject of her two most influential works—tracing the establishment of legal fact through the institutions of witnesses, testimony and credibility. Not only did the growth of a legal culture lead to a systematized process of establishing legal facts, it also spread this concept of fact to a relatively wide public throughout England, as legal proceedings became a facet of everyday life. In turn, Shapiro asserts, historical studies echoed law. Figures such as Thomas Blundeville, Francis Bacon and Gilbert Burnet sought criteria and methods for establishing historical truths. Growing alongside historical studies, antiquarianism reflected a fact-driven historical consciousness, based on philology and the assessment, collection, and presentation of material evidence.

More than just the growth of professional and intellectual disciplines, a fact-based culture spread throughout England *via* the expanding practices of social and geographical observation, or, to use the technical term, "chorography." Explorers, ambassadors, and natural historians began surveying the world around them, writing reports and publishing studies that described geography, topography, soil, climate, antiquities and even ethnographic traits. William Camden traveled across the entire country to write his study, *The Britannia* (1695), providing maps, genealogies, and surveys of such things as manufactures. Along with travel logs and reporting, the old genre of political observations flourished, as works such as Edward Chamberlayne's *Anglia notitia: or, the Present State of England* (1669) attempted to describe the English state. Even religion knelt at the authority of fact as faith became a question of "rational methods of proving" religious truth. At all levels, England was subject to learned surveillance.

On this rich backdrop of widespread observational culture stood the eminent Royal Society. The authority and influence of this institution led to a more systematized process of establishing the idea of fact as Restoration natural philosophers, such as Robert Boyle, grounded the existing concept of natural facts in observational methodology. As in law, facts were established by witnesses, whose observational testimony was judged by standards of credibility, skill, expertise, and impartiality. In their quest to identify facts, natural philosophers also relied on scientific instruments and varied practices of collection, classification, and presentation. By the eighteenth century, "matters of fact" became ever more accepted and systematized in epistemological treaties such as *An Inquiry into the Human Mind and the Principles of Common Sense* (1764) by Thomas Reid, who hailed Bacon and Newton and embraced a clear inductive, experimental method.

As in any ambitious venture, there are risks in trying to cover a vast amount of material in a relatively concise study. But there is a reason for the sweeping scope of *A Culture of Fact*. Clearly, Professor Shapiro feels an urgent need to counter the historians of science, Steven Shapin and Simon Schaffer, whose popular work, *Leviathan and the Air Pump*, argues that social status was a determining factor in the establishment of scientific fact. Did scientific truth rely on social status? Did a gentleman's credibility weigh heavily in determining what would be considered factual and true? Is it possible to write an entirely social history of truth? While Shapiro agrees with the idea that gentlemanly status could indeed help establish the credibility of a witness, it was by no means the only criterion in legitimating testimony: "Expertise, experience, opportunity, number, disinterest, and impartiality were other criteria" (140). Indeed, in much the same spirit as the early experts in *materia medica*, Garcia d'Orta and João d'Acosta, who took eyewitness accounts of Asian plants from Jews and infidels, some members of the Royal Society sought out the testimony of seamen and common travelers to establish natural and geographical facts. And of course, in the legal courts, truth was not necessarily based on social status as gentlemen argued against gentlemen and judges followed fairly strict testimonial procedures. In light of Shapiro's convincing argument and interdisciplinary evidence, the sometimes reductionist social history of truth needs to be reconsidered in a wider historical perspective.

If the culture of fact did indeed spread across the spectrum of the learned world, it seems unlikely that it grew primarily from a single tradition, in this case law. The history of knowledge is elusively complex, for legal culture was intertwined with the essentially interdisciplinary culture of humanism, which itself was based on the Aristotelian helix of ancient rhetoric, history and natural philosophy. Thus Shapiro never really gives a convincing genealogy of the idea of "fact." To do so would entail beginning in the classical world and actually tracing the origins of the word itself into the sixteenth and seventeenth centuries. Surely the definition of "fact" evolved over time. Fact, and the culture of observation, did not emerge in one place, but were rather fostered by humanists—the great missing players in this book—the learned Latin masters who excelled as philologues, rhetoric teachers, historians and lawyers all at the same time. Surely it was the convergence of these learned traditions that engendered "factual" consciousness.

In the end, what seems extraordinary is that it took the rationalist culture of fact so long to arise, for many of its key elements had been present for so long. Oddly, there is no mention of those who battled against the culture of fact. Indeed, the opponents of epistemological rationalism and induction were surely key figures in the process by which the culture of fact emerged. Thus what held the early modern period together was not so much the unified march toward "fact," but rather the ongoing struggle around this evolving concept that threatened traditional

Christian cosmology and so shaped the beginning of the modern age. Professor Shapiro's book forces us to examine these questions and furthers the debate at the center of the growing field of the history of truth and knowledge.

Jacob Soll
Rutgers University, Camden

Jean S. Yolton, editor, *John Locke as Translator: Three of the "Essais" of Pierre Nicole in French and English* (Oxford: Voltaire Foundation, 2000). Pp. xix + 266. ISBN 0-7294-0708-X. £49.00.

Writing to Samuel Pepys in February 1690 the diarist John Evelyn gives a most enthusiastic précis of the contents of the latest book he has read, Locke's *Essay concerning Human Understanding*. Evelyn claims that he has never encountered someone "who has Vindicated, and Asserted the Existence of God Almighty in all his Attributes, with more solid, and incontestable Argument." This contemporary response to the *Essay* is not perhaps one that we would expect today. Yet it comes from an era that valued arguments for the existence of God more highly than our own. It is of interest therefore to learn that one of the earliest sources of stimulation for Locke's ruminations on the existence of God was a short essay penned by one of the writers of the Port Royal *Logique*, Pierre Nicole. In fact, this comprises one of three essays from Nicole's *Essais de morale* which Locke translated out of French in the mid-1670s and that are transcribed for us by Jean Yolton in a charming new volume in the Studies on Voltaire and the Eighteenth Century series.

Locke purchased Nicole's *Essais de morale* while travelling in France in the mid-1670s and around that time he set himself the goal of translating some of them. Perhaps this was with a view to improving his French or rather as a sign to himself that his French was now respectable. Perhaps he was genuinely delighted by the content of the essays he chose and saw in them a reflection of the wife of his patron, the Countess of Shaftesbury, to whom his translation is dedicated. Whatever his reasons, it is clear that the *Essais* were a cause for reflection by Locke because he discusses them in his Journal. He finds Nicole's theistic proofs "very clear and cogent" yet "not perfect demonstrations."

Jean Yolton's edition is a parallel French/Locke version of the three essays which Locke translated; "Discourse on the existence of God," "Discourse on the weaknesse of man," and "Treatise concerning the way of preserving peace." The volume contains an extended Preface by John Yolton that provides the reader with helpful background discussion of

Nicole and the content of his essays and gives a brief review of scholarly interest in Locke's translation of the *Essais*. Jean Yolton's Introduction sets out a brief history of the translation, provides a discussion of the French text and editions of the *Essais* as well as a detailed description of the manuscript of Locke's translation now housed in the Pierpont Morgan Library, New York.

Locke translates quite loosely at times. Indeed he often paraphrases and adds his own clauses. The exercise, in his mind, seems to be more one of presenting a handbook of moral and theological reflection than a test of grammatical and lexical skill. In fact, it is often when Locke departs from the text or adds his own material that the "translations" are most interesting. There are familiar turns of phrase which reappear in the *Essay*, there are tidbits here and there, such as Locke's use of the term "texture" to translate "pour être differemment arrangée" and there are important continuities between aspects of Nicole's outlook and Locke's as expressed in the earlier Drafts of the *Essay* and the finished work. For example, Nicole's development of the analogy between our sight and our minds plays upon the fact that "Our eyes peirce not into the inside of things" (79). This must have resonated with the corpuscular scepticism that Locke seems to have imbibed from Thomas Sydenham and which plays such an important role in the *Essay*. But it must be said that there are no "finds" here. There are no crucial thoughts, no revelations or turning points in Locke's thought as a result of encountering Nicole's moral essays. Nicole is not a major influence on Locke. In spite of those thoughts and literary motifs as well as the general tenor of the *Essais* which Locke found congenial, Nicole's Jansenism and Cartesianism marked him as a thinker of a different cast. Therefore the real value of the essays lies in what we can glean from them about Locke's own intellectual development and predispositions during the mid-1670s, particularly in contrast to the views expressed in the *Essay* of 1690.

I do have some misgivings about the volume, however, in so far as it aspires to be a scholarly edition of Locke's manuscript and Nicole's text. In the first place, there is no indication that Yolton has checked her transcription against the 1712 edition of Locke's translation. The reader needs to be assured that this first published edition of Locke's translation was transcribed from the same manuscript as the presentation copy now in the Pierpont Morgan Library. It is unlikely that they differ, but the publication history of some of Francis Bacon's posthumous works is a salutary reminder that different versions of manuscripts can be in circulation at the same time. Furthermore, when editing early modern manuscripts an informal collation with pre-existing transcriptions often serves to eliminate errors and could have improved this edition. Take for example a phrase in Yolton's transcription of "Discourse of the weaknesse of Man," section 38. Her transcription reads "it comes to passe often, that a truth ~~mistaken~~ imperfectly understood, being, by mistake, though sufficient to direct us, leads us out of the way." While the word "though" makes sense in this context, the word "thought" is a more natural reading. Hancock's transcription has "thought" and the French reads "étant prise par erreur comme suffisante pour nous conduire" which would more naturally be translated as "by mistake, thought sufficient to direct us...." It would be interesting to know how the 1712 edition transcribes the word. Anyway, if "though" appears in Locke's manuscript, then Yolton should add a "t" to "though" as an editorial insertion.

A second point has to do with the editorial conventions that Yolton employs. It is claimed that they follow those of Peter Nidditch in the Clarendon edition of the *Works of John Locke* and to a limited extent they do. However there are significant differences: first Yolton leaves her editorial marks in the text, whereas Nidditch locates them in footnotes; second, unlike Nidditch, Yolton does not expand "côn" for "tion"; third, as illustrated in the quotation above, Yolton uses a strike-through for scribal deletions where Nidditch does not. Fortunately, Locke's text is relatively clean and Yolton's editorial insertions are fairly unobtrusive, though when she writes "[*illegible deletion*]" (e.g. 169) in the text one would surely prefer a discreet footnote. I highlight this feature of Yolton's editorial style because it is symptomatic of a wider and increasingly pressing problem in editing early modern manuscripts. The fact is that there is, as yet, no standard set of editorial conventions. Until a standard can be agreed upon, scholars will have to bear with a plethora of sets of conventions that are not always consistent with one another.

A third and more serious point has to do with Yolton's choice of copy texts for the French version of Nicole's *Essais*. She tells us that she used the 1672 Elzevier piracy (and I assume the 1677 second volume containing the "Discourse on the existence of God"). However, it is almost certain that Locke used the 1671 first edition of volume I of the *Essais* to translate essays two and three and the 1675 first edition of volume III for the first essay. We cannot therefore be certain that the French text that Yolton supplies is identical to that which Locke used. This may seem like a minor point, but for a scholarly edition it would be far wiser to use the version that is closest to that which Locke used, especially given the unreliability of pirated texts in the early modern period.

Furthermore, when listing the editions of the *Essais* that Locke owned in her Introduction, Yolton tells us of volume II that Locke owned the 3rd edition of 1678 (3). However, she seems unaware that Nicole's *De l'education d'un Prince* (1670) was reissued as volume II of the *Essais* in 1671. Locke's Journal tells us that he had purchased this work, along with volume III, by April 1677 (as Yolton earlier informs us, 2). Therefore, Locke appears to have acquired the first three volumes of the *Essais* by April 1677, having purchased what was probably volume I on 30

September 1676. Furthermore, Locke left his translation and his copies of the *Essais* themselves in Paris with Mme Herinx on 2 and 7 July 1678 respectively, just before he resumed his travels. It is most likely then that he had completed the translation by 2 July 1678 rather than April 1679 as Yolton claims (2).

This leads me to a fourth and final criticism of the volume and that is its neglect of detail. In the "Discourse on the existence of God" Nicole mentions Pliny the Elder's account of the use of mills giving the reference to Pliny's *Natural History* as "18. Livre, Chap. 10" (32). However, a quick check in Pliny reveals that in modern editions, which use revised chapter divisions, the discussion is actually in the section numbered XXIII of book 18. An explanatory footnote here would have been most welcome. John Yolton in his Preface (ix) refers to Maurice Cranston's reporting of Voltaire's high opinion of the third essay "Peace among men" providing a reference to Cranston ("Marshall" in note 11 should read "Cranston"). But Cranston gives us no reference. Another quick search reveals that the comment is made in Voltaire's *Le Siècle de Louis XIV*. Again, notes 3 and 4 (30 and 32) to the "Discourse on the existence of God" refer to the French text as the 1672 edition, but this essay was not published until 1675. Yet Yolton nowhere tells us that she is using, at least as I presume, the 1677 pirated edition of volume III of the *Essais* as her copy text for this essay. Finally, in a note to "Discourse of the weaknesse of Man," section 41, Yolton mentions concerning the first translator of the *Essais* into English that "Hancock conjectures that this is Robert Boyle" (85). However, it was not Hancock, but the nineteenth-century editor of the *Christian Observer*, Samuel Wilks, who made this conjecture on the basis of Boyle's proficiency in French, his (supposed) partiality to Jansenist writers and the correspondence between the contents of the essays and Boyle's thought. None the less, there is no known connection between Robert Boyle and Pierre Nicole's *Essais*.

In spite of these misgivings, I find *John Locke as Translator* an enjoyable volume to read in its own right and an informative source on Locke's intellectual development. The parallel translation gives us a deeper insight into the Locke of the mid-1670s than we have from his Journal alone or from previous editions of his translation of the *Essais*. Yolton's volume certainly supersedes Hancock's edition that was reissued in 1991 by Thoemmes Press. While it could have been more carefully edited, it is a useful addition to the literature on Locke.

Peter R. Anstey
University of Sydney

James Moore and Michael Silverthorne, editors, *Natural Rights on the Threshold of the Scottish Enlightenment. The Writings of Gershom Carmichael* (Indianapolis: Liberty Fund, 2002). Pp. xvii + 405. ISBN 0-86597-320-2 (pbk.). $12.00.

Gershom Carmichael (1672-1729) taught philosophy at the University of Glasgow from 1694 until 1729, first as a regent (tutor), and latterly, from 1727, as the first Professor of Moral Philosophy. He was, without doubt, the ablest Scottish philosopher of his generation; and he established the reputation of his chair, whose subsequent holders in the eighteenth century included Francis Hutcheson, Adam Smith and Thomas Reid. This volume is the first modern edition and translation of his published works, all of which were written to aid his teaching. It is the fruit of an unusually congenial scholarly partnership, which has already contributed a series of articles establishing Carmichael's importance in the histories of Natural Jurisprudence and of the Scottish Enlightenment. A short foreword by James Moore outlines Carmichael's biography and approach to teaching, and indicates the context in which his thinking should be understood. The translations themselves are the work of Michael Silverthorne, who has previously published translations of both Hobbes and Pufendorf. Here as there his translations are distinguished for the clarity with which he renders complex arguments without recourse to excessive modernization of idiom. In Silverthorne's hands, Carmichael is a pleasure to read. The accessibility of the texts is further enhanced by editorial annotation that is equally informative and unintrusive. As the first in what promises to be an important and very valuable series by the Liberty Press devoted to Natural Law and Enlightenment Classics, under the general editorship of Knud Haakonssen, this volume sets a high standard.

The first and longest work in the edition is Carmichael's *Supplements and Observations upon the two books of Samuel Pufendorf's On the Duty of Man and Citizen according to the Law of Nature, composed for the use of students in the universities* (1724). Since the "Supplements" and "Observations" were commentaries on Pufendorf's text, and were originally published alongside that text, the editors have had to decide how best to present them as a free-standing work. Their solution is a division into chapters, following as far as possible the order in which, in an appendix (here chapter 23), Carmichael himself indicated moral science should be studied. The four longer essays (Carmichael's "Supplements") are either presented as separate chapters, or included in chapters alongside relevant notes (Carmichael's "Observations"). The result is that the chapter numbering differs from that of Pufendorf's work; but the reproduction of Carmichael's system of references means that it is a straightforward matter to identify the passages in Pufendorf to which the notes apply: the *Supplements and Observations* can conveniently be read alongside the edition of Pufendorf's *On the Duty of Man and Citizen* by James Tully, likewise translated by Michael Silverthorne, in the series Cambridge Texts in the History of Political Thought (1991).

Carmichael's "Preface" (Chapter 1) reveals him as a conscious exponent of what Richard Tuck has characterized as "modern" natural jurisprudence. Esteemed by the ancients, but subsequently "buried under debris" by the scholastics, this approach to morals had been restored to its "pristine splendor" by Grotius. After Selden's mistaken attempt to trace the Law of Nature to the "so-called books of Noah," and Hobbes's brazen attempt to corrupt it, the Grotian endeavor had been resumed and brought to a higher state of perfection by "that most distinguished man, Samuel Pufendorf." Pufendorf had explained how the doctrine of natural law was distinguished from both moral theology, or casuistry, and civil law, neither of which could supply, as natural jurisprudence did, the basis of moral science. But Pufendorf had made one serious error: he had separated study of the law of nature from natural theology. Carmichael's first and second supplements (chapters 2 and 5) explained the mistake. The Law of Nature is the will of God, declared by the constitution of human nature. As man is able to recognize God as the source of all good things, his obligations should be deduced from "the existence, perfection, and providence of the supreme being." The first Law of Nature, accordingly, is that God is to be worshipped; the second, that each man should promote the common good of the whole human race, being the universal system of rational creatures who can rise to knowledge of God. From the second law followed two subordinate precepts, that each man should promote his own interest without harming others, and that he should cultivate sociability. Carmichael's insistence that the whole human race were the subjects of natural law led to some radical conclusions. There was no justification for slavery, "for men are not among the objects over which God has allowed the human race to enjoy domination" (140). Against both Grotius and Pufendorf, Carmichael also upheld a right of resistance, since no man has an unlimited right against another man (164-5). But Carmichael was anything but a teacher of subversion. He was confident that it was ignorance of "the true principles of natural right" which had led evil citizens to unsettle the public happiness enjoyed by these nations under their Hanoverian king.

The second work included in this volume is the *Synopsis of Natural Theology* (1729), which Carmichael prepared for publication when he became Professor of Moral Philosophy and found his teaching limited to courses in these subjects alone. As his commentary on Pufendorf had made clear, an understanding of natural theology was the foundation of moral philosophy. It was "far from my aim," he ingenuously admitted, to say anything new. He merely wished to provide his students with a compendium that would not be out of line with "the present state of philosophy." Even so, he believed that the doctrines of the scholastics, once rid of their obscure, ambiguous, and deceptive terminology, were more correct than those that were now opposed to them. The *Synopsis* consists of four chapters, devoted to the existence of God, his incommunicable and his communicable attributes, and his operations. The third work to be included here, *A Short Introduction to Logic* (1722), was dedicated solely to the use of students. An adaptation of the famous Port Royal logic, it was primarily for use in the first year; Carmichael had evidently prepared a version of it at least ten years previously. The editors suggest that it be read as an introduction to Carmichael's two sets of *Philosophical Theses* (1699, 1707), which form Part IV of this volume. The theses were assigned to students for public discussion, in Latin, on the occasion of their graduation, and thereafter Carmichael continued to use them in his own teaching. This and much else about Carmichael's teaching emerges from the final, fascinating item in the volume, an unpublished account, apparently prepared as a report to the Faculty in 1712, of the four-year program of studies through which he took his students as a regent.

　　This excellent edition of Carmichael's writings will be invaluable to scholars on at least two accounts. At one level the volume provides an unusually integrated set of teaching materials, and thus offers remarkable insight into the form and content of teaching in a Scottish university in the early decades of the eighteenth century. At the center of the program was moral philosophy, in the form of natural jurisprudence. It is well known that Pufendorf's *On the Duty of Man and Citizen* provided Europe's northern Protestant universities with a convenient textbook: with Carmichael's *Supplements and Observations* we can see just how the Lutheran Pufendorf was adapted for a Calvinist university system, and absorbed into a neo-scholastic didactic tradition. At the same time the *Synopsis of Natural Theology* and the *Logic* supply the framework in which students were prepared for moral philosophy. As Carmichael's account of his teaching method underlines, the demands of such a four-year program, on the regent or professor as well as the student, were not light. The printed word cannot reveal how a teacher like Carmichael developed and illustrated his points in class: for that vital dimension of the experience we remain dependent on limited anecdotal evidence. But Carmichael's writing is at least suggestive of the character of his teaching: he had a gift for clear exposition, but also saw it as his purpose to challenge his young students (who would have been in their mid teens) to engage with serious, sometimes complex, philosophical argument. It cannot be assumed that Carmichael was typical; David Hume remembered learning nothing but languages at Edinburgh in the 1720s (though he went to college even younger than the usual student), and wrote of professors at the time with contempt. But Carmichael's achievement at Glasgow was lasting. Such was his demonstration of the disciplinary value of natural jurisprudence for teaching moral philosophy that his successors followed suit, even when it was not the idiom in which they wrote for publication. Though he had been a student at Glasgow, Francis Hutcheson turned in the 1720s to the philosophy of Shaftesbury, effectively the antithesis of Carmichael's; but when he succeeded Carmichael in his chair in 1730, Hutcheson immediately reverted to the discipline of natural jurisprudence. The same pattern recurred in the case of Adam Smith: Hutcheson's pupil in the late 1730s, Smith continued the teaching of natural jurisprudence into the 1760s.

At another level, the volume is revealing of the state of Scottish intellectual culture in the period immediately before the flowering of Enlightenment. It is clear from the *Philosophical Theses*, the earliest texts in the collection, that Carmichael was abreast of many of the most important developments in contemporary philosophy in the 1690s. The first set of theses carried an epigraph from Malebranche, and showed familiarity with the debates between him and his critic Arnauld, as well as with the ideas of Locke and Newton. Carmichael's natural jurisprudence was likewise up to date: he was familiar with Leibniz's criticism of Pufendorf, and corresponded with the greatest contemporary exponent of both Grotius and Pufendorf, Jean Barbeyrac, (though he thought that Barbeyrac was repeating Pufendorf's mistake of discounting natural theology). His last published text, the *Synopsis of Natural Theology*, engaged with Malebranche, Leibniz, and Samuel Clarke, as well as recent exponents of reformed dogmatics. But there were limits to Carmichael's willingness to apprise his students and readers of "the present state of philosophy." Acknowledging that "schemes which utterly divorce morality from religion" had recently been put before the public, he declined to engage with them for fear of attracting the ire of other "very grave men" who "go in quite different directions." In other words, he would not respond to Shaftesbury and Hutcheson, in order to avoid exposing himself to criticism from the stricter Calvinists. Still less would Carmichael discuss Epicureanism, except to associate it with atheism. But the greatest single absence from Carmichael's writings is Bayle. Arguments that Bayle had exposed to searching criticism, such as the invocation of universal human consent to support the existence of a supreme deity, were repeated by Carmichael without the least indication of their vulnerability. It is hard to believe that Carmichael, the correspondent of Barbeyrac, was ignorant of Bayle and of the arguments that had made him notorious. But if Carmichael did know, he was not going to alert his readers to their potential interest by mentioning them, let alone attempting to refute them. For the ablest Scottish philosopher of his generation, it was a singular act of reticence. It may have been pedagogic prudence; but it is indicative of an intellectual culture that was not yet fully open. Little wonder, perhaps, that when, a few years later, the young David Hume found himself unable to work out his "new Scene of Thought," he had to discover Bayle for himself, and leave Scotland for France.

John Robertson
St Hugh's College, Oxford

Jonathan Edwards, *The Works of Jonathan Edwards.* Volume 19, *Sermons and Discourses, 1734-1738.* Edited by M. X. Lesser (New Haven: Yale University Press, 2001). Pp. xiv + 849. ISBN 0-300-08714-4. $85.00.

American intellectual historians generally recognize Edwards, along with Charles Peirce, as an authentic world-class thinker, although Europeans do not share this evaluation with respect to Edwards, and many Americanists still regard him as simply the quintessential fire-and-brimstone Calvinist. Some fifty years ago now a group of scholars devoted to Edwards began to publish a modern edition of his writings, which got off to a slow and straitened start. In the last ten years, the Yale Edition has taken off and over two-thirds of the anticipated twenty-seven volumes are in print. The other *half* of Edwards' writings will be obtainable in electronic format. The wide availability of the *corpus* of Edwards's work will substantiate—indeed, is already substantiating—the claims of his admirers.

When complete, the non-electronic Yale Edition will contain a large selection of sermons (six volumes); several volumes of his connected thoughts on speculative matters (known as the "Miscellanies"); correspondence; editions of his major books; and a variety of volumes on thematic subjects.[1] The volume under review is typical of the quality of the edition and displays some of Edwards' power as a thinker.

Volume 19 consists of thirty-two sermons or lectures that Edwards delivered over five years in the mid to late 1730s. Some were printed during his lifetime, and were thus polished and rewritten for a reading audience. This number represents, according to the Yale editors, about one-twelfth of the number of discourses Edwards prepared in this period. An annotated list at the end of the volume describes the 187 that are dated and extant. There is also a careful and comprehensive index, and a final index of cited biblical passages. Alert readers will quickly come to

---

[1] For more detail about the shape of the Yale edition and its history see my "Review Essay: An Edwards for the Millennium," *Religion and American Culture* 11 (2001), 109-17.

understand the editorial policy that has been used in the preparation of the volume, but they are also directed to Volume 10, the first of the six volumes of sermons, which contains an introduction to Edwards' sermonic practice and an overview of all the remaining sermons. But Max Lesser, the editor of Volume 19, has provided a useful and comprehensive account of Edwards' life in the 1730s and his mode of preparing his lectures. There is a brief, helpful report on each of the selected sermons, although this volume and the Yale Edition in general demand serious readers.

The distinctive aspect of this book is that it covers the period during which Edwards led a revival in his Northampton, Massachusetts, parish. This local set of events is considered to be the precursor of what was later called "the Great Awakening," which swept southern New England in the late 1730s with Edwards in command and precipitated the crisis in American religion between evangelical Protestants and their more conservative, and often socially more prosperous, brethren. Edwards's sermons are not directly concerned to document the course of the Northampton Awakening but he was aware of the tradition of revivals over which his predecessor (and grandfather) Solomon Stoddard had presided. Edwards did not minister with the view that the larger awakening was in the offing but did see himself, sometimes portentously, as participating in events of singular historical significance. Reading the sermons in chronological order gives an idea of Edwards's increasing sense of his revivalist power and his belief that some special dispensation was occurring. As a preacher and minister he is concerned, in turn, with the initial "dullness" of his flock; the potentiality of the young to lead a harvest of souls; a growing religiosity among his congregants; backsliding; the glories of grace; and declension from an emotional crest. Edwards is not much good at dealing with psychological variation in religious affections, and in this instance he was lucky that his small revival was followed by a larger one, validating his hopes and satiating his need for sustained communal piety of a high level.

Not all the sermons show Edwards at what some of his admirers think to be his best. Both the lack of piety and the possibilities of its occurrence call forth displays of his self-righteousness and his priggishness. The title "Fast Days in Dead Times" delivered in April, 1734 is a dead giveaway to its contents; and "Youth and the Pleasures of Piety"—preached a month later and often repeated—takes up the favored Edwardsean theme of exhorting adolescents to be godly and displays his emphasis on the evangelizing of the young. "The Justice of God in the Damnation of Sinners" of mid-1735 hails divine sovereignty and simultaneously berates human depravity and threatens eternal suffering, joining three typical Edwardsean revival themes.

In addition to reading of the denunciation of human weaknesses, the reader is also witness to the first stages of Edwards's developing style—extended metaphors and a rich imagery that expresses his sensuous empiricism. Even presiding over his own revival, however, Edwards is interested in more than bringing people to Christ through descriptions of torment or bliss. In this volume "Justification by Faith Alone" indicates Edwards's interest in theological niceties. Originally delivered as a lecture, it is here published in the extended form it took in a collection of discourses of 1738. "Justification by Faith Alone," which occupies one hundred pages of this text, shows Edwards's abilities as a Calvinist exegete of the King James Bible, and his familiarity with the technicalities of the themes of Pauline Christianity.

Volume 19 of the Yale Edition of Edwards is not of primary importance in the body of Edwards's works—it does not rank with *Freedom of the Will* (Volume 1) or the first volume of *The "Miscellanies"* (Volume 13), which has an extraordinary editorial account of Edwards's writing practices. But *Sermons ... 1734-1738* does effectively show the minister on the hustings, being prepared for his entrance onto the larger colonial religious stage.

Bruce Kuklick
University of Pennsylvania

William Clark, Jan Golinski, and Simon Schaffer, editors, *The Sciences in Enlightened Europe* (Chicago: University of Chicago Press, 1999). Pp. xiv + 566. ISBN 0-226-10940-2 (pbk.). $27.50.

For a long time, historians of eighteenth-century science tended to treat its subject either as a remnant of the seventeenth century or an anticipation of the nineteenth. In addition, the relationship between science and the intellectual phenomenon known as the Enlightenment was far from clear: many, even a majority, of works on the Enlightenment made no mention of science. Thomas Hankins's volume on eighteenth-century science in the Cambridge History of Science series only appeared in 1985, fourteen years after R. S. Westfall's account of the scientific revolution. Hankins's book signaled that a change in historiography was afoot; already in 1980, Roy Porter and George Rousseau's edited volume, *The Ferment of Knowledge*, provided the first inkling that the eighteenth century, far from being a way station between two illustrious ages of science, was in fact a period rich with incident and full of interest. The past twenty years have seen an outpouring of historical writing about the eighteenth century, and not only in the history of science. The eighteenth century is hot.

The editors of this volume self-consciously see themselves as "open[ing] up new paths for historical writing on the sciences in Europe during the 'long eighteenth century.'" Despite the perhaps unconscious evocation of Roy Porter in the phrase, "long eighteenth century," these new paths are not ones followed by Porter and he and his work are curiously missing from this book. Rather than Porter's coupling of science with politics and popular culture, Clark, Golinski, and Schaffer emphasize three very different organizing principles: one is technology, instruments, and what they call "body discipline." A second revolves around changing concepts of human nature, while the third focuses on place.

Underlying these three themes are concepts that are by now familiar to most scholars of the seventeenth and eighteenth centuries: sociability, the growth of the public sphere, and the role of patronage. In contrast to Porter's raucous and raging eighteenth century, Clark, Golinski, and Schaffer present a society straining toward genteel decorum and polite utility. The editors' selective survey of the historiography of Enlightenment science in their introduction culminates with Michel Foucault and his ideas about the relationship between knowledge and power, discipline, and control. These ideas, they claim, provide the theoretical underpinning for the essays in this volume.

These essays tell a very different story about Enlightenment science than the familiar one of the gradual triumph of Newtonianism. They also cover a wide geographical area, from Prussia to the Baltic to Russia to Italy and the Netherlands—all unjustly neglected areas in the historiography—while not neglecting England and France, although Scotland makes no appearance. In addition, many of the essays look at new topics and provide succinct summaries of their authors' larger research projects. Andrea Rusnock's excellent account of political arithmetic, Ken Alder's look at French engineers during the Revolution, and Emma Spary's analysis of French natural history, among others, fall into this category.

In her brief prefatory essay, Dorinda Outram offers a pointed and welcome critique of the Horkheimer-Adorno thesis that identified in the Enlightenment the origins of technological and, ultimately, totalitarian society. Outram argues that seeing the Enlightenment merely as a predecessor to ourselves obscures its own unique identity. The first section of the volume, "Bodies and Technologies," presents the theme of disciplining the human body via statistics (Rusnock's essay on political arithmetic), instruments (Jan Golinski's on the barometer), and technology (Alder on French engineers). Simon Schaffer offers the ultimate in disciplined bodies in his essay on automata, but it is unfortunate that he did not take note of Jessica Riskin's work on this topic.

The organizing theme for the second section, "Humans and Natures," seems less well-defined and the section ranges widely in topic. Michael

Hagner's account of monsters is well-written but diffuse in its attempts to summarize the entire century. Both Marina Frasca-Spada and Emma Spary look at polite culture, the former by examining the science of human nature through English novels, the latter looking at natural history. Frasca-Spada blunts her argument by avoiding discussion of religious motivations, especially in the work of Samuel Richardson. Spary's excellent essay places natural history at the center of Enlightenment culture. Mary Terrall offers a sophisticated argument for the replacement of metaphysics by mathematics as the language of natural knowledge in eighteenth-century France.

The final section looks at places deemed peripheral to the mainstream. Paula Findlen's fine essay on the Newtonian Cristina Roccati tells us much both about the role of women and about the organization and practice of science in the provinces, adding to a growing historiography of eighteenth-century Italian science. Lissa Roberts nicely sums up the Dutch scene, while Lisbet Koerner opens up a fascinating new world in her account of the Baltic states. Like Terrall, William Clark is concerned with the declining status of metaphysics in the eighteenth century; but his densely argued essay did not convince me that Prussia was indeed provincial or that this provinciality helps to explain Kant's work. It is unfortunate that this volume's attention to place did not extend to the science of geography.

I learned a lot from this volume, but I must confess I was also somewhat disappointed. While the individual essays are of high quality, their attention to the local and the particular left me feeling that opportunities were lost for a much broader and deeper account. Of course it is impossible to touch on everything in the space of a single volume, but many areas are slighted or ignored in this one, most notably religion, imperialism, and medicine. The lack of attention to religion is particularly telling, revealing how much this new story of Enlightenment science owes to the old story of progress. There was more to religion in this period than natural theology. The authors carefully eschew any grand scheme, but I was left wanting more of a conclusion than was provided by the final two essays. Nicholas Jardine returns the argument to Foucault in his account of the end of the Enlightenment, while Lorraine Daston seems to concur that the Enlightenment was about enlightened individuals and not about any bigger theme. In their introduction, the editors argue that by displaying diversity they will reveal the underlying unity of Enlightenment science, but this goal remains unfulfilled.

This volume certainly fulfills its aims of marking out new pathways for historical writing, but it also reveals the limitations of its analytical scheme. Far from being new, the themes of power and sociability have been around for at least thirty years. Both of these themes have value as analytic tools, but both have also unnecessarily narrowed our view of the eighteenth century. The best current work in eighteenth-century studies is more interdisciplinary, employing multiple methods, ideas, and points of view. In my view, the best of the articles in this volume—Spary's, Findlen's, and Alder's—succeed insofar that they transcend the limitations of the volume and provide evidence of a broader, cross-disciplinary frame of analysis.

Anita Guerrini
University of California, Santa Barbara

Stephen Buckle, *Hume's Enlightenment Tract: The Unity and Purpose of "An Enquiry Concerning Human Understanding"* (Oxford: Clarendon Press, 2001). Pp. xi + 351. ISBN 0-19-825088-6. $55.00.

Stephen Buckle's new reading of Hume's *An Enquiry Concerning Human Understanding* has two major purposes. The first, which comprises the second and largest, section of the book, is to show that the *Enquiry* must be read as a coherent whole, and not merely as a piecemeal abridgment of Hume's earlier *Treatise of Human Understanding*. The second major aim, most explicitly divided between the first and third sections, is to demonstrate that the *Enquiry*, once taken as a whole, is a tract that supports Enlightenment principles over both Academic philosophy and "all forms of religion worthy of the name." That is, the *Enquiry* is to be read as a work whose purpose is to show how experimental philosophy, founded on skeptical principles, can triumph over dogmatism.

The first of Buckle's three sections endeavors to clear the way for a close reading of the *Enquiry*. The "popular view" that Buckle targets has two parts. First, there is the charge that the Hume of the *Enquiry* is more concerned with literary fame than with serious philosophy. This view is not without merit. Buckle observes that Hume himself expressed a desire for literary fame to the point of confessing that desire to be a "ruling passion" (17). However, Buckle argues, this love of fame is not to be regarded in the shallow way that we consider contemporary celebrities to love fame, but rather should be viewed as an expression of Hume's desire to be widely regarded as a serious man of letters.

The second component of the "popular view" is that in the *Enquiry* Hume regards himself as a popular conversationalist whose task is to water down serious philosophy for the masses. Buckle's response to this charge is that Hume's popular project is to improve *both* philosophy and the common understanding. The world of common affairs can be improved by having access to philosophical theories, and the world of philosophy can avoid stagnation through close contact with real human affairs. It is partly in this sense that Buckle regards the *Enquiry* as an Enlightenment tract, meaning that it is an Enlightenment project to make philosophy a vehicle for genuine human progress. For Buckle, Hume intends to show how "true philosophy and its fruit, civilized social order, can flourish" (329).

The middle section of the book is a commentary on the *Enquiry*. Buckle develops Hume's views on association, skepticism, probability, necessary connection and liberty in order to show just how, for Hume, philosophy can contribute to a better social order. When we can obtain adequate standards of proof, for example, then we can dismiss reports of miracles and other religious revelation. Further, when we recognize that regularities in human behavior—regularities that inform what we do and can expect of others and ourselves—are on a par with regularities in natural phenomena, then we can begin to reconcile the tension between liberty and necessity. Human motives and inclinations are fully natural phenomena, and "liberty" becomes a power to act or not act, according to choice, within a range of circumstances. Hume's Enlightenment philosophy, then, is able to answer questions about the place of human beings in nature.

Buckle sums up his thesis as follows:

> When read sympathetically—that is, in its own right—the work reveals a unified argument with a polemical purpose: it moves from the implications of the new natural philosophy for perception, and for the doxastic processes of human nature, to the criticism of religion and the practical principles built thereon. Along the way, it affirms the possibility of social improvement through experimental enquiry, and affirms human standards as the only rightful standards. This is the outlook of the Enlightenment: *An Enquiry Concerning Human Understanding* is Hume's Enlightenment tract (329).

I have one major reservation about Buckle's book. Philosophers who study Hume, on reading Hume's own writings about the *Enquiry* and his intellectual and literary aspirations, might well be tempted toward the tenets of what Buckle calls the "popular view." Still, Buckle's case that these targets are in fact embraced by many scholars and teachers, or that they constitute the most influential reading of Hume, is not as well documented as it might be. This is not to say that Buckle's target is weak, because it is very plausible, and is likely a view that most readers of the

Enquiry have encountered. To be sure, Buckle's arguments in this section do not at all weaken his later commentary on the *Enquiry* itself. Yet it would be good to have a more solid sense of the influence of the popular view, if only better to clear the air prior to Buckle's close reading.

That being said, *Hume's Enlightenment Tract* is otherwise well documented and is well written—indeed, it is a pleasure to read. Buckle's commentary on the *Enquiry* is compelling, and the manner in which he situates the *Enquiry* in its historical and intellectual context is likewise engaging. This book clearly presents the roles of philosophical thought in the various phenomena constituting the Enlightenment, and so will be of value to scholars and students of Hume, and will be of special value to people who are teaching the *Enquiry* for the first time and desire to understand how it all "hangs together."

Katherine Bradfield
Washington University

Richard Yeo, *Encyclopaedic Visions. Scientific Dictionaries and Enlightenment Culture* (Cambridge: Cambridge University Press, 2001). Pp. xx + 336. ISBN 0-521-65191-3. $60.00.

In a world such as ours, at risk of drowning beneath the ever rising tide of information, the Encyclopaedia represents a lingering belief that knowledge can be drawn into an accessible and comprehensible synthesis. Post-modernists might argue that knowledge is multiple, culture bound and variously understood, but encyclopaedias continue to bear testimony to the assumptions of a modernist view deriving from the Enlightenment that human learning is universal and ultimately unitary.

It is the great merit of *Encyclopaedic Visions* that it adds significantly to our understanding of the Enlightenment by focusing on the encyclopaedia as a cultural phenomenon. The importance of the study derives in part from its wide chronological sweep, since it traces the trajectory of the genre of encyclopaedias from its pre eighteenth-century origins to the early nineteenth century. While there have been major studies of the great *Encyclopédie* of Diderot and D'Alembert, the merit of Yeo's work is that it embraces a range of encyclopaedias—chiefly, though not exclusively, drawn from Great Britain. By doing so, the study is able to draw out the important ways in which encyclopaedias embodied basic assumptions about knowledge and its social functions.

Thus, in Yeo's hands, the encyclopaedia becomes a lens that magnifies and gives clearer definition to a number of the more significant features of Enlightenment culture. In the first place it emphasizes the extent to which the eighteenth century shared our concern about an "information explosion" turning to encyclopaedias as a way of drawing together all branches of knowledge into an accessible whole. In other words, encyclopaedias represented an assertion of the unity of knowledge, and with it a confidence in the extent to which all branches of learning could be made available to a person of culture.

To some degree the growing use of alphabetical organization, with its strange juxtaposition of topics, was a concession to the increasing difficulty of drawing knowledge into a tightly organized overall structure. But such seeming arbitrariness was offset by the eighteenth-century encyclopaedists' use of prefatory maps of knowledge that provided order and system in the face of the apparent randomness of the alphabet.

Such an alphabetical arrangement, Yeo convincingly argues, can be traced back to the phenomenon of the commonplace book with its roots in Renaissance humanism. The keeping of such commonplace books was urged on students as a way of assimilating their reading and, in particular, their reading of the Ancients. By having some of the more telling *bons mots* readily available in an organized manner such learning became part of the stock of an individual's conversation and writing. So, too, the alphabetical organization of an encyclopaedia made possible ready access to society's large store of knowledge. Alphabetization may have appeared to have atomized knowledge but the intent was to make it more readily available in ways which would assist the convergence rather than the divergence of learned discussion.

And such discussion was meant to transcend national boundaries—a tribute to the Enlightenment's cosmopolitanism and its belief that learning was universal, whatever its cultural origins. Eighteenth-century encyclopaedias might be written in different languages, but it was not until the nineteenth century that different nationalities emphasized the need to put their particular cultural inflection on the body of knowledge encased within the encyclopaedia. One instance of the cosmopolitan character of the eighteenth-century encyclopaedia was the way in which the great French *Encyclopédie* began as a translation of the English Ephraim Chambers' *Cyclopaedia: or, An Universal Dictionary of the Arts and Sciences* of 1728. The French venture developed a character of its own but it still took as one of its mentors the Englishman, Francis Bacon. Moreover, the *Encyclopédie* was a work read and admired well beyond the borders of France.

Eighteenth-century encyclopaedias, as Yeo shows, needed patrons and preferably royal patrons, but this did not imply that the knowledge that they presented was not of value to any domain within the broad Republic of Letters. Such patrons assisted, it was hoped, in protecting the rights and the financial investment of the compilers of encyclopaedias but knowledge was not generally subject to the prevailing mercantilist assumption that wealth and power were best pursued by denying one's rivals access to valuable national commodities.

By the beginning of the nineteenth century, however, many of the assumptions that underlay the encyclopaedic project of the Enlightenment had come under question. In the first place it could no longer be so readily assumed that the whole realm of knowledge should in principle be open to any learned citizen of the Republic of Letters. In the sciences in particular, the need to accumulate a specialized body of expertise cordoned off some branches of learning from learned society more generally. In some of the early nineteenth-century British encyclopaedias this problem was compounded by the way in which articles on major scientific subjects promulgated recent findings and theories—in effect making encyclopaedias part of the world of specialized journals which were beginning to fragment the wider reading public. Tellingly, by the early nineteenth century the *Encyclopaedia Britannica* was prefaced with a disquisition on why it was not possible to present any overall map of knowledge.

Encyclopaedias were, of course, to survive and in many respects to prosper but in their passage from the eighteenth century they also lost much. Less and less did they reflect the current state of learning in all fields and less and less did they perform the task of diffusing knowledge as more specialized avenues of learned inquiry became ever more significant. The sheer weight of learning—oppressive even in the eighteenth century—made attempts to draw clear maps of knowledge ever more difficult. The eighteenth century still thought it possible to draw knowledge into a synthesis—later ages were less and less inclined to try. The notion of a Republic of Letters became more and more difficult to combine with the strident nationalisms of the nineteenth and twentieth centuries but is perhaps more suited to the twenty-first with its increasingly global communications.

But the most basic legacy of all of the Enlightenment, which underlay the project of the encyclopaedists, is the belief that knowledge is coherent, unifiable and, ultimately, an agent of progress—assumptions that are increasingly difficult to sustain in a culture preoccupied with pluralism, diversity and the corrupting effects of power which knowledge makes possible. It is the achievement of *Encyclopaedic Visions* to uncover the cultural roots of a tradition still distantly visible in the encyclopaedias that represent the continuing impulse to dam and contain the oceans of knowledge that surround us.

John Gascoigne
University of New South Wales

Index

404